Kim is the fast and furious one. She's a small Asian-American child who speaks both English and Chinese. Her energetic nature characterizes her from toddlerhood to adolescence. She has a mind of her own and knows what she wants and how to get it. She is bright, well-liked, and socially oriented.

Nicky is a ''difficult'' baby and a ''difficult'' older child who lives with his mother in a single-parent family. He is small for his age but has a tough quality due to his difficult life. In school, he is hyperactive and aggressive and is unpopular with teachers and children his own age.

Carlos was born in Puerto Rico. He speaks both English and Spanish. A first-born child, Carlos wants to do the right thing, but somehow has trouble, especially during early adolescence.

(continued at back of book)

Scamper: Games for Imagination Development
Robert F. Eberle   ISBN 0-914634-50-X
1977 DOK Publishers Inc
Buffalo NY   14214

Child Development and Relationships

Child Development and Relationships

Carol Flake-Hobson
University of South Carolina, Columbia

Bryan E. Robinson
University of North Carolina, Charlotte

Patsy Skeen
University of Georgia, Athens

Addison-Wesley Publishing Company
Reading, Massachusetts • Menlo Park, California
London • Amsterdam • Don Mills, Ontario • Sydney

This book is in the Addison-Wesley series in Education

Sponsoring Editor: Linda C. Fisher
Developmental Editor: Linda J. Bedell
Production Editors: Stephanie Argeros-Magean and Lorraine Ferrier

Text Designer: Marie E. McAdam
Illustrator: Oxford Illustrators, Ltd.
Cover Designer: Hannus Design Associates, Richard Hannus
Cover Photographer: Mike Mazzaschi / Stock, Boston
Art Coordinator: Kristin Belanger

Production Manager: Karen M. Guardino
Production Coordinator: Peter Petraitis

The text of this book was composed in Garamond by TKM Productions.

Library of Congress Cataloging in Publication Data

Flake-Hobson, Carol.
  Child development and relationships.

  Includes index.
  1. Child development.   2. Interpersonal relations.
I. Robinson, Bryan E.   II. Skeen, Patsy L.   III. Title.
RJ131.F49   155.4   81-4428
ISBN 0-201-04092-1   AACR2

ABCDEFGHIJ-HA-898765432
ISBN 0-201-04092-1

*To our families
and our relationships
with them.*

And to Jim Collins -- a
man who is a true gift
from the universe. May you
walk in joy and peace
and love.

♡ Carol Flake-Hobson
     July 22, 1983

Preface to the Instructor

As both students and teachers of child development for many years, we approached the writing of this book with several goals in mind. We wanted students to understand children and their relationships with others. We wanted them to have a sound foundation based on a comprehensive and interdisciplinary review of research and theory. Most of all, we wanted students to be able to *use* this information to improve their personal and professional lives. We hoped to write a book that would be both fluid and interesting to read.

With these goals in mind, we have developed this text to serve beginning education, home economics, psychology, and nursing students at the college level. We have tried to use down-to-earth language and to balance research and theory with many practical examples and applications. We believe that this approach, in combination with the emphasis on parent-child relationships, makes this book appropriate for parenting classes as well.

Organization of the Text

Our organization is primarily chronological. Physical, language, cognitive, social, and emotional aspects of the child are considered separately within each age period, but these aspects are integrated into a view of the whole child. However, because these aspects are considered separately within age periods, you can easily use this text topically, as illustrated in the topical outline shown here.

Suggested Topical Outline

History, Theory and Research in Child Development	Chapter 1 and Epilogue
Conception and Prenatal Development	Chapter 2
Birth and the Neonate	Chapter 3
Physical-Motor Development	Chapters 2,3,4,5,8,11, and 13
Perceptual Development	Chapters 3,4,5, and 8
Cognitive Development	Chapters 4,6,9,11, and 13
Language Development	Chapters 4,6, and 9
Moral Development	Chapters 11 and 13
Social Development	Chapters 3,4,7,10,12, and 14
Emotional Development	Chapters 3,4,7,10,12, and 14
Development of Parent-Child Relationships	Chapters 3,4,7,10,12, and 14
Sex-Role Development and Relationships	Chapters 4,7,10,12, and 14
Cross-Cultural Development and Relationships	Chapters 2,3,4,7,10,12, and 14
Exceptional Development and Relationships	Chapters 2,3,4,5,9, and 11

Using This Text

Although you can use this book in conventional ways, you might elect to use the empathetic approach to case analysis, in which students systematically analyze cases drawn from real-life situations. This approach encourages students to consider both facts and feelings when describing, explaining, and predicting real-life behaviors and relationships.

EMPATHETIC ANALYSIS OF CASE STUDIES

The empathetic approach to case analysis is a developmental learning process. As a case is analyzed, students move from consideration of personal reactions, to emotional empathy, and finally to cognitive empathy. Expressing personal reactions requires that students identify and analyze their feelings, thoughts, and behaviors. Emotional empathy involves "feeling like" the people in the case. Cognitive empathy emphasizes the application of knowledge gained from research and theory in explaining and predicting the behavior of the people in the cases.

Students usually find it difficult to analyze a case at the cognitive empathy level before they have analyzed it at the personal reaction and emotional empathy levels. Therefore you might choose to emphasize personal reactions and emotional empathy early in the term, moving increasingly toward an emphasis on cognitive empathy as the term progresses.

To the extent that the empathetic approach is used, this book has advantages not found in most child development texts. The empathetic approach encourages students to go beyond recognition and recall to the higher levels of application, analysis, and beginning synthesis and evaluation. As students actively explore personal feelings, values, and attitudes and use factual information to solve real-life problems, the material becomes personally relevant. Students also better understand the whole child and the reciprocal relationships of the child in family and community through this approach.

Special Features

Empathetic Prologue.   A prologue discussing the empathetic approach presents a step-by-step explanation of this unique approach.

Star Children.   Children of both sexes, several races, low and middle income levels, developmentally typical and atypical are followed from birth through adolescence, allowing students to see development of ''real'' persons over the years.

Case Studies.   Case studies are used throughout the text to stimulate student interest and to provide opportunities for instructors to implement the empathetic approach if they wish.

Learning Activities.   At the end of each chapter, six activities are presented. Each is designed to help students reach a specific goal including: (1) getting in touch with their feelings, (2) thinking about theory, research, and/or application, (3) observing in an observation school, home, or public place, (4) applying information to describe, explain, and/or predict behavior, (5) considering the whole child, and (6) considering relationships.

Parent-Child Relationships.   Reciprocal relationships between parents and children are emphasized throughout the book. That is, a bidirectional relationship is presented in which both the effects of parents upon children and the effects of children upon parents are examined.

Cross-Cultural Development and Relationships.   A section on cross-cultural development is included within each age period, so that students can gain an understanding of how the broad social system influences development and relationships.

The Father's Role.   The often-neglected role of the father in child development is given special attention throughout the book.

Exceptional Development and Relationships.   Exceptional development is integrated developmentally within each age period rather than in a single chapter.

Spotlights.   In each period of development, special material concerning educational implications, current issues, research and theory, and practical implications is set off from the text and discussed. Examples include obesity and malnutrition, bilingual children, effects of day care, prosocial behavior, learning to read, expectant fathers, test tube babies, divorce adjustment, anorexia nervosa, adolescent parenthood, wage earning mothers, and male preschool teachers.

Racial, Sex-Role, and Socioeconomic Level Balance.   The presentation of material is balanced with respect to race, sex, and socioeconomic level. Particular care was used to avoid sexist terminology. Sex-role development and relationships are presented developmentally from infancy throughout adolescence.

Flexibility of Learning Style.   Additional special features are designed to motivate students, make learning easier, and allow this text to be used in either self-directed or teacher-directed courses:

1. Abbreviated chapter outlines.
2. Numbered summaries at the ends of each chapter that detail key concepts.
3. Annotated bibliography of related readings for each chapter.
4. Terms defined when used in the text.
5. Glossary of terms.
6. Headings to help students understand the organization of the book and to point out major concepts.
7. Down-to-earth language that avoids jargon and abstraction.
8. Practical consideration of problems that students will encounter in dealing with children and families, along with possible solutions.

Illustrations.   We wanted this text to appeal not only to students' minds, but to their eyes. Toward this end, we have made every effort to supplement the text material with appropriate figures, graphs, photographs, and tables and to present a visual chronology of child development. Of special note are the illustrations of the star children on the endpapers and in the chapter openings. We hope these unique portraits will help convey what for us remains the ever-fascinating world of children.

Supplementary Materials.   The *teacher's manual* was written to help the teacher use a minimum amount of effort while providing an outstanding learning experience for students. Suggestions for lectures, films, games, reference books, journals, term paper topics, additional student learning activities, and guidelines to help students in doing observations are presented. An outline, a summary, and key terms are provided for every chapter. Additional cases, along with a detailed discussion of how to use cases and the empathetic approach, are also included.

A comprehensive *test item file* is provided in the teacher's manual. Multiple-choice, true-false, and matching questions are presented in addition to essay questions.

The *student guide* is designed to help students understand and apply material from the text and to become personally involved as much as they or their instructor desire. Outlines, key terms, short-answer questions, essay questions, annotated bibliographies, and cases with questions to help students analyze the cases are provided. Each chapter also has an overview. Activities involving thought, feelings, observation, and research (data analysis as well as securing and synthesizing information from a variety of sources) are included.

Acknowledgments

Without the aid and assistance of many colleagues, friends, and family members this book would not have been possible.

We received many helpful comments from our reviewers:

Donalene Andreotti, El Camino College

Jeanne Armstrong, Lane Community College

Charles A. Austad, Bemidji State University

Ann Bingham-Newman, California State University at Los Angeles

Thomas Bond, Thomas Nelson Community College

Robert Bradley, University of Arkansas at Little Rock

John Stewart Dacey, Boston College

Donna Dempster, Cornell University

Marlene Evans, Arizona Western University

Susan Wanska George, Kansas State University

Bernard Gorman, Nassau Community College

Marilyn Hallisey, Diablo Valley College

Elizabeth Henry, Old Dominion University

Richard E. Hult, Jr., University of South Carolina at Columbia

Afra Katzev, Portland Community College (Oregon)

Janet Kelley, Rio Hondo College

Janet Kilbride, University of Delaware

Dene Klinzing, University of Delaware

Judith L. Kuipers, Oregon State University

Michael Lamb, University of Utah

Garrett Lange, University of North Carolina (Greensboro)

Rosina Lao, East Carolina University

Judith A. Powell, Oklahoma State University

Ester Rolnick, Bronx Community College

Gin Sgan, Fitchburg State College

Jane Stormer, Cuyahoga Community College

Susan Taylor, St. Thomas Aquinas College

Nancy P. White, Pine Manor College

Special thanks to Professor Rebecca Smith at the University of North Carolina, Greensboro, for her inspiration and early guidance in the use of the empathetic approach to case analysis. Appreciation to Dr. Emily Pou, Dean of the College of Home Economics at the University of Georgia for her steadfast personal and administrative support.

Thanks to Dr. Ruth Highberger, Dr. Keith Osborn, and Dr. Jim Walters for helpful suggestions, especially those concerning how to work with publishers.

We also benefited from the suggestions of Milda Baker, Jamey McCullers, Sharon Bono, Anda Cochran, Diane Carpenter, Scott Loftin, Freda Nicholson, Sue Swick, Carol Yoeman, and of Dr. Hobson's graduate class at Coastal Carolina College, summer, 1980.

The technical assistance of Glenda R. Loftin, Lara McLester, Pat Robinson, Alisha Sides, Georgie Skeen, and Fannie Wilson is much appreciated. And Gail Carter, Judy Durham, Pat Geiser, Charlotte Johnson, Janie Jones, Margaret Robinson, Ethel Sikes, and Ginger Vickery typed draft after draft with dedication and skill.

We also want to thank the staff and our editors at Addison-Wesley—particularly Damon Gardner, whose excitement, creativity, and belief in us helped us get this book off the ground, and Linda Bedell, whose patience and skillful guidance helped us finish it.

Finally, special thanks to our families, who always gave support and cheerfully weathered holidays without us.

All three authors contributed equally to the writing of this book; their names appear in alphabetical order.

Columbia, South Carolina　　　　　　　　　　　　　　　　C. F. H.
Charlotte, North Carolina　　　　　　　　　　　　　　　B. E. R.
Athens, Georgia　　　　　　　　　　　　　　　　　　　P. L. S.
September 1982

Contents

II The Importance of a Good Beginning

2 Conception and Prenatal Development   45

III Toddlerhood

5 Toddlerhood: Physical-Motor and Perceptual Development   169

IV Early Childhood

8 Early Childhood: Physical-Motor and Perceptual Development

VI Adolescence

13 Adolescence: Physical and Cognitive Development

Child Development and Relationships

I **Introduction to Child Development**

Prologue: The Empathetic Approach

Having worked with college students term after term, each of us has dreamed of writing a textbook that would help students understand children and their relationships with others. We wanted to write a book that would be less than boring to read—perhaps even fun! We thought that students should be able to use the information they learn in school to improve their personal and professional lives.

We have written this book with the idea in mind that you should not be asked to learn an assortment of unconnected facts about children that will be forgotten after the final exam. Instead, we have provided ways for you to learn facts and to apply them in explaining and predicting human behavior and relationships. But we also believe behavior and relationships cannot be understood unless both facts and feelings are considered. The empathetic approach to case analysis is one way for you to use both. Before we can discuss how to use the empathetic approach, though, we need to define some important terms we will be using throughout this book.

What Are the Important Terms?

CASES

Cases are descriptions of real events drawn from newspapers, magazines, books, movies, tape recordings, and personal experiences. For example, the following case is based upon anthropologist Margaret Mead's (1952) research.

In this text, we will use some short cases to illustrate points and promote discussion. We will examine other cases in more detail. We believe that abstract concepts and theories about children and their relationships with family, school, and society are easier to learn when you apply them to cases.

The Case of Omblean

Pidgin likes to busy herself with quarreling, fishing, climbing coconut trees, and preparing food while the men of her tribe plot and fight. She is a member of the Mundugumor tribe of New Guinea, a tribe of cannibals who live on the banks of a swiftly flowing river. Like all Mundugumor women, Pidgin views the bearing and rearing of children as a most unwelcome task. Omblean is her newborn child.

Omblean is carried around in a rough basket, separated from the touch of his mother's skin. He lies exposed to the tropical heat, scratched by the abrasive basket that is his home. Omblean is constantly hungry because his mother does not like to feed him. When Pidgin does decide to breastfeed her newborn infant, she remains standing in a nonsettling, transient position—in the manner of all nursing Mundugumor women. Pidgin does not position herself so that Omblean can mold to her body. Once Omblean's hunger is minimally satisfied, he is immediately and harshly pushed away from Pidgin's breast.

Omblean will grow up in a hostile and aggressive world. A typical daily meal will consist of a captured enemy who will be cooked and served while Omblean's father and other hunters humorously recount the events leading up to the capture of their meal. Even in lovemaking, the adults of Omblean's tribe scratch and bite each other in a form of sex play.

THE EMPATHETIC APPROACH

The **empathetic approach** is a method that allows you to use both facts and feelings in explaining and predicting behavior. Using this approach involves three steps: personal reactions, emotional empathy, and cognitive empathy.

Personal Reactions.   The first step in using the empathetic approach is being able to identify and analyze **personal reactions,** which include feeling, thought, and behavior. Feeling can be viewed as an emotional, ''gut-level'' reaction; thought as ideas, facts, and information; and behavior as what you actually do in response to feelings, thoughts, and situations.

What were your feelings as you read the case of Omblean? Were you horrified and angry that a parent would treat a baby that way? What were your thoughts? ''That poor baby!'' or ''What will happen to him?'' How did you behave? Did you just continue to read? Did you talk to a friend about the case? Such feelings, thoughts, and behaviors are personal reactions. Personal reactions are never identical. They vary in response to different situations and also because each individual has a unique heredity and a unique set of previous experiences. List some key words that describe your personal reactions to the case of Omblean.

Emotional Empathy.   Take a few minutes to consider how Omblean felt as he lay in his rough, scratchy basket: How did Pidgin feel? Can you identify with the feelings of the people in this case? If so, you are experiencing emotional empathy. **Emotional empathy** requires that you actually feel the same feelings that another person experiences (Clark, 1980).

Cognitive Empathy.   Two distinct types of empathy—emotional and cognitive—have been identified by researchers (Stotland, 1969; Mehrabian and Epstein, 1972). As already discussed, emotional empathy involves experiencing the feelings of another person. **Cognitive empathy** involves using information derived from research and theory to explain and predict the behavior of people in a particular situation. Let's look more closely.

Read the case of Omblean again. Omblean's mother places him in a rough, scratchy basket. She doesn't hold him, cuddle him, or feed him whenever he's hungry. Can you explain why Pidgin did these things? Perhaps some information about behavior can help you explain Pidgin's actions. Parents usually rear their children the same way they were reared. Mundugumor women don't like to bear or rear children. Omblean's grandmother quarreled, fished, and climbed trees, ignoring her daughter, Pidgin, who was also placed in a scratchy basket. All the other women in the Mundugumor tribe did the same. Pidgin learned to mother in the same way as her mother and the other women in her culture. As the case of Omblean shows us, child-rearing customs around the world may sound odd or harsh when judged against our cultural standards. But all such early parent-child relationships prepare children for later survival in their own particular society.

Can you predict what might happen to Omblean? Erik Erikson (1963), an important theorist, provides us with the following useful information: One of the most important accomplishments of an infant is the establishment of a sense of trust in people and the world. Success or failure in feeling safe and trusting others forms the basis of the child's personality. Children are successful in this task when the adults around them are affectionate and when they recognize and respond to the infant's needs consistently. When the infant is deprived of love, or is neglected or abused, a sense of mistrust is established. Such failure at this stage could result in a mistrustful attitude for the remainder of the child's life. Based on Erikson's information, make predictions about Omblean's future. If you are interested in how Omblean turned out as an adolescent, read the section on cross-cultural development and relationships in Chapter 14.

In addition to explaining and predicting behavior, cognitive empathy also involves the realization that you, with a different background and experiences, may behave differently from the people in the case. For example, how will your parenting behavior compare with Pidgin's? Explain any differences in behavior related to background and experiences.

How Do You Use the Empathetic Process?

Learning to do an empathetic analysis of a case is a developmental process. Your skills will develop gradually as you read and analyze the cases found in this book and in other sources. You will be analyzing cases in a different manner when you finish this book. In the first place, you will gain more and more information about child development as you read and study. You will be able to use this new information in thinking about a case. You will be better able to recognize your personal reactions and feel more comfortable sharing them with others. In addition, you will improve in your ability to empathize both emotionally and cognitively. Figure P.1 outlines the empathetic process. The case of Alan and his teacher gives you an opportunity to begin to use the empathetic process in case analysis.

I. Personal Reaction Level

    A. Read the case and identify your immediate reactions.

    B. Note information about personal experiences that might explain your reactions.

II. Emotional Empathy Level

    A. Try to "feel like" the individuals in the case. Choose one person at a time and identify with the feelings of that person. Be careful not to condemn or judge, just describe.

    B. Compare your personal feelings with the feelings of an individual in the case. Begin to consider why those feelings are alike or different.

III. Cognitive Empathy Level

    A. Identify the major problem areas in the case.

    B. Gather as much information as possible that seems to apply to the identified problems. You may obtain information from your textbook and from many other sources.

    C. Apply the information to the case. Use it to understand and explain the behavior of the people involved.

    D. Predict the future behavior of the individuals and families in the case. Avoid judging. Base your predictions on information.

    E. Think about how you might have behaved the same or differently from the people in the case. What in your background and experience would cause your behavior?

Figure P.1 Outline of the empathetic process

The Case of Alan and His Teacher

He always wanted to say things. But no one understood.
He always wanted to explain things. But no one cared.
So he drew.

Sometimes he would just draw and it wasn't anything. He
   wanted to carve it in stone or write it in the sky.
He would lie out on the grass and look up in the sky and
   it would be only him and the sky and things inside
   that needed saying.

And it was after that, that he drew the picture. It was a
   beautiful picture. He kept it under the pillow and would
   let no one see it.
And he would look at it every night and think about it. And when it
   was dark, and his eyes were closed, he could still see it.
And it was all of him. And he loved it.

When he started school he brought it with him. Not to show anyone,
   but just to have with him like a friend.

It was funny about school.
He sat in a square, brown desk like all the other square, brown desks
   and he thought it should be red.
And his room was a square, brown room. Like all the other rooms. And
   it was tight and close. And stiff.

He hated to hold the pencil and the chalk, with his arm stiff and
   his feet flat on the floor, stiff, with the teacher
   watching and watching.
And then he had to write numbers. And they weren't anything.
   They were worse than the letters that could be something
   if you put them together.
And the numbers were tight and square and he hated the whole thing.

The teacher came and spoke to him. She told him to wear a tie like
   all the other boys. He said he didn't like them and
   she said it didn't matter.
After that they drew. And he drew all yellow and it was the
   way he felt about morning. And it was beautiful.

The teacher came and smiled at him. "What's this?" she said.
   "Why don't you draw something like Ken's drawing?
   Isn't that beautiful?"
It was all questions.

After that his mother bought him a tie and he always drew airplanes
   and rocket ships like everyone else.
   And he threw the old picture away.
And when he lay out alone looking at the sky, it was big and blue
   and all of everything, but he wasn't anymore.

He was square inside and brown, and his hands were stiff, and
   he was like anyone else. And the thing inside him
   that needed saying didn't need saying anymore.

It had stopped pushing. It was crushed. Stiff.
Like everyone else.*

PERSONAL REACTION LEVEL

Take some time to reflect about *your* personal reactions to the case of Alan and his
teacher. (Remember to include feelings, thoughts, and behaviors.) Now move to
the next part of the personal reaction level: explaining your reactions. What things

---

* "About Schools," *Colloquy,* January 1970. Reprinted by permission. Since the poem was
published, the publishers have learned that it was written by R. Mukerjii, a Japanese University
student.

in your background and experience would cause you to react differently from someone else? One college student reported that when she was in elementary school, she was required to wear a uniform consisting of a red jumper and hat. She still remembers the anger she felt in being required to wear that hat and she can identify strongly with Alan's feelings of not wanting to wear a tie. As a teacher, she plans to allow children to dress as they choose.

Compare your reactions and recollections with those of other students. Since each of us has a unique personality, background, and set of experiences, we all may react in different ways to the same situation. Remember that everyone's feelings and thoughts are valid. At this point the important thing is to understand with accuracy your own reactions and those of others, not to reach agreement on anything.

EMOTIONAL EMPATHY LEVEL

Now that you have begun to identify your personal reactions and to understand their origins, you can move on to the level of emotional empathy. The goal at this level is to begin to ''feel like'' the people in the case, not to judge or to blame them. It might be easy for you to feel like or to identify and understand Alan's feelings since you and he are both students. Say to yourself, ''I am Alan, I feel. . . .'' Also try to feel like the teacher in the case. Say to yourself, ''I am the teacher. I feel. . . .''

Compare your personal feelings and reactions with those of Alan and the teacher. Consider the probable values, attitudes, and beliefs of each person and compare them with your own. This will help you to understand why they behaved as they did and why you would or would not behave in a similar way.

COGNITIVE EMPATHY LEVEL

Having progressed through the personal reaction and emotional empathy levels, you are ready to begin to use the information derived from theory and research in the cognitive empathy level of the empathetic process.

Identifying Problem Areas.　It is important to begin by identifying the issues or problem areas in a case. In Alan's case, one problem area is that Alan does not express himself well verbally. Instead, he expresses himself best through creative art and in this particular classroom such independent, creative expression is not rewarded. A problem area that is not mentioned in the case but that may be inferred is that there might be administrative pressures forcing the teacher to closely control the children's behavior. She may be expected to teach a large group of students and to maintain rigid quiet and order in the classroom. Make a list of any other problem areas that you can identify.

Gathering Related Information.　Cognitive information includes facts or general truths that are established in the development of a science. Such information can be used to understand, explain, and predict behavior. Gather as much information as possible that seems to be related to the problems you identified in the case.

Many children find it easier to express themselves through art than in words.

Textbooks, periodicals, personal experiences, and other academic courses can be used as sources.

For example, the following information about human behavior can be related to the case of Alan:

1. Research has shown that when adults are high in control and do not permit independence, children are likely to be more well-behaved, withdrawn, passive, and conforming, but less happy, inquisitive, original, and fanciful than children in democratic settings (Baldwin, 1949; Baumrind, 1971; Lewin et al., 1939).

2. If a behavior is rewarded, it will occur more often (Skinner, 1957).

Applying Information.   You should now present a nonjudgmental explanation of the behavior in the case based on the information you have gathered. Apply the first piece of information stated above. The teacher did not permit independence. She asked Alan to conform in his dress and in the way he drew pictures. Alan became well-behaved, withdrawn, and conforming but less inquisitive and original. Why do you think this happened? What was the teacher's role? What about the influences of parents, class members, and Alan himself?

Now apply the second piece of information. The teacher rewarded children who wore ties, drew airplanes and rockets, and sat at their desks with their feet flat on the floor. At first Alan did not want to do these things, but when he saw the other children being rewarded for meeting the teacher's expectations, he began to wear a tie and to draw airplanes and rockets. Such behavior began to occur more often as a result of the teacher's rewards.

This second piece of information can also apply in the teacher's case. She might have graduated from a teacher education program in which value was placed on allowing children the freedom to make independent choices about their own learning. When she started teaching, she might have been criticized by her principal, curriculum supervisor, or another teacher if her pupils were away from their desks or if her classroom was noisy. Or the principal and curriculum supervisor might have rewarded her by saying what a good teacher she was when her classroom was highly teacher-controlled and orderly. Perhaps parents bragged to her about the children's art work when they drew ''real'' things like airplanes and rockets and criticized her when their drawings were free-form. The teacher's behavior—insisting on structure and order and requiring ''real'' pictures—would then occur more often because she was being rewarded for that behavior.

Making Predictions Based on Information.   Try to locate other information that will be helpful in making predictions about the people in this case. Considering the information given here, one prediction you might make is that if Alan's life continues as described in the case, he probably will become withdrawn, well-behaved, passive, and conforming, but not very curious or creative as an adult. If he continues to gain rewards for drawing airplanes and rockets, then he may decide to become an aircraft designer or, since he does appear to have artistic interest, a technical artist. What other predictions can you make based on the information that you have gathered?

Comparing the Effect of Background and Experiences.   Compare your own background and experiences with those of the people in the case. Think about how you would have behaved in the same situation. How would your behavior be affected by your background and experience?

Why Use the Empathetic Approach to Study Child Development?

If you are now working with children, or if you plan to work with them in the future as a teacher, nurse, therapist, caseworker, or parent, having information about children as well as being able to apply that information in your work will help you to be more effective. This book presents factual information based on research and theory, just as other textbooks do, but it also examines feelings about children, just like the feelings you had while reading about Omblean and Alan. Feelings accompany and interact with thoughts and influence behavior (Zajonc, 1980). Recognizing and expressing these feelings is as important as using factual knowledge if you are to build satisfying relationships with children. The empathetic approach to case analysis is designed to help you use both facts and feelings in dealing with people in real-life situations (Klemer and Smith, 1975).

1 Studying Child Development and Relationships

15

The Case of Babies in the Mill

I used to work in factories when things was moving slow
When babies worked in cotton mills, each morning had to go
Every morning just at five the whistle blew on time
To call those babies out of bed at the age of eight or nine
Get out of bed you sleepyheads and get you a bit to eat
The factory whistle's calling you, there's no more time to sleep
To their jobs those little ones was strictly forced to go
They had to be at work on time through rain and sleet and snow
Many times when things went wrong their bosses often frowned
Many times those little ones was kicked and shoved around
Our children they grew up unlearned, they never went to school
They never learned to read and write, they learned to spin and spool
Many times I close my eyes and see that picture still
When textile work was carried on with babies in the mill
Oldtimer can't you see that scene way back in years gone by
When babies had to go to work the same as you and I
Aren't you glad that things have changed and we have lots of fun
As we go in and do the jobs that babies used to run*

A Historical Perspective

There is an old, abandoned factory in the area of Gainesville, Georgia, where visitors may note several sharp wooden pegs protruding from the top of the banister on the stairwell. During the early 1800s, it was common for five- and six-year-old children in the United States to work sixteen hours a day in a factory. The purpose of the sharp pegs was to keep those young factory workers from sliding down the banister.

Today most adults would think that children who are still interested in sliding down banisters are too young to work in factories. But in the past, people thought of children as miniature adults, so it was logical that children should work in factories; after all, adults did. Old photographs depicted children as little adults, not children, and even children's toys reflected this idea. Children whose families could afford them were given real china tea sets, ornately carved wooden soldiers, and china or wooden dolls that looked like adults. If you look in a department store or toy catalog today, you will see that children have a variety of toys designed especially for them. Most dolls look like babies and the tea sets are metal or plastic.

---

* Words and music by Dorsey Dixon, Sr. Used with permission from Dorsey Dixon, Jr.

Childhood was not always a carefree time. During the early part of the Industrial Era in the United States, children often worked long hours to help supplement the family income.

The further back in history you go, the more you discover that children were likely to be abused, abandoned, beaten, terrorized, sexually molested, and even killed (DeMause, 1974). In ancient Greece and Rome, infanticide, the killing of infants, was a common practice. Children were seen not as persons but as the unwanted result of sexual activities (Aries, 1962). As Christianity spread through the ancient world, the practice of infanticide came under question. Christians believed that children were persons with souls and that infanticide was murder. In A.D. 318, the Roman emperor Constantine declared infanticide a crime and offered payment to any family that would take in an unwanted child. But infanticide continued.

In 1784, the Austrian government passed a law forbidding young children to sleep with their parents, since a common practice of that time was for parents to "accidentally" roll over and suffocate their sleeping child. During the 1800s, nurses were often hired to dispose of babies, a practice called baby farming (Osborn, 1980). Infanticide was gradually outlawed and condemned by most people, but it was not until 1963 that the state of Colorado passed the first strong legislation against child abuse in the United States.

In addition to being mistreated in these ancient, and not-so-ancient, times, children were viewed as evil creatures born in sin. Adults literally tried to ''beat the devil'' out of children. During the 1700s, dunking children in cold water until they turned blue was thought to be a suitable disciplinary technique (Osborn, 1980). In 1979, as the International Year of the Child drew to a close, the International Labor Organization announced that 41 million of the world's children are still exploited by their familes, required to work in mines and factories and on farms just to survive. In our society today, most people believe that children are basically good and innocent. No longer viewed as miniature adults, most children spend their time in school and play, not working in factories. Throughout this book, we will discuss many modern-day children, but our particular focus will be on the lives of the twelve children introduced on the inside cover of this text.

THE NATURE-NURTURE CONTROVERSY

At three o'clock Mary Hopkins and Susan Abel sat down with cups of coffee to plan for the next day's kindergarten class. ''I just don't know what to do with Nicky Thomas,'' Susan began. ''He wants to talk all the time. He uses dirty language. And he's so unruly! I can't get him to listen for a minute.''

''Well, he probably inherited that from his mother,'' Mary replied, ''Every time I've chatted with Mrs. Thomas, I couldn't complete a single sentence without her interrupting.''

Susan countered, ''I don't know. I don't believe behavior is caused by heredity. I think children learn most behavior from the way they're brought up. Nick didn't inherit his talking, he just copied it from his mother. With that kind of home environment what else would you expect him to do but talk?''

People have always wondered about what causes children to behave and develop as they do. Do you think Nicky's unruly behavior is caused mostly by inherited characteristics or by environmental factors? You may, like Mary Hopkins,

PEANUTS ®   **By Schulz**

TITLE—Peanuts, Reg. U. S. Pat. Off.

Whether human behavior is the result of heredity, environment, or both has been a subject of debate for centuries.

argue that hereditary factors (inherited characteristics) are most important. Or you may agree with Susan Abel, and argue that environmental factors such as learning from adults and other children are most important. This controversy, "**nature versus nurture,**" or heredity versus environment, has lasted for centuries.

We can trace the argument back to 1690 when John Locke, a British philosopher, revived the philosophy of Aristotle. Like Aristotle, Locke took an extreme environmentalist position in describing the mind of an infant as a blank slate, a **tabula rasa.** Locke believed that a child's experiences inscribed the slate, that the child was a passive receiver, a lump of clay, easily shaped by environmental forces. If we accept Locke's view, the burden of responsibility falls on parents, educators, and society to provide an environment that enables the child to develop "in the right way."

The opposing view, that behavior and development are primarily determined by heredity or nature, was advocated by Jean Jacques Rousseau, a French philosopher. In his book *Emile,* which was published in 1762, Rousseau described children as active participants in their own development. The child was viewed as a busy, self-directed explorer, with nature or heredity ensuring the child's healthy growth. Rousseau's let-nature-take-its-course philosophy placed less responsibility for the child's development on parents and teachers than did Locke's philosophy. Instead, Rousseau thought a child's natural goodness unfolded best according to nature's plan, without the interference or corruption of societal influences.

There is still much argument about the causes of behavior, but most people now agree that neither position alone sufficiently explains behavior and development. In fact, the nature-nurture controversy is really a naive argument because the definitions of "nature" and "nurture" are unclear and incomplete and the "either-or" argument ignores the interplay between nature and nurture. Spotlight 1.1 describes some ways heredity and environment interact in influencing behavior and development.

Child Development as a Scientific Field of Study

If someone is holding an apple and lets it go, you can predict that it will fall. Your prediction would be based partly on your past experience. If someone pressed you to explain why the apple fell, you would probably remember that the apple's falling has something to do with the gravitational pull of the earth. Your explanation and prediction that the apple would fall down and not up could be made on the basis of your knowledge of Sir Isaac Newton's theory. A theory is defined as a group of general truths or principles that are related in an organized way and allow people to explain past and present behaviors and to predict future behaviors. Newton discovered a general truth about gravity as he sat under an apple tree. When an apple dropped to the ground near him, Newton wanted to know why it fell down and not up. Most of us would not ask such an obvious question, but good scientists ask and conduct objective studies designed to answer the obvious,

❋ Spotlight 1.1: Maturation and Learning

Can you explain the appeal of fictitious characters such as Superman, the Jolly Green Giant, Popeye, Wonder Woman, and the Incredible Hulk? One explanation may be that they break the biological barriers of strength and growth that limit ordinary humans.

To illustrate, there is a limit to how large a baby the prenatal environment can accommodate, so growth rates of potentially large babies are held back during prenatal development. After birth, an automatic catch-up mechanism allows infants to grow rapidly according to their genetically determined growth pattern (Tanner, 1963). This catch-up mechanism also operates before or after birth if a child's unique growth pattern is slowed down by unfavorable factors in the environment. In Zambia, infants that were conceived and developed in an inadequate intrauterine environment were immature at birth but showed rapid recovery from this immaturity after birth (Brazelton et al., 1976). A poor environment can slow growth and prevent children from developing their full genetic potential and, in contrast, an enriched environment can assist them in reaching their full genetic potential. But the environment cannot change heredity so it is impossible for children to grow as tall as the Jolly Green Giant or as strong as Popeye, no matter how many green beans or how much spinach they eat!

Although height is primarily controlled by heredity, it is also influenced to some degree by environmental conditions. Did you ever stoop down to walk through the doorway of a historic castle or ancient fort? The doors did not shrink, people have just grown taller over the last hundred years. This **secular trend,** the tendency for today's children to grow taller and reach their adult height earlier than children who lived a century ago, is due to environmental factors such as better nutrition, increases in caloric intake, and decreases in childhood diseases (Roche, 1979; Tanner, 1970).

Jun, a Hopi Indian, spent much of the first nine months of life tied to a cradleboard, as is customary for Hopi infants. Jun couldn't raise his body, roll over, or move his arms, except in the evenings when he was held or allowed to play on the floor. Scotty, a baby reared in typical Western fashion, spent his daytime hours in his crib, playpen, and baby carriage. In what ways would you expect Jun and Scotty to differ in their motor development?

Because physical changes occur at a fairly regular rate in all children, motor development has traditionally been attributed to maturation more than learning. **Maturation** refers to inherited patterns of growth that occur at about the same time in all people. Children cannot learn a motor skill before their muscles, bones, and nervous systems are developed to a certain point. Parents will find that practice in motor skills such as walking and toilet training is effective only when the child, as a result of maturation, is biologically ready to perform these skills anyway.

With this information in mind, how would you compare Jun and Scotty? Those who emphasize inherited factors such as biological maturation, would say Scotty and Jun would walk at the same time; others who emphasize environmental factors would say that Scotty would learn to walk before Jun because Scotty had more opportunities to practice and learn motor movements. To resolve this conflict, Dennis (1940) conducted a study in which he compared a group of Hopi infants reared like Jun with a group of Western infants reared like Scotty. The study showed that the physical restraint of the cradleboard did not affect the age at which the babies started to walk. More recently, Chisholm (1978) compared age of walking in the Navajo cradling culture with a small group of Caucasians in the same geographic region. He found that amount of cradleboard use had no effect on the age at which children walked. In other cultures in countries such as Guatemala (Kagan and Klein, 1973), Zambia (Goldberg, 1972), and Mexico (Brazelton, 1972), where various physical restrictions are practiced in early infancy, no permanent lags in motor development have been reported. In some instances children experienced lags but they soon caught up with age-mates in the United States when given opportunities to practice motor skills.

Research on identical twins sheds further light on the roles of maturation (heredity) and learning (environment). Because identical twins have the same heredity, any changes that occur in one twin but not in the other are assumed to be the result of environmental influences. Gesell and Thompson (1929) trained one identical twin in motor skills such as climbing stairs and manipulating blocks. They found that this training had no effect and that the development of motor skills in the "trained" twin and the "untrained" twin were the same.

Another famous twin study is that of Johnny and Jimmy conducted by McGraw (1935). Johnny was given early training in certain motor skills; Jimmy was given no practice until twenty-two months of age. Johnny's early practice in walking, grasping, and creeping had no special effect on his motor development; he developed these skills at the same age as his twin brother. Johnny, drilled in climbing and buttoning, learned these everyday skills earlier than Jimmy, but such differences were temporary and disappeared within a few days or weeks. When Johnny was taught to ride a tricycle before he reached the necessary maturation point, it took him ten months to learn, a much longer time than it took Jimmy, who learned to ride in a matter of weeks. Jimmy acquired the tricycle-riding skill more quickly because he had reached the necessary maturation point for mastering that skill. McGraw concluded that Johnny had trouble learn-

Learning to ride a tricycle takes practice, but children cannot do so until their bodies are ready.

ing to ride a tricycle because he formed poor habits that were the result of being trained at too young an age.

We can conclude from these research studies that physical growth and motor development are governed by both hereditary and environmental factors. Practice given before children are biologically ready, as was the case with Johnny's climbing, can have temporary but not lasting advantages, and forcing children to learn before muscles, nerves, and bones are appropriately developed can even be harmful, as Johnny's tricycle experience indicates. Maturation must occur before infants are biologically prepared to acquire certain physical-motor skills. Once that point is reached, opportunities for practice are important so children won't lag behind in motor development. When children are allowed to explore and practice motor skills in an enriched environment, they can develop to their fullest, within their biological limitations.

and the less obvious, questions. Newton soon figured out the answer to his question, and so developed his theory on gravity. Newton later explained and made predictions about the behavior of the earth, planets, moon, sun, stars, and asteroids. He based his explanations and predictions on the principle of gravity and a few related general truths.

American psychologist Arnold Gesell was a pioneer investigator who helped turn the study of child development into a science when he used scientific studies to answer questions about children. The science of child development uses research studies to systematically ask and answer two kinds of questions about children: *Questions that ask what.* What are children like? What do they do? In what ways do they change over time? *Questions that ask why.* Why are children like they are? Why do they do what they do? Why do they change over time? Answering the "what" questions involves *descriptions* of children's behavior and development; answering the "why" questions involves *explanations* about the causes of behavior and the process of behavioral change (Thomas, 1979). Like many early investigators, Gesell was interested in answering the "what" questions. The child development researchers of today focus less on description and more on explanations, the "why" questions.

Both theory and research help us increase our understanding of children. Gesell studied many children as he developed his maturational theory, which states that physical growth and motor development follow an orderly sequence. Spotlight 1.2 illustrates how Gesell used research studies to verify this theory.

Theories of Child Development

Many parents, teachers, nurses, biologists, psychologists, sociologists, home economists, and social workers would like to be able to explain and predict the behavior of children and adults. Unfortunately, theories of child development and human development are not as well developed as theories in the physical sciences. To date, no single theory provides a comprehensive view of child development, so students interested in children and relationships must study several theories to obtain a true picture of the subject. We will discuss five major theoretical approaches, each focusing on different aspects of the child. *Psychoanalytic theory,* which was developed earliest, deals with people's emotions and interpersonal relationships, sometimes called personality development. *Cognitive theory* deals primarily with thought or the processes of acquiring knowledge of the world. *Behavior theory* is primarily concerned with how people learn to behave as they do. *Biological theory* emphasizes the behavior of animals and humans in natural environments. *Humanistic theory* views the whole person as a unique individual striving for personal fulfillment.

Spotlight 1.2: Dr. Gesell's New Science

I remember Arnold Gesell well!* We first met in 1927 in New Haven, Connecticut, when I was just a baby. I visited Dr. Gesell at his clinic off and on until I was about ten. Dr. Gesell always chatted with my mother about me and wrote down what she said to him. (My father never came with us.) People in the clinic put me in a huge dome and made the biggest fuss over me! I couldn't see out, but they could see in, which I didn't know at the time. They let me play all sorts of games. And when I learned to talk, they asked me questions, too.

Dr. Arnold Gesell, one of the pioneers in the study of child development, is shown here observing an infant in his laboratory at the Gesell Institute of Child Development.

I was one of hundreds of infants who were studied at the Yale Clinic of Child Development, which Dr. Gesell founded in 1911. I had the good fortune to participate in the most extensive series of research studies on child and infant development in history. Now I am as old as Dr. Gesell was at the time we met. My early relationship with him is very special to me because I, too, am a child development specialist. I now know that those "chats" with my mother were interviews about my behavior at home and school. The playing I did was recorded by motion picture cameras rigged to metal tracks on the dome. The games and questions were a series of tests designed to find out how different I was each time I visited the clinic. This information was collected on all the other children, too, and kept in a case record that grew to considerable size before the end of Dr. Gesell's research.

Using information from his research, Dr. Gesell developed his maturational theory, which concluded that from infancy onward certain behaviors occur at common ages. By observing and studying us, he identified some average behavior sequences. At five months, the majority of us could support most of our body weight; by ten months, we were pulling ourselves to a standing position, and by twelve months, most of us were walking. Gesell described these average sequences of behavior, which he called **developmental norms,** in two famous books: *The First Five Years of Life* (1940) and *The Child from Five to Ten* (1946). He called his method of studying children the biographic-clinical approach. Gesell continued his studies until his death at what is today known as the Gesell Institute of Child Development, named in his honor in 1950.

*The events in this case are true, the narrator is fictional.

PSYCHOANALYTIC THEORY

Freud's Theory.   Sigmund Freud, the founder of psychoanalytic theory, was most interested in personality development. Freud explained behavior in terms of biological drives, instincts, and unconscious motives in interaction with early family experiences. It was his belief that practically everything that happens to us is stored in the unconscious mind. We are not consciously aware of many of the reasons for our behavior—they are hidden from us.

Freud identified three components of the human personality, each having separate functions: the id, superego, and ego. The **id** is the inborn component that contains basic instinctual drives and is pleasure seeking. It is composed of the **libido,** positive, loving, sexual impulses (with "sexual" being defined broadly by Freud to mean pleasure seeking rather than the current, narrow definition of actual sexual activity), and the **thanatos,** destructive, aggressive impulses. The **superego** is similar to what is typically referred to as our conscience, the rules of right and wrong that are primarily learned from and enforced by parents. What the id drives us to do and what the superego permits are often in conflict, a conflict that according to Freud causes **anxiety** (nervousness or tension with no real or logical basis). It is the **ego,** the rational or reasoning part of the personality, that helps to reduce the conflict between the id and the superego by devising socially acceptable ways to satisfy the desires of the id. For example, Nicky's classmate becomes angry with him, feels an urge to hit him (id), but knows that she should not hit others (superego). She resolves her conflict and handles her anger in a socially acceptable way (ego) by saying, "You make me mad, Nicky!" and by pounding her clay. The id, superego, and ego do not usually work at cross-purposes. Instead, they work as a team under the administrative leadership of the ego.

Freud also believed children go through five stages of psychosexual development and that the way they progress through these stages is a major influence on their adult personality. In each stage, the concerns of the child and society are focused on a specific pleasure-giving area of the body.

Anna and Sigmund Freud

Sigmund Freud (1856–1939) was born in Freiburg, Moravia, which is today a part of Czechoslovakia. He lived for more than eighty years in Vienna. In 1938 he left Vienna for London, when the Nazis overran Austria in World War II. Freud was Jewish, a fact that influenced not only his decision to leave Austria but also earlier decisions regarding his career. Scant pay, limited opportunities for Jews to advance academically, and a growing family forced him to abandon his first goal—to be a research scientist—and to establish a private medical practice. Freud's interest in neurology led him to specialize in nervous disorders. His continual cigar smoking may have contributed to his later battle with cancer of the jaw, which tormented him for over fifteen years. Freud is shown here with his daughter, Anna, a famous child psychologist, who continued in the psychoanalytic tradition begun by her father.

1. **Oral stage** (birth to two years). The infant's world centers on the mouth. Excessive gratification during the sucking stage can lead to an unreasonably self-assured adult, while an unpleasant or unsatisfactory sucking period can produce an overly dependent adult. You may know adults who are verbally aggressive or sarcastic, or who overeat, chew their nails, talk a lot, smoke, or chew gum excessively. Freud would say these adults were fixated (stuck) in the oral stage of development.

2. **Anal stage** (two to three years). These are the toilet-training years, attention being focused on the anal area and elimination. People who pass successfully through this stage become flexible, generous, and tidy adults. But harsh toilet training can produce compulsiveness, overemphasis on cleanliness, sanitation, and order, and insistence on excessive rules and rituals. In contrast, a messy, negative, and dominant adult may emerge if parents are too lax in toilet training.

3. **Phallic stage** (four to five years). This is the period when children explore their sexual organs and masturbation often occurs. During this stage the child becomes attracted to the opposite-sex parent and hostile to the same-sex parent. This situation and the conflict it produces are called the **Oedipus complex** in boys and the **Electra complex** in girls. Children who pass successfully through this stage resolve the conflict through **identification** with the same-sex parent. They pattern their behavior after that parent, boys identifying with fathers and girls with mothers. Boys who have difficulty at this stage are said to become timid, passive, and sometimes effeminate adults. Freud believed that women experience the Electra complex throughout life in a modified fashion—wishing they had a penis and wanting to have a male child to replace the lost penis.

4. **Latent stage** (six to twelve years). The libido is not concentrated on any particular body part during this stage. This is a quiet period when sexual feelings lie dormant. At this time, as a result of identification, children learn the rules of their society.

5. **Genital stage** (twelve to eighteen years). The focus again returns to the sexual organs, usually in relation to members of the opposite sex.

Freud placed little emphasis on the latent and genital stages. In fact, he believed the basic adult personality is established by five or six years of age. He suggested that if the oral, anal, and phallic stages are successfully passed through, a healthy adult personality would most likely result and that an unhealthy adult personality would occur if there are problems at these stages. When children experience a traumatic event or too little or too much gratification in one of these three stages, they may become fixated, that is, they may retain aspects of that stage as a permanent part of their personality.

Erik Erikson

Erik H. Erikson was born in 1902 in Frankfurt, Germany. His parents separated soon after his birth, his mother later marrying Erik's pediatrician. The family lived in Karlsruhe, Germany, where entertainment at home often involved his mother's friends from the arts and his stepfather's friends from the world of medicine. Erikson ignored his stepfather's wish that he attend medical school to become a pediatrician. Searching for his "identity" Erikson dropped out of school and left home. He began a career in the arts, a "young man with some talent but nowhere to go (Erikson, 1956, p. 40)." At age twenty-five in Vienna, Erikson was hired to teach art to American children whose parents had come to work with Freud. This experience focused Erikson on children and their development. Anna Freud accepted Erikson for psychoanalytic training and, as Erikson explains, "admitted me to the kind of training that came as close to the role of a children's doctor as one could possibly come without going to medical school (1970, p. 744)." Erikson proceeded to study children in their everyday lives and cultures. He came to the United States and taught at the University of California and the San Francisco Psychoanalytic Institute while continuing his studies and writing. He later taught at the University of Pittsburgh and the Massachusetts Institute of Technology. Eventually, this high school dropout with no formal academic career and only a Montessori teacher's certificate became a professor at Harvard University, retiring from there in 1970.

Erikson's Theory.   Erik Erikson, like Freud, believes that a healthy adult is one who is able to satisfy personal developmental needs and the desires of the self, as well as the demands of society. For example, young adults need to find work that not only suits their own interests and abilities but also meets society's ideas about what is "acceptable."

Figure 1.1 presents Erikson's eight *psychosocial* stages in personality development. You will recall Freud's stages were called *psychosexual*. The "sexual" label reflects Freud's emphasis on sexual or biological pleasure, while the "social" label reflects Erikson's emphasis on social, historical, and cultural influences. Each of

STAGE	APPROXIMATE AGE
Basic trust versus basic mistrust	Birth to 1 year
Autonomy versus shame and doubt	1 to 3 years
Initiative versus guilt	4 to 5 years
Industry versus inferiority	6 to 11 years
Identity versus role confusion	12 to 18 years
Intimacy versus isolation	Young adulthood
Generativity versus self-absorption	Middle adulthood
Integrity versus despair	Older adulthood

Figure 1.1 **Erikson's eight stages of personality development**

Erikson's stages is characterized by a crisis specific to that stage. If the crisis is to be resolved, a particular type of personality development must occur. Erikson says every person continues through all eight stages as long as they live. When people fail to resolve a crisis in a particular stage, they will still go on to the next stage, but they won't be able to completely resolve the crisis in this new stage until they have resolved the crises in the earlier stages. It is possible to ''go back'' at a later time and resolve crises that should have been resolved earlier, but it is more difficult. Each of Erikson's stages will be discussed in greater detail in this book as we study children's social-emotional development.

COGNITIVE-DEVELOPMENTAL THEORY

Piaget's Theory.   Cognitive-developmental theory has been most completely developed and described by Jean Piaget, a Swiss scientist, and Lawrence Kohlberg, an American psychologist. Kohlberg's theory of moral development will be discussed in detail in Chapters 11 and 13. Piaget placed relatively little emphasis on emotions, personality development, and individual differences in children, focusing instead on thought processes or intellectual development in explaining behavior change. He was very clear in pointing out that children think differently from adults, and that they are active, self-motivated participants in their own intellectual development. According to his theory, the ability to think logically follows a pattern of development beginning in the early days of life and systematically changing until young adulthood.

Piaget believed that cognitive skills develop naturally as a child matures and explores the environment. A great deal of children's behavior that we adults call ''play'' is in fact part of the child's important work of exploring people and things

Jean Piaget

Jean Piaget (1896–1980) was born in Neuchatel, Switzerland and raised in Geneva. By age ten, he had published his first scientific paper—on an albino sparrow he observed in a park. At fifteen he had developed such a reputation for his knowledge of mollusks that he was offered, sight unseen, the job as curator of the mollusk section of a Geneva museum. At the age of twenty-one, Piaget received his Ph.D. in natural sciences from the University of Neuchatel. While later studying in France, he was assigned to do intelligence testing with French school children. His fascination with their incorrect rather than their correct answers led Piaget to devote the rest of his life to understanding children's intellectual development. Detailed notes about the mental growth of his own three children—Jacqueline, Lucienne, and Laurent—formed the basis of his early theory building. For more than fifty years, Piaget spent his summers working in a mountain retreat in the Alps. Each autumn, he would come down the mountain with material for books and articles. He died in a Geneva hospital on September 16, 1980.

in the environment (Piaget, 1952a). Such "learning by doing" is necessary if children are to have normal cognitive development and become effective and competent adults.

According to Piaget, people progress through four major periods of cognitive development: sensorimotor (birth to two years), preoperational (two to seven years), concrete operational (seven to eleven years), and formal operational (from eleven or twelve through adulthood). Some children pass through the periods more slowly or more quickly than others. You will read about each of these periods in later chapters when Brad's cognitive development is discussed.

BEHAVIOR THEORY

Like John Locke, who described the mind of a baby as a blank slate inscribed by the environment, behavior theorists think behavior and development are controlled mostly by environmental influences. John B. Watson has been called the "father of behaviorism" because of statements such as this famous quotation:

> Give me a dozen healthy infants, well-informed, and my own special world to bring them up in and I'll guarantee to take any one at random and train him to become any type of specialist I might select: doctor, lawyer, merchant, chief, and yes, even beggar-man and thief, regardless of his talents, penchants, tendencies, abilities, vocations, and race of his ancestors (Watson, 1925, p. 104).

How did Watson propose to produce a specialist of his choice? Given the appropriate environment, a child could *learn* to be either a doctor or a thief.

Three Kinds of Learning. According to behavior theory, we are what we learn. In fact, since learning is emphasized so much by behaviorists, many people call them "learning theorists." Learning theorists believe that learning shapes behavior throughout life but they do not believe that behavior develops in a series of stages, as Freud, Erikson, and Piaget suggest. Instead they have identified three major types of learning: classical conditioning, operant conditioning, and observational learning.

CLASSICAL CONDITIONING. **Classical conditioning** is the simplest type of learning. It emphasizes involuntary reflex behaviors that are inborn in animals and human beings. The learner simply responds automatically to a stimulus in the environment and is then taught to respond in the same way to a different stimulus. Let's see how a nine-month-old infant, Little Albert, learned to fear a white rat through classical conditioning. John B. Watson and Rosalie Rayner (1920) observed that Albert was afraid of a sudden loud noise but not of a furry white rat. When he heard the noise (stimulus), his body automatically jerked, he raised his arms and legs, and he soon began to cry (response). Both the startle reflex and the crying are automatic, unlearned behaviors exhibited by infants in response to sudden loud noises. In behavior terminology the loud noise is called an **unconditioned stimulus** and the startle reflex and crying are **unconditioned responses** to that stimulus.

Watson and Rayner asked a crucial question: Could Albert be conditioned (or learn) to fear and respond to the white rat in the same way he had automatically responded to the loud noise? When the white rat was presented to Albert, he reached for it. As soon as his hand touched the animal, a sudden loud noise was made behind his head. The first time he was startled; the second time he cried. After the loud noise was repeatedly paired with the white rat, Albert began to cry when he saw the white rat alone. In behavior terminology the white rat is called the **conditioned stimulus** and the crying in response to the white rat is called the **conditioned response**. Albert had been conditioned (had learned) to ''fear'' the white rat. He showed the same type of fear of a furry white rabbit and a Santa Claus mask, even though he had not been directly conditioned to fear these things. Such a reaction, Albert's fear of things resembling the rat, is called *generalization*. You will later see that generalization also occurs in the other two types of learning.

This experiment may strike you as unfair to Albert. Certainly it would not be acceptable today under the guidelines established by the American Psychological Association and Society for Research in Child Development. First, it was unethical to teach Albert to fear the rat; second, Watson and Rayner should have planned a way to ''undo'' what they had done. They shouldn't have left Albert terrified of rats. See the Epilogue for a discussion of ethics.

OPERANT CONDITIONING.   Suppose your instructor told you that your entire grade in a course would be determined by your ability to teach a rat to press a bar located at the side of its cage. How would you go about doing this? You might first turn to the writings of B. F. Skinner.

Skinner described a kind of learning called **operant conditioning**, in which behavior is controlled by the consequences—negative or positive—of that behavior. For example, in some of his experiments, Skinner trained rats to press bars that were mounted on the sides of their cages by giving them food pellets as soon

---

Born in 1904, B. F. Skinner was reared in Susquehanna, Pennsylvania, in a warm, stable family setting, the son of a small-town lawyer. As a child he describes himself as ''always building things. I built roller-skate scooters, steerable wagons, sleds, and rafts. . . . I tried again and again to make a glider in which I myself might fly'' (Skinner, 1967, p. 388).

After graduating from Hamilton College with a major in English, Skinner set out to be a novelist. When he failed at creative writing, he decided to study psychology at Harvard, where he received his Ph.D. in 1931. After completing a five-year postdoctoral program at Harvard, he worked for nine years at the University of Minnesota and spent a short time at Indiana University before returning to Harvard, where he remained on the faculty until his retirement. Today he continues his lecturing and writing.

B. F. Skinner

as they pressed the bar. First, the rat had to operate or act freely on something in the environment (the rat pressed the bar). Second, the rat was given an immediate reward when it did what Skinner wanted (the rat received a food pellet). The next time you go to the circus, carefully watch the animals and their trainers. Their amusing behaviors have been learned through the same operant conditioning process used by Skinner to teach his rats to press bars. What do rats pressing bars and circus chimps riding bicycles have to do with children? Children also learn much of their behavior through methods used in operant conditioning, especially reinforcement and punishment.

Reinforcement is defined as any stimulus that increases the likelihood that a behavior will be repeated. Reinforcement can be positive or negative. A **positive reinforcement** is any consequence that is pleasurable or satisfying to the subject and serves to increase the behavior it follows. Skinner's rats continued to press the bars because the consequence, receiving food pellets, was positive. **Negative reinforcement** occurs when the removal or avoidance of some aversive (unpleasant) stimulus serves to increase the behavior it follows. Suppose you get into your new car, sit in the driver's seat, and hear a loud, buzzing noise. Since you probably find this noise unpleasant, you buckle your seat belt so that the buzzing will stop. Because the buzzing is removed when your seat belt is fastened, you will probably fasten your seat belt more often in the future. Your seat-belt-fastening behavior has been increased by the removal of an aversive stimulus—the loud, buzzing noise.

Skinner and others have also found that punishment affects behavior (learning). By **punishment** we mean any stimulus that serves to decrease the behavior it follows. The operant conditioning terms of punishment and negative reinforcement are often confused. In punishment, something unpleasant is *administered* or something pleasant is taken away in order to discourage or decrease a particular behavior. In negative reinforcement, something unpleasant is *removed* in order to encourage or increase the rate of a particular behavior.

Skinner emphasizes the use of positive reinforcers instead of punishment because of the negative effects of punishment. He believes that positive reinforcers are more effective in controlling behavior and that punishment should be avoided whenever possible.

Ignoring behavior also affects future behavior. When a behavior is ignored, it tends first to increase and then to decrease in frequency. If Nicky's teachers and everyone else ignored, that is, refused to respond in *any* way to, Nicky's "dirty language," you would expect the language to first increase and then decrease in frequency. Nicky is used to getting attention for this language. When his language is ignored, he just uses more bad words to try to get the attention he received in the past. When he learns that there will be no attention, he stops.

OBSERVATIONAL LEARNING.   You've probably heard parents talk about how important it is to "set a good example" in front of children, or as a social scientist would say, to "model appropriate behavior" for children. Both phrases mean the

Sometimes parents ignore appropriate and reinforce inappropriate behaviors of children.

same thing. Albert Bandura, an American psychologist, recognizes the importance of learning through classical and operant conditioning, but he believes most learning occurs through observation of parents, peers, and other individuals in a person's social world. Because Bandura and his colleagues see a person's social world as being so influential in learning, they are called *social learning theorists*. In **observational learning** (also called learning through **modeling** or **imitation**), we copy behavior that has been observed without receiving direct rewards or punishment—for example, when a child "pretends" to be a doctor after a visit to the doctor's office, after watching another child play doctor, or after seeing a doctor on television. Throughout their childhood, children remember information about many behaviors they have observed without actually engaging in these behaviors. But if they have observed others receiving rewards for a behavior, they are more likely to copy that behavior. Children are also more likely to copy the behavior of significant people in their lives and people they admire, rather than "unimportant" people or people they fear.

BIOLOGICAL THEORY

Ethology.   Suppose we want to know about the effects of parental absence on the development of children, or how attachments are formed between babies and parents. It would be cruel (not to mention unethical and unlawful) to deliberately deprive a group of babies of their parents' love during their first few days of life just so we could see what would happen. And naturally occurring cases of child deprivation are not always at our fingertips. One science that has helped solve such research problems is **ethology**, the study of animals and humans in their natural environments. Ethologists are especially interested in determining which animal and human behaviors are biologically based (influenced by heredity), and which are learned (influenced by the environment).

The well-known ethologist Konrad Lorenz applied the term **imprinting** to instinctual early learning that occurs during **critical** or **sensitive periods** when environmental influences have their greatest effects on development. An example of imprinting would be how newborn ducklings will automatically follow the first moving object they see. Perhaps you've seen a row of ducks, mother in front, four or five ducklings behind, walking toward a pond and staying in their row during an afternoon swim. But have you ever seen a row of ducklings following a man (see Fig. 1.2)? Lorenz found that ducklings can imprint on people or any moving object. Once imprinting on another object occurs, it is useless to try to get the baby duckling to follow its natural mother.

Lorenz theorizes that human infants, ducklings, and babies of all species are born with certain **fixed action patterns,** biologically determined behaviors commonly called **instincts**. Ethologists believe these fixed behaviors have been built into our hereditary makeup because of their survival value. It seems that many things in the natural environment, such as spiders, snakes, and lightning, that were feared by our prehistoric ancestors, continue to cause the most fear in people today. Fears of spiders, snakes, and lightning are not inborn, but some ethologists believe that humans are biologically prepared to learn to fear some things more than others (Scarf, 1974). Little Albert learned to show extreme fear of the white rat—but ethologists doubt Albert could have been conditioned to fear a pair of eyeglasses or a book. Ducklings who follow their mother will be more likely to survive and reproduce than ducklings who don't have the "following response." Fixed action patterns are biologically ready to occur as soon as contact is made with the proper stimulus in the environment. If hook-ups are not made with the proper stimulus within the critical period, the fixed action patterns may cease to operate. If contact is made with a different stimulus, unexpected hook-ups may occur, such as ducklings following a human rather than the mother duck.

The ethological theory of imprinting has caused researchers to consider the critical periods concept when studying attachment and deprivation in children. Bowlby (1958), an English ethologist, and Klaus and Kennell (1976), American pediatricians, believe there is a critical period early in life when the potential for parent-child attachment is highest. Bowlby believes that if children are deprived of their parents during this critical period, they will have difficulty in forming in-

Figure 1.2
Imprinting. Baby ducklings imprinted on Konrad Lorenz and followed him as if he were their mother.

timate and lasting parent-child relationships. Klaus and Kennell say the first ninety minutes after birth is an optimum period for attachment between parent and infant. Ethologists have extensively studied parent-infant "bonding" and attachment processes in animals and humans, which we will discuss later.

Sociobiology.   **Sociobiology** is "the systematic study of the biological basis for all social behavior" (Wilson, 1975, p. 4). Sociobiologist Edward O. Wilson, a professor at Harvard University, believes that a wide variety of human social behaviors, including sex-role differences, aggression, and even religion, are strongly influenced by heredity. To illustrate, sociobiologists claim that the reason we help and care for others is not because we learned these behaviors but because the tendency to help those in need is carried in our genes, a type of insurance policy that enables our species to survive (Dawkins, 1976). This theory has much in common with ethology, and both views run counter to the behavior theorists' notion that environment is the primary determinant of behavior. We will talk more about sociobiology in Chapter 2.

HUMANISTIC THEORY

As we explained earlier, Rousseau believed that children are born with a natural goodness and are capable of self-direction. These beliefs characterize the thinking of humanists and the five major assumptions they share:

1. People are free agents, capable of determining personal growth and development. They are influenced by, but not at the mercy of, biological urges, unconscious thoughts and feelings, or events in the environment.

33

2. People are thinkers and active planners. Their ability to reason enables them to choose what is best for themselves.

3. All people do not fit into the same "average" mold. Each person is unique.

4. Positive characteristics such as goodness, normality, health, and excellence should be the focus of a science of human development. (This is in direct opposition to the psychoanalytic emphasis on depression, abnormality, and sickness.)

5. People are motivated to develop their unique inner potential to its fullest (to become self-actualized).

Humanists ask such questions as "What are humans capable of becoming?" and "How can human beings develop to their fullest potential?" In this section we will discuss Abraham Maslow's theory of humanism since he is the most closely connected with the development of the theory.

Maslow's Theory.   Abraham Maslow, the founder of humanistic theory, was fascinated by psychoanalytic theory early in his career and was convinced that Freud had the answers to human behavior. But when Watson introduced behavior theory in the early part of the century, Maslow switched his views:

> I had discovered J. B. Watson and I was sold on behaviorism. It was an explosion of excitement for me. . . . Bertha [Maslow's wife] came to pick me up and I was dancing down Fifth Avenue with exuberance; I embarrassed her, but I was so excited about Watson's program. It was beautiful. (Maslow, 1968, p. 37).

At that time, behaviorists were in their laboratories trying to better understand human behavior by studying how rats learn.

When Maslow's first child was born, he saw huge, gaping holes in psychology. He felt that the psychoanalytic view of children driven by biological urges and filled with conflicts did not describe his infant. When he looked at his baby,

Abraham Maslow

Abraham Maslow (1908–1970) was born in Brooklyn, New York, to Russian-Jewish immigrants. The son of a barrel maker, Maslow was a shy young man, a fact that he attributed to the anti-Semitic attitudes experienced during his childhood years. He retreated from these unpleasant times through his hunger for knowledge. He grew up reading about the American Revolution and the lives of famous patriots like Thomas Jefferson, George Washington, and Abraham Lincoln. His interests in democracy are reflected in his theory: Give people the freedom to make decisions about their lives and provide a society for the development of human potential. Maslow, the shy young boy, grew into Maslow, the brilliant but shy theorist. Maslow attended classes at City College of New York and Cornell University, but did not become interested in academics until he took a course in psychology at the University of Wisconsin, where he ultimately earned a degree in psychology. After receiving his Ph.D., Maslow taught at Brooklyn College and Brandeis University.

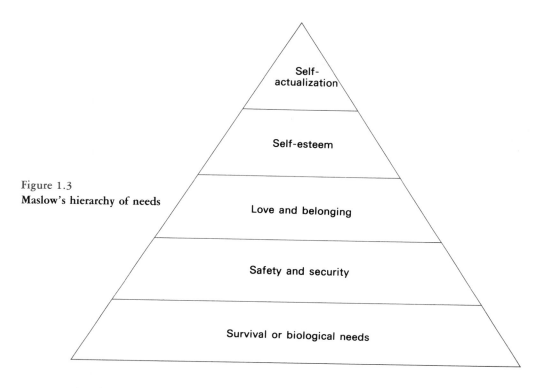

Figure 1.3
Maslow's hierarchy of needs

he observed more than just an organism who responded automatically to environmental stimuli. Maslow thought psychology had become too cold and objective. In his view, behaviorists stressed rigorous scientific studies so much and were so concerned with small details of behavior that they ignored the wholeness of the human being.

To fill these gaps, Maslow coined the term ''the third force,'' which referred to the impact on psychology of the humanistic movement, officially begun in 1962 when the Association for Humanistic Psychology was established. The third force was a reaction against the other two theoretical views or forces dominating the field: psychoanalytic theory and behavior theory. Maslow combined some parts of the first and second forces but with a new focus on uniqueness and positiveness. The third force was Maslow's way of putting the human element back into psychology.

According to Maslow, all individuals are motivated to satisfy five levels of needs (see Fig. 1.3). The first level includes biological necessities for survival—food, air, water, sex, and the like. Only when these needs are adequately met can we progress to the next level, the need for safety and security. We cannot expect a child to spend the day in self-fulfilling activities such as drawing, developing readiness skills in reading, or forming close peer relationships if the basic needs of hunger and security are not met. When our survival and our safety and security needs are met, we can then progress to meeting our needs for love and belonging, self-esteem, and **self-actualization,** which is the development of an individual's unique inner potential to its fullest. By self-actualizing, we become more healthy, autonomous, creative. We are better problem solvers, more accepting of ourselves and others, and more successful in building satisfying interpersonal relationships and doing something we really believe in (Maslow, 1968). But the self-actualization level is difficult to reach and, in fact, one that most people never reach. Even those who do achieve self-actualization cannot remain at that level all the time because self-actualization is a process, not a final state.

The Whole Child: A Systems Approach

In attempting to understand child behavior and development, researchers and theorists often consider the physical, cognitive, social, and emotional parts of the child separately and study children in laboratory settings, apart from their real-life environments and relationships (Bronfenbrenner, 1977a; 1979). A systems approach helps us see how all the aspects fit together.

Suppose you wanted to know how the cardiovascular (circulatory) system works. How would you study it? You might go to a medical laboratory, locate a heart and the attached blood vessels then carefully dissect and study them. In this way you would learn something about the basic structure of the cardiovascular system, that the heart has four chambers and a number of valves. But you would still not know how these chambers and valves work because the heart would not be functioning. Only by studying the cardiovascular system while it is functioning in a living person would you see how the chambers and valves pump blood through the body. But if you were studying the cardiovascular system by itself, you still could not completely understand how this system works. What happens to the heart while you are running? You can't answer this question without studying the cardiovascular system in relationship with the whole body system. While running, the muscles of your body require more oxygen than they do at rest and your heart beats faster to supply the oxygen. This example illustrates that you cannot really understand the cardiovascular system without studying how it and all its parts function in relation to the whole body system.

A **system** is defined as a set of parts (**subsystems**) and the interactions or relationships among those parts. You are a system composed of all your subsystems. As a psychological system, you have physical, cognitive, social, and emotional subsystems. A biologist would think of you as a biological system containing subsystems of skin, skeleton, muscles, nerves, and so on.

Even though you can be thought of as a biological or a psychological system, you can also be thought of as a *subsystem* of the larger social system. For instance, you are also a subsystem of your family. Your family is, in turn, a subsystem of society. Other societal subsystems you may belong to are churches, schools, government, and so forth.

A systems approach compels us to consider the whole child in relationship to people, such as family and friends, and institutions, such as churches and schools. Because the roles of these people and institutions are unique in each child's development, we cannot understand a child until we look at the youngster's relationships within family, school, society, and the rest of the physical environment.

The lives of children whose parents hold two or more jobs, commute long distances, move frequently, or have a high economic status will be different from those children whose parents usually stay home, live in a single home for long periods of time, or have a low income. The family makeup—one versus two parents, stepparents, birth order, siblings, grandparents—are important influences on development and relationships. Schools affect children directly (teaching them academic skills needed later in adult jobs) and indirectly (influencing their parents and the community). A school might offer classes to teach parents how to help their children with math problems, or the community might be made aware of the importance of funding education. Governments make and enforce legislation, such as child labor laws, and develop welfare systems and other policies that affect the lives of children.

Physical surroundings in the home, school, and community are also important. Colors, temperature, space, room arrangement, available food, and cigarette smoke can affect a child's behavior and development (Perkins, 1979). Pediatricians tell parents that if they smoke, their children will be more likely to have respiratory infections than children whose parents don't smoke. Air pollution, the availability of parks, geographic location, climate, quality of medical care, traffic patterns, and the need for transportation are important community influences. Researchers have suggested, for example, that noise in the community can affect children's health and behavior in the classroom (Cohen et. al., 1980).

INTERACTION AMONG SYSTEMS

The physical, cognitive, social, and emotional subsystems of a person are constantly interacting (or working together) to influence behavior and development. Consequently, dividing children into these subsystems in order to study them is an artificial separation. Just as we cannot fully understand the cardiovascular system without considering the *whole* body system, we cannot fully understand the child's behavior, development, and relationships without considering the *whole* child system. To illustrate, suppose Eve and her third-grade classmates are taking their annual achievement tests. If Eve is *physically* tired or hungry during the test, she might not be able to solve problems (*perform cognitively*) as well as she could if her physical needs were met. Poor test (cognitive) performance might cause her to feel *emotionally* upset. She might express her emotions by yelling at her friend Caroline or by withdrawing and refusing to talk about the test with the gang (*social*).

Larger systems also influence Eve's test performance. If her parents and her teacher (*family and school*) put excessive pressure on her to make a high score (as

A Systems Approach: The Whole Child

The cognitive system

The physical system

The social system

The emotional system

A Systems Approach: The Larger Systems

The physical environment

The school system

The social system

The peer group

The family system

well-meaning adults sometimes do), she could become overly anxious and do poorly on the test. A too cold or too hot testing room or one polluted by aircraft noise (*physical surroundings*) could result in poor test performance.

We have organized the chapters of this book according to subsystems in the child—physical, cognitive, social, and emotional—but throughout the book we will discuss the subsystems together with the larger systems of family and society. We will also consider how these systems interact to affect children's behavior, development, and relationships.

Summary

1.   Children have been viewed throughout history as miniature adults, as creatures born in sin needing severe discipline. The further back in history we go, the more we find that children were likely to be abused, abandoned, beaten, terrorized, and sexually molested, and even killed.

2.   The nature-nurture controversy presents opposing explanations of behavior and development. One argument claims that inherited traits (nature) are the most important influences on behavior and development; the other claims that the environment (nurture) is the most important. Today, most people agree that heredity and environment interact in influencing children's development and behavior.

3.   Researchers of child development use scientific studies to describe children's growth and activities and to attempt to supply reasons for their behavior.

4.   Sigmund Freud's psychoanalytic stages of development explain personality development in terms of biological factors interacting with early family experiences. Erik Erikson's psychoanalytic theory, which was influenced by Freud's ideas, stresses the psychosocial stages of development that humans pass through from birth to death. Jean Piaget's theory suggests that cognitive growth takes place as individuals pass through four periods of development. Behavior theory emphasizes the environment as it influences behavior and development through three types of learning: classical conditioning, operant conditioning, and observational learning. Ethology is a biological view of development that is concerned with the behaviors of human beings and other animals in their natural environments. Sociobiology is the systematic study of the biological basis for all social behavior. Humanistic theory stresses free will and is concerned with the positive growth of individuals in becoming more healthy, creative, and fully developed.

5.   The systems approach provides a framework for thinking about the whole child at once. This holistic approach is particularly useful in understanding the behavior and development of children since all subsystems are examined. The systems approach also allows us to view the child in interaction with the larger systems of family, society, and physical surroundings.

Empathetic Activities

- What feelings did you have as you read "Babies in the Mill"? How do you think the children felt? How did their parents and employers feel?

- Watson and Skinner believed that behavior theory can be used to make our society anything we want it to be. Can we really use learning to create any society we want? If so, what kind of society do you think most people would choose? How would you use behavior theory to change society?

- Make arrangements to observe a preschool or elementary school teacher in the classroom. Note the teacher's use of positive reinforcement and punishment. Before you begin, carefully define both terms by listing specific behaviors. For example, positive reinforcement might be defined as the teacher smiling at a child, making positive comments, joining in the child's play, or giving a reward such as a star, check mark, or extra play time. Punishment might be defined as making unfavorable comments, spanking or isolating the child, or taking away privileges such as play time. Count the number of times the teacher uses each example of positive reinforcement and punishment.

- Using the information presented in the section on behavior theory and the three kinds of learning, explain Nicky's unruly behavior.

- Begin a reference notebook for your personal use containing information about child development. Include cases and articles from newspapers, magazines, television, movies, and filmstrips. Establish a section that will include all the information you can find on the *Whole Child*.

- How do the parent-child relationships of today differ from those of the past? Base your answers on the information presented in the historical perspective section of this chapter.

Related Readings

Crain, William C. *Theories of development: Concepts and applications.* Englewood Cliffs, N.J.: Prentice-Hall, 1980. An in-depth treatment of theories discussed in this chapter. Emphasis on basic concepts and application makes this an excellent and relevant resource. Easy and interesting to read, an unusual combination.

Evans, Richard I. *Dialogue with Erik Erikson.* New York: E. P. Dutton, 1969. Erik Erikson answers questions about his theory of psychoanalysis. Interesting and understandable.

Milhollen, Frank, and Forisha, Bill E. *From Skinner to Rogers: Contrasting approaches to education.* Lincoln, Nebr.: Professional Educators Publications, 1972. Implications of the theories of Skinner and Rogers for classroom teaching.

Piers, Maria W. *Infanticide.* New York: W. W. Norton, 1978. A widely acclaimed work that has been translated into many languages. Traces the nature and incidence of the killing of infants.

Rogers, Carl R. *Freedom to learn.* Columbus, Ohio: Charles E. Merrill, 1969. An interesting application of the humanistic approach to the classroom.

Salkind, Neil. *Theories of human development.* New York: D. Van Nostrand, 1981. An overview of the major theories and theorists of human development. A good reference for students in nursing, education, home economics, and psychology who are looking for a clear, straightforward presentation.

II The Importance of a Good Beginning

The Prenatal Period (conception and birth)

The Neonatal Period (the first four weeks of life)

Infancy (the first year of life)

2 Conception and Prenatal Development

The Case of the Expectant Parent

Dear Sis,

Thanks for your letter. I know I didn't make much sense when I called to tell you about my pregnancy. I still feel ambivalent at times about having the baby even though Bill and I thought and planned for a long time before we made our decision. We considered not having children at all. We worried about the total commitment a baby will take—and for so many years. Bill and I have a good relationship now, but the baby will take time away from us as a couple. And I worried about the effect a baby would have on my career. You know how I love my job as a reporter on the newspaper. We worried about money too. Let's face it, children are a tremendous added expense.

I don't want you to think I'm selfish. I'm already beginning to feel a strong commitment to be a good parent. As soon as we found out for sure I was pregnant, Bill and I checked out an armload of books on conception and prenatal development and parenting from the library.

I do worry that the baby won't be normal. I don't think I could cope if anything goes wrong. I have done everything I know to be sure. I eat the right food and get exercise and rest. I'm not drinking or smoking. I wonder if there is any way to tell whether the baby will be normal and healthy?

You asked how I feel. Sometimes I feel sick in the mornings, but mostly I feel great. The baby will be born in about six more months. One part of me can't wait and the other part wants to call the whole thing off!

Love,
Doreen

Introduction

Conception and prenatal development are controlled by hereditary factors and affected by environmental influences, a subject we will discuss in later sections. But first let's look at how Doreen and Bill's baby is growing and developing during conception and prenatal development and how Doreen and Bill are being affected by the pregnancy, too. Their concerns and shifting feelings are typical of many expectant parents.

Conception

In one of her books on childbirth, Doreen read about Clarence Gray, a West Virginian in his early sixties better known in his community as "Catfish, man of the woods." Catfish has spent his entire life on the banks of the Ohio River where he has used his knowledge of folk medicine, handed down from his great-great-grandfather, to treat people in his community (Green, 1978). The following list contains some of Catfish's ideas about conception:

- Women can become pregnant only during the few hours of a heat cycle that occurs midway between menstrual periods.
- A woman feels hot from head to toe when she is in her heat cycle.
- If women do have intercourse during their heat cycle, petroleum jelly, inserted into the vagina, will cause the sperm to slide right back out of the womb!
- A seed formed in a woman's right ovary produces a female child; a seed for a male child is produced in the left ovary.

Doreen quickly learned that modern-day scientists look upon such theories as pure folklore. And couples who try Catfish's birth control technique with petroleum jelly may well have to agree since conception is the likely result! As she continued her reading, Doreen became fascinated by the story of what took place in her body during conception and prenatal development.

The miracle of Doreen and Bill's baby began at the moment of **conception,** or **fertilization,** when a single **sperm** penetrated a single **ovum,** or egg, to form a **zygote** (see Fig. 2.1).

Figure 2.1
Fertilization. Photo of a sperm penetrating an egg, taken with a scanning electron microscope.

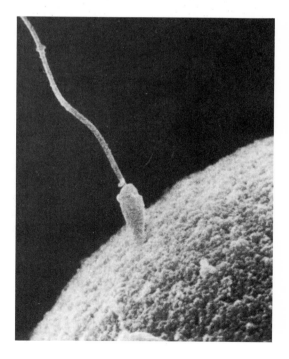

During **ovulation,** a single ovum (or sometimes more than one) is expelled from one of a woman's two ovaries and begins its one or two day journey through a **fallopian tube** toward the uterus or womb (see Fig. 2.2). Ovulation occurs about midway through a woman's menstrual cycle (around the fourteenth day) and usually goes unnoticed—a woman does not feel hot from head to toe! A mature ovum, which is about one-fourth the size of the period at the end of this sentence, is the largest cell in the human body, containing enough food to sustain a new life for almost two weeks after an egg is fertilized.

The sperm cell is the tiniest cell in the human body. Enough sperm to repopulate the entire world would fit into a container the size of an aspirin tablet. The testes of a healthy male produce several hundred million sperm cells each day. When sperm cells are ejected during sexual intercourse, millions of them land directly at the entrance to the cervix. A sperm can journey through the cervix and the uterus to join the ovum in one of the fallopian tubes in about ninety minutes.

Once the ovum is produced, it must be fertilized within one or two days or it will disintegrate. If a woman is sexually active without an effective birth control method during ovulation or the two or three days before ovulation, pregnancy is likely to occur. The reason for this is that sperm can stay alive and vigorous for two

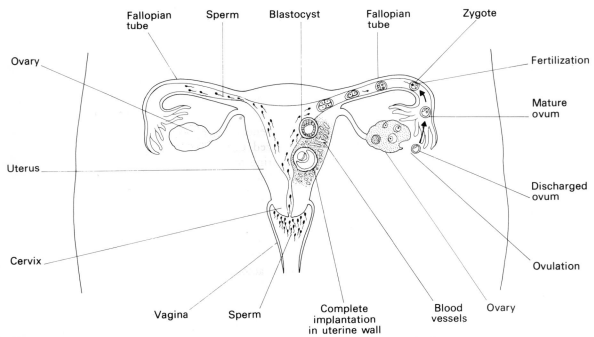

Figure 2.2 Conception. Ovulation, fertilization, and implantation of a human egg in the female reproductive system.

or three days or even longer. Consequently, during each monthly menstrual cycle there is a total of four or five days around the time of ovulation when conception can occur. Although conception usually occurs as a result of sexual intercourse it can now also occur in a test tube!

❖ Spotlight 2.1: Test Tube Baby

If Babygirl Brown, when she grows up, is ever curious about the when and how of her conception, she won't have to ask her parents. She can read all about it in a history book.

Nov. 10, 1977. In a petri dish—or, more popularly, a test tube.

Her mother, Lesley Brown, lay on an operating room bed, under anesthesia, in a small institution quaintly named Dr. Kershaw's Cottage Hospital, outside Oldham, England. Her father, Gilbert, waited in an adjoining laboratory.

Two doctors, gynecologist Patrick C. Steptoe and physiologist Robert G. Edwards, hovered between the two as chaperones in surgical masks.

They started with Mrs. Brown, infertile in ten years of marriage because of a blockage in her Fallopian tubes—a condition she shared with an estimated thirty-five percent of women unable to bear children.

By Nov. 10, fertility hormones, like those responsible for the rash of multiple births of recent years, had had their desired effect. Mrs. Brown's ovaries contained numerous mature eggs.

To get at them, the silver-haired Dr. Steptoe utilized an optical technique he pioneered, laparoscopy. A long, thin telescopic device inserted through an incision near Mrs. Brown's navel allowed Dr. Steptoe to view the inside from outside while he drew eggs from the ovary with a hollow needle.

The eggs were put aside in a small glass dish of salts, nutrients, and blood serum.

The doctors turned to her husband. His sperm, obtained by masturbation, had to be capacitated, or primed for fertilization, in a salt solution.

Then quickly so neither the eggs nor the sperm would die, they were added to the dish with the eggs.

For the mysterious ingredients of life to divide and create a cluster of cells, called a blastocyst, from which an embryo might develop, conditions had to be just right. It had been the intricacies of this step that had eluded researchers for decades.

For two days, the petri dish was maintained in a rigidly controlled, contaminant-free environment in the lab's incubator.

Cambridge University's Dr. Edwards was in charge for the next crucial step—implantation. The doctors had reported sixty previous efforts without success beyond nine weeks.

Mrs. Brown, having received more hormone treatments to prepare her uterine lining to accept a fertilized egg, returned to the Cottage Hospital operating room.

The egg-sperm combination—no larger than a pencil point—was picked out of its culture with a hollow tube and reinserted into her reproductive tract.

From then, nothing was a scientific certainty. From then, pregnancy would follow or would not follow according to the laws of nature.

"It's a Girl!" by John Murche, *New York Post,* July 26, 1978. Reprinted by permission of the *New York Post.* © 1978, New York Post Corporation.

When the sperm penetrates the egg, an immediate chemical change occurs in the wall of the egg and a barrier is formed that prevents other sperm from entering. The newly formed zygote divides into two identical cells and continues to the uterus. Sometimes one zygote splits into two identical zygotes that develop into two children who have exactly the same heredity—**identical** or **monozygotic twins.** Identical twins are always the same sex because they originate from the same zygote. But if two eggs are released during ovulation and are fertilized by two different sperm, two different zygotes, which may or may not be the same sex, will be formed—the result being **fraternal** or **dizygotic twins.** Because such twins are formed by different zygotes, their heredity is as similar or different as that of any other brothers and sisters.

Prenatal Development

PERIODS OF GESTATION

Development, from conception to the much awaited birth, is called the **gestation period.** It requires about 266 days or nine calendar months and can be divided into three periods: the *ovum,* the *embryo,* and the *fetus.*

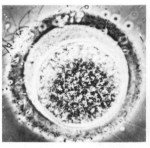
Ovum at the moment of fertilization.

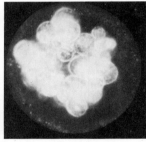
Ovum three and a half days after fertilization

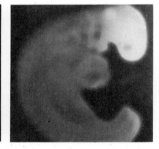
Embryo at twenty-eight days.

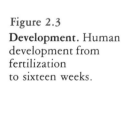
Figure 2.3
Development. Human development from fertilization to sixteen weeks.

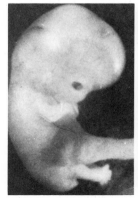
Embryo at eight weeks.

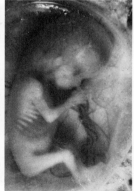
Fetus at fourteen weeks.

Fetus at sixteen weeks.

The Ovum (conception to second week). The cells of the zygote continue to divide rapidly as it moves through the fallopian tube toward the uterus—a journey requiring several days. At this stage the zygote is transformed into a **blastocyst**—a fluid-filled, bubble-like ball about the size of a pinhead. During the journey to the uterus, the rapidly dividing cells of the blastocyst begin to differentiate, to develop into tissues that will serve different functions. Cells from one part of the blastocyst will develop into the amniotic sac, placenta, and umbilical cord —organs that provide protection and nourishment during prenatal development; cells from another part will develop into the baby itself.

While the blastocyst journeys to the uterus, the mother's menstrual cycle proceeds as usual. The uterine wall is thickened with blood in preparation for the blastocyst. When it enters the uterus, the blastocyst will contain about two hundred cells. It will float freely for a few days and then begin to implant, or attach itself to the uterine wall. Before implantation, the independent, free-floating blastocyst is nourished by the nutrients in the egg. After implantation, it burrows itself among the blood vessels of the uterine wall and begins to draw nourishment directly from the mother. When implantation is completed—at about ten to fourteen days after conception—the blastocyst is called an **embryo**. About two days following implantation, the mother's menstrual period will be due, but it will be prevented from coming by a hormone produced by the tiny, new embryo.

The Embryo (second week to end of second month). Cells continue to differentiate rapidly during the embryonic period. The amniotic sac, placenta, and umbilical cord develop completely in this period and sustain the embryo's life. Enough cells develop by the end of this period to make the tiny embryo recognizably human.

The **amniotic sac** surrounds the embryo like a watertight balloon filled with fluid. It provides moisture and protection from injury and also helps maintain a warm and constant temperature.

The disk-shaped **placenta** begins to develop during the second and third weeks of prenatal development, and by the twenty-seventh day after conception, it has started to function. A remarkable organ, the placenta does the work of the unborn infant's lungs, kidneys, intestines, liver, and hormone-producing glands. The embryo is now quite dependent on the mother for oxygen and for such nutrients as sugars, fats, and certain proteins. Waste products such as carbon dioxide from the embryo pass through the placenta into the mother's blood system. The placenta also produces hormones essential to maintain pregnancy, prepare the breasts for milk production, and stimulate uterine contractions at the time of birth.

The **umbilical cord**—the lifeline of the unborn baby—has two arteries that carry blood containing waste matter from the embryo to the placenta, and one vein that carries blood containing such things as oxygen and nutrients from the placenta to the embryo. Blood from the mother's arteries flows into the maternal side of the placenta, and blood from the embryo flows into the other side through the umbilical cord. The mother's blood does not mix with blood from her baby during pregnancy. Instead, the placenta acts as a partial barrier. Exchanges of oxy-

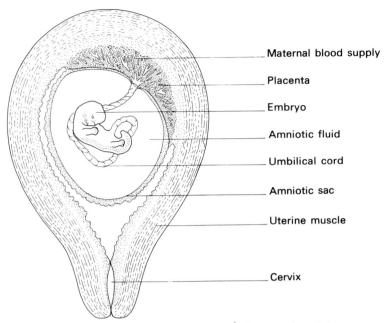

Maternal blood supply

Placenta

Embryo

Amniotic fluid

Umbilical cord

Amniotic sac

Uterine muscle

Cervix

Figure 2.4 **Life-support systems for the embryo.** Cross-section of the uterus showing those structures in the mother's body designed to support the development of the embryo and the fetus.

gen, nutrients, and waste occur through thin, permeable cell membranes that act like very fine screens. Some things are permitted to go through, while relatively large structures, such as blood cells, are blocked. We once thought that the placenta completely prevented harmful agents from reaching the unborn baby, but research has now proved that this is not so. As we will see, many things, such as viruses, nicotine, alcohol, caffeine, and drugs, can cross the placental barrier and can harm the developing baby.

By the fourth week after conception the embryo is about a quarter of an inch long. Despite its minute size, the one-month-old embryo contains the beginning of all the vital organs and features of an adult—from a well established nervous system to a primitive mouth. The thickened cell mass that once formed the original blastocyst has developed into three layers: the ectoderm, the mesoderm, and the endoderm. The ectoderm, or outer layer, will later become various outer layers of the body—the skin, hair, nails, parts of the teeth, skin glands, sensory cells, and the nervous system. The mesoderm, or middle layer, will become the muscular, skeletal, and circulatory systems, and the excretory organs. The endoderm, or inner layer, will become the lining of the stomach and intestines, the salivary and thyroid glands, and the pancreas, trachea, lungs, and liver. During this period the embryo's development proceeds with incredible speed. On the twenty-fourth day after fertilization, the embryo has no arms or legs. By the twenty-sixth day, knob-shaped arm buds appear. Two days later, each knob has developed into an arm. Within three more days, each arm has developed a sort of paw that will eventually become a hand.

At the beginning of the second month of development, only two weeks after the mother's first missed period, the unborn baby, who is no bigger than a pea, has a beating heart. The brain is growing rapidly at this time. Six weeks after fertilization a skeleton is formed but at this point is made exclusively of cartilage. By the end of the second month, bone cells have started to develop. The embryo is about one and a half to two inches long and weighs about two thirds of an ounce.

The Fetus (third month until birth). At the beginning of the third month of prenatal development, the developing baby is called a **fetus.** The mother has missed a second period and is probably certain she is pregnant. Her uterus is just beginning to stretch in size. Since conception, her unborn baby has grown 240 times in length (to three inches) and one million times in weight (to one ounce). Its arms are long enough to touch its face and it already has fingerprints. The two halves of the roof of the baby's mouth will fuse during this month, and the whole face will begin to look more human. The fetus can open its mouth, and inhale and exhale. Once the ability to swallow appears, it will begin to drink **amniotic fluid,** the liquid that fills the amniotic sac, eventually drinking several pints every day.

The graceful, weightless movements of the fetus attached to the umbilical cord resemble the movements of an astronaut in space—a resemblance that together with fetal swimming, twisting, turning, and somersaulting has inspired some people to call the fetus an intranaut (Apgar and Beck, 1972)! This liquid environment allows the fetus to move about and, more importantly, to exercise its muscles. But no matter how much the fetus moves, its body is still too little and its movements too gentle for the mother to feel.

Growth during the fourth month is rapid. The fetus grows to be eight to ten inches in length or about one half of its length at birth. Nails appear on fingers, and hair grows in the place where eyebrows will be. Bone cells grow rapidly at this time, causing **ossification,** the hardening of cartilage into bone. The four-month-old fetus is now even capable of sucking its thumb!

At the beginning of the fourth month, Doreen sent a note to her sister:

Dear Sis,

I tried to reach you on the phone today, but you weren't in. I'm so excited! I just got back from the doctor's office. I heard the baby's heart for the first time! Bill went with me and I think he was even more thrilled than I was. I've begun to realize that this child soon will be a real person—separate from me. It seems like a miracle. The doctor says that by the end of the month Bill will be able to hear the baby's heartbeat without a stethoscope!

Love,
Doreen

The baby's tiny heart pumps blood through the developing circulatory system and through the umbilical cord into the placenta at a rate of four miles per hour. The blood makes this trip and returns to the infant's body in about thirty seconds. It flows through the two arteries passing from the heart to the umbilical cord. This continual pumping keeps the umbilical cord rigid, much like a garden hose might be when you water your garden.

Rapid growth in size and refinement of structures characterizes the fifth and sixth months of pregnancy. The fetus grows about another two inches in the fifth month and two or three more inches during the sixth month. The nervous and respiratory systems are developing rapidly but are not mature enough to keep the baby alive outside the mother's body. Skin thickens and becomes covered by fine, downy hair called **lanugo**. Skin glands start to secrete an oily substance that combines with the dead outer skin cells to form **vernix,** a waxy, waterproof cream that coats the fetus during the last months of pregnancy and is visible at birth. Fingernails and toenails harden and grow rapidly. In fact, Doreen and Bill's baby had fingernails so long they had to be cut immediately after birth to prevent the baby from scratching itself. The developing fetus can now hiccup, and it can also hear sounds. Doreen noticed that her baby was startled by the loud noise when she dropped an armload of pots and pans.

Every fetus works out a favorite position and makes adjustments to stay in that position. Doreen's mother said the baby would be a girl since Doreen was carrying it high—a popular myth that Doreen and Bill learned there is no truth to.

By about the seventh month, Bill can see a bump in Doreen's abdomen when a tiny fist, foot, or head moves, and he can even feel the fetus shifting around. Doreen's baby is rocked and lulled while she moves about, and just when she lies down for some much-needed rest, the baby begins to do its own exercises. A friend said that because Doreen's baby was active, it would be a boy. But evidence does not support the myth that boys are more active than girls during prenatal development.

During the last months of pregnancy, **antibodies** produced by the mother pass through the placental barrier. These antibodies attack disease and other foreign agents and provide the newborn infant with some immunity to disease. This is also a time for rapid gains in weight and height. Seven months after conception, the fetus weighs about four pounds and is about sixteen inches long. It grows about one pound heavier and two inches longer in the eighth month. Weight gain during the last three months consists mostly of a layer of fat that develops just under the skin and serves as insulation that maintains the baby's body warmth after birth. Growth of the fetus during the last month is slower than at any other time before birth, but it is still very rapid compared to its growth after birth. If the baby continued to grow as fast after birth as it did during the last month of pregnancy, it would weigh almost 160 pounds on its first birthday!

The fetus has grown so large by the end of pregnancy that being upside down is the best way for it to get the most space in the inverted, pear-shaped uterus

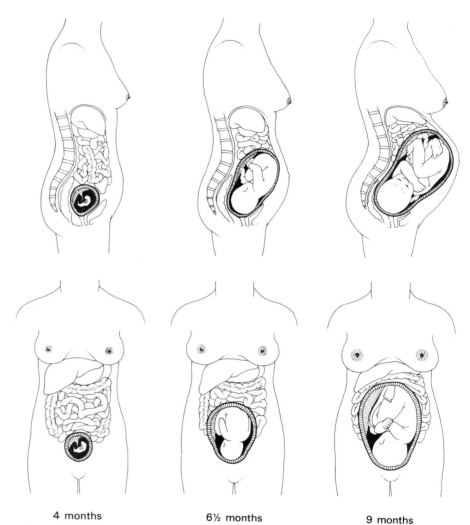

| 4 months | 6½ months | 9 months |

Figure 2.5 **Physical changes in pregnancy.** Changes in the woman's body shape and changes in fetal position from four months to full term.

(see Fig. 2.5). So the fetus usually settles into an upside-down position until birth. During the last two weeks of pregnancy, the fetus moves toward the bottom of the mother's pelvic area. Doreen experienced her baby's settling as a ''lightening'' of her heavy load—the pressure against her diaphragm was lessened and she could breathe more easily. By the ninth month after conception the fetus is so big it can hardly move in its cramped space. If the fetus were to grow any larger, its head could not be pushed through the mother's bony pelvic ring at birth. Fortunately, the fetus can now survive independently in the outside world—the baby is ready to be born.

We will be describing the birth of Doreen and Bill's baby in Chapter 3—but first let's consider how pregnancy affects parents and how heredity and the environment influence prenatal development.

EFFECTS OF PREGNANCY ON PARENTS

Expectant mothers and fathers cannot experience pregnancy without having certain physical and psychological reactions. Doreen began to have physical reactions as soon as the blastocyst was implanted, and when her pregnancy was confirmed both she and Bill had psychological reactions. Already we begin to see that parents and children are a system with reciprocal influences—child to parent and parent to child.

Physical Changes. Like many pregnant women, Doreen experienced breast changes—swelling, fullness, a darkening of the nipples, and extra sensitivity—even before she missed her period. She felt tired and needed extra sleep in the first months of pregnancy, and until about the third month, she felt nauseated in the mornings. Doreen's reproductive system changed in size and in other important ways. Muscle fibers grew in length and the cervix softened (see Chapter 3). Hormones from the placenta caused her breasts to increase in size, lose fat, and develop glandular tissue in preparation for the production of milk. The volume of blood in her circulatory system increased by one fifth, with an increased supply of blood going to the uterus and breasts. Doreen's kidneys worked hard to get rid of the wastes from her body and that of the fetus.

Psychological Changes.   Pregnancy is often a time of emotional ups and downs and increased anxiety for both parents. Even the most stable mother-to-be will worry that she won't succeed as a parent—a worry also shared by many expectant fathers. Bill was even more worried than Doreen since he had less preparation for child rearing than she did. Expectant couples worry about the well-being of their baby and they usually have financial adjustments to make. In Doreen's case, her salary would be lost temporarily and Bill would assume the financial responsibility of caring for his wife and new child. They have not yet decided whether or not Doreen will return to work after the baby is born—a possible source of conflict in the future.

The amount of stress on the expectant parents depends, of course, on their attitudes toward the pregnancy, the time it occurs, and their resources. A couple who has been having difficulties in their relationship may see pregnancy as ''a last chance'' or as a burden. Even a couple with a good relationship may view pregnancy with ambivalence—both as a blessing and as the end of their carefree existence. When resources such as money, space, and psychological maturity are present, the couple is more likely to view the pregnancy in a positive way, but when these resources are lacking, their view may be a negative one.

Hereditary Influences

We have already described how Doreen and Bill's unborn baby grew from the tiny pinpoint of a single, fertilized egg cell into a seven-pound baby having all of the physical features of an adult. This marvelous transformation is mostly under the control of hereditary influences. Environmental influences are also important as you will later see.

MECHANISMS OF HEREDITY

Chromosomes, DNA, and Genes.   Hereditary influences begin the moment the sperm and egg combine. Both sperm and ovum contain twenty-three microscopic, rod-shaped particles called **chromosomes.** When the sperm joins the egg, the chromosomes from the father pair with the chromosomes from the mother to form a new cell containing a total of forty-six chromosomes arranged in 23 pairs, all of which are contained in the nucleus of this and all future cells. Each chromosome is made up of a chemical called **DNA (deoxyribonucleic acid)**, a large molecule containing sugars, phosphates, and nitrogen bases arranged to resemble an extremely long and twisted microscopic ladder.

The segments of a chromosome are called **genes.** Each gene consists of a five-hundred to two-thousand rung long chunk of the DNA ladder. Because of the unique duplicating ability of DNA, genes can direct heredity, instructing each cell on what to make and what to become. They are the master blueprint for the body's growth and development from conception to death. The information coded in the genes of a single chromosome exceeds that contained in several sets of encyclopedias (Apgar and Beck, 1972). Most of the information carried by genes is similar for all humans; it directs all humans to develop like all other humans—not like dogs, monkeys, trees, or flowers.

A small portion of the genes provides information that accounts for individual differences. **Heredity** is the term used to refer to genetic characteristics that differ in individuals and that are transmitted from parent to child. Bill is a tall, blue-eyed, fair-skinned man with curly, blonde hair. Doreen is a tall, dark-skinned woman with straight, black hair and brown eyes. Their child will assume some physical characteristics from each of them. The development of all physical characteristics is guided by each individual's unique heredity. Scientists have long debated the extent to which genes influence behavior and which personality differences may be explained by heredity. For example, why do some babies like to be cuddled, while others do not? Why are some children passive and some active?

❖ Spotlight 2.2: Sociobiology

A wide variety of human social behaviors, including sex role differences, aggression, and even ethical and religious behavior, are shaped not just by cultural traditions but by inherited genetic controls common to all people, according to Edward O. Wilson's book *On Human Nature*.

Some scientists, ideologically opposed to any hint that human social behavior is subject to genetic determinism, were poised to attack the book when it came out. Some others, with less ideological objection, contend that Wilson's views are based on little or no evidence.

Sociobiology, despite a common misinterpretation, does not hold that human behavior is governed by the same genes that control animal behavior. Neither does it hold that all human behavior is determined by genes. Rather, sociobiologists suggest that some forms of human behavior are influenced by genes, and that these genes evolved under the same pressures of natural selection that shaped all other genes, human and animal.

Among the conclusions Wilson reaches are the following:

Human beings do not appear to possess a generalized instinct to be aggressive under all circumstances. We are, however, genetically predisposed to partition other people into categories of friends or aliens and to respond with unreasoning hatred or violence when threatened under certain conditions by those we perceive as aliens.

Men and women are born with predispositions to slightly different temperaments that suit them for certain sex role specializations. Also men are, on the average, larger and stronger than women. While neither of these genetically controlled factors necessarily makes for male dominance, cultural evolution in industrialized societies has exaggerated the expression of genetic factors into situations of extreme male dominance over females.

The primary biological purpose of sex among human beings is not reproduction. It is love which serves to keep the parents together long enough to ensure that children are raised well. Reproduction could be achieved perfectly well if men and women became sexually attracted only during brief periods of fertility, as is the case with other mammals. Instead, women have no estrous period and are sexually receptive at all times, including the infertile periods between ovulations. Continuous sexual attraction, which builds a mutual commitment, binds the couple. Love and sex, Wilson concludes, are biologically linked.

The capacity to make personal sacrifices for the good of others, even to give one's life, does not necessarily arise from some divine or transcendental impulse. Altruism among animals has been found to be genetically controlled. Although the sacrifice of one's life would, at first, seem to eliminate genes for altruism from a species and, therefore, not favor their natural selection, it is now known that this is not the case. If the sacrifice is for one's close kin, who share many of the same genes, their chances of survival are improved. Thus genes like altruist's will be more likely to survive than if there had been no sacrifice. The "moral imperative" that ancient philosophers such as Plato tried so hard to isolate as an entity within the mind may, as sociobiologists see it, reside in the chromosomes.

"Religion, Morality Carried in Genes?" by Boyce Rensberger, *New York Times*, October XX, 1978. © 1978 by The New York Times Company. Reprinted with permission.

Children in the same family may have strikingly similar physical characteristics—such as facial shape and coloring—due to their common heredity.

Sex Determination. Twenty-two of the twenty-three pairs of chromosomes—the **autosomes**—contain genes that carry instructions for all traits except sex. The twenty-third pair of chromosomes determines the sex of a baby. A normal female's twenty-third pair contains two X chromosomes (XX), so called because of their shape; a normal male's twenty-third pair contains an X and a Y chromosome (XY). Since women carry only X chromosomes, the twenty-third chromosome in the egg is always an X. The twenty-third chromosome in the sperm is an X in roughly half the cases and a Y in the other half. If a sperm containing an X chromosome combines with the egg, the resulting zygote will have an XX pair and the baby will be a girl. As you can see, the "seed" or sperm from the father, not the "seed" from the mother determines the sex of the baby.

Genetic Inheritance.   Look at Fig. 2.6, a photograph of a woolly-haired woman and her straight-haired husband. What kind of hair do their children have? Why do some of their children have woolly hair and some straight hair?

A few hereditary traits in humans, such as woolly or straight hair, are determined by a single pair of genes. Genes are paired because they are located on chromosomes, which also occur in pairs. Remember, each pair of chromosomes that a person receives contains one chromosome (with attached genes) from the mother and one from the father.

When one gene is **dominant,** it outranks the other gene of the pair in controlling heredity. The outranked gene is called **recessive** and will only affect a trait when it is paired with another recessive gene. The gene for woolly hair is dominant (D), and the one for straight hair is recessive (d). So children will have woolly hair if they have two dominant genes (DD) or a dominant and a recessive gene (Dd). They will have straight hair only if they have two recessive genes (dd).

An inherited genetic pattern such as DD, Dd, or dd is called a **genotype,** or **gene type**. The actual appearance of the genetic pattern in physical traits or behavior is known as the **phenotype,** or **body type**. In Fig. 2.6, half of the children have the phenotype of woolly hair and half have the phenotype of straight hair. The

Figure 2.6 **Effects of recessive inheritance.** The woolly and straight hair textures of the children in this family are the result of their mother having one gene for woolly hair and one for straight, while their father has two genes for straight hair.

father has the phenotype of straight hair so he *must* have the genotype dd. If he had Dd or DD, he would have had woolly hair! The mother's hair is woolly so she could have either the genotype DD or Dd. If the mother had the DD genotype, she would have passed on the D gene to all of her children and each of them would have had woolly hair. But since some of her children have straight hair (dd), the mother *must* have the Dd genotype.

Some human genes do not indicate dominant or recessive traits so clearly, and most traits result from several gene pair combinations—not just one pair as is the case in hair texture. For example, in height determination, several gene pairs combine with each other to produce a taller or a shorter person. Because many gene pairs usually work together as well as in interaction with environmental factors to influence traits, we can understand why many children differ in noticeable ways from both of their parents.

GENETIC DEFECTS

The majority of babies are born healthy. But according to the National Foundation of the March of Dimes, approximately 7 percent of the babies born in the United States have birth defects. About one fifth of these defects are inherited and another one fifth are caused by environmental influences. The remaining number is accounted for by the interaction of heredity and environment. We will discuss environmental and interactional effects later. Now let's look at birth defects caused by hereditary influences: autosomal inheritance, X-linked genes, and defective chromosomes (see also Table 2.1).

Autosomal Inheritance.   The dominant or recessive nature of genes is not very important when we are talking about eye color or hair texture, and most parents don't care if their children have brown or blue eyes or woolly or straight hair. But the subject is important when you consider that almost a thousand illnesses or birth defects—including cystic fibrosis, PKU, sickle cell anemia, and Tay-Sachs disease—are thought to be transmitted through autosomal recessive genes (Hendin and Marks, 1979). **Autosomal recessive genes** are carried on autosomes and can be outranked by dominant genes. A normal human carries from two to eight autosomal recessives genes that could produce serious birth defects. But these **carriers** only ''carry'' the recessive genes. They do not show the defect themselves because their dominant gene (D) outranks their dangerous recessive gene (d).

How is the birth defect resulting from an autosomal recessive gene passed on to the children of carriers? First, *both* parents must be carriers of the defective recessive gene (Dd). Second, the affected child must receive *two* recessive genes— one from each parent. The genotype of such a child would be dd. If a child of carrier parents received a genotype of either Dd or DD, the normal dominant gene would prevent that child from being affected by the autosomal recessive birth defect (see Fig. 2.7).

Table 2.1
Some Genetic Defects

DEFECT	CAUSE	EFFECTS	PROGNOSIS, TREATMENT
Autosomal Inheritance			
Cystic fibrosis	Recessive gene	Glands controlling production of mucus, sweat, tears, and saliva function incorrectly. Sticky mucus makes breathing difficult. Cough, recurring pneumonia, large appetite, small size, and enlarged fingertips are symptoms.	Used to be fatal at an early age, but early diagnosis, antibiotics, and other medications now allow many victims to lead nearly normal lives. At this time there is no prenatal test.
Phenylketonuria (PKU)	Recessive gene	Newborn lacks ability to process the amino acid phenylalanine that is found in meat protein and milk. When phenylalanine accumulates in the body, it poisons brain cells causing mental retardation.	No foods containing phenylalanine may be consumed. With such a diet, physical effects are minimized.
Sickle-cell anemia	Recessive gene	The red blood cells are sickle-shaped and lack the ability to carry oxygen. Results in poor physical growth and secondary infections such as pneumonia.	Affected persons usually die at an early age. Blacks are particularly susceptible. No known cure or means of prenatal detection.
Tay-Sachs disease	Recessive gene	Deterioration of brain and nervous system because of enzyme deficiency. Normal development stops at 6 months.	Usually fatal by age 5. East European Jews most susceptible. No cure or treatment known. Prenatal detection by amniocentesis.
Huntington's chorea	Dominant gene	Jerking movements, lopsided gait, progressive insanity likely. Effects appear in middle age or later, so defect may be passed on to children unknowingly.	Premature death. No known cure or means of prenatal detection.
Marfan's syndrome	Dominant gene	Gaunt, bony appearance, lack of fatty tissue, high incidence of heart defects.	No known cure or means of prenatal detection.
X-Linked Inheritance			
Color blindness	X-linked recessive gene	Red-green color blindness.	No known cure.
Hemophilia	X-linked recessive gene	Commonly known as "free bleeding." Blood lacks an important clotting agent.	A "clotting factor" obtained from healthy blood donors can prevent death from bleeding. No known cure or means of prenatal detection.

DEFECT	CAUSE	EFFECTS	PROGNOSIS, TREATMENT
X-Linked Inheritance (continued)			
Muscular dystrophy (childhood form)	X-linked recessive gene	Symptoms begin in first years of life, starting with enlargement of leg muscles. Other muscles follow and eventually waste away.	Confinement to wheelchair and finally to bed. Eventually results in premature death. No known cure.
Defective Chromosomes			
Cri du chat syndrome	Number 5 chromosome is broken and the broken part is missing.	Newborn's crying sounds like cat mewing. Effects include abnormal head development, retarded physical and cognitive development.	No known cure.
Down's syndrome (mongolism)	Extra chromosome associated with the twenty-first pair.	Heart abnormality, physical and cognitive retardation. Happy, with loving natures.	No known cure. Medical advances have lengthened the life span of many children. Prenatal detection through amniocentesis is possible.
Klinefelter's syndrome	Extra X chromosome (XXY)	Males have small testes, usually unable to produce sperm, and feminine appearance. Some individuals also exhibit some mental retardation. Usually not discovered until adolescence.	Administering male sex hormones at adolescence masculinizes body characteristics and increases assertiveness.
Turner's syndrome	Missing X chromosome (XO)	The only disorder known in which a human can survive with only 45 chromosomes. Female will have little development of reproductive organs and no mammary glands because of a lack of female hormones. Abnormally short in height. Personality traits include being relaxed, pleasant, and not easily upset.	Treatment with hormones at adolescence leads to normal sexual appearance, but affected females remain sterile.
XYY syndrome	Extra Y chromosome	Taller than average male (over 6 feet) with normal sex organs but abnormal brain patterns causing seizures. More likely to have acne. Impulsive.	No known cure.

Adapted from Erlich, Holm, and Brown, 1976; Apgar and Beck, 1972; Hendin and Marks, 1979.

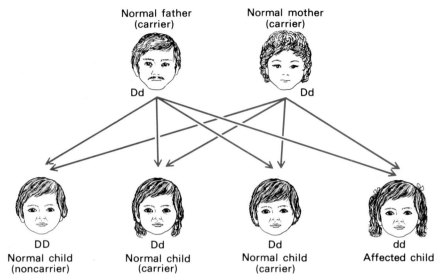

Figure 2.7 **Autosomal recessive inheritance**

Defects also result when only one or both genes in a pair are defective but dominant genes (Dd or DD). **Autosomal dominant genes** are carried on autosomes and outrank recessive genes. They are known to cause such disorders as Marfan's syndrome and Huntington's chorea, as well as extra fingers or toes (Hendin and Marks, 1979). A person cannot be a carrier of a dominant gene—you are either affected or don't have the gene at all. People can only "carry" recessive genes without themselves being affected. So autosomal dominant genes do not usually cause serious disorders. When a dangerous dominant gene is present, the affected person may die before reproducing or may be aware of its presence and the effects of the gene and decide not to have children.

X-Linked Inheritance. Sometimes dominant or recessive genes are carried on the sex chromosomes. As you remember, the twenty-two pairs of autosomes carry genes that always occur in pairs. But the twenty-third pair—the sex chromosomes—are different. All of the genes on the sex chromosomes of the female (XX) *do* occur in pairs, but dozens of genes on the X chromosome of the male (XY) are *not* paired with genes on the shorter Y chromosome because the Y chromosome does not carry matching genes. The dozens of single genes on the X chromosome, which have no counterpart on the Y chromosome, are called **X-linked genes** and these genes cause X-linked genetic defects, such as **hemophilia** (free bleeding), a disorder in which the blood does not clot properly. The term X-linked genetic defects is used because the defect is "linked" or carried on the X chromosome.

Boys are much more likely than girls to have hemophilia, color blindness, and other X-linked defects. Why? Females have two X chromosomes containing genes that affect these traits. The recessive gene for hemophilia is usually out-ranked by a dominant gene for blood clotting on the other X chromosome. There-fore a female will not have these genetic defects very often and will be a free bleeder only if she receives *two* recessive genes—one from *each* parent. This means that her mother must be a carrier of the gene for free bleeding and that her father must be a free bleeder if she is to inherit the trait. The female will, however, be a carrier if she inherits one recessive gene for free bleeding.

Defective Chromosomes. A human needs twenty-three pairs of chromo-somes—no more and no less—with the usual configurations of gene pairs to develop normally. Defective chromosomes—either missing ones, extra ones, or broken ones—lead to birth defects. Such gross chromosomal abnormalities as a missing or extra chromosome are usually fatal to the unborn baby. For example, in a study of 166 miscarriages, 39 percent were found to have a missing or an extra chromosome (Geisler and Kleindbredt, 1978).

But there are cases, Down's syndrome being one, in which a person with an incorrect number of chromosomes does survive (see Spotlight 2.3). These persons have varying degrees of abnormality.

GENETIC COUNSELING

Many couples are now asking for help in trying to determine whether their future children will have birth defects. One source for this help is from **genetic counselors** who may be family doctors, obstetricians, pediatricians, or genetic specialists. Their job is to discover the cause of any defect in the couple's living children or blood relatives, the patterns for inheritance of the defect, and the chances of trans-mitting the defect to future children. In their attempt to help couples have healthy babies, genetic counselors use karyotypes, amniocentesis, and ultrasound.

Karyotypes. The chromosomes of each living child can be studied using **karyo-types.** Body tissue cells, such as blood or bone marrow cells, are grown in a cul-tured medium, and the chromosomes from the cell nucleus are then photo-graphed. The pictures of individual chromosomes are arranged on a chart called a **karyotype** (see Fig. 2.8). Genetic counselors can study karyotypes and give parents information about their own genetic makeup and their chances of having an abnormal child.

The genetic counselor's role is to provide information—not advice—about what to do with the available evidence. If a couple with a high probability of hav-ing abnormal children decides to go ahead and have a baby, or if there are other reasons to suspect genetic defects, amniocentesis and ultrasound can be used to determine the existence of problems.

Amniocentesis. When a woman is about fourteen to sixteen weeks pregnant, **amniocentesis** may be done to determine evidence of abnormalities in the unborn child. In this procedure, a long, hollow needle is inserted through the woman's

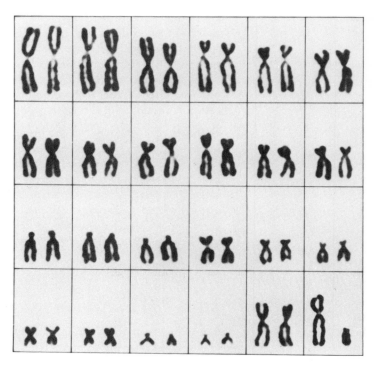

Figure 2.8
Karyotype. This karyotype shows the genes of a normal human male. If the last pair were composed of two Xs (XX) rather than an X and a Y, the subject would be female.

abdominal wall and into her uterus. Some amniotic fluid is withdrawn, cells are cultured, and a karyotype of the chromosomes is made. Since the fetal cells contain the same chromosomes as the unborn child, genetic counselors can examine them to identify many genetic abnormalities.

Ultrasound.   Another procedure involves using an ultrasound technique developed by the U.S. Navy. The **ultrasound** scan employs a special device responding to sound waves, which instantly transmits a visible outline of the fetus on a video screen. A continual record of the ultrasound outline is kept by instant photographs. This technique can determine such things as the age and growth rate of the fetus, as well as information on the health of the heart, blood system, and kidneys.

Ultrasound is used as a standard part of prenatal care in Germany and some medical personnel are recommending this be made the policy in the United States (Schuman, 1980). Others warn of the possible long-range effects on the developing child since it is known that lengthy exposure to high levels of ultrasound can damage cells and tissues. Although the low levels used in obstetrics do not appear to have any adverse effects, precautions should be taken here as in all situations involving the rapidly developing fetus.

✤ Spotlight 2.3:
Genetic Counseling and Down's Syndrome

Because I am a genetic counselor, Joe and Catherine came to me for help when Catherine was pregnant for the fourth time. "We want you to tell us whether this child will be normal," said Joe. "Our first child is a perfectly normal and healthy child. But two years after Eddie was born, we had a baby who died. Then Jane was born and she has Down's syndrome. She is still not toilet trained and, even though we love her, she has been quite a burden. Now Catherine is pregnant again. Will this baby be mongoloid too?"

Down's syndrome—sometimes called **mongolism** because afflicted children like Jane have eyes that are slanted like the eyes of people of the Mongoloid race—is the most common and best understood birth defect caused by a chromosomal disorder (Apgar and Beck, 1972). I told Joe and Catherine that Down's syndrome occurs when there are too many chromosomes, a condition that can happen two different ways.

The first way Down's syndrome can occur is by accident, when a mistake in cell division causes an extra number twenty-one chromosome to be placed in the mother's egg cell, the extra chromosome being put there just before the egg is fertilized. Environmental factors that make the eggs of older women less well-formed than those of younger women appear to be the major cause. The risk of Down's syndrome increases rapidly as mothers age. For all mothers, the risk is one in 600, but for mothers between forty and forty-five the risk is one in 400. Recent studies have shown that there is also a greater risk of Down's syndrome when fathers are

over fifty-five (Hendin and Marks, 1979). Improper cell division in the sperm causes perhaps 25 percent of the cases of Down's syndrome (Magenis, 1977). If Jane's disorder was caused in this way, it would be unlikely that the new baby would have the same defect.

The second type of Down's syndrome occurs when the extra chromosome is stuck onto one of the other chromosomes in the twenty-first pair. Called piggy-back mongolism, this disorder can be inherited.

My next step as a genetic counselor was to do a complete physical examination of the living family members. I was especially interested in Jane and took blood from her and sent it to a lab where the chromosomes were stained and a karyotype (see Fig. 2.8) was made. This showed that Jane had the piggy-back type of Down's syndrome. I gave my report to Joe and Catherine with the conclusion that their chances of having another Down's syndrome child were one out of three (Apgar and Beck, 1972).

Joe and Catherine were not satisfied with this news of their chances. They asked me if I could tell them for sure. I then arranged for Catherine to undergo amniocentesis. The test showed that the child Catherine was carrying definitely suffered from Down's syndrome—the piggy-back type.

When I made my report to Joe and Catherine, they were naturally upset. Joe turned to Catherine. "What should we do?" he asked in despair.

While most children with Down's syndrome are mentally retarded to some degree, they can learn to do many things and play an active role in family life.

GENETIC EXPERIMENTATION

Scientists are already using technology to modify the genetic structure of cells. They may soon be able to correct defects such as Down's syndrome through **corrective gene therapy**. Another type of genetic experimentation is **cloning**, the creation of a whole new organism from just one cell of one parent. Since all the genetic material in the new organism is identical to the genetic material in the parent, the offspring would be an exact but younger twin of the parent. Spotlight 2.4 discusses an instance of human cloning.

Environmental Influences

When Doreen was five months pregnant, she and Bill flew home to visit his parents. At a family gathering, Doreen was cautioned to be careful about what she ate, drank, and even looked at. She was warned that drinking ginger root tea would cause the fetus to abort naturally; that being scared by birds or snakes would cause her baby to be marked; that eating strawberries would cause strawberry marks; and that lifting her hands over her head during the last months of pregnancy would cause the umbilical cord to become wrapped around the baby's throat and cause choking.

❋ Spotlight 2.4: Clones Again

Colleagues winced when Dr. Landrum B. Shettles put out a book purporting to tell couples how they could choose the sex of their children at conception. They groaned when he tried to produce a test tube baby, an experiment that resulted in his leaving New York's prestigious Columbia-Presbyterian Medical Center. And last week, the sixty-nine-year-old researcher made a claim bound to dismay them once again: He reported a successful first step in the cloning of a human.

If the claim is true, Shettles has pulled off a feat unprecedented in reproductive biology. In the respected *American Journal of Obstetrics and Gynecology,* he describes experiments performed on male and female volunteers over a three-year period at Gifford Memorial Hospital, Randolph, Vermont. The women were patients undergoing a variety of gynecologic procedures; the men were having surgery for testicular problems.

According to his report, Shettles withdrew eggs from the women's ovaries with a syringe and placed them in lab dishes. Using a microscope and ultra-thin glass needles, he teased out the nucleus of each egg. Next, Shettles removed spermatogonia—precursors of sperm cells—from the testes of the male volunteers. Unlike the nuclei of sperm, spermatogonia nuclei contain the full complement of 46 chromosomes. Detaching these nuclei, Shettles gently inserted them into the incubating ova. In three of many attempts, he says, the eggs divided and, over a period of three days, grew into multicelled blastocysts, the stage at which a normally fertilized ovum leaves the fallopian tube and becomes implanted in the womb.

Shettles destroyed the blastocysts. "I was only interested in seeing if I could get to this stage," he says. But the implication of his experiment is clear. Such a developing group of cells could be implanted into the uterus, as was done with the husband-wife laboratory-fertilized ovum that produced Louise Brown, the British test tube baby last summer. But in this case, the result would be a baby genetically identical to the male donor. In short, a clone.

Shettles's previous research has often raised professional eyebrows. At a trial last summer that stemmed from his earlier test-tube-baby experiment, expert witnesses testified that Shettles had once used the same picture of a human egg to illustrate papers describing two different laboratory fertilization procedures.

Experts maintain that Shettles's latest paper contains several flaws. Dr. Luigi Mastroianni, Jr., fertility specialist at the University of Pennsylvania School of Medicine, notes that mature ova can be obtained from a woman only after careful monitoring of her ovulatory cycle, and there is no evidence that Shettles did that. Dr. Joe Leigh Simpson of Northwestern University Medical School raises another objection. A blastocyst would have to be analyzed to determine that each of its cells contained forty-six chromosomes matching those of the donor male before anyone could say that it was the beginning of a clone. Shettles admits that he didn't perform such an analysis. In any event, his claim—like any other researcher's—cannot be accepted until someone else duplicates the feat.

Doreen became worried and referred to a book her doctor had recommended. She learned that the environment does have an effect on prenatal development and that the timing of environmental influences is important. An environmental agent that may have a severe effect on development during one stage of pregnancy will have little or no effect during another stage. As we mentioned in Chapter 1, the times when environmental agents have their greatest effects are called critical or sensitive periods (see Fig. 2.9).

As Doreen read on, she learned that such environmental factors as the mother's physical and emotional state, the family's economic status, and teratogens can affect prenatal development in negative ways. Doreen found not one shred of evidence that drinking ginger root tea, being scared by birds or snakes, eating strawberries, or raising her hands over her head would affect her baby. She and Bill decided that the ideas expressed by his relatives were more folklore.

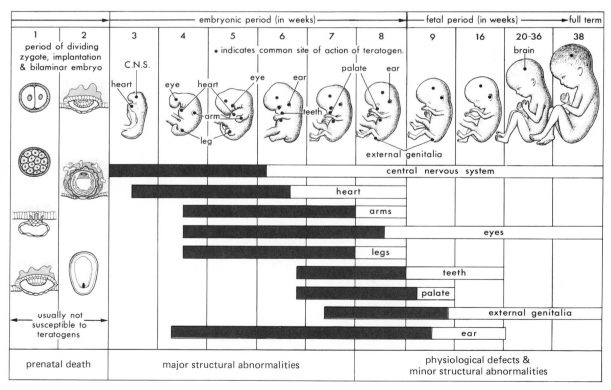

Figure 2.9 **Critical (sensitive) periods in prenatal development.** The areas in color are most sensitive; those in white, less so.

MOTHER'S PHYSICAL STATE

Age and Childbearing Patterns. You may not think an eighteen-year-old woman is especially young, or a thirty-five-year-old woman is particularly old. Nonetheless, women who are under eighteen and over thirty-five can have problems bearing children for several reasons. Since teenagers have notoriously poor diets in our society and their own growth is rapid, the extra nutritional needs of the baby are likely to put a strain on the mother's body. Younger mothers are also less likely to receive the needed prenatal care. The older woman faces different problems, her reproductive system having passed its prime. As a woman gets older, her ova, all of which are present at birth, are likely to deteriorate. Older mothers—especially those having their first baby—also seem to have more problems and illnesses during pregnacy and longer labors. In light of all of these difficulties, younger and older mothers have increased chances of miscarriages, premature births, birth difficulties, and health problems during pregnancy. Their babies are more likely to have low birth weights or Down's syndrome, or to be retarded or stillborn.

Childbearing patterns are also related to risk. The likelihood of problems for both mother and baby are increased when babies are spaced less than two years apart and as the number of children increases.

Toxemia. A very small number of pregnant women (less than 10 percent) develop toxemia, or poisoning. Toxemic women suffer from fluid retention (resulting in swelling and weight gain) and high blood pressure. Protein is generally found in the urine of women with toxemia.

Although the causes of this condition are unknown, its effects are obvious and often severe. The stress put on the mother's system can result in convulsions, coma, and even death for her. Toxemia can also endanger the unborn child's blood and oxygen supply and may result in premature deliveries and low-birth-weight infants (Beal, 1980).

There is currently no cure for toxemia (other than ending the pregnancy), but strict bed rest, sedatives, and drugs to lower the mother's blood pressure can control the symptoms—and thus the negative effects—of toxemia.

Nutrition. Doreen had been wanting to lose ten pounds, but her doctor immediately vetoed her plan to diet while pregnant. It was once thought that an unborn baby would take whatever necessary from the mother's body. If the mother did not have proper nutrition, it was supposed the baby would take what it needed and the mother would get what was left over. Now we know that this is not true. Restriction of calories may harm both mother and baby. The recommended weight gain for pregnant women is now about twenty-eight to thirty pounds and the timing of the weight gain is thought to be important. Weight gain for the first three months should be from two to four pounds. During the last six months, nearly one pound per week is the recommended gain since the baby is growing so rapidly (Pitkin, 1977). Doreen's doctor recommended that she eat a well-balanced diet including plenty of protein and 2200 to 2300 calories per day. She was also told to limit fats and carbohydrates.

Nutrition is important to the life of a baby long before it is conceived or born. In fact, when women are subjected to starvation during a famine or war, they are less likely than well-nourished women to conceive at all (National Research Council, 1970). A woman's nutritional patterns during her own growth will influence her preparedness for childbirth—her final body height and pelvic width, both of which are related to infant prematurity, birth complications, and infant death (McWilliams, 1980). So it is important to start thinking about good nutrition even before pregnancy.

Malnourished mothers usually give birth to low-birth-weight infants. Low birth weight is associated with high death rate and more illnesses early in a child's life. The low-birth-weight infant of a malnourished mother also has poorer brain development and may have behavior problems (Languis et al., 1980). When dietary supplements are given to pregnant, malnourished women, birth weights of their babies increase (Lechtig et al., 1975) and babies are more active (Restak, 1979).

If a fetus does not receive adequate nourishment, the rate of brain cell division slows down. A severely deprived fetus may have 20 percent fewer brain cells than normal. If the baby is malnourished *both* prenatally and during the first six months of life, the results are especially serious, contributing to long range effects such as lowered IQ and poor school performance (Kaplan, 1972; Richardson, 1972).

Lack of specific nutrients has severe effects. Mothers whose diets are deprived of iodine often produce babies who suffer from **cretinism**—a thyroid disorder that produces physical and mental deficiencies (Kaplan, 1972). Lack of calcium contributes to poor bone and teeth formation and lack of iron can lead to anemia in both mother and child. When maternal diets were deficient in phosphorus and vitamins B, C, and D, their babies were more likely to be malformed than babies of well-nourished mothers (Murphy, 1947).

In conclusion, it is important for pregnant women and those who think they might become pregnant to eat a well-balanced diet containing adequate amounts of protein, vitamins, minerals, and calories. Pregnancy is not the time for overweight women to try to reduce.

Rh Factor.   The **Rh factor** is a component of the blood found in 85 percent of whites and 95 percent of blacks living in the United States (Rugh and Shettles, 1971). If the factor is present, the person is said to have Rh positive blood; if it is not, the blood is said to be Rh negative. When one parent is Rh negative and the other is Rh positive, there is a strong likelihood that their baby will be Rh positive because the Rh factor follows the autosomal dominant inheritance pattern.

When the mother's blood is Rh negative and the unborn baby's is Rh positive, there may be problems for the fetus. A first baby is not likely to be harmed since no blood cells cross the placental barrier except in very rare circumstances. But during an abortion or a birth, the mother's blood may become mixed with the baby's when the placenta pulls away from the uterine wall. When this happens, the mother's blood will begin to develop antibodies to destroy the Rh factor. Antibodies are manufactured to destroy any foreign bodies in the blood—whether the foreign body be a virus, a bacteria, or the foreign Rh factor present in an Rh positive baby's blood. In later pregnancies, the antibodies can pass through the placenta and destroy the Rh factor in the baby's red blood cells. This can cause spontaneous abortion, deafness, cerebral palsy, mental retardation, or stillbirth (Stern, 1973).

So, if the Rh negative mother has a second child who is Rh positive, that baby could be in serious danger during the pregnancy and at birth. Amniocentesis can determine if the blood of the unborn baby is Rh positive and the mother's blood can be tested for the presence of the antibodies that destroy the Rh factor. If a problem does exist, the baby can be given a complete blood transfusion immediately after birth, or even before birth through the uterine wall.

Fortunately, an Rh vaccine was developed in 1968. Rh negative mothers receive an injection of this vaccine within seventy-two hours after the birth or abortion of an Rh positive baby to prevent formation of antibodies that would harm future babies.

MOTHER'S EMOTIONAL STATE

An apparently healthy baby, born to a healthy seventeen-year-old mother, vomited blood and died twenty-one hours after birth. An autopsy revealed three peptic ulcers. It was later learned that the mother had been under extreme stress during her pregnancy. She was coerced by her parents into marrying the child's father—an alcoholic wife-abuser. Even though she returned to live with her parents, her husband continually visited, trying to persuade her to return to him. Could the baby's peptic ulcers have resulted from the mother's stress (Spezzano, 1981)?

One case certainly does not prove that maternal stress can cause ulcers in a newborn baby, but it does provide justification for more research. We already know that prolonged stress during pregnancy carries with it an increase of many risks: premature delivery, long or difficult labor, miscarriage, and nausea and vomiting during pregnancy (Sameroff and Chandler, 1975). When pregnant mothers were under emotional stress, fetal body movements increased (Sontag, 1944). Recently, Sontag expressed his continued confidence in his earlier findings: "I definitely feel maternal emotions during pregnancy have both an immediate and a long-term impact on the child (Spezzano, 1981, p. 51)." Babies of anxious mothers seem to be more irritable and "colicky," and to cry more immediately after birth than other babies. Anxiety during pregnancy is also related to irritabili-

Although most women report feeling especially tired only early in their pregnancy, proper rest and nutrition are important for all expectant mothers.

ty, hyperactivity, and feeding problems in infants (Davids et al., 1961). But no lasting effects have presently been identified.

TERATOGENS

It was once thought that the placenta filtered all harmful agents from the mother's blood and prevented them from reaching the unborn baby. Research indicates that this is not so. Some harmful agents are filtered but many can cross the placental barrier and harm the developing baby. Environmental agents that disturb fetal development are called **teratogens**. These include disease, drugs, chemicals, and radiation. As scientists identify more teratogens and begin to understand their effects, a greater number of birth defects can be prevented.

Disease. Most disease agents that affect the mother are too large to pass through the placental barrier and infect the fetus. Chicken pox, hepatitis, poliomyelitis, and smallpox are exceptions. If a pregnant woman contracts one of those diseases, her baby may be born with the disease. There are a wide variety of diseases—including rubella, syphilis, and diabetes—that can have a particularly severe effect on the fetus.

RUBELLA. Commonly known as German measles, rubella is a viral infection, which can be so mild in an adult it may go unnoticed, but it can cause serious problems in some—but not all—developing fetuses if infection occurs during the first three months of pregnancy. During this sensitive period the effects of rubella on the development of the fetus can be grave: heart disease or malformation, a smaller-than-normal head, retardation, defective eyes or ears, and even death. Fortunately, Doreen was vaccinated against rubella before she became pregnant. All children should be vaccinated and adult women having no immunity and wanting to be vaccinated should first find out whether or not they are pregnant.

VENEREAL DISEASE.   Although the number of babies infected with rubella is decreasing, the number born with syphilis is increasing rapidly in the United States. Syphilis is a disease passed from the mother to her unborn infant. When the organisms causing syphilis infect the fetus, they multiply rapidly and invade almost all tissues and organs, with marked damage occurring in bones, liver, blood vessels, and lungs. About 50 percent of syphilis-infected babies die before or shortly after birth. If the baby lives, pneumonia may develop and eye damage will probably be permanent. Syphilis can easily be detected in a pregnant woman. If she is treated before the fourth month of pregnancy, the infant will not be affected by the disease.

Other venereal diseases, such as gonorrhea and herpes simplex 2 can infect the baby as it passes through the birth canal during birth.

DIABETES.   Babies of diabetic mothers are about three times as likely as other babies to have abnormalities. Diabetic-related problems include stillbirths, missing vertebrae, skeletal abnormalities, and respiratory problems. The diabetic mother may also produce a larger-than-average baby, making labor and delivery more difficult. Since so many infants of diabetic mothers die in the last weeks of pregnancy, many doctors induce labor in order to deliver the babies early. Less serious effects are encountered when diabetic mothers receive medical attention.

Drugs.   Stop and count the number of drugs and pills you have taken in the last week. Have you smoked a cigarette or some marijuana? Did you drink a beer, a cocktail, or a cup of coffee? Did you take an aspirin for a headache, or pills to keep you awake to study for a big exam, or tranquilizers to make you relax, or appetite suppressants to help you lose weight? Many of these common, over-the-counter remedies can cause serious damage to unborn babies. Even prescription drugs can cause problems.

Pregnant women take drugs for the same reasons you do—for relaxation, headaches, illness, depression, and sleeplessness. And it was for just these same reasons that thousands of pregnant women in West Germany took thalidomide as a tranquilizer in 1960 with tragic results. Hundreds of babies came into the world with no arms and legs or with flipper-like limbs; many had sight and hearing defects and a score of other abnormalities. Only 20 percent of the fetuses of pregnant mothers who took thalidomide were abnormal. Perhaps the mothers of the lucky 80 percent did not take the drug during a sensitive period. Or perhaps some of the developing babies were just resistant to the harmful effects. Whatever the reasons are that the majority of the babies escaped harm, the tragic minority who were harmed should sensitize us all to the best rule for pregnant women to follow when they are thinking about taking drugs: Don't—unless health is threatened and then only under the direction of a doctor. No drug is absolutely safe—especially during the first few weeks of pregnancy (Bowes et al., 1970).

ALCOHOL.   "If mama boozes, baby loses." This slogan was used to kick off the state of South Carolina's media campaign to educate people about **fetal alcohol**

syndrome (FAS), a condition which results from maternal consumption of alcohol. Babies with FAS are usually quite small at birth, slow to develop physically, irritable, and retarded in intellectual performance. They also have heart defects, disturbed sleep patterns, unusually small heads, and facial abnormalities (Streissguth et al., 1978). Infants with FAS are born addicted and their withdrawal from alcohol is a further problem (Pieroy et al., 1977). Recent findings indicate long-term behavioral effects at age four (Landesman-Dwyer et al., 1979).

FAS was discovered in 1973, but it is still not known how alcohol causes this syndrome. Neither is it known exactly how much alcohol must be consumed before FAS will occur. The National Institute on Alcohol Abuse and Alcoholism suggests that pregnant women should not consume more than two alcoholic drinks in any one day. ''Binge drinking'' should especially be avoided. Alcohol is thought to have its most serious effects during the first months of pregnancy. This can be a real problem for women who drink regularly because they may be consuming alcohol without knowing they are pregnant.

NICOTINE.   We have known for some time that the fetal heart rate increases shortly after the pregnant woman smokes. Nicotine also causes fetal circulation to slow down—particularly in the eighth month. No one knows for sure what long-range effects these occurrences have.

In 1979, the Surgeon General of the United States issued a report on smoking containing some thought-provoking statements about the effects of smoking on prenatal development. The average weight of babies born to smoking mothers was seven ounces less than that of babies whose mothers did not smoke. Maternal smoking was also correlated with increased risk of spontaneous abortion and increases in both fetal and neonatal death rates. The report found growing evidence that children of smoking mothers experience deficiencies in physical, cognitive, and emotional development. Finally, children of smoking parents are more likely to have bronchitis and pneumonia during the first year of life (Office on Smoking and Health, 1979). Some other researchers found that the effects of maternal smoking lasted until at least age four (Landesman-Dwyer et al., 1979).

But the Surgeon General's report was contradicted by Richard Naeye, a professor at Pennsylvania State University who found *no* evidence that retarded intelligence was associated with maternal smoking during pregnancy or that prenatal problems associated with smoking mothers were permanent (Naeye, 1978; 1979). A later report by Lefkowitz (1981) also found no physical, intellectual, social, or emotional differences between ten-year-old offspring of mothers who smoked or did not smoke during pregnancy. So the long-term effects of smoking during pregnancy continue to be debatable.

ADDICTIVE DRUGS.   Babies born to mothers who are addicted to codeine, heroin, or morphine are born addicted and are also more likely to be born prematurely than babies of nonaddicted mothers. These newborn addicts show such withdrawal symptoms as irritability, sleep disturbances, convulsions, and vomiting, and sometimes death will occur. Even when infants are cured of their addiction, there may be long-term effects. Usually, addicted infants are less alert and responsive than nonaddicted babies. They also cry more but cuddle less. As we will see, such crying and lack of cuddling can affect parents negatively and get parent-child relationships off to a bad start.

MARIJUANA.   Animal research with marijuana has shown that fetal malformations can be caused by heavy dosages of marijuana administered experimentally. No relationship has been found between human fetal abnormalities and marijuana smoking. Even though there is no clinical evidence that marijuana causes problems in pregnancy, the best advice in this situation remains the same as with all drugs: Don't!

LSD.   The effects of lysergic acid diethylamide (LSD) on pregnant women and their babies is hard to separate from effects caused by other events in the environments of LSD users. One group of women who took LSD also used other drugs, suffered from various infections, and were malnourished. Many users of LSD may get impure mixtures. One group of researchers showed that the chromosomes of some species of rats showed damage as a result of experimental dosages of LSD, but there were great individual differences in the extent of damage among the rats studied (Dishotsky et al., 1971). These researchers concluded that *pure* LSD is not a teratogen in humans—but its use should still be avoided by pregnant women.

HORMONES.   Female sex hormones in the form of oral contraceptives (estrogen and progesterone) taken just before or shortly after pregnancy may also harm the developing embryo. Male sex hormones (androgen) can bring about masculinization of the female fetus and female hormones the feminization of the male fetus. DES (diethylstilbestrol), a hormone given to women in the 1960s during their first trimester of pregnancy to prevent miscarriage, has been related to vaginal cancer in daughters after adolescence (Herbst et al., 1972). The uterus can also be poorly formed making it difficult for some of these women to have children. If they do conceive, stillborn or premature babies are likely (Edwards, 1980). Evidence also suggests that males whose mothers took DES show more sterility and abnormalities of the testes than other males. Both men and women whose mothers took DES should have frequent medical checkups.

Chemicals.   Mercury, chemical sprays, herbicides, insecticides, fungicides, cosmetic ingredients, food additives, and air pollutants have all been found to affect chromosomes in a negative way. Herbicides, insecticides, and fungicides are related to abortion, stillbirth, and birth defects in animals and possibly in humans, and cause damage to the egg or sperm or to the fetus after conception. When a great number of infants with mental retardation and birth defects were born in a single community in Japan, medical detective work tracked the cause of the defects to mercury contained in the fish the pregnant women were eating. The families in the community caught their fish in a local bay that was contaminated by industrial wastes containing mercury (Apgar and Beck, 1972).

Radiation.   Before she knew she was pregnant, Doreen was not feeling well. Her family doctor thought she might require diagnostic X rays but he suggested that they would wait until just after her menstrual period to take them. This practice of waiting until just after menstruation to x-ray a woman's abdominal region was adopted in Denmark and is becoming common in the United States.

Why is it important to avoid all X rays at a time when a woman might be pregnant? If radiation damages even one chromosome of the unborn child, normal development can be thrown off course because each chromosome must exactly duplicate itself for growth and development to proceed normally. The first two to six weeks after conception are critical for the embryo, which is considerably more susceptible to radiation than a fetus is in the last two or three months of pregnancy. This is because the principal structures affected by radiation—the central nervous system, brain, and spinal cord—are growing most rapidly during this time. To prevent damage to the fetus, X rays of a pregnant woman's abdomen must be avoided. Studies of unborn babies who were exposed to atomic radiation at the time of the attacks on Hiroshima and Nagasaki show leukemia, cataracts, microcephaly (abnormally small heads), stunted growth, and other abnormalities that might have been caused by the excessive radiation.

FATHER'S INFLUENCE

New evidence increasingly points to the need for fathers as well as mothers to avoid exposure to teratogens. In one well-documented case, birth defects were more frequent when fathers were exposed to anesthetic gases during their work in hospital operating rooms (Ad Hoc Committee, 1974). And high concentrations of lead and radiation cause abnormal sperm production in exposed men (Landcranjan, 1971; 1975). Men who have been exposed to carbon disulfide and DES in their work may suffer from sexual impotence—the most decisive influence of all on potential offspring (Landcranjan, 1971; Wasserman, 1971).

A Systems Approach: Heredity and Environment

Doreen was beginning to think that with so many causes of birth defects, they must be hard to prevent. As she continued to read, she learned that most babies are born healthy and normal and that fewer than 10 percent are born with defects. And when parents follow certain precautions (see Fig. 2.10), their chance of having a child with a birth defect is further reduced.

- Ask for genetic counseling if you have a close relative with an inherited disorder.
- Plan to have children when the mother is between twenty and thirty-five years of age.
- Remember that even though new sperm are manufactured each day, birth defects are more likely to be avoided if the father is under forty-five years of age.
- Space babies at least two years apart to give the mother's body time to recover and prepare itself for a new pregnancy.
- Remember that each child after the third brings an increasing risk of stillbirth, prematurity, and birth defects.
- Obtain good prenatal care from qualified medical personnel.
- Be sure to be immunized against rubella before you become pregnant.
- Avoid exposure to contagious diseases.
- Don't eat rare meat and avoid contact with cat feces while pregnant in order to prevent toxoplasmosis—a disease causing birth defects that can be transmitted to the unborn baby.
- Don't take drugs unless they are essential.
- Don't permit X rays, smoke cigarettes, or drink alcohol.
- Eat a nourishing diet both before and during pregnancy.
- Be sure to check for the Rh factor.
- Do not try to lose weight during pregnancy.
- Be in good health.

Figure 2.10 **Preventing birth defects**
(Adapted from Apgar and Beck, 1972).

Cross-Cultural Development and Relationships

Anthropologist Margaret Mead describes some rather astounding cultural beliefs related to conception and prenatal development (1952). The Rossel Islanders near New Guinea claim the father lays an egg in the mother to achieve conception; the Arapesh of New Guinea say the baby sleeps until ready for birth and then dives out; and the Iatmul believe the fetus can hurry or delay birth, as it wishes. The Ifugao of the Phillipines believe that the expectant father's behavior affects the welfare of the fetus just as much as the mother's does (Mead, 1967) so food and activity restrictions are observed by both parents throughout pregnancy. For example, because an Ifugao husband cannot cut or kill anything during his wife's pregnancy, relatives cut wood, and the expectant father is permitted to carry it home.

In some societies, such as that of the Trobriand Islanders of Melanesia, no connection is made between sexual intercourse and conception (Malinow-

Margaret Mead, whose observations of other cultures revealed some surprising differences in how children are raised, is shown here on a visit to the Manus tribe in the Admiralty Islands in 1953.

ski, 1966). "Conception" is thought to occur when a deceased ancestor swims into the mother as she bathes and swims in a particular pool of water. Because the Trobrianders do not recognize the father's part in conception, the only adult male who is considered blood-related to the child is the mother's brother, since he and the child's mother have the same mother. So children look upon their fathers as "the husband of my mother" and refer to them as outsiders in discussions of family relationships. The "husband of my mother" acts as the family's loving protector and shares in child care duties such as feeding, carrying, and bathing children, but not in discipline, which is usually the responsibility of the mother's brother (Lynn, 1974).

The Kpelle of Liberia believe a child is the offspring of each man with whom a pregnant woman has intercourse. They also claim the child will resemble each man in proportion to the number of times the mother has had intercourse with him (Bledsoe, 1980). Because children are needed to help support the family financially, success at reproduction is highly valued among the Kpelle and sterility of husband or wife is grounds for divorce. Because of the economic importance of children, lovers as well as husbands sometimes try to claim children whose fatherhood is in doubt (Bledsoe, 1980).

In contrast, women in China are encouraged to practice birth control during the childbearing years. Neighborhood health workers make information on birth control readily available, and abortion and children born outside of marriage are practically nonexistent. Planned birth is emphasized by the government to strengthen the political values of the country. "Birth is a direct contribution that every young couple can make to the building of China. (Sidel, 1972, p. 57)."

For the sake of clarity, we have discussed separately the influences of heredity and environment on development. Of course in reality, these influences form a continually interacting system in which all parts affect growth and development. A gene merely provides the potential for a certain trait to develop. If the environment is especially beneficial or especially adverse, then a genetically determined trait may not appear at all.

Consider the effects of a beneficial environment on the genetically determined PKU defect. If a PKU baby is fed protein from animal sources, such as breast or cow's milk, then the accumulation of phenylalanine in the baby's body will begin to destroy brain cells. But if the baby's diet (nutritional environment) is kept free of the harmful protein, severe mental retardation can be prevented.

In contrast, if the environment is adverse, growth may not occur. For example, human height is controlled by several pairs of genes. Although you may have the genes that would allow you to grow to be six feet three inches tall, adverse environmental factors, such as a protein or calcium deficiency or a serious disease, might cause you to be much shorter than the limit set by your genes. There are, of course, many more hereditary and environmental influences that form the complex system that affects all growth and development. No single influence ever operates alone. Hereditary influences establish the potential; environmental influences control the extent to which this potential is reached.

Summary

1. Conception occurs when a single sperm from the father penetrates a single ovum, or egg, from the mother.

2. Gestation is divided into three periods. During the period of the ovum (conception to second week), the zygote moves down a fallopian tube and attaches itself to the uterine wall. During the period of the embryo (second week to end of second month), all the major body organs and systems begin to develop. During the period of the fetus (third month after conception until birth), bone cells are formed and organs, muscles, and body systems start to function.

3. The physical symptoms a woman experiences during pregnancy include the absence of menstrual periods, breast changes, and for some, nausea. Both parents may experience psychological reactions such as emotional ups and downs and increased anxiety.

4. Hereditary influences begin the moment the sperm and egg combine. Chromosomes from the father pair up with chromosomes from the mother to form twenty-three pairs. Genes are segments of chromosomes that direct heredity, instructing each cell on what to make and what to become.

5. The sperm, not the egg, determines the sex of the child. If the twenty-third chromosome in the sperm is an X, the baby will be a girl. If it is a Y, the baby will be a boy.

6. Genes are paired because they are located on paired chromosomes. When a gene is dominant, it outranks the other gene of the pair in controlling heredity. The outranked gene is called recessive.

7. Exceptionalities in development caused by genetic defects include cystic fibrosis, PKU, sickle-cell anemia, Tay-Sachs disease, Huntington's chorea, color blindness, hemophilia, muscular dystrophy, Down's syndrome, Klinefelter's syndrome, and Turner's syndrome. Such defects are the result of autosomal inheritance, X-linked inheritance, or defective chromosomes.

8. Genetic counselors use various procedures—karyotypes, amniocentesis, and ultrasound—and they look at family history in order to inform couples about their chances of having a child with birth defects.

9. Environmental influences that can adversely affect prenatal development include maternal age and nutrition and teratogens such as disease, drugs, chemicals, and radiation.

10. Hereditary and environmental influences do not operate alone. All influences are a part of an interacting system that continually affects growth and development. Heredity sets the limits, and the environment affects the extent to which these limits are reached.

Empathetic Activities

- Read Aldous Huxley's *Brave New World*. Do an empathetic analysis of the case in the first chapter of that book. Following the steps outlined in the Prologue of this text (see Fig. P.1), answer these questions:
  - What are your *personal reactions* to the mechanized way babies are produced in the Central London Hatchery and Conditioning Center?
  - Using *emotional empathy*, consider how the people felt about giving up their ovaries and sperm to be used by the state.
  - Using *cognitive empathy*, describe the hereditary and environmental influences on prenatal development that were used to control the development of the babies in the bottles. What effects might the X rays have on the unborn infants. What about the effects of the chemicals that were injected into the bottles?
- Re-read Spotlight 2.3 and answer the following questions:
  - If you were the genetic counselor, what would you do next? Remember that the genetic counselor is only supposed to provide information, not to advise.
  - What would you do if you were Joe or Catherine?

- Analyze the case of the expectant parent following the outline in Fig. P.1. Be sure to consider the following questions:

  - Emotional empathy: If you were pregnant, do you think you would feel the same way Doreen did? Would you also have second thoughts? Why or why not?

  - Cognitive empathy: After reading this chapter carefully, write a letter to Doreen telling her the things that can affect her unborn child in a positive or negative way. Try to give her some helpful suggestions to follow while she is pregnant.

- Discuss how hereditary and environmental influences work together to influence the growth and development of the *Whole Child*.

- How might the effects of pregnancy on parents influence their relationship with each other and with their newborn baby?

Related Readings

Apgar, Virginia, and Beck, Joan. *Is my baby all right? A guide to birth defects,* rev. ed. New York: Trident, 1973. A fascinating book. Explains birth defects—what causes them and how to prevent them. Cases included in almost every chapter make you want to read on and on.

Guttmacher, Alan F. *Pregnancy, birth, and family planning: A guide for expectant parents.* New York: Viking, 1973. Specific information for prospective parents about pregnancy and family planning. Also contains information about abortion, labor, delivery, multiple births, infertility, and the newborn baby.

Huxley, Aldous. *Brave new world.* New York: Harper and Row, 1932. A fascinating and frightening account of what can happen when "test-tube babies"—babies grown in bottles and "decanted" rather than born—become the rule rather than the exception.

Nilsson, Lennart. *A child is born: The drama of life before birth,* rev. ed. New York: Delacorte, 1977.

Nilsson, Lennart. *How was I born? A photographic story of reproduction and birth for children.* New York: Delacorte Press, 1975. Both books by Nilsson contain beautiful pictures of prenatal development and birth. We have read the children's book to the little ones in our lives with a great deal of joy for all.

Rugh, Roberts, Shettles, Landrum B., and Einhorn, Richard. *From conception to birth: The drama of life's beginnings.* New York: Harper and Row, 1971. Yes, this is the same Shettles who has reported the cloning of a human ovum. But this book is solid, not speculative. Contains an in-depth description of prenatal development, along with lovely pictures.

3 Birth and the Neonate

The Case of Doreen and Bill's Childbirth Experience

As soon as Doreen felt the first gush of water, she called to her husband who slept heavily in the bed beside her. When he was finally awake, he was just as excited as she was. The long-awaited time had come. Bill and Doreen had felt their baby's movements for months. Soon they would hold him or her in their arms! Bill carried the already packed suitcase to the car, and they were on their way to the hospital to participate in the arrival of their first baby.

The labor continued for ten hours. Bill provided support and helped Doreen use the relaxation techniques they had learned in their prepared childbirth classes. The most thrilling moment came when Dr. Hallman examined Doreen and announced it was time to go into the delivery room. Soon Doreen and Bill were there together. Doreen thought Bill looked hilarious in his green cap and gown, with his blue eyes peering out over the top of the gauze mask.

Things were proceeding rapidly now. When Doreen felt a contraction beginning, she would push hard when Dr. Hallman told her to. Doreen and Bill were soon able to see the baby's head in the mirror that was provided at the end of the table. "One more push and we'll have it." Dr. Hallman announced. "It's a boy!" Bill and Doreen could see the slippery, wrinkled baby as the doctor held it up by the heels. This was Brad, the baby they had planned and prepared for all those months. This day was the happiest day of Bill's life. Tears welled up in his eyes from the joy inside of him. Doreen's exhaustion disappeared. The hours of labor were forgotten as she experienced the excitement and happiness of the moment.

Soon Dr. Hallman was placing Brad on Doreen's chest and Doreen and Bill were looking in amazement. "Oh, you adorable baby!" Doreen was saying in a high-pitched voice. "You have all of your toes and all of your fingers! They are so tiny! You look like a doll!" Brad was looking at Doreen; he appeared to be staring directly into her eyes. And Doreen stared into Brad's eyes as she continued to talk to him in a high-pitched voice that she had never used before.

A hospital orderly took Brad and Doreen to a bonding room as Bill followed by their side. They had arranged to "room in" with Brad, so he could remain with them in the hours immediately following his birth. Bill noticed Brad's body seemed to move to the rhythm of Doreen's voice. He had a very special feeling of pride and love for his wife and his new baby. He wished Brad's grandparents could be here to share in the joy. But even this modern hospital wouldn't permit other family members to be present during childbirth.

Bill stayed with Doreen and Brad and watched their interaction. Doreen would touch Brad's legs and arms with her fingertips. Then she would use the palms of her hands to stroke the rest of his body. Bill knew he was witnessing an important moment in their relationship. He joined Doreen in stroking Brad's soft body. He was feeling something important and new beginning inside himself.

Birth

Until recently, a woman giving birth in a hospital was treated as a passive, uninformed patient. But today more and more expectant mothers and fathers, like Doreen and Bill, are active and informed participants in the birth of their child. By attending the prenatal classes offered by hospitals or health-care agencies, they learn how to minimize fear and pain by becoming familiar with all aspects of the birth process. They have access to much information that will help them make decisions about one of the most significant events of their lives. Doreen learned breathing techniques designed to keep her body relaxed and to focus her attention away from the contractions of her uterus during labor and delivery. Expectant parents also learn that labor, like pregnancy, has three distinct stages, each with its own characteristics.

STAGES OF LABOR

The first stage of labor is usually the longest—generally about ten hours for a woman's first baby, but only three or four hours for later babies. The amniotic sac breaks, causing a discharge of fluid or "breaking of waters." Contractions may begin and then suddenly stop. When the **cervix** (the opening of the uterus) begins to dilate or open, we know that the first stage of labor has truly begun. At first, contractions are brief and occur at irregular intervals. As labor progresses, the contractions become increasingly stronger and closer together. The first stage of labor ends when the opening of the cervix measures about ten centimeters, or about the width of a hand, and is large enough for the baby's head to pass through.

The second stage of labor—which may last from thirty minutes to two hours for a first baby and from five to thirty minutes in later births—ends with the baby's birth. By now, the baby's head has descended so that the top of it is visible—a condition known as **crowning.** During this stage, the physician often makes an incision called an **episiotomy** in the area between the vagina and rectum to allow for a quicker delivery and to eliminate the possible tearing of vaginal tissues.

The third stage of labor occurs after the birth of the baby and lasts only a few minutes. At this time the umbilical cord is clamped and cut. Delivery is complete when the umbilical cord and the attached placenta, now called the **afterbirth**, are expelled.

CHILDBIRTH METHODS

There is much controversy about the appropriate place and roles of parents and technology in the birth process. Today, parents have more childbirth choices available to them than ever before. There are no right or wrong answers on how to bring children into the world. It is a decision that rests with the expectant couple and one that requires them to examine their feelings and personal beliefs. While

In some cultures, childbirth is primarily a social event. In Termoli, Italy, for example, all the members of the family gather outside the mother's hospital room. Parents, grandparents, and several other relatives will have kissed the baby within five minutes of the birth. The birth and sex of the baby are officially announced when a blue or pink rosette is placed on the front door at home. Visits by acquaintances, neighbors, and distant relatives quickly begin (Klaus and Kennell, 1976).

Whether childbirth should be a surgical or a social event has become a very controversial issue in the United States. Many critics claim that modern technology has done more to dehumanize the birth process than it has to improve it. Many couples to-day are put off by the sterile and impersonal atmosphere in most hospitals, so they are shopping around and seriously deliberating on how they will birth their child. At first, Doreen and Bill were reluctant to have a hospital birth because they felt they would be too removed from the intimacy of their family and loved ones. And they feared Doreen would become lonely, depressed, and alienated in a sterile hospital setting. They decided on a hospital childbirth when they discovered that many hospitals, yielding to consumer demands, now emphasize the social as well as surgical aspects of the birth process. Some hospitals have set up **birthing rooms**—homelike, warm, and intimate labor and delivery rooms, just steps away from all

many couples continue to prefer a conventional delivery in the hospital, others are opting for changes—from special birthing or bonding rooms and special staff to the Lamaze, Leboyer, and husband-coached methods and even home birth.

Conventional Childbirth. For the past forty years, conventional childbirth in Western society has often been a surgical event. To prevent infection, every effort is made to keep mother and baby in a germfree environment. During the first stage of labor, the mother stays in a labor room. As she enters the second stage, she is moved into a well-scrubbed delivery-room—a sterile, brightly lit room where the actual delivery takes place. There are many sounds as people call out to each other and move around. A normal, healthy baby is expected to cry. The umbilical cord is cut quickly. Silver nitrate is placed in the baby's eyes to prevent blindness in case the mother has venereal disease. After the birth, the baby is taken to a carefully supervised nursery and will remain there during the first days of life.

Generally, the mother is alone with medical personnel during childbirth while other members of the family wait elsewhere. Pain-relieving drugs are routinely administered. Sometimes mothers are lightly sedated with *analgesics* so they can relax; other times they are heavily drugged with *general anesthesia*, which makes them totally unconscious. Or a *regional anesthesia* may be injected into the spinal canal, which causes a loss of feeling in the lower half of the body. A fourth option, injection of *local anesthesia* into the vaginal area, results in a lessening but not complete loss of feeling in that area.

the technological advantages a hospital can offer. There are no stirrups and a firm bed is used instead of a delivery table. More progressive hospitals also have **bonding rooms**—where mother, father, and newborn can be alone immediately after birth to get acquainted with no outside interference. **Rooming in** arrangements allow the newborn to stay in the mother's hospital room instead of the nursery. Mother, baby, and perhaps father can establish feeding routines and begin to adjust to each other in a relaxed atmosphere.

Nurse midwifery is being practiced in some hospitals. A qualified nurse who has had special training in obstetrics, the **nurse midwife** delivers babies in problem-free births under the supervision of an obstetrician and aids in family planning, education, counseling, and post-natal advice. Maternal and infant mortality rates across the United States have been reduced in those areas where nurse midwives have been employed (Litoff, 1978).

Many expectant couples in larger cities plan to deliver their baby in a **home birthing center**—a clinic with a homelike atmosphere where nurse midwives and obstetricians are on hand to assist as needed in the birth process. This way, the stay is brief and medical costs are cut in half, plus other family members—parents and older children—are sometimes permitted to share in the joy of the childbirth experience.

Lamaze Prepared Childbirth. **Lamaze childbirth** involves preparation, limited medication, and active participation by both parents. Dr. Fernand Lamaze, a French obstetrician, developed this method of prepared childbirth to reduce expectant parents' fear and pain through education. In Lamaze classes, parents gain a realistic understanding of the childbearing process. Each mother learns several breathing exercises and other techniques that she will use during the three stages of labor. The husband or coach learns these techniques, too, and helps the mother use them. By concentrating on the things she has learned, her attention is distracted from her contracting uterus. This concentration helps her to relax and work with, rather than against, the labor. It also reduces the discomfort associated with the contractions, and it provides the opportunity for parents to work closely together to bring their baby into the world. The husband-wife and parent-infant emotional bond is perhaps the greatest advantage of the Lamaze method (Horn, 1977).

Leboyer Childbirth. Perhaps the most revolutionary and controversial new childbirth method is the one introduced by Dr. Frederick Leboyer, a French obstetrician. The **Leboyer method** is supposed to be a gentle process designed to ease the baby's transition into the world. Parents who choose Leboyer almost always use Lamaze or a similar preparation. But there are differences. In Leboyer there are no slaps and the infant is not turned upside down. The Leboyer delivery room is dimly lit and no one speaks above a whisper. The newborn is placed on the mother's warm abdomen in the fetal position. Doctor and mother gently massage

❋ Spotlight 3.2: Expectant Fathers

Actor Donald Sutherland describes his childbirth experience:

> It was the most incredible, wonderful, terrifically joyful, sexual, sensual, loving time of our lives. It was so intensely personal that it's hard to believe we didn't discover it all by ourselves. But it is as common as dying, or making love, or being born. It's what the hospitals categorize as "normal childbirth," and it was extraordinary for us because we did it together. . . .
>
> We chose Robert A. Bradley's husband-coached childbirth method because it seemed to ensure our mutual participation more than any other. We took classes together for three months; we exercised together every day. We found a doctor, a hospital, and a truly dedicated nursing staff that eagerly supported both Bradley and ourselves. They assured us certain freedoms: There would be no medication, no shaving of the pubic hair, no legs in stirrups, no tied-down wrists, no premature breaking of the bag of waters. We would be able to conduct privately, in a darkened room, the first stage of labor; work together with the staff in a quiet delivery room during the second stage; and while Francine was still on the delivery table, I would be able to place our new-

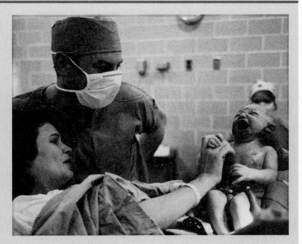

"He was a boy, and we couldn't stop saying how beautiful he was, and counting his fingers and toes," said actor Donald Sutherland of the birth of his son.

born child on her breast for the first feeding. And then, when everybody was dressed, all three of us would go home.*

---

*From "Childbirth Is Not for Mothers Only" by Donald Sutherland, *Ms. Magazine,* 1974, vol. 11, p. 47. © *Ms. Magazine,* Corporation, 1974. Reprinted with permission.

---

the baby for up to six minutes before the umbilical cord is cut. Then the newborn is bathed in water that is the same temperature as the intrauterine environment.

Babies born in the Leboyer tradition are usually very quiet. And many smile right after birth (Hamilton, 1979). Leboyer enthusiasts say that children born by this method experience a smoother transition into the world and are more advanced in physical development than children born by more traditional means (Trotter, 1978). Leboyer babies are supposed to be more trusting and serene than other children and to show more interest in the world around them. But recent research disputes many of these claims. In two separate studies, Leboyer babies reacted to their first bath with irritable crying (Hamilton, 1979; Nelson et al., 1980). Canadian obstetricians found the Leboyer procedure had no advantages over conventional methods of delivery at least through the eighth month after birth (Nelson et al., 1980). Perhaps the major advantage to the Leboyer method is that it may strengthen parent-child relationships and improve parents' compe-

Traditionally, childbirth and child care have been exclusively the woman's role in our society. The father's role has been to support his wife but to take little part in the birth experience or rearing of children. But today the importance of a father in his child's development is recognized (Lamb, 1979). Some think the expectant father's early involvement in childbirth has an important effect on mother, father, and baby as individuals and as a family unit (Parke, 1981).

More and more fathers are expressing a desire to participate in the birth of their children. A survey of unmarried college men reported that 90 percent felt fathers should participate in childbirth and infant care (McIntire et al., 1974). Under pressure from expectant parents, hospital policies that once excluded expectant fathers from the delivery room are being changed, and most hospitals now allow fathers to actively participate throughout the birth process. Some even allow them to room in with their newborns.

Prepared childbirth classes have become popular for many expecting couples. It is no longer unusual for fathers, like Donald Sutherland, to coach their wives in breathing, to help make them comfortable during labor, and to give them emotional support. This also allows mothers to give their husbands emotional support rather than leaving them pacing the floor. Fathers now participate in the birth process just as they did in conception. One research study showed that fathers experienced a "high," increased self-esteem, and closer ties to their newborns after childbirth participation (Greenberg and Morris, 1974). Not only do fathers share the highs, they share the lows too. A recent study of new fathers indicated that 62 percent experienced post-birth blues or depression similar to the emotional letdown reported by 89 percent of new mothers (Zaslow and Kramer, 1981).

Societal changes are helping fathers adjust in their new role. Special classes aid expectant fathers in their transition to parenthood (Resnick et al., 1978). Child development experts also recommend that more businesses and industries institute paternity leave so that fathers can become more involved in childbirth and child care and that hospitals and schools help fathers learn to be effective parents and provide advice and assistance when families have problems (Parke, 1981).

tence because of their active participation in the birth process (Berezin, 1980; Duff, 1980).

Husband-Coached Childbirth. Many parents are choosing **husband-coached childbirth,** sometimes called the **Bradley method** after its developer, Dr. Robert Bradley, an American physician. Expectant parents take classes to learn about nutrition, exercise, and physiology, and how to select childbirth services. They decide where the birth will occur and who will help during the process. Like Lamaze, the Bradley method is husband coached, but unlike Lamaze it opens up many more labor-delivery options. Couples are encouraged to find their own labor-delivery "style." For example, mothers might choose to walk, sit, or squat during labor—whatever is comfortable for them. During childbirth, mothers "tune in" to the experience instead of using breathing techniques to draw their mind away from the pain. Spotlight 3.2 describes a delivery by the husband-coached method.

Home Birth.   "Oh! My God! The baby is choking to death!" cried the gray-haired grandmother as she waved her arms in the air. "He's already turning blue!"

After screaming these words, the grandmother calmed herself. Then she carefully reached down and unraveled the umbilical cord from around the newborn baby's neck. She laid the baby on his mother's stomach. She then turned to greet the rotund, cigar-smoking country doctor who had arrived too late to deliver the baby.

This vignette describes the actual birth of one of the authors of this book. Earlier in this century, it was common for babies to be born at home. Even though most medical personnel say that home delivery is quite unsafe, this delivery practice is being revived in the United States (Litoff, 1978). Recent statistics show that 15 percent of all births in California occur at home (Wertz and Wertz, 1977).

Home birth is a social event. Intimate, family-centered maternity care is emphasized. Advocates of the home delivery method believe that sophisticated equipment and obstetric techniques and the high costs they entail have transformed a natural and joyous social event into an unnatural and much-feared surgical ordeal (Arms, 1975).

Lay midwives often assist in delivering babies at home. Because lay midwives have no formal medical training, they have been severely criticized by the medical profession. But today there are better controls than in the past. In 1975, twenty-two states had licensing laws for lay midwives and others issued "permits" to practice. Some authorities believe that legally recognized lay midwives will help to ensure that safe home childbirth programs are established (Sousa, 1977).

DRUGS AND CHILDBIRTH

Despite renewed interest in alternatives that stress childbirth without drugs, drug administration during birth is on the rise (Brackbill, 1979). These drugs pass directly through the placental barrier into the fetal bloodstream and newborns are born groggy. Some people claim the rate of infant death in this country in the latter part of this century is related to use of medication during delivery. Other effects of drugs during childbirth are presented in Fig. 3.1.

EXCEPTIONAL CHILDBIRTH

Although most births occur without complications, much like Brad's, occasionally there are problems such as prematurity, anoxia, and breech birth and techniques such as cesarean surgery and forceps delivery are necessary.

Premature Babies.   On November 29, 1979, Russell Williams made history. Today a healthy child, he is remembered as the smallest premature newborn to survive in the United States. He weighed only 1.01 pounds at birth and only eight

- When drugs are given to mothers during labor and delivery, effects are later observed in infant behavior:
    - Lags in motor, muscular, and mental development.
    - Depressed bodily functions, such as poor circulation and slowed heart and breathing rates.
    - Decreased physical-motor activity, sensory alertness, and muscular strength.
    - Lowered food intake, weight gain, and sucking rate and strength.
    - Delayed mental functioning, such as poor attention and concentration.
    - Increased quiet sleep; decreased active states.
- Medication effects are dose-related. The greatest effects on infants occur when mothers receive high-potency drugs or high doses of certain drugs.
- Drug effects may last a long time—anywhere from one day to one year. In some cases, medication effects remained just as strong months after birth.
- There is no evidence that drugs affect boys or girls differently, or that their effect is related to race, ethnic background, or socioeconomic class.

Figure 3.1 **Using pain-relieving drugs during childbirth**
(Adapted from Brackbill, 1979)

pounds at six months of age—what some normal babies weigh at birth. **Premature** babies are either born too early (preterm infants) or are born full term but are underweight (low-birth-weight infants). **Preterm** infants have a gestation period of thirty-seven weeks or less, instead of the usual forty full-term weeks. **Low-birth-weight infants** weigh less than five and a half pounds (2500 grams) at birth.

It's hard to make generalizations about premature infants because each case is so different. Some premature babies are healthy and stay that way, while others are too underdeveloped to survive. Death rates are highest for the very lowest birth weight babies (Kopp and Parmelee, 1979). Most premature infants are not physically ready to function independently from their mothers. They are more susceptible to infections, they usually have respiratory problems and delayed reflexes, and they lack enough fatty tissue to stay warm. Because of these and other problems, premature babies typically stay in the hospital longer than healthy babies.

It used to be the practice of hospitals to isolate premature babies from human touch because of their fragile health. Often placed in incubators, the young ones remained under close hospital supervision, separated from the warmth of their mothers' arms. But with the discovery that premature newborns thrive on human contact and stimulation, these earlier practices have been reversed (Kopp and Parmelee, 1979). Today, parents are encouraged to visit the intensive care nursery as often as they wish. There they can caress, cuddle, and fondle their babies and take part in feeding and changing routines sooner than usual. Not only does this aid in establishing closer parent-infant ties, it also builds parents' confidence in their ability to care for their new baby. Waterbeds, which simulate the prenatal environment by permitting rotation and more flexible movement, are now being used by some hospitals to provide additional stimulation.

The absence of mother's early physical contact and care are believed by some experts to interfere with and have later negative effects on the mother-infant relationship. Generally, mothers of preterm babies do not cuddle and smile at their newborns as much as mothers of full-term babies do (Leifer et al., 1972). And above average incidences of abuse have been reported among premature babies where early parent-newborn interaction had been interrupted (Egeland and Vaughn, 1981).

In general, the more physically immature newborns are, the more likely they are to have long-lasting problems (Kopp and Parmelee, 1979). Research shows that preterm infants can distinguish familiar people and events from new ones, but they are slower in mentally processing these differences than full-term babies (Rose, 1980; Werner and Siqueland, 1978). During their first two years of life, premature children also perform lower on tests of mental and motor development than full-term youngsters (Field et al., 1979). While differences in motor and mental development vanished by the fourth birthday, differences in hearing and language ability lingered. Nevertheless, the number of premature infants affected by lasting intellectual or neurological defects has been reduced—from between 10 and 40 percent in the past to between 5 and 15 percent (Drillien, 1975). Early in-

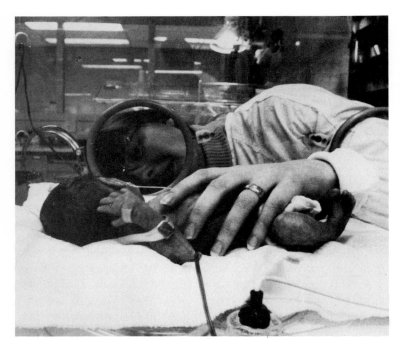

Because newborns thrive on early human contact and stimulation, hospitals now encourage parents of premature infants to visit them as often as they wish and, especially, to touch them.

fant care, including improved diet, early sensory stimulation, and monitoring of the newborn's vital signs, account for these reductions (Kopp and Parmelee, 1979).

Anoxia. If the oxygen flow through the umbilical cord is cut off, **anoxia**, or oxygen loss, can result. Extreme pressure during prolonged labor can cause a blood vessel in the baby's brain to rupture. Or the umbilical cord can become tangled or squeezed during the birth process, cutting off the oxygen supply before the baby is breathing independently. When anoxia occurs, the baby may suffer brain damage. When the damage is severe, the brain can be reduced to one-third or one-fourth its original size (Csermely, 1972). And although most babies who experience anoxia are not mentally retarded, the percentage of anoxic babies who are retarded as infants and preschoolers is higher than that for nonanoxic babies (Goldstein et al., 1976; Gottfried, 1973).

Breech Birth. Most babies are born in a **vertex presentation**—head first and facing their mother's back. But in 3 percent of deliveries, the baby's feet or buttocks emerge first, called **breech birth**. Breech births usually last longer than head-first deliveries. As the baby journeys through the birth canal, pressure against the umbilical cord reduces the oxygen flow from the placenta. The fetus is endangered because the head is the last part to emerge and the oxygen supply can be cut off for too long, causing permanent brain damage.

Cesarean Birth. Today, most babies who would be breech births are delivered by a surgical procedure known as **cesarean birth**—delivery of the fetus by abdominal surgery instead of the normal vaginal route. A father from Portland, Oregon, describes his daughter's cesarean birth:

> Her scream pierced the air as soon as her head poked out of her mother's abdomen—heralding a natural phenomenon no less staggering to me than the eruption of a volcano forty-five miles away. And unlike many men before me whose wives had given birth by cesarean section, I was able to witness the miraculous event from a seat at the head of the operating table. With my wife coping with chest pains, intravenous feeding, oxygen hoses up her nose and bright lights in a room filled with four doctors, two nurses and assorted medical paraphernalia, it was not a perfect experience. Still, Vicki was awake and able to hear her child's first cries. And, gratefully, I was there too.*

A cesarean operation takes about one hour, although the baby is born in the first five minutes. Cesarean babies don't have warped heads and they look better than babies who squeeze down the vaginal canal in a normal delivery. Before the twentieth century, cesareans were very dangerous and often ended in death for mother and infant. Today, with improved medical techniques, cesarean delivery is

---

* "Cesarean Birth a Joyous Event for Mom, Dad" by B. Baum, *The Charlotte Observer*, June 17, 1980. Reprinted by permission of the Associated Press.

practical and safe. In fact, in many instances—for example, if the space between the mother's pelvic bones is too small to accommodate her baby's head—it is decided well in advance of the actual birth that a cesarean delivery is a better choice than a vaginal delivery.

Nationwide, the number of cesarean births tripled between 1970 and 1980 (Bottoms et al., 1980). Why the increase in cesarean births? For one thing, more older women are having babies, and they are more likely to have cesarean deliveries. Mothers who deliver their first child by cesarean usually have repeat cesarean births—a group accounting for 23.1 percent of the increase in cesarean births (Bottoms et al., 1980).

Forceps Delivery.   Sometimes problems during a delivery make mechanical aids necessary. Slowed contractions or danger signs from the mother or fetus may make a quick delivery necessary. **Forceps delivery**—birth assisted by a double pronged surgical instrument that eases the newborn from the birth canal—may be selected in such instances. Forceps are placed on either side of the head while the baby is still in the uterus, and the handles are joined. Then the baby is pulled, turned, and forced out of the womb. Although forceps pressure can cause permanent brain damage, usually no harm is done. Typically, there is only a temporary warping of the baby's delicate head and some bruising on the head and cheeks.

APGAR SCALE

It was only sixty seconds after delivery. Nicky lay limp and lethargic in the warmth of his mother's arms. His bluish skin coloring alerted the doctor that he was experiencing oxygen loss or poor circulation. He barely responded as the doctor quickly checked him using the Apgar Scale.

The **Apgar Scale** is routinely used to assess the condition of newborns right after birth and again five minutes later. Developed by Dr. Virginia Apgar, the scale is a screening test that rates the new baby's adjustment to the world outside the mother's womb so that problems can be detected and lifesaving measures can be employed immediately (Apgar, 1953). The scale yields a score based on color, heart rate, muscle tone, reflex, and respiration. Two points are given for each feature, allowing a total of ten possible points. Most normal babies score seven or more points. More boys than girls have low Apgar scores (Apgar, 1953). Newborns like Nicky who score four points or less are in immediate need of life support systems. Low Apgar scores at birth seem to indicate lower performance in later infancy. Babies with Apgar scores from zero to three at one minute after birth had significantly lower eight-month mental and motor scores than infants who scored between seven and ten (Serunian and Broman, 1975). In addition, high Apgar scores at birth have been associated with better language development in childhood (Jordan, 1980).

The Neonate

Newborn babies are called **neonates** during the first four weeks of life. The neonatal period is one of transition from the sheltered environment of the mother's womb into a demanding world. The experiences in these first moments, days, and weeks of life establish the foundation for all later life. Knowledge of the neonatal period is important for a better understanding of children and the relationships that they will come to establish.

PHYSICAL CHARACTERISTICS OF THE NEONATE

Ask any new mother or father. They will tell you that their newborn is beautiful. But those of us who have a more objective view might see things differently. The skin of the neonate is wrinkled, soft, and blotchy. The flesh is firm and elastic. All infants are pale, even those who will eventually be very dark. There may be an abundance of soft, fine hair, or none at all. Many neonates have fine hair on their ears and on the lower backsides of their bodies. Their eyelids are puffy. Eye color is grayish but changes to a permanent color at a later time. On the average, the newborn weighs about seven and a half pounds and is twenty inches long at birth.

BODY SYSTEMS OF THE NEONATE

The fetus usually enjoys a perfect environment: constant temperature, regular oxygen supply, and nutritional benefits maintained and regulated by their mother's body. But at birth, the conditions under which neonates live change drastically. Separated from the mother, neonates are exposed to a new environment in which temperature, physiological functioning, and nutrition are different. They can no longer live passively and must depend upon their own body systems to regulate body functioning. In short, the neonate makes the first giant steps toward being an independent human being.

Skeletal System.   At birth, parts of the neonate's skeletal system remain undeveloped. The new bones are pliable. The baby's head may appear lopsided from the birthing process because of the softness of the bones. **Sutures**—gaps running between the bones of the skull that look like crevices or gulleys—exist in the skull before the bones fuse together. The skull is also characterized by **fontanelles** (see Fig. 3.2). These consist of soft, connective tissue that covers depressions in the skull where it has not yet connected. Some people call fontanelles "soft spots." The fontanelles appear to be diamond-shaped and they vary in size. The sutures and fontanelles permit the skull bones to overlap and make the head more adaptable during the birth process. You may have heard that extreme care must be taken not to bump the soft spots in a baby's head. This is really not true, since they are protected by a covering of cartilage.

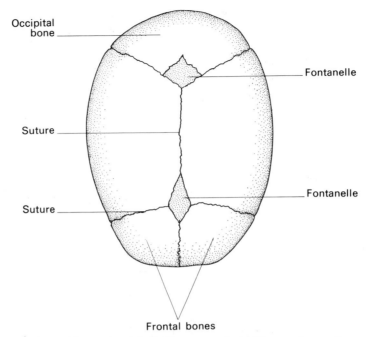

Occipital bone

Fontanelle

Suture

Fontanelle

Suture

Frontal bones

Figure 3.2 **The neonatal skull.** The neonate's skull bones, fontanelles, and sutures as seen from above.

Respiratory System.   During prenatal development, the fetus receives oxygen through the umbilical cord, but at birth respiration becomes an independent activity. After birth, the breathing of the neonate is irregular, rapid, and shallow with the abdomen doing more work than the chest. Babies make wheezing and snorting sounds as they breathe because the breathing mechanism is still underdeveloped and some fluid still remains in the lungs.

Circulatory System.   Before birth, the baby's blood flows to and from the placenta, transporting oxygen and nutrients to the baby and taking away waste products that will be eliminated by the mother's body. But once the umbilical cord is cut, the baby's original source of oxygen and nourishment is lost and circulation to the placenta is shut down as the opening leading from the fetal heart to the placenta closes. This shutdown causes the infant's circulatory system to begin operating independently from the mother's by forcing increased blood flow through the newborn's lungs. The neonate's blood contains hemoglobin, which carries oxygen to other parts of the body.

An opening between the right and left ventricles, present since prenatal life, slowly closes during the first seven days after birth. The neonate's heartbeat remains fast and irregular until about the second week, with faster heart rates reported when the baby is awake and slower ones during sleep.

Digestive System. Once born, the neonate no longer passively receives nourishment from the mother's blood. Food is taken from bottle or breast into the mouth and stomach. Some babies are nursed immediately after birth while others are not fed until twelve hours later. The first food from the mother's breast is called **colostrum**. This fluid has a laxative effect and contains antibodies that protect the newborn from many diseases.

After one day of life, neonates pass their first stool. Called **meconium**, this stool contains intestinal secretions, bile, mucus and products of cellular breakdown that accumulate before birth. As the bowels and bladder become full, the sphincter muscles automatically open and bowel movements occur. The stool of the newborn varies in color and consistency, depending upon the type of food that is received. The breastfed baby has a soft, yellowish stool that is curd-like in appearance, while the bottlefed baby has a darker, firmer stool.

ACTIVITIES OF THE NEONATE

Neonates are active creatures. They fall into and out of sleep easily, exhibit many reflexes, and are capable of a great deal of learning.

Sleeping and Waking. Neonates sleep lightly and are easily awakened. With equal ease, they fall back to sleep. Six different states or variations in neonatal activity have been identified (Wolff, 1966):

Regular sleep. The baby's eyes remain closed. There is slow, even breathing and the infant's facial muscles are relaxed.

Irregular sleep. The respiratory pattern is uneven and faster than during regular sleep. The newborn's eyes are closed and there is frequent twitching of the muscles. The irregular sleep state is sometimes called **rapid eye movement sleep (REM sleep),** which is characterized by a rapid fluttering of the eyeballs under closed eyes. In adults, REM sleep is a signal that they are dreaming. We aren't sure what it signals in newborns.

Drowsy state. The baby's eyes have a dull, glazed appearance. Breathing is irregular and there are slow body movements. Drowsiness occurs when babies are on the verge of sleep or right after they have awakened.

Alert inactive state. This state is similar to a state of conscious attention in the adult. Babies appear spellbound as they focus and stare at different objects and events, while at the same time moving their heads, arms, or legs.

Waking activity. A lot of motor activity involving the baby's entire body characterizes this state. Eyes are open and there is irregular breathing.

Crying state. The baby cries and fusses for the remainder of the waking time, although some babies will spend more time than others crying.

The neonate sleeps seventeen to twenty hours a day. A small part of this time is spent in regular sleep. And seventy-five percent of sleeping time is spent in ir-

Babinski Reflex. Fanning or separating the toes and turning the foot when the sole of the foot is stroked.

Babkin Reflex. Turning the head and opening the mouth when pressure is applied to the palm.

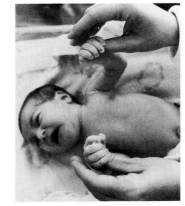

Grasping Reflex. A reflex observed when the palm of the hand is stroked. Babies make very strong fists and cling to objects in their palms. The grasp is surprisingly strong. Newborns can have as much as two pounds of pulling power in each hand (White, 1975). This reflex disappears after the first six months of life.

The grasping reflex

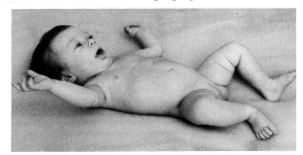

Moro Reflex. Throwing out the arms and legs and bringing them together again in response to loud noises. Similar behaviors occur when babies are gently dropped into a crib.

The Moro reflex

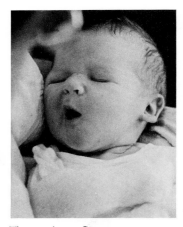

Rooting Reflex. When the cheek is stroked, turning the head to the side which is touched. This is one means by which newborns locate their source of food.

The rooting reflex

Figure 3.3 **Reflexive behaviors of the newborn**

Swimming Reflex. The occurrence of well-coordinated, involuntary swimming movements when neonates are placed in a prone position on the stomach.

Walking Reflex. The making of step-like motions that resemble well-coordinated walking when babies are held under their arms, with bare feet touching a flat surface.

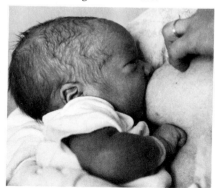

Sucking Reflex. This reflex is activated after the rooting reflex is achieved. Babies begin to suck once the source of nourishment is located, usually the nipple. Some suck outright while others are stimulated when the nipple is moved around in the mouth.

The sucking reflex

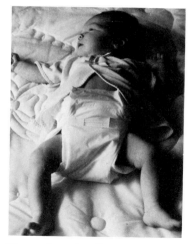

Tonic Neck Reflex. Sometimes called the ''fencer's pose'' because it resembles the stance assumed in the sport of fencing. When placed on the back, the head is turned to one side, usually the right side, with both hands fisted. The arm and leg on this same side are extended and the opposite limbs are flexed.

The tonic neck reflex

Withdrawal Reflex. Jerking away the legs when the soles of the feet are tickled. Withdrawal may also take the form of protective movements with the hands, as the upper portion of the body is touched.

The withdrawal reflex

regular sleep (Hutt et al., 1969). Newborn sleep is broken by short, waking periods caused by pain, hunger, or internal discomforts. Average neonates are awake from four to seven hours a day. During two or three of these hours, they are awake and quiet; they are active for the remaining two or more hours. The amount of time which newborns spend in each of these states varies greatly from infant to infant (Thoman, 1975). Newborns are just as different in behavioral states as they are in individual personalities.

Reflexes.   When you blink your eyes, jump from fright, or jerk your hand from a hot oven, you do not stop to think about it. You do it automatically because of reflexes. **Reflexes** are automatic, inborn behaviors. The newborn baby has many reflexes. Called "primitive" reflexes, they are described in Fig. 3.3 on pages 100 and 101.

Although the primitive reflexes disappear within the first year of life, other reflexes—such as the startle reflex, the eyeblink, the knee jerk, yawning, coughing, gagging, and sneezing—persist throughout life. There is a clear relationship between brain maturation and disappearance of the primitive reflexes. The reason for this disappearance is that primitive reflexes are controlled by the *midbrain*—the first part of the brain to develop and the part that is most like that of lower animals. As the cerebral cortex—the more advanced, grey area of the brain—matures, more of the nervous system comes under its control. The primitive reflexive behaviors that are controlled by the midbrain disappear. Through a medical examination of an infant's system of reflexes, it is possible to determine if the brain and nervous system are developing normally. So presence or absence of primitive reflexes is a good indicator of neurological growth.

Learning.   Until recently, most people thought that neonates were not capable of much learning. But current research increasingly shows that newborns are remarkable creatures with sophisticated learning capacity.

In classical conditioning (see Chapter 1) experiments, neonatal learning has been observed as early as three weeks of age (Papousek, 1967). The stroking of the newborn's cheek causes a reflexive turning of the head. In one study this stroking was paired with the sound of a bell. After many instances of pairing, babies turned their heads at the sound of the bell alone (Papousek, 1967). As their perceptual and cognitive abilities mature and experience increases, older infants learn more easily than newborns through classical conditioning (Sameroff and Cavanagh, 1979).

The ability of newborn infants to learn has also been observed in studies of operant conditioning. In one experiment, two groups of neonates were given a sweetened solution as a reward for turning their heads (Siqueland, 1968). These infants increased the number of times they turned their heads. When a third group was rewarded with the sweetened solution when they kept their heads still, the amount of time they kept their heads still increased.

Another way babies learn is through observational learning, a process not dependent on any rewards. A capacity for imitating some simple motor acts and simple sounds already exists in the newborn's makeup at birth. Two-week-old neonates will imitate human gestures—such as opening the mouth, sticking out tongue and lips, and moving fingers one at a time—that they have observed (Meltzoff and Moore, 1977; Parton, 1976). Imagine a new father's surprise when he sticks out his tongue playfully at his new baby and the infant copies his gestures (see Fig. 3.4)!

Newborns also have the ability to **habituate** or get used to repeated stimuli or events. As newborns habituate to a new event, they pay less attention to or ignore familiar events. For example, Brad's father noticed that he listened intensely at first to the sound of a new rattle. But after a while, he ignored the sound of the rattle in favor of a new music box sound or the sound of his father's voice.

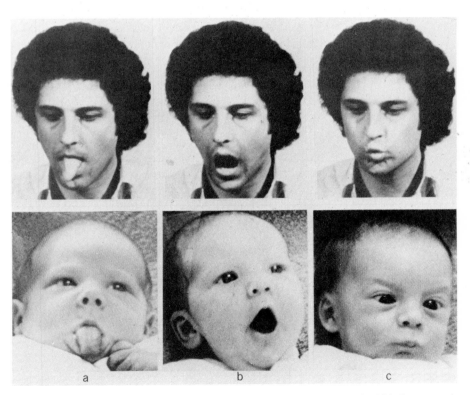

a   b   c

Figure 3.4 **Observational learning in neonates.** These two- to three-week-old infants can already imitate an adult sticking out his tongue, opening his mouth, and protruding his lower lip.

By studying habituation in neonates, researchers have been able to learn more about their learning and responses. One way to measure the newborn's habituation is to monitor the heart rate. A decline in heart rate indicates that the newborn is paying attention. If heart rate becomes stable, that means the newborn has habituated (Horowitz, 1972; Sameroff, 1973). When Brad repeatedly watches a toy car roll down an incline, his heart rate becomes stable. If the car is stopped on the incline, his heart rate will slow down—indicating he has noticed this new event.

PERCEPTUAL CAPABILITIES

William James (1890) said, "The baby, assailed by eyes, ears, nose, skin, and entrails at once, feels it all as one great blooming, buzzing confusion" (p. 488). Most people used to agree with James that the neonate's view of the world was hazy and disorganized. But modern research techniques have shown that neonates have extensive perceptual capabilities that include seeing, hearing, smelling, touching, and tasting (Kessen, 1973). Some researchers now believe that the neonatal period is the most significant four weeks in an entire lifetime for exercising and developing perceptual capabilities.

Seeing.   Although the eyesight of the newborn is not fully developed and the retina and optic nerve are immature, the neonate is capable of sophisticated visual activity (Cohen et al., 1979). Focusing is evident within the first week of life, and newborns can focus both eyes on the same point when objects are placed approximately eight to ten inches away (Slater and Findlay, 1975). Newborns can respond to different levels of brightness or light intensity (Peiper, 1963). Parents observe that babies will avoid a sudden bright light by turning their heads or closing their eyes. Neonates can also accurately follow or track objects with their eyes (Gregg et al., 1976; Kagan, 1970). In general, newborns prefer to watch bright and moving objects rather than stationary ones (Fantz, 1967). Newborns can discriminate (tell the difference) between many objects, patterns, and colors. Using his specially designed "looking chamber" (see Fig. 3.5), Fantz (1961) found that neonates prefer to look at striped and checkerboard patterns over solid colors and that they can discriminate between color and black and white (Fantz and Nevis, 1967). They also prefer to look at unusual rather than familiar objects (Milewski and Siqueland, 1975), large patterns rather than small ones, and curved lines rather than straight ones (Cohen et al., 1979). Newborns pay more attention to complex rather than simple things (DeLoache et al., 1978; Haaf and Brown, 1976). Their visual perception is also developmental in nature, that is, the skills improve as they get older (Goldblatt et al., 1980).

Hearing.   Neonates can discriminate among various sounds and voices (Papousek, 1967) and they can detect changes in frequency and intensity of tones. By four weeks, they can recognize different speech sounds (Ungerer et al., 1978). At birth, neonates can coordinate looking and listening. When they hear a sound, they will turn their eyes to the spot where the sound came from (Field, J., et al., 1980). Such early coordination has led some researchers to suggest that certain connections among the five senses, called **sensory linkages**, are inborn (Bower, 1977). Other research on sound-vision linkage shows that not only will babies look toward the source of a sound, they will also follow its movement with their eyes. This has been interpreted to mean that sound activates the inborn tendency to scan and serves as a guide to direct babies where to look (Mendelson and Haith, 1976).

Smelling. Certain experiments, such as one using the strong odor of anise and the offensive odor of asafetida, have shown that newborns can discriminate between strong odors (Lipsitt, 1966). Respiration changes have been used as an indication of a newborn infant's ability to smell (Self et al., 1972). Studies have shown that body activity and rate of respiration increase when infants are exposed to a solution with a distinct smell. Neonates as young as sixteen hours of age turned away from an ammonium hydroxide odor source more frequently than they turned toward it (Reiser et al., 1976).

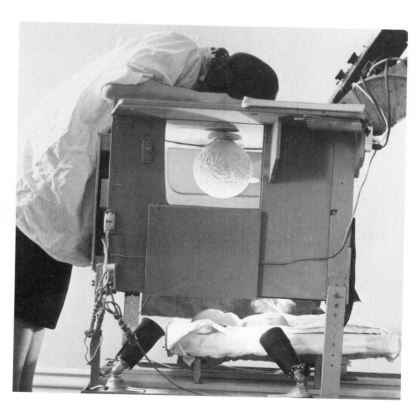

Figure 3.5

The Fantz looking chamber. This device allows researchers to show infants different pictures, patterns, and designs and to record what babies prefer to look at and for how long.

Touching.   The sense of touch begins while the baby is still in the uterus. An eight-week-old fetus responds reflexively to a touch on the skin (Hooker, 1952). Neonates react to cold, pain, heat, and touch. After the first few days of life, they become more sensitive to touch and pain (Lipsitt and Levy, 1959). Early studies suggested that female neonates are more sensitive to touch and pain than male neonates (Arganian, 1973), but more recent research disputes these findings. When neonates' feet were stimulated by stiff, nylon bristles, no differences were found between males and females (Jacklin et al., 1981). A summary of research on this topic concludes that the sexes do not differ in sensitivity to touch (Maccoby, 1980).

Tasting.   Neonates can discriminate between the four basic tastes of sour, bitter, salt, and sweet (Jensen, 1932 ; Engen et al., 1974). When given sour, bitter, and salty solutions, some infants grimace and suck slowly and some reject salty tastes altogether (Crook, 1978; Pratt et al., 1930). Some researchers believe this early discrimination protects neonates against the intake of poisonous fluids-—which typically have bitter tastes (Crook, 1978). New babies are equipped with a ''sweet tooth.'' They are fond of sweet solutions—the sweeter the better (Nowlis and Kessen, 1976; Burke, 1977). Researchers think that newborns probably savor and enjoy sweet solutions— such as breast milk (Crook and Lipsitt, 1976)—just as you would an ice cream cone.

NEONATES AND ADULT RELATIONSHIPS

The neonatal period is an important time in which parent-child relationships are established.

Bonding.   Research suggests that right after delivery a period of high sensitivity exists for parents—especially mothers—to form close ties with their babies (Kennell et al., 1979). In their studies of newborns and their mothers, Marshall Klaus and John Kennell (1976) reported that an innate bonding mechanism exists in humans. **Bonding** is the formation of a strong close relationship between individuals. Klaus and Kennell believe a critical or sensitive period (see Chapter 1) occurs in the first ninety minutes after birth and may be the best time for parents to bond with their babies. These researchers found that most mothers who give birth without anesthesia are elated when their babies are born, and newborns are in a very alert state for the first hour of life. The elated state of the mother and alert state of the baby combine to make mother and infant particularly receptive to each other at this early period in their relationship. When they were allowed to hold their infants in the delivery room, mothers spent nearly three fourths of the time looking into the eyes of their newborn babies. The babies also looked into their mothers' eyes. Once they had experienced this mutual gazing, mothers reported feeling much closer to their infants. In fact, Kennell (1977) found that *anyone*—fathers, grandparents, and siblings—present during birth can form a special bond with the baby.

In a series of studies, Klaus and Kennell compared early-contact mothers with late-contact mothers. Early-contact mothers were allowed to hold and touch their naked newborn infants skin to skin for one hour immediately after birth and for five hours (in addition to the usual feeding time) on each of the next three days. Late-contact mothers followed the usual hospital procedure—glancing at the baby after birth and holding the child only at feeding times for the next three days. One month after discharge, mothers who had early contact with their newborns behaved differently than mothers who did not have the early contact (Klaus et al., 1972). Early-contact mothers were more likely to stand near and watch infants during a physical examination, soothe them if they cried, fondle them during feeding, and avoid leaving them in someone else's care. Long-term observations after five years also showed differences between children of early-contact mothers and late-contact mothers (Spezzano and Waterman, 1977). Presumably as a result of maternal bonding, children of early-contact mothers were breastfed longer, gained more weight, cried less, laughed and smiled more, had higher IQs and were more advanced in language development than were babies of late-contact mothers.

More recent and better-controlled studies have failed to confirm Klaus and Kennell's findings that early mother-neonate contact has any special advantages (Schaller et al., 1979; Svejda et al., 1980). As a result, many researchers question the existence of a sensitive period for parent-infant bonding or that early contact produces any special long-term effects (Bronfenbrenner, 1979). But early contact and interaction certainly allow parents and infants to tune in to each other's signals, the first stage in parent-child relationships.

Parent-Infant Synchrony

Doreen noticed that whenever Bill came into the room, Brad started smiling and following him with his eyes. Bill, in turn, drew closer to Brad's crib, and Brad's continued gazing and smiling caused Bill to pick him up and play with him—sometimes for as long as an hour. When Bill mimicked Brad's cooing, Brad returned the message; sounds and glances were batted back and forth like a tennis ball! "I've never seen a boy and his father so close to each other!" Doreen told her mother.

Parents have claimed for a long time that their babies try to speak or communicate when they are only a few weeks old. It is true that in early weeks of life, infants enter into exchanges with adults through gestures, facial expressions, and vocalizations. At birth newborns appear to be genetically "programmed" to com-

❊ Spotlight 3.3: Do Neonates Really Differ?

At this point you might be thinking that all neonates are just alike. Sometimes parents think this, too, and worry unnecessarily when they discover their second baby is so different from the first. While newborns *are* similar in the many ways we've described, T. Berry Brazelton, a famous pediatrician, observes that babies are also unique from birth:

> There are as many individual variations in newborn patterns as there are infants. Each newborn varies in an infinite number of ways from another—in appearance, in feeling, in reaction to stimuli, in movement patterns, in capacity to develop his own individual pattern. . . . Many a mother will remark after holding her second, third, sixth, or eighth child for the first time, "How can he be so different from all the rest!" (1969, p. 1)

Perhaps new parents will find it reassuring to know that some newborns enjoy physical contact and some don't. Cuddlers snuggle up to the person holding them, but noncuddlers don't like to snuggle. Newborns also show individual differences in sucking strength, their reactions to stress, the amount of energy they have, and how irritable they are. Some babies react to changes quickly and vigorously while others react slowly and without vigor (Bell, 1960; Kessen et al., 1961).

A group of researchers studied 141 new babies to find out more about infants' **temperament** —their unique styles of interacting with others (Thomas et al., 1970). They found that the temperament of 65 percent of these babies could be described as "easy," "difficult," or "slow-to-warm-up" (Thomas and Chess, 1980). The "easy" infant was characterized by regularity of such biological functions as hunger, sleep and eliminating; a positive approach to new people and situations; easy adaptation to new situations or changes in routines; and mild, mostly positive moods. "Difficult" babies were described as irregular in biological functions; negative and withdrawn toward new people and situations; not able to adapt to change easily; and intense, mostly negative in mood. "Slow-to-warm-up" infants had mildly negative responses to new people and situations, but they showed slow adaptability after repeated contact. The remaining 35 percent of the babies had a mixture of traits from the three categories. The researchers continued to study these children for the next ten years and found that many of the behaviors were stable over time (Thomas and Chess, 1977). Babies rated as "difficult" in early infancy were more likely to have behavior problems in early and middle childhood (Thomas and Chess, 1980).

You might be wondering what would cause such variations in temperament. Such things as genetic differences, the mother's emotional condition before and after birth, the neonate's physical condition, the type and duration of birth, and perhaps early bonding experiences combine to cause people to develop temperamental differences. It was once believed that the behavior of parents toward their infant was the only cause of temperamental differences. Irritable mothers were thought to cause irritable babies. Scientists now believe that babies affect parents just as parents affect their babies from the beginning of life (Bell and Harper, 1977; Lewis and Rosenblum, 1974; Parke, 1979a).

Patterns of parent-infant interaction are established during the first few days of life, with both neonate and parent contributing to the patterning (Osofsky, 1976). Recent evidence suggests the newborn's temperament can influence the early parent-newborn relationship (Bell, R. Q., 1979). An irritable baby can cause a parent to react in irritable ways, while a contented neonate who is easy to care for can cause parents to be gentle and contented

Parent-infant relationships are reciprocal. Infants are sensitive and react to the calm or anxious state of their parents, just as parents become concerned when their baby is fretful and relax when their baby is contented.

(Huntington, 1979; Segal and Yahraes, 1978). Research has also shown that alert and responsive newborns tend to have more responsive and sensitive mothers (Osofsky, 1976), and that adults pay more attention to happy, pleasant babies than to somber ones—by smiling back, talking, or picking up the baby (Maccoby, 1980).

The newborn's physical condition also influences the responses of nurses and parents. Nurses' reactions to premature infants were influenced by the infant's appearance. Nurses experienced in caring for premature infants rated them as more attractive than did nurses without this experience (Corter et al., 1978). In a study of mother-infant interactions in a hospital nursery for premature babies (Minde et al., 1978), it was shown that the way mothers behaved toward their premature newborn was partly determined by the size and medical status of the infant.

Some studies report more positive attention, social interaction, and care given to babies because they are considered high-risk—that is, premature or suffering from some kind of obstetric problem (Beckwith and Cohen, 1978; Zeskind, 1980). Differences in the cries of high-risk babies and low-risk (healthy) babies might make a difference in the kind of care they receive. Cries from high-risk infants called forth more immediate, tender and caring attention than low-risk infants did from a group of parents—even though parents knew nothing about the infant's conditions (Zeskind, 1980). Researchers speculate that high-pitched cries, typical of infants with a wide range of medical conditions, may be a survival signal to ensure adult care and protection (Lester and Zeskind, 1979).

In sum, infant signals set off a reciprocal relationship with adults around them. Such infant signals trigger additional attending behaviors from adults. These interconnected behaviors between adults and babies each influence the other and eventually result in closeness of adults to infants and infants to adults.

Cross-Cultural Development and Relationships

As you saw in the case of Omblean (see Prologue), childbirth and neonatal customs around the world may sound odd or harsh when judged against our cultural standards. If you think Omblean was abused, keep in mind that these early parent-neonatal relationships prepare him for later survival in his aggressive society. Child-rearing practices in every culture serve important social functions in the lives of parents and children. And Margaret Mead (1952) observed that childbirth and child-rearing customs are as different as the cultures in which they are found.

MOTHERS' PARTICIPATION

In some cultures, the mother kneels, squats, or holds on to two poles or a piece of rattan hung from the ceiling during delivery. In others, she is held around the waist by her husband or strapped to a modern delivery table. Among the Samoans, Mead (1928) notes, there was no privacy during childbirth:

> Convention dictates that the mother should neither writhe, nor cry out, nor inveigh against the presence of twenty to thirty people in the house who sit up all night if need be, laughing, joking, and playing games. The midwife cuts the cord with a fresh bamboo knife and then all wait eagerly for the cord to fall off, the signal for a feast. . . . Then the visitors go home, the mother rises and goes about her daily

tasks, and the new baby ceases to be of much interest to anyone. (p. 20–21)

FATHERS' PARTICIPATION

As we have seen, more and more men in our culture now participate in childbirth. But in some cultures fathers have been actively involved for hundreds of years. On Easter Island, fathers have their wives recline against them during labor and delivery (Metraux, 1940). In Sweden, more than 60 percent of expectant fathers take advantage of recent laws allowing them a period of paid paternity leave from their jobs after their infant is born (Parke, 1981).

Mead (1967) reported that out of sixty-four cultures, eighteen tribes observed a custom called the **couvade**, in which the husband shows some of the symptoms of pregnancy, goes into seclusion, or restricts activities during childbirth. Sometimes fathers report having real labor pains. And sometimes the symptoms are so realistic that the father lies beside his wife resting after the birth (Mead, 1952). Marco Polo (1938) reported the following account in Chinese Turkestan:

> And in this province the custom is that when the ladies have been confined and have given birth to a child, they wash him and wrap him up in clothes, and the lord of the lady gets into bed and keeps the infant that is born with him and lies in the bed forty

municate with their caregivers as they ''dance'' or move in rhythm to the sounds of adult speech (Condon and Sander, 1974; Stern, 1974). Slow-moving pictures of this beautiful activity resemble a graceful ballet dancer moving to the rhythm of an orchestra. Through these interactions, newborns become synchronized to adult speech. New babies respond with reciprocal vocalizations to their mother's high-pitched voice more than they do to their father's (Brown, 1979).

Although these early gestures, expressions, and vocalizations are reflexive

days without getting up from the bed except for important necessary duties. (p. 282).

The couvade is still practiced among the Black Carib of British Honduras. Almost every man interviewed by a research team reported pregnancy symptoms during his wife's pregnancy—food cravings, daytime sleepiness and fatigue, vomiting, headaches, fever, dizziness and toothaches (Munroe et al., 1973). Among the Wogeo of New Guinea, males were as apt to suffer from morning sickness as their wives (Munroe et al., 1973). And in our own culture, an expectant father sometimes reports episodes of morning sickness or other physical and psychological complaints during his wife's pregnancy (Gearing, 1978). These symptoms usually fade after childbirth.

Some scientists say the couvade strengthens the legitimacy of the child's need for the father (Munroe et al., 1973). Others believe it provides emotional satisfaction because men cannot bear children (Bettelheim, 1954).

NEONATAL RELATIONSHIPS

In the United States, early bonding and parent-neonatal interaction are stressed. Many other cultures also emphasize experiences such as breastfeeding, which encourages early bonding. Breastfeeding was found to exist in fifty-one primitive societies (Whiting and Child, 1953). In almost every case, mothers were relieved of other duties to make this a full-time practice. Mead (1952) reported that Samoan neonates are nursed generously, fed when hungry, carried when tired, and allowed to sleep at will. The Chenchu Tribe of India do not wean their children until five or six years of age. And the Lepcha allow the youngest child to nurse up until the time of puberty (Whiting and Child, 1953).

In contrast, the early parent-child activities in other societies interfere with early bonding. The Marquesans of the South Pacific nurse their children irregularly, for short time spans, and sometimes unwillingly. They feel if they provide lengthy nursing, children will become ''spoiled'' and hard to raise (Whiting and Child, 1953). Besides, these women take great pride in the firmness and beautiful shape of their breasts—which nursing is thought to ruin. The Hausa of Africa avoid interacting with their first-born children from birth (Leiderman et al., 1977). Hausa mothers do breastfeed their babies, but they never play with them, maintain eye contact with them, or refer to them by name. As a result, first borns are not as close to their mothers as later borns who are allowed more interaction with their mothers.

rather than adult-like communications, they are important in establishing a relationship between parent and infant. One research team (Strain and Vietze, 1975) called early mother-infant vocalizations a ''joining in'' pattern in which infant vocalizations affect the mother's talking and the mother's speech affects the infant's vocalizations. As you will see in Chapter 4, these ''joining in'' or ''tuning in'' behaviors form the basis for later relationships (Stern, 1974). Similar interactions occur between infants and fathers, as you saw with Brad and his Dad.

Development of the Parent-Child Relationship

Relationship	Developmental Period
Parent-Newborn Synchrony—Parents and their newborns begin tuning in to each other's signals. Grown-ups respond to neonate smiles and verbal sounds by such actions as moving near them, returning a smile, talking to them, or picking them up. In turn, body gestures, vocalizations, facial expressions, smiles, and other signals are activated from the babies.	Newborn (birth–4 weeks)
Parent-Infant Attachment	Infancy (birth–12 months)
Parent-Toddler Dependency	Toddlerhood (1–3 years)
Parent-Preschooler Partnership	Early Childhood (3–6 years)
Parent-Child Detachment / Children's Same-Sex Friendships	Middle Childhood (6–12 years)
Parent-Teenager Individuality / Crowd Formation	Adolescence (13–18 years)

A newborn's cry also causes an increased blood flow to the mother's breast stimulating milk production (Spezzano and Waterman, 1977). A baby's sucking triggers the release of two hormones, *oxytocin* and *prolactin,* in the mother. Oxytocin causes the mother's uterus to contract, which reduces bleeding after delivery; prolactin stimulates her breasts to produce milk and it may act to promote the formation of a bond between mother and newborn. It is also interesting to note that prolactin acts as a love hormone in birds. As you can see, infants have a lot of say in their social interactions with adults. And with increasing age, young ones initiate social interactions more and more.

Summary

1. There are three stages of labor: the first and longest begins with the dilation of the cervix and ends when full dilation is reached; the second is characterized by more frequent contractions, hard labor, and birth; in the third stage, the umbilical cord and placenta are expelled.

2. Although the surgical environment of traditional childbirth is still found in some hospitals, many hospitals are humanizing the birth process through birthing rooms, bonding rooms, rooming in, and midwifery. Other options for expectant parents include Lamaze prepared childbirth, Leboyer childbirth, the Bradley method, and home birth.

3. Drugs given to the mother during childbirth pass directly into the fetal bloodstream. Research suggests that medication, especially high-potency drugs or high doses of certain drugs, can have long-lasting effects on the infant.

4. More expectant fathers are becoming involved in their baby's birth by participating in prepared childbirth classes, coaching their wives in breathing, making them comfortable in labor, giving and receiving emotional support, and bonding with baby and mother as a family unit.

5. Prematurity, anoxia, breech birth, cesarean birth, and forceps delivery are exceptionalities in childbirth that can make birth more complicated than usual.

6. The Apgar Scale—a measure of the neonate's heart rate, muscle tone, reflexes, breathing, and skin color—is administered immediately after birth and again five minutes later.

7. The neonatal period—the first four weeks of life—is a time of transition as babies move from a perfectly balanced environment in the womb into a demanding world.

8. At birth, newborns must depend upon their own body systems to regulate body functioning. Although still underdeveloped, the neonate's skeletal, respiratory, circulatory, and digestive systems function independently from the mother's and continue to mature during the neonatal period.

9. Although neonates spend the majority of their time sleeping, six different states or variations in neonatal activity have been identified: regular sleep, irregular sleep, drowsy state, alert inactive state, waking activity, and crying state.

10. Healthy babies are born with many reflexes, among them the Babinski, Babkin, grasping, Moro, rooting, sucking, swimming, tonic neck, walking, and withdrawal. Many of these reflexes will disappear during the first year of life, as the lower parts of the brain yield to the maturity of the higher brain center.

11. Newborns have a considerable capacity for imitating and learning to discriminate through classical and operant conditioning. They are also well-equipped with sophisticated sensory capabilities—seeing, hearing, smelling, tasting, and feeling. They can track objects; they can discriminate between colors and patterns and between sounds and voices; they react to strong odors, solutions tasting sour, bitter, salty, and sweet, cold, pain, heat, and touch.

12. Both neonate and parent contribute to the two-way parent-infant interaction pattern that is established within the first few days. Bonding, neonatal temperamental differences, and the newborn's physical condition affect the nature of parent-infant synchrony.

Empathetic Activities

- What feelings did you have as you read the following?
  - Doreen and Bill's childbirth experience
  - Donald Sutherland's experience
  - The Portland, Oregon, father's cesarean birth experience
- If you were going to participate in childbirth today, which method would you choose and why?
- Interview a new mother and father. Ask them how individual family members have been affected by the birth of the new baby and how the total family system has been affected.
- Use information from this chapter to do the following:
  - Describe how you think Brad might look and behave when his parents take him home from the hospital.
  - Predict what you think his sensory capabilities will be during his first few weeks of life.
  - Explain the important relationship development that was going on between Brad and his parents right after his birth.
- How is knowledge of the childbirth and neonatal period important for a better understanding of the *Whole Child?*
- What kinds of long-lasting effects do childbirth and neonatal experiences have on children and their relationships with others?

Related Readings

Brazelton, T. Berry. *On becoming a family: The growth of attachment.* New York: Delacorte, 1981. A well-written account of early relationships between parents and their newborns. Taking on the myth of instant bonding, the author shows how parent-infant ties are learned and develop over time.

Dick-Read, Grantly. *Childbirth without fear,* 4th ed. New York: Harper and Row, 1978. The author's view on how women can prevent fear and pain in childbirth by learning how to relax.

Gresh, Sean. *Becoming a father: A handbook for expectant fathers.* New York: Butterick Publisher, 1980. A practical guide for expectant fathers on what to expect in their new role.

Klaus, Marshall, and Kennell, John. *Maternal-infant bonding: The impact of early separation or loss on family development.* St. Louis: C. V. Mosby, 1976. An important book. Shows how family-centered childbirth and special provisions for premature infants are said to facilitate maternal-infant bonding.

Leboyer, Frederick. *Birth without violence.* New York: Knopf, 1975. Describes the controversial Leboyer method of gentle childbirth with many photographs of Leboyer deliveries. Fun to read.

Litoff, Judy Barrett. *American midwives: 1860 to the present.* Westport, Conn.: Greenwood Press, 1978. The history of midwifery, including the lay midwife versus nurse midwife controversy. Suggests that the education and training of midwives is one way to reduce the number of maternal and infant deaths in the United States.

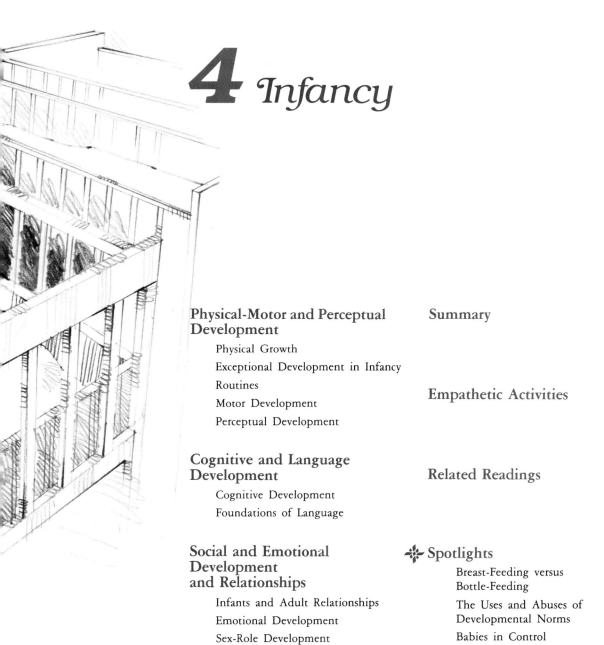

4 Infancy

The Case of Velma and Thelma

Identical twins Velma and Thelma were separated from their parents and each other immediately after birth and placed in different "homes." Thelma was taken to a "real" home. Her parents had planned and looked forward to the day they could adopt a baby. When Thelma arrived, they showed their affection and love by holding her, cuddling her, and playing with her a lot. They especially liked holding their newborn when they fed her and talking to her when they bathed her. Thelma's new parents made her an attractive, colorful room with a beautiful crib mobile. The room was bright and cheery, with plenty of things to look at and play with. Thelma was rocked and sung to frequently. Her new parents took her for a walk in the stroller each afternoon. They took her lots of places, talking to her about the things they saw. As a result of all this care and attention, Thelma thrived and became closely attached to her parents.

Velma was placed in a different kind of home—an orphanage—where there were many babies. She was fed, bathed, and kept warm and dry. But no one smiled at her, talked to her, or cuddled and played with her—they were too busy caring for all the other infants. Velma never knew who would be the next person to hurriedly change her, bathe her, or give her a propped-up bottle and then rush off into the night to care for some other unattended baby. Velma didn't have things to look at and play with. She was alone in a stark, white crib in a stark, white room. At first, Velma's only reaction to her new surroundings was to cry and cry. Sometimes her caregivers would be so busy they would not come when she cried, so she cried herself to sleep. When she realized crying brought no relief, she did what any other baby would do. She gave in. She became apathetic. And she began to wither away.

Physical-Motor and Perceptual Development

In Chapter 3 you saw how well developed and capable neonates are during their first month of life. But many necessary accomplishments still lie ahead during infancy—the first year of life—before babies become full-fledged toddlers between one and three years of age. For one thing babies are not born as completely developed human beings. A great deal of physical-motor and perceptual development takes place during this period. Infancy is also a time of adjustment for new babies—they must get used to the routines being established by parents and their various schedules for sleeping, eating, weaning, and nutrition.

PHYSICAL GROWTH

On that bright summer day when Thelma's parents first brought her home, they were greeted by Thelma's new aunts, uncles, grandparents, and assorted well-wishers. Proud family members pinched her tiny cheeks, picked her up, and passed her back and forth. They noted she was lighter than a gallon of milk (about eight pounds) and at just twenty inches long could stretch out comfortably on a hand towel. But a year from now Thelma's loved ones won't be passing her around with as much ease. She'll weigh almost as much as three gallons of milk and stand as high as the kitchen table by the time she enters toddlerhood. That's because the most rapid physical growth takes place between conception and the end of the first year of life. This development can be observed through changes in height and weight, growth patterns, and structural development of the bones, teeth, muscles, and nervous system.

Height and Weight.   Body height and weight are the best and most commonly used indicators for measuring physical growth. Infants usually increase their birth length by one half during their first year, double it by four years, and triple it by thirteen years of age (Beal, 1980; Pipes, 1977).

Weight gain in the first year of life is dramatic. At birth, water makes up 75 percent of body weight. Right after birth, typical neonates lose weight due to water loss, but by the tenth day, they regain their birth weight. After this period, weight gain in infancy continues at a rapid, but steadily decreasing pace. By four months of age, infants double their birth weight and by the end of the first year, they triple it (Beal, 1980; McWilliams, 1980). So the infant who weighed seven pounds at birth would weigh about twenty-one pounds at twelve months of age.

Growth Patterns.   At first glance babies might look like small adults to you but any such physical resemblance is amazingly deceptive. Infants are not the well-proportioned miniature adults so often pictured in medieval art. A baby's head is out of proportion to the rest of the body because all physical growth begins with the head and proceeds toward the lower part of the body—as is stated in the **cephalo-caudal principle.** The infant's head region—including the muscles, brain, skull, eyes, and ears—develops earlier and is proportionately larger than other parts of the body (Tanner, 1970). Upper body control appears before lower

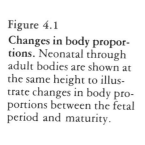

Figure 4.1

Changes in body proportions. Neonatal through adult bodies are shown at the same height to illustrate changes in body proportions between the fetal period and maturity.

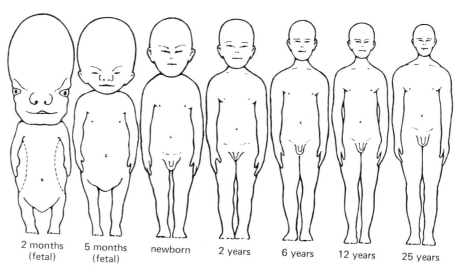

| 2 months (fetal) | 5 months (fetal) | newborn | 2 years | 6 years | 12 years | 25 years |

body control. Thelma could lift her head first, then she could lift her shoulders and control her arms. Months later she gained control over her legs.

Physical growth also follows the **proximo-distal principle,** which states that physical development begins along the innermost parts of the body and continues developing toward the outermost parts. Newborn Thelma has control of her shoulders but randomly waves her arms and lacks control over other muscles in her arms and hands. In the months to come, Thelma will develop the ability to grasp objects placed in her palms, to reach out and brush at objects, and eventually to reach out and grab objects in her palm with consistent skill. But she will not be able to pick up an object with her thumb and forefinger until she is nearly nine months old. This observation—that babies will swipe or bat an object before they can pick it up between thumb and forefinger—represents a third growth principle. This is the principle of **general movements to specific movements,** which states that generalized physical movements develop before a specific, controlled physical movement.

Structural Development.   The infant's bone structure differs from that of the adult (see Fig. 4.2). It will be some time before the baby's bones completely harden, or *ossify* (see Chapter 2), a process that you will remember began during prenatal development. The ossification of some of the hand and wrist bones reaches completion early in infancy. But ossification of the entire skeletal system is not complete until the end of adolescence. This gives infants tremendous flexibility—they have no trouble sticking their toes in their mouths.

Teeth begin to form during the sixth week of fetal development (Watson and Lowrey, 1967). All twenty baby teeth and the first permanent teeth are already developing at birth. Some infants are actually born with one or more teeth, while others do not get their first tooth until eighteen months of age. But the average age for the first tooth is seven months. Baby teeth act as guides to help the permanent teeth position themselves.

Newborns come into the world with all of the muscle fibers they will ever have. But their muscles are small, watery, and under developed (Eichorn, 1979). Muscles continue to grow in thickness and length. By maturity, muscle weight is forty times more than what it was at birth. Incomplete muscle and bone development in early infancy prevents babies from supporting themselves or holding objects or from directing their limbs and fingers precisely.

The incompletely developed nervous system of infants also affects their abilities. At three or four weeks after birth, the infant's legs are still making reflex crawling movements while arms, already under the control of higher brain centers, do not make any reflex movements. During the period from birth to four years, the nerve cells in the cortex increase in number and size (Tanner, 1970). As nerve cells grow, more connections are made among the cells. The brain soon increases in size so that by six months the cortex has completed 50 percent of its total growth (Tanner, 1970). At that time the cortex begins to take control and many of the neonatal reflexes disappear. By twelve months, the baby's brain has already grown to 60 per cent of its adult weight.

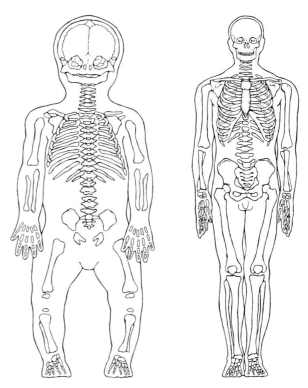

Figure 4.2
Changes in skeletal structure.
Neonatal and adult skeletons are shown at the same height to illustrate the differences between skeletal development at birth and that at maturity.

Babies are born with an important material called myelin. **Myelin** is a soft white substance that coats each nerve cell, insulating it and allowing messages to be transmitted from the brain to other parts of the body. This coating process—called *myelinization*—is not complete at birth and, in fact, will not be complete until age six. Incomplete myelinization explains the newborn's inability to control the lower parts of the body. By six months, many of the nerve fibers leading from the cortex have been coated with myelin (Tanner, 1970).

EXCEPTIONAL DEVELOPMENT IN INFANCY

From birth, every child is different from every other child. But some children are so different from the average child that they require special attention. These **exceptional children** are developmentally delayed or handicapped or developmentally advanced or gifted. For the average baby, development is smooth-sailing during the first year. But there are exceptions to normal infant development that can cause parents, medical professionals, and caregivers concern.

Sudden Infant Death Syndrome. It was much like any other morning for Mary Hopkins, a young teacher, and her husband, Jack, except on that day they overslept. Depending on the regular morning cries of their seven-month-old, they hadn't needed an alarm clock since his birth. The haunting quiet that fell over the house that morning caused them to leap from bed and hurry into the nursery. Covered by his blanket, their son lay face down, still, and cold. He had died of **Sudden Infant Death Syndrome (SIDS)**, sometimes called **crib death.**

This mysterious disorder is the largest killer of infants between one week and one year of age. Affecting two or three out of every 1000 newborns, SIDS accounts for more than 10,000 deaths each year—most often between the second and fifth month of life (Lipsitt, 1979). The disorder gets its name from the suddenness with which it claims its victims, usually male, who by all outward signs appear to be healthy.

SIDS most often strikes babies whose mothers are less than twenty years old or who received inadequate prenatal care (Beckwith, 1978). Infants who suffer crib death are usually premature, have low gestational weight, and come from low income families (Deal and Bordeaux, 1980). They lag behind in growth, length, weight, head circumference, and size of major organs (Valdes-Dapena, 1978), and they received low Apgar scores at birth (Lipsitt et al., 1979).

Unfortunately, because there are no warning signals, SIDS cannot be prevented, and medical experts remain baffled by the mysterious occurrence of the disorder. Suffocation from bedcovers or clothing (Deal and Bordeaux, 1980) and choking or strangulation from vomiting (Beckwith, 1978) have been ruled out as possible causes.

Some British scientists believe SIDS is partly due to a vitamin B-complex deficiency, triggered by mild stress such as infection, excessive heat or cold, or a missed meal (Johnson et al., 1980). But the most promising clues to date have been the linkage of SIDS with problems in respiratory centers of the brain (Bosma and Showacre, 1971; Lipsitt et al., 1979). Some researchers believe that a respiratory virus may predispose infants to SIDS (Deal and Bordeaux, 1980), since autopsies have shown that many crib death babies had upper respiratory infections. When asleep, all normal infants (and adults too) experience **apnea**—periods in which they stop breathing. There is evidence to show that a lengthy apnea episode during sleep could be a factor in SIDS (Deal and Bordeaux, 1980; Lipsitt, 1979). Prolonged apnea complicated by a respiratory infection could result in severe oxygen loss and death.

Recent breakthroughs by a Rutgers medical team may help doctors predict which parents are likely to have babies susceptible to SIDS (Schiffman et al., 1980). Tests showed that parents of crib death babies don't inhale powerfully when their breath is cut off. Instead, they had significantly lower breathing responses than a comparison group of normal couples. These results suggest that the failure to automatically breathe harder when oxygen is cut off might be an inherited link in many cases of SIDS. Although this poses no problem for adults, researchers think it could be a fatal defect if passed on to children. The discovery of a hormonal imbalance in SIDS babies might also lead to a test that could identify and save victims of the ailment (Chacon and Tildon, 1981). Researchers found that forty-four out of fifty SIDS babies studied had unusually high levels of the hormone T-3, which regulates body functions such as breathing and heartbeat.

Those infants experiencing prolonged apnea who have been revived in time are classified as "near miss" infants. This means their chances of succumbing to SIDS are higher than average. As a precaution, some parents of "near miss" babies use home monitors (see Fig. 4.3), which are attached to infants during sleep and will alert parents in case of breathing difficulty (Favorito et al., 1979).

But what about the unfortunate parents of babies who succumb to SIDS? SIDS can happen to anyone. Robert Redford and his wife, Lola, lost their firstborn to SIDS. A medical team from Children's Hospital Medical Center and the Boston SIDS Center reported that SIDS can have a shattering effect on the family system—including the ending of some marriages (Mandell et al., 1980). They observed that fathers show anger, self-blame, and aggression in an attempt to remain tough and unemotional. In contrast, mothers become depressed, withdrawn, and absorbed in grief.

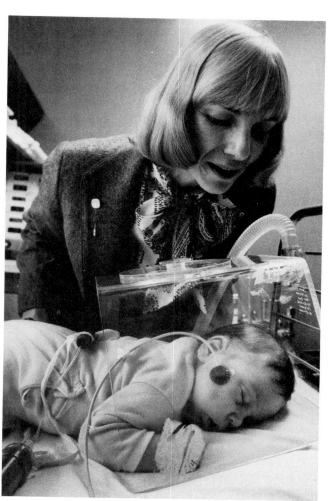

Figure 4.3

Breathing monitors. Special monitors attached to "near miss" babies during sleep can alert parents to breathing difficulties in time to revive the infant.

Many SIDS parents need professional counseling to help them cope with their feelings and understand more about this mysterious disease. To lighten the burden, the National Sudden Infant Death Syndrome Foundation in Chicago has nationwide chapters to assist parents, educate the public about crib deaths, and promote SIDS research. The International Guild for Infant Survival in Baltimore also provides public information on SIDS and counseling to SIDS families and promotes research into the mystery of its cause.

Failure to Thrive Syndrome.   At the age of six months, Velma was taken to the hospital. On admission, she was listless and didn't smile. She was severely underweight and in serious need of life-support systems. She was suffering from **Failure to Thrive Syndrome (FTTS)**—failure of an infant to achieve a normal physical growth rate, despite the absence of any neurological or physical abnormality (Lipsitt, 1979). Approximately 5 percent of pediatric admissions include this kind of growth failure (Rosen, 1977).

The onset of FTTS usually occurs during the first six months and most babies are hospitalized by six to twelve months of age (Lipsitt, 1979). But like SIDS, FTTS carries no warning signs. Some sort of feeding disturbance is usually associated with FTTS babies. Their intake of food is less than normal babies. Certain physical and emotional problems also accompany FTTS. Delayed language development, poor physical motor development, little smiling, lack of cuddliness, no fear of strangers but extreme watchfulness and listlessness are other symptoms (Lipsitt, 1979).

Spitz (1946) described FTTS as a type of depression—usually occurring in institutionalized infants like Velma during their first year of life. He blamed emotional deprivation and lack of adult nurturance and stimulation for this condition. More recently, research has linked FTTS in noninstitutionalized babies to poor mother-infant relationships—usually little two-way interaction and lots of stress during feeding (Lipsitt, 1979).

It is interesting to note that physical and emotional problems of FTTS infants fade and growth resumes when they are placed in an environment different from the one they were in at the time of hospitalization (Niven, 1977). Such was the case with Velma. Three weeks after admission, alert and smiling and having gained eight ounces, Velma went home with her adoptive parents. She thrived in her new surroundings because now she had a ''real'' home too—just like her sister, Thelma.

ROUTINES

Thelma demands the total attention of her parents. She needs them to feed her, change her diapers, keep her warm, and cuddle her. And she needs them now! Thelma's parents don't want her to be hungry or upset, but they would like to sleep through the night again some day. So like most new parents, they are concerned about getting Thelma on some type of schedule. Areas of particular concern for new parents include sleeping, eating, weaning, and nutrition.

Sleeping.   By their first birthday, infants have spent over one half of their life asleep. During the first two months, they sleep about seventeen hours a day, but by three months, this time has dropped to fourteen hours. Between four to six months, average babies begin to sleep through the night, much to the delight of weary parents.

Infants have their individual patterns of sleeping. Some sleep in short snatches. Others nap for two or three hours at a stretch. Some babies are easily disturbed by noises when asleep, while others can sleep through a Mount St. Helen's volcanic eruption! Common events that disrupt sleep—such as a soiled diaper, internal discomforts, pain, hunger, or sudden changes in their surroundings—will affect one baby more than another.

Eating.   Getting infants to eat on schedule can be difficult, especially those babies that wake up at irregular times and require different amounts of food. But rigid scheduling won't solve any problems. When parents force eating, they make infants eat before they're hungry. So they might take too little food or be fussy and difficult to feed. They might also wake up early for the next feeding.

Babies have built-in biological clocks that help them to stabilize their eating and sleeping patterns. The best advice for parents who want to establish an eating routine is to be aware of the times the baby gets hungry and to feed at those times. This is called a **self-demand feeding schedule.** It is important to get the schedule

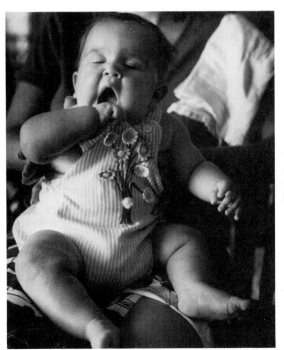

Though infants vary in their individual patterns of sleeping, most three-month-olds sleep about fourteen hours a day.

❖ Spotlight 4.1: Breast-Feeding versus Bottle-Feeding

Throughout history, breast-feeding has been the most commonly used method of infant feeding. In Russia most mothers breast-feed and in China virtually all mothers do. Chinese mothers take newborns to work, leave them in a nursing room, and breast-feed them during work breaks (Sidel, 1972). Existing cultural conditions greatly influence the decision of whether to breast-feed or bottle-feed. Modern technology and mobility have permitted bottle-feeding to replace breast-feeding as the most prevalent form of infant feeding in Britain (Vulliamy, 1972), Canada, and the United States (Maslansky, 1974).

Sometimes bottle-feeding is the only alternative. In some cases, mothers have illnesses such as tuberculosis or breast cancer or take drugs that would harm the child. In others, the baby might not be able to digest mother's milk or cow's milk because of a genetic deficiency. One example is the PKU baby who must be bottle-fed with food derived from vegetable sources. In other situations, breast-feeding is the best option. When formula milk has been introduced into underdeveloped nations, a variety of problems have arisen. Many mothers in these countries are illiterate and cannot read directions for formula preparation. Mothers who lack the money to buy enough formula milk often water it down. Poor hygiene, unclean water, and lack of refrigeration can lead to infection and make bottle-feeding unsafe. For these reasons the World Health Organization in 1981 wholeheartedly endorsed the superiority of breast-feeding over bottle-feeding, especially in underdeveloped nations.

Aside from these cultural and health restrictions, bottle-feeding versus breast-feeding becomes an issue of individual choice. Physical factors, parent-child relationships, and convenience all influence the new parents' choice.

Physical Factors.   Mother's milk is natural for human babies. It provides extra resistance to infection. Babies seem to have less colic and fewer allergic reactions and digestive problems when mother's milk is used for feeding (Vulliamy, 1972). The American Academy of Pediatrics (1980) declares that the nutritional elements in human milk suit the baby's immature digestive system better than any alternative and may even provide built-in protection against obesity. Cow's milk has a relatively high salt content (Vulliamy, 1972) and has been linked with such disorders as skin rashes, diarrhea, and cramps.

Parent-Child Relationships.   Physical contact through breast-feeding is believed to strengthen the psychological bond between mother and newborn (Klaus and Kennell, 1976). An advantage of breast-feeding is that mothers must hold their babies when they feed them. Bottle-fed babies might have less contact with their mothers since they can be fed while propped on pillows or in an infant seat. On the other hand, bottle-feeding allows greater participation by the father. Increased father-baby contact during feeding facilitates a bonding between father and newborn similar to that of mother and infant (Klaus and Kennell, 1976).

Convenience.   Mother's milk is free and is always readily available at the right temperature whereas formula must be prepared, heated, and placed in a clean bottle. Since babies must be fed every few

Bottle-feeding as well as breast-feeding are now found all over the world. Here, two mothers feed their infants while waiting to see the doctor at a clinic in Togo.

hours, breast-feeding may be inconvenient for mothers who work outside the home or want to be away from home for a day or longer.

It cannot be proved that one method of infant feeding is better than the other. For example, a study that compared breast-fed babies with bottle-fed babies reported no significant differences between the two groups (Schmitt, 1970). When deciding which infant feeding method is desirable, the crucial factor seems to be the quality of parent-infant interaction during feeding rather than the method itself. Parents, friends, pediatricians, nutritionists, and organizations like the La Leche League (which promotes breast-feeding) may all offer advice and information, but ultimately parents must determine which feeding method is best for both themselves and their baby.

going early and to maintain it by consistently offering food at the times when the baby is usually hungry. When self-demand scheduling is followed, infants adjust to a regular schedule earlier than they do when they are fed on a rigid schedule during the first year (Breckenridge and Murphy, 1969).

Feeding times can be an important period for building parent-infant relationships. Feeding an infant with a propped bottle should be avoided. Whether the infant is breast-fed or bottle-fed, touching, stroking, and eye-to-eye contact are important for the baby's emotional growth (and as we will see later in this chapter, for the development of parent-infant attachment). Spotlight 4.1 contrasts breast and bottle feeding. Some nutritional experts believe that when fathers (or small children supervised by a parent) participate in feeding the baby, it can draw the family closer together (McWilliams, 1980).

Weaning.   As the period of infancy draws to a close, babies have developed some of the skills needed for adult-like eating. The transition from breast- or bottle-feeding to drinking from a cup and eating solid foods is called **weaning.** The age of weaning and the method used is determined by the culture. Among underdeveloped cultures, the average age for weaning is two and a half (Whiting and Child, 1953). To discourage nursing, the custom of daubing a bitter or peppery substance on the breast is widely reported. In the United States, we begin to wean babies at about nine months of age. Weaning can be an emotionally difficult time for both mother and baby. For the mother, it is a landmark in the development of her baby's independence. She must face the fact that her baby is gradually growing less dependent on her. Mothers who breast-feed may become slightly depressed at this time due to hormonal changes (Caplan, 1973).

In certain parts of Africa, one day is chosen in advance for weaning and the child is abruptly deprived of the breast (Leiderman et al., 1977). In the United States, weaning is more successful when it is gradual rather than sudden. The noon breast- or bottle-feeding is usually dropped first, the evening feeding next, and the early morning feeding last (Caplan, 1973). Often the first step is to give the child a small amount of liquid from a cup each day. The amount of table food is gradually increased while breast- or bottle-feeding is decreased. Eventually, breast- or bottle-feeding is omitted altogether and the baby drinks from a cup at each meal. Bottle fed infants are usually completely weaned by twelve to eighteen months whereas some breast-fed babies nurse until they are two years old. Because introducing too many changes in the routine at once can be confusing and unsettling for infants, it is not advisable for parents to wean when other important events, such as a move across the country, toilet training, or the birth of a new baby, might conflict with the process.

But before they give up the breast or bottle for a cup, most infants in this country have started to eat solid food. When children should first be introduced to such foods is a topic of much debate among those involved in child care. Many pediatricians recommend introducing solid food to infants as young as four weeks of age. Others believe the infant's digestive system is too immature to handle solid foods before eight weeks of age (Beal, 1980). They point out that food allergies are more common among children who receive solid foods in the early months (Eichorn, 1979).

A recommended pattern for introducing solid foods is to delay spoon feeding until four to six months of age (Beal, 1980). Pureed fruits and vegetables, egg yolks, and strained meats can be introduced over a period of time (McWilliams, 1980). Nutritionists suggest offering only one new food at a time and not more than one teaspoon at first (Beal, 1980). By about one year, most babies in the United States are on a three solid meal a day schedule.

At about nine months, infants try to feed themselves. They have the ability to use the thumb and forefinger to pick up foods. Some children attempt to feed themselves with a spoon but do not have the coordination to get the spoon to their mouths. Even when the spoon makes it to the mouth, it's often empty by the time it gets there. Infants also enjoy exploring and experimenting with their food, so as you can imagine, this is a messy but important learning experience for babies.

Nutrition. Good nutrition is of utmost importance for the infant's physical, cognitive, social, and emotional health. Energy comes from the chemical changes of fats, carbohydrates, and proteins. The energy from fats and carbohydrates provides fuel to keep the infant's body functioning and to ensure activity and growth. Protein provides the infant's body with essential amino acids and nitrogen. Amino acids help in the development of new body tissues. And nitrogen assists in the growth of already existing body tissues. Iron, which is quickly depleted by the body, is one of the earliest nutritional needs and can be met through iron-fortified cereals (Beal, 1980).

Nutritional habits established during the first year set practices that are apt to be continued throughout life. By twelve months of age, infants should have been introduced to all the foods that form the basis of an adequate diet (Breckenridge and Murphy, 1969). A well-balanced diet should include foods from the basic four food groups: bread and cereals; fruits and vegetables; meat, nuts, and poultry; and dairy products. Infants should be encouraged to eat a wide range of foods without overeating. The intake of milk should be limited to thirty-two ounces a day to leave room for the other important foods (McWilliams, 1980).

MOTOR DEVELOPMENT

In Chapter 3, we referred to reflexes (involuntary movements) that babies are born with. By the end of their first year, infants have begun to make many voluntary movements as the cortex matures. They roll over, sit up, crawl, and creep—movements using the large body muscles (usually arms and legs) and generally called **gross motor activity.** Babies can also pick up objects with thumb and forefinger, an example of **fine motor activity** (movement using the small muscles, usually the separate fingers and toes). Infants are mostly involved with gaining gross motor control through **locomotor movement**—the ability to move about. Some fine motor development also occurs as a result of eye-hand coordination, but most fine motor refinement takes place later on in childhood.

Rolling over

Sitting alone

Locomotor Movement in Infancy

Creeping

Crawling

Pulling self to stand

131

Locomotor Movement.   Locomotor movement involves a sequence of maturational stages. Thelma will lift her head, raise her chest from her crib, roll over, sit up, crawl, creep, and ultimately pull herself to a standing position before taking her first step. One or two stages are occasionally skipped, but most infants progress through them all. Locomotion begins when infants lift their heads during the first week of life. During the second and third months, infants begin to raise their chests from their cribs (Shirley, 1933). Other babies may at this time be moving from one end of their crib to another by kicking their legs and moving their arms. Rolling over requires infants to use their entire body—something they won't be able to do until the fourth month of age. Rolling over sets the foundation for later locomotor movements such as standing and walking.

Most infants first sit with support after being placed in a sitting position. But by nine months, they can get into the sitting position by themselves and remain in it for ten minutes or longer (Gesell and Amatruda, 1947). Crawling and creeping are preliminary walking movements. **Crawling,** seen between six and eight months, is locomotor movement in which a baby's stomach remains on the floor. A baby's arm and leg muscles are not strong enough to support the total body weight until about ten months, at which time they begin to creep (Shirley, 1933). When **creeping,** infants use their hands and knees to move about. Creeping is a more advanced skill than crawling because more coordination of arm and leg muscles is needed. By the time infants are creeping, they have already developed most of the skills necessary for walking. The ability to stand carries them a step closer to walking. But walking alone is not usually achieved until the first year. The charts in Spotlight 4.2 show the average ages at which many locomotor movements are accomplished.

Eye-Hand Coordination.   Eye-hand coordination also follows a series of maturational steps. Thelma's parents noticed she could wave her arms and swat at the butterfly mobile that dangled above her crib before she gained the precision of carefully taking hold of a single butterfly between her thumb and forefinger. During the neonatal period, the infant's grasp is reflexive, and most experience with objects is visual, not manual. At around two months of age, infants begin to swipe or swat at objects with a closed fist, combining visual and manual abilities. But they usually don't hit the objects because they have trouble keeping their eyes focused and they can't control their arm muscles very well. At two months of age, babies can grasp objects placed into their hands and bring them to their mouths, but not accurately or directly.

At four months of age, infants can stretch their arms in the general direction of an object. Their eyes may shift from object to hand and back again. These repeated glances between the target object and the hand help four-month-olds make comparisons of two locations (White et al., 1964). At five months, infants develop the **visually guided reach,** that is, they can keep their eyes on the object target and reach for it directly (White et al., 1964). The appearance of this ability

By five months of age, most infants have developed visually guided reach and can grasp objects securely.

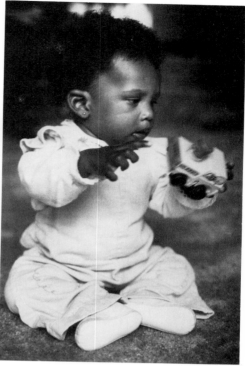

signals that eyes and arms are coordinated and the infant's visual-motor systems are now well integrated. Adult-like, rapid, and direct reaching along with accurate grasping of the target object are now possible.

At about nine months of age infants can use their thumbs and forefingers to pick up small objects (Bayley, 1935). Now they can begin to feed themselves small pieces of food such as peas or cubes of cooked carrots. They can also be observed hitting, shaking, tearing, pulling, and squeezing toys and anything else they can get their hands on. Between ten and eighteen months, children can successfully manipulate objects that require the use of both hands (Ramsay et al., 1979). Many infants even indicate right or left hand preference at this time. By the end of their first year, infants have learned to throw objects, often to the dismay of their parents.

PERCEPTUAL DEVELOPMENT

Thelma's perception improves dramatically throughout her first twelve months. As a result of experience with objects in her environment and maturation of her brain and eyes, the amount of information her perceptual system can handle in-

❖ Spotlight 4.2: The Uses and Abuses of Developmental Norms

As we discussed in Chapter 1, *developmental norms* are average ages at which certain behaviors appear. These norms can be useful yardsticks in observing infant and child development. Understanding the regularity of development can help those who care for children establish the best physical and psychological conditions to foster the child's development. Serious developmental delays can also be noted by the use of norms. If an infant is far behind the norm, the parent or caregiver is alerted to a possible developmental problem.

Several well-known infant tests have been devised from developmental norms for use by pediatricians and child development specialists. For example, *The Brazelton Behavioral Assessment Scale* (Brazelton, 1973) measures the maturity of the neonate's central nervous system and how well the newborn interacts with others. *The Cattell Infant Intelligence Scale* (Cattell, 1947) rates perceptual and motor abilities of babies between the ages of two and thirty months. And *The Bayley Scales* and *Caldwell's Inventory of Home Stimulation* are useful in predicting later cognitive and language abilities and delays at two years of age (Siegel, 1981).

Unfortunately, certain drawbacks regarding developmental norms must be kept in mind if they are to be used profitably. First, norms stress the *uniformities* in development among children and say nothing about individual *differences*. Since norms are only averages, the ages at which individual children acquire skills will vary. Generally, it is only the *sequence* of the skills that remains the same. Second, norms vary as much as one or two months from scale to scale. In 1933 Shirley reported that infants had the ability to sit alone at seven months, while in 1935 Bayley reported the average age for sitting alone to be eight and one-half months.

A third drawback is that several of the developmental norms (for example, Gesell, Shirley, and Bayley) were researched in the 1930s. Normal motor development for children of the 1980s may not be the same as normal motor development for children fifty years ago. Notice that in Fig. A the older Shirley scale reports pulls to stand at twelve months, while in Fig. B the newer Frankenburg and Dodds scale reports that behavior at ten months. Can you find other differences in the norms reported in the two scales?

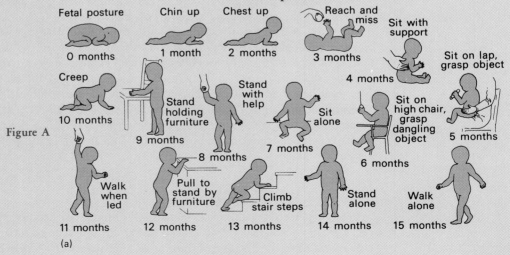

Figure A

(a)

Furthermore, norms do not reflect racial or cultural differences. Black infants in Africa and the United States are more advanced in physical and motor development than white infants (Ainsworth, 1967; Bayley, 1965; Goldberg, 1972). Central American Indian and Asian children are also ahead of Caucasian children (Werner, 1979). But these racial differences are not reflected in most norms. The American Academy of Pediatrics (1973) has called for separate norms for black and white babies to account for these differences.

Sometimes norms are abused by well-meaning parents and professionals. Adults sometimes get the idea that children should perform certain behaviors "on schedule." Parents have been known to panic if their child is on the slower side of the norm and to think their child is a genius when performance is noted on the faster side of the norm. Of course, neither of these extreme assumptions is accurate. Individual children do not begin their physical-motor skills right on schedule according to the norms because they all have unique, biological clocks that regulate the same skills at different rates. Sometimes norms seem to encourage negative comparisons between infants. Parents whose babies are "behind" the norms in development may feel embarrassed or even guilty and may place undue and harmful pressures on children who lag behind.

Infant and preschool developmental programs exist for children who have developmental delays or who are likely to experience developmental difficulties. These programs measure the child's developmental level, review medical and developmental history, and plan with the family for treatment and additional services from other community agencies. Repeated evaluation of these types of programs show they are effective in stimulating children's development—especially during the first three years of life (Beller, 1979). If parents suspect that their child is lagging behind in certain developmental areas, experts recommend that they consult a pediatrician or contact a local infant-preschool stimulation program. Preschool teachers, in cooperation with parents, can also refer children for appropriate treatment.

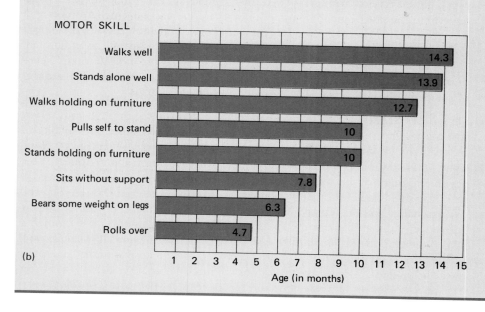

Figure B

(b)

creases and her world comes more into focus. Table 4.1 shows some developmental landmarks in perception during the first year of life.

Vision.   While all the infant's perceptual abilities are developing, nowhere are the changes more dramatic than in the visual sense.

VISUAL COMPLEXITY.   The newborn's attraction to visual complexity increases as he or she gets older (McGurk, 1972). Above all else, two-month-old infants prefer the face and eyes, presumably because of facial contours and high contrasts (Fantz, 1961). Preference for unfamiliar (more complex) faces increases with age (Sherrod, 1979) and three-dimensional masks of faces are preferred over flat pictures of faces (Haaf, 1974).

CONVERGENCE.   Although neonates are able to coordinate their eye muscles and to track moving objects and people, **convergence**—the process in which both eyes turn slightly inward to see a near object—is still inaccurate, inconsistent, and poorly refined (Aslin, 1976). By three months of age, convergence has developed enough so that infants can achieve **binocular vision**—the ability to perceive a single image with both eyes (Aslin, 1976).

OBJECT-SOUND LINKAGE.   How would you react if your instructor gave tomorrow's lecture standing at the front of the room but with his or her voice coming from the back? Probably with great surprise, even shock! As adults, we link the source of a sound to its visual location. Infants also learn to link sounds with objects. At four months of age, infants link the sound of their mother's voice with her face (Spelke and Owsley, 1979). This linkage was shown in an experiment in which infants became distressed when the recorded sound of their mother's voice came from the side of the room opposite to where she was standing (Aronson and Rosenbloom, 1971). Infants also link the sound of a familiar object with the object itself, and they become upset when a familiar sound is heard but an unfamiliar object accompanies it (Lyons-Ruth, 1977). These behaviors indicate that as perception and memory develop, certain sounds and sights become united as aspects of the same object (Lawson, 1980; Spelke and Owsley, 1979).

OBJECT CONSTANCY.   The image of an airplane that you see through your *retina* (the part of the eye that receives the image formed by the lens) becomes smaller as it leaves the ground and flies into the distance. As the plane disappears from sight, you know that it and all people on board did not shrink and disappear. You are able to perceive this because you have **object constancy**—the ability to recognize that size, shape, or other attributes remain the same, even though they appear to change and the retinal image does change. For example, in your mind you still perceive the airplane in the air as the same huge airplane you saw moments ago on the ground. Although the image changed because of viewing distance, you retained the constancy of its size. Size constancy is present at six months, and some researchers suggest it exists as early as four months (McKenzie et al., 1980). Shape constancy is present between eight and ten months (Cohen et al., 1979).

Table 4.1
Developmental Landmarks in Infant Perception

AGE	CAPABILITY
Neonatal period	■ Sound-vision-motor linkages—indicated by turning head and eyes toward sounds. ■ Tracks movement of objects and people. ■ Discriminates mother's smell from smell of others.
1 month	■ Recognizes different speech sounds.
2 months	■ Has two-color vision. ■ Begins to respond to relationships among parts—not just the parts themselves.
3 months	■ Has binocular vision and peripheral vision. ■ Recognizes mother's face from a photograph. ■ Hears and imitates a variety of high- and low-pitched sounds.
4 months	■ Links mother's voice with her face and the sounds of a familiar object with the actual object. ■ Discriminates mother's and father's voices from a stranger's. ■ Discriminates between objects in upright and nonupright positions. ■ Discriminates between flat pictures and three-dimensional objects.
5 to 6 months	■ Discriminates different nonupright positions—such as upside down from sideways.
6 months	■ Discriminates mother's face from that of a stranger. ■ Achieves size constancy.
6½ months	■ Prewired visual-motor system is activated to aid in depth perception as infants begin crawling.
8 to 10 months	■ Achieves shape constancy.
10 to 12 months	■ Recognizes objects by touch—without looking at them. ■ Discriminates by touch between familiar and new objects in the dark.

Data from Aslin (1976); Barrera and Maurer (1981); Brown (1979); Cohen et al. (1979); Fagan and Shepherd (1979); Field (1976); Field, J. et al. (1980); Fouts and Atlas (1979); Gottfried and Rose (1980); Gregg et al. (1976); Kessen et al. (1979); Lawson (1980); Maurer and Lewis (1979); McKenzie et al. (1980); Rader et al. (1980); Russell (1976); Soroka et al. (1979); Spelke and Owsley (1979); Ungerer et al. (1978); Werner and Wooten (1979).

DEPTH PERCEPTION.   Psychologists, Eleanor and James Gibson were vacationing at the Grand Canyon with their infant daughter. James Gibson, a specialist on depth perception, insisted that their crawling daughter would be safe at the brink of the canyon because she could see the drop-off and would avoid it. Eleanor Gibson wasn't convinced and would not let her baby venture to the edge of the canyon. But years later she conducted a now-famous study at Cornell University to try to answer the fascinating question about depth perception that had been suggested to her on that family vacation: "Can infants perceive depth?"

Thirty-six infants ranging in age from six to forty-six months were tested by means of a "visual cliff," as shown in Fig. 4.4 (Gibson and Walk, 1960). The experiment involved a large sheet of heavy glass laid across a checkerboard pattern. On one side of the apparatus, the checkerboard pattern was directly beneath the glass (the surfaced side). On the other side, the pattern was placed several feet below the glass (the deep side), which gave the visual illusion of a cliff. A wide board also covered with this checkerboard pattern was laid over the glass along the brink of the "cliff."

When the babies were placed in the center of the board, their mothers coaxed them, first from the surfaced side and then from the deep side. Most of the babies would quickly crawl across the surfaced side, but only three of them crept off the wooden board onto the "deep" side. Some of the infants crawled away when their mothers coaxed from the deep side. Others cried but refused to cross the deep side. The experiment supported the notion that infants can perceive depth as they begin to crawl since they avoided the "drop-off" of the visual cliff.

A more recent study using the visual-cliff apparatus addressed the question of whether depth perception is inborn or learned (Rader et al., 1980). The researchers concluded that the visual-motor system is biologically prewired and activates at six and one-half months, thereby giving crawling infants a "feel" for different distances and levels and causing them to avoid the cliff.

Nonvisual Perception.   In the past, researchers have spent less time studying the nonvisual senses. But now they are becoming more interested in how the senses of hearing, smell, touch, and taste develop during infancy.

HEARING.   The infant's ability to discriminate sounds improves after the neonatal period. At four months of age, for example, babies can tell the difference between their mother's and father's voices from that of a stranger (Brown, 1979). Between three and six months, they can hear and imitate a variety of high- and low-pitched tones (Kessen et al., 1979). Experiments show that infants are startled by high-pitched tones and calmed by low-frequency, rhythmic sounds, as evidenced by their slowed heartbeat and breathing (Brackbill, 1970). No wonder the rhythmic, soft sounds of the lullaby sung by Thelma's mother soothed Thelma and lulled her to sleep!

SMELL.   At only one week of age, Thelma can recognize her mother by smell. Breast-fed babies distinguish and prefer the smell of their mother's milk to that of another mother. In one experiment, for instance, breast fed babies were more

Figure 4.4

The visual cliff. Like most infants studied, this baby will not crawl across the "deep" side of the visual cliff.

quickly awakened by the smell of a fabric worn by their mother under her bra than by the odor of fabric worn by another breast-feeding mother (Russell, 1976).

TOUCH.   The baby's sense of touch seems to be developed more than any other. Crying babies are easily soothed or quieted when swaddled or wrapped securely in a blanket or when cradled snuggly in the arms of a loved one. By the end of the first year, infants can recognize objects solely by their feel and discriminate between familiar and new objects in the dark (Gottfried and Rose, 1980; Soroka et al., 1979).

TASTE.   Infants develop preferences for certain tastes during the first year. Pediatrician T. Berry Brazelton (1969) reports that breast-fed babies sometimes develop a distaste for formula bottle milk and will gasp and cough to inform mothers of their displeasure.

Cognitive and Language Development

As with perception, the baby's cognitive and language skills undergo significant change during infancy. Cognitive and language development are inseparable because language is the means by which thought is represented. Neonates "think" in primitive ways that are tied to their senses and motor actions, and so they communicate through simple sounds, not words. But as motor and perceptual skills advance, so do cognitive and language abilities. Twelve-month-olds emerge from infancy "thinking" in purposeful and deliberate ways and ready to "speak" their first word.

COGNITIVE DEVELOPMENT

Newborn Brad could grasp his father's finger moments after birth. At nine months he has learned to grasp a one inch square block his Grandma Rachel gave him. He can grasp his bottle, his rattle, and his mother's hair. And Brad can also grasp a small red ball about the same size as his block. One day Brad's father placed a spoonful of green peas on the high chair tray in front of Brad. Brad tried to grasp the peas by using his familiar whole hand grasp. He was astonished when his familiar grasping pattern failed. With much deliberation, Brad touched a pea with his index finger. Then he slowly bent his thumb and touched the other side of the pea. Very pleased with himself, Brad carefully picked up a pea and popped it into his mouth.

Brad's actions might seem rather unimportant to most people, but Jean Piaget saw the basis for all kinds of thought in this simple act. He came to believe that the tendency to organize information in specific ways is inborn, that babies are born with **schemes**—organized patterns of behavior that guide the ways individuals act on and organize information. Children's earliest schemes involve motor reflexes (such as sucking, crying, and grasping) and sensory abilities (such as looking and hearing).

Piaget also examined the ways in which children expand on and change these early schemes as they interact with their new environment—how Brad's grasp of his father's finger later expanded to picking up blocks and balls and then to picking up peas. He found that children use **assimilation** when they can fit new information into an existing scheme without having to change that scheme (when Brad found he could use his whole hand to grasp not just his father's finger but hair, rattles, and blocks). But he found that they use **accommodation** to change the scheme so that different or contradictory information can be taken in (when Brad learned to pick up peas with his fingers).

Of course, children do not use only assimilation or only accommodation to learn about the world. Instead, they use assimilation and accommodation together in a balancing process Piaget called **equilibration**—organizing actions and information and adapting to changing demands of the environment. For Piaget, intelligence is measured by the child's ability to adapt to increasingly complex environments.

Piaget's Stages of Sensorimotor Development.   The **sensorimotor period** is so named because infants have not mastered language and have no mental pictures for words. Their learning about people and objects is limited to information they gather through their senses and random motor movements. Gradually, these external actions become internalized, as when older children can explore ''in their heads'' what infants must do through sensorimotor exploration. There are six stages in the sensorimotor period, four of which we will discuss here. The last two will be discussed in Chapter 6.

STAGE 1: PRACTICING REFLEXES.   Shortly after his birth, Doreen made the following notations in Brad's baby book:

November 5: When an object is placed in Brad's hand, he will immediately grasp it. He grasps my finger, a rattle, a blanket, and even my hair all in the same way. He will suck on my finger when I touch it to his lips. In fact, I noticed that he will suck on any object placed near his mouth. He reacts to loud noises, bright lights, and rapid movements with crying.

Can you name the reflex actions (see Chapter 3) that Brad's mother described? During the first stage of the sensorimotor period (which occurs between birth and one month) practically all learning occurs through these and other reflex-motor actions and the five senses. Newborn infants grasp objects placed in their palms, and they suck on any object placed near their mouths—rattle, pacifier, thumb, nipple, or blanket. Almost all neonatal behavior involves assimilating objects through the inborn reflex scheme of sucking.

Piaget believes children practice whatever skills they have in every period of development. The neonate has very few skills—only reflexes. So it is natural that these reflex skills would be repeated over and over again. Neonates cannot differentiate between objects and so they act on all things in the same way.

STAGE 2: PRIMARY CIRCULAR REACTIONS.   By two months of age, Brad's behavior is no longer purely reflexive.

January 5: Brad has developed a mind of his own! He can tell the difference between sucking on the nipple and on his blanket. When he's hungry, he'll push the blanket away, preferring to nurse at my breast. He began to discover his fingers after he repeatedly moved them to his mouth. He has also started sucking his thumb quite a bit! (I wonder if I should be concerned about this?) As I go about the room, Brad's eyes follow me as if he was watching my every move.

As you can see, Brad has begun to accommodate to his surroundings, which characterizes Stage 2 of the sensorimotor period (occurring between one and four months). Brad's mother gave three clues that accommodation was taking place. First, the appearance of habitual thumb sucking signals the development of hand-mouth coordination. According to Piaget (1952b), this sequence of behaviors involves more elaborate schemes than the reflexes of Stage 1. Before this stage, thumb sucking is accidental, but now Brad deliberately directs the coordination of his hand to his mouth so that the end result (thumb sucking) takes place.

The second clue that Brad was accommodating occurred when a hungry Brad preferred his mother's breast to his blanket. Infants like Brad learn that some things on which they suck produce milk, and others do not. They develop different schemes for milk-producing objects and for non-milk-producing objects, and they can tell the difference between the two. So when Brad gets hungry, he rejects his non-milk-producing rattle or blanket in favor of his mother's breast.

Putting thumb into mouth is learned early and for many infants, like this one, seems to be a source of great contentment.

A third clue to Brad's development is that he moved his head in the direction of sounds his mother made. He followed her with his eyes as she moved about the room. This behavior signals the coordination between Brad's hearing and vision. It is also a sign that Brad like other infants in this stage has developed the ability to center or focus on objects and people. But when Brad's mother leaves the room or when his favorite toy dog is hidden from sight, Brad acts as if they no longer exist.

STAGE 3: SECONDARY CIRCULAR REACTIONS. At this stage (which occurs between four and eight months), infants do things on purpose and their behavior becomes more deliberate. Schemes developed in earlier stages are now combined. For example, at six months of age Brad had a musical apple that, when moved, would chime out a musical sound. He accidentally moved the apple and realized that it would play music. When the apple was still, he noticed it made no noise at all. Somehow, Brad understood that there was an association between his movement of the apple and the music it made, as Brad's father noted:

May 5: Brad will roll the apple over and giggle with delight at the sound it makes. He will continue this play until he grows tired of it. When he gets excited over a newly performed feat, he will pant and squeal at his sense of accomplishment. Then he will repeat the act.

As in Stage 2, behaviors at this stage are produced accidentally at first. But when an event is pleasurable, the baby will try to repeat it. Notice that the objects in this stage are more related to the infant's surroundings, such as the musical apple, rather than around the baby's own body, as in Stage 2.

You saw that infants in Stage 2 acted as if objects outside their field of vision didn't exist. But toward the end of Stage 3, infants begin to develop some notion of object and person permanence. **Object permanence** or **person permanence** is the understanding that objects and people exist even though they cannot be seen. Infants realize that, even though a toy is placed out of sight or Mommy goes into the next room, the toy still exists and Mommy has not disappeared forever. At eight months of age, Brad's development of object permanence did not go unnoticed by his mother:

July 5: An interesting thing happened when Brad was playing with his block. As I was straightening his bed, I accidentally pushed the block under his blanket. Before I could reach down and pick it up, Brad pulled back the covers and retrieved it himself! I was astonished because I had never seen him do this before.

Person permanence is developed before object permanence if babies have a warm, intimate relationship with their mothers (Bell, 1970). But if mother-infant relationships are not warm and intimate and if babies spend more time with objects, they develop object permanence first. Object and person permanence become more complete in Stage 4.

Babies in Stage 3 can also anticipate the positions that objects will pass through when in motion. For instance, Brad's mother often entertained Brad with his wind-up toy dog. One day as Brad sat in his infant seat, the toy dog marched behind the left side of a nearby chair. His mother observed that Brad reached out for the dog on the right side of the chair, where seconds later it reappeared. This is in contrast to Stage 2 when Brad, lacking object permanence, would not reach for his toy dog when it was hidden from sight.

STAGE 4: COORDINATION OF SECONDARY SCHEMES. Purposeful and deliberate behaviors are further refined at this stage (which occurs between eight and twelve months). Infants coordinate the two old schemes of means and ends to make something new happen. In the following example, Piaget's daughter, Jacqueline, devised a *means* (pulling the strings of her bassinet) to achieve an *end* (obtaining a cigarette case). Pulling the strings and obtaining the cigarette case are two schemes that Jacqueline already had. When these two old schemes were coordinated, Jacqueline could perform a new behavior. She intentionally pulled the strings so that she could get the cigarette case.

[At eight months and twenty days] Jacqueline tries to grasp a cigarette case which I present to her. I then slide it between the crossed strings which attach her dolls to the hood [of her bassinet]. She tries to reach it directly. Not succeeding, she immediately looks for the strings . . . in which the cigarette case is entangled. She looks in front of her, grasps the strings, pulls and shakes them, etc. [means]. The cigarette case then falls and she grasps it [ends]. Second experiment: same reaction, but without first trying to grasp the object directly. (Piaget, 1952b, p. 215)

Infants at this stage also show signs of anticipating events. Piaget (1952b) described Jacqueline's frightened and tearful reaction when alcohol was applied to a minor scratch. Two days later she began to cry as soon as she saw the bottle brought out, anticipating what would again take place.

FOUNDATIONS OF LANGUAGE

The word "infancy" is derived from Latin and means the period without speech. Even though true language is not present in infancy, this is an important time in which the foundations of language are laid. Babies build the foundation for true language as they practice and experiment with sounds through "meaningless" repetitions of crying, cooing, and babbling sounds (Frost, 1971).

Crying. At birth, crying is the only means Eve has to communicate. Her first cry results from a reflex action produced as air is expelled from her lungs. By one month of age she cries to communicate many messages—hunger, discomfort from a wet diaper, pain from colic or teething, anger, or desire for attention. Sometimes it is a difficult job for Eve's parents to interpret the meaning of her many cries.

Cooing. At about two to three months of age, Eve begins to experiment with **cooing**—sounds usually characterized by extended vowel sounds such as "e-e-e-e-e" or "o-o-o-o." Researchers describe cooing as "vocal play" and say it occurs when the baby has no discomfort (Lewis, 1975). Eve's parents view her cooing as an indication that Eve is happy and content.

Babbling. Six-month-old Eve increases the type and number of sounds she makes as she begins **random babbling,** adding consonant sounds such as "buh" and "h" to prelanguage skills. These consonant sounds require more control of the tongue and lips than cooing. Combinations of vowel and consonant sounds such as "ba-ba-ba-ba" or "da-da-da-da" are frequent. These babbling sounds are unsystematic and lack meaning but are important because babies are practicing and refining their speech. At first, deaf infants will make cooing and babbling sounds identical to hearing infants but later some deaf infants stop vocalizing altogether while others produce limited babbling sounds (Lenneberg, 1964a). One explanation for this change in deaf infants' behavior is that they lose interest in vocalizing because they cannot hear the sounds made by themselves or others (Clifton, 1970).

When Eve was eight months old, her parents took her to church where the other adults showed a great deal of interest in her. As friends spoke to her, she babbled to them, frequently repeating certain sounds as if she had developed some favorite expressions. Even though she wasn't using words, her babbling sounded just like real talking.

Eight-month-old infants begin **advanced babbling** as they begin producing the sounds of their own language. When crying, cooing, or random babbling, all babies make the same sounds regardless of their native tongue. But in advanced babbling, the influence of the environment on language becomes apparent. English babies begin "speaking" English, German babies speak German, and so forth. As they imitate others in their culture, babies repeat sounds over and over as

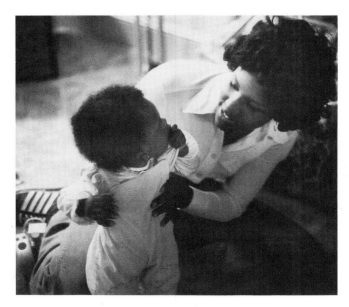

The bidirectional nature of language is evident before the first words are spoken. Many parents report ''knowing'' what their children want from the sound of their cries or tone of their gurgling. And babies respond early to different tones in their parents' speech.

if playing a game, even though they don't understand the meaning of the sounds. This repetition or echoing of what is heard is called *echolalia*.

The advanced babbling stage continues until children begin to use words in a meaningful way—at about one year. By this time they have learned the sounds of their language and can reproduce them whenever they desire. The foundations of language have been laid and true language can now begin.

How Language Is Bidirectional.   Language development is reciprocal in nature. Eve influences her parents' speech just as they influence hers. Infants on the verge of speech cause mothers to alter their language. Mothers of four-month-olds tend to comment mostly about their infant's well-being, but mothers of eight-month-olds adjust what they say to the on-going activities of their babies (West and Rheingold, 1978). When infants are about nine or ten months old, just before they speak their first words, parents begin to speak very distinctly to them. They also begin to use more auxiliary verbs. The usual grammatical errors typical of adult speech disappear. So next time you feel your grammar needs improvement, find an infant to talk to!

Social and Emotional Development and Relationships

Parents do not instinctively ''love'' their babies (Robson and Moss, 1970), and babies do not instinctively ''love'' their parents the minute they're born. During the neonatal period, newborns and their parents become attuned to each other's signals. And after a few weeks of exchanging looks, smiles, and vocalizations with their babies, most mothers report feeling love for their newborns (Robson and Moss, 1970). But for infants these feelings emerge later in the first year as they develop their relationships with adults, express their feelings with more specific emotions, and begin to learn about their sex roles.

INFANTS AND ADULT RELATIONSHIPS

Throughout the first twelve months, infants continue to become better acquainted with parents and other important persons in their social environment. The two most important accomplishments during this period are the establishment of a sense of basic trust and the formation of attachments to loved ones.

Basic Trust versus Basic Mistrust.   How would it feel to live in a clean, white institution like Velma did from the time she was born? How do you think Velma viewed her world? These are difficult questions to answer, but we can make some fairly accurate predictions based on Erik Erikson's theory. Consider an infant's world. Babies are dependent on adults to gratify their needs for food, security, love, and touching. According to Erikson (1968), infants are struggling with the conflict of **basic trust versus basic mistrust** during this helpless first year of life. Whether or not this conflict will be resolved successfully depends upon the quality of the parent-infant relationship.

If infants are fed when hungry, if their cries are answered within a reasonable time, if their discomforts are removed, and if they are loved, cuddled, played with, and talked to, they will begin to know that the world is a safe place and that they can trust others to care for them. When their needs are not met in a loving adult-child relationship, they will grow to mistrust their world.

But what about Velma's world? Her needs for food and warmth were met, but she was never talked to or kissed and caressed. She was allowed to lie in her crib and cry until she fell asleep from exhaustion. According to Erikson's theory, she would perceive her world as an unsafe place and be fearful and mistrustful of others because her need for a loving relationship with an adult was not met in her earliest days. As a result of distrusting her world, Velma might be more easily upset and have more difficulty in social relationships than her sister, Thelma, who lived in a loving home where her needs were generally met from birth. During her first year, Velma, like all infants, needed opportunities to interact with her world to become trustful of its permanency. But while in the institution, her life was temporary. And she sensed this about her daily surroundings. Fortunately, as we saw earlier in this chapter, Velma's story had a happy ending.

Erikson does not mean that parents must be superhuman. The needs of infants don't have to be satisfied immediately all of the time. And Erikson doesn't say that babies should never be allowed to cry. Parents with other children to care for may not get to their infants the instant they begin to cry. New parents may be clumsy in fondling their infant or interpreting the meaning of some cries. Children who are generally well cared for and loved can certainly tolerate occasional lapses on the part of their parents. In fact, infants who are developing a basic sense of trust learn to tolerate occasional delays or discomfort because they know or trust that someone will come soon. It's important for Velma to have a reasonable amount of mistrust. But if her sense of basic mistrust outweighs her basic trust, she is in for a rough life ahead!

Attachment.   The relationship between infants and parents undergoes changes at this time.

During Thelma's first three months of life, her parents noticed that their daughter was the life of the party, socializing with anyone and everyone. Between three and six months, she began to recognize certain familiar faces. After six months, Thelma became very choosy about whom she interacted with. In some respects you might say she became a social wallflower—preferring the company of her mother and father to that of strangers. Thelma's parents were mystified by these sudden changes but the pediatrician told them it was merely because their little girl had become attached to them.

As we mentioned in Chapter 3, some researchers suggest that right after delivery a period of high sensitivity exists for parents to form close ties with their babies (*bonding*). But infants do not become attached to adults until the second half of their first year (Yarrow, 1963). **Attachment** refers to the establishment of an intimate tie that is formed in later infancy between a baby and another person, binding them together and lasting over time. Spotlight 4.3 shows how babies contribute to the attachment process. *Dependency* is the label traditionally given to describe a close relationship between older children and adults (Martin, 1975) and will be discussed in later chapters.

PHASES OF ATTACHMENT.   Three phases of attachment have been identified that describe how infants gradually develop emotional ties with their loved ones (Ainsworth, 1967; Bowlby, 1969).

In the first phase, infants from birth to three months seek nearness with anyone, whether they are familiar or not. Young babies are ready to interact with anyone in any way. They use their signals—smiling, vocalizing, and following someone with their eyes—to achieve this end. And they show no anxiety when mother is exchanged for a newcomer (Schaffer, 1963). One reason young babies do not discriminate in relationships or experience anxiety when mother leaves is that they still do not recognize their mothers as separate beings. Although the infant might cry or whimper when put down, the identity of the caregiver doesn't seem to matter.

In the second phase, infants between three and six months gradually learn to discriminate familiar from unfamiliar people. For example, six-month-olds can discriminate between their mothers and strangers (Fouts and Atlas, 1979). And

❖ Spotlight 4.3: Babies in Control

Ethologists have contributed to our understanding of child development through their studies of parent-infant attachment and their attention to early inborn patterns of infant behavior. In Chapter 1, you read about the imprinting of ethologist Konrad Lorenz's baby ducklings. John Bowlby (1958), another ethologist, believes that certain fixed action patterns of infants, such as smiles and gazes, increase interactions between parents and infants in somewhat the same way that the duckling's following response attracts the mother duck to the baby duckling. These signals are said to get the adult to care for and attend to the infant. Clearly these signals serve as biological safeguards ensuring care and survival—infants who can get adults to care for them have a greater chance of surviving than do rejected infants.

Experimental studies report that during reciprocal parent-infant interaction, physiological reactions occur. For example, one study (Emde et al., 1978) showed that five- and nine-month-old infants became so actively involved during smiling that their heart rate and motor movement increased. In another study (Frodi et al., 1978), infant smiles caused little change in parents' blood

pressure or skin conductance, but infant cries caused parents' blood pressure to jump and skin conductance to increase. Parents were drawn to babies in both instances, to prolong the smiling and to stop the crying.

One of the more interesting views of some ethologists is that adults are biologically programmed to respond to the features of a baby. Lorenz described ''babyness'' in 1943 (Fullard and Reiling, 1976). *Babyness* consists of characteristics that are true of animal as well as human babies: the head and forehead are large in proportion to the body and face, the eyes are below the midpoint of the head, the cheeks are round and protruding. Lorenz suggests that these ''baby'' characteristics cause adults to prefer babies (over adults) and activate fixed action patterns of caregiving in adults.

Fullard and Reiling (1976) studied Lorenz's idea. They discovered that young children (grades two through six) preferred to watch slides of adults, but that older girls (grades six through eight) started preferring the slides of babies. Boys began to prefer the slides of babies about two years later than girls. These researchers believed that the

their mothers are more positively reinforcing than strangers, so they begin directing more of their signals toward their mother figure. Thelma could distinguish her mother from her grandmothers, and she directed her vocalizing and smiling toward her mother more than anyone else. But she was still friendly and playful with her grandmothers.

By the third phase, seven- or eight-month-old babies have developed the abililty to distinguish one person from another and person and object permanence, so they become very choosy about whom they interact with. Infants usually develop their first meaningful attachment to specific people between seven and eight months (Ainsworth, 1967; Schaffer and Emerson, 1964). Most babies become attached to their mothers and another familiar figure such as father,

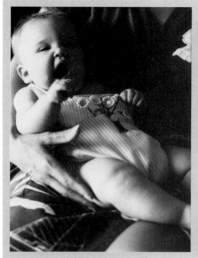  

change in preference suggested a biological influence since the time of the shift from preferring adults to preferring babies occurred at about the time of puberty. Other studies have shown that babies with babyish characteristics—short and narrow features, large eyes and pupils, and a large forehead—more often elicit ''cute'' ratings from adults than infants without these characteristics (Hildebrandt and Fitzgerald, 1979).

People do seem to react in a certain way when they see young animals. Watch others the next time you are around young babies—humans, kittens, or puppies. Many people talk to babies in high-pitched voices, smile, and comment on how cute the child or animal is. Do you think these behaviors could be termed fixed action patterns? What feelings, attitudes, or behaviors do the pictures of infants shown here trigger in you?

grandmother, or older brother or sister. Specific attachment indicates the first formation of true social relationships. When specific attachment occurs, the friendly and undiscriminating reaction to everybody else stops. Infants begin to fear being separated from their parents and become anxious when newcomers approach them. Thelma treats strangers, like her baby-sitter, with caution and gets very upset if her parents leave her with a sitter for an evening. Along with specific attachments, infants attempt to maintain physical contact and proximity (nearness) with their parents. They will follow a departing mother, greet her on her return, and use her as a security base from which to explore (Ainsworth, 1973; Maccoby and Feldman, 1972). This proximity-seeking dependency carries over into the toddlerhood period and will be discussed in more detail in Chapter 7.

ATTACHMENT AND FEEDING.   It was once believed that infants form attachments with their mothers because of the association of the mother with feeding times. But attachment studies with monkeys have shown that feeding is not required nor is it even the most important factor in forming attachments. Psychologist Harry Harlow (1958) constructed several cages, each containing two imitation monkey "mothers" made of wire mesh. One of the "mothers" in each cage was a simple, wire frame. The second "mother" was covered in terry cloth. Both monkey "mothers" had monkey-like heads. Newborn monkeys were observed as they interacted with these "mothers." Even when fed by a nipple affixed to the wire mothers, all the babies spent time between feedings clinging to and cuddling with their cloth-covered mother (see Fig. 4.5). When frightened, they would run to the cloth mother, not the wire mother, even when the wire mother was the source of food. Harlow concluded that such *contact comfort* was more important for forming attachments than feeding itself. Monkeys that received the contact still didn't develop normally due to lack of social stimulation. As a result of this and other investigations, researchers have concluded that social interaction and contact comfort are critical to human attachments (Rheingold, 1961; Rutter, 1979). Spotlight 4.4 presents the effects of institutionalization on infants who do not receive constant social interaction and contact comfort from a loved one.

Figure 4.5
Attachment and feeding. Proving that feeding alone does not cause attachment, this young monkey clings to its cloth "mother" even when feeding from its wire "mother."

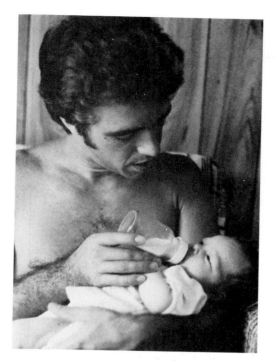

We now know that infants attach themselves to fathers as well as to mothers, and that fathers are just as sensitive and attached to infants as are mothers.

ATTACHMENT TO FATHERS.   Seven-month-old Thelma whimpered and clung to her departing father like a vise when the new baby-sitter came to stay with her for the evening. Thelma was attached to her dad. For many years we thought infant attachment was confined mostly to mothers (Bowlby, 1969), but now we know that it is not confined to mothers alone. Infants can attach to other adult women (Leiderman and Leiderman, 1974), to brothers, sisters, and grandparents (Schaffer and Emerson, 1964), and, of course, to fathers (Lamb, 1977c). Little research has been done on infant attachment to these other adult figures. But more and more research is being done on attachment to fathers as fathers increase their involvement in childbirth and child care. Most studies have reported that babies are more attached to their fathers than they are to strangers (Cohen and Campos, 1974; Lamb, 1977a). The results of recent studies have shown that when given the opportunity, infants attach to fathers as strongly as they do to mothers (Lamb, 1977c).

Some researchers have found that fathers interact differently with their infants than mothers do. Mothers are more likely to hold their babies to feed and change them. But fathers are more likely to pick up their babies to play with them or simply because the child wants to be held (Lamb, 1977a). Fathers also play more touching games and physically arousing games, while mothers usually play

❖ Spotlight 4.4: Institutionalized Infants and Relationships

Velma and other infants living in institutions like orphanages often don't get necessary social stimulation and affectionate physical contact such as smiles, pats, and caresses with one, consistent adult. In contrast to infants in a home setting, the physical needs of institutionalized infants are sometimes met, sometimes not. And these infants receive little sensory stimulation since such objects as toys or mobiles are absent from their cribs. This lack of adequate social and sensory stimulation causes infants who are institutionalized at an early age to be delayed in motor development, cognition, and language development, and in establishing relationships with others. Cases have also been documented in which the height and weight of infants living in a negative emotional environment—whether they live at home or in an orphanage—become stunted (Gardner, 1972; Widdowson, 1951). Known as **deprivation dwarfism**, this condition results when a child's body reacts to emotional distress by switching off the growth hormone (Gardner, 1972).

Infants separated from their mothers and institutionalized between six and twelve months of age—a time when specific attachments reach their peak—suffer more emotional upset than children institutionalized at other ages (Bronfenbrenner, 1979). If institutionalized infants are deprived of one stable relationship with one caregiver, they are unable to form close attachments (Yarrow et al., 1972). They are also unable to distinguish between strangers and familiar caregivers (Yarrow, 1961). They do not develop stranger anxiety or specific attachments either, like home-reared babies do (Schaffer and Callender, 1959). In fact, they become as detached and apathetic towards others as their caregivers are towards them. This poor social stimulation and lack of attachment also accounts for the fact that institutionalized infants reach their peak of smiling seven weeks later than home-reared infants (Ambrose, 1961).

A long-term study (Tizard, 1977; Tizard and Hodges, 1978; Tizard and Rees, 1975) observed English children living in long-stay residential nurseries where close, personal relationships between staff and children were discouraged and the care of children passed through different hands. The researchers reported a developmental pattern of behaviors in infancy, early childhood, and middle childhood associated with institutionalization. At age two, toddlers in institutions were more clinging and less attached to one person than children reared at home. By age four, institutional children continued their excessive clinging, were still missing any deep attachments, became overly friendly with strangers and spent lots of time in attention-getting behaviors. By the time institutional children reached eight years of age they had difficulty in their relationships with adults and other children in school. Few children were closely attached to their housemothers but they sought affection more than "attached" children. Compared with children brought up at home, institutional children were more restless, quarrelsome, attention seeking, irritable, disobedient, and unpopular at school.

Still, institutions need not be so harmful to a child's development. When social stimulation in the form of warm, loving relationships is established and when sensory stimulation is provided, it does make a difference. Institution-reared infants in one study were given small amounts of extra handling during their first week of life. Later, they showed more visual interest in their environment than those who were not handled (White and Castle, 1964). Korner (1964) suggested that when babies are picked up to the shoulder, they usually

The sensory stimulation provided by bright-colored toys is important to the developing motor and visual abilities of infants.

stop crying, become visually alert and have an opportunity to look around. Picked-up babies have more chances to get acquainted with their world than do infants who are left crying in their cribs. Two groups of six-month-old institutionalized in-

fants were held, cuddled, and played with for eight weeks by a consistent, mothering figure. Afterwards, the babies became more socially responsive and vocalized more than a group of orphans remaining under regular conditions (Rheingold, 1956). Sensory stimulation such as mobiles, bright colors, and pictures projecting from the crib along with extra cuddling and stroking enabled orphans to be more advanced in motor and visual abilities than orphans who didn't get this stimulation (White, 1967).

Despite the negative effects of institutions, all hope is not lost for children such as Velma. Negative effects of institutionalization can be reversed when children are placed in environments that include opportunities for locomotion, objects to use in spontaneous activity, and a parent figure with whom the child can develop a close attachment (Bronfenbrenner, 1979). In one study mentally handicapped two-year-olds were taken from orphanages and placed in a setting where each one had a regular caregiver—an older mentally handicapped child. Twenty years later, it was reported that those children with a consistent caregiver were more advanced in cognitive development than children who had remained under regular orphanage conditions (Skeels, 1966). Other studies have shown that even though foster children spend their infant years in institutions, when they are later placed with foster parents, they tend to be more emotionally secure, better adjusted, and higher in intelligence than those children who remain institutionalized (Goldfarb, 1945).

Development of the Parent-Child Relationship

Relationship	Developmental Period
Parent-Newborn Synchrony	Newborn (birth–4 weeks)
Parent-Infant Attachment—During their first few months, infants seek proximity with anyone. Between 3 and 6 months, they learn to discriminate familiar from unfamiliar people. After 6 months, babies attach to specific persons in the environment—usually the mother, father, or both. They will try to maintain nearness to parents if parents leave them or if a stranger appears.	Infancy (birth–12 months)
Parent-Toddler Dependency	Toddlerhood (1–3 years)
Parent-Preschooler Partnership	Early Childhood (3–6 years)
Parent-Child Detachment/Children's Same-Sex Friendships	Middle Childhood (6–12 years)
Parent-Teenager Individuality/Crowd Formation	Adolescence (13–18 years)

verbal games such as peekaboo (Flaste, 1976; Lamb, 1977c; Clarke-Stewart, 1978). Given a choice, infants in one study (Clarke-Stewart, 1978) preferred their fathers to mothers as playmates—probably because of the livelier nature of their fathers' play.

Ross Parke (1981), a noted researcher on fathering, reports that in his studies, fathers touch, look at, talk to, and kiss their newborns just as often as mothers. And new fathers are just as skillful and gentle as mothers in the way they handle their infants. In some cases fathers were apt to hold their infants and gaze at them more often than mothers. Fathers are also just as sensitive and responsive as mothers to infant signals during feeding—an essential for the development of secure parent-infant attachment (Ainsworth, 1973).

STRANGER ANXIETY.   Infants' behaviors with other adults also undergo changes.

Brad has two grandmothers who compete for his favor. At five months of age, Brad would cry to be picked up. When his visiting Grandma Rachel would pick him up, he would immediately stop crying and begin smiling. Of course, this pleased Grandma Rachel greatly and made her feel special. Three months later, Grandma Bonnie attempted to soothe Brad on her first visit with him. Every time she approached his crib, Brad would scream and wail as if he was terrified. But when his mother and father tried to quiet him, he became immediately calm and playful. Grandma Bonnie felt rejected by her eight-month-old grandson. For years after that, Grandma Rachel bragged to family and friends that little Brad liked her better than Grandma Bonnie!

Would you agree with Grandma Rachel's analysis of these social interactions? Probably not. What if the visiting times of the grandmas had been reversed? If Grandma Bonnie had visited Brad when he was five months of age she would have been just as well received as Grandma Rachel. And if Grandma Rachel had visited the eight-month-old Brad, she might have had little to brag about because she would have been greeted by Brad's wails. As we see from Brad's behavior, the same infant who will respond with familiarity to strangers during the first five or six months of life, will react with much anxiety to strangers at around seven or eight months of age. What mysterious developmental events occur to cause such an abrupt change in infant behavior?

Brad was experiencing **stranger anxiety**—crying and signs of distress in the presence of newcomers. Sometimes babies also show stranger anxiety by crawling away from a new person. Stranger anxiety emerges in infants at about seven or eight months of age—although the age varies for each baby (Ainsworth, 1973; Schaffer and Emerson, 1964), and not all babies show signs of stranger anxiety.

There appears to be a strong relationship between attachment and stranger anxiety—the more intense the attachment, the greater the fear of strangers (Schaffer and Emerson, 1964). Rise of attachments and the onset of stranger anxiety, which begin at about the same age, has been explained in terms of *object permanence* (Ainsworth, 1973). When infants like Brad realize that mother still exists even though she cannot be seen, they often attempt to prolong contact or bring about mother's return (Ainsworth, 1967). In addition, by seven months of age, infants develop schemes for the familiar people and objects in their world. And they have difficulty assimilating new people and objects that do not fit into their existing schemes. The infants are now able to distinguish between mother, self, and strangers. As a result, when strangers or unfamiliar objects appear, they may become frightened. For this reason, eight-month-old Brad became fearful upon meeting his unfamiliar Grandma Bonnie.

As infants act on their environment, they add to their schemes by experiencing people and objects. More numerous and varied schemes develop and they have an easier time assimilating unfamiliar events and people. Stranger anxiety declines. So, if both Grandma Rachel and Grandma Bonnie attended Brad's first birthday party, he would probably receive them with equal affection.

It is also important to bear in mind that infants do not show stranger anxiety in every situation. Stranger anxiety usually occurs only when a stranger tries to communicate with the baby (Schaffer, 1971), as Grandma Bonnie did. The manner in which a stranger approaches an infant also determines the anxiety level. When strangers remain at a distance rather than seeking close contact with the baby, it is less likely that the infant will be afraid (Lewis and Brooks-Gunn, 1972). Strangers who rapidly approach infants are more likely to be perceived as threatening. On the other hand, when an infant has time to observe and evaluate the characteristics of the stranger, the infant shows less anxiety and sometimes smiles (Trause, 1977). Sometimes infant reactions to strangers include both smiling and crying—indicating interest in a new person (novel stimuli) and at the same time, fear of the unknown and possible threat (Yarrow, 1979).

Based on this information, what is a good way to approach a new baby? A gradual warming up will do better than an abrupt appearance. But if you're too passive a stranger, you may not be received well either. When newcomers *gradually* get involved by talking, gesturing, or offering toys, infants are apt to engage in sociable, reciprocal interactions.

EMOTIONAL DEVELOPMENT

One-month-old Roosevelt is unhappy. And he wants everybody within earshot to know it! He belts out a shrill cry, tightens his little body, and flaps his arms and legs in what adults might interpret as a fit of rage. But is it really rage? Or is it pain, fear, frustration, or something else?

It's hard to tell because newborns don't have specific emotions, like adults. According to an old but famous study by Bridges (1932), infants have general, global emotional states called *generalized excitement or distress.* All other emotions are born from generalized excitement. Emotions differentiate or move from generalized excitement to specific emotions as infants get older. By the end of his first year, Roosevelt will replace generalized cries with specific utterances about his displeasure.

Development of Specific Emotions.   Before infants develop specific emotions, they begin to recognize the emotions of others. They are sensitive to the positive and negative feelings of their caregivers and respond to their fears and anxieties (Yarrow, 1979). Research shows that three-month-olds can distinguish between surprise and happiness (Browne et al., 1977). And between four and six months of age, infants begin to discriminate between pictures of adult facial expressions of joy and anger, and neutral expressions—preferring to gaze at joyful expressions (LaBarbera et al., 1976). At seven months of age, infants can tell whether an adult is happy or afraid (Nelson et al., 1979). Once infants learn to make these distinctions, they begin to develop specific emotions of their own.

Positive emotions such as smiling or laughter appear before negative emotions such as anger or fear—suggesting that babies can handle positive emotions before negative emotions (Sroufe, 1979). Still, by nine months of age, infants have been found to show interest, joy, surprise, sadness, anger, disgust, contempt, and fear (Izard et al., 1980).

Expressing Emotions. Crying and smiling are two chief ways infants express their emotions. Generally, crying is a negative emotional response—indicating displeasure; smiling is a positive emotional response—usually indicating no displeasure.

CRYING. Although we mentioned how difficult it can be to interpret infant cries, crying is distinctive. Wolff (1969) identified four different patterns of infant cries: hunger cry, ''angry'' cry, pain cry, and frustration cry. Reasons for crying change with age. Very young babies cry for physical reasons such as discomfort or hunger. Older infants cry for psychological reasons such as boredom or the desire to be held. It takes new parents a while to learn the distinction between different types of cries. Thelma's mother has now learned to distinguish a hunger cry from a boredom cry and no longer has to use her ''mind reading powers'' to care for Thelma's needs.

SMILING. One of the most appealing emotional responses of infants is their smile. Like most significant landmarks in development, smiling is a developmental process that begins as a simple reflex in the first few days after birth. The early smiles of newborns are called **reflexive smiles** and are associated with the neonate's internal state (Sroufe, 1979). Newborns sometimes smile spontaneously during

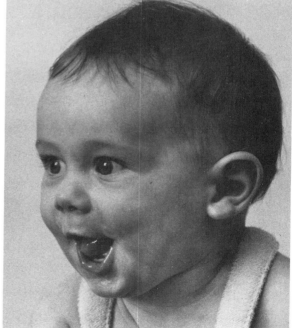

Babies use crying and smiling to express a wide range of emotions, from fear to pain and from contentment to glee.

certain states—such as REM sleep (Emde et al., 1976). Practically any stimulation to the neonatal nervous system will get babies to smile, especially during a drowsy or sleep state. When Thelma's mother gently brushes the cheeks of her drowsy newborn, Thelma reflexively smiles back.

Simple, reflexive smiles develop into **social smiles** toward human faces and voices at two to eight weeks of age (Gewirtz, 1965). These smiles occur when the infant is alert and they are more vigorous and last longer than reflexive smiles (Wolff, 1963). They also aid the parents' attachment to their baby.

At three months of age, Thelma smiles at her mother's face because of its familiarity and association with pleasure. When infants see toys, objects, or faces over and over again, they smile as they recognize these stimuli (Kagan, 1971). During the third month, infants will vigorously smile and coo when they manage to master complex problems in their environment—such as making a mobile move because of their own actions (Watson, 1972). This pleasure from control is also observed in blind infants who smile and coo when they gain control over an auditory mobile (Bower, 1977).

Infants begin to laugh at four months, usually when playing social games such as peekaboo or being bounced on the knee of a loved one. Toward the end of the first year, infants will smile and laugh when they can make things happen. Twelve-month-old Thelma, for example, laughed uproariously as she batted her butterfly mobile and made it spin round and round!

Social scientists disagree about the cause of smiling. A likely explanation is that smiling begins as an inborn reflex but becomes gradually influenced by shifts in cognitive development and increases through reinforcement and social interactions with others (Etzel and Gewirtz, 1967).

SEX-ROLE DEVELOPMENT AND RELATIONSHIPS

One Saturday Roosevelt's mother was making plans for a joint garage sale with Caroline's mother. The two women busied themselves pricing objects for the sale while ten-month-old Roosevelt and Caroline occupied themselves on the floor with some of their favorite toys. From time to time, Roosevelt would bang his block on the floor and Caroline would make a shrill sound—both trying to get their mother's attention. Caroline's mother would look up, smile, and nod. Then Caroline would go back to play. Roosevelt's mother would also look up, speak to him, and continue her work. But that wasn't enough for him. His banging got louder until his mother picked him up for a brief time or gave him more of her attention. Why was Roosevelt so much harder to please?

Sex Differences.   Sex differences in behavior have been documented during the first year of life. Research suggests that as early as ten months, boys are more persistent in demanding their mothers' attention than girls (Martin, 1981). Goldberg and Lewis (1969) observed sex differences in behaviors of thirteen-month-olds when a frustrating barrier was placed between them and their mothers. Boys more actively tried to get around the barrier to rejoin their mothers. Girls just stood where they were placed and cried. When the barrier was not present, these same girls touched and talked to their mothers more than boys did. Another study reported that girl infants were more socially responsive than boy infants when their mothers spoke to them. Girls also initiated more reciprocal interactions with their mothers than boys did (Gunnar and Donahue, 1980). Besides these observed differences in reactions to parents and to frustration, boys play more actively than girls. Boys are also more aggressive than girls in almost every culture and this difference persists throughout life (Maccoby and Jacklin, 1974). This has led some researchers to suggest that boys are biologically predisposed to being more aggressive than girls because of sex hormones (Maccoby, 1980). A recent study also suggests male neonates are stronger than females. When placed face down on a flat surface, boys raised their chins higher and had a stronger grasp than girls (Jacklin et al., 1981).

Sex Typing.   How can we explain these early sex differences? Besides biological factors, which influence such things as aggression, adults have different ideas about what behaviors are appropriate for each sex. Sometimes the labeling of an infant's behavior as "masculine" or "feminine" begins before birth. Active fetuses are rumored to be males and the less active ones females. Sometimes parents will behave differently toward the child before birth according to the child's imagined sexual identity—by furnishing the child's room with certain toys and choosing clothes with the supposed sex of the unborn child clearly in mind.

Treating babies differently because of their sex is called **sex typing.** A good illustration of how it works can be found in a study in which a group of adults were asked to rate the emotional behavior of nine-month-old infants (Condry and Condry, 1976). One half of the adults were told that the infant was a boy and the other half was told they were observing a girl. The same infant was thought to display different emotions and different levels of emotional arousal depending on whether the observers thought the infant was a boy or a girl. When presented with a jack-in-the-box, "girls" were thought to be displaying *fear* reactions and "boys" were judged to be showing *anger.*

In another study (Frisch, 1977), adult strangers interacted with fourteen-month-olds. In one session, each child was introduced as a boy. In a second session, the same child was introduced as a girl. Adults encouraged more activity and tended to choose male toys when playing with children they thought were boys, while they showed more interpersonal interaction and nurturance toward children designated as girls.

The existence of sex typing in crying and in the caregiving treatment of infants in a nursery for newborns showed that nurses gave more attention to fussing, crying boys than they did to fussing, crying girls. Nurses also gave male infants more attention than female infants during periods when the babies weren't crying or fussing (Lyberger-Ficek and Sternglanz, 1975). (Text continues on p. 162.)

Cross-Cultural Development and Relationships

Cultures around the world have different views and customs about the care of infants. In most societies, infants are constantly carried by their caregivers (Goldberg, 1972). But in the United States infants have traditionally been placed in a crib, baby seat, or playpen. As babies become more mobile, varying degrees of physical restrictions and permissiveness can be observed from culture to culture. Practices range from a high degree of physical restraint to almost total freedom of movement.

CARE OF INFANTS

Among African nations, mothers do not pay much attention to caring for the infant's psychological and social development. Instead, they give major attention to physical well-being and survival. LeVine (1977) compares the different patterns of care practiced by African parents with Western parents:

> The infant is on or near a caretaker's body at all times, day and night. Crying is quickly attended to and becomes rare relative to Western infants. Feeding is a very frequent response to crying. There is, by Western standards, little organized concern about the infant's behavioral development and relatively little treatment of him as an emotionally responsive individual (as in eye contact, smile elicitations, or chatting). (p. 23)*

During their first year of life, infants in rural Guatemala are kept inside a small, dark, windowless hut to make the job of child care easier (Kagan and Klein, 1973). Infants are not allowed on dirt floors, and the outside sun, air, and dust are considered harmful. Mothers stay busy preparing food and weaving, and infants are seldom spoken to or played with. Besides the mother's body or the infant's own clothing, the only available objects for play are oranges, ears of corn, and pieces of wood or clay. Because of these child care practices, Guatemalan infants often lag behind their agemates in other countries developmentally. Guatemalan infants are also more fearful, quieter, and smile less. According

_____
*Reprinted by permission.

to Kagan and Klein, these early restrictions do not permanently impair Guatemalan children, who catch up with their agemates in the United States by eleven years of age. Once they become mobile at fifteen months, they have left the dark huts and are playing with other children.

The ancient custom of swaddling has been or still is practiced in almost every part of the world (Moss and Solomons, 1979). Russians continue to practice swaddling so babies won't harm themselves. The Polish swaddle infants to strengthen legs and toughen the baby through suffering (Moss and Solomons, 1979). Swaddling in Poland and Romania has been practiced to keep a distance between ''clean'' and ''dirty'' parts of the body—the face, feet, and genitals.

CARRYING PRACTICES

As you saw with Jun in Chapter 1, Hopis, Navajos, and members of other American Indian tribes have traditionally swaddled babies on cradleboards for portability, the cradleboard serving as both carriage and crib. A baby can be taken to the fields where a mother works, strapped to the mother's back as she walks, or hung from a tree limb (Moss and Solomons, 1979). Among the Navajo Indians, cradling becomes less frequent as the baby grows older. The amount of time on the cradleboard averages sixteen hours a day at three months, but amounts to only nine hours a day by twelve months (Chisholm, 1978).

Susan Goldberg (1972) studied the Zambian culture in Africa. She noted that Zambian infants are carried upright in a sling on their mother's back. In that position, contacts with the world are wide and varied. Infants participate in all of mother's daily activities—routine housework, trips to market, gardening, trips to bars and movies, and social gatherings. Goldberg observed that as a rule, physically restricted Zambian infants receive more physical stimulation than most American babies and have more chances to use their muscular control than the relatively free American crib babies. Constant physical contact allows the Zambian mother to determine the state and needs of her infant by the "feel" of what is happening on her back. There is no need for her to listen or go and look in another room the way American mothers do.

EFFECTS OF CARE AND CARRYING PRACTICES

Little or no permanent lag in development has been reported in cultures where physical restrictions are imposed during the care and carrying of infants. Nevertheless, in our culture the trend is to give infants as much physical freedom as possible. Nonrestrictive clothing is used to foster sensorimotor development. In fact, the practice of restricting movements runs counter to our "liberal" ideas about child-rearing. But the practice of temporary swaddling for short periods of time is being revived by the nursing profession in this country as a means of soothing irritable, fretful, or "difficult" infants (Moss and Solomons, 1979). After years of baby buggies and strollers, the use of front and back infant carriers has become a current trend in the United States. In addition to the physical-motor and perceptual advantages for the baby, parents find that this practice makes it easier to attend to their baby during housework, shopping, or leisure walks in the park. This just goes to show what we can learn from observing other cultures and what useful practices we can borrow to enrich our own.

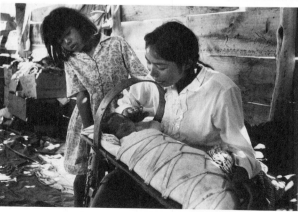

Infants throughout the world are usually carried in slings, cradleboards, or some type of carrier. Some parents in the United States have borrowed the practice of transporting their babies in front and back carriers.

Mothers of girls touched their six-month-olds and talked to them more than mothers of infant boys (Goldberg and Lewis, 1969) and mothers imitated sounds to their daughters more than they did to their sons (Moss, 1967). In other studies, mothers talked to, sat on the floor with, and played more with their daughters than with their sons. And fathers engaged in these same activities more with sons than daughters (Weinraub and Frankel, 1977).

Sex Similarities. Despite the existence of early sex differences, there are also many similarities between the sexes. In fact, as Maccoby (1980) points out, there are many more similarities than differences:

> When the behavior of individuals is examined, it becomes clear how misleading sex differences in average scores can be. Many individual girls delight in rough-and-tumble games, and many individual boys prefer more tranquil and rule-governed pursuits. Similarly, many individual girls are negativistic and difficult to control, while many individual boys are easygoing and tolerant of frustration. So, even if group sex differences are found in a given behavioral domain—physical, cognitive, emotional, or social—the behavior of individual members of the two sexes is often very similar. Men and women, boys and girls are more alike than they are different. (p. 223)

In view of these similarities, attempts are being made to avoid sex typing infants and adults. Although some people argue that there are natural differences between boys and girls that predispose them to certain adult roles, others claim that tightly defined sex roles limit children's opportunities right from the beginning of life.

Summary

1. The most rapid physical growth occurs from conception to the infant's first birthday. Body proportions alter and the bones, teeth, muscles, and nervous system develop.

2. For most babies development is smooth sailing during the first year but there are exceptions. Some babies are struck by Sudden Infant Death Syndrome, a mysterious disorder that kills more babies during the first year than any other illness. Other infants suffer from a Failure to Thrive Syndrome—the failure to achieve normal physical growth rates.

3. Getting used to routines is an important adjustment for new babies whose parents are concerned with getting them on some type of schedule for sleeping and eating. As infants are weaned from the breast or bottle, parents must help them establish proper nutritional habits.

4. Rolling over, sitting with support, crawling, creeping, and standing are maturational steps that set the foundation for later locomotor movement such as walking. Eye-hand coordination also follows a series of maturational stages, progressing from reflexive grasping at birth, to the visually guided reach at five months, to the use of thumb and forefinger between seven and nine months.

5. The ages for developmental norms vary from scale to scale. Many norms were established fifty years ago and stress uniformities in development instead of individual differences. But despite these shortcomings, norms are useful guideposts for observing and recording the development of children.

6. During the first twelve months, maturation of the infant's perceptual system and experience with objects brings the world more into focus, as desire for visual complexity, convergence, object-sound linkage, object constancy, and depth perception appear. The senses of hearing, smell, touch, and taste also improve dramatically within the first year.

7. According to Piaget, the schemes babies are born with guide their actions and help them organize information from their world. Assimilation allows infants to fit new informaton into an existing scheme without having to change that scheme. Accommodation enables babies to change schemes so that contradictory information can be taken in. Infants use assimilation and accommodation together in a balancing process of equilibration, which helps them organize actions and information and adapt to changing environmental demands.

8. In Stage 1 of the sensorimotor period in Piaget's theory of cognitive development, reflexes dominate neonatal behavior; in Stage 2, accommodation occurs and new patterns of behaviors are accidentally coordinated; in Stage 3, pleasurable behaviors are intentionally repeated and object and person permanence develops; and in Stage 4, object and person permanence and intentionality are further refined.

9. During infancy, important foundations of language are laid through crying, cooing, and babbling. Language development is reciprocal, with both infants and parents influencing each other's speech.

10. Generally, infants establish a sense of basic trust when their caregivers are affectionate and when they recognize and respond to the infant's needs consistently and effectively. But if an infant is deprived of love, neglected, or abused, a sense of basic mistrust can be established.

11. There are three phases of attachment: The infant seeks proximity with anyone; the infant learns to discriminate familiar from unfamiliar people; and the infant attaches to specific persons and maintains nearness to those persons. Social interaction and contact comfort form the basis for human attachments—not the feeding situation. And infants attach as strongly to fathers as they do to mothers.

12. Stranger anxiety, appearing at the same time infants develop object permanence (seven months), represents the beginning of specific attachments to one or a few important persons.

13. When institutions are poorly staffed and minimal social interaction and intellectual stimulation is provided for children, the effects can be damaging. But providing sensory stimulation and one constant adult with whom to attach minimizes these effects.

14. Infants develop positive emotions before negative ones, and by nine months of age interest, surprise, sadness, disgust, contempt, anger, fear, and joy have all

been developed. Infants express their emotions by crying, smiling, and eventually laughing.

15. While there are differences between male and female infants, many sex differences in infancy are due to sex typing by many parents and other caregivers. There are more similarities than differences between boys and girls.

Empathetic Activities

- What feelings did you have as you read about the following?
    - The case of Velma and Thelma
    - The sudden death of Mary and Jack Hopkins's infant
    - Brad's cognitive development
- As a parent, what special things would you do (and not do) to ensure that your infant develops a sound sense of trust and attachment?
- Pretend you are Roosevelt's parent. Select and cut out from a mail-order catalog wallpaper, draperies, blankets, bedspreads, toys, and accessories for his room. When finished, read the discussion section from the following article: H. L. Rheingold and K. V. Cook, "The contents of boys' and girls' rooms as an index of parents' behavior." *Child Development,* 1975, *46,* 459–463. Evaluate your selection for Roosevelt's room based on this discussion.
- Suppose we reversed Grandma Rachel's and Grandma Bonnie's trips to visit their grandson, Brad. Predict what differences in social interactions would occur when Brad is five months, eight months, and twelve months of age. Use information from the discussion on stranger anxiety to support your thoughts.
- How does the onset of object permanence and stranger anxiety at approximately seven months illustrate the *Whole Child?*
- How are parent-infant relationships important in the establishment of trust, attachment, and sex-role development? How does the child's whole social network (grandparents, caregivers, and others) contribute to the infant's early relationships?

Related Readings

Caplan, Frank. *The first twelve months of life.* New York: Bantam, 1978. A beautifully illustrated, detailed, practical guide to baby's growth during the first year of life. Easy reading.

Gonzalez-Mena, Janet, and Eyer, Dianne. *Infancy and caregiving.* Palo Alto, Calif.: Mayfield, 1980. A practical application of theory and research using short cases about everyday situations. A must for infant caregivers.

Jackson, Jane, and Jackson, Joseph. *Infant culture.* New York: Thomas Y. Crowell, 1978. Presents the latest scientific research on infancy in such a way that you'd think you were reading a novel. Recommended for parents and child development practitioners.

Lewis, Michael, and Rosenblum, Leonard, eds. *Origins of behavior, Vol. I: The effect of the infant on its caregiver.* New York: Wiley, 1974. An interesting reversal of the old belief that adults do all of the controlling! A comprehensive review of reciprocal relationships showing what infants do to cause their caregivers to behave in certain ways towards them.

Maccoby, Eleanor. *Social development: Psychological growth and the parent-child relationship.* New York: Harcourt Brace Jovanovich, 1980. Outstanding! The best synthesis of current research on social development we've seen.

Spock, Benjamin. *Baby and child care.* New York: Meredith, 1972. Information about the day-to-day lives of children from birth to adolescence. Provides parents with the answers to all the questions they used to ask Grandma.

III Toddlerhood

(ages 1 to 3)

5 Toddlerhood: Physical-Motor and Perceptual Development

The Case of the Typical Toddlers

Scene 1: You are at the supermarket shopping for a party you are giving that night. The outside temperature is ninety-five degrees and the air is humid. The market aisles resemble a freeway on a holiday weekend. You are almost finished with your shopping, enjoying your solitude in spite of the crowd.

Action: As you round the corner from paper products to dry cereals, you are startled by the rapid approach of a small child on the run. She manages to cover the distance of the aisle length with amazing speed, even though her gait is uneven and her legs widespread. Frequently glancing over her shoulder, she looks like a freight train with no brakes. In hot pursuit is a young woman—clutching a baby in one arm and barely controlling a grocery cart with the other.

"Kim!" the woman shouts, apparently unaware of her large audience. "You stop right now! You hear me? When I catch you, I'm going to . . ." Kim, laughing gleefully, toddles on, taking the turn at the end of the aisle with ease if not grace. Rounding the bend, Kim, aged twenty-four months, crashes headlong into your grocery cart, causing you to swerve into a shelf of mayonnaise jars. Several jars topple onto the floor. Amazingly enough, only one breaks but it splatters all over you. The noise summons the store manager who appears experienced and skilled where toddlers are concerned. He catches Kim as a first item of business. She is returned to her embarrassed mother and placed in the infant seat of the shopping cart. All the while Kim is kicking, screaming, and frantically moving her body in a sort of frenzied last attempt to escape her captors.

Scene 2: Later the same evening, you have worked hard to make your living room look attractive for the party. Magazines are carefully arranged on the coffee table, flowers are placed here and there, and a variety of interesting objects decorate the room.

Action: Guests have begun to arrive on time. The doorbell rings. Close friends are at the door with Scotty, their two-year-old son. The babysitter backed out at the last minute and rather than miss the party, they decided to bring their toddler. They were sure you wouldn't mind. But after your earlier experience in the supermarket, you're not so sure. You don't want to be rude and so decide to give it a try. At first Scotty is a perfect angel. He spends a time at his mother's knee, quietly assessing the situation. Then he ventures away from her briefly and silently. After awhile, he seems to gain a sense of confidence and courage as he begins to explore the environment—all of it! In a quick, one-handed operation, a magazine cover is ripped off, while the other hand picks up a nearby ashtray. Magazine and ashtray are dropped suddenly in favor of the debris on the floor from the ashtray. Then, for his grand finale, Scotty stands in your great-grandmother's antique rocker and makes it slide from one end of the room to the other. Scotty's father tries to divert Scotty's attention while his mother attempts to redeem the situation.

Scene 3: The party finally ends. You throw your ripped magazine into the trash, sweep up the broken ashtray, and survey the damage to your rocking chair.

Action: Actually, there is no action. Feeling flushed, you collapse into a nearby chair. As your hair streams down your face, you detect bits of dried mayonnaise streaked throughout. You sit there staring helplessly into space, silently vowing to yourself. . . .*

Physical Growth

Toddlerhood has been called ''the first adolescence'' (Strang, 1969)—a transition from babyhood to childhood, just as adolescence is a transition from childhood to adulthood. While infancy is characterized by rapid physical growth, toddlerhood is characterized by refinement in height and weight and structural development as physical growth slows down but remains faster than it will be again until adolescence.

HEIGHT AND WEIGHT

Each time Kim and Scotty visited their pediatrician for their regular checkups during toddlerhood, they got a clean bill of health. And their parents got an important progress report on their toddlers' growth in height and weight. The height of these typical toddlers was thirty inches at one year of age, thirty-four inches at two, and thirty-eight inches at three. Their weight increased from seven pounds at birth to twenty-one pounds at one year, twenty-seven pounds at two years, and thirty-two pounds at three years of age.

By two years of age, toddlers weigh about one fifth of their total adult weight. And by two and a half, they have quadrupled their birth weight (Vaughan, 1964). Weight has now stabilized and will increase at a slower rate until adolescence, when a growth spurt results in another rapid weight increase.

Generally, girls reach about 53 percent of their adult height and boys 50 percent by two years of age. But boys tend to be slightly taller and heavier after age two, and they will be substantially taller and heavier at maturity than girls.

Some children are tall and heavy while others are short and light. And some youngsters mature more quickly than others. Genetic makeup influences the height, weight, and rate of maturation of children more than environmental factors do (Garn, 1966; Mittler, 1971). Children grow at much the same rate and to about the same size as their parents. This is especially true for mothers and daughters and for fathers and sons. The general rule is that shorter parents will have

---

* Adapted from a case written by Jeanne Armstrong, instructor of child development at Lane Community College, Eugene, Oregon.

shorter children, and taller parents will have taller children. Weight is more influenced by environmental factors than is height. Exercise, illness, emotions, and the amount and kinds of foods consumed by children influence their weight gain.

STRUCTURAL DEVELOPMENT

Despite the active nature of Kim and Scotty, most people find their cherub-like appearance delightful. Their "baby faces" result from the small lower jaw and large cranium that must accommodate a proportionately large brain. The abdomen and chest are almost identical in size at age two, but by age two and a half, the chest has become larger. Abdomens protrude and backs appear swayed because all the toddler's internal organs must be housed in such a short trunk. The cephalocaudal principle (see Chapter 4) is seen in all of this development as well as in the proportionately large arms and short legs. Because of the large head and long arms, toddlers have a center of gravity high in the trunk, making them top heavy. But at two and a half to three years of age, legs catch up with arms and the rest of the body—becoming more adult-like in proportion.

A toddler's brain has reached about four fifths of its adult weight by the end of the second year (Nelson et al., 1975). By age three, the brain is closer to its mature growth than any other part of the body.

The calcification and ossification of bones begun in infancy continues in toddlerhood. The fontanelles of the skull are beginning to close and the spine is hardening and changing from the "C" shape of infancy into the "S" shape characteristic of adults. Small bones are combining to form larger ones and new bones are

By age two and a half, most children have their full set of deciduous teeth, but they still have a baby face and other infant-like characteristics.

developing from cartilage in wrists and ankles, but the toddler still has a larger proportion of cartilage than hard bone. So at age two, the child's bones are still soft and are particularly subject to the effects of disease, dietary deficiencies, and deformation. A toddler's joints are more flexible than an adults and ligaments and muscles are still loosely attached.

Specialists can tell if a child's growth is progressing normally by examining the number, thickness, and shape of the small bones in the hand and by measuring head circumference. In fact, skeletal maturation is used as an overall measure of the maturation of other body systems (Teeple, 1978).

By two and a half years of age, most children have their full set of twenty *"baby"* or *deciduous teeth.* And cavities are already a problem for some children. About 5 percent of one-year-olds, 10 percent of two-year-olds, and 40 percent of three-year-olds have cavities. For this reason Kim's parents make sure she brushes her baby teeth. Another potential problem concerns growth of the jaws. Imbalance of the face and problems with chewing can occur if the upper and lower jaws do not meet properly. So, just like her older siblings, Kim sees the dentist for checkups twice a year.

Muscle tissue develops at a much slower rate during the second year (Breckenridge and Murphy, 1969). In fact, the development of muscle tissue is slower than other tissue growth during the early years and does not catch up until adolescence.

Fat, which developed rapidly in the first nine months, decreases—rapidly until two and a half years, then more slowly until age five and a half. This loss of fat gradually helps turn the plump, toddler's body into the more slender physique characteristic of the preschool child.

Motor Development

It should be obvious to you after reading the Case of the Typical Toddlers that toddlers are physical in their approach to the world. During toddlerhood, gross and fine motor skills are refined. Children develop more control over their bodies, with the use of hands and arms developing ahead of the use of legs and feet. Although walking is the milestone of locomotor movement, hand dominance and other motor refinements and coordination also take place during this period.

LOCOMOTOR MOVEMENT

As Kim rounds the corner in the supermarket, it's hard to believe that less than a year ago she couldn't even stand alone! Like most toddlers, Kim's ability to get around is developing rapidly.

Once infants crawl, creep, and pull to a standing position, they begin to take their first steps. Most children walk without help between fourteen and fifteen months—some earlier and some later (Frankenburg and Dodds, 1967; Shirley, 1933). Toddlers get their name from the unsteady toddling movements they make as they begin to walk. Because they are top heavy, they must spread their feet wide

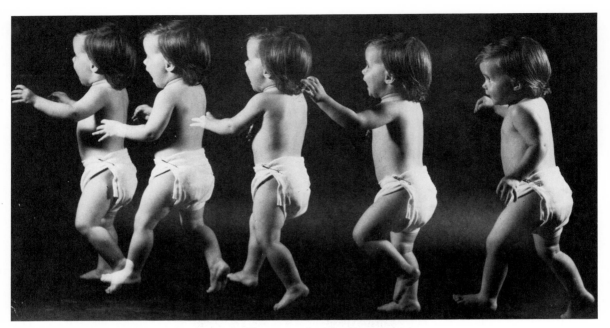

Figure 5.1 **Toddler walking.** Strobe photos of a fifteen-month-old walking show the arms held forward and toes turned outward as this toddler tries to achieve body balance.

and "toddle." They have a forward tilt to their posture, with knees and elbows slightly bent, arms held forward, and toes turned outward (see Fig. 5.1).

It is easy to tell how much locomotor experience toddlers have had. With practice the spread between the legs narrows, balance becomes more steady, hands drop to the side, and additional motor movements are combined with walking—stopping, turning, bending over (Brazelton, 1974). Eventually, they lose their forward tilt, become less clumsy, and their toddle disappears. As walking is refined, toddlers begin to place their feet straight ahead with the heel of one foot directly in front of the toes of the other foot—the steps of two-year-old toddlers measuring about half the length of adult footsteps (Cratty, 1970). So at the grocery store, Kim must take two steps to her mother's one. But when Kim is on a rampage, running through the store, the shoe is on the other foot! Kim's mother feels like she must take two steps to match one of Kim's strides! No wonder they invented toddler seats on shopping carts!

HANDEDNESS

During lunch, Scotty managed to drink his milk with his right hand only. He lifted the cup, raised it to his lips, and lowered it. He held his spoon in his right hand, using his fingers now and then. Finally, he put the spoon down and used both hands to lift his food from the plate. He ate with his left hand once in a while, sometimes using both hands to wield his spoon.

Like all motor development **handedness**—a preference for using one hand more often than the other—is a developmental process. At first, infants and

Fine coordination becomes refined enough between twenty-four and thirty months so that toddlers can hold a crayon much like adults do—with the thumb on one side and the fingers on the other.

young toddlers use both hands interchangeably to manipulate objects in their environment. In the early months, the two hands work together as if they hadn't yet separated in their function. And both hands are used with equal frequency and ease. Children begin to show hand preferences as early as six months. But most are twelve to fifteen months old before handedness is fully developed (Breckenridge and Murphy, 1969). Children continue to switch hands in new and unfamiliar activities, with right-handedness increasing until seven or eight years of age. Hildreth (1949) found that more toddlers between two and three used their right hand to throw a ball and catch than to shovel or mark with crayons. Left hands were used more for eating with fingers or drinking from a cup. But as our frenzied partygiver found, left hands can be used for picking up fragile ashtrays while right hands simultaneously and skillfully rip off magazine covers!

In the United States, 90 percent of all children are right-handed. The general agreement is that right- or left-hand dominance results from a combination of inherited and environmental influences. Scotty's parents might encourage right-handedness by offering him objects and food in his right hand. But trying to "break" a child of left-handedness—a common practice in this country even in this century—can be emotionally harmful to toddlers, perhaps leading to stuttering or reading problems. Most authorities now advise parents and teachers to let nature take its course by allowing children to use the hand with which they are most skillful.

MOTOR REFINEMENT

When Mom and Dad played march music on the stereo, Scotty amused everyone with his attempts to march. The toddler tried to march, manipulate his baton (a stick with beads attached), and turn his head to see what Mom and Dad were doing—all at the same time. This caused him to become unsteady and to stumble occasionally. As he marched, his tongue protruded slightly as if to indicate the challenge of his difficult task. When the music and the marching stopped, Scotty celebrated his triumph with a loud "Hooray!"

As motor development becomes more refined in toddlerhood, children develop the ability to combine other motor movements with walking. Scotty was able to perform three motor tasks at once: marching, shaking his baton, and turning his head to see other happenings in the room. But if he had dropped his baton, he would have had difficulty bending at the waist and picking it up without falling. This skill doesn't develop until between twenty-one and twenty-four months.

By eighteen months, toddlers can judge the weight of an object by its size. They assume if it's big it's heavy and if it's small it's not. And their reaching and grasping become smoothly coordinated action (Willemsen, 1979). These developments allow toddlers to skillfully manipulate objects in their environment. They delight in using their newly found thumb and forefinger grasp to pick up tiny specks off the ground and floor. By the end of toddlerhood, children can run, jump, kick, and throw. Sudden starts, stops, and turns are smoother but are still difficult even though toddlers enjoy the challenge. As Table 5.1 indicates, there are other fine- and gross-motor behaviors toddlers practice just for the pure pleasure it brings. This holds true for climbing, romping, or something a bit more exotic—like sailing a neighbor's antique rocker through a sea of shredded magazine pages and cigarette butts!

Changing Routines

Along with the physical changes in toddlerhood comes the need for changes in everyday routines. Toddlers and parents are glad when feeding, dressing, and toileting can finally be done without parental help. But acquiring such self-help skills is a real struggle for toddlers and often tests the patience of the most tolerant parent. Parents should realize the importance of being patient while their child struggles for what seems like forever to button a jacket the parent could have done in a minute. Now that toddlers are walking and climbing about on their own, certain safety measures must be taken because they cannot always make the best judgments.

SAFETY

Houses are not built for the safety and comfort of toddlers, whose constant moving and exploring is not only a trial for parents but a danger to themselves. So child proofing the house and setting reasonable limits is important. Child proofing includes the removal of all breakable, dangerous, or heavy items from the child's reach—even things that can be reached only by climbing. Although fed-

Table 5.1
Motor Refinements During Toddlerhood

AGE	FINE MOTOR	GROSS MOTOR
12–15 months	Marks on paper with crayons	Walks alone
	Inserts object into hole—clothespin into bottle for example	Creeps up stairs
	Holds spoon, brings it to mouth	Throws objects in clumsy way
	Removes hat and shoes	Pushes and pulls large toys
15–18 months	Turns pages of book (2 to 3 pages at once)	Walks sideways and backward
		Climbs onto furniture
		Walks up and down stairs with help
		Throws large ball 4 to 5 feet
18–21 months	Imitates scribbling	Walks up and down stairs alone, both feet on one step at a time, holding rail
	Makes painting strokes	
21–24 months	Opens door by turning knob	Kicks a large ball
	Strings 3 or more beads	Bends at waist to pick something up without falling
	Turns pages of book one at a time	
24–30 months	Holds crayon with fingers (thumb on one side, fingers on the other)	Stands on one foot and balances (briefly, no outside help)
		Stands on tiptoes
		Alternates feet going up stairs
		Rides small tricycle using pedals

"Language, motor, and socioemotional development from twelve to thirty months" by C. Christensen, C. Frederickson, and J. McNeil. Unpublished manuscript. Institute for Family and Child Study, Michigan State University, 1978. Reprinted by permission.

eral law requires that containers of harmful substances be child-proofed, it is still a good idea to lock substances such as drugs, cleaning fluids, and gardening supplies in a high cabinet. Sometimes children open child-proof tops more easily than adults! Electrical outlets should be covered, loose electrical cords fastened, yards fenced, stairways blocked, pot handles turned in while cooking, and unused refrigerators locked or their doors removed. Floors should be constantly checked for small objects that a child might gleefully pick up and swallow. Out of seven million poisoning accidents reported during 1980 to poison control centers (where emergency calls are handled by medical personnel), 80 percent involved young-

Even with the new "child-proof" tops on medicines and cleaning products, locking such substances up is the best assurance of toddler safety.

sters five years of age or under. And in most of these cases, a parent was nearby when the accident occurred. When parents are sure their toddler is safe, they don't have to say no as often, the child's exploratory efforts are not frustrated, and everyone is happier. Of course, it may not be easy to find a safe place for Great-grandma's rocking chair.

TOILET TRAINING

Kim's parents dreamed of the day they could turn her diapers into dust cloths. All Kim had to do was learn to use the toilet. What could be simpler? But toilet training doesn't always turn out to be a simple matter. When parents begin to toilet train before a toddler's first birthday, they are usually setting themselves and their child up for a long, difficult process and frequent failures. The muscles necessary for control of the elimination process have not fully developed before age one.

As a rule of thumb, children are most easily toilet trained at eighteen to twenty-eight months of age. But toileting is developmental and unique for each child. Many toddlers whose training begins around eleven months are fully trained by eighteen months (Sears et al., 1957). When allowed to make their own choices about toileting, 80 percent of children are trained by about twenty-seven months (Brazelton, 1974). Most children are both bowel and bladder trained by 27.7 months on the average. But regardless of when the training occurs, bowel control usually comes before bladder control.

Being toilet trained brings many toddlers feelings of accomplishment and great pleasure.

Bladder control during sleep remains a problem a bit longer than daytime control because it requires unconscious control. Brazelton's (1974) research indicated that most children sleep through the night without bedwetting by thirty-three months. But soiling and wetting accidents are common for children, even after they are well in control of their toileting needs. These incidents usually come about because of a break in daily routines—the child gets overly excited, becomes ill, or is fearful of something. In any case, adults should expect and tolerate accidents. Shaming or humiliating young children in these instances is extremely harmful. When parents expect and tolerate toileting mistakes, children will soon establish regular toileting patterns.

In fact, attitude is the single most important factor in the family's approach to toilet training and pressure the single greatest barrier. When parents become impatient, apply too much pressure, or give unusual amounts of attention to toileting, they only make matters worse. In these instances, toddlers will sometimes rebel and become negative: "No! No! No!" will be their response.

Fortunately, a sound relationship exists between Kim and her parents. Instead of using force, Kim's parents took the most sensible approach to toileting. She was free to observe parents, siblings, and older playmates model toileting behaviors, and she was praised when she expressed a readiness to participate in the process. Kim's readiness signals, which included straining, squatting, and grunting, led to a regular schedule of bowel movements. And Kim's ability to tell her parents she needed to go to the toilet was the best cue of all. In an attempt to please her parents, Kim was fully toilet trained by twenty-five months of age. The independence and feelings of success that accompanied this achievement gave Kim great pleasure. And her parents were able to take those old diapers and turn them into dust cloths—a dream come true at last!

179

EATING

By twelve months of age, most babies in the United States are eating three meals a day. Formulas and bottles are replaced by milk and juice from a cup. Kim and Scotty have graduated from baby foods to table foods, and they enjoy feeding themselves.

Self-feeding is usually a messy time because toddlers are still learning how to balance a cup and hold a spoon. Food is mashed, mixed, tossed, and smeared. Sometimes Kim adds chunks of food to her beverage and blends beverage with food. Her parents sometimes complain that more food ends up on the floor, in the seat, and on her face than in her mouth. Nonetheless, the self-feeding experience is a valuable one. Children at this age are practicing motor control and eye-hand-mouth coordination. They are also exploring and experimenting with their food—taking in sensory information. Providing finger foods, accepting messiness, and allowing plenty of time to finish helps toddlers learn to do things for themselves. Although children differ in their readiness to feed themselves, most children have mastered this task by twenty-four months of age and before long will be doing it with ease if not "grace."

NUTRITION

Regardless of "how" toddlers eat, "what" they eat is crucial. Well-balanced meals are of utmost importance. Nutritionists recommend that parents use the basic four food groups throughout toddlerhood and the preschool years (McWilliams, 1980). Milk continues to be a necessary source of calcium and phosphorus for bones and teeth, and nutritionists recommend that children between one and five years of age consume a minimum of two cups and preferably three cups per day. Younger children who cannot chew sometimes do not eat an adequate amount of meat. A helpful rule of thumb is to give toddlers about one tablespoon of meat (or fruits or vegetables) for each year of life (McWilliams, 1980). Eggs and cheese are additional rich protein sources for the young child. As an infant, Scotty had a large appetite, but now that he is a toddler he actually eats less. Nutritional demands aren't as great in the second year since body growth doesn't occur as rapidly as it did during the first year.

Sometimes parents become upset about a toddler's loss of appetite or refusal to eat new foods. Such parental concern can lead to well-intentioned but harmful demands that may force a child to eat more food than is needed.

Most nutritionists advise against forcing children to eat, especially new foods, as this can cause unpleasant associations and turn the child off certain foods and make meals a dreaded time of conflict and tension for both parent and toddler.

Yet, when it comes to food preferences, toddlers are experimenters. They will sample practically anything placed before them. Attractive, tasteful, and textured foods served in a pleasant manner—such as apple, banana, orange, and cheese slices shaped into smiling faces or other imaginative shapes—are particularly appetizing to children. In these ways parents and preschool teachers can capitalize on the toddlers' curiosity and expand food choices to include new and nutritious foods.

SLEEPING

All people need to sleep—and all people have individualized sleeping routines. Some people like to go to bed late and get up late. Others are of the "early to bed, early to rise" variety. Toddlers also have individualized sleeping routines. Some go to bed early and fall asleep easily—others do not. During infancy children have the luxury of sleeping whenever they need or want to. But toddlers are expected to adapt their sleeping habits to those of the family—often with little adult understanding of the child's feelings.

There are ways in which parents can help toddlers adjust to a reasonable bedtime schedule. Instead of roughhousing with children before bedtime, parents can provide a transition time to help toddlers "shift gears" from the busy day to quiet sleep. Listening to relaxing records and stories (not monster stories), looking at picture books or talking quietly about the events of the day can help children relax and give them the attention they need. Development of independence and cooperation are fostered when children can choose the records or stories they want. Bedtime routines help toddlers know what is expected and help quiet fears. For example, every night Scotty's parents do exactly the same things and in the same order. They give him a bath, put on his pajamas, let him go to the toilet, read him a bedtime story, give him a hug and kiss, tuck him in, and turn out the lights. Night-lights, open bedroom doors, teddy bears, stroking and patting provide additional night-time comforts for youngsters.

After a busy day, the bedtime story can give children a chance to wind down with a good book and their loved ones.

Spotlight 5.1: Obesity and Malnutrition

Most children in the United States are within the normal range for weight. But an estimated 40 percent of American children are *obese* or overweight (Galton, 1978). And while malnourished children are uncommon in the United States, one quarter of the people in the world today (more than a billion people) are or have been malnourished (Warren, 1973).

OBESITY

Because of poor eating habits, obesity is more common among the poor (Garn and Clark, 1976). It also develops more often among babies who are bottle-fed. Overprotective or overanxious mothers often feed their babies every time they cry. And sometimes mothers overfeed infants as a substitute for love they are unable to give the child (McLaren and Burman, 1976).

Infants who are overfed develop more fat cells than normal weight babies. And some overweight children develop adult-sized fat cells by two years of age. These excessive fat cells are difficult to remove by weight loss in adulthood, so obese babies tend to be obese adults (Eichorn, 1979; Knittle, 1975).

Overweight preschool children also eat faster than their normal-weight agemates (Drabman et al., 1979), a difference that is noticeable around the time of the first self-feeding. Some research even traces obesity to birth. Heavier babies are born to heavier mothers, and heavier neonates will suck

harder for sweet solutions than average weight newborns (Engen et al., 1978).

Childhood obesity can be successfully managed when parents abide by some of these practices:

1. Avoid overfeeding children during infancy and toddlerhood.
2. Provide youngsters with nutritionally balanced meals during the first year of life.
3. Decrease the ratio of fat to nonfat foods served.
4. Encourage children to cut food into small pieces, eat slowly, and take small bites.
5. Have overweight preschool or school-age children put eating utensils down between bites.
6. Plan lots of time for meals so children are not rushed when eating.
7. Never use obesity as a measure that children are nutritionally healthy. Chubby toddlers are neither healthier nor happier!
8. Avoid using food as a reward or punishment.
9. If possible, encourage physical exercise such as walking or biking, involving the entire family.

MALNUTRITION

A nine-month-old baby was admitted to a hospital in Great Britain, very thin, feeble, and swollen. He was malnourished. His parents explained that they had joined a new cult that allowed them to eat only raw vegetables. Severe malnutrition such as this can result when children are put on fad diets (Roberts et al., 1979).

Malnutrition can be caused by a variety of other factors—low income, cultural biases against foods, poor eating habits, and lack of information about proper nutrition. The problem is most severe in the underdeveloped nations of Africa, Central and South America, and Asia, where food shortages regularly lead to starvation. During 1979 and 1980, the plight of Cambodian children was a familiar one to the American public.

Malnutrition exists in the United States, too. The most common nutritional disease among infants and toddlers in the United States today is iron deficiency anemia (Eichorn, 1979). Riboflavin, protein, and vitamin A deficiencies are more common among children of Hispanic backgrounds. Overall, poor health and malnutrition occur most frequently among blacks, Mexican-Americans, whites from Appalachia, and migrant workers of all races (Eichorn, 1979; Winick, 1976).

Malnutrition can have permanent effects upon physical growth, particularly infant height and weight (Tanner, 1970). Babies who are malnourished are shorter and weigh less than well nourished infants (Pipes, 1977). Malnourished Navajo children were found to be behind well-nourished white children in skeletal development—about two years for girls and one year for boys (Reisenger et al., 1972). Brain development is affected too. During infancy and toddlerhood, malnutrition is re-

lated to reduced brain cell growth and slowing of myelinization (Kelin and Pertz, 1978; Winick, 1976), conditions that may be associated with developmental lags. In fact, Lester (1976) found a similarity between the cries of malnourished infants and those of brain-damaged infants. Both have initial longer sounds and higher pitch, which suggest that malnutrition affects the function of the central nervous system.

Malnourished children usually play less, are less active and curious (Languis et al., 1980), and are lower in intelligence than well-nourished children (Hoorweg and Stanfield, 1976). Iron-deficient children are more irritable, have trouble paying attention, and perform poorly on cognitive tasks (Honig and Oski, 1978).

Some early effects of malnutrition can be reversed with prompt intervention (Zeskind and Ramey, 1979). Developmental delays among iron-deficient infants and toddlers were reversed with early doses of iron. After iron treatments, these undernourished children had higher mental test scores, were more alert, and showed better gross and fine motor coordination than before (Honig and Oski, 1978). When poverty-level children were provided an enriched diet, they became six to seven times more active than their undernourished agemates (Restak, 1979). So, as is the case with obesity, it is important to begin nutrition education and the development of good eating habits during the early years.

Perceptual Development

"We have a lost child about two and a half years old, named Kim. Will her parents please come to the informaton counter at once!" How many times have you heard similar announcements over a loudspeaker while shopping? Lost toddlers in public places are not unusual. When Kim strayed from her mother and got lost, her limited perceptual ability prevented her from recognizing her mother's face or voice in a large crowd. Let's examine why this is so.

MATURATION OF SENSORY ORGANS

As early as one year, the fibers in the pupils of the eye are fully developed (Cratty, 1970). By two years of age, the perceptual system has matured in many ways. Although the eyeball has not reached adult size, its size and weight are similar in dimension to that of adults. Most toddlers are well coordinated in tracking objects moving at various speeds and angles (Cratty, 1970). They can also tell the difference between horizontal and vertical lines (Rudel and Teuber, 1963). Kim's favorite pastime is watching a blinking neon sign showing a soft-drink bottle emptying its contents into a glass, over and over again.

Despite these maturational improvements, Kim's perceptual development is not complete. Like most toddlers she has difficulty in form discrimination. A two-year-old is just as likely to look at pictures and figures upside down as rightside up (Rudel and Teuber, 1963). The complete integration of the visual and motor systems still hasn't occurred by toddlerhood. Accuracy of vision and hearing are also limited to short-range distances. This is why it was difficult for Kim to locate her mother in the supermarket.

Toddlers' inefficient scanning ability also causes them to make incomplete and inaccurate judgments (Rosinski, 1977). They are unable to perceive both the whole and its parts at the same time. So when Kim looks for her mother, she can't scan the sea of faces to identify her. Instead, she gets stuck on one face at a time (part) or becomes immersed in the sea of faces, ignoring details altogether (whole). Obviously, the chances of Kim ever finding her mother are lessened with such an inefficient scanning strategy. With maturation and experience, older preschool children and school-age children can process and organize larger chunks of incoming data and can fit the whole and its parts together (Cratty, 1970; Elkind et al., 1964). For now, Kim must wait until her mother hears the announcement over the loudspeaker and comes to get her.

EXCEPTIONAL PERCEPTUAL DEVELOPMENT

A relatively small percentage of children suffer from perceptual handicaps. Children with faulty hearing or vision perceive the world differently through an altered perceptual system. Hearing handicaps may result from genetic defects, maternal disease during pregnancy, childhood disease, or injury. Prenatal influences cause half of all cases of blindness in children (DeMott, 1978). Visual handicaps can also result from postnatal disease or injury to the eye.

Hearing is especially important because it is the sense used by infants and children to perceive and learn language. Through language, they learn about the accumulated knowledge and customs of their society. And, just as important, they use language to think. Children with even minimal hearing dysfunction can be severely impaired in their language and cognitive development if measures are not taken to correct the problem.

Blind infants are born with the same potential for movement as other children and they progress through the same sequence of motor development skills. But since they cannot see, blind children are not motivated to reach and examine objects. These objects that are reached for are limited to those that the blind infant can identify through sounds (Fraiberg, 1977).

Concepts such as skyscrapers, clouds, or rainbows are also difficult—if not impossible—for blind children to grasp since they cannot be perceived except through sight. Self-awareness is delayed since such activities as visually comparing one's own height or size to others, looking in mirrors, or noticing which facial expressions accompany which verbal expressions are impossible. Parents of blind children must take special precautions to help their toddlers use motor skills to explore an unseen world so that motor and cognitive retardation will not occur (see Spotlight 5.2). Primary goals for parents and teachers of the blind include teaching children to be mobile, encouraging them to use all senses to the maximum, and translating visual events into a form that they can perceive (Bateman, 1967).

MOTOR DEVELOPMENT, PERCEPTION, AND COGNITION

Motor development, perception, and cognition are closely tied together and constantly influence each other. Maturation of the brain and motor actions causes the restructuring of cognitive schemes, which in turn improves perception. Kim and

Climbing, a favorite toddler sport, allows this young boy to perceive the world from a new angle.

❖ Spotlight 5.2: Visually Impaired Children

As we have noted, perceptually handicapped children need special, often intensive stimulation if they are to develop to the full extent of their capabilities. Unfortunately, they do not always receive such attention, especially when they are very young.

Visually impaired infants, for example, may be quite content to lie on their backs in their cribs and be ministered to by their parents. After all, they know no other way of life. Parents may not be aware—or may not want to believe—that their infant cannot see. They may attribute their child's inability to sit or stand when other children do to be an individual growth pattern. They wait eagerly, and more and more anxiously, for their baby to make the first move. A child may reach the age of eight or ten months before the now-despairing parents seek professional help.

Even when special training is delayed, it can still be of enormous benefit to perceptually handicapped children. First, however, long-established, counterproductive behavior patterns between parents and child must be altered. Parents must learn that helping their child adjust to and cope with the world can be a painful process for all concerned. But, as you can see in the following cases of visually impaired children, the skills and abilities that can be gained more than offset the difficulties involved.

WAYNE

Wayne was eighteen months old when we first met him and his family. He was the typically limp, passive, understimulated blind infant. His parents were most eager to make up for lost time, but Wayne was not so keen on the new routine, and preferred to lie on his back forever. But it is never too late to start the baby moving. He has been permitted to do as he liked for months and he will loudly and fiercely object to attempts to change him. Get him down on the floor on his stomach and sell him on the idea that he is going to learn to like it. If he can, he will insist on lying on his back and doing nothing.

Wayne lay happily on clothes pins, golfballs, and even some building blocks fastened to his back to make it uncomfortable for him just to lie there. Then his father tied a toy telephone to Wayne's back that actually rolled him over onto his side every time the child tried to lie on his back. This was too much for Wayne and he gave up the struggle and learned to lie on his stomach. Six weeks later he was creeping, and eventually walked at two years, putting up token resistance at every new demand that he become independent. Finally he learned that life could be more fun if he moved around than it had ever been lying on his back on one spot.

DICKIE

Three-year-old Dickie, who had no useful vision, was presented to a staff training session at a children's rehabilitation center by the parent counselor as an example of a competent blind child. One of the staff asserted that blind people could tell colors just by feeling them. When told that this was not so, she turned to Dickie and asked him what color his overalls were. Dickie promptly replied that they

Scotty perceive their world in different ways than infants do. Now that their motor development allows them to remain upright and to move about, they can perceive their environment from many different angles. And the more sensory information they perceive, the more cognitive development occurs. Like all beginning walkers, Scotty and Kim must constantly watch what their feet are doing and look for obstacles in their path. But by three years of age, these visual checks aren't necessary. With walking come newly freed hands that can be used to touch and grasp objects

were red and everyone was most impressed. Then the counselor spoiled it all by asking Dickie how he knew that his new overalls were red. Quick as a flash, he said, ''My mum told me!'' In time, Dickie would learn that the overalls with the smooth buckles on the straps were red ones, and that his old brown ones had buttons on their straps. Then his mum would not have to tell him which ones he had on.

MYRNA

Myrna, a four-year-old deaf and blind child, had exhausted the patience of her family and the staff at a child development center. When she was admitted to hospital, the nurses, physiotherapists, and occupational therapists all had a try at toilet training, but Myrna still refused to use the toilet. It became obvious that there was more than stubbornness involved. It was suggested that maybe she did not know what was expected of her and perhaps one of the staff should take her hands and show her. After one demonstration, Myrna, with a big grin, hopped on the toilet and performed. She finally understood what all those people wanted her to do.

IAN

Five-year-old Ian learned to use his sonar so skillfully that he could walk down a street and call out each time he passed a parked car or a lamp post without missing a single one. Next time you are downtown, listen to your footsteps as you walk along a building and notice how the sound changes

A visually impaired toddler using his ''sonar'' for walking.

as you pass the entrance to each store or reach a corner. That kind of information is very useful to a blind person but is ignored by those who see. It is not necessary to keep the floor clear for a blind toddler; for some strange reason they seem to enjoy walking across a room strewn with toys. Maybe the obstacles add a little suspense to an otherwise dull trip.

From *Can't your child see?* by Eileen P. Scott, James E. Jan, and Roger D. Freeman, University Park Press © 1977. Used with permission.

that can be smelled or tasted. Freed hands allow toddlers to experiment with and learn more about things in their environment than they were able to do when hands were required for locomotion. And using hands and eyes toddlers touch and see their bodies and those of others. Through motor and perceptual exploration, they develop an awareness of toes, hands, eyes, nose, genitals and learn the names of most of these body parts. It is at this time they first begin to understand that there is a ''me'' and everybody else is not part of ''me.''

Summary

1. During toddlerhood, growth in height and weight slows down, while body proportions and structures become more similar to those of adults.

2. Walking is the milestone of locomotor movement and hand dominance the milestone of manual movement during toddlerhood. Gross- and fine-motor skills are refined, and the toddler can perform several motor tasks at one time.

3. The increased mobility of toddlers means parents must take special precautions to ensure their safety.

4. During toddlerhood children must adjust to new routines, become toilet trained, and learn to feed themselves. Early establishment of good nutritional habits can prevent obesity and malnutrition. To make mealtime enjoyable and nutritious for toddlers, nutritionists recommend the Basic Four Food Plan and colorful, textured, and flavorful foods served in a pleasant manner.

5. Toddlers can track objects moving at various speeds and angles, and they can tell the difference between horizontal and vertical lines. But their perception is limited to short-range distances and they are unable to perceive both the whole and its parts at the same time.

6. Matured motor development allows toddlers to perceive their world from different angles than before and frees their hands to experiment and learn more about things in their environment—something they could not do when their hands were required for locomotion.

7. Although a relatively small percentage of children suffer from perceptual handicaps, those who do may require special education to offset developmental delays.

Empathetic Activities

- What feelings did you have as you read the Case of the Typical Toddlers? What feelings do you think the supermarket manager had? The partygiver? Kim and Scotty? Their parents?

- If you were responsible for a toddler for one day, what safety precautions would you take to child proof your kitchen area and what kinds of meals would you prepare?

- Visit a nursery school. Choose a toddler and observe him or her on the playground. Make a list of all the motor skills this child can perform. Compare your list with Table 5.1.

- Use information from this chapter to do the following:
  - Describe Kim's structural development and motor development.
  - Based on Kim's perceptual development, predict what would happen if she got lost in the supermarket.

■ What are some specific ways in which perception, cognition, and physical-motor development interact during toddlerhood to influence the development of the *Whole Child?*

■ In the Case of the Typical Toddlers, you saw how the toddler's physical approach to the world influences the nature of adult-toddler relationships. Complete the partygiver's thoughts in terms of future relationships with toddlers: ''You sit there staring helplessly into space, silently vowing to yourself . . . .''

Related Readings

Brazelton, T. Berry. *Toddlers and parents: A declaration of independence.* New York: Delacorte, 1974. Facts on the physical and social development of toddlers. A blend of practical knowledge and case studies illustrates the content and brings it alive!

Caplan, Frank, and Caplan, Theresa. *The second twelve months of life: A kaleidoscope of growth.* New York: Grosset and Dunlap, 1979. Sequel to *The first twelve months of life;* equally well-illustrated and easily read. Detailed, month-by-month summaries describe the toddler's growth and development and emerging self-help skills.

Endres, Jeannette, and Rockwell, Robert. *Food, nutrition, and the young child.* St. Louis: C. V. Mosby, 1980. An excellent and easy to read resource. Discusses food and nutrition developmentally, with chapters on the infant, toddler, and preschooler. Additional sections on food service management and nutrition education relate food and nutrition to the educational curriculum.

Ridenour, Marcella V., ed. *Motor development: Issues and applications.* Princeton, N.J.: Princeton Book, 1978. A readable little handbook, exploring motor development and related issues in detail. Motor development principles are applied to children's play spaces, curricula, and evaluation methods.

Scott, Eileen P., Jan, James E., and Freeman, Roger D. *Can't your child see?* Baltimore: University Park Press, 1977. A useful book that answers many questions about blindness: What are children with little or no sight really like? Can they grow and develop like other children? Where do they go to school?

6 Toddlerhood: Cognitive and Language Development

The Case of Brad's First Birthday Party

Today Brad is one year old! Doreen and Bill wanted their son's first birthday to be a perfect occasion, but unfortunately it didn't turn out that way. At first things were great. They had a beautiful cake with one candle and sang happy birthday. It was a joyous celebration, and everybody was having fun. They gave Brad a piece of cake and a spoon to eat it with. Then the fun ended! The minute the cake was placed before Brad, he started pinching off the chocolate icing and dropping it from his high chair onto the floor. Then he threw chunks of cake across the room and mashed handfuls onto the table, wall, and himself. As if that weren't bad enough, he began dropping his spoon from his high chair. At first Brad's parents thought it was accidental. But after he dropped his spoon the fourth time, they were exhausted and almost ready to call it a day. Covered with chocolate cake from head to toe, the three of them headed for the bathroom. Doreen and Bill looked at each other in wonderment as if to say: "And this is only the beginning. What will happen next?"

Once Doreen, Bill, and Brad were cleaned up, it was time for Brad to open his presents. Gifts had been sent from Grandmas Bonnie and Rachel, but Brad's favorite turned out to be the one from Mom and Dad—a blue and white toy soldier that marched when wound up. But there was only one problem. At first, Brad was more interested in throwing his toy soldier from his playpen than in winding it up. After many throws, Doreen and Bill became tired of throwing it back. So Brad tried to pull the toy in through the bars of his playpen. But because he was holding it horizontally, the toy was too large to pull through. After a series of trials and errors, Brad finally turned the soldier vertically and it slipped through the bars. Much to his parents' surprise, Brad could now throw and retrieve his toy all by himself! After his first success, his second and third attempts to recapture the toy soldier grew progressively shorter. Finally his attention was drawn to making the soldier march—much to the relief of his parents.

While Brad's first birthday party began as a busy and somewhat messy time, it ended on a pleasant note. Brad was delighted because he had discovered how to retrieve his toy soldier, which unknown to him, marked the beginning of his first true thoughts. Now Brad was ready to celebrate this occasion and sing "Happy Birthday" one more time!

Cognitive Development

As was the case with infants, sensorimotor actions continue to guide the way toddlers think. The Case of Brad's First Birthday Party illustrates how Brad's gross- and fine-motor refinements and matured perceptual development aid him as he makes strides in cognitive development. Brad's ability to move about more freely, to perceive the world from different angles, and to better coordinate his senses and motor actions enable him to experiment and learn more about the world around him. Still, Brad the Toddler is a sharp contrast to Brad the Infant. Let's see why this is so.

SENSORIMOTOR INTELLIGENCE IN TODDLERHOOD

As children move into toddlerhood, we can see the beginnings of simple experimentation as they try to solve problems by trial and error. They also begin to use mental images to refer to and think about objects and people not present. Vivid imagination and pretend play accompany this new development. The toddler's use of trial and error experimentation and mental images is the first step along the road toward the adolescent's ability to use systematic, abstract reasoning as a scientist might.

In Chapter 4, we saw infants in the beginning stages of "thought." During Piaget's Stage 1 of the sensorimotor period, practically everything they do is reflexive. But these primitive thought forms soon develop into more advanced ways of "thinking" in Stage 2 when accommodation appears. In Stage 3, babies begin to intentionally repeat activities that bring them pleasure and people and objects in their world take on a permanent existence. As this happens, infants lose some of their egocentrism. In Stage 4 they begin to coordinate old schemes to solve simple problems and to anticipate what will happen before it actually takes place.

Stage 5: Tertiary Circular Reactions.   Actually, Brad's parents shouldn't be too disappointed over the birthday celebration. What seemed to be a disaster to them was quite typical behavior for a one-year-old. During Piaget's fifth stage of the sensorimotor period (which occurs between twelve and eighteen months), the child becomes a curious scientist, forever exploring and trying out new things. Although his behavior is taxing to his parents, Brad, like other children at this stage, is *experimenting* with the chocolate cake and spoon. He deliberately applied the cake in as many places as he could—on the floor, table, wall and himself. And he was looking for new experiences with his spoon. He tried various ways of dropping it and listened to the different sounds it made each time it fell. The repetition of such new experiences is an end in itself. Toddlers like Brad are very intent on seeing how objects "behave" in new situations (Wadsworth, 1979). Through constant testing of their surroundings, they learn to solve simple problems through trial and error.

Brad's behavior with his toy soldier demonstrates how children at this stage don't simply coordinate old schemes to solve new problems as they did in Stage 4. Instead, both new schemes and new coordinations are present. As a result of accommodating his behavior, Brad developed a new means (the scheme of turning the soldier vertically rather than horizontally) to an end (the scheme of pulling the soldier back into his playpen). Brad's discovery marks the beginning of true thought. He has genuinely adapted (accommodated) himself to unfamiliar situa-

Children in Stage 5 of the sensorimotor period are constantly experimenting with new ways to use objects in their environment.

tions by finding new means for dealing with them. Before this stage, almost all behavior was the result of assimilation to reflexive schemes.

The object concept becomes further developed at this stage. In Stage 4, infants search for hidden objects. But they don't always look in the right place. They search where the object was found last, whether they saw it put there or not. Remember back in Stage 4 when Brad's block kept getting pushed under his blanket? Suppose his block was hidden under his pillow for a change. In Stage 4, he would continue to search for it under his blanket because that's where he had always found it before. But in Stage 5, he would search for it in the last spot he saw it—not just in the places it is usually put. So Brad will now look for his block under his pillow, blanket, sheet or wherever he saw it last.

Stage 6: Invention of New Means Through Mental Combinations. Before this stage, children's cognitive behavior is totally dependent on taking information through the senses and motor action. But Stage 6 (which occurs between eighteen to twenty-four months), signals the beginning of **symbolic thought**—the ability to use mental images to represent objects. We can see this in children's ability to imitate actions or objects that are not present. For example, Brad's mother reported that at nineteen months of age, Brad's favorite words were "cookie" and "thank you." He liked to pretend he was handing his mother a cookie. In return he expected her to say "thank you." This exchange of imaginary cookies for thank you's was a delightful game to Brad. But to us, it shows Brad was thinking symbolically. He imagined an object (cookie) was present when it really wasn't. And he symbolized an action (handing his mother a cookie) without actually performing it with a real cookie.

At about the same time, Brad's mother noticed that he was solving problems differently.

September 5: Brad and I were in the backyard today. I watched him go to the swinging gate and try to push it open. But it was held back by a tricycle on the other side and it wouldn't move. He tried to use force, but it just wouldn't budge. He looked up at the gate, and swayed from side to side, as if to predict the direction of its swing. Suddenly, he seemed to have a brainstorm! He walked beside the fence and through the side door. Quickly returning to the outside of the stubborn gate, he moved the tricycle that was blocking it and pulled the gate toward him. As the gate slowly swung open, his eyes followed its path and got wider and wider. He emerged from behind the fence with an expression of triumph!*

Toddlers in Stage 6 can also solve problems without the trial and error experimentation they relied on in Stage 5. Instead, they can think through solutions without the aid of actual objects that characterized problem solving in previous stages. But using images instead of real objects to think through solutions is a *gradual* process that develops over about a two-year period. Brad and other toddlers his age are just beginning to use symbols for thinking. They still cannot mentally carry out the entire process. We can tell this because Brad continues using motor actions. Swaying from side to side helped him imagine swinging the gate open from the outside before he actually did it. These accompanying physical behaviors are still part of the cognitive process that helps toddlers find solutions to their problems.

The conclusion of the sensorimotor period is an important milestone in children's cognitive development. The sensorimotor period sets the foundation for language development in toddlerhood and for other cognitive skills that develop in the next major period—the preoperational period. Sensorimotor development does not end, but from here on, intellectual development is dominated by symbolic rather than motor activity. Although the preoperational period begins in toddlerhood, it spans the preschool years as well. So, we will rejoin Brad as a preoperational thinker in Chapter 9.

---

* Piaget (1974) described a similar incident with his son, Laurent.

❋ Spotlight 6.1: Play and the Sensorimotor Period

INFANTS

Suppose you are interested in buying a toy for Thelma. You might complain that you are not sure what she would like. Even though Thelma and other infants can't tell you directly, research results on infant play can give you a clue on purchasing toys.

In the first month of life (Stage 1 of the sensorimotor period), play occurs through simple, reflex actions. So newborn babies like toys that allow them to practice their reflexes—for example, pacifiers for sucking, rattles for grasping, and complex, patterned, high-contrast crib mobiles with visual appeal for scanning. But toys don't always have to be purchased. Sometimes the taste of her own little fist or the feel of her toes keeps Thelma entertained for a long time. These first play activities of observing and handling the parts of the body and watching and touching their parents' faces, hands, and bodies enable infants to distinguish between the boundaries of self and others. As Thelma gnaws on her fists, she feels something in two parts of her body—hand and mouth. But when she sucks her mother's fingers, she has sensations in her mouth only. Realizing where her personal boundaries begin and end eventually gives her a concrete recognition of her own personhood—a person different and separate from all others.

Between one and four months (Stage 2 of the sensorimotor period), as the coordination of hands and eyes takes place, toys that can be seen *and* touched become important. Now the black and white contrast of a mobile is not only fun to look at, but it is also fun to swipe, batt, kick, and twirl. Child development expert Burton White (1975) recommends a nonbreakable mirror placed over the baby's head about seven inches away from the eyes: "Babies tend to engage in modest flirtations and then mild love affairs with their own mirror image

during this particular time of life. It is all part of their growing sociability" (p. 53).

At four to eight months (Stage 3 of the sensorimotor period), babies enjoy making things happen now that they understand cause and effect. Thelma can retrieve a rattle and knows that if she shakes it, it makes a "fun" sound. According to Piaget (1952b), pleasurable activities are repeated in order to experience the pleasure over again. At eight months of age, Thelma is at the pleasurable repetition stage. If the toy you select for her makes a sound and is easily manipulated (such as a toy that squeaks when squeezed, a bell that rings when hit, or a ball that plays music when rolled), more than likely she will be very pleased with her gift!

Infants between eight and twelve months (Stage 4 of the sensorimotor period) can now coordinate old schemes to make something new happen. So they will try out a wide variety of actions on objects. These actions take the form of exploration—banging, mouthing, throwing, spinning. A strainer or small pots and pans from the kitchen are fun to bang and clang. Burton White (1975) suggests waterplay toys, toys with knobs, or a collection of thirty to forty objects of various sizes and shapes placed in a large container such as a suitcase. He also recommends any ball from eight to twenty-four inches in diameter because the ball's path is unpredictable and it enables the child to throw and retrieve. And now that infants anticipate events, their sense of curiosity and anticipation is aroused by jack-in-the-box toys.

TODDLERS

As you've already seen in the case of Brad, toddlers do not respond to objects as infants do. While infants spend most of their time exploring objects (sensorimotor behaviors), toddlers show more creativity, imitation, and imagination in their play (Weisler and McCall, 1976).

At the beginning of the first year (Stage 5 of the sensorimotor period), toddlers have developed an awareness of how objects in the environment are physically related and fit together to serve certain functions. A good illustration of this was Brad's recognition of the physical and functional relationship between his toy soldier and the bars on his playpen (see The Case of Brad's First Birthday Party). Infant Brad didn't recognize this relationship; he obtained the toy only when he accidentally turned it horizontally. But once Toddler Brad recognized the relationship, he immediately turned the toy horizontally.

Objects in the toddler's world also take on new meaning (Fein, 1979). Interest in cause and effect relationships brings a fascination with wind-up toys, push-button devices, switches, and hinges (Fenson et al., 1976). Brad appreciates his wind-up toy soldier now more than ever!

Play becomes more developed during the second year of life (Fein and Apfel, 1979; Nicolich, 1977). At about eighteen months, toddlers recognize the use that many objects have in their culture and symbolic play emerges. A cup that was once used for visual and tactile exploration and to obtain nourishment now holds ''pretend'' water and is one of many props that can be used in symbolic play. Scotty now drinks ''pretend'' water from an empty cup and may even offer his mother some. Kim now realizes that dolls can be ''fed'' and put to bed, just like a ''real'' baby. But the props children use at this age must be similar to the real-life object—usually miniature replicas of real objects (Weisler and McCall, 1976). Brad must sweep

This sand-and-feathers structure can be many things—a boat, a castle, a bird—it's up to the toddler's active imagination.

with a broom-like toy broom, a stick wouldn't do! And his cup must be cup-like.

But children between eighteen and twenty-four months (Stage 6 of the sensorimotor period) can use mental symbols, so their play is less dependent on exact replicas of objects. This loosening of requirements for likeness comes about because of the development of mental symbols (Vygotsky, 1967). A broom no longer must be broom-like—a stick or a variety of other objects will do. Blocks and boxes are also used to represent real-life objects in the child's play at this age.

EGOCENTRISM

The inability to differentiate between objects causes infants to be **egocentric**—to see things only from their own point of view, unable to take the point of view of others. As cognitive growth occurs at each stage of development, children are freed from the egocentrism characteristic of the previous stages, but they simultaneously take on new forms of egocentrism (Elkind, 1976). We will explore the various types of egocentrism as they occur within each period.

Infants don't understand that they are separate and distinct from the world around them. Brad had no notion of where his personal boundaries left off and the boundaries of others began. He considered himself the cause of all activity, all situations, and all results. He believed that his thoughts and his actions controlled the world. When Bill or Doreen came to hold or feed him, he "caused" them to appear.

But now that Brad is a toddler, he's not so sure. He is beginning to view himself as separate from others and to realize that some things happen quite apart from his own desires—much to his disappointment at times. And other people exist in their own right—sometimes having needs that are different from his own. He no longer sees himself as all powerful and the cause of all things. But Brad is still egocentric in the sense that he assumes everybody perceives and understands the world as he does. In time, he will learn that this is not so. And one very important element in his discovery of the outside world will be his acquisition of language.

Language Development

Language is a critical link between children and the people around them. It fosters toddlers' thinking abilities and allows them to express their wants as well as their imaginations. As you read on, you'll see how language is structured, as well as how and in what patterns toddlers around the world acquire language.

LANGUAGE MEANING

Every language is structured by **grammar**—a set of rules governing all the basic parts of a language and ensuring that the meaning of sentences can be understood. These rules serve very important functions. They determine how we combine words to build phrases and sentences (**syntax**) and they determine the meanings of words (**semantics**).

Syntax.   Anyone trying to learn a language must learn rules about how words are put together to form phrases and sentences—the rules of syntax. Without syntax, words would be separate and unrelated. Of course, there is no syntax when children use only single words. But as soon as they combine two words in their first sentences, syntax is present in their speech.

But using words appropriately in sentences is more complex than just understanding meaning or defining words correctly. For example, you would not use the sentence: "The giggling house caught the frisbee tossed by the horse." Even though the right words are used in the right places, it is not a *meaningful* sentence. In our language, houses don't giggle or catch frisbees nor do horses toss them. So this "sentence" violates the *semantic* rules of our language.

Semantics. Semantics is concerned with the meaning of words. Children understand meanings conveyed in language long before they can speak (Ervin, 1964; Huttenlocher, 1974). When Eve's father calls her over to change her diaper, she frowns, turns, and toddles down the hall as if to escape the "undesirable" experience. She has heard the same words and word combinations often enough in similar circumstances to understand Dad's meaning immediately.

As soon as children use their first words, they show some knowledge of word definitions. One of Eve's first words was "kitty." For her, kitty referred to an animal that "meows" and has fur and four legs. But her word definition for kitty was not the same as an adult definition. When Eve saw a tiger at the zoo, she also called it a kitty. Children's knowledge of word definitions increases as their experience increases.

Why can children understand meanings before they can speak? How do they develop word definitions? And what rules allow children to produce grammatical and sensible sentences they never heard before? These are questions studied by psychologists and language experts interested in semantic development. We will present some ideas about the answers to these kinds of questions in the section on theories of language development. But first let's look at Eve's growing ability to use language.

STAGES OF LANGUAGE DEVELOPMENT

Eve Learns to Talk

Scene 1 (July 4): Dad thought he heard twelve-month-old Eve, who was alone in her room, talking to someone. When he crept to the door and peeped in, he saw her playing with her toes and uttering a string of words that sounded like language. He listened carefully, but what Eve was saying made no sense to him at all.

Scene 2 (two days later): Eve was wearing a bandage on her finger. When a neighbor asked her what happened to it, she replied, "Hurt." The neighbor understood Eve's finger was hurt and the bandage was to help the cut, but she didn't know what Eve actually meant by her one-word phrase "hurt."

Scene 3 (three months later): The following one-word statements were used by Eve during a thirty-minute period:

blocks	Daddy	cake
girl	shirt	phone
wagon	dog	rabbit
purple	socks	carrots
sleep	hurt	kitty

Scene 4 (New Year's Eve): Eve watched her mother and father dress and start out the door to a party. As soon as the door was opened, Eve shouted her first two-word phrase "Eve go!"

Jargon.   The unintelligible jabber Eve's father heard in Scene 1 is called **jargon.** It appears around twelve months and increases until about eighteen months. Intonations of the jargon make it sound like actual conversation at first. Upon closer listening, the sounds can be recognized as merely a string of nonsensical utterances with pauses and inflections like sentences. Toddlers like Eve who have only a few real words in their vocabulary seem to use jargon to mimic the rushing speech and rhythmic flow of adult language.

Real words also start to appear along with jargon at twelve months. The appearance of single words is considered a developmental milestone for children (Bloom, 1978). In both the one- and two-word stages, toddlers use simple one- and two-word statements to communicate the same meaning we adults express through an entire sentence.

One-Word Stage: Twelve Months.   First words are heard as toddlers begin labeling objects and people in their worlds. Or they use words to express wants, either negative or positive. So it's only natural that toddlers' first words are usually nouns, followed by verbs, adjectives, adverbs, and pronouns (Ausubel et al., 1980).

When Eve answered "hurt" in response to her neighbor's question, what she probably meant was "I hurt my finger this morning" or "It hurts." Such one-word sentences are called **holophrases.**

You will notice that each object Eve names in Scene 3 is related to her personal behavior. Nelson (1973) found the same trend in her research. She studied the first fifty words spoken by each of eighteen toddlers (see Fig. 6.1). Most of their first words were names of objects. But mere exposure to words and objects did not determine which words were learned first. These earliest words were labels for objects children could act on (ball) or which moved or changed on their own (car). Because action objects are different in each child's environment, each child develops a unique vocabulary of first words. For example, Eve named objects she could play with or manipulate (blocks, wagon, socks), objects that moved in interesting ways (dog, kitty), or objects that made an interesting noise (telephone). Eve

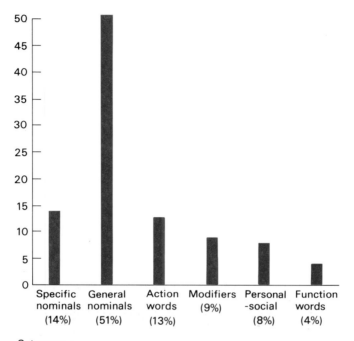

Category:

1. Nominals (words that name)
   a. Specific — used for only one member of a class of people (Dada); animals (Lassie); or objects (car).

   b. General — labels for classes of people (girl, he); animals (doggie); and objects (ball, car).

2. Action words — describe (go, bye bye); demand (up, out); or accompany action or express or demand attention (hi, look).

3. Modifiers — refer to properties or qualities of things or events (big, red, pretty, all gone, mine).

4. Personal-social — express feelings and social relationships (want, ouch, please, no).

5. Function words — fulfill grammatical function only (what, where, is, to, for).

Figure 6.1 **Categories of toddlers' first words.** Adapted from Nelson (1973).

would not be likely to use such first words as watch, wall, and pants. Even though these were present in her environment, she didn't act on them nor did they themselves move or change.

Once toddlers learn to use a word in one situation, they soon extend it to refer to something totally different in another situation. Bloom (1978) tells about Allison, who had always heard the word "more" at mealtime when someone asked for "more food." At sixteen months she began using "more" at the dinner table. Two days later she used the same term to ask her baby-sitter to tickle her again. Allison continued to use this one word in days to come to communicate many different messages or requests. As you can imagine, children's use of holophrases sometimes keep parents busy trying to figure out the wants and desires of their young ones.

Two-Word Stage: Eighteen Months.   "Car broken down . . . wallet lost . . . send money American Express Paris." What this telegram means is "My car has broken down and I have lost my wallet; send money to me at American Express in Paris." But the more words, the more expensive the telegram. So the sender is short and to the point, using only essential words to convey the message. Brown (1973) used this telegram to illustrate the two-word language stage. Around eighteen months of age, toddlers begin speaking in **telegraphic speech**—two-word sentences that, like telegrams, consist of only essential words (Bloom, 1970; Bowerman, 1973; Brown, 1973).

When Eve wanted to go with her parents to the New Year's Eve party, she yelled, "Eve go!" Her real meaning was something like "I want to go too!" And when Scotty said "Truck by!" his full message was "A truck is going by!" Toddlers' telegraphic speech, consists mostly of nouns and verbs with an occasional adjective and adverb (Brown, 1973).

Telegraphic combinations are unique from child to child because all children invent their own combinations. Nevertheless, two-word sentences show consistent patterns and are governed by rules (Braine, 1976; Brown, and Bellugi, 1964). When Eve says "He runned" instead of "He ran," she shows that she has learned the rule that past tenses required "ed" on the end. But she hasn't learned about the exceptions to the rule—irregular verbs. So in attempting to apply the rule of syntax, she adds "ed" to an irregular verb—a grammatical error known as *overgeneralization* (Brown, 1973).

Braine (1976) studied the two-word combinations of his son, Andrew, which demonstrated the use of rules (see Fig. 6.2). Some of Andrew's combined word inventions are "No down" for "Don't put me down" and "More car" for "Drive around some more." Andrew used a few words such as "all," "more," "no," and "see" over and over again. These words, known as *pivot words,* almost always appear in the same position and never show up by themselves (McNeill, 1972). They are usually used in conjunction with noun *X words,* which refer to a large variety of words used along with pivot words, such as "car," "bed," and "milk." In Fig. 6.2, note that the pivot words "no" and "more" always appear first.

In attempting to explain beginning speech, Braine (1976) identified three patterns in early word combinations:

1. *Invented Patterns.* Word combinations that are *invented* by the child—not learned from adults. For example, Andrew's "More high" is an invention for "There's more up there."

2. *Learned Patterns.* Word combinations in which positions of pivot words are *learned.* It is not likely that the many combinations Andrew made with "all" resulted from imitation. Instead, Andrew learned that the pattern position for "all" should come first in word combinations. Then he learned an association between the pivot word "all" and each of the different words occurring with it.

More car[a]	No bed	Other bib	Boot off	See baby
More cereal	No down[c]	Other bread	Light off	See pretty
More cookie	No fix	Other milk	Pants off	See train
More fish	No home	Other pants	Shirt off	
More high[b]	No mama[d]	Other part	Shoe off	Hi Calico
More hot	No more	Other piece	Water off	Hi mama
More juice	No pee	Other pocket	Off bib	Hi papa
More read	No plug	Other shirt		
More sing	No water	Other shoe	Airplane all gone	Airplane by[h]
More toast	No wet[e]	Other side	Calico all gone[f]	Siren by
More walk			Calico all done[f]	Mail come
Outside more	Down there		All done milk	Mama come
	Clock on there		All done now	What's that
All broke	Up on there		All gone juice	What's this
All buttoned	Hot in there		All gone outside[g]	Mail man
All clean	Milk in there		All gone pacifier	Mail car
All done	Light up there		Salt all shut	Our car
All dressed	Fall down there			Our door
All dry	Kitty down there		Byebye back	Papa away
All fix	More down there		Byebye Calico	Look at this
All gone	Sit down there		Byebye car	Pants change
All messy	Cover down there		Byebye papa	Dry pants
All shut	Other cover down there		Calico byebye	
All through	Up on there some more		Papa byebye	
All wet				

Figure 6.2 Andrew's word combinations

a. Drive around some more.
b. There's more up there.
c. Don't put me down.
d. I don't want to go to mama.
e. I'm not wet.
f. Said after the death of Calico the cat.
g. Said when the door is shut: "The outside is all gone."
h. A plane is flying past.

Telegraphic speech keeps adults busy figuring out toddlers' full messages.

3. *Groping Patterns.* Word combinations in which the child is still *groping* to express a meaning. Groping patterns appear before a significant set of rules for expressing meaning have been acquired. Because Andrew didn't always know rules for ordering words, his word orders were sometimes one way and sometimes a different way. To illustrate, sometimes Andrew said "Airplane all gone" with the pivot last. Other times the pivot word came first as in "All gone juice." With groping patterns, word order varies because no order has yet been learned.

Bloom (1971) disagrees with Braine's explanation of pivot and X words. She suggests that Braine's analysis is a good description of what we hear children say. The problem is that Braine has given no consideration to the meaning children intend in their two-word combinations. Bloom (1975) argues that children combine words a certain way because of the meanings they want to convey. And the same two-word combination can have numerous meanings depending upon the context. As an illustration, "Mommy sock" is a combination of two X words. In one situation it might convey ownership—"Mother's sock." In another situation, a subject-object relationship is intended—"Mommy put on her sock," or even

"Mommy I want my sock." Brown (1973) also suggests that meaning is important in explaining language development and points to the complexities of early speech. He identified eleven different forms of meaning contained in two-word combinations of children in the sensorimotor period. Through two-word combinations, toddlers express a complexity of meaning and inference that can only be understood in the context of the situation.

Complete Sentences.   The transition from telegraphic speech to adult-like speech is not a sudden shift but a gradual process. At about the age of three, children speak in complete three- or four-word sentences that contain most parts of speech. The plurals, past tenses, and prepositions that were notably absent in earlier stages are gradually incorporated into their speech. For instance, English-speaking children begin to add prepositions and plurals early. Irregular verbs (went, saw) come next, with possessive and auxiliary verbs (am, do) developing later. But overgeneralization continues to characterize children's speech throughout the early childhood years.

VOCABULARY GROWTH

Children typically have a vocabulary of about ten words at sixteen months of age. By twenty months, the number of words increases to fifty (Nelson, 1973), and by twenty-four months, it is more than two hundred (Bowley, 1963). Two-year-olds can understand many more nouns and verbs than they can vocalize (Goldin-Meadow et al., 1976). Although word production gets off to a slow start, it proceeds rapidly once underway. But the difference between the vocabulary of a thirteen-month-old and that of an eighteen-month-old is more than just an increase in the number of words. Children of thirteen months don't use syntax—at nineteen months they do (Bloom, 1978). In addition, certain words are used for a time and then dropped, only to reappear several months later in different forms. For example, at thirteen months Eve might use "dog" to refer to her pet and at nineteen months, the same animal might be labeled "bow wow." By the age of three, toddlers Eve's age have a vocabulary of between nine hundred and a thousand words (Lenneberg, 1967).

THE LANGUAGE ENVIRONMENT

The language environment in which children are reared has a lot to do with their becoming competent speakers. Generally, environments that are rich in language stimulate development, those that are poor hamper it. Associations between the quality of language stimulation in an infant's early home environment and language development at three years of age have been clearly established (Elardo et al., 1977). By this age many youngsters become competent speakers and develop intellectual and social competence as well. Spotlight 6.2 describes why some toddlers gain competence in these areas and others do not.

Culture also influences language development. We already mentioned that children of all cultures learn language in similar ways. Evidence suggests that toddlers the world over go through a one-word stage, a two-word stage, and a complete sentence stage (Bowerman, 1973; Dale, 1976). For example, Eve's "more milk" is expressed as "yesche moloko" by Lev, a Russian toddler, and her "where ball?" is expressed as "missa pallo" by Seppo, a Finnish toddler. Children everywhere also show similar development of meaning (Slobin, 1971) and use of rules in language acquisition. And all over the world children learn grammatical patterns whether or not anyone corrects their speech (Ervin, 1964). They also overgeneralize just like English-speaking children (Slobin, 1977).

THEORIES OF LANGUAGE DEVELOPMENT

Even though language authorities agree that children learn language in similar ways, they don't agree on the process by which language is acquired. In fact, the

upset because he tore the pages out of her coloring book.

Families chosen for the study covered a wide variety of socio-economic, educational and ethnic backgrounds. From four hundred preschoolers the researchers picked fifty-one children who were studied to determine what factors in their home life led to the development of competence. What makes a six-year-old successful?

Rejecting academic tests as too narrow for their purpose, researchers came up with their own definition of what a competent child is: a youngster who can "cope in superior fashion with anything he meets, day in and day out."

He can gain and hold an adult's attention in socially acceptable ways, express both affection and hostility toward his accomplishments, can compete with his peers and express both affection and hostility toward other youngsters. He speaks articulately, uses grammar and vocabulary well and, intellectually, can detect discrepancies.

The mothers who reared competent children, researchers found, had many common traits.

Though busy, they still talked often to the child at a level he could handle. They kept many small objects—ranging from baby-food jars to toys—within his reach. They were generally permissive and indulgent, encouraging exploration and "teaching on the fly" as the child expressed curiosity.

Mothers of the less competent youngsters, however, tended to restrict their child's activity. They let the child learn most of his language from television and radio. They are more meticulous housekeepers than the other mothers but seem to derive less real pleasure from their children.

"Most women are capable of doing a fine job with their one-to-three-year-old children," the study concludes. Nor does she need a diploma or substantial economic assets. "In these statements we see considerable hope for future generations."

"Researchers discover how children gain competence" by David Fortney. Copyrighted, *Chicago Tribune*. Used with permission.

issue of language acquisition has aroused many a firey debate. Some theorists argue that language ability is learned through positive reinforcement and imitation (*behavior theory*). Still others insist that children learn rules of grammar on their own (*rule-learning theory*). Another group claims the ability to acquire language is programmed into the brain from birth (*biological theory*). Let's look at each of these theoretical positions more closely.

Behavior Theory.   According to behavior theory, individuals in the child's environment determine how children acquire language (Mowrer, 1960). Positive reinforcement and imitation of adults and peers in the social environment are seen as the essential requirements for language acquisition. According to Skinner (1957), children are reinforced for speaking correctly—but not for speaking incorrectly. For example, when Eve points to her bottle and says, "See bottle," her father's reply of "Yes, that's right, *bottle*" is a positive reinforcer for Eve's vocalization. During snack time, a teacher might ask each child to say "cheese." When they correctly repeat (imitate) the word, they receive a square of cheese (positive reinforcement). In this way, imitation and reinforcement are combined. Research supports the usefulness of reinforcement in learning to speak (Rheingold et al., 1959; Strain and Vietze, 1975; Weisberg, 1963).

Obviously, imitation also plays a role in the development of language. German children learn to speak German and Chinese children to speak Chinese. And the first words children speak are people's names or objects that have been labeled for them. There is research to bear out these observations (Bloom et al., 1974; Whitehurst and Vasta, 1975). For example, young children smile and vocalize more when adults smile and speak during routine activities such as feeding, bathing, and diaper changing. And between nineteen and twenty-three months, toddlers imitate sounds fairly directly and accurately (Ryan, 1974).

But can the acquisition of language be completely explained by behavior theory? Increasing research indicates reinforcement and imitation do not offer a complete explanation of language acquisition. In fact, children learn correct grammar despite a lack of reinforcement for its accuracy.

On a visit to a nearby zoo, three-year-old Eve pointed to a group of animals grazing and said, "See sheeps." Her father, leaning over, responded, "No, those are goats, Eve," ignoring her misuse of "sheeps" for "sheep." And later, when they reached the sheep pen, Eve again remarked, "See sheeps," to which her mother replied, "Yes, I see the *sheeps*"—actually imitating and reinforcing Eve's incorrect grammar.

Roger Brown and his associates at Harvard found that most parents act in much the same manner as Eve's parents. That is, they reinforce children for factual, but not for grammatical accuracy (Brown and Hanlon, 1970). In one study, mothers imitated children—even when they were *wrong*—three times as often as children imitated mothers (Brown and Bellugi, 1964).

Behavior theory also fails to explain how children can make up word combinations they have never heard before (Braine, 1976). Children utter so many sounds it would be impossible for them to hear every one before they make it. Such creative combinations as "All gone juice" or "Salt all shut" obviously are not imitations of adult speech. In fact, one researcher flatly states that "there is not a shred of evidence supporting a view that progress toward adult norms of grammar arises merely from practice in overt imitation of adult sentences" (Ervin, 1964, p. 172). Lenneberg's studies (1962) of exceptional children cast further doubt on the behavior theory of imitation. He describes the case of a boy having a physical disability that prevented him from imitating adult speech. Yet the boy learned to understand complex grammar and word meanings. In addition, cases have been reported of mentally impaired children who spoke frequently, despite their trouble in imitating (Lenneberg et al., 1964).

When parents talk to children during routine activities such as feeding, children increase their vocalizations in response.

Rule-Learning Theory.   Rule-learning theory holds that children's language acquisition cannot be explained simply through reinforcement and imitation. Instead, children extract general rules from the speech they hear. Such general rules eventually enable children to produce words and sentences they have never heard before. Sometimes children make mistakes in applying rules they've heard from adult speech (Brown, 1973). One example is the grammatical error of overgeneralization that we discussed earlier. Through trial and error, children practice, edit, and correct their speech.

> They string words together and then play substitution games, taking out one word and putting in another, adding on phrases to build up longer sentences, and systematically changing the forms of sentences to make them into questions or negatives and back again into statements. (Clark and Clark, 1977, p. 402)

In these ways—through rule learning, misapplication, and revision—children eventually construct on their own the rules of their language (Weir, 1962). Before you know it, they have mastered adult forms of speech and say grammatically correct things, such as "I fell down and hurt myself."

There is a good deal of research support for rule-learning theory. Although different children use the same words in different ways, they develop similar rules for syntax at an early age (Brown, 1957). In fact, studies have shown the earliest two-word utterances by toddlers are systematic and governed by rules (Brown, 1973; Brown and Bellugi, 1964).

But there are problems with rule-learning theory, too. Adult language patterns are incredibly complex. To assume that toddlers are capable of figuring them out may be overestimating their abilities. Their task is complicated further when adults ''break'' the rules of grammar by speaking in incomplete sentences and making grammatical errors.

Biological Theories. Biological theorists, led by Noam Chomsky, argue that language is not a direct result of environmental influences. They insist language is too complex to learn through reinforcement, imitation, or rules picked up from the speech of others. Instead, language acquisition is controlled by a combination of biological and environmental influences. Chomsky (1965) thinks that we are biologically prepared from birth to develop language. That is, we are born with an innate ability for language analysis that allows us to automatically understand some of the rules of grammar. The rules we can automatically understand are those universal to all languages.

You might be wondering why some of us speak German and some of us English if all have the same inborn universal language rules. Chomsky explains this difference as the result of different environmental inputs in different languages. That is, each language has, in addition to inborn universal language rules, language rules that are unique to the language and learned by children from their environment.

In elaborating his view, Chomsky (1957) set forth the theory of **transformational grammar.** This theory proposes that every sentence has two different levels of syntax or structure, a surface structure and a deep structure. **Surface structure** refers to the way in which words are ordered in a sentence. **Deep structure** refers to the basic meaning or idea the sentence conveys.

The following two pairs of sentences from Dale's (1976) discussion of Chomsky's theory should help you better understand these concepts:

John is easy to please.

John is eager to please.

The dog bites the man.

The man is bitten by the dog.

The first pair of sentences has an identical surface structure. That is, the subjects, verbs, etc., are placed in the same order. But their deep structure is different because they convey different meanings. In the second pair, the surface structure is different because the two sentences have different subjects, verb tenses, objects, etc. But both sentences have the same deep structure because they have the same meaning.

According to Chomsky, the way in which deep and surface structures are related is determined by rules of transformation. Let's look at the third sentence again:

The dog bites the man.

By applying rules of transformation, we can transform this sentence into different surface structures while keeping the same deep structure (meaning). For example, possible transformations are "The man is bitten by the dog" or "Is the man bitten by the dog?" But if we violate certain transformational rules when changing the surface structure, we lose the intended deep structure meaning as we can see in the following sentences:

The dog is bitten by the man.

The man bites the dog.

Is the dog bitten by the man?

Chomsky (1957) and McNeill (1970) have suggested that we can better understand the acquisition of language if we think of the child's brain as a computer with a prewired (inborn) **Language Acquisition Device (LAD)** that contains all the universal rules governing language behavior. In other words, children are preprogrammed to tell the difference between surface and deep structure. They can automatically understand that language has certain rules for changing sentences from statements into questions, making negatives, making the subject active or passive, and so forth. The prewiring aids children as they acquire rules of syntax and semantics. Information about language in a child's specific environment comes into and interacts with the LAD. This interaction produces the rules that guide a child's language development.

There is support for the biological point of view. For example, a common set of rules does underlie all human language (Greenberg, 1966). And all children in the world go through similar stages of language development. Research also confirms that a portion of the left part of the human brain is devoted to language learning (Lenneberg, 1967).

The biological theory remains controversial, however, because it is difficult to study an innate structure such as the LAD. But this viewpoint has caused researchers to shift their emphasis away from counting the numbers of times children say nouns, verbs, and other parts of speech at different ages. Now they are much more concerned with the function of children's speech and the regular rules they use to speak and understand.

A Systems Approach to Language Learning.   There is wide agreement that babies throughout the world have the capacity to make all speech sounds at birth. The universal aspects of language clearly indicate biological influences. And as you have already seen, the environment is an important source of stimulation for language development. In addition, children on their own, form sentences and phrases they have never heard. This suggests that some type of internal learning of rules occurs, perhaps unknown to the child. Although there are no clear answers to

The observation that children of all cultures learn language and communicate with adults in similar ways lends support to the belief that humans are "prewired" to learn language.

this mystery, evidence indicates that all three components (environment, the child's own activity, and biology) are operating to some extent in helping children acquire language.

Thought and Language

Which comes first: the chicken or the egg? Answering this riddle is difficult, if not impossible. Actually, we posed the riddle because it illustrates a similar and equally puzzling problem scholars are trying to solve about the thought/language relationship. Which comes first: thought or language? We know that significant changes in children's thinking go hand in hand with their ability to use language (Greenfield and Smith, 1976). But the nature of the relationship is unclear. So far, more questions than answers exist. Does Eve's language control what she thinks? Or do thought and language develop independently of each other?

PIAGET: A COGNITIVE-DEVELOPMENTAL VIEWPOINT

Piaget (1952a) claims that early forms of thought develop from action—not language. Language begins to emerge late in the sensorimotor period—not as a cause or predecessor of thought but as a means of representing thought. Children's use of words reflects their stage of sensorimotor development (Bloom, 1975). For example, Eve shows object permanence when she drinks her milk and declares, "Milk gone." Then when her mother gives her more she exclaims, "More milk!" In fact, in Piaget's view, language is only one of several ways we express thought (Piaget, 1970); thought is also expressed when we dream. For Piaget, a child's competence in producing and understanding language proceeds according to periods of cognitive development, through interaction between mental structures (schemes) and the environment. For example, toddlers between twelve and twenty-four months can accurately put objects such as sticks into categories based on a common physical dimension such as size or shape. But these toddlers don't have the language ability to label the categories or the relationships between the objects. So, before children speak, they are building schemes for organizing and understanding their world—even though they cannot express this cognitive growth through language. And deaf children who cannot hear or talk can still think and solve problems (Furth, 1971). So, according to this view, language is useful, but not essential, for thought.

WHORF AND SAPIR: A CROSS-CULTURAL VIEWPOINT

In contrast to Piaget's approach, anthropologists Benjamin Whorf (1956) and Edward Sapir (1958) studied the relationship between thought and language in a number of cultures. Their findings support the belief that our language often determines how we think and behave. Simply stated, the Whorf-Sapir hypothesis says that the language and vocabulary of each culture restricts how people think about the world around them. Each culture has its own unique word and concept patterns. So when children of different cultures begin to talk, they reason and view the world differently because of these patterns.

For example, in the English language we have many words to describe colors—pink, orange, yellow, purple, and so forth. But many societies have far fewer color descriptions in their language. People in these societies use fewer color words, and as a result they see fewer colors than we do. In the same way, Eskimos have many words to describe snow, while the English language has only a few. So the Eskimo sees and thinks about more kinds of snow than the English-speaking person.

So far this theory has received little experimental support. In fact, the opposite view is receiving support—that perception is fairly uniform rather than different from culture to culture, regardless of the spoken language (Rosch, 1973).

VYGOTSKY: A RUSSIAN VIEWPOINT

Russian psychologist Lev Vygotsky (1962) believes that language and thought first develop separately and later along parallel lines. For example, children develop sensorimotor thought before they are able to understand or use language. At the same time children are developing sensorimotor thought, they are learning the sounds of their language. At about the age of two, thought and language join together. At this point, "thought becomes verbal and speech rational" (Vygotsky, 1962, p. 44). This can be observed as toddlers become curious about words, trying to label everything in their surroundings. Their vocabulary increases daily and they become aware of the symbolic property and uses of language. The two threads, thought and language, are now intertwined as one.

CONCLUSION

It appears that language ability cannot entirely account for cognitive ability. Thought either comes before or accompanies language—at least in the preschool years. But language becomes increasingly important in cognitive skills such as memory and problem solving, especially as children get older. Language allows children to express their imagination, ask questions, give directions, accept or refuse something, and demonstrate knowledge. Language also enables youngsters to express emotions to someone else, which greatly affects the development of social relationships, as you will see in Chapter 7.

Summary

1. In Stage 5 of the sensorimotor period in cognitive development (twelve to eighteen months), toddlers use trial and error experimentation to solve problems; they accommodate new situations by developing new means to an end; and they demonstrate the object concept as they search for missing objects in the last place they saw them instead of where they're usually kept.

2. In Stage 6 of the sensorimotor period in cognitive development (eighteen to twenty-four months), toddlers use symbolic thought and mental images to represent actions and objects. Trial and error experimentation gives way to mental solutions to simple problems without the aid of actual objects.

3. Egocentrism characterizes children's thinking during the sensorimotor period. In contrast to infants, who have difficulty understanding they are separate and distinct from the world around them, toddlers begin to view themselves as separate from others and to realize that some things happen apart from their own desires. But they continue to assume everyone sees the world as they do.

4. Language meaning emerges from the rules of grammar that govern syntax (how words are combined to build phrases and sentences) and semantics (the meanings of words).

5. During toddlerhood, toddlers sometimes use unintelligible jabber called jargon as they begin to speak their first words. The meaning of an entire sentence is conveyed through holophrases in the one-word stage and telegraphic speech in the two-word stage (at which time children begin to use pivot and X words). Children then move to complete sentences that sound more like adult speech.

6. A rich language environment stimulates and a poor language environment hampers a child's development. Children in all cultures pass through the one-word, two-word, and complete sentence stages of language. All languages contain syntax and semantics. Regardless of their native tongue, toddlers overgeneralize the rules of their language.

7. Behavior theorists suggest language ability is learned through positive reinforcement and imitation; rule-learning theorists believe that children learn the rules of grammar on their own; and biological theorists claim language ability is wired into the brain from birth.

8. Conflicting viewpoints exist regarding the relationship between thought and language—with Piaget at the one extreme viewing language as a reflection of thought, and Whorf and Sapir at the other extreme viewing thought as a product of one's native language. In between these extremes is Vygotsky, who thinks language and thought originate as separate systems, eventually joining to produce higher levels of thought.

Empathetic Activities

- What feelings did you have as you read The Case of Brad's First Birthday Party and Eve Learns to Talk? What feelings do you think Brad and Eve had? Their parents?
- What things could you do to foster a toddler's cognitive and language development?
- Pretend you are Brad's parent. Using a mail order catalog, select some toys that Brad would enjoy at sensorimotor Stages 5 and 6. Compare your selections with the suggestions made in Spotlight 6.1.
- Re-read Eve Learns to Talk.
  - Count the nouns, verbs, adjectives, adverbs, and pronouns used by Eve. What percentage of Eve's words falls into each part of speech?
  - Look at Fig. 6.1. Categorize Eve's holophrases using Nelson's six categories: (1) specific nominals, (2) general nominals, (3) action words, (4) modifiers, (5) personal-social words, (6) function words. How do Eve's first words compare with those of the eighteen toddlers Nelson studied?
- What are some specific examples of how the thought/language relationship illustrates the concept of the *Whole Child?*
- How do the advances toddlers make in cognitive and language development change the nature of their relationships with adults?

Related Readings

Bloom, Lois, ed. *Reading in language development.* New York: Wiley, 1978. A collection of professional journal articles written in a rather technical style by authorities in the area of language development. A good overview of the various methodologies and theories used in studying language acquisition.

Dale, Phillip S. *Language development: Structure and function,* 2nd ed. New York: Holt, Rinehart and Winston, 1976. The most authoritative source around on syntax, semantics, phonology, transformational grammar, and general study of language development.

Pulaski, Mary Ann. *Understanding Piaget: An introduction to children's cognitive development,* rev. ed. New York: Harper and Row, 1980. Further discussion of Piaget's stages of sensorimotor development. Clear and easy to read.

Wadsworth, Barry J. *Piaget's theory of cognitive development,* 2nd ed. New York: David McKay, 1979. The simplest, clearest, and most concise explanation of Piaget's theory that we know of.

7 Toddlerhood: Social and Emotional Development and Relationships

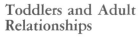

The Case of Noah Time

It was another busy morning for twenty-two-month-old Noah and his mother, Jean Time. Noah's boundless energy and hungry curiosity kept his mother on her toes that day. Noah spent most of the morning in his favorite sport of climbing. He climbed everywhere—onto the kitchen cabinets and onto tables and chairs. When he ate his lunch, he insisted on doing everything himself and took great pride in the mess he made. When potty time came, Noah resisted, but finally lost the struggle to his mother. After getting Noah down for his afternoon nap, Jean was ready for a long-overdue rest, too. No sooner had her head touched the pillow than she drifted into a deep sleep.

Suddenly, she saw herself sitting in a court of law filled with curious onlookers. She heard the rumbling sounds of voices, followed by the clanging of the judge's gavel calling the court to order: "We are gathered here today to hear the case of Noah Time versus Jean Time. We will hear the mother's defense first."

Jean testified that she wanted to change her toddler's name from "Noah Time" to "No All the Time" because that's what he says—"no" all the time! Jean explained how strong-willed Noah is and described his busy and sometimes hair-raising activities. She explained that Noah had a temper tantrum during lunch—throwing himself onto the floor, screaming and banging his fists—because he wanted to feed himself. And when she tried to console him, Noah spit carrots on her.

Just as it came time for Noah's defense, Jean woke up in a cold sweat to find her carrot-spitting youngster toddle over from where he had been sleeping. Noah covered his mother with his blanket and gave her a wet kiss. That morning, Jean's first impulse had been to "give him away." But now, on second thought, she decided to keep both him and his name just as they are!

Toddlers and Adult Relationships

Noah, Kim, and Scotty, like typical toddlers, are full of energy, curiosity, and a desire for independence—a combination that often gets them into trouble. Day by day toddlers are developing abilities to do new things for themselves. You have already read about how they are developing physically and how they are beginning to dress and feed themselves, and to become toilet trained. You also read about how their cognitive capacities are unfolding as they experience new things each day and how they are gaining exciting new language skills. Toddlers' relationships with adults are influenced by their new physical and cognitive skills. The ways in which people—adults and peers—react to toddlers influence how toddlers behave and feel about themselves.

But toddlers have their point of view too. Suppose Noah was to testify in The Case of Noah Time. He might argue that climbing is his favorite pastime but that his parents demand he stay off kitchen cabinets and get down off the sofa. Or he might complain that his parents make him sit on the potty, eat without making messes, nap when he wants to play and other "unreasonable" requests too numerous to mention. As you can imagine, given the nature of toddlers and demands of their parents, toddlerhood can be a difficult time for everyone. But through the process of socialization and the establishment of autonomy within limits, children come to control their impulses.

SOCIALIZATION

Through the process of **socialization,** children learn to behave in ways considered acceptable by their society. Toddlers decide for themselves what is socially acceptable. But as you saw in The Case of the Typical Toddlers and The Case of Noah Time, toddlers don't always make the best judgments. They are not concerned with the rules of society, which make no sense at all to them and, in fact, seem unreasonable! What's wrong with dumping ashtrays on the floor, running through supermarkets, or climbing on kitchen cabinets? Those are fun things to do! The guidance parents must give in response to such "fun" things is a major task. But through successful guidance, Kim will soon learn she must walk, not run, through the aisles of a supermarket, Noah will realize he cannot climb onto furniture, and Scotty will be taught he cannot "destroy" someone else's home and possessions. And they win approval from family, supermarket personnel, and partygivers!

Some toddlers begin to internalize their parents' rules as early as twelve months of age (Stayton et al., 1971). Once rules are internalized, children can begin to control some of their impulses. Signals that the child is internalizing the rules and expectations of adults will reveal themselves in various ways. For example, Kim might be heard to say, "Not run, not run!" as she toddles around the supermarket. And Noah might reprimand himself as he starts the forbidden climbing with, "No! No! No!" Toddlers contribute to their socialization by signaling to adults the need for lots of attention and guidance (Bell and Harper, 1977). In this way, toddlers control, to some extent, how parents and teachers behave toward them. As we examine this cycle of adult-toddler interactions in more detail, you will see that socialization is a two-way street.

AUTONOMY VERSUS SHAME AND DOUBT

Noah's negativism is typical of many toddlers. Many parents describe their toddlers as willful, which is a good description of what is happening at this age. Children begin to develop a will of their own, a sense of what Erik Erikson calls *autonomy.*

According to Erikson (1968), just as infants face a conflict of trust versus mistrust, toddlers face a conflict of **autonomy versus shame and doubt.**

Autonomy is a form of independence in which toddlers struggle to develop a will of their own. It is no accident that struggles for emotional autonomy accompany changes in physical, cognitive, and language development. Toddlers no longer need to depend on adults to carry them or push them in a stroller. They can move about by themselves and climb, push, and pull to get things without asking. And instead of crying for something desirable, they use their newfound gift of language to ask for it or demand it! They are even beginning to use the toilet and to feed and dress themselves. These autonomous behaviors represent toddlers' new freedom from their former infant-like dependence on adults for need satisfaction.

Autonomy is also evidenced by a toddler's desire to make independent choices and decisions. ''I want to do it myself, my way, and in my time!'' says Noah (though perhaps not in so many words). Unwanted help or demands from an adult are met with negativism and resistance from the toddler, as was the case with Noah. Conflicts centering around the basic routines of eating, sleeping, and elimination are unavoidable at this age.

Developing Autonomy.   If children are to achieve a sense of autonomy, they need patience and support from loving adults—especially during conflict situations. Praising a child for using self-control and making good choices is an adult's best approach. Telling children you understand and accept their anger or frustra-

Parents of toddlers must constantly balance their concern for their children's safety with the need to encourage developing skills and curiosity.

tion and providing a constructive outlet for this rage are additional ways of showing support and understanding. For example, you might let the child kick and scream for a few minutes or pound clay. Children should also be encouraged to explore their environment, exercise their will, make decisions, and be responsible for things they can do, such as feeding and dressing themselves.

But toddlers are usually not able to make responsible decisions and control their own behavior. "Outer control at this stage, therefore, must be firmly reassuring," says Erikson (1963, p. 252). Reasonable limits must be set *consistently* by loving adults. For instance, if Noah's mother allows him to climb on the cabinets one day and punishes him for the same behavior two days later, he will not know which behavior is and is not acceptable. Everytime Noah climbs on the cabinets and tables, he must be stopped, or perhaps redirected to his outside climbing equipment. When encouraging decision making, Noah's parents can give him safe, limited choices. He can decide whether or not to have a second helping of mashed potatoes, to play with blocks or paint, or to stay with Daddy or go with Mommy, or whether to use the toilet now or later. Such limits guide toddlers like Noah toward wise decison making and self-control, and let them know where they stand.

Limit setting and arranging a suitable environment also keep toddlers safe. Suppose Noah's mother wanted to give him lots of room to play in the yard, but feared he would toddle into the street. She might fence in a large grassy area for him to play in. Inside spaces might also be arranged in various ways. "Coffee-table psychology" is another means of protecting toddlers from their mistakes in judgment. Toddlers don't place value on objects that are important to adults. Removing precious breakables from tables and replacing them with objects that toddlers can safely handle and manipulate is a good compromise for child and adult. Noah can assert his autonomy by playing with the unbreakable objects. And his parents can protect their valuables.

Developing a Sense of Shame and Doubt. A positive sense of self develops when adults encourage autonomy while lovingly and consistently setting firm, reasonable limits. Toddlers develop a sense of shame or doubt about their abilities when their newly discovered independence is restricted, discouraged, or poorly guided. For example, shame develops when a child is frequently scolded or criticized for making poor choices or mistakes. Excessive criticism of Noah when he soils his pants, breaks a toy, drops his spoon from the high chair, or spills his juice, can lead to feelings of shame. Or if Noah's parents were to make all of his decisions for him and not provide him with adequate opportunities to make choices and develop self-control, Noah could become doubtful or uncertain about his abilities and fail to develop autonomy. Furthermore, when they make rigid demands that he meet their expectations about time, place, facilities, and cleanliness, they are not considering his emerging sense of control over and management of his own body. Such rigid demands lead to self-doubt in children—doubts about their ability to function independently.

According to Erikson, not only parental guidance but also play becomes important during the autonomy versus shame stage. Play serves the child as a ''safe island where he can develop his autonomy'' within his own set of rules and boundaries (Maier, 1978, p. 97). Noah decides where in the sandbox he wants to build a road for his truck and then struggles to build it. He can pour water in and out of containers without worrying about spills. Old familiar play things are a comfort when faced with the pressures of his real world. Through such play activities children build autonomy and confidence in their abilities—thus, avoiding shame and doubt. Says Erikson, ''The small world of manageable toys is a harbor which the child establishes, to return to when he needs to overhaul his ego'' (Erikson, 1963, p. 194).

While this is a trying time for parents and toddlers, changing Noah's name won't change his game. Instead, the support and positive attitudes of his parents can help him get through this period of negativism and on with the task of becoming a responsible adult.

PARENT-TODDLER DEPENDENCY

Noah has been going with his mother to the pediatrician for regular checkups. On the last two visits, Noah's mother noticed that Noah behaved differently in the doctor's office than at home. In the stranger-filled waiting room, Noah didn't say much. Instead, he stayed quietly seated—clinging to his mother's side and gazing around him. This was a far cry from the rambunctious Noah she was used to at home!

As youngsters become more autonomous during toddlerhood, separation from their parents is unavoidable. Toddlers spend more time away from their parents exploring their environment and playing with toys—and sometimes other children—than they did in infancy (Heathers, 1955). But they are still dependent on adults for their main source of social interaction. And they continue to show signs of attachment or dependency through clinging to, following, and staying near their parents, especially in unfamiliar situations like the doctor's office. Toddlers use their mothers as a security base from which to explore new and strange surroundings (Maccoby and Feldman, 1972).

Because of their egocentrism, toddlers' relationships are a bit one-sided in their favor. It is difficult for them to postpone something they want. And they usually cannot consider the wishes of others. Relationships with parents are grounded in the here and now and are based on physical proximity and contact. So when Noah's mother's intentions don't fit with his, he tries to achieve his end in physical ways—such as pushing or pulling her in the desired direction. But toward the end of toddlerhood, dependency bonds become weaker. After age three, parent-child relationships take the form of a partnership as children mature cognitively and continue to move out into the world (Marvin, 1977).

Toddlers spend more time away from their mothers but still show signs of attachment, such as clinging, especially in unfamiliar situations.

Development of the Parent-Child Relationship

Relationship	Developmental Period
Parent-Newborn Synchrony	Newborn (birth–4 weeks)
Parent-Infant Attachment	Infancy (birth–12 months)
Parent-Toddler Dependency—Toddlers continue to show signs of attachment or dependency through desire for, clinging to, and being near their mothers. They still return to her periodically to make sure their security base is still there.	Toddlerhood (1–3 years)
Parent-Preschooler Partnership	Early Childhood (3–6 years)
Parent-Child Detachment/Children's Same Sex Friendships	Middle Childhood (6–12 years)
Parent-Teacher Individuality/Crowd Formation	Adolescence (13–18 years)

SEPARATION ANXIETY AND ATTACHMENT

In Chapter 4, you saw how infants experience stranger anxiety as they become attached to their parents. Another type of fear that normally accompanies attachment and emerges between eight and twelve months is called **separation anxiety,** the distress or anxiety a youngster feels during the absence of a parent or customary caregiver. Stranger anxiety can occur in the presence or absence of the parent but disappears by twelve months of age, while separation anxiety persists well into toddlerhood. Separation anxiety reaches a peak at eighteen months, diminishes gradually and levels off by age three, usually disappearing in the preschool years (Weinraub and Lewis, 1977). This progression is shown in Fig. 7.1. When two groups of toddlers eighteen to twenty-four months and twenty-four to thirty months were separated from their mothers and left in day care facilities, the older children cried less due to the separation (Wynn, 1979). Separation anxiety is a universal pattern that has been found in such diverse countries as the United States, Uganda (Ainsworth, 1967), Guatemala (Lester et al., 1974), and Israel (Bettelheim, 1969).

As long as toddlers know their mothers are nearby, they will continue with their play and exploration (Corter, 1976). But when mothers leave, toddlers almost always stop playing with toys that moments before had captivated their attention. They might cry, cease moving about, follow the parent to an exit, and call for the parent to return (Weinraub and Lewis, 1977). Toddlers observed in the

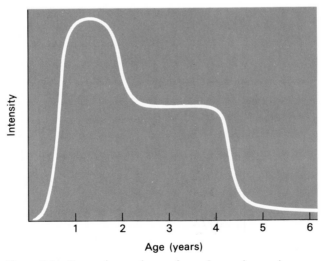

Figure 7.1 **Separation anxiety and age.** Separation anxiety reaches a peak at eighteen months of age, diminishes gradually, and by age three, begins to level off, usually disappearing in early childhood.

presence of mothers, during separation from her, and upon reunion cried most during the separation period (Coates et al., 1972).

According to Kagan (1976), children react to separation with anxiety because they are faced with discrepant (unfamiliar) events that they can't understand or deal with. The more discrepant the separation experience from prior separations, the more difficulty the child has in assimilating the new separation experience. Hence, the more likely the child is to be upset. A number of studies have found that the more familiarity (and so the less discrepancy) the child has with events surrounding the parents' leaving, the less the child will show anxiety. For example, children are less likely to be upset when parents leave them in a familiar place such as their own home than in a strange place such as a laboratory setting or a friend's home (Ross et al., 1975). Ainsworth and her research team found that the degree to which children show dependency behaviors during separation from their parents is also associated with the quality of mother-infant attachment established during the first twelve months (Ainsworth, 1979; Ainsworth et al., 1978). Spotlight 7.1 discusses some of the effects of separation on emotional security.

LENGTHY SEPARATIONS

The brief, day-to-day separations we have been discussing are not the same as prolonged absences such as those caused by hospitalization or war. Long-term separations between parent and child can be quite harmful to children and even to parents. How do we know this?

Harry and Margaret Harlow (1966) observed that when baby monkeys were raised *without mothers* in groups of three or more, they clung to each other in a "choo-choo" pattern, "a chain of infants, one in the lead and one at the end with intermediate infants clinging to the back of the infant in front of it" (p. 67). When only two of the baby monkeys were reared together (but apart from their mothers), they clasped and clung to each other, stomach to stomach. If the monkeys were reared alone—without mothers or other baby monkeys—they developed seriously abnormal behaviors. For instance, they would sit in their cages and rock back and forth, demonstrating extreme fright when approached by a human and violence when placed in contact with another monkey. The Harlows concluded that the behaviors of the infant monkeys resulted from the lack of an attachment figure. The monkey's behavior is startlingly similar to the behaviors of children who are separated from their parents at a young age and deprived of a stable adult caregiver with whom to form an attachment.

As we mentioned in Chapter 4, research has found that institution-reared two-year-olds are more clinging and less attached to specific persons than children from ordinary families (Tizard and Rees, 1975). Difficulty in establishing relationships with others remained a problem for these youngsters throughout childhood. But perhaps the best illustration of these behaviors in children is the effects of war separation on a group of orphans studied by Anna Freud and her associates (Freud

❧ Spotlight 7.1: Separation and Emotional Security

As a toddler, Thelma has developed a secure attachment with her mother. She is secure enough to venture away from her mother and explore new surroundings—occasionally checking to see if her secure base is still there. When her mother is present, Thelma spends time smiling, vocalizing, and seeking physical contact and interaction with her. In her mother's absence, Thelma frets very little. And when her mother returns, Thelma welcomes her with open arms—embracing her and showing her the new toy she discovered while she was gone.

Ainsworth and her research team observed that children could be classified as securely attached or anxiously attached (Ainsworth et al., 1978). **Securely attached** toddlers like Thelma show healthy signs of attachment, cry less, are less angry, and more cooperative than anxiously attached youngsters. Anxiously attached toddlers are of two types. The first is the **anxious-ambivalent** child, a category that fits Velma. Velma stays anxious and emotionally distressed even on her mother's knee. She demands her mother's attention and is extremely upset when her mother leaves. And when her mother returns, Velma is emotionally ambivalent—on the one hand, seeking close contact, yet on the other hand, angrily resisting her mother's contact and interaction by pushing her away. Nicky represents the second type of anxiously attached child—the **anxious avoidant.** He shows few signs of being attached to his mother at all. He has more anger than other children. He seldom cries when his mother leaves, and when she returns, he ignores and avoids her altogether.

Mothers of securely attached babies are usually more gentle and sensitive to their offspring's signals than mothers of anxious babies (Londerville and Main, 1981). Secure children develop a general "feeling" that their caregivers are accessible and responsive, while those who are anxiously attached seem unsure that their caregivers will be there when they need them, which was Velma's experience in the orphanage. Perhaps Velma is anxious because she does not yet know what to expect from her new parents. Mothers of anxious-avoidant youngsters seem to dislike close body contact, are angrier and withhold emotions more than mothers in other groups (Ainsworth, 1979).

The securely attached infant sounds very much like the infants Erikson (1968) described as having an early sense of trust in their caregivers, in contrast to anxiously attached children who perceive their world through mistrustful eyes. Some research suggests anxious-ambivalent children may have been "difficult" newborns (Waters et al., 1980)—a type described by Thomas and Chess (1977).

As a rule, the type of attachment pattern established in the first twelve months remains stable. That is, children secure or anxious at twelve months, will show the same pattern at eighteen months (Waters, 1978). In fact, attachment patterns at twelve months are associated with personality traits two, three, and six years later (Ainsworth et al., 1978).

Compared to anxiously attached children, securely attached youngsters like Thelma become more cooperative, positive, and less aggressive and avoidant toward adults (Londerville and Main, 1981). They tend to be more competent and sympathetic in social interactions with peers. And they are more curious, enthusiastic, and persistent in problem-solving matters. Being more curious and self-directed, they also score higher on developmental tests and are more advanced in language. In contrast, anxious-avoidant children like Nicky continue to be more angry, aggressive, avoidant, and uncooperative. And anxious-ambivalent children like Velma are easily frustrated, less persistent, and generally less competent.

As you continue to read about Thelma, Nicky, and Velma throughout this book, look for their personality differences. You will notice that many of them are related to the emotional security each child developed in the first year.

and Dann, 1951). Six infants were brought together in a concentration camp when they were six months old. Their parents had died in the camps soon after these children were born. Like Harlow's monkeys, the orphans had no stable adult figure to care for them, so they became close to and emotionally dependent upon one another. They developed no signs of warm, intimate relationships with any adult. In fact, adults and other children were treated as outsiders. The attachments among these children remained high, and they experienced anxiety when they were separated from one another.

A more commonplace but still frightening experience for children is long-term hospitalization. This can be a shocking experience at a young age because it involves separation, change of environment, and threat of physical pain (Wolman, 1978). Bowlby (1960) observed that toddlers between fifteen months and thirty months go through three stages of separation anxiety during lengthy separations. At first they *protest* their parents' absence. Then they experience *despair* and become inactive and withdrawn. Finally, they go through *detachment* and show disinterest in their loved ones. They accept care from practically any provider, sometimes ignoring parents upon visitation. Many children react this way to lengthy separations, but there are individual differences in the ways children respond, and how parents treat the situation can have an important effect.

Rutter (1971), who spent years studying children separated from their parents, concluded that "children can be separated from their parents for quite long periods in early childhood with surprisingly little in the way of long-term ill effects" (p. 238). Of course, as with brief separations, the way in which parents prepare the child for lengthy separations can make a difference in their effects. When possible, parents should remain in the hospital with the sick child and bring in something familiar such as a favorite stuffed animal or a security blanket. In

Like many toddlers, this boy seems to find great security in the company of his teddy bear and favorite blanket.

✤ Spotlight 7.2: Effects of Day Care

When both parents work outside the home, or when they just need a break from the rigors of parenting, substitute care must be found. In-home care with neighbors or relatives is one possibility. The family day-care home in which five or six children are taken care of in a private home is another. But about 15 to 20 percent of the care young children receive is provided by day-care centers.

Regardless of the type of setting, it is essential that children receive good quality day care, where provisions are made for plenty of stimulation in the physical, cognitive, social, and emotional areas of development. Consistent, well-trained caregivers who have a warm, loving relationship with each child must also be available. Quality care is directly related to a low adult-child ratio (Rowland, 1980).

Research conducted in good quality day-care centers reveals that day care is not harmful to children or the attachment between parents and child. For example, one of the pioneer studies on the effects of infant-toddler group care was conducted at the University of North Carolina at Greensboro (Keister, 1970). Three years were spent observing children and collecting data. The results showed no negative effects on youngsters in good group day care when compared with those reared exclusively at home. About six years after the Greensboro study, Dr. Jerome Kagan and his associates at Harvard University conducted a five year study comparing infants and toddlers at home with those who were in good day care centers for seven hours a day, five days a week (Kagan et al., 1976). No major differences were found on such measures as language

development, attention span, and peer relationships. As a result of these findings, Kagan concluded that good day care is not harmful to infants and toddlers. Another study also found that toddlers who were used to being in day care showed less separation anxiety than home-reared toddlers to whom the experience was not as familiar—that is, more discrepant (Wynn, 1979). When placed in an unfamiliar situation with a peer, day-care toddlers ventured a greater distance from their mothers, spent more time away from her, more time out of her eyesight, and more time in exploratory play than toddlers used to being at home.

A particular fear that experts have had is that putting children into day-care centers would interfere with parent-infant attachment. But studies have shown no reduction in parent-infant attachment (Caldwell et al., 1970; Farran and Ramey, 1977; Masters and Wellman, 1974; Portnoy and Simmons, 1978). In fact, children in day-care centers showed clear attachment preferences for their mothers over other familiar caregivers (Ragozin, 1980), though children did prefer stable to nonstable caregivers in their day care centers (Cummings, 1980).

In good day-care centers, the research is conclusive on three points: 1. There are no damaging effects upon the intellectual development of the child; 2. there are increases in the child's positive and negative interactions with agemates; and 3. there is no disruption in mother-child attachment (Belsky and Steinberg, 1978). But good day-care centers are hard to find.

strange situations, toddlers will rely on objects like blankets for security, about as much as they would rely on their parents (Passman and Weisberg, 1975). Of course, in times of extreme distress, blankets can never equal the warm presence of the child's mother or father, but they can provide some comfort. Pacifiers (Halonen and Passman, 1978) and color films of mothers (Passman and Erck, 1978) have also reduced toddler stress during a parent's absence.

Unfortunately, there are many poor quality day-care centers where children's needs are not met properly. Child development specialists have good reason to warn parents that poor quality day-care centers are harmful to their offspring. What is the best way to choose a day-care center? What should parents look for? And what questions should they ask?

Parents often base their choice on reports by friends and professionals, newspaper ads, the Yellow Pages, or convenient location (Bradbard and Endsley, 1979). Richard Endsley and Marilyn Brad-bard (1981) developed and tested a checklist of items based upon current research and professional opinion to help parents select a good quality center. They had young women rate centers of poor and good quality. The women who used the guide made judgments of center quality much like the judgments of local day-care experts. In contrast, women who did not use the guide made judgments that did not match the expert's evaluations. A checklist like the one shown in the figure can help parents choose quality day care.

A Day-Care Checklist

- Adequate space and adequate staff (35 to 50 square feet per child and adult/child ratio of 1 to 4)
- Attractive center developed with the child in mind (child-sized furniture, adequate materials, various interest areas, toys, and equipment)
- Meals and snacks that are tasty, nutritious, and attractive
- Sensitive and friendly teachers
- Flexible space arrangements
- Equipment for large and small muscle movement
- A variety of activities and materials
- Choice among activities
- Children interested and involved in ongoing activities
- A stable, safe environment

- Provisions for special needs of individual children (sickness, etc.)
- Encouragement and praise for children
- Periods of time for active play alternating with quiet periods
- Parent involvement opportunities
- Regularly scheduled parent conferences
- Elements of novelty in the program (a special uniqueness)
- Safe plan for the arrival and departure of children
- Teachers trained in child-care education
- Regular staff development program
- Children treated with care and respect

From *Infant-toddler guidebook* by Bobbie H. Rowland, p. 19. Copyright © 1980 by Graded Press. Reprinted by permission.

Because studies of institutionalized infants showed that children who are separated from their mothers at an early age are often negatively and severely affected (Bowlby, 1958; Yarrow, 1964), many parents and child development specialists believed, until recently, that it would also be harmful to put babies and young children in day-care centers. But as Spotlight 7.2 shows, research conducted in *good* quality day-care centers has not supported this belief.

Toddlers and Peer Relationships

Elihu (at thirteen months) saw Maria playing with a "surprise box"—a contraption that requires the child to push a button, turn a wheel, or flick a switch in order to cause a door to open and an animal's head to pop out. Elihu quickly joined her, and soon the two were busily working side by side, each of them patterning some of their actions after those of the other. Later, Elihu and Maria, neither of whom could yet walk without assistance, toddled around together while holding on to opposite sides of a toy cart. Whenever one of them took a step that propelled the cart in a particular direction, the other had to take a corresponding step in order to stay upright. In these episodes, Elihu and Maria did not look directly at one another in anything but the most fleeting way. Nevertheless, the surprise box and the toy cart provided opportunities for the toddlers to make contact with one another, to imitate each other's actions, to take turns and to coordinate their behaviors. (Rubin, 1980, p. 18–19).

As toddlers separate themselves more and more from their parents during the second year of life, social interactions with adults decrease and children gradually begin to interact socially with one another (Holmberg, 1980; Rubenstein and

Toys provide a common ground for toddlers to develop their first social interactions with peers.

Howes, 1976). For example, a toddler's play is more likely to involve a peer instead of the child's own mother even when both are present (Eckerman et al., 1975; Rubenstein and Howes, 1976). Although both infants and toddlers still prefer to interact more with their day-care teachers than peers, toddlers spend more time interacting with their playmates than do infants—who prefer adult relationships almost exclusively (Finkelstein et al., 1978).

Contacts made in the play group around objects such as the toy cart are starting points for the development of social interaction among toddlers (Mueller and Lucas, 1975). Once contact is made, toddlers like Elihu and Maria will imitate each other's actions and coordinate their behaviors. Sometimes as many as five toddlers will play in a group around one toy (Mueller and Rich, 1976). Although these encounters are usually brief ones, they mark the first true social relationships between children of the same age. As toddlers develop the ability to reciprocate social behaviors and to use language, their interactions with peers increase (Finkelstein et al., 1978; Holmberg, 1980). When toddlers begin to interact socially, they praise each other, share toys, and show concern when a playmate is hurt. Success in getting along with playmates is related to the security and satisfaction toddlers have experienced in their relationships with parents (Easterbrooks and Lamb, 1980). Toddlers who are securely attached to their parents make better social partners in peer relationships than do toddlers who are anxiously attached. (Pastor, 1981).

Emotions

Toddlers develop a wide range of emotions towards others—from love to rage—as you saw in The Case of Noah Time. In this section, we will look at some important emotions that appear during the toddler's impelling drive toward autonomy, and we will consider some ways of dealing with them.

AGGRESSION AND TEMPER TANTRUMS

It's not surprising that toddlers' interactions with others sometimes bring out their best—such as caring for others (see Spotlight 7.3). But sometimes social interactions bring out undesirable behaviors such as aggression. Aggressive behaviors are virtually unseen between birth and two years of age, except for an occasional temper outburst (Maccoby, 1980). These outbursts are not aggression in the sense of attacks directed against another person. But toward the end of toddlerhood (between ages two and a half and three), full-blown aggression appears—focused on specific targets and accompanied by threatening gestures (Maccoby, 1980). Goodenough (1931) found that toddlers between two and three years of age were usually aggressive after conflicts with parents in which parents exercised their author-

❖ Spotlight 7.3: Caring about Others

Eighteen-month-old Kim sees her mother drop her book. She toddles over and, after much effort, picks it up and gives it to her mother.

Fourteen-month-old Scotty toddles about the house, drinking his juice. He makes his rounds, offering some of his drink to his mother, his father, a visiting neighbor, and even the family dog.

Noah's mother was bending over to play with her fourteen-month-old son in his crib when Noah's hand suddenly hit a picture hanging overhead. The picture fell off the wall, hitting Noah's mother on the head. Seeing his mother grab her head, Noah began to cry. Minutes later, nestled in his mother's arms, Noah watched her apply cold compresses to the wound. Noah leaned his head against his mother's and stroked her hair, as if to console and soothe her. Noah knew his mother had been hurt and was trying to comfort her.

Toddlerhood is a time in which important patterns of showing concern for others (or ignoring other's troubles for that matter) are established (Pines, 1979a). These patterns of concern are called **prosocial behaviors**—''a child's potential helping, sharing, and comforting'' (Yarrow and Waxler, 1975). Between one and a half and two and a half years of age, children begin to behave in prosocial ways (Yarrow and Waxler, 1977). Behaviors like those shown by Kim, Scotty, and Noah are examples of prosocial behaviors. By eighteen months (or younger for some children), sharing is common among toddlers (Rheingold, et al., 1976). Sharing occurs without prompting, direction, or praise—but it can be *increased* through reinforcement and modeling. Toddlers will naturally share whatever interesting objects they discover in their play surroundings with mothers, fathers, unfamiliar persons, or even the family dog—just as Scotty did his juice. Oftentimes, specific emotions such as em-

pathy or distress accompany prosocial acts (Zahn-Waxler et al., 1979). But to what extent are prosocial behaviors inborn or learned? Various theories address this question in different ways.

SOCIOBIOLOGICAL THEORY OF PROSOCIAL BEHAVIOR

Some social scientists believe that concern for others is inborn (Hoffman, 1975b), resulting from primitive feelings of distress upon seeing distress in others. According to this view, empathetic distress is so unpleasant that children are motivated to help others in order to relieve it. And sociobiologists believe children are genetically programmed to help others—a kind of insurance for the survival of their species (Dawkins, 1976).

LEARNING THEORY OF PROSOCIAL BEHAVIOR

It is likely that many prosocial acts have been learned from parents and do not require empathy. We know, for instance, that children's prosocial behaviors can be increased the same way as aggressive behaviors—as a result of observational learning (Masters, 1972; Mussen and Eisenberg-Berg, 1977; Staub, 1971) and rewards (Aronfreed, 1968). For example, children who observe another's generosity, become more generous themselves and children who are praised for giving, tend to give more.

COGNITIVE-DEVELOPMENTAL THEORY OF PROSOCIAL BEHAVIOR

Showing concern for others is not only a social-emotional function. It also involves cognitions. Traditionally, cognitive theorists have believed that children must be capable of putting themselves in the place of others in order for prosocial behavior to occur. For this reason, the idea that eighteen-month-olds are capable of showing concern for the feelings of others challenges Piaget's notion that youngsters at this age are self-centered and egocentric, and therefore unaware of other's needs. But recent studies suggest that children can experience empathy before they cognitively realize that others exist apart from themselves. For instance, prosocial behaviors exist in primitive form in early infancy when newborns cry when they hear another infant cry (Sagi and Hoffman, 1976; Simner, 1971). This could be a reflexive reaction or the result of classical conditioning in which distress cues from another person become associated with the infant's own previous experiences with distress.

Toward the end of the first year, toddlers begin to see themselves as separate and distinct from others. At the same time, when confronted with upset or distress, they become aware that it is the other person and not themselves who is in need. Consequently, they can feel distress when others are distressed and show helping or caring behaviors (Pines, 1979a). But at this age, concern for others is sometimes shown in primitive ways. A toddler who observes a little girl fall off her tricycle might offer her the remainder of his cookie by way of comfort instead of helping her up or checking to see if she is physically hurt.

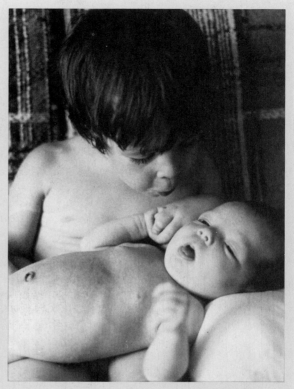

As this toddler imitates his parents' actions with his baby sister, he is learning caring behaviors he will carry with him into adulthood.

FOSTERING PROSOCIAL BEHAVIOR

When parents deliberately teach caring behaviors by helping another person in distress, children are apt to imitate these behaviors at a later time. Parents can also teach an empathetic orientation toward others by showing intense concern when one child hurts another (Zahn-Waxler et al., 1979). Parents who wish to rear prosocial children should start setting examples early. For example, they should model helping and sharing behaviors clearly and frequently; talk about their own and other's feelings and emotions; use reason during discipline; help children accept responsibilities for others; and maintain high standards for behavior and carefully explain them to the child (Mussen and Eisenberg-Berg, 1977). Such teaching is especially important during toddlerhood—a critical time in which children's discovery of the separateness of another's pain can lead to concern for others or to selfishness. Toddlers who are noted for their concern for others at two and a half still behave in caring ways at seven years (Pines, 1979a).

ity. In contrast, preschool children between four and five years old become more aggressive after confrontations with siblings or playmates. This shows again the shift begun in toddlerhood from exclusively adult relationships to peer relationships.

Brief conflicts over toys are common in toddler's play. On two different occasions, eighteen-month-old Scotty showed aggression while playing with another boy. When his playmate tried to grab his toy, Scotty pushed him away. Scotty then got up, walked away, and continued playing with the toy. Another confrontation occurred when Scotty and his friend had a ''tug-of-war'' over a toy truck they both reached for at the same moment. Scotty whacked his friend on the head with the truck and walked away, leaving him in tears. Some people might consider Scotty a selfish child. But toddlers like Scotty are not ''selfish'' in the adult sense. They simply just view their toys as exclusively their own and because of their egocentrism, they find it difficult to share and consider the needs of others. Besides, part of learning how to *share* is knowing how to *possess*.

Things don't always go according to plan in the toddler's world. The frustrations and clashes that occur can cause toddlers to respond with emotional outbursts called **temper tantrums**—expressions of anger springing from lack of inner control. Toddlers and temper tantrums go together—tantrums are a toddler's ordinary reaction to child socialization practices. Tantrums flourish when outside parental rules or expectations go against the child's will (Keister, 1973), as when Noah spit carrots on his mother. And when Kim was apprehended and restrained from her ''shopping spree,'' she began ''kicking, screaming, and frantically moving her body in a sort of wild rhythm.''

Temper tantrums also occur when demands for attention are not met. One minute Noah twists to get away from an unwanted hug. And minutes later he comes running back, demanding hugs from his mother. Being the toddler that he is, Noah wants attention from his mother on *his* terms. But when she is busy and doesn't comply with his wishes, Noah reacts with shouting, stomping, crying, falling on the floor, and kicking his feet. Jealousy over a sibling, a pet, or a friend can also lead to tantrums. The child's physical world is also a source of tantrums, especially when objects won't do what toddlers want them to do. The inability to open a door, for example, can throw a toddler into a furious rage.

Giving in to the child during tantrums is no help at all. It is important to be firm and hold your ground when reasonable limits have been set. If parents pay too much attention to temper tantrums, toddlers may discover that this behavior gets them what they want. The undue attention acts as a positive reinforcer so tantrums will increase in frequency and intensity. One good approach is for parents to ignore tantrums when possible. But the most important ingredient of all is to pick the child up and offer love and comfort after the tantrums are over. When adults handle temper tantrums appropriately, they decline after age two and disappear by four years of age (Goodenough, 1931). But aggressive acts continue throughout the early childhood years (Maccoby, 1980).

FEARS

Noah's mother, Jean, had always worn her hair straight, hanging down her back. One day she decided to get a new look—a permanent. Jean was excited about her new image and eager for her family's approval. When she returned from the hair salon to surprise her toddler, it was she who was surprised! Upon seeing his mother, Noah stood motionless, staring wide-eyed at her new hairdo. Then, as Jean greeted him and tried to pick him up, he began to scream and cry. In her wonderment Jean asked herself, "Do I really look that bad?"

Of course, it wasn't Noah's disappointment over the hairdo that caused all the commotion. Noah's response to his mother's hairdo is an example of the fear of the unfamiliar—changes or transformations in familiar things. For adults, objects and people have an identity that is maintained, despite surface changes (Hyson, 1979). But this does not hold true for toddlers. Surface changes in familiar objects and people cause toddlers to see them as unfamiliar and fearful things. Noah could not be sure his mother was the same person because her new hairdo transformed her surface appearance.

When sights or events are impossible for the child to assimilate, fear occurs (Kagan, 1975). A full-bearded man, for example, can scare the daylights out of a twenty-month-old toddler if this is the first time the child has ever seen a man with a beard. We have already mentioned the anxious effects of separation and strange events caused by discrepant schemes. But once the child accommodates to the strange event and fear is mastered, the event can bring laughter instead of fear (Rothbart, 1973). Stroking the beard of the newcomer can eventually be amusing play for the child.

Toddler fears extend beyond the infant fears of loud noises, sudden movements, falling, and fear of strangers (Jersild and Holmes, 1935) because perceptual and cognitive abilities have matured and the number and variety of experiences have increased. As perceptual abilities improve, toddlers note that things do disappear and so may often fear that they themselves will disappear, too. They may be afraid of a draining bathtub or the flushing of a toilet, believing they will go down with the water (Wolman, 1978). Halloween masks, wigs, new glasses, a doll with a missing arm or a slowly collapsing balloon are examples of transformations especially scary for toddlers (Hyson, 1979). Many toddlers are also afraid of going to sleep and of animals and engines.

Learning to Fear.   A certain amount of fear can be a good thing. If toddlers don't learn to fear ovens, large dogs, or speeding cars, they may be in serious trouble. But sometimes adults teach children needless fears, either accidentally or on purpose. If a parent is terrified of electrical storms and hides in the nearest dark closet with the child whenever lightning strikes, the child will quickly believe that electrical storms are to be feared. Siblings and peers may also serve as models for fear.

When parents and others model fear in this way, children learn through observation to be afraid in the same or similar situations (Hagman, 1932). And sometimes children's everyday interactions with the world may arouse fears. For example, a bad experience with the next-door-neighbor's cocker spaniel can cause the child to be afraid of all dogs for a period of time.

Occasionally, uninformed adults take advantage of the child's tendency to fear in order to manage the child more easily. A parent who is having trouble controlling a toddler might keep the child from other rooms in the house by threatening, "The bogeyman will get you!" or "Santa Claus will put switches in your stocking if you don't behave!" Adults who use such convenient but harmful techniques are teaching children irrational fears that may last throughout life. Such use of fear threats is usually a sign that parents have no control over the situation and are desperately grasping for some power beyond themselves to enforce their rules. But such external control will never get at the inner controls that toddlers need to develop.

For the toddler, the world can be a frightening place sometimes, but parental support can help youngsters conquer their fears.

Learning Not to Fear.   Usually, toddler fears like Noah's disappear in a matter of time without special treatment. As he acquires more sophisticated ways of thinking, Noah will realize that a mask or new hairdo won't transform the whole person, that the vacuum cleaner won't gobble him up, and the flushing toilet won't whisk him away. When handled properly, irrational fears disappear with age and the child learns to tell the difference between what is reasonable to fear and what is not. Parental impatience, irritation, or anger will only make the child feel rejected and perhaps worsen the fears (Wolman, 1978). Overprotection is not the answer, either. It can only convey to the child that perhaps there is something to worry about after all—the world is unsafe. And forcing children to face fears before they are ready only makes matters worse. Name calling and telling the child not to act like a baby about spiders or whatever, just causes more fright. Casual reassurances won't work either. A gradual introduction to the fearful experience and allowing the child to devise individual means for dealing with fears is a good practice (Wolman, 1978).

Adults can play a more active role helping children unlearn fears by the examples they set. Sensible, calm reactions during electrical storms can prevent the child from being unnecessarily afraid of storms in the first place. The fearless behavior of an adult or peer holding a cocker spaniel, petting it, and scratching its stomach, can reduce a child's fear of the dog (Bandura et al., 1967). Sometimes book reading and dramatic play with puppets or dolls can help children deal with their fears or prepare them to deal with fearful situations. These activities give children a chance to master scary feelings in ''safe'' situations (Erikson, 1959a; Garvey, 1974). In addition to setting good examples, adult patience, understanding, and warm reassurance are usually enough to soothe most toddler fears, at least at this stage.

THUMB SUCKING

Noah's parents were concerned when he started sucking his thumb. ''Try some black pepper on the thumb,'' a friend told them. ''That'll stop him!'' But instead, they talked with their pediatrician, who put them at ease when she told them about an important study on thumb sucking. The study reported that 50 percent of all children below four years of age suck their fingers (Traisman and Traisman, 1958). Ordinarily, thumb sucking does not harm teeth formation, unless it persists into the elementary years when permanent teeth begin to erupt. In fact, for some children thumb sucking seems to serve a purpose similar to a security blanket. It provides comfort during moments of hurt or fear. Putting pressure on children to stop thumb sucking usually increases the need for comfort which, in turn, increases thumb sucking. A good approach is for parents to ignore the behavior and to try to remove sources of anxiety or tension, which usually causes thumb sucking to disappear.

❖ Spotlight 7.4: Do Daddies Make Good "Mothers"?

Until recently, the American father was totally ignored in the study of children and families (LeMasters, 1974). In fact, for a long time fathers were thought to be unimportant in the development of the child. Strong emphasis on the mother's role caused us to equate "parenting" with "mothering." Remnants of this one-sided view can still be seen. The term "mothering," used in reference to the father's parenting role, indicates an inadequate vocabulary to properly refer to "fathering." Early studies of motherless babies referred to "maternal deprivation," but cases of fatherless children spoke of "father absence"—the two terms reflecting the greater emphasis placed on the role of mother in child development.

It was not until the 1970s that research addressed the issue of father involvement. In fact, the second half of the 1970s was nicknamed "the era of paternal rediscovery": "Social scientists now recognize that for biological and social reasons, most children have two parents—one of either sex" (Lamb, 1979, p. 938).

The father's traditional roles as breadwinner and achiever are changing. Women are seeking careers for themselves, spending more time away from home, and depending more on men to share in household tasks such as cooking and cleaning. And as more divorced men share custody of their children, fathers are called upon to be "mothers" as well. Men are sharing in the nurturing and rearing of children more than ever before.

The amount of father participation in child rearing is related to how **androgynous** the father is—that is, the degree to which his personality blends both masculine and feminine traits (Bem, 1974). Androgynous females pump their own gas as well as wash dishes. Androgynous males change diapers and play football. Androgynous fathers are more nurturant, are more involved in everyday child activities, and interact more with their children than fathers who have only "masculine" traits (DeFrain, 1979; Russell, 1978). Androgynous fathers are also more child-centered but less firm with their children, while masculine fathers are firm, demanding, and positively reinforcing, and leave the direction of daily activities to their wives (Baumrind, 1982). In a recent study, every father interviewed felt that husbands should take part in

Sex-Role Development and Relationships

Three-year-old Caroline and Roosevelt were pounding clay at the day-care center they attend. Roosevelt reached for some of the clay from Caroline's pile. The following exchange took place:

Caroline: Stop that! That's mine!

Roosevelt: I can have some too!

Caroline: I'll beat you up! I'm strong. See! (She exerts her strength by pounding the clay.)

Roosevelt: No you're not! Girls aren't strong. Boys are strong!

SEX-ROLE IDENTITY

In three short years, Caroline and Roosevelt have learned that girls are "supposed to be" one way and boys another. Most of this knowledge is learned through *sex typing* (see Chapter 4), which begins in infancy and continues throughout child-infant care and that men are important to the emotional needs of their children (Cordell et al., 1980).

To help fathers fit into their new role, Ross Parke and his associates set up training sessions for new fathers, featuring education about infants and toddlers and modeling of child care and social interaction (Parke et al., 1979). Trained fathers were more involved in caring for their youngsters and helping with housework three months later. In contrast, untrained fathers and their wives rarely saw themselves as having any choices other than the traditional roles of female caregiver and male breadwinner.

As you can see, we can never again accept the view that fathers are not important in their children's growth and development. One modern-day father comments on his fathering role:

> More than contributing something unique, my hope is that male involvement with young children will feminize, and therefore sensitize, men and boys to their betterment and that mutual sharing of child care responsibilities with women will provide them opportunities to expand the scope of their lives. (Podolner, 1978, p. 11).

As the importance of fathering has been recognized, many men have felt free to show their affection for their children.

hood. By the end of toddlerhood, most children know they are either male or female. They have also begun to develop their **sex-role identity**—an understanding that each sexual classification (male or female) carries certain behavioral requirements. That is, some behaviors are categorized as boy behaviors or girl behaviors (Kuhn et al., 1978). Toddlers also know that crossing these sex-role lines is to be avoided at all costs (Kohlberg, 1966), though boys are more likely to avoid ''sissy'' behaviors than girls are to avoid being tomboys (Maccoby, 1980). By age three, children play more with playmates of the same sex rather than the opposite sex (Jacklin and Maccoby, 1978). And they can accurately label others as ''male'' or ''female''—basing their judgments on physical traits such as facial hair, clothing, or strength (Ullian, 1976, 1979).

The adult-child relationship is an important influence in acquiring sex-role identity. See Spotlight 7.4 for a look at the importance of fathers. Research by Lamb (1977b, 1979) indicates that at the beginning of the toddler's second year, fathers begin to pay special attention to their sons and withdraw from their daughters. As this happens, boys channel their attention toward their father's behavior and girls toward their mother's. Mothers in Lamb's research made no distinc-

Formo, a toddler, plays confidently with knives, axes, and fire—and he doesn't get hurt. Despite the fact that Formo manipulates such dangerous objects, he handles them safely and they are never taken away by adults. In fact, Formo's play is not even supervised by adults. Occasionally, when he feels uncertain, Formo will toddle to his mother. But his mother's nod of encouragement and approval sends him back to playing with his "tools of life."*

Formo is a member of the Fore (pronounced *for'ay*) people of Papua New Guinea, described by Sorenson (1977). Before the influence of Western technology, the Fore were successful hunter-gatherers and subsistence gardeners. Toddler Formo is allowed unlimited exploration of his world without adult interference. As he begins to crawl and toddle, literally no restraints are placed on his movement. So he examines and manipulates whatever is around. As he takes his first experimental steps in walking, no one urges him on. He makes it on his own. And he can go anywhere in the village his curiosity takes him. Sometimes, he even ventures beyond the village into the forest. Formo, like all Fore toddlers, is

not expected to adjust to adult schedules or routines. His rules and schedules are his own. He is encouraged to follow his interests and whims wherever they lead.

The sense of touch is a central part of the Fore culture. As a baby, Formo remained in constant body contact with his mother. His basic needs were always satisfied immediately. His mother's lap was the perch where he nursed, slept, and played with his own body and his mother's. From his perch, Formo was able to observe and test his world. Formo's mother never put him aside for the sake of other activities such as preparing food or building fires. Instead, she carried him while she did all her tasks. This close physical contact taught Formo to communicate all his feelings and needs through body language even before he could talk. Once he felt confident, he was free to crawl down and to go and come at will—exercising absolute autonomy to be where and with whom he pleased. Fore infant-handling practices—early, close physical stimulation and touching—sharpened Formo's sense of touch so much that he was able to handle knives, axes, and fire casually and with skill even before he could walk.

Clearly, Fore child-rearing practices differ greatly from those of our society. The idea of tod-

*This case is based on a detailed description of the Fore people by Sorenson (1977).

---

tion in responding between sons and daughters. Through this channeling, children prefer to interact with the same-sex parent—increasing the likelihood that boys will identify with fathers and girls with mothers. Lamb believes that preference for the same-sex parent is a major factor in the child's acquisition of sex-role indentity.

Research on father absence supports the idea that sex-role identity develops within the first two or three years and that fathers are important in this process. If father absence occurs before the boy's fourth birthday, the child is apt to be less masculine, more dependent on peers, less assertive, and less involved in competitive physical contact sports. But father absence after age four has little effect on the boy's sex-role development (Hetherington, 1966). Effects of father absence on girls doesn't show up until adolescence, at which time females have difficulty adjusting to the female role and interacting with men (Hetherington, 1972).

Because of accidents or other medical reasons, rare cases have been reported in which a baby boy has been made into a girl or a baby girl into a boy. John

Formo played with knives, axes, and fire even before he could walk.

dlers playing with weapons such as knives and axes certainly is not accepted in Western culture, nor is such total autonomy. But the Fores are not unique in allowing their toddlers great freedom. In Kenya, Okinawa, and India, toddlers are allowed to fend for themselves in the company of an older sibling (Whiting and Whiting, 1975).

Nowhere is the difference in toddler-rearing more striking than in how toilet training is handled. The East African Digo believe that infants can learn toilet training soon after birth. They begin motor and toilet training in the first weeks of life. Night and day dryness is accomplished by five or six months of age (deVries, 1977). In the Soviet Union,

toddlers are expected to develop full bowel and bladder control by eighteen months (Bronfenbrenner, 1978). In China, toilet training is begun between twelve and eighteen months. Up until age three, toddlers wear pants that open in the back so they can squat and relieve themselves anytime—even in the streets (Sidel, 1972). But in nursery school, toilet training is collective. "After breakfast, children sit on white enamel potties and all have their bowel movements together! In another nursing room we visited, we were told that the children all sit on potties after lunch as well" (Sidel, 1972, p. 96).

Money (1975) reported a case in which a seven-month-old identical twin lost his penis during a circumcision accident. Upon advice from their physician, the parents decided to raise the boy as a girl. The child was given a new name, clothes, and hairstyle that matched his new sex. And adults began to react to the child in terms of his new identity. By three years of age, the child had learned to view himself as a girl and to behave in ways typical of the female sex.

Research on other cases of sex reassignment shows that before age three, children will accept either a male or female sex-role identity without psychological harm, but after age three, children who are reassigned sexual identities will be psychologically harmed (Money et al., 1957).

As you have seen, the first three years of a child's life is an important time for learning sex-role identity. While biological factors play some part in this process, children like Caroline and Roosevelt discover what sex they are and what sex-role identity is appropriate mostly by what they learn through important relationships with others (Maccoby, 1980).

241

Summary

1. Socialization is the process through which toddlers and older children learn to behave in ways considered acceptable by their society.

2. Patience and support from loving adults are necessary if toddlers are to develop a sense of autonomy. A reasonable setting of limits guides toddlers toward wise decision making and self-control and keeps them safe from physical harm. A sense of shame or doubt results when independence is restricted, discouraged, and poorly guided or when toddlers are punished or humiliated for their efforts.

3. Toddlers continue to show signs of dependency through clinging to and staying near a parent, usually becoming anxious when that parent leaves them—for whatever reason. Separation anxiety peaks at eighteen months of age and then gradually disappears. Lengthy separations during wartime or hospitalization can harm children more than brief, day-to-day separations.

4. Social interaction between peers gradually occurs during the second year of life, and play is the medium in which toddler-peer relationships are formed. Toddler play is more likely to include a peer instead of a parent even when both are present.

5. Aggression is seldom seen before two years of age. But toward the end of toddlerhood, full-blown aggression appears, usually in confrontations with playmates over toys or in temper tantrums when toddlers don't get their way.

6. As perceptual and cognitive abilities mature, the number and variety of toddler fears increase. These include the fear of the unfamiliar, separation, going to sleep, animals, and engines, and the overriding fear of "disappearing."

7. By three years of age, toddlers know they are either male or female, and their *sex-role identity*—the knowledge that certain behaviors are expected of them because of their sex label—begins to develop.

Empathetic Activities

- What feelings did you have as you read about The Case of Noah Time? Kim, Scotty, and Noah and their prosocial behaviors? Formo and his upbringing? What feelings do you think each child had? Their parents?

- What things do you believe are important to remember when toilet training toddlers? When dealing with separation anxiety for short periods and lengthy periods? When dealing with thumb sucking and temper tantrums?

- Observe toddlers in a nursery school and on a playground. Write a profile of the emotions you see, using the following guidelines:

  - Describe any toddler fears that are expressed.

  - Calculate the percentage of children that sucked their thumbs.

- Describe incidents of aggression or temper tantrums.
- List prosocial behaviors observed.
- Review the information contained in The Case of Noah Time. Pretend you are Noah's attorney and prepare a defense on his behalf justifying Noah's strong will and negativism during toddlerhood. Then provide some ''limit-setting techniques'' Noah's mother can use to help deal with his negativism.
- In what ways do social, emotional, and cognitive development interact as children play to develop the *Whole Child?*
- How will Formo's relationship with his mother affect his development of dependency, attachment, and separation anxiety?

Related Readings

Butler, Annie, Cotts, Edward, and Quisenberry, Nancy. *Play as development.* Columbus, Ohio: Charles E. Merrill, 1978. A practical, readable examination of the developmental nature and function of play. Many helpful hints on how parents and teachers can stimulate and guide children's play to enhance learning and development.

Endsley, Richard, and Bradbard, Marilyn. *The wise guide to quality day care: A guide for parents and students.* New York: Spectrum Books, 1981. Everything you always wanted to know about selecting good quality day care. Comprehensive checklists based on the authors' research guide the reader on what to look for when making this important decision.

Mussen, Paul, and Eisenberg-Berg, Nancy. *Roots of caring, sharing and helping: The development of prosocial behavior in children.* San Francisco: W. H. Freeman, 1977. A synthesis of research on how prosocial behavior develops and how children are socialized in prosocial ways. Environmental and hereditary conditions considered as determinants of helping, sharing, and comforting, with emphasis on socialization experiences as crucial factors.

Parke, Ross. *Fathers.* Cambridge, Mass.: Harvard University Press, 1981. An excellent picture of the modern-day father who has become involved in his child's development. Addresses in a readable way the consequences of this involvement for children, wife, the life of the family, and the father himself.

White, Burton. *The first three years of life.* Englewood Cliffs, N. J.: Prentice-Hall, 1975. Easy-to-read, yet comprehensive description of young children in the first thirty-six months of life. Suggestions on child-rearing practices, parenting strategies, and the selection of toys and equipment.

Wolman, Benjamin B. *Children's fears.* New York: Grosset and Dunlap, 1978. An encyclopedia of various types of childhood fears presented developmentally. Chapters on infancy, toddlerhood, preschool years, middle childhood, and adolescence.

IV Early Childhood

(ages 3 to 6)

8 Early Childhood: Physical-Motor and Perceptual Development

The Case of the Parents' Day Picnic

It was a warm September afternoon—a special day for Kim, Scotty, and Nicky because it was Parents' Day at their nursery school. The children's families had gathered for a picnic under the shade trees behind the school. The teachers looked forward to the day as it gave them a chance to get to know the parents and to see how the children interacted with each other and their parents.

Some parents spent the entire day fanning themselves and watching the children play. "Kim is growing up so fast," her mother remarked. "She doesn't look like my baby anymore." "I know what you mean," Scotty's mother replied. "Scotty's getting to look more like his Dad every day," she said, gesturing to the lanky man beside her. "And he seems determined to keep up with the older boys. I must, say, though, he's getting better at catching that ball."

Several feet away a group of children and some parents were playing catch, running far across the lawn to retrieve the ball when, as was often the case, it missed the intended receiver. Another group of children was gathered around a teacher telling a story, while some other children played on the swings and slides. But one child, Nicky Thomas, ran from one group to another until finally, spotting a tricycle, he jumped on and began to ride in wide circles.

"There he goes again," remarked Mary Hopkins, Nicky's teacher, to another teacher. "Sometimes I think riding that tricycle and painting are the only things that interest Nicky. Some days he'll paint for a while and then run over to show me what he's done. When I smile and comment on how pleased I am, he runs back to paint more pictures for me to see. He seems starved for attention!"

According to the school's records, Nicky's mother had left Nicky's father when the child was two years old. A man described by Nicky as "my mother's boyfriend" delivers him to school every day. "He sort of pushes the youngster in the door," Mary said. "Then Nicky just stands there, ignoring everybody and everything." There appeared to be some question of physical abuse. Nicky frequently came to school with large welts on his legs, which his mother had explained as an allergic reaction to some of the foods he eats. As Mary casually talked with Nicky's mother during the picnic, Ms. Thomas mentioned that although Nicky liked most foods, it was hard to get meals—especially breakfast—into him. "But Nicky always drinks a lot of juice," she said. Noting what Nicky ate that day, Mary saw that his "juice" was one of those high-sugar-content fruit drinks and that his lunch consisted of a sandwich, a doughnut, and a can of chocolate pudding.

The teachers learned a lot at the picnic from their observations of children and conversations with parents. They looked forward to the remainder of the year and the work to be done with parents and children.

Physical Growth

During early childhood (ages three to six), the physical appearance of preschoolers is changing, but growth does not occur by leaps and bounds. In fact, the rate of growth is slower between ages two and five than in the first two years of life (Lowrey, 1973). Kim and Scotty's physical growth during early childhood is more a process of smoothing out and shedding the infant-like characteristics of toddlerhood.

HEIGHT AND WEIGHT

By age three, most boys have grown to be about thirty-eight inches. Three-year-old girls continue to be slightly shorter than boys (Tanner, 1978), Kim trailing behind Scotty by an inch or so. Three-year-old Scotty, like average boys his age, will grow eight more inches by age six—reaching about four feet, two inches (Watson and Lowrey, 1967). Preschool girls will continue to grow two or three inches each year until they surpass their male agemates shortly after age eleven. The typical boy weighs about thirty-two pounds at age three but about forty-eight pounds by age six (Watson and Lowrey, 1967). Girls usually lag behind boys their age by about a pound but catch up by adolescence.

STRUCTURAL DEVELOPMENT

As their mothers noted, Kim and Scotty are not just growing taller and heavier but are changing shape to more closely resemble the lean, lanky look of school-age children. This happens as different rates of growth occur in various parts of the body and proportions change during early childhood. As a result, the top-heavy appearance that Kim and Scotty had during toddlerhood is lost and they move about with more confidence and ease.

Other body structures such as the brain and nervous system are also developing, although these inner changes are not as easily observed as outward changes. The brain grows larger, becomes more convoluted or wrinkled, and gets thicker during early childhood. At maturity, the adult brain weighs about three pounds and is the size of two fists held together (Languis, et al., 1980). By age five, the brain of the preschool child is almost 90 percent of its adult size. At this time, the brain is closer to its adult weight than other body parts (Tanner, 1978). Researchers believe there is a continuing increase in both the size of nerve cells and the number of connections forming between nerve cells in the cortex and other parts of the brain and nervous system (Tanner, 1970). There is also evidence that myelinization is more complete in five-year-olds than three-year-olds.

The brain is divided into two hemispheres that appear to have different functions. Left hemisphere functions are concerned with language and skilled motor acts. Perception is a function of the right hemisphere and includes visual-spatial abilities and nonverbal sounds such as music. Connections between the two hemispheres remain immature during the early preschool years (Crinella et al., 1971), but communication between the two brain hemispheres does improve between ages three and five (Languis et al., 1980).

Some studies suggest that brain development may differ in boys and girls. For example, the earlier dominance of the left hemisphere of girls may explain their superior verbal ability (Hutt, 1972). There is also speculation that boys demonstrate superior spatial abilities because the left hemisphere becomes dominant later and more completely in males than females (Witelson, 1976).

The toddler's soft cartilage becomes hardened bone during early childhood. Bones of the skeletal system also grow larger. Environmental factors such as malnutrition and fatigue can damage the preschool child's skeletal system. *Bone maturation*—the thickness, shape, and number of small bones—is retarded and head circumference is smaller among malnourished preschoolers from poor countries (Scrimshaw, 1967).

As we mentioned in the toddlerhood section, most two-year-olds have their full set of "baby" teeth. These baby teeth start falling out by five years of age but usually not before age four. And by six or seven the first permanent teeth have begun to appear. Premature loss of the baby teeth because of accident or tooth decay can affect the alignment of permanent teeth. Baby teeth guide the permanent teeth into position, aid digestion by breaking up food, and help the development of teeth and jaws.

Muscle development makes up most of Kim and Scotty's weight gain during early childhood. Boys have more muscle tissue than girls while girls generally have more fat tissue than boys (Tanner, 1970). At age five and a half, fat is half as thick as it was at nine months, so Kim and Scotty have become leaner as preschoolers. By about age three, children have the total number of fat cells they will have as adults (Guthrie, 1975). Increases in fat at later ages are caused by an increase in the size, not the number, of fat cells. Muscle tissue develops differently, growing at a slower and slower rate throughout childhood and remaining behind other tissue growth until the growth spurt begins in adolescence.

EXCEPTIONAL PHYSICAL DEVELOPMENT

Mary Lou attends a preschool for developmentally delayed children. She is physically handicapped and confined to a wheelchair because of cerebral palsy. Her movements are uncontrolled, jerky, and irregular and she lacks coordination and balance. Because she cannot speak or write, her teachers experiment with other ways to communicate with her.

Cerebral palsy is responsible for the largest number of physically disabled children in special education classes (Bigge and Sirvis, 1978). It is caused by damage to or improper development of the brain. Prenatal influences, prematurity, difficult labor, or lack of oxygen at birth can all be causes of cerebral palsy. Children may also be physically handicapped because of muscular dystrophy, hemophilia, cystic fibrosis, sickle cell anemia, or cancer. Early education is especially important for physically handicapped children. Many of these children require special training to learn self-help skills such as toileting and eating, and to develop a means of mobility if they cannot walk. Teachers and parents can also provide psychological support and educational activities to help the physically handicapped child maintain a positive attitude.

Sometimes adults become so protective of children who have handicaps that opportunities for exploration and social interaction are restricted even more than necessary. When parents experience prolonged feelings of guilt, anger, and grief over their child's handicap, the parent-child relationship further deteriorates because of these barriers. Sometimes counseling can reduce these conflicts and help adults develop a healthier outlook.

Child Abuse

Severe restrictions of physical movement and physical abuse can have long-lasting and damaging effects on a child's physical growth and motor development. Spotlight 8.1 describes the effects of prolonged abuse on Rebecca Holmes, a child who was hidden away and abused by her parents for many years.

The incidence of **child abuse**—''any action against or neglect of a child that harms or threatens to harm the welfare of that child''—is widespread (Cook and Bowles, 1980). Authorities estimate that two or three million children are the victims of physical abuse and neglect each year. And these are low estimates because many professionals never report cases and abused children are usually afraid or ashamed to talk. Some children even believe their punishment is deserved. No wonder it was so hard for Nicky's teachers to tell if he was being abused.

Child abuse ranges from physical and sexual assault to neglect and failure to provide protection. About two thousand children die annually as a result of their circumstances (Spar, 1980). As you can see in Spotlight 8.1, despite persisting physical problems, Rebecca's life was spared. Although the physical effects of abuse are often the most obvious, abuse has far-reaching effects in the cognitive, social and emotional areas as well.

Since the 1970s, the problem of child abuse has received increasing attention, but abuse and neglect of children has existed for centuries. It was not until 1962 that social scientists coined the term ''the battered child syndrome'' to rally professionals to take action. The first laws requiring medical and educational personnel to report child abuse and neglect were implemented in 1967 in various states. The federal government became involved in 1974 when it passed the Child Abuse Prevention and Treatment Act, which made it illegal for professionals to fail to report child abuse. In 1979, an estimated 19 million dollars was spent on public education, research, treatment centers, and professional training.

Spotlight 8.1: The Abuse of Rebecca Holmes*

The tip that ultimately led to Becky's release was one of hundreds received by Sergeant Miriam Travis of the child abuse unit of the Los Angeles County Sheriff's Department. The street to which she went with three deputies was like any other in the working-class suburb of Paramount, south of Los Angeles. And the house, a pastel-colored stucco dwelling, seemed neat, well-maintained, and as unprepossessing as the neighboring single-story homes that uniformly evoke a Mexican heritage in the neighborhood.

Perhaps the most unusual thing about this particular case was that the sergeant had been warned about the terrible temper of Daniel Holmes, thirty-three. She and her deputies were afraid that the sturdily built head of the household would get violent at their arrival; as Sergeant Travis put it, "We didn't know what to expect."

They went up to the front door with some caution, but the officers needn't have worried. Holmes was not there, and though his common-law wife gave the deputies no reason to think so at the time, she was the one who ruled the household. The woman, Alice Hernandez, made only a token effort to rebuff the deputies and surprised them by letting them inside her tidy home without a search warrant.

A plant lover, the sergeant noticed that the living room was filled with greenery. One of the deputies, John Rondina, noticed something else: One wall was covered with family snapshots showing Holmes with Hernandez and two children —Alice, thirteen, and Danny, nine.

Not shown in any of the twenty-five photographs was the child the officers had come to see, eight-year-old Rebecca. Rondina asked the Hernandez woman whether they could see the girl. Eyeing the two peace officers suspiciously, the slight and stolid mother tried to put them off. The girl, she said, was sleeping. Sergeant Travis replied that they wanted to see Rebecca anyway. "Would you take us to her?" she asked firmly. The woman simply turned and slunk down a short hall, past a sitting room and a girl's bedroom to a place where the kitchen, master bedroom, and bathroom were situated. She reached for the bedroom door. "As she opened the door," Sergeant Travis recalls, "the smell from inside just about bowled me over. I had to hold my breath because it was so overpowering. It was definitely a urine smell." Rebecca, however, was nowhere in sight.

Asked where the child was, the mother motioned to a screen set up near the closet. Moving it aside, Sergeant Travis beheld a grotesque sight. Asleep on a green, vinyl-covered cot was the little girl. She was not lying down. She was not covered. She slept sitting up, unsupported, her legs outstretched stiffly before her. "I said, 'This is Rebecca?' " the sergeant recounts, her voice rising with persisting incredulity. "Here was this tiny, tiny, tiny little girl."

Sergeant Travis, a slim grandmother whose blonde, pixie-styled hair belies her age, picked up the astonishingly small eight-year-old. Becky's overflowing diaper slid to her ankles, revealing a crimson rash so bad that the girl's skin was peeling. The sleeve of the trim blue suit Sergeant Travis was wearing got soiled, so she put the child down on the cot again. She then noticed what she calls a classic sign of child abuse: Becky looked up at her mother and resumed her original submissive pose, eyes closed, hands clasped on her thighs, quiet, sore, and uncomplaining.

The deputies were also interested in seeing the closet in the bedroom, for it was here, they were told, Becky was kept. The floor of the closet measured roughly two and a half feet by four feet. There appeared to be a space where someone had been sitting for a long time. Besides women's clothes hanging inside, the closet contained a dirty pillow without a pillowcase, a broken doll, and what Rondina took to be the crumbled remains of old disposable diapers. Feces were smeared on one wall. It was in this closet that a niece of Alice Hernandez had found Becky while investigating a noise in the presumably empty house. To her, the girl inside looked like a two-year-old, but the young woman knew that the child must have been her long-forgotten cousin born to her aunt years earlier.

When the deputies found Becky on April 18, 1978, she weighed twenty-four pounds and stood thirty-two inches high. These measurements are about half the usual height and weight of a child her age, and her mother understated the girl's birth date by two full years either out of forgetfulness or as an attempt to conceal the extent of Becky's deprivation. In addition, Becky was unable to walk; she propelled herself by scooting along on her backside. Nor did she speak more than a handful of words. Nor did she eat normally; she initially rejected foods like meats and bananas, possibly because they were new to her. She would, however, attempt to eat cat food whenever she had the chance. She craved doughnuts and peanut butter. According to the foster mother with whom she was placed, she would make a meal out of a mere cornflake. Strangely, though, despite her size, Becky displayed no signs of malnutrition in medical tests performed after she was discovered and taken from her parents.

In the year since she was freed, Becky has grown more than twice as fast as is usual for a child her age, thanks to the devoted nurture of her foster mother. In just the first six months, she grew six inches; she now weighs more than forty pounds. She has outgrown three or four sizes of clothes and has gone from infant's-size to children's-size shoes. She is toilet-trained. She eats normally. She has developed a vocabulary of several hundred words and can carry on a simple conversation. She recog-

nizes characters from Sesame Street. She no longer shrinks from the closet near her crib. Nor does she wake up nights screaming in terror.

Yet she still lines up her dolls around the edge of the crib, as if to make more room for herself. Also, she still needs to wear uncomfortable braces at night to correct completely the dislocations of her knees and hips. And she still cries when her foster mother leaves the house.

For all she has been through, Becky has a quick and sunny smile, which she beamed at a recent visitor who gave her a present. "Look at that, Mom," she laughed, tearing off the gift wrap. Inside was a game that she learned rapidly. Then she went outside, to a world that continues to fascinate her; an earthworm, for instance, caught and held her attention as she toddled along the sidewalk.

No one can speculate with any certainty what will happen to her now. The foster mother, who has cared for six handicapped children during the past three years, is optimistic. She says children can recover from abuse and neglect.

Dr. Widelitz is less sanguine. It is, he says, "quite likely" that Becky will be intellectually and physically retarded. Although she has progressed through almost two years' development in only one year's time, she would have to maintain that rate of growth for years to catch up to, and stay with, her age group. "It is too late for her to catch up. I think she will be a very small, retarded adult. But," the pediatrician continues, "kids do amazing things sometimes."

For her parents, the bizarre case of Rebecca Holmes all but ended in Compton Superior Court last January. Alice Hernandez was sentenced to a maximum of three years in prison on her felony conviction of child endangering. Daniel Holmes was sentenced to a year on the same charge. They will lose mere months. But Rebecca Holmes has lost a childhood and—who knows?—the likelihood of a happy and productive future life.

Nine-year-old Becky with her foster mother.

Despite all this recent attention, experts know very little about the causes of child abuse. There is no single explanation. Usually it results from an interaction of many factors: "The particular child, his or her parents and their psychological characteristics, social forces impinging on the family, institutions, and the total character of our society must be considered" (Starr, 1979, p. 874).

UNIQUE CHARACTERISTICS OF ABUSED CHILDREN

One explanation for child abuse may involve the unique characteristics of the child. For example, infant temperament and health can cause parents to react in certain ways towards their babies. Crying infants are more likely to be abused than quiet infants because crying is perceived as an arousing, unpleasant stimulus. In a recent study, child abusers reacted to infant cries with a faster heartbeat and greater skin conductance, indicating more distress than non–child abusers (Frodi and Lamb, 1980). A high percentage (23 to 31 percent) of premature children are abused (Bell, R.Q. 1979). Because these children are harder to care for and soothe, their parents feel unsuccessful. Higher than average incidences of abuse are also found among children with physical handicaps (Gaines et al., 1978). Bonding experts suggest high incidences of abuse result from early deficiencies in bonding (Klaus and Kennell, 1976; Egeland and Vaughn, 1981).

FAMILY SYSTEM

The family system is also said to contribute to child abuse. Many parents who abuse their children were themselves abused as children. Most were deprived of basic mothering—"a lack of the deep sense of being cared for and cared about from the beginning of one's life" (Steele and Pollock, 1974, p. 98). Like their own parents, abusive parents have unrealistic expectations for their offspring and little understanding of normal child development. They might, for instance, view naughty behavior as a deliberate attempt by the child to "get them." Or they might take it personally when a child spills food or breaks something. Abusive parents often expect their child to respond in far more mature ways than the child is capable of. Many times abusive parents view their children as the cause of their problems. As a result of their own unpleasant childhoods, abusive parents often suffer from fear of rejection, poor self-concept, insecurity, and low tolerance for frustration. They expect their child to act as a source of reassurance, comfort, and love for them: "It is hardly an exaggeration to say the parent acts like a frightened, unloved child, looking to his own child as if he were an adult capable of providing comfort and love" (Steele and Pollock, 1974, p. 98).

SOCIAL SYSTEM AND PHYSICAL ENVIRONMENT

In addition to the family system, the larger social system is also a contributing factor to child abuse. Child abuse can be found among *all* social classes. But more cases are reported among low-income families where unemployment, family stress, isolation, and other social and economic pressures are commonplace (Pelton, 1978). Some social scientists suggest that the mistreatment of children is related to our society's routine tolerance of high levels of violence (Gelles, 1978). Recent research lends support to the concept of neighborhood "risk." Even where income levels are the same, some neighborhoods are at higher risk for fostering child abuse than others. Families in high-risk neighborhoods evaluated their neighborhood more negatively as a place for rearing children and were more socially impoverished than families in low-risk neighborhoods (Garbarino and Sherman, 1980). In high-risk neighborhoods, houses and families are more "run down", little giving and sharing exist, and needy neighbors compete for scarce social resources.

TREATMENT AND PREVENTION

It has now been recognized that abusive parents need help and understanding. Programs to help potential child abusers have been established. Parents Anonymous, an organization operating on principles similar to Alcoholics Anonymous, provides a supportive atmosphere for parents who need help in dealing with their problems or who feel they might take their anger out on their children. Toll-free numbers have been established for the organization throughout the United States. And many states have a twenty-four-hour hotline for emergency needs. Family counseling and abuse shelters have also sprung up in many regions of the country. Additional information on the prevention and reporting of child abuse can be obtained from The National Center on Child Abuse in Washington, D.C., the National Committee for Prevention of Child Abuse in Chicago, Illinois, and the Citizens Committee for Children and Parents Under Stress in Chicago, Illinois.

Motor Development

As the Parents' Day picnic progressed and the heat lessened, Susan and Mary lay their fans and lemonade aside. They formed a circle with a small group of children among which were Kim and Scotty and played a game of pitch with a ball. Meanwhile, Nicky spent his time on a tricycle, circling round and round the small group. As the children played, a lot of important advances could be observed in their motor development.

Motor development, following the *cephalo-caudal principle* (see Chapter 4), is concentrated on the body below the waist and involves activities such as running, skipping, and jumping. And following the *proximo-distal principle* (see Chapter 4) preschoolers' motor development is concentrated on development of smaller muscles in the arms and hands—drawing with a crayon or cutting with scissors.

Nicky has spent literally dozens of hours of his preschool life on his tricycle. Once he had the skill of riding down pat, he wanted to do it faster and faster and to try out all sorts of imaginative stunts, much to the delight of his peers and worry of his teachers! Between the ages of three and five, children continue to refine their motor skills and coordination (Terry et al., 1979). Children first get the basic movement of a motor act, such as throwing a ball or riding a tricycle. Although their movements are still jerky at first, with practice, they become smoother and better coordinated. That's why you'll see preschoolers practice throwing a ball, riding a tricycle or other motor skills over and over again.

Although preschool children are likely to sit still longer than toddlers, they continue to be busy and vigorously on the move. The parents at the picnic could attest to this as they sat back with their fans and lemonade, while Kim and Scotty continued a game of pitch and Nicky zoomed around on his tricycle.

LOCOMOTOR DEVELOPMENT

Strength, speed, and coordination—the components of all motor activity—are much improved after toddlerhood. As children grow during the preschool years, they complete motor activities with more speed and require less body and mind reaction time. Three-year-old Kim's legs now stay closer together when walking, so she doesn't have to look at her feet to see what they are doing anymore. She can run better than she did at age two, and she can stop and start suddenly, turn corners, and jump up and down. By age four, balance is more developed (Terry et al., 1979). Some five-year-olds even manage two activities at once—for example, throwing a ball while running.

Children develop skills such as running, jumping, climbing, balancing, and throwing by spontaneously participating in these activities—not through direct instruction or teaching of the skill. But more complicated skills such as swimming, skating, skiing, or shooting marbles can improve as a result of formal instruction (Breckenridge and Murphy, 1969; Sinclair, 1973).

FINE-MOTOR MOVEMENT

Scotty, a typical three-year-old, can draw with a crayon, feed himself, unbutton most of his clothes, and put on his shoes. At four years of age, his improved eye-hand coordination will permit fine-motor skills such as zipping, turning knobs, and cutting with scissors. Scotty can tell the front and back of his clothes and put them on fairly well—buttoning and unbuttoning them. He can also pour milk, wash his face and hands, and brush his teeth. By age five, buttoning and zipping will be easy for Scotty and he will even have learned to tie his shoes.

From these descriptions, you can see that fine-motor movements develop from clumsy, inaccurate efforts to smooth, precise movements in the same way that gross-motor movements develop. Figure 8.1 describes gross- and fine-motor skills that are developed during early childhood.

Changing Routines

SELF-HELP SKILLS

During the preschool years, routines change as children continue to acquire the ability to do more things for themselves, largely as a result of their improved motor development and coordination. Of course, they will continue to require adult supervision, support, and guidance for many years to come.

NUTRITION

Good nutritional habits continue to be important in the preschool years. About 1800 calories per day are required by the four- to six-year-old child. When children are given the type of "junk food" Nicky brought to the picnic—high-sugar-

3 YEARS

Runs well but will stumble or fall occasionally.

Can change speed, direction, or style of movements at signal from teacher, e.g. shifting from a fast run to a walk.

Can walk a straight line (1-inch line for 10 feet).

Can throw a ball without losing balance.

Can make a standing broad jump.

Rises from prone to standing position without turning.

Jumps from bottom step (12 inches).

Alternates forward foot going up stairs.

Can ascend and descend vertical ladder.

Rides tricycle with no difficulty.

Can use hands and feet simultaneously, e.g. stamping foot while clapping hands.

Handles most of dressing; puts on own shoes.

May be able to unbutton some front buttons; side buttons with difficulty.

Feeds self; spills little.

Can drive nails into wood with hammer.

Handles kitchen utensils such as small pitcher in pouring milk.

May be able to use scissors.

Can copy a circle reasonably well.

May be able to copy a crude cross (a simple line cross, using a vertical and a horizontal line—line *must* intersect at some point).

Adds two parts to incomplete man.

Makes tower of ten blocks or cubes.

Completes simple puzzles.

Can unzip clothing.

3½ YEARS

Runs smoothly with acceleration and deceleration.

Skillful in balancing on toes, can run on tiptoes.

Turns sideways to adjust to narrow opening.

Stands on one foot for two seconds.

Briefly hops on one foot.

Heel-to-toe walk.

Catches bounced ball (hands held in viselike position, elbows extended).

May shift body weight to throw (may not ''step out'' until five years of age).

Can erect self from squatting position.

Removes wrap without assistance.

Marked shift to bilaterality.

Hand tremor when fine coordination is required.

Can make a circle and a cross.

May be able to imitate a crude square (the square will be lopsided with ''dog-eared'' or rounded corners).

4 YEARS

Easy balance in walking.

Can run, stop, start, turn with ease.

Can accomplish running or standing broad jumps.

Balances on one foot for 4 to 8 seconds.

Skips ''lame duck'' on one foot.

Likes rhythm and can march in time.

Descends stairway with alternating feet (may need some help).

Oriented in space—can go to a certain point and stop; can go in a certain direction; not get in way of others.

Touches tip of nose with eyes closed.

Grasps cube neatly with thumb and middle finger.

Still lacks poise in reaching.

Imitates square (vertical lines usually longer).

Completes eight-piece formboard puzzle.

Matches geometric forms.

May draw six-part man (head, body, two arms, two legs).

Makes crude designs, some letters.

May button front buttons.

Uses scissors and attempts to cut on a straight line.

Enjoys using a hammer and nails; holds hammer near the head.

Visual ''tracking,'' right-left.

Lateral tongue movements; tongue-tip elevation.

Figure 8.1 **Gross- and fine-motor development in early childhood**

4½ YEARS	5 YEARS
Backward heel-to-toe walk.	Smoother control of general bodily activity.
Hops on nondominant foot.	Two-hand catch (often fails to catch ball).
Can jump quarter turn to right and left.	May bounce ball in place, catch each bounce.
Can cross feet over midline of body.	Hops on one foot for 15 feet.
Can lace shoes; tie bow-knot.	May be able to hit a swinging ball.
May print some letters, large and irregular, some reversed; may write from right to left.	Skips smoothly.
Smooth visual tracking.	Can walk the balance beam (2 inches × 4 inches × 6 feet).
Leaps over objects 10 inches high.	Uses roller skates.
Hops forward three hops, maintains balance (knees should flex slightly).	Rides junior bicycle.
Can turn somersault.	Skips rope.
Stands on one foot, hands on hips, eyes open, for ten seconds.	Shifts body weight to throw ("steps out" with foot opposite throwing hand).
Dresses self except for tying shoes.	Can move with the contrasts in music—loud, soft, high, low.
Imitates six-block bridge.	Can execute simple dance steps.
Draws six-part man.	Reaching and grasping becoming one continuous motion.
May copy a recognizable triangle (sides will not be equal, nor will base be parallel to edge of paper).	Hand dominance established.
Usually shows unilateral right-hand dominance in most activities.	Differentiates between square and rectangle.
	May be able to imitate a rectangle.
	Can manipulate buttons well.

Figure 8.1 (continued)

content drinks, doughnuts, or other foods high in calories but low in nutritional value—they will develop a taste for this kind of food. But when they are given foods such as raw celery, carrot sticks, natural fruit juices, fruit slices, and other foods high in nutritional value, they are more likely to develop a preference for this kind of food. A wide selection of such nutritional foods can be consistently introduced to preschoolers over a period of time. This keeps youngsters naturally curious and interested in a variety of tastes, textures, and colors.

Protein is a nutrient of great importance during the preschool years since muscle tissue is being developed. And optimum development of muscles occurs only with adequate protein. Two glasses of milk, an egg, and one meat serving per day will provide the necessary protein for preschool children. But obtaining iron is a tricky business. Meat and eggs are good sources of iron as are iron-fortified breakfast cereals.

Maintaining a reasonable daily schedule for meals will allow the child to have the best appetite. A light midmorning and afternoon snack are useful in preventing hunger and irritability between meals. The digestive process of preschoolers is

Balancing

Locomotor Movement in Early Childhood

Kicking

Hanging

Throwing

Climbing

Running

261

This child is gaining experience in coordinating her sense of sight, touch, hearing, smell, and even taste as she makes a cake.

similar to that of adults but their stomach has less than half the capacity of an adult stomach (Breckenridge and Murphy, 1969). Since their stomach is still a small organ, it is easily irritated by spicy foods and those with high roughage content.

Preschoolers are not too young to learn about nutrition. And sometimes nutrition can be used to teach them other concepts. The pleasing bright colors of fruits and vegetables can be used to introduce colors to children. A tray containing green grapes, pepper, pickles, parsley, and lettuce can provide a good introduction to the color green. Parents can also talk about the basic four food groups and help children learn to categorize foods accordingly. The purpose of seeds and peelings, the different shapes, colors, and textures of foods, and food production processes are good discussion topics for curious preschoolers. Such foods as raw turnip slices can be cut into interesting shapes and radish roses or cauliflower are appetizing when served as finger foods (McWilliams, 1980). Children also enjoy helping out in cooking projects. Cooking not only is a good opportunity for learning science, math, language, and social skills, it also improves the appetite. Nothing is as good to three-year-old Nicky as his own biscuits—no matter how hard or misshapen they are.

Perceptual Development

During the preschool years, eyesight improves and children are able to see finer details at a distance. The eyeball is short and shallow until the child turns six, causing farsightedness (Breckenridge and Murphy, 1969). This makes it hard for preschoolers to focus on close materials such as cutting out "perfect" designs.

Preschool children are better than toddlers at coordinating their senses of sight, touch, and hearing, and by five or six they become as skilled as adults at co-ordinating the senses. Shifts in perceptual preferences and abilities also occur at about five years of age. Three- and four-year-olds prefer to explore an object such as a new toy by touch, but by six or seven years of age visual exploration is preferred. And when given problems to solve, three- and four-year-olds notice the color and size of an object more than its shape. At age six, children (like adults) notice shape more (White, 1965). And as you will see, preschoolers still differ from adults in their abilities to pay attention to and to discriminate among stimuli.

ATTENTION

We live in a world with many different sights, sounds, smells, textures, and tastes. If we tried to attend to all of these things at one time, we would be overwhelmed. So we develop **selected attention**, that is, we attend to or respond to some things and shut out others, depending on our interests, needs, and abilities.

Preschool children have trouble attending to one particular task and shutting out unwanted or irrelevant information—especially when a lot of complex activity is going on at once (Gibson, 1969). For example, when Kim was four, her mother gave her a surprise birthday cake. Kim's eight-year-old friend suggested they count the candles together. While her friend counted all the candles, Kim became sidetracked by the bright red roses and the flickering candle flames atop the cake.

The features that attract children's attention undergo a major shift between ages three and six (Wright and Vlietstra, 1975). The three-year-old attends to prominent features of an object—exploring it quickly, impulsively, and playfully. In contrast, the older child focuses on the informativeness—not the promi-nence—of an object's features. Older children—being more focused, task-ori-ented, and slower than the younger children—consider the object more systemat-ically. Wright and Vlietstra (1975) suggest that children's cognitive abilities will suffer unless they can learn to attend systematically and selectively so they are not continually distracted by objects and events in the environment.

Children between four and six are less effective than eight-year-olds in deal-ing with situations in which sustained attention is required. As perception im-proves, cognitive development occurs and motivation increases. A preschooler's **attention span**—the amount of time spent paying attention to an activity—also increases gradually. Still, there are individual differences. Nicky's attention span

New objects and experiences hold the young child's attention for longer periods of time than do objects children are used to.

is much shorter than that of the average five-year-old, while Scotty's is more typical of that age. Scotty's attention span developed as follows in the years from three to five:

Age three: Scotty's longer attention span makes possible short group experiences such as story time or music time. He is also able to spend more time at one activity.

Age four: Scotty usually finishes activities that he begins. He sometimes spends a good deal of time planning an activity before he begins. He enjoys more group activities. He can listen as well as share in story time and music time.

Age five: Scotty enjoys group activities. He enjoys planning a project in detail and is generally patient and enthusiastic about completing his work even though the activity may extend over a period of several days. It becomes important to him to complete work he has begun.*

DISCRIMINATION

Remember the difficulty toddler Kim had locating her mother in the supermarket (see Chapter 5)? Now that she's five years old, Kim is more skilled at picking her mother out of a crowd—partly because of past experience and partly because her ability to discriminate has matured since toddlerhood. Children between ages five

---

* Data from North Carolina Office of Day Care Licensing, Raleigh, North Carolina.

and nine scan more completely and thoroughly than children between ages two and four and a half (Vurpillot, 1968). As a result, five-year-old Kim now has an easier time of finding her mother. She can scan the mass of women around her and notice details as she looks. She can pick out her mother from all the rest because her brown-haired mom is wearing a red dress and is toting Kim's baby brother in a back carrier. While refinements in scanning and part-whole discrimination become more fully developed around the beginning of the school years, they continue to mature and improve into adulthood (Rosinski, 1977).

As you will see in Chapter 9, preschoolers learn that objects can be transformed (changed) in some ways yet still remain the same object. A face, for example, is still a face whether it is rotated (slanted, upright, upside down) or reversed (as in a mirror image). Since objects in the everyday world can be transformed in these ways without changing their identity, imagine the confusion that results when children learn to discriminate letters of the alphabet. Both rotation and reversal alter the identity of letters such as b, p, d, and q—each letter being just a rotation or reversal of the other.

Kim's mother noticed she reversed her b's and d's. She worried and asked Mary Hopkins, Kim's preschool teacher, about it. Mary assured her that children frequently reverse letters when they first learn to read or write. Gibson (1963) notes that certain cues are more important and helpful than others. In a study of discrimination of differences in letters of the alphabet, she found that children could more easily discriminate between open and closed curves (q and c) than they could between reversed (b and d) or rotated (p and d) letters. The ability to discriminate between letters such as b and d, p and q remains faulty until age seven, at which time confusions occur less often.

By age five, children can discriminate between lateral, vertical, and horizontal lines (Cratty, 1970). These distinctions enable children as young as three to carry out simple map reading skills. This skill further improves by age five with the ability to rotate maps and view them from different angles (Bluestein and Acredolo, 1979). Improved discrimination permits improvements in the child's ability to categorize objects and patterns. Children use similarities and differences to categorize like and unlike objects and patterns (Smith, 1979).

PATTERN PERCEPTION

Pattern perception improves as children mature in the preschool years. Gibson (1969) suggests this improvement occurs as children develop more efficient and systematic abilities to extract information from visual events. Studies also show that with practice, pattern perception does become more efficient, which allows children to compare more features in a given time, as well as more systematic, which allows children to move from a random approach to a systematic, pair-by-pair comparison (Rosinski, 1977; Von Mickwitz, 1973).

Children could not learn to read if they did not have the ability to compare patterns and notice their similarities and differences. During the preschool years,

A child's ability to perceive similarities and differences in patterns is critical in the process of learning to read and write.

the ability to discriminate among patterns improves, and the stage is set for learning to read and to take part in other school work (see Spotlight 8.2).

FUNDAMENTALS OF READING AND WRITING

Five-year-old Scotty runs to meet his mother at the end of the day. He has had many experiences at nursery school today. He manipulated objects at the woodworking table and in the art, music, and block centers. He dug in the sand and climbed a tree. Pretending to be a firefighter with two playmates and later dictating a story about firefighters to the teacher was great fun. He also listened to stories and looked at books. Scotty's mother was pleased he enjoyed his preschool experiences because she knew these activities would prepare him to eventually read and write.

But Nicky's mother held a different attitude. During a parent-teacher conference with Mary Hopkins, she commented: "Nicky loves school, but I'm concerned. He's already five years old and he just plays all day! I want him to learn something—especially to read and write! Why don't you sit these children down and teach them to read and write?"

During the preschool years, young children develop the fundamentals that prepare them for reading and writing. Whatever the activity—art, science, outdoor play, field trips, lunch, building, or dramatic play—parents and teachers can use it as an opportunity to help children develop the fundamental abilities that underlie reading and writing skills.

Oral Language Usage.   Children must be able to use oral language and feel that it is important to communicate if they are to find reading and writing satisfying (Mattingly, 1979; Nurss, 1980). Games and other forms of play provide opportunities for children to use oral language as an aid to beginning reading and writing.

Listening Skills.   "Listening skills are basic in learning to read and should be developed early as children lose the ability to distinguish sounds as they grow older" (DeChant, 1970, p. 127). Listening to stories and records, and games such as "Simon says" and "hot and cold" (which require differentiated listening) can help a child develop such skills.

Remembering in Sequence.   Children should be encouraged to remember in sequence (Jensen and Hanson, 1980). Having children talk about their day's activities can help, as can leading them through a series of pictures of a familiar activity or asking them to name the people who live in the houses on their block.

Left-to-Right Eye Movement.   Children should have some practice in developing eye movement from left to right since individual words and the placement of words on the page proceed in this direction (Jensen and Hanson, 1980). Songs and games that emphasize left and right give children such practice. And running a finger across the page under the words while reading to a child not only accustoms the child to the left-to-right pattern but associates such movement with reading.

Games that call for children to know their left from their right provide practice in skills they will need for reading.

"Reading is FUNdamental," says the slogan of an organization aimed at getting children "into" books. Allowing even very young children to select books and to help tell the story by "reading" the pictures can go a long way toward making books—and reading—a pleasurable part of growing up.

Scotty and his Mom are driving across town. When they stop for a light, Scotty suddenly yells, "Look Mom! There's McDonald's!" Three-year-old Scotty has taken his first step in learning to read.

Learning to read begins long before children reach kindergarten or first grade. The process begins the first time children make sense of print (Smith, 1979). Before five years of age, most children growing up in a literate culture naturally become aware that certain printed symbols have special meaning (Clay, 1977). They can read signs on fast food restaurants and department stores; brand names of favorite cereals, soft drinks, clothing, toys and cars; traffic signs, exit signs, and signs on restroom doors. Children naturally learn to read all kinds of things that have meaning for them (Goodman, 1976).

Pushing children to read is not advisable. They will begin to read when they are ready. Some children need more time than others. Just as children learn to talk when they are ready to communicate and to interact with other people, they will learn to read when reading becomes important. Some children just take longer to discover that reading is important for them. Adults can help children learn to read through the same natural process used in learning to talk (Goodman, 1976; Lundsteen, 1977).

Making use of the wealth of printed material that surrounds us will help children learn to read. It is important that both children and parents become aware of all the things that can be read in everyday situations. Questions that call attention to the meaning and function of print in the environment help to encourage readiness for reading: "What do you think that sign says?" "Why do we have signs on street corners? On doors? In stores?"

Children need to be read to regularly. Enjoying books and hearing others read books to them help youngsters better comprehend stories when they too become readers (Chomsky, 1972). Children should be allowed to choose from a wide selection of story and picture books that interest them.

Auditory Discrimination. Children must hear differences before they can visualize them or speak, read, and write (DeChant, 1970). Stories and fingerplays with rhymes and identifying familiar sounds on a tape recorder can help children learn to make such discriminations.

Recognition of Beginning Sounds. When reading, children must recognize the beginning sounds of words. Activities that emphasize such sounds include nursery rhymes and game books (Dr. Seuss books, for example). Guessing games also link sounds with objects. For example, "I am thinking of something in the kitchen that is red and white. I wear it when I cook and it begins with an "a" sound. What is it?"

Visual Discrimination. Visual discrimination of letters and words is necessary for reading and writing (Jensen and Hanson, 1980). According to DeChant (1970, p. 184), "a child must be able to discern and verbalize similarities and differences in the form of objects, pictures, words, and geometric forms before he can read effectively." Sorting objects according to particular visual clues and playing card games such as pairs and fish improve visual discrimination.

Children can be encouraged to apply what they know about oral language to the process of learning to read. It is helpful to use books with natural-sounding language, not the stilted "Look, look. See Bob go" variety found in dated pre-primers. Research has shown that such language, intended to make reading easier for children, actually makes learning to read more difficult (Goodman, 1967; Smith, 1979). Children cannot predict the order of such language and so cannot use what they have learned about oral language in learning to read.

Choosing books with predictable, repetitive sections is helpful—for example, *The Three Little Pigs, The Three Billy Goats Gruff,* or *Chicken Little.* When reading aloud, adults can pause before a predictable word, phrase, or section. Children can supply the missing parts or "read" whole sections after the book has been read aloud a few times.

Children can be made aware of the need they have for reading when the written language is used in natural, helpful ways. Older siblings can write letters for preschoolers to family or friends who will respond. Adults can read aloud simple directions for making something, cooking a favorite treat, or following clues for a treasure hunt.

It is important to use children's language as a part of the early reading experience. Children learn the relationship between spoken and written language when they dictate stories or experiences about things that interest them. The dictation can be written on charts or in small, personal books that youngsters can illustrate and then share with others.

In summary, children can learn to read as naturally as they learn to talk when they are provided with a rich, literate environment where reading is meaningful and enjoyable.

"Learning to Read as a Natural Process" by Dr. Gail M. Huffman, Associate Professor of Human Development and Learning, University of North Carolina, Charlotte. Reprinted by permission.

Letter Discrimination. Discrimination of the letters of the alphabet is an indicator of a child's readiness for reading and writing. Being able to recognize letter names is an important predictor of first-grade reading achievement (Silberberg, et al., 1968). As Nicky watches his teacher print his name on his latest art masterpiece, he is learning about letters. So is Kim as she looks from her name tag to that of her classmate's.

PERCEPTION AND OTHER AREAS OF DEVELOPMENT

It is important to remember that perception develops not in isolation but in interaction with other processes such as cognitive development, growth in language, and motivation. For example, if four-year-olds say aloud the names of figures, they can remember them better (Yussen and Santwik, 1974). And when children are interested and motivated, they will spend more time paying attention. Scotty was particularly fascinated with dinosaurs and spent long periods of time painting and modeling clay dinosaurs and pestering teachers to read about them "just one more time!"

Summary

1. During early childhood, growth in weight and height continues to slow down and body proportions more closely resemble those of adults. Refinements in the nervous system and development of the brain, bones, muscles, teeth, and other body systems continue.

2. Gross-motor skills such as running, jumping, climbing, balancing, kicking, and throwing develop as children naturally participate in these activities. Improved eye-hand coordination permits fine-motor skills such as buttoning, unbuttoning, zipping, turning knobs, and cutting with scissors.

3. The incidence of child abuse and neglect is widespread—ranging from physical and sexual assault to neglect and failure to provide protection. Abuse results in problems in the physical, cognitive, social and emotional development of the child. Contributing factors are the child's unique characteristics, family background, and the social and physical environment in which the child has been reared.

4. Preschool children make strides in dressing and feeding themselves when parents provide encouragement and guidance. It is important that mealtime be nutritious and pleasant, and that it provide learning experiences for the preschool child.

5. Perceptual abilities improve during early childhood. Attention span lengthens and scanning, part-whole discrimination, and pattern perception are refined. But the preschooler still has trouble shutting out irrelevant information and discriminating letters of the alphabet.

6. Fundamentals of reading and writing include oral language, listening, memory, left-to-right eye movement, auditory discrimination, discrimination of beginning sounds, visual discrimination, and letter discrimination. Children acquire these skills through their everyday interactions with the world around them and particularly through their games.

7. Perception develops not in isolation but in interaction with other processes such as cognitive development, growth in language, and motivation.

Empathetic Activities

- What feelings did you have as you read The Case of the Parents' Day Picnic? What feelings do you think Nicky had? What about Mary Hopkins and Susan Abel?

- What feelings did you have as you read The Abuse of Rebecca Holmes? What feelings do you think Rebecca had? Her mother and father? Sergeant Travis?

- What activities would you provide preschoolers to help them develop eye-hand coordination and a perceptual foundation for reading and writing?

- Visit a nursery school. Observe groups of three- four- and five-year-olds playing outside and inside.

- Make a list of the gross-motor abilities found at each age level.
- Make a list of the fine-motor abilities found at each age level.
- Make a list of the activities and types of equipment used by each age group.
- Compare your lists with Fig. 8.1.
- Use information from this chapter to discuss the following:
  - What factors might be associated with Nicky's short attention span and his fast pace?
  - What factors might be associated with Rebecca Holmes' physical size and motor abilities and what she will be like as an adult?
- In what ways do the physical, cognitive, social, and emotional aspects of development interact to affect abused children as a whole? How does a child's whole system contribute to child abuse (for example, unique characteristics of children, family system, and social and physical environment)?
- What are some specific ways in which learning to read requires the development of the *Whole Child*?
- How do Nicky's active physical-motor behavior, nutritional habits, and short attention span affect his relationships with his preschool teachers and classmates?

Related Readings

Flinchum, Betty M. *Motor development in early childhood: A guide for movement education with ages 2 to 6.* St. Louis: C. V. Mosby, 1975. Information about movement activity and motor development emphasizing teaching strategies and learning activities. Easy reading.

Languis, Marlin, Sanders, Tobie, and Tipps, Steven. *Brain and learning: Directions in early childhood education.* Washington, D.C.: National Association for the Education of Young Children, 1980. An excellent and concise book on the growth of the brain and learning during early childhood. Systems approach to implications for teaching preschool children on the basis of brain research.

McWilliams, Margaret. *Nutrition for the growing years,* 3rd ed. New York: Wiley, 1980. Information concerning nutrition requirements along with many practical suggestions for making eating times a positive learning experience. Covers prenatal development through adolescence. Easy reading.

Skinner, Louise. *Motor development in the preschool years.* Springfield, Ill.: Charles C. Thomas, 1979. Easily read guide for parents and teachers. Lists motor abilities every six months from two to five years. Many activities for enhancing motor development.

Walk, Richard D. *Perceptual development.* Monterey, Calif.: Brooks/Cole, 1981. An in-depth look at the development of the senses from infancy to older adulthood. The most comprehensive and up-to-date coverage we've found.

Williams, Gertrude, and Money, John. *Traumatic abuse and neglect of children.* Baltimore: Johns Hopkins University, 1980. An encyclopedia of facts and case studies on abused and neglected children and their families.

9 Early Childhood: Cognitive and Language Development

The Case of Brad's Rainbow Discovery

Breathless and flushed, four-year-old Brad rushed into the house to find Doreen, who was busily setting the dinner table. "There's a rainbow in the sky!" he yelled. Brad had seen pictures of rainbows but had never seen a real one before. Doreen encouraged Brad's excitement: "Wow! Help me finish here and then show it to me!" Doreen had set everybody's place but her own. Encouraging Brad to be her helper, she faced him across the table. Then she asked Brad to reach across the table and put her fork and spoon on her place mat. Doreen was both surprised and amused when Brad arranged the utensils as if *he* would be using them—facing himself instead of his mother.

When they had finished setting the table, Brad took his mother's hand and pulled her next door to his friend's house, where he had "discovered" the rainbow. When they arrived at the right spot, Brad's little finger pointed skyward, "See, there it is!"

"What a beautiful rainbow," Doreen said, adding with a smile, "Did you know there's a pot of gold at the end of the rainbow?" Brad's eyes widened. "Can we find it?" he asked. But before his mother could answer, Brad's thoughts jumped to something else: "Let's bring Daddy and show him too!" he urged.

Cognitive Development

It seems only yesterday that breathless, excited preschooler Brad was just a bundle of reflexes. In only two years, Baby Brad had turned into curious, problem-solving Toddler Brad. Remember how Brad impressed his mother by using symbolic thought to solve the "stubborn gate" problem without hesitation (see Chapter 6)? This shift from motor activity to symbolic activity marks the beginning of the **preoperational period**—the second period of cognitive development (age two to seven years) described by Piaget, in which symbolic representation characterizes the child's thought.

PREOPERATIONAL THOUGHT

As a toddler, Brad had begun to use symbols for thinking, but he still couldn't carry out an entire process in his head. We could see this when he used sensori-motor actions like swaying from side to side to help him figure out the stubborn gate problem. During the preoperational period representations become more internalized and such sensorimotor behaviors no longer accompany cognitive solutions. Brad starts thinking through problems—planning and remembering. Instead of swaying his entire body from side to side, he might only move his arm. With time, we might see the signs of sensorimotor action through the slight movement of Brad's tiny fingers. In fact, some adults still move their fingers slightly when adding! Eventually, as sensorimotor actions become more internalized into

Preschool children sometimes use traces of sensorimotor action—such as sticking their tongues out—to help them concentrate on challenging motor and cognitive tasks.

mental images, no significant movement can be observed. This is a sign that the symbolic function has matured.

As Brad moves into early childhood, we can observe more and more instances of symbolic thought. No longer must preoperational children see actual objects to think about them or compare them with other things. Symbolic thought allows children to think and make comparisons in their minds. Preoperational children can use symbols and concepts to aid them in their thinking. Spoken words can be used to represent objects or people not present. For example, Brad can think about and tell others about the rainbow he discovered without having to see the rainbow each time he refers to it. And as we saw in Chapter 6, children often imitate the behaviors of their parents and other adults in their play. This ability to reproduce mental images at a later time also makes it possible for preschool children to imagine themselves in many different roles during pretend play.

CHARACTERISTICS OF PREOPERATIONAL CHILDREN

Although preoperational children have made many cognitive advances, they still have not achieved adult-like, logical thought, as you can see from The Case of Brad's Rainbow Discovery. Egocentrism, centration, inability to follow transformations, and irreversible thought are characteristics of preoperational thinking, identified by Piaget, that prevent preschoolers from thinking logically.

Egocentrism.   We said earlier that toddlers are egocentric because they view the world of events and objects as revolving around themselves. But preschoolers are egocentric, too. Preoperational children don't realize that there are many points of view different from their own. And as a rule, they cannot see things from another person's point of view, which explains why Brad arranged his mother's placemat for himself instead of for her. He believes that everyone thinks the same things and in the same way he does. Like all preoperational children, Brad's egocentrism characterizes his way of thinking and his interpersonal relationships. Brad's mother noticed that he talked to himself while others were around. Piaget (1952a) called this **egocentric speech**—talking aloud to oneself without attempting to convey a message to anyone. Sometimes preoperational children will initiate self-centered conversations by telling about an event from the middle instead of from the beginning—as if the listener's mind centered on the same thoughts as theirs.

Centration.   Egocentrism causes **centration**—Piaget's term for the tendency of preoperational children to center their attention on just one dimension of an object or event, instead of looking at all dimensions simultaneously. Doreen had read about the simple experiments Piaget used to observe obstacles to logical thinking in preoperational children. To test this theory, Doreen put two equal-length rows of six buttons in front of four-year-old Brad (see Fig. 9.1). Brad agreed that both rows had the same number of buttons. But when his mother spaced the buttons in the bottom row farther apart, he told her there were more buttons in that row. Despite his mother's attempts to logically explain that nothing had been added or taken away, Brad insisted on his same answer every time. Brad focused or centered on only one aspect of the problem—the *length* of the rows, while ignoring the more important dimension—the *number* of buttons.

Not only did Brad center on length, but he also centered on self in interpersonal relationships. As far as Brad was concerned, his answer was the only possible, correct answer. Because it never occurred to him he might be wrong, he never questoned his self-centered thoughts—even when his mother tried to convince him otherwise. To show his mother the rainbow, Brad centered on the exact, same spot where he first saw it. Thinking others could see the rainbow only if they stood where he stood, Brad took his mother next door where he first discovered it. He didn't realize he could see the same rainbow from inside his house, from his backyard, or even from Grandma Bonnie's house a mile away.

Unknowingly, Brad's mother was observing everyday instances of centration when she wrote about Brad's ''peculiar'' eating habits:

October 6: During snack- and mealtime, Brad's eating has become peculiar. He asks that his food be broken apart. Yesterday during afternoon snack, I gave him a cracker and some juice. But he insisted on breaking his cracker into small pieces before eating it. And instead of his usual short, wide cup for juice, Brad asked for a tall glass. Nowadays, when I serve hot dogs, I have to go through a ritual of cutting his hot dog in half. Otherwise, he whimpers and refuses to eat at all!

Brad is demonstrating centration in each of these instances. He thinks if his cracker and hot dog are broken up, he'll have more to eat. In making these demands, he centers on the parts or pieces instead of the wholes of the food. And he thinks a tall, slender glass holds more juice than his short, wide cup—even though he sees his mother pour the same amount of juice directly from the short container into the tall one. He gets sidetracked by the height of the juice in the container, losing sight of the container's thinner width. In each of these situations, Brad centrates on one dimension of what he sees. Bound by his perception, he takes in only limited parts of his visual field. So he makes judgments on how things *appear* to be—not on how they actually *are*. To him three pieces of a cracker *look like* and therefore *are* more than the whole cracker. Two halves of a hot dog are more than a whole hot dog. And a tall glass holds more to drink than a shorter but wider cup.

Inability to Follow Transformations. Preoperational children cannot follow **transformations**—the process in which one state is changed to another. They don't focus on the process when something is transformed from an original state to a final state. Instead, they can only produce correct mental images of static situations. So they concentrate on the state—or end result—not the transformation (Ginsburg and Opper, 1979). Piaget uses the example of a child watching a motion picture. The child sees each frame of a motion picture as a separate and unrelated picture. But an adult sees a continuous, related story.

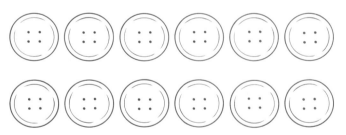

9.1A   When the buttons are spaced equally, Brad agrees that both rows have the same number of buttons.

Figure 9.1
Conservation

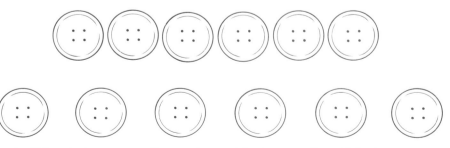

9.1B   When the bottom row of buttons is spaced further apart, Brad thinks there are more buttons in that row.

In the button experiment, Brad didn't focus on the transformation of the buttons as they were spread apart. Instead, he observed the widely spaced pattern of buttons as if it was independent of the original, closely spaced pattern of buttons. Because of his inability to focus on the transformation, Brad made judgments based on perception—what things looked like. At that moment in time, the buttons in the bottom row looked like more, so they must be more.

Perhaps now you can understand better why Toddler Noah was terrified when his mother came home with a new hairdo (see Chapter 7). Noah could not be sure his mother was the same person because he fixed his attention on two different states (long, straight-haired woman and short, curly-haired woman)—not on the transformation that caused these changes.

Irreversible Thought. When thought is reversible, children can backtrack their line of reasoning to where they started. Or they can reverse a logical operation in their mind. But preoperational children have **irreversible thought** and are unable to reverse their thinking. Because preoperational children cannot attend to processes, as illustrated by the button experiment, they cannot *reverse* the process of moving the buttons apart in their mind. The button experiment was impossible

Gray, 4 legs, moves, long tail. Pretty doggie

Preoperational children have made great strides cognitively, but they are still apt to focus on the wrong elements in a situation and so draw erroneous conclusions.

for Brad to solve because he could not reverse or think backwards. In other words, he could not mentally envision the widely spaced buttons being put closely together as they were to begin with.

In discussing Piaget's notion of preoperational thought, Wadsworth (1979) points out:

> Piaget's concepts of egocentricism, centration, transformation, and reversibility are closely related. Early preoperational thought is dominated by the presence or absence of each of them. As cognitive development proceeds, these characteristics gradually subside in unison. A deterioration in egocentricism permits (requires) the child to decenter more and attend to simple transformations. All this in turn helps the child in his construction of reversibility. (p. 82–83)

REASONING AND CONCEPT FORMATION OF PREOPERATIONAL CHILDREN

As you can see, the characteristics of egocentrism, centration, inability to follow transformations, and irreversible thought are roadblocks to logical thought. Although these roadblocks are a necessary step in the formation of logical concepts, they cause preoperational children to think in a qualitatively different way from adults. Piaget noted that these differences can be observed in the way preschoolers reason about the world around them and in the way they solve everyday problems.

Transductive Reasoning. Logical thought is based on two types of reasoning: *deductive* and *inductive*. **Deductive reasoning** moves from the general to the particular. For example, "All humans have eyes. I am a human. Therefore, I have eyes." **Inductive reasoning** moves from the specific to the general. Suppose for instance that you are a Martian and have just landed on Earth. You notice that unlike yourself, every Earthling you meet has two round circles in their heads called eyes. So you conclude that all Earthlings have eyes.

According to Piaget, preoperational thought is somewhere in between deductive and inductive reasoning and is called **transductive reasoning**—reasoning from the particular to the particular, without reference to the general (Ginsburg and Opper, 1979). In transductive reasoning, children associate; they think that two unrelated events are connected just because they occur at the same time. The result is often illogical reasoning. For example, Brad thought the rainbow could be seen only from one spot—from where he originally discovered it. In this case, Brad's thoughts associated standing in the right spot next door (the first particular) with seeing the rainbow (the second particular). So Brad concluded that in order to see the rainbow, he had to go next door—an illogical conclusion.

Conservation. Experiments like the one with the buttons were developed by Piaget and are called conservation problems. **Conservation** is the understanding that basic properties of objects (such as mass, number, quantity, area, etc.) stay the same (are conserved) even though their outward appearance changes. Preoperational children do not show the ability to conserve. As an illustration, Brad could not conserve the number of buttons in the experiment. His insistence that the widely spaced row of buttons contained more buttons indicated that he could hold one dimension constant (conserve the original number of six buttons) in the midst of changes in the length of rows. Instead, he centered his attention on the appearance of the lengthened row. Once Brad becomes a conserver, he will understand that when nothing has been added or taken away, outward changes such as wide or narrow spacing do not increase or decrease the number of buttons. As a conserver he will have developed new schemes that will enable him to decenter his perceptions, attend to transformations, and reverse his thinking to the original spacing of the buttons. While children begin to grasp the concept of conservation at this age, they do not master it until the concrete operational period (ages seven to eleven).

One-to-One Correspondence.   What if Brad's mother modified the button experiment a little bit? Suppose she presented Brad with a row of six buttons, then set up a pile of six more buttons and asked Brad to make a row equal to hers. What do you think would happen? Probably, Brad would succeed in making a row the same length. But he would use only four or five buttons, instead of six. And he wouldn't use **one-to-one correspondence**—the ability to match items one

The inability of preoperational children to put objects in sequential order except by trial and error is evident in this young girl's attempts to reassemble a nest of boxes.

to one, with those of a model. According to Piaget (1967), if there is one-to-one correspondence with four- or five-year-olds, it is accidental—not deliberate. School children master this concept as they learn to think logically.

Seriation.   **Seriation** is the ability to order objects in a sequence or series along some dimension. Given a pile of different-length sticks, children four or five years old can pick out the largest and smallest stick from the pile (Piaget, 1952b). But suppose they are shown ten sticks, ordered by length from smallest to largest. Then the series is demolished, and they are asked to reorder the sticks from smallest to largest. Four-year-old children couldn't do it. That's because preoperational children cannot see relationships between more than two elements at a time, and they do not have the schemes to mentally order events in a series. "They may add a long one and a short one, another long and short one, and so forth; arrangements may be entirely random." (Wadsworth, 1978, p. 60). Five- and six-year-old children would also have difficulty reconstructing the series from memory. Although they are sometimes able to seriate the sticks by trial and error, their approach is not systematic. But after age seven, concrete operational children acquire the necessary schemes to correctly solve the seriation problem. Seven-year-olds have no difficulty seeking out and choosing the smallest stick from the pile, then the next smallest, and so forth (Wadsworth, 1978). Without using trial and error, they can correctly arrange the ten sticks from smallest to largest, in a systematic and coordinated way (see Fig. 9.2).

Classification

It was Christmas time! Brad and his father were making popcorn strands for their Christmas tree. Altogether they popped three bags of popcorn for the occasion. They colored two bags red and one bag green. Brad poured all the popcorn pieces into a large cardboard box to cool. Once the tree was put in place, Brad helped separate the colored popcorn by putting all the red pieces in one bowl and all the green pieces in another bowl. Brad's behavior showed that he understood the classification "red" and "green." Four-year-olds like Brad can easily make such simple **classifications** (Piaget, 1952b)—grouping objects into categories based on some common characteristic such as color or shape.

Figure 9.2

Seriation. Children between ages four and six have difficulty reconstructing a series from memory. But after age seven, they acquire the necessary schemes to correctly solve the seriation problem.

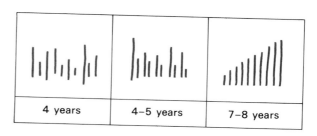

| 4 years | 4–5 years | 7–8 years |

Once the classes of all the popcorn were clear, Brad's father asked him: "Which would make a longer strand for the Christmas tree, all the popcorn pieces or the red pieces?" Brad answered, "The red pieces, because there are more red pieces than green pieces." Brad was unable to think of the strands as being both popcorn (the whole) and colored pieces (part of the whole) at the same time.

Class Inclusion.   In Chapter 8, you saw that preoperational children do not think of parts and wholes at the same time. This is partly because they cannot take into account two kinds of classes at once. And they cannot perform the process of **class inclusion**—they do not realize that the sum of the subclasses equals the whole class (red pieces + green pieces = popcorn). As happens in the conservation problems, preoperational children *center* on only one dimension (color) and ignore the common characteristic of *popcorn*, which all the colored pieces share.

Judgments of Age, Time, and Distance

AGE.   Preoperational children have learned that a person's age and size are somehow related. But Brad has difficulty judging someone's age. Like all preoperational children, his perceptual orientation to life causes him to *center* on a person's size. So the larger a person is, the older that person is. These errors diminish with the onset of the concrete operational period, when children consider factors in addition to size in judging age (Kratochwill and Goldman, 1973).

TIME AND DISTANCE.   When Grandma Bonnie called, Brad excitedly told her about the rainbow he saw "yesterday." Simple time concepts such as "today" and "yesterday" are beginning to be understood by preoperational children. But the concept of time is not fully mastered until much later. For example, children do not understand the relationship between time and speed until they are ten or eleven (Piaget and Inhelder, 1969). Instead, they equate time with distance because distance can be seen—it is more tangible than speed. Brad's mother noted this inability in his baby book:

January 5: We had a wonderful ski weekend in the mountains! On our first day on the slopes, Brad and I boarded the scenic tram to the top of the mountain. Brad's father took the tram for skiers, running parallel to the scenic tram with the same destination. Seeing that both trams covered the same distance, Brad figured it would take the same time for each tram to reach the top of the mountain. He did not consider that the ski tram moved faster than the scenic tram. So he was confused when he saw his father waiting for him at the top.

From his mother's description, we can tell that Brad's use of visual cues caused him to make errors in judgment of time. He *centered* on the fact that the trams covered equal distances. But he did not take into account an important second dimension—the speed of the tram.

Animism.   Preoperational children have difficulty telling the difference between reality and fantasy. You will remember that Brad took his mother seriously when she suggested that there was a pot of gold at the end of the rainbow.

Preoperational thinking is also characterized by what Piaget called **animism**—attributing life or human qualities to nonhuman objects or animals. For instance, Brad believes that snowmen can dance and sing and that teddy bears can talk. Animism explains why young children are charmed by animated characters such as Mickey Mouse and Big Bird. That's why they believe in the Easter Bunny and the Tooth Fairy. But such beliefs also have their drawbacks. Animism is most likely to occur with things that move, radiate heat, or make noise—that's why children might fear that cars or vacuum cleaners will gobble them up. A young child viewing horror films and violent television shows may not be able to separate what is real from what isn't. Demons, witches, and ghosts can also produce very real and serious fears. Again, we can see the relationship between developing thought and emotions. For this reason, it is important for parents to monitor the television viewing and movie going of their youngsters. Animism slowly fades as children enter middle childhood.

Animism: This child really believes that once he and his father place a hat on their snowman, it will dance and sing.

Language Development

As we discussed in Chapter 6, children do not merely parrot what they hear or rely solely on parental corrections and reinforcements to learn language. Instead, they construct sentences according to rules that they extract from the language they hear. Although 90 percent of the job of learning speech and language skills is complete by early childhood (Leitch, 1977), many advances still occur in the young child's language development. Vocabulary and sentence length continue to increase. But most language advances involve developing, discarding, and refining language rules as the use of complex grammatical rules increases.

VOCABULARY GROWTH AND SENTENCE LENGTH

Vocabulary continues to grow rapidly (see Fig. 9.3), jumping from an average of 1500 words at four years of age to over 2000 by age five (Leitch, 1977; Lenneberg,

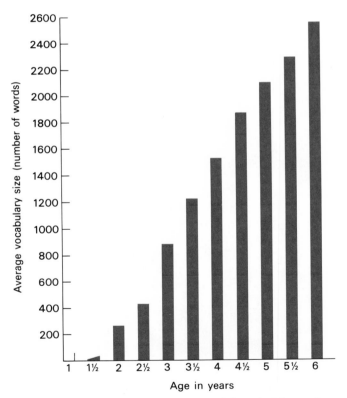

Figure 9.3 **Vocabulary growth.** (Adapted from Smith, 1926).

1967). But children are still a long way from the average adult vocabulary of 12,000 to 13,000 words (Leitch, 1977).

Children learn concrete word meanings before abstract ones (Anglin, 1970). So words such as *table* appear first, and words such as *happy* emerge by age five. Preschool children's sentences are longer, too, and their use of different parts of speech increases (Brown and Hanlon, 1970). The two-year-old's use of single nouns gives way to noun phrases, serving the same grammatical functions but expressing richer meanings. In other words, two-year-olds will speak of dog, but three- and four-year-olds expand this to *that big dog* or *Mrs. Brown's dog* or *the dog with the wiggly tail* (deVilliers and deVilliers, 1978). Listeners have a much easier time interpreting the speech of a four-year-old than a two-year-old.

GRAMMATICAL RULES

To really understand preschool children's language advances, you must also look at their increasing understanding of syntax and grammatical rules as they move from toddlerhood into early childhood. It will be helpful to refer to Table 9.1 on page 286 throughout the following discussion of language development.

Three-year-old Eve can speak in complete sentences. This is quite an advance over her cooing and babbling in infancy and the holophrases, telegraphic speech, and beginning questions she asked during toddlerhood. But like most children her age, Eve's understanding of sentence structure is limited to simple declarative sentences in which the actor appears before the action and the object of the action appears after the action—actor-action-object (Bellugi, 1970). So if she hears *The truck bumped the car,* she believes the truck crashed into the car. But three- and four-year-olds do not understand *passive sentence structure,* where the actor-action-object relation is reversed. They are not sensitive to the use of words like *by* or *was,* which signal the passive (deVilliers and deVilliers, 1978). Upon hearing a passive sentence like *The truck was bumped by the car,* Eve treats it as identical in meaning to the first, active sentence, *The truck bumped the car.* Word order, not the inflection of the passive voice, governs children's understanding at this age.

Correctly forming both questions and negatives is difficult for preschool children. Eve has trouble switching the word order of subject and verb to form questions. And it is difficult for her to insert negatives in the right place. But by the end of early childhood, she learns to apply complex grammatical rules and to speak in more complicated sentence forms.

By five years of age, Eve can understand passive sentences (Potts et al., 1979) and she has learned to ask questions by switching the word order of subject and verb. She can also use future tenses and adult-like speech containing *embedded sentences*—one sentence within another. Conjunctions and prepositions are common among preschoolers (Brown, 1973). They also use clauses joined by *because,*

Table 9.1
Overview of Language Development from Infancy Through Early Childhood

AGE	LANGUAGE SKILL	EXAMPLES
2–3 months	Through *cooing*, infants experiment with vowel sounds.	"e-e-e" or "o-o-o"
6–10 months	Infants *babble*—making consonant sounds and combinations of consonant and vowel sounds.	"ga-ga-ga-goo"
	By the end of the first year children say their first word.	"papa"
12 months	Single words or *holophrases* are used to convey the meaning of an entire sentence.	"Hurt"
18 months–2 years	*Telegraphic speech* or two-word combinations serve as sentences.	"Eve go!" "Airplane by"
	2-year-olds use declarative sentences with a rising tone to ask a question. The subject-verb-object order is not reversed.	"Daddy home?"
	Wh-questions—questions that begin with *what, why, where, who, when*—appear, with subject and verb order firmly held in place.	"Where Daddy is?"
3 years	Helping verbs and negative contractions are blended together. Sometimes emphasis on forming negations results in the addition of extra negatives.	"I don't want more cookie." "I don't never want no more cake!"
	Sentences become longer and ideas more complex. But the subject and verb order in questions remains unswitched.	"When the clowns will come?" "Why he can't go?"
	Children have difficulty understanding passive sentences because for them word order governs meaning.	"The cart is pulled by the horse."
4–5 years	Reversing order of subject and verb appears and questions sound more adult-like. The future tense is also used.	"When will the clowns come?"
	More complex sentence structures, such as *embedded sentences*, are formed.	"Carlos sang what I like to hear."
4–5 years	Clauses, conjunctions, and prepositions are used to join simple sentences.	"I like the shirt because it is red." "John went shopping and bought a toy."
	Tag questions appear, indicating knowledge of more complex grammatical rules.	"The cake is finished, isn't it?"

and, or *but.* But conditional clauses (joined by *if* and *so*) do not appear until early elementary school (Pflaum, 1974).

Tag Questions.   Another sign that more complex grammatical rules are being applied is the appearance of *tag questions*—requests for a confirmation, which usually appear at the end of a statement. For example, Bellugi (1970) described four-and-a-half-year-old Adam's use of tag questions in which Adam supplied the correct pronoun to match the subject of each sentence:

"The *man's* not bad, is *he?*"

"*Me* and *Jim* are working, aren't *we?*"

Adam was also able to copy the helping verb in the sentence or use a form of do:

"He *can* say Adam, *can't* he?"

"Adam winned, *didn't* he?"

As you can see, the form of the tag is determined by the syntax of the statement it follows. According to Bellugi, "The grammatical processes that form tag

THE FAMILY CIRCUS®   **By Bil Keane**

"Grandma said I'm very nautical today and I was tryin' to be good!"

Sometimes preschool children don't understand the meaning of adult words.

questions are complex and rest on basic operations of English: the rules for changing nouns to pronouns, for making assertions, negating and questioning'' (p. 66). Because children produce many tag questions they've never heard before, Bellugi suggests that this is further evidence that they derive rules from language they hear.

Overgeneralization.   ''Scotty has the mostest!'' seven-year-old Eve complained when her playmate was given more clay than she was. Her mother responded. ''Scotty has the *most,* Eve. There is no such word as mostest.'' ''But there is biggest . . . tallest . . . smallest . . .'' Eve replied. ''Why can't there be mostest?''

Eve was trying to make the English language more regular than it is. Four-and-a-half- to five-year-old children have developed the major grammatical rules of their native language. But they continue to *overgeneralize* (see Chapter 6) as they slowly learn exceptions to grammatical rules. Three- and four-year-olds would say *eated* or *goed.* But five- and six-year-olds who have learned the irregular past tense form are just as likely to say *ated* or *wented* as *eated* or *goed* (Kuczaj, 1978). Older children are more concerned with using past tense than with avoiding the past tense repetition. Carol Chomsky also found that ten-year-olds showed confusion over the subject in more complicated sentences like ''John asked Bill what to do.'' She concluded that an understanding of more difficult sentence structures continues to develop throughout the elementary school years (Chomsky, 1969).

THE DEVELOPMENT OF SOCIAL SPEECH

Another important milestone in children's language use is the development of **social speech**—speech in which an attempt is made to communicate. Based on his observations of children's conversations, Piaget (1952a) contrasted *social speech* with *egocentric speech,* which is not communicative. For the most part, preoperational children's speech is egocentric, but it gradually becomes more social at the beginning of the concrete operational period. Brad's mother notes that Brad sometimes carries on long conversations with himself, usually when others are nearby. But he makes no effort to involve those around him in his conversations, nor does he try to communicate information to them. Piaget called children's lengthy conversations with themselves in the presence of others *collective monologues.* He believed language development during the preoperational period is ''a gradual transition from egocentric speech characterized by *collective monologue* to socialized intercommunicative speech'' (Wadsworth, 1979, p. 72).

Vygotsky believed egocentric speech directs childrens' thoughts and actions, helping them to perform tasks before they can use language silently to themselves as adults do (Zivin, 1979). For example, Brad might say, ''Me close gate'' as he attempts to do so.'' Piaget suggested that egocentric speech disappears at six or seven years of age. But Vygotsky argues that it is just taken inward. Here it is fused with thought and transformed into what he calls **inner speech**—thinking in word meanings or using language as a tool for reasoning (Dale, 1976). Inner speech serves the same purpose in adults as egocentric speech does in children. When thought and language fuse, the child attempting to open a gate guides his action silently through inner speech and no longer needs to guide action verbally by saying "Me close gate."

THE LANGUAGE ENVIRONMENT

Clearly, children learn language by figuring out rules and putting together sentences and phrases. Despite universal similarities in language development, differences occur because of varying language environments. Socioeconomic and racial groups can also influence language development, though there are problems with the research on these effects. Bilingualism can also affect language development (see also Spotlight 9.1).

Socioeconomic Class.   Socioeconomic class differences can affect language development. For example, children from middle-income families have larger vocabularies and use more complex sentences than children from low-income families. Some research suggests that middle-income level children have richer and more stimulating language experiences than children from poverty-income levels (Bee et al., 1969; Hess and Shipman, 1965). For example, middle-income mothers talk to their infants more and understand the importance of these interactions more than poverty-level mothers (Tulkin and Kagan, 1972). Middle-income mothers have also been described as more involved, more accepting, and less controlling of their children than lower-income mothers (Jay and Farran, 1981).

In his studies of speech patterns, British sociologist Basil Bernstein (1972) found that lower- and middle-class mothers use different verbal interaction patterns with their children. Lower class mothers are more likely to use a **restricted code**—a mode of speaking in which sentences tend to be short, grammatically simple, and concerned with the present. This simple language has little reference to cause, intent, feelings, or abstract ideas. In contrast, middle-class mothers tend to use an **elaborated code** in which sentences are long, grammatically complex, and precise. Cause and effect, intent, feelings, and abstract ideas are often referred to and are not tied to the present. Hess and Shipman (1965) illustrate the two codes by describing two mothers who are trying to quiet a noisy child while talking on the telephone. Low-income mother: "Be quiet." Middle-income mother: "Would you keep quiet a minute? I want to talk on the phone."

Elaborated language is thought to promote problem-solving abilities, communication skills, and the development of a flexible language—all important in managerial jobs and social situations in our society. Bernstein points out that low-income children can learn to use elaborated language when given the opportunity. And in fact, as the number and richness of verbal interactions increase, the low-income child's ability to solve problems by verbal means improves (Jay and Farran, 1981; Radin and Kamii, 1965).

❖ Spotlight 9.1: Bilingual Children

Kim and Carlos are *bilingual*, that is they understand and speak two languages. Kim is learning her native language of Chinese as well as English. Carlos can speak Spanish equally as well as he speaks English, and eventually he will learn to read both languages. There are many American children like Kim and Carlos who will become fluent in two languages. In 1970, for example, the Japanese, Chinese, Filipino, Vietnamese, Korean, Hawaiian, and Samoan population in the United States numbered over one and a half million, with the count steadily rising (Kitano, 1980). In 1980, Spanish-speaking Americans—primarily Mexicans, Puerto Ricans, and Cubans—became the largest minority group in the United States.

But bilingualism is not a new idea. Bilingualism as well as *multilingualism* (proficiency in more than two languages) have historically been the usual language patterns in the world. The existence of common national languages only began in the nineteenth century (Feitelson, 1979). Usually, two languages are welded together as bilingual children speak their first words and phrases (Garcia, 1980a). The sorting out of two separate languages begins at about age three (Albert and Obler, 1978). In a national study of bilingual children four, five, and six years old, Garcia (1980b) discovered that young children switch from one language to the other before acquiring two independent language systems.

Language switching used for emphasis and elaboration has been observed among three- and four-year-old bilingual Mexican-American children (Lindholm and Padilla, 1979) and eight-year-old Puerto Rican children (Zentella, 1978). But clear separation of two languages takes place at about age seven, at which time bilingual children can keep the two languages separate, yet maintain fluency in each (Albert and Obler, 1978).

Brain development is clearly reflected in the learning of two languages. For most people, the language center of the brain is located in the left cerebral hemisphere. But recent evidence indicates that among bilingual children, cerebral dominance for the first-learned language shifts from the left to right hemisphere as the second language is learned (Albert and Obler, 1978; Languis et al., 1980).

Garcia (1980a) summarized current findings on bilingual children as follows:

1. Acquisition of more than one language during early childhood is a documented phenomenon.

2. The acquisition of two languages can be parallel but need not be. One language may lag behind, surge ahead, or develop equally with the other language.

3. Bilingual language acquisition may very well result in the child's development of an interlanguage, incorporating the aspects . . . of both languages.

Black English.   **Black English** is a dialect spoken mostly by blacks living in low-income areas. A debate exists among language experts over whether this dialect is a bona fide language form or simply illiterate speech. Table 9.2 on page 292 presents many of the differences between Black English and Standard English. Potts and his associates (1979) noted that these differences begin between ages three and five as children put final touches on their language. Among white children, the use of auxiliary words increases with age and omissions decrease. In contrast, black children omit more auxiliary words—especially verbs such as *is*.

Some proponents of the **language-deficit hypothesis** argue that Black English is inferior or lacking some of the essential characteristics that exist in the language of middle-class white children (Deutsch, 1965).

4. Acquisition of two languages does not developmentally hamper the acquisition of either language. (p. 55–56)*

Nevertheless, children reared in homes where a foreign language such as Spanish, Chinese, or American-Indian predominates can face serious educational problems as they enter preschools and elementary schools where English is the language of instruction. For instance, one study reported that Asian-American children could distinguish forms, figures, letters, and numbers. But these children had difficulty matching verbal labels to letters and numbers in English (Kitano, 1980).

Research indicates that a bilingual experience in early childhood education does not necessarily retard cognitive or language development and may, in fact, foster cognitive flexibility (Garcia, 1980a). In an effort to help bilingual children truly master English and other language skills, many communities have established programs of **bilingual-bicultural education**, which incorporate the language and culture of the non–English-speaking child into the English-language and middle-class school curriculum. Bilingual-bicultural education programs aid children in learning basic academic skills, build cultural pride and identity and maintain cultural traditions by accepting the child's native tongue as a vehicle to learning.

This young Cuban refugee will have to learn to speak a second language, English, as one step in adjusting to his new life in the United States.

*Eugene E. Garcia. ''Bilingualism in early childhood. Research in review.'' Reprinted by permission from *Young Children,* vol. 35, November 4 (May, 1980) pp. 52–66. Copyright © 1980, National Association for the Education of Young Children, 1834 Connecticut Ave. N.W., Washington D.C. 20009.

In opposition to this theory are the advocates of the **language-different hypothesis.** They suggest that those using Black English are not deficient in language but merely use rules different from Standard English (Baratz and Baratz, 1970). Black ghetto English has been found to be just as complex, rich, and grammatical as standard middle-class English (Labov, 1970). Baratz (1973) presents a clear summary of this viewpoint:

Although one dialect may be chosen as the standard language, it is important to realize that this is an arbitrary, or at most, social decision which has nothing to do with that particular dialect's linguistic merits. That is to say, the dialect chosen as standard is no more highly structured, well formed, or grammatical than any of the other dialects. (p. 126)

Table 9.2
Differences in Syntax
Between Black and Standard English

BLACK NONSTANDARD ENGLISH	STANDARD ENGLISH
He goin'.	He is going.
John cousin.	John's cousin.
I got five cent.	I have five cents.
John he live in New York.	John lives in New York.
Yesterday he ain't had no money for the bus so he walk home.	Yesterday he didn't have any money for the bus so he walked home.
He run home.	He runs home.
She have a bicycle.	She has a bicycle.
I'm a go home.	I will go home.
I ask did he do it.	I asked if he did it.
It ain't no cat can't get in no coop nohow.	No man can get in a coop.
He ain't go.	He didn't go.
I want a apple.	I want an apple.
Us got to do it.	We have to do it.
He book.	His book.
He over to his friend house.	He is over at his friend's house.
He teach Francis Pool.	He teaches at Francis Pool.
He be here.	He is here all the time.
He been ate the chicken.	He ate the chicken a long time ago.
No, he don't.	No, he isn't.
He done been gone.	He had left.
He might could go.	He might go.
What it is?	What is it?
I drunk the milk.	I drank the milk.

"Language abilities of Black Americans, review of research" by J. C. Baratz. In K. Miller and R. Dreger, eds., *Comparative Studies of Blacks and Whites in the United States*. New York: Academic Press © 1973, p. 144. Used with permission.

Drawbacks in Research.   There are problems with the studies that have been conducted on socioeconomic class, Black English, and language development. First, many studies use measures such as number of vocabulary words but overlook other important factors such as language complexity and function. Second, most of the studies of black mother-child interactions were conducted in laboratories, school classrooms, or waiting rooms—unnatural settings that can distort research findings (Bronfenbrenner, 1979). According to Wyatt (1977), such settings create self-con-

Many aspects of preschoolers' play help children to develop their language skills.

sciousness for the low-income mother who is afraid her child might upset toys or other materials in a strange environment. Third, scholars challenging these studies argue that the language abilities of poverty-level children are judged by middle-class standards, which "sets them up" to fail. So as you can see, we must be careful when drawing conclusions about language differences based on socioeconomic class and racial dialects.

LANGUAGE DIFFICULTIES

Your child may repeat a sound (*S-S-Sammy*), a syllable (*la-la-lady*), or a word (*the-the-the*). He may hesitate before the next word in the sentence, saying, "uh, uh, uh, Mary did that." He may start the sentence halfway through it or decide to rephrase it. He may prolong one sound longer than ordinary, such as *m-mmmommy* (Leitch, 1977, p. 66).

Grammatical errors, mispronunciations, hesitations, and stuttering all occur naturally as children learn to speak. Such language imperfections should be expected and accepted during early childhood. But the possibility that a youngster is developing a speech problem can become a stark reality. Five percent of all school children show some type of language difficulty. Delayed language accounts for 12 percent of all childhood language difficulties. Articulation errors and stuttering make up the remaining 88 percent (deVilliers and deVilliers, 1978).

Delayed Language.   Delayed language is usually noticed when children are late in acquiring their first word and slow in grasping rules of syntax and use of sentence structure. Late appearance of language sometimes occurs for no obvious physical, emotional, social, or intellectual reasons. It may be a simple matter of a child's slower rate of development. There are documented cases in which children have not spoken their first word until three years of age! But this is more the exception than the rule. So when children's speech appears delayed, consulting with a speech specialist may be called for.

Articulation Errors.   Articulation errors involve trouble in sounding out words correctly. Some children omit sounds from words as in *es* instead of *yes* or *ooe* for *shoe*. Other children distort words by incorrectly using phonemes. For example, an *r* sound may be replaced by a *w* sound (*wed* for *red*). And children who lisp have trouble making *s* sounds. Articulation errors account for most referrals to speech specialists.

Stuttering.   *Stuttering*—the hesitation, repetition, and stammering of words, phrases, and sounds—has been called a disorder of childhood. That's because in practically all cases, stuttering starts during the early childhood years (Wingate, 1976). The onset of stuttering ranges anywhere from eighteen months to twelve years, with the majority of cases beginning by four years of age (Dickson, 1965, as cited in Wingate, 1976). Today, there are an estimated two million stutterers in the United States, with males outnumbering females four to one (Jonas, 1977).

Stuttering rarely worsens with age. In fact, most preschool stutterers gradually outgrow the problem without professional help (Jonas, 1977; Wingate, 1976). In one study those who recovered on their own did so before eight years of age (Johnson, 1955). Of course, those who do not may need the professional services of a speech therapist.

Although the cause of stuttering remains a mystery, many speculations have been made. Neurological defects, emotional problems, social pressures for proper speech, faulty learning experiences, stressful experiences, and various combinations of these factors have been cited as causes (Jonas, 1977).

Help for Language Difficulties.   When children are suspected of having a language problem, the earlier they are referred to a speech specialist, the greater are their chances for improvement (Leitch, 1977). Speech and language services are usually available from university clinics, clinics run by the Easter Seal Society for Crippled Children and Adults, public schools and kindergartens, Head Start Programs, private speech therapists, and rehabilitation centers for crippled children and adults (Leitch, 1977). The American Speech and Hearing Association in Washington, D.C., also provides information on community resources throughout the country.

Language Difficulties and Relationships.   When children have trouble with language, relationships with others are affected.

> What I remember most acutely about my stuttering is not the strangled sound of my own voice but the impatient looks on other people's faces when I had trouble getting a word out. And if their eyes happened to reflect some of the pain and frustration I was feeling, that only made me uneasy. There was nothing they could do to help me, and I certainly didn't want their sympathy. I was nine or ten at the time. Like most people with a stuttering problem, I had already learned to live by my wits in a way that normally fluent people cannot begin to appreciate. (Jonas, 1977, p. 3).

Although a language difficulty may not be emotional in origin, emotional problems can erupt as a side effect of frustration or embarrassment. Children may avoid verbal contact. Or they may become very shy about speaking in certain situations or around certain persons (Speech Foundation of America, 1962). In addition to speech therapy, a positive and supportive relationship between adult and child can make a difference in the child's willingness to overcome a speech difficulty. And parents and teachers who listen with a patient ear can be the child's biggest help!

Summary

1. The cognitive development of preoperational children is characterized by symbolic representation, which enables them to think about and compare things in their minds without having to see the actual object.

2. Egocentrism, centration, inability to follow transformations, and irreversible thought are characteristics of preoperational thinking. This prevents preschoolers from solving conservation problems, achieving one-to-one correspondence, systematically seriating objects, classifying, and accurately judging age, time, and distance. It also underlies the transductive reasoning and animism typical of this age.

3. Transductive reasoning is reasoning from the particular to the particular, without reference to the general. Conservation is the understanding that basic properties of objects stay the same. One-to-one correspondence is the ability to match items one to one with those of a model. Seriation is the ability to order objects in a sequence or series along some dimension. Classification is the grouping of objects into categories based on some common characteristic. Animism is attributing life or human qualities to nonhuman objects or animals.

4. Vocabulary size and sentence length continue to increase in early childhood, but most language advances involve developing, discarding, and refining language rules.

5. Toward the end of the preoperational period, children begin to use social speech to communicate with others, rather than the egocentric speech that characterized their language during most of this period.

6. Despite universal similarities in language development, differences occur because of varying language environments. Language differs in different socioeconomic groups, Black-English-speaking families, and bilingual families.

7. Delayed language, articulation errors, and stuttering sometimes naturally occur as children learn to speak. But when these problems persist, children should be referred to a speech specialist early.

Empathetic Activities

- What feelings did you have as you read The Case of Brad's Rainbow Discovery and other descriptions of Brad's preoperational thinking such as popcorn strands for the Christmas tree and the ski weekend? What feelings do you think Brad had? His parents?

- List activities you could provide to foster a preschooler's cognitive and language development.

- Observe a three-year-old and a five-year-old at nursery school in a free play situation. Compare their language abilities on the following points:
  - Number of vocabulary words used
  - Length of sentences
  - Use of grammatical rules (passive sentences, questions and negatives, embedded sentences, tag questions, overgeneralization)
  - Egocentric and social speech

- Recreate the button experiment Brad's mother carried out with a four- or five-year-old child you know. Then try your hand at the seriation and classification problems discussed in this chapter. How did your findings compare with those presented here?

- How does the interaction of thought and language during early childhood illustrate the *Whole Child* concept?

- How does preoperational thought influence the preschooler's relationships with others?

Related Readings

Carew, Jean, Chan, Itty, and Halfar, Christine. *Observing intelligence in young children.* Englewood Cliffs, N.J.: Prentice-Hall, 1976. Daily experiences of eight preschool children show how relationships with others influence the development of intelligence and personality. Case studies over a two-year period illustrate content.

Donaldson, Margaret. *Children's minds.* New York: Norton, 1979. A readable account of the development of the child's mind in early and middle childhood. Rejects certain features of Piaget's theory, specifically the degree of egocentrism among preoperational children, based on more recent evidence.

Forman, George E., and Hill, Fleet. *Constructive play: Applying Piaget in the preschool.* Monterey, Calif.: Brooks/Cole, 1980. A practical guide for applying Piaget's theory of cognitive development in the preschool classroom. Over one hundred simple activities derived from Piaget's theory, appropriate for children aged two to five.

Forman, George E., and Kuschner, David S. *The child's construction of knowledge: Piaget for teaching.* Monterey, Calif.: Brooks/Cole, 1977. A practical approach for understanding the implications of Piaget's theory for early childhood education curriculum. Based on Piagetian theory, explains how ordinary experiences benefit children's learning.

Leitch, Susan M. *A child learns to speak: A guide for parents and teachers of preschool children.* Springfield, Ill.: Charles C. Thomas, 1977. An excellent resource for parents and teachers. Covers language development from birth to five years. Unlike most language books, it presents language development in a clear, concise and readable format, without sacrificing content.

Wadsworth, Barry J. *Piaget for the classroom teacher.* New York: Longman, 1978. A simple, straightforward approach for applying Piagetian concepts in the preschool and elementary classroom. Emphasis on application to traditional subject and skill areas such as reading, math, science, and history.

10 Early Childhood: Social and Emotional Development and Relationships

The Case of the Parent-Teacher Conference

"Nicky has been nothing but trouble since school started," Mary Hopkins reported to Susan Abel, another teacher, only two months after the Parents' Day picnic. "Nicky's very aggressive. He hits and shoves the other children and takes their toys away. He doesn't participate in any of our group activities unless he can be the center of attention. He won't sit in the circle with the other children at story time. And every time my head is turned, he gets into one thing or another.

"Why, just yesterday I was working with a group of children at the science center. Suddenly, my aide called out to me, 'Come quickly Ms. Hopkins, Nicky's killed the hamster.' When I went over, I saw that Nicky had taken the hamster from the cage and had squeezed it until it was dead. I don't think Nicky killed the hamster on purpose. But when I asked him about it he just appeared sullen and wouldn't respond.

"Frankly, I've had all I can take! It's impossible to manage with him and all the other children. If we can't figure out some way to help Nicky, he'll just have to be removed from my classroom."

Susan attempted to calm Mary down a bit. Then she suggested that Mary have a conference with Nicky's mother before doing anything else.

The suggestion seemed to be a good one at the time Susan made it. Three weeks later, Mary wasn't so sure. She became more nervous every minute as she waited for Nicky's mother to arrive. How would Ms. Thomas react to her concerns about Nicky? "The children almost never approach Nicky any more and Kim is actually afraid of him," Mary had explained to Susan. Just then Ms. Thomas came hurrying into the room.

After sharing with Ms. Thomas several of Nicky's paintings and some of the stories he had dictated, Mary Hopkins nervously asked the young mother about his behavior at home. "I just can't understand why Nick is such a bad child," his mother replied. "I certainly have done my best to make him behave at home. He's always been a difficult child, impossible to manage—so hostile and unruly. Once he used such dirty language I had to wash his mouth out with soap. Then he complained that his mouth was blistered and I had to make him eat his meals. He'll be sick if I don't make him eat, won't he? We're always rushed in the mornings, but I always see that Nicky has a box of cereal or a breakfast cake to eat on the way to school, anyhow."

Ms. Thomas seemed anxious to pour out her difficulties with Nicky and her plans and her ambitions and everything else about her life to Mary Hopkins that afternoon. In a way, Nicky's mother seemed more interested in herself and in her own interests than in Nicky's problems in school. When questioned about her son's early development and his eating habits, she wanted to talk about herself rather than respond to the questions. After much questioning, she finally reported she couldn't remember much about Nicky's infancy. She did remember that he had walked before he was a year old. She also remembered she had a lot of difficulty with toilet training. He was continually plagued with constipation. She had taken him to a doctor who told her she was just too demanding of Nicky. That hurt her feelings so she never went back to that doctor. She reported she just kept giving Nicky prune juice and apple juice and the problem eventually disappeared.

"I really want the best for Nick," Ms. Thomas continued, "I want his life to be easier than mine. You know, my boyfriend is sending me back to school to study for a degree in nursing. The only reason I'm going is so I can afford to send Nicky to college. Of course, my studies keep me pretty busy. Nick used to bother me with questions all of the time. I got so frustrated with his constant questioning, I finally told him to entertain himself. 'Watch television while I'm trying to study,' I said. 'Don't keep bothering me.' Now, he doesn't bother me much at home. He loves to watch television. He especially likes war stories."

Suddenly, Ms. Thomas asked with near desperation in her voice, "What can I do to help Nicky behave better in school?"

Preschoolers and Adult Relationships

The ways in which preschoolers Nicky, Kim, and Scotty interact physically and mentally with their worlds are changing. The ways in which they interact with others are different, too. Rigid identification with parents lessens as peers, teachers, and other individuals outside the family become increasingly important. Preschoolers also have more control over themselves, so they are better able than toddlers to cooperate with others in working toward common goals.

INITIATIVE VERSUS GUILT

Toddlers who have successfully resolved the autonomy-versus-shame-and-doubt conflict know they are a separate person and feel a positive sense of self. This new independence combined with increasing physical, cognitive, social-emotional and language skills, gives children a feeling of power, and they set about showing great initiative in exploring their physical and social worlds with optimism and high energy. But at the same time they want to explore, children must also internalize and adhere to the rules of their society. For example, parents now ask children to assume more responsibility for supervising themselves, their pets, and their toys. Stealing and hitting others are prohibited. Such rules are internalized in the child's conscience. Trouble typically arises as free-spirited, initiating children must learn to control their own behavior and follow the rules of society. According to Erikson (1963), this conflict is at the center of the **initiative versus guilt stage.** That is, new abilities permit children to think about and initiate behavior that they may not be able to control or which is forbidden by parents and society—causing fear and guilt.

Children feel guilty when they do not live up to what they perceive are parent expectations and when they infringe upon the rights of others (as they frequently do). They cannot always control their new power. No doubt Nicky's sullenness after killing the hamster was caused by fear and perhaps guilt over his uncontrolled power gone astray. A child may also fear imagined acts such as hitting a parent. "He cannot avoid frightening himself with what he himself has dreamed and thought up" (Erikson, 1959b, p. 75). During this stage children must also move from a strong attachment to the opposite sex parent to an identification with the same sex parent. This process can also be a source of guilt (Erikson, 1963).

Children who resolve the conflict between initiative and guilt gradually assume responsibility and take pleasure in exploring their social and physical worlds. They learn to meet their needs and express themselves in ways acceptable to both themselves and their particular society. Failure to resolve this stage successfully results in children and adults who overcontrol themselves—obeying all the rules of their restrictive consciences without meeting their own needs in order to avoid guilt. Such persons are also often intolerant of others who do not rigidly adhere to their strict set of rules.

When children believe they are a bother, feel guilty about initiating activity, experience repeated failure, and receive frequent criticism and severe punishment from parents, they will be unable to resolve this stage successfully. Fortunately, children with proper guidance can resolve it successfully. Erikson noted that children have boundless energy that helps them forget failure quickly. They are "ready to learn quickly . . . and are willing to find ways of channeling their ambition into socially useful pursuits" (Erikson, 1963, p. 258).

Parents can help by encouraging children to explore a safe and stimulating environment in which they can experience frequent success. Answering questions and allowing children to contribute to meaningful projects such as cooking and planning activities are also important. Encouraging children to talk about their feelings and understanding their guilt is beneficial. Children also need firm but reasonable limits that will encourage them to control their own behavior. And consistently concentrating on the positive—what children can do instead of what they cannot do—also helps.

As was the case in toddlerhood, play is an extremely important factor in the resolution of this stage. Children need opportunities to play alone and to daydream. And play with other children allows them to work out mutual problems and learn the rules and roles of their society.

PARENTING STYLES

Huntington (1979) wrote about a sign, hanging in a Washington, D.C., toy shop, which reflects changing childrearing advice decade by decade:

1910—Spank them   1920—Deprive them

Parents and teachers who adopt an authoritative style stand firm in the face of children's whims, pleas, and temper tantrums, but allow children to express their position.

1930—Ignore them   1960—Spank them lovingly

1940—Reason with them   1970—The Hell with them!

1950—Love them

Fads in parenting styles have come and gone over the years as adults search for *the* best method of bringing up their children. But according to researcher Diana Baumrind (1975), there is no such thing as *the* best way to rear children. Baumrind (1967, 1971) studied parenting practices and their relationship to preschool children's personalities. From her observations of three- and four-year-old nursery school children, she identified three personality types of children that were traced to three different styles of parenting.

Authoritative Parents / Energetic-Friendly Children. **Authoritative parents** use affection and positive reinforcement but little punishment. They demand mature behavior from children and give support and attention to youngsters. But they are firm and unyielding to the child's whims and pleas. They give reasons for disciplinary actions, while also allowing children to express their position. Their reasonable yet firm approach appeared to help children develop responsible, mature, internalized standards of behavior. Their children tend to be more energetic, self-reliant, self-controlled, self-content, interested, and curious. They also have more harmonious peer relationships than children in the other groups.

Authoritarian Parents/Conflicted-Irritable Children.   **Authoritarian parents** believe children have few rights and should adhere unquestioningly to authority. So youngsters are not allowed much choice or disagreement during disciplinary actions. Authoritarian parents use power and firm disciplinary controls without reason or explanation. Disapproval, physical punishment, and fear techniques are routinely administered. Authoritarian parents are generally more detached, less approving, and less affectionate in relationships with children. Their harsh and controlled practices lead children to develop behaviors governed by external controls of guilt or fear of being punished—not by an internalized set of standards. These children are usually more withdrawn and hostile, easily upset, moody, unhappy, mistrustful, apprehensive in times of stress, and less competent in peer relationships than children of authoritative parents.

Permissive Parents/Impulsive-Aggressive Children.   **Permissive parents** exercise practically no control over their children. They provide little guidance, allowing children to act on impulse and to do anything they wish without demanding responsible, mature, and independent behaviors in return. Discipline is lax and inconsistent. If a child's behavior becomes too unbearable, permissive parents typically overreact in desperation—resorting to ridicule, withdrawal of love, and violent temper outbursts. Permissive parents' freewheeling and inconsistent practices lead to children without inner controls or knowledge of proper standards of conduct. They typically avoid new and unfamiliar experiences out of fear and uncertainty over whether or not they will make right decisions. These impulsive-aggressive children are immature and discontent and even less self-reliant and self-controlled than the children of authoritarian parents.

Parenting in the 1980s: Reciprocal Relationships.   While there is no magic formula for parenting, we can add to our toy shop sign a few ideas from modern-day experts. There is a growing realization that children's behavior influences parenting styles and that reciprocal influences are an inescapable part of family interactions (Baumrind, 1980; Bell, R. Q., 1979). Reports of parental disciplinary approaches to different misdemeanors by their children indicate that most parents use multiple discipline techniques. Such techniques are associated with the adult's sex, age, and experience in parenting and with what children do—not by some consistent, child-rearing approach followed by the parents (Carter and Welch, 1981; Grusec and Kuczynski, 1980).

Acknowledgment of this reciprocity allows parents to regulate the power relationship between themselves and their children based on the developmental status of each child. In Baumrind's (1980) view, the rights and responsibilities of children are complementary—not identical—to those of adults. So authority should be uneven in favor of adults—gradually shifting from complete parental authority to increasing autonomy for children as they grow and mature. According to Baumrind, authoritative parents come closest to this ideal:

> Authoritative parents see the balance between the rights of parents and those of children as a changing function of the child's stage of development as well as an expression of the norm of reciprocity by which they operate and which they wish their children to adopt (p. 641).

PARENT-PRESCHOOLER PARTNERSHIP

When toddler Scotty attended a birthday party for a playmate of his, he had little to do with the other children. He sat near his mother and started to cry when she left him to help in the kitchen. But at a birthday party two years later, four-year-old Scotty wasn't at all upset when his mother went into the kitchen. After a wave to her he went back to playing with all the presents and the other kids.

After age three, there is a major change in how children handle dependency and separation. Now that the preoperational child's cognitive development is dominated by symbolic rather than motor activity, the child's attachment relationship changes from one based on physical clinging and closeness to one based on a parent-child *partnership*. This partnership is characterized by increased cooperation and consideration for the other person's feelings, goals, and plans (Bowl-

---

Development of the Parent-Child Relationship

Relationship	Developmental Period
Parent-Newborn Synchrony	Newborn (birth–4 weeks)
Parent-Infant Attachment	Infancy (birth–12 months)
Parent-Toddler Dependency	Toddlerhood (1–3 years)
Parent-Preschooler Partnership—During early childhood, children's dependency shifts from maintaining nearness to seeking attention and approval. As more distant relationships are formed, interaction centers around occasional eye contact, coordination of plans, and mutual agreements between parent and child.	Early Childhood (3–6 years)
Parent-Child Detachment/Children's Same-Sex Friendships	Middle Childhood (6–12 years)
Parent-Teenager Individuality/Adolescent Crowd Formation	Adolescence (13–18 years)

by, 1969; Marvin, 1977). Their newly acquired ability to use symbols enables preschoolers to mentally represent their relationship with parents just as they do objects in the environment. As a result, the parent-child relationship becomes an enduring one that can be maintained whether parent and child are together or apart (Marvin, 1977).

As we mentioned in Chapter 7, toddlers begin to separate themselves from their parents. But three- and four-year-olds become increasingly detached—putting more distance between themselves and their parents (Maccoby and Feldman, 1972; Marvin, 1977). The child's attachment shifts from maintaining nearness to mother to bids for attention—such as glancing at mother, smiling at her, showing her a toy or speaking to her (Maccoby and Feldman, 1972). Children now play longer away from their parents on their own or with peers. And they settle down with toys for longer periods of time.

Preschoolers have an easier time orally communicating their goals and wishes. They are also able to delay carrying out their intentions until their efforts can be coordinated with those of their parents. As they lose their egocentrism, preschoolers begin to see that their mothers and fathers are separate individuals with thoughts, goals, and plans independent of their own. But the parent-preschooler partnership is put to a real test when both parents work outside the home (see Spotlight 10.1).

Preschoolers and Peer Relationships

Toddlers spend most of their interaction time with parents and teachers, while preschoolers spend more time interacting socially with their peers. For example, by the age of three or four, children begin to interact with their peers as often as they do with their teachers (O'Connor, 1975). Such peer interaction helps preschoolers loosen strong ties with parents. It also helps them become physically separate as well as socially and emotionally independent. By age three, previous experience in interacting with peers increases the child's competence in social situations with peers (Lieberman, 1977). And infants and toddlers with prior day-care experience have more positive interactions with peers at ages three and four than youngsters with no previous experience (Meyer, 1979). In this section we will discuss sibling relationships, the first important peer interaction for many children. We will also look at play in some detail because it is the most important avenue for the development of peer relationships during early childhood.

SIBLING RELATIONSHIPS

The first real social experience with other children comes through relationships with *siblings*—brothers and sisters. In many cases, the older sibling acts as a model for the younger child. Studies show that younger children will watch and imitate older brothers or sisters and play with toys abandoned by their older siblings

Sibling relationships are important because they are the first peer relationships many preschoolers will have.

(Lamb, 1978c). Sibling relationships include both aggressive and prosocial interactions that prepare children for later relationships with the many types of people they will meet outside the home (Abramovitch et al., 1979).

Because of their lengthy and close early relationships, siblings usually become closely attached to one another. But **sibling rivalry**—antagonism or resentment toward a brother or sister—can also erupt when one child feels left out. Sibling rivalry occurs most often with the arrival of a new baby. A new sibling is associated with changes in the patterns of interaction between firstborn children and their mothers (Dunn and Kendrick, 1980). For example, a new brother or sister means less attention from mother and father and in some cases a need to share daily routines, toys, and other personal belongings. This can be an emotionally upsetting time for firstborn children who have always had their parents' undivided attention. They may view their new sibling as an intruder. Adjustment problems are sometimes shown through aggressive, attention-getting behaviors, loss of appetite, baby talk, and even relapses in toilet training.

Spotlight 10.1: Wage-Earning Mothers

Wage-earning mothers are a real part of American family life. Caroline's mother is a lawyer; Kim's mother is a sixth-grade teacher; Roosevelt's mother works at a bank. Only Brad's mother works full-time in the home.

Between 1960 and 1975 employed (that is, wage-earning) married women with children under the age of six more than doubled in number (Bell, R. R., 1979). In 1979, the work force included 37 percent of all mothers with children under six (about 6.4 million women) and 33 percent of mothers with children under two (Haskins et al., 1979; Zigler and Heller, 1979). As of March, 1980, almost 57 percent of mothers who had children under age eighteen worked outside the home. The number of employed mothers is expected to increase to 10.5 million by 1990—at which time only one in four married women will be a full-time housewife and mother (Zigler & Heller, 1979).

Why are so many mothers entering the work force? Most women work outside the home because they need more money (Bell, R. R., 1979). There has been an increase in the number of families headed by women—from 9 percent of all families in 1950 to 13 percent of all families in 1976 (Craig, 1977). Many women who have working husbands need the wages from a second income to maintain the standard of living they desire. But in a national survey on wage-earning women, 76 percent said they would continue working outside the home even if they didn't have to. Their reason was "to

Working mother Diana Ross with her daughters, Rhonda Suzanne, Chudney Lane, and Tracee Joy.

fill the time'' (Dubnoff et al., 1978), although many of these women are committed to careers for personal fulfillment.

Experts no longer believe that constant mothering by the actual mother is required for optimal development of children. With respect to motor and mental development or social interactions with their mothers, children of mothers who work outside the home do not differ from children of mothers who stay at home (Hock, 1980). Current research suggests that the *quality* of the parent-child relationship—rather than hours of contact—is most important for normal social-emotional development (Anderson, 1980). The mother's satisfaction with her role was found to be more important for quality parenting than whether or not she stayed

---

Sibling rivalry is sharpest when children are closely spaced and of the same sex. As a rule, preschool children (about three years old) have an easier time adjusting to a new sibling than younger children because preschoolers can do more things for themselves. But the adjustment process depends greatly on how parents handle the situation. Maladjustment can be reduced when preschoolers are prepared for the arrival of their new sibling and allowed to help plan for the newcomer. They can be made to feel they will gain rather than lose from the experi-

home (Hock, 1980; Hock et al., 1980). In other words, when mothers enjoy their work, they make better mothers. Both employed and nonemployed mothers who feel satisfied and competent in their employment or homemaking roles have more positive relationships with their children than do unhappy employed or nonemployed mothers (Hartley, 1966; Hoffman, 1961). So mothers and fathers who provide their children with good quality care while they are working need not feel guilty or worried.

In fact, there are some advantages to having mothers employed outside the home. Maternal employment can have positive modeling effects on children (Barahal, 1978). In families where fathers are participating more in housework and child care (Hoffman, L.W., 1979), children are able to see both parents involved in caring for them and in occupational roles. Children also have a greater opportunity to select their own future child care and occupational roles. In fact, girls whose mothers work outside the home typically plan to work outside the home after marriage. These girls tend to have higher self-esteem (Baruch, 1972; Hartley, 1966). When mothers are wage-earners, daughters (Gold and Andres, 1978) and sons (Derdiarian and Snipper, 1979; Romer and Cherry, 1978) have less stereotyped sex-role ideas than children of mothers who stay at home. Maternal employment also encourages peer interaction, independence, and responsibility—especially for boys (Zambrana et al., 1979). Middle-class children of wage-earning mothers usually set higher educational and occupa-

tional goals for themselves (Stein, 1973). When mothers do not feel guilty about working outside the home, they are apt to encourage their children to be independent at an earlier age (Hock, 1978; Hoffman, L.W., 1979). This early independence training leads children to participate more in household duties than children of nonemployed mothers.

But there can be problems, too. In many homes, fathers do not assume more responsibility for child and home care. This places the employed mother in a position of assuming all child care and home care responsibilities as well as those of employment (Zambrana et al., 1979). In other words, she is expected and expects herself to be superhuman—mother, wife, and career woman—a role combination that produces great stress. The largest role conflict and marital disruption is felt by wage-earning mothers of young children. Hiring help for household tasks and child care can reduce the stress, but this can be expensive and hard to find.

Yet these problems are not insurmountable. Children can be cared for by individuals such as fathers, grandparents, and day-care teachers as long as the youngsters' psychological and physical needs are met. Once stable and predictable substitute care is found, employed mothers can achieve career satisfaction with an absence of excessive guilt and worry. If suitable child care is found, and warm, quality parent-child relationships are maintained, there should be no negative effects on children. The whole family can be happy!

ence. Through their new role as ''big brother'' or ''big sister,'' youngsters can share in caring for the new baby in simple ways such as bottle feeding or getting a diaper for mother. In this way they will feel like an important insider in the new experience rather than an unimportant outside observer. But the role of helper is not enough. The older child still needs time alone with mother and dad every day. Everyone will be happier if the family can share in the care of the new baby but also show concern for each family member's need for attention and love.

PLAY AND SOCIAL DEVELOPMENT

A Case of Dramatic Play

At nursery school one day Mary Hopkins watched four-year-old Caroline and Roosevelt go over to the doll corner. Caroline is wide-eyed and eager. Roosevelt trails behind her, less purposefully. Caroline goes to a doll buggy with a Raggedy Ann doll in it. She wheels the buggy round and round. Roosevelt looks on, a bit bored. Suddenly Caroline turns to Roosevelt and says decisively, "I'm the mommy, you can be the daddy." Without waiting for an answer she pushes the buggy into the corner, takes the doll out, seats the doll at the table and starts setting three places. "We gotta eat now," she blurts out urgently. "Time for dinner." She puts out three spoons, three plates, two cups. Unable to find a third cup, she uses a plastic flower pot as a substitute.

Roosevelt doesn't pay much attention to the domestic scene. He finds a box half-filled with blocks and climbs into it, pretending he is a chauffeur with an imaginary steering wheel. Suddenly he climbs out of it, bends over, and looks at the side of the box. Frowning, he says, "Shucks, got a flat; gotta change the tire. Dumb tire." With an air of importance, he goes through the motions of tire-changing, using a spoon for a tool.

Caroline glances at him, says, "No, Roosevelt, you're supposed to eat now." She goes to the shelf, gets a piece of clay, squashes it, pounds it, and then cuts it. She puts a piece of clay on the doll's plate, saying, "There, eat your meatloaf." She then picks up the rag doll and starts scolding her angrily. "Wet again; you wet your pants and spilled your milk. I'm going to have to spank you." She slaps the doll hard, then puts her in the bed and says, "You go to bed now, cause you were bad."

Roosevelt approaches her with a tray full of blocks and says, in a grocery-boy tone of voice, "Here are your potatoes, Ma'am." But Caroline walks off with the self-satisfied expression of one who has done her job well. And, indeed, she has. So, for that matter, has her young friend and playmate.*

Categories of Preschool Play. In what is now considered a classic study, Mildred Parten (1932) examined the social participation of preschool children aged two to five. She discovered that as children get older, they play alone less and become more socialized in their play. She classified six types of preschool play:

1. **Unoccupied behavior:** the child is not playing but is occupied with anything that happens to be of fleeting interest.

---

* Written by Glenda Riddick, instructor, Orange Coast College, Costa Mesa, California. Used by permission.

2. **Onlooker play:** the child spends time watching others play—often asking questions, giving suggestions to other children but rarely entering into play.

3. **Solitary play:** the child plays alone and independently with toys, sometimes within speaking distance of others.

4. **Parallel play:** the child plays independently but alongside other children.

5. **Associative play:** the child plays with peers who are engaged in similar activities, although each child acts as he or she wishes. Sharing, borrowing, and lending play materials is typical. Roosevelt and Caroline's behavior in A Case of Dramatic Play is typical of associative play.

6. **Cooperative play:** the child plays in groups organized for the purpose of making some material product or attaining some common goal. When Roosevelt and Caroline work together to build a house in the block corner and prepare a ''gourmet clay dinner'' as a team, they will be engaging in cooperative play.

Parten concluded that the isolated types of play (unoccupied, onlooker, and solitary) were more characteristic of young toddlers, while the social types (associative and cooperative) were more typical of older preschool children. More recent research confirmed the developmental nature of preschool children's play (Rubin et al., 1978). Increased amounts of group and dramatic play among older preschoolers is possible because of their greater ability to decenter and to understand reciprocal relations in social situations.

Dramatic Play.   Preschoolers enjoy a type of play called **dramatic play**—acting out scenes they observe from everyday life. Most preschool classrooms have an area especially designated as the housekeeping corner or dramatic play area. Props such as dress-up clothes, empty soup cans and cereal boxes, and dolls are usually on hand to help stimulate dramatic play.

As preschoolers imagine themselves in lots of different situations, they get a chance to ''rehearse'' for later adult life by learning the rules and roles of society. They become doctors, pirates, firefighters, mothers, daddies, and even babies. They also get an opportunity to work through fears and to practice give and take as they work out mutual problems with their peers.

The preschool child's dramatic play becomes more complex and organized than in toddlerhood. Toddlers are more apt to imitate simple, domestic themes such as telephoning, rocking the baby, driving the car, or having dinner. But older preschool children weave the simple themes into more complex, sustained dramas placed in exotic as well as commonplace settings—pirate ships, service stations, airports, outer space, grocery stores, or their own house. Their fantasies carry them into exciting adventures as they fly over buildings, save those in peril, or in a moment's notice transform themselves into dogs, horses, trains, flowers, doors, snakes, and back to themselves again! They can travel into the past. Or they can project themselves into the future, describing adventures, places, and dimensions never recorded by humankind.

Dramatic Play in Early Childhood

Adult guidance during dramatic play can help children sharpen their questions, clarify issues, and explore alternative courses of action (Butler et al., 1978). By joining in doll play, for instance, adults can model successful ways of handling interpersonal conflict or dealing with fears, simply by acting out a situation—not by telling children how to behave. But usually it's not necessary for adults to be a part of children's play. In fact, bossy adults make play less effective for children. It is important that children be given as much freedom as possible to explore, create, and solve problems in their play environment. Meanwhile, adults can help by *responding, consulting,* and *supporting*—but not by *directing*.

Imaginary Playmates. Play does not always involve "real people." Sometimes preschool children invent imaginary playmates—especially when they have few real friends, have no siblings, or are firstborn children (Manosevitz et al:, 1973). They get emotional satisfaction from carrying on lengthy conversations and sharing toys with these "unseen friends."

Four-year-old Caroline has a friend named Elizabeth whom no one else can see. Caroline talks, plays, and shares toys with her invisible friend. One day Caroline's mother "thoughtlessly left" Elizabeth on the corner as she and Caroline crossed the street. Caroline began to scream that Elizabeth was left all alone. Onlookers wondered at mother's "cruelty" and then her sanity as she and Caroline went back to get Elizabeth and help her across the street too. Such imaginary playmates are not unusual for preschool children. One investigation reported that 65 percent of the three- and four-year-olds studied had imaginary playmates (Pines, 1978). Maybe you even had one yourself!

Preoperational children can create make-believe companions because of their new cognitive ability to form mental images. This ability fits their animistic and magical view of the world. Children who have imaginary companions are not mentally sick. They are totally aware of the unreality of the fantasy, despite its vividness. In fact, highly intelligent and creative children are more apt to produce vivid imaginary friends and more detailed stories about them. Girls create make-believe companions three times more often than boys do (Kay, 1980).

Imaginary playmates help children reduce loneliness, cope with fears or unsatisfactory relationships, and find an outlet for anger and hostility (Kay, 1980). Most imaginary playmates appear between the ages of two and a half and ten but disappear as children enter school or meet other friends to play with (Nagera, 1969; Manosevitz et al., 1973).

Emotions

As preschoolers move from interaction mostly with parents, which was typical of toddlerhood, toward interaction mostly with peers, their emotions are increasingly influenced by this larger social world. In this section, we will discuss how play helps children deal with their emotions. We will also consider aggression and prosocial behavior, childhood psychoses, and helping children cope with death.

PLAY AND EMOTIONAL DEVELOPMENT

Play serves not only as a workshop for development of social skills but also as an important aid to emotional development. Through play, children often deal with reality in a nonthreatening and satisfying way. Play helps children deal with fears aroused by trauma such as hospitalization. The following case illustrates how one five year old used play to master fears of intrusive hospital procedures after being struck by an automobile:

> A week had elapsed from the time he received his last injection to the time of the first play session; however, memory of the painful injections was revealed in his play. In the first play session, Jason picked up Moofy, his stuffed bear. He indicated a syringe contained inside a clear plastic box next to him and said, "This is a special kind of needle; it doesn't hurt." He put Moofy down and began examining other pieces of equipment. Later in the same play session, while holding a vial of solution, Jason said "I like shots. I don't like the way they feel." In the second play session, Jason picked up a stethoscope and said, "I'm not scared of this, but I am scared of shots." Immediately, Jason gave the bear an injection and, in the bear's voice, screamed "Ouch" then in his own voice, "There's your shot." He laid both bear and syringe aside. At the end of this play session, Jason announced "I hate shots."*

Dreams also begin during the preschool years. In dreams, as in play and language, children reproduce mental images of objects, people, and situations. The first reports of nightmares also occur among preschoolers—sometimes the result of a scary movie or being in a strange situation (Wolman, 1978). Play can also be an avenue to work out fears aroused by nightmares, television, movies, and frightening stories as well as hospitals.

As we have just indicated, play is important to social and emotional development. In Chapters 8 and 9 we pointed out that play is vital to physical and cognitive development as well. The role of play in preschool education has been varied. Some schools de-emphasize play but others, such as most Head Start programs, emphasize it greatly (see Spotlight 10.2).

AGGRESSION AND PROSOCIAL BEHAVIOR

Brad's mother observed the following scene at the parents' day picnic when Brad was four. Brad and Scotty were building a road with their earth movers. Brad's mother suddenly heard loud angry voices. "Stupid head!" Scotty yelled. "The road can't go that way!" "It can too!" replied Brad. After a few more exchanges, an angry Brad ran his earth mover over Scotty's road tearing it up. An indignant Scotty responded by hitting Brad. A fight ensued and Brad began to cry. Before Brad's mother could get to the scene Kim arrived and put her arm around a frightened Brad while Scotty glared at them both.

---

* "One Five-Year-Old Boy's Use of Play" by L. T. Acord, *Maternal-Child Nursing Journal*, 1980, vol. 9, p. 30. Reprinted by permission.

❋ Spotlight 10.2: Choices in Preschool Education

Kim's mother felt that going to preschool would be a good experience for Kim. She started to get information on just what type of preschool experiences were available. Day-care programs (see Chapter 7) are full-day programs operating daily that enroll infants of a few months to children of preschool age. Preschool programs serve the needs of children between the ages of three and six and usually last for only part of the day. Early childhood programs have existed for many years and vary greatly, some emphasizing one philosophy or theory more than another. Some programs are primarily based on a learning theory approach. Others take a cognitive approach, a social-emotional approach, or basic skills approach. In this section, we will discuss two preschool programs—the Montessori preschool, which takes a basic skills approach, and Head Start, which is more multidimensional, emphasizing physical and social-emotional aspects as well as cognition and basic skills.

MONTESSORI PRESCHOOLS

The ideas and ideals of Dr. Maria Montessori (1870–1952), Italy's first female physician, are the foundation of the many Montessori preschools in the United States today. These schools are carefully prepared environments in which children make choices of what to work with from specifically designed equipment and materials such as sandpaper letters and perceptual blocks. These prepared materials carry the burden of instruction, with the teacher's role being one of support, not direct instruction.

The schools offer varied programs that include practical life exercises such as sweeping, buttoning, and other everyday activities; sensory exercises, math activities, language materials that emphasize sensory experience and spoken language as well as writing and reading; and cultural subjects such as science, history, and geography. Housekeeping centers and role playing activities are not permitted in the traditional Montessori school. Most of the activities are done individually or in a small group, although some large group activities such as singing and games are included.

Critics claim that Montessori's emphasis on individualized learning deprives preschoolers of opportunities for social interaction and the development of social skills. Some claim that the learning materials stifle creativity and problem-solving skills. But Montessori advocates argue that their school prepares children to enter everyday life with confidence, independence, a sense of purpose, contributions to others, and joy.*

HEAD START

During the 1960s, there was great concern that poor children were being denied the opportunity to succeed in school and eventually assume a productive role in society. In an attempt to break the crippling effects of the poverty cycle and to give children between the ages of three and five a "head start" in life and school, the Head Start program was established under the Economic Opportunity Act of 1964. By 1975, over 5 million children—including handicapped as well as economically disadvantaged children—had taken part in the Head Start program (Cryan and Surbeck, 1979). Central to the idea of Head Start is the concept of a Total Child Development Center. Transportation, comprehensive health care, and nutrition as well as educational opportunities involving the social, emotional, cognitive, and physical aspects of the child are emphasized (Osborn, 1980). Parental and community participation in the form of volunteerism, education about child development, and participation in program policymaking are also stressed. As you can see, the Head Start program

*Adapted from information provided by Kathryn McGarry, The Charlotte Montessori School. Reprinted by permission.

deals with the whole child in the family and community systems.

Has Head Start been successful? Research findings have been mixed, but overall they indicate that it is generally a valuable experience for children and families (Mann et al., 1977). When compared to non–Head Start children, Head Start children had better health and fewer were held back in school or put in special education classes (Schweinhart and Weikart, 1981). Head Start also appeared to facilitate child socialization (Mann, et al., 1977). The results of a twenty-year study of children in the Perry Preschool Project in Ypsilanti, Michigan indicated that children were more highly motivated in school, did more homework and engaged in less delinquent behavior than a group of children who did not attend the Perry Preschool (Schweinhart and Weikart, 1981). A review of early results indicated significant gains in language and I.Q. development (Osborn, 1980). But the first major study of Head Start showed that these gains in I.Q. seem to "wash away" when children moved into the primary grades (Westinghouse, 1969). Some researchers said intervention should begin much earlier than age three. Others questioned the research results claiming that there were problems with the methods used. For example, centers of poor, medium, and good quality were all lumped together. Still others complained about problems with the tests used in the research.

Changes were made as a result of this research. Parent-child centers for families with children under three were started. Between 1972 and 1975, Home Start, a Head Start type program, was set up in private homes primarily by paraprofessionals, members of the community who had been especially trained to work with parents and children. Project Follow Through was begun for children who had been in Head Start or similar programs (Haney, 1977). In this program the Head Start idea of comprehensive services to the child and heavy parent participation was continued into the pri-

The Montessori classroom's individualized approach is designed to make use of the preschooler's "absorbent mind," which Montessori compared to a sponge—constantly absorbing the content of the immediate environment.

mary grades. In 1980, 69,000 children in 150 different locations were being served in nineteen different types of educational programs (Wilson, 1980). Planned Variation, which involves different types of educational experiences, is another change in Head Start and Follow Through programs. It deals with the problem of quality and type of program by trying several different theoretical and philosophical approaches.

It cannot be said that any one theoretical approach is best for all children. But parent involvement is vital in any program at any age. Research indicates that the long-term effects of school achievement and performance on I.Q. tests is linked to parental involvement (Levenstein, 1971; Gordon, 1969). Bronfenbrenner (1974b) also concluded that active parental involvement is essential in maintaining the cognitive skills gained in Follow Through programs.

As you can see, aggression as well as fear are often a part of children's play. Throughout the preschool years, a pattern can be seen in the development of aggression (Maccoby, 1980). During infancy and toddlerhood, children have generalized temper outbursts. But true aggression is not observed until the preschool years (about age three) when aggressive acts and threatening gestures are focused on particular persons. Preschoolers like Scotty will attack and intentionally hurt someone else—usually another youngster during struggles over toys or control of play space. Once aggression reaches a peak in early childhood, it begins to rapidly decline among normal children. As children get older, aggressive acts or physical attacks are more likely to take the form of verbal abuse such as name-calling or "biting" criticism.

Childhood aggression is likely to be the product of a combination of biological and learning factors. Because aggression is present among all animals, most scientists believe that there is a biological basis for it in humans. The fact that its onset follows a built-in timetable also indicates a biological basis. Research also shows that children learn aggression. Aggression is transmitted through observational learning (Bandura et al., 1961). Some children learn aggression from peers. And some learn to aggress by exposure to family violence. Children like Nicky who are unusually aggressive often come from homes in which aggression is the accepted way of settling disputes. These children are reinforced for conforming to these aggressive standards because it usually gets them what they want. And as you can see in Spotlight 10.3, television viewing is also an important influence.

During the preschool years, children become more prosocial—more cooperative, caring, empathetic, and willing to share (Yarrow & Waxler, 1976). Pre-

During the preschool years, children's first aggressive acts appear, accompanied by threatening gestures. But prosocial behaviors exceed aggressive acts in preschoolers' relationships with each other.

schoolers are becoming aware that others feel differently from themselves, and that they can, like Kim, do something appropriate in response to the other child's feelings (Strayer, 1980). This increase in prosocial behaviors helps lessen aggressive behaviors.

A review of research indicated that "friendly behaviors exceed negative, aggressive behaviors by a considerable margin in most of the groups of young children that were observed, and that the proportion of total social interactions that are positive increases with age throughout the preschool years" (Moore, 1977a, p. 73). Parents can help preschoolers in their transition from aggressive to nonaggressive means for resolving social disputes by teaching positive social skills and helping youngsters become sensitive to the feelings of others (Maccoby, 1980).

CHILDHOOD PSYCHOSIS

Five-year-old Jamey wanders aimlessly around his preschool classroom. He looks "through" or around his teacher and classmates, seemingly unaware of them. He makes meaningless flapping gestures with his hands—over and over again. When there is a sudden change in routine, Jamey gets very upset—crying and banging his head against the concrete wall and showing no signs of pain. Jamey suffers from a form of **childhood psychosis,** a severe emotional disturbance in which a child loses or refuses contact with reality.

For some unknown reason, childhood psychosis is three times more common in boys than girls (Paluszny, 1979). And it is more frequently reported among upper-middle-class families (Schopler et al., 1979). Although psychotic children share some of the ·same symptoms, experts have isolated two types—*infantile autism* and *childhood schizophrenia.*

Children with **infantile autism** are totally withdrawn from the outside world and do not communicate meaningfully with others. Listless behavior may be the first sign of autism in infancy (Rimland, 1964). It may not be until the child is eighteen months to two years that parents become seriously concerned about their child's lack of communication and seek help (Wing, 1972). It is usually at this point that autism is diagnosed.

The withdrawal of autistic children from the world is usually extreme. They may sit for hours motionless and staring into space. They will not respond to the words or eye contact of others. Emotional attachment is poor and human contact is avoided or resisted. Autistic children often remain stiff and rigid when being carried or held. But they are often unusually attached to objects in their environment and become furious if their objects are bothered or their routines changed.

The child may be mute or have limited or impaired speech and may make grunting noises and unclear sounds. Like parrots, autistic children sometimes mechanically repeat what they heard minutes before—nursery rhymes, television commercials, or everyday conversations recited verbatim. Because of these symptoms autistic children are often initially diagnosed as being deaf, retarded, or brain-damaged.

❖ Spotlight 10.3: The Effects of Television on Young Children

Nicky sat motionless, eyes fixed on the twenty-five-inch color television screen, watching "The Road-runner," his favorite cartoon. A researcher's analysis of a six-minute segment of this particular cartoon described what befell the coyote:

> In minute one, a cannon blew his head off; in minute two he was pushed under a boulder; in minute three, he fell a long, long way to plop in a puff of dust to the canyon floor; in minute four, he fell again and was later crushed by a rock; in minute six he was run over yet again to total eight alleged deaths in six minutes (Kaye, 1979, p. 80).

Preschoolers watch an average of four hours of television a day (Osborn and Osborn, 1977). By the time children graduate from high school, they have spent 15,000 hours watching television (Kaye, 1979). Out of the 15,000 hours, the average child has observed more than 13,000 violent deaths (Gerbner and Gross, 1978). What effects do large amounts of television viewing in general and violence in particular have on preschoolers like Nicky?

AGGRESSIVE AND ANTISOCIAL BEHAVIOR

Television has had a powerful impact on children's socialization since it made its way into millions of homes in the 1950s. As a result of observational learning, children will repeat what they see and hear on television (Bandura, 1978). Cases have been reported in which small children have jumped from windows or tried to fly like their television heroes. In the first televised trial in history, a youth was tried for the murder of an older woman—the crime supposedly inspired by an episode of *Kojak*.

In 1972, the Surgeon-General's Report produced five volumes of research reports that found indicators of a causal relationship between television violence and aggressive behavior.

Evidence from research has shown that when children watched a lot of television violence, they were more prone to act aggressively than children who did not watch such violence (Stein and Friedrich, 1975; Rubinstein, 1978). For example, Liebert and Baron (1972) showed one group of children violent scenes from *The Untouchables*—two fist fights, two shootings, and a knifing. A second group of children viewed a neutral videotape of a track race. Afterwards, observers of the violent program were more aggressive in their play and more willing to hurt another child than observers of the neutral program. When asked to press a button that could either help or hurt another child, the aggressive group pressed the hurt button earlier and longer. Nursery school children who watched *Batman* and *Superman* became more aggressive in interpersonal relationships, were less patient, and less likely to obey school rules than children watching neutral TV shows such as animal films (Friedrich and Stein, 1973). A link has also been discovered between the classroom aggression of third-grade boys and the amount of violence they observed on TV (Lefkowitz et al., 1972). Some researchers suggest that the aggressive behaviors that were observed in this study might be temporary. When this type of study was done over an extended period of time in natural settings, the findings were contradictory (Friedrich and Stein, 1973).

Other findings indicate that heavy viewers of violence also became emotionally desensitized toward aggression (Murray, 1980). And heavy viewers are also more apt to believe that violence is an effective and bona fide means of solving everyday problems (Stein and Friedrich, 1975).

As we have seen, most studies show that there is a link between television violence and aggression in children. So it is probably a good idea for Nicky's mother to restrict his viewing of violent television programs. But as in all areas of development, individual reactions are often different. While Nicky's aggressive behavior may increase after viewing war stories, Brad, who has good social skills and is generally not aggressive, will probably be less affected. Some would argue that children like Brad might be less aggressive because they can vent their feelings vicariously with the TV character instead of behaving aggressively themselves (Feshbach and Singer, 1971). But Murray (1980) suggests caution in drawing this conclusion: "the most viable interpretation is the suggestion that although for *some* children under *some* circumstances, viewing televised violence may enable the child to discharge some of his or her aggressive feelings, for *many* children under *many* circumstances, viewing aggression on television leads to an increase in aggressive feelings, attitudes, and behavior." (p. 38).

PROSOCIAL BEHAVIOR

Although television has its disadvantages, it also has some positive points. Television stimulates prosocial behaviors through observational learning in the same way it produces aggressive behaviors. Exposure to prosocial TV shows has a strong short-term effect in reducing aggression in preschoolers' free play (Bankart and Anderson, 1979). The *Mister Rogers' Neighborhood* series has been the focus of much research because it was designed for preschool children and is concerned with friendliness, cooperation, emotional empathy, and other prosocial behaviors. Nursery school children viewing *Mister Rogers* were more likely to tolerate delays, observe rules, and show friendliness and cooperation during play than children who watched neutral films (Friedrich and Stein, 1973).

ACADEMIC LEARNING

By the time children graduate from high school, they have spent 11,000 hours in educational instruction, compared with 15,000 hours watching television (Kaye, 1979). So it's no surprise that there is an association between large amounts of television viewing and lower grades in school. Gadberry (1977) explained that children who watch a lot of television generally spend less time on their schoolwork. When a group of first-grade children was restricted in their TV viewing, their academic performance, reading time, and developmental test scores improved (Gadberry, 1980). But she found (1977) that much depends on the kind of television shows children watch—watching commercial television was linked to poor schoolwork, while watching educational programs was related to higher grades in school. The success of *Sesame Street, The Electric Company,* and *The Big Blue Marble* illustrates the impact television can have on the development of basic educational skills (Lesser, 1974).

Children's behavior is especially influenced by television advertising (Feshbach et al., 1979). The average television-viewing child observes over 20,000 commercials per year (Adler, 1978). Preschoolers pressure their parents to purchase products they have seen advertised on television (Stoneman and Brody, 1982). And children prefer food products which they have seen advertised even

✤ Spotlight 10.3: The Effects of Television on Young Children (continued)

more if peers also prefer the products (Stoneman and Brody, 1981). After exposure to commercials for high-sugar-content foods, young children will usually select sugared foods. But when children are exposed to public service announcements advocating more nutritional foods, they are more likely to select unsugared snacks (Goldberg et al., 1978). This is a good illustration of how a larger social system (the advertising industry) affects a child's social-emotional development.

REFORMS IN CHILDREN'S PROGRAMS

In the late 1960s, ACT (Action for Children's Television) started questioning the effect of television on youngsters. From expert testimony, ACT concluded that television is a major educator of young children, but that, as a rule, its lessons are poorly planned and the needs of broadcasters and advertisers are placed above the needs of children (Kaye, 1979). ACT's demands for change have stopped some of the worst abuses, reducing commercial time on children's programs by forty percent and no longer aiming ads for fireworks and vitamins directly at children. The pros and cons of television for children and what, if any, regulation of television should be carried out are still hotly debated issues.

ADULT GUIDANCE

Meanwhile, specialists recommend that parents take an active role in their children's television viewing by helping children select appropriate programs, viewing them together, and whenever possible, conducting a follow-up discussion about the program content and an evaluation of its quality

"...NO, HE CAN'T REALLY FLY... NO, THE BAD GUYS DON'T REALLY HAVE A RAY GUN... NO, THIS CEREAL REALLY ISN'T THE BEST FOOD IN THE WHOLE WORLD... NO, IT WON'T MAKE YOU AS STRONG AS A GIANT..."

(Brazelton, 1979). A calm adult watching TV with a child can counteract the effects of violence and help youngsters distinguish between make-believe and real life (McCown, 1979). And the impact of prosocial television is greater when parents or teachers are present to label televised activities or expand on their content. Children who have been exposed to the experience of an adult mediator are more likely to have more positive social interactions such as helping, sharing, cooperation, nurturance, and empathy (Cofer et al., 1979). And adult mediation during televised viewing has educational benefits because it helps children remember more of what they see (Watkins et al., 1980) and helps them make more nutritional food choices (Galst, 1980). Adult presence and guidance during television viewing also provides a time for meaningful sharing and gives a more human dimension to an otherwise isolating experience.

Like autism, **childhood schizophrenia** is usually characterized by a withdrawal from reality, although typically it is not as severe as it is in autism. Other symptoms include ritualistic, repetitive actions like Jamey's repeated flapping of his hands, poor language skills, rigid posturing, temper tantrums, and an intolerance for changes in the environment. But unlike autism, childhood schizophrenia follows a period of healthy development. It appears later in childhood than autism—usually after five years of age.

Failure to use language is characteristic of some schizophrenic children, but more often they talk continuously. But their language generally makes little sense to others. Hallucinations and disordered thought are common for schizophrenia but rare in autism (Hanson and Gottesman, 1976).

To date, there is still no clear-cut cause or cure for either disturbance. But several theories have emerged. Some blame cold, rejecting parents or an emotionally unstable home atmosphere. Others believe childhood psychosis results from a genetic tendency for the disturbance that is triggered by emotionally unstable surroundings. Another belief is that childhood psychosis results from improper biochemical functioning of the brain. The child has difficulty organizing thoughts and feelings into a meaningful whole, has trouble sorting incoming information, and perceives a hazy and confused world. But a growing number of experts believe that there is no single, universal cause underlying childhood psychosis. Instead, many are persuaded of multiple causes that are associated with a genetic defect, coupled with neurologic impairment of some type (Piggott, 1979).

The chief method of treatment for psychotic children is to place them in classrooms run by teachers trained in special education for emotionally disturbed children. Teachers use physical exercises and games to help children develop an awareness of others, to increase motivation to explore their environment, to improve intellectual and social functioning, and to overcome perceptual-motor impairments. The use of operant conditioning techniques and involving parents as co-therapists have shown promising results (Schopler and Reichler, 1971). Parents are also often asked to participate in child-rearing counseling or some type of psychotherapy. Certain drugs are commonly used to reduce the symptoms of schizophrenia, though they are rarely successful with autism. Unfortunately, the outlook for most autistic children is poor (Paluszny, 1979), especially if the autism is moderate or severe. While some autistic children show little progress, many master basic self-help skills and some progress enough to attend public schools.

HELPING CHILDREN COPE WITH DEATH

One night as four-year-old Brad lay in bed waiting for his routine hug and bedtime story, he heard the telephone ring several times and the sounds of muted whispers. He would later find out that Grandma Rachel had died that evening.

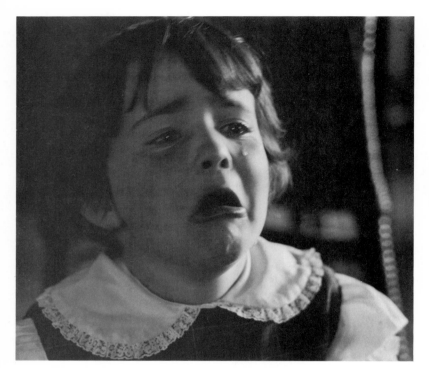

The death of a loved one or pet can be a difficult time for a child, cognitively as well as emotionally.

The next day, realizing that Brad must be told, Doreen explained that Grandma Rachel had died. Brad wanted to know if Grandma Rachel would play ball and read him stories again. Bill and Doreen explained that dead people cannot play ball and read stories. Then Bill read him a children's story about death. Brad asked with concern, "Who'll take care of her garden while she's away?" Soon he was ready to go outside and play.

Death is an abstract concept difficult for children to fully grasp. How well they understand death depends on their level of cognitive development (Koocher, 1971; White et al., 1978). Because of egocentrism and centration, preschoolers cannot significantly share the experiences of others, cannot grasp the irreversibility (permanency) of death, and cannot comprehend that it happens to everyone (Koocher, 1971). Brad's query "Who'll take care of her garden while she's away?" indicates he expects Grandma to return.

After a cognitive shift at age five to seven (see Chapter 9), children show a clearer understanding of the concepts of dying and death (Weininger, 1979). By age nine or ten, Brad will better understand the permanency of death and that it involves an end to body functions. His lessened egocentrism will help him see that death is universal and will happen to him (Weininger, 1979; White et al., 1978).

Death is an emotionally difficult time for adults. The experience is magnified when death must be explained to a child (Koocher, 1974). Unsure of what to say, many well-meaning adults provide false explanations, like "Grandma is just asleep." This explanation often causes children to be afraid to go to sleep. Others attempt to shield youngsters from the mourning process altogether. Children are usually eager to talk about death, so it need not be a mystery (Koocher, 1974).

Avoidance or silence teach children that the subject of death is forbidden. Evasive, incomplete, or false information can prevent children from clarifying their feelings and thoughts about death or cause them to react with undue anxiety. Children might think they did something wrong to cause the disappearance, or feel that Grandma left because she didn't love them anymore.

But it's also important not to provide more information than children ask for or can handle cognitively and emotionally. Simple, direct answers to questions are best. Drawing from familiar experiences, such as the loss of a pet, can make death more understandable and produce the least possible confusion (Koocher, 1974). Because of the preschool child's magical, animistic, and egocentric interpretation of the world, it is important to ask children to repeat what they have heard. That way, any confusion can be corrected. "It is far better to explore and respond to the child's ideas, than to allow magical or unspoken fears to play upon a child's imagination" (Koocher, 1974, p. 410).

Death education with kindergarten and first-grade children can be a rewarding experience (Bowen, 1977). The death of the class pet hamster, dead leaves in the fall, and discussions of the food chain help children see that death is a normal part of the life cycle (Crase and Crase, 1976). A number of good children's books have been written to help youngsters learn about death. Informal reading and open dialogue with adults can encourage children to express their feelings. When information is presented in a factual, honest, and sensitive way, children are able to understand facts about death that match their unique personal experiences and their cognitive ability (Bowen, 1977; Weininger, 1979).

Sex-Role Development and Relationships

Roosevelt's parents were pleased when his grandparents bought him a small rubber football for his birthday. But when Caroline's favorite aunt bought her a doll and carriage for her birthday, Caroline's parents did not approve. As we mentioned in Chapter 4, some people argue that there are natural differences between boys and girls that predispose them to certain adult sex roles. And parents like Roosevelt's believe we shouldn't go against society's standards in socializing children. Others, like Caroline's parents, claim that tightly defined sex roles limit children's opportunities right from the beginning of life.

In previous chapters, you saw that parents and adults treat boys and girls differently. And even though some differences between boys and girls are influenced by biological factors (aggression, for example), most appear related to socialization by parents and others.

SEX-ROLE STEREOTYPES

Sex-role stereotyping is the belief that it is only natural and fitting for males and females to adhere to traditional sex-role patterns. Stereotyped ideas about behaviors for boys and girls are held by parents (Fagot, 1974; Rheingold and Cook, 1975) and preschool teachers (Robinson et al., 1980). During early childhood, sex-role stereotypes are not only transmitted by parents and teachers but also through media such as television (Ruble et al., 1981; McGhee and Frueh, 1980), children's books (Koblinsky et al., 1978), peer interaction (Lamb and Roopnarine, 1979), and other influences in the child's expanding social system. As early as two years of age, youngsters have a lot of knowledge about sex-role stereotypes (Kuhn et al., 1978). And from three years of age, peers reinforce one another for sex-appropriate behavior and punish one another for sex-inappropriate activities (Lamb and Roopnarine, 1979).

Preschoolers persistently hold on to their sex-role stereotypes. One research team (Cordua et al., 1979) showed five- and six-year-olds films of a man and woman in an occupation characteristic of the opposite sex (such as male nurse or female physician). When asked who had been the physician and who had been the nurse, children usually reversed what they had just seen. They said the man had been the physician and the woman had been the nurse. There was a stronger tendency for children to relabel the male nurse than the female physician. The researchers explained the persistent mislabeling in terms of children's everyday exposure to stereotyped roles.

Some authorities say stereotyping is a necessary stage in the course of sex-role development—but not the final stage (Rebecca et al., 1976; Pleck, 1975). Some believe the stereotyping stage parallels the child's cognitive development (Garnets and Pleck, 1979; Kohlberg, 1966; Ullian, 1976). For example, preoperational children view the world in dichotomies—big/small, long/short and so forth. They learn to classify people in the same way as male/female—just as Brad made simple classifications of red and green popcorn for his Christmas tree (see Chapter 9). Asked to think in terms of a variety of sex-role choices for people, preoperational children are hampered by their rigid way of thinking. Of course, the stereotyped stage is the end of the road for some children—depending on their social environment. But others will have an opportunity to examine more flexible sex roles (see Spotlight 10.4).

ANDROGYNY

Sex-role stereotypes were the norm until quite recently and parents didn't question them. But today some parents are calling for an end to sex-role stereotyping. In fact, some psychologists argue that androgyny (see Chapter 7) is a more human

Many people are calling for an end to sex-role stereotyping in all
areas of our lives and culture.

standard of psychological health (Bem and Lenney, 1976) than sex-role stereotyping. Parents like Caroline's who want androgynous children believe that socializing them to be exclusively feminine or masculine doesn't prepare them for today's
world. Reflecting this attitude, it has become more acceptable for boys to play
with dolls and girls to participate in active games and compete with male playmates. Once committed to an androgynous view, many parents and teachers allow
children to explore both masculine and feminine roles, give rewards for androgynous behaviors, and set examples for children by modeling androgynous behaviors. The aim is not to make boys and girls the same. Instead, androgynous parents
are more interested in giving their sons and daughters the freedom to blend masculine and feminine traits—to be themselves.

❉ Spotlight 10.4: Male Preschool Teachers

During the 1940s it was unheard of—even prohibited—for men to work in child care or kindergarten classes. As one educator put it: "Men should not be asked to play nursemaid to young children. . . . No man should be assigned to teach children below the fifth grade level." (Kaplan, 1947, p. 368). Another educator expressed a similar view: "One could hardly imagine a situation in which a man would be in his element teaching a class of kindergartners. He would immediately become suspect." (Tubbs, 1946, p. 394).

But the men of the 1980s are quite different from the men of the 1940s. Over the past four decades, our society has redefined what is meant by masculinity and femininity. Both men and women have crossed sex-role lines and adopted nontraditional jobs and behaviors—a situation that has liberated women as well as men.

So today, along with increasing awareness of the importance of men in the rearing of children, we have become more aware of their importance in caring for the young. The critically acclaimed film *Kramer versus Kramer,* clearly demonstrated that when a contemporary man is placed into a traditional female role of caring for a child, he can not only cope but do well. In much the same way, we have progressed in our views of males nurturing young children. In the past, few men have chosen to work with young children. In 1974, for instance, male child care workers—also called male caregivers—comprised only 4 percent of the total number of workers in this nation (Drive to open, 1974). Among the 1,170,000 elementary school teachers in the United States in 1979, only 15 percent were men (Phillips, 1979).

With the loosening of gender-based sex roles, more nurturant men are on the scene. In fact, male caregivers have become well organized. They have established the National Men's Child Care Caucus as part of the National Association for the Education of Young Children and they have founded a national newsletter—*Nurturing News*—dedicated to increasing male involvement in the lives of young children on all levels in the home and on the job. The Nurtury—a predominantly male-staffed child care center in California serving a population of single-parent children—was founded to give children from father-absent homes consistent, nurturing relationships with men (Brody, 1978).

Research shows that men who choose to work with young children are different from the male stereotype in at least two important ways. First, when asked why they entered child care, one group of full-time caregivers didn't give the same reasons as men in traditionally male jobs. Instead of money, prestige, or power, the men said they selected their jobs because of altruistic concerns. They mentioned such reasons as love and enjoyment of working with children, the appeal of the content of the day-care program and curriculum, and the desire to make a special contribution to the preschool age group (Robinson, 1981).

Second, when the personalities of male caregivers were compared with those of men in traditionally male jobs such as engineering, it was discovered that male caregivers possess more "feminine" traits than men in traditional job types (Robinson and Canaday, 1978), possibly because work with young children requires both male and female (or *androgynous*) orientations. Male caregivers are expected to be sensitive to young children's needs but also to be assertive and show initiative where situations demand such a stance. Some children need help learning to potty, while others just need to be held. Children need caregivers—men and women—who can be nurturant and warm, qualities that historically have carried "feminine" labels.

Male caregivers can provide children with an androgynous role model, which teaches them
firsthand that caring for the young can be a woman's or a man's job.

In her most recent work, Baumrind (1982) observed that sex-typed parents
are more traditional but more firm and authoritative in their child-rearing practices. In contrast, androgynous parents practice a more permissive, child-centered
upbringing, resulting in lax parental authority. Children of sex-typed parents are
more socially assertive and generally competent than children of androgynous parents. Baumrind (1982) explains why: ''It is probably because androgynous parents
tend to be child centered, and children from child-centered homes tend to be less
competent than children from firm or traditional homes'' (p. 68). But androgynous parenting remains somewhat ''experimental'' in nature and additional research needs to be done in this area.

Parenting styles are unique from culture to culture—ranging from restrictive to permissive and from harsh to nurturant. Fear, anger, and aggression are universal, but cultures view them differently. What do the Pygmies of the Ituri Forest in Africa, the Tahitians in the South Pacific, the Senai of Malaysia, the Eskimo of the Arctic Circle, the Bushmen of the Kalahari Desert in Northwest Africa, and the Tasaday of the Phillippines all have in common? They are very unaggressive people who are very gentle and loving toward their children (Montagu, 1978). In contrast, Whiting (1963) reported that over 80 percent of the Nyansongo mothers of Kenya, Africa, punish children between three and six with *caning*—beating on the legs and buttocks with a tall weed or branch. And in that culture, fear is an ordinary means of parental control: "I'll throw you out in the dark and you'll be eaten by hyenas." As we saw in the case of Omblean (see Prologue), the Mundugumor people of New Guinea view the bearing and rearing of children as an unwelcome task. They are aggressive with children, and infants are treated roughly and encouraged to be aggressive.

Generally, our society discourages aggression—especially violence towards children. Parents and caregivers in the United States emphasize the democratic ideal in child rearing, providing children toys of their own. But in countries like Russia, the notion of common property is adhered to. One doll might be given to a group of children, and one large playpen may be used for several infants. Similar practices are followed in the kibbutzim of Israel. As the following account indicates, value is placed on group living and upbringing, and competition and private property are discouraged.

GROWING UP ON A KIBBUTZ

Imagine, if you can, the urban atmosphere of Tel Aviv, a short, dusty bus ride, a winding road through orange and grapefruit groves, and the first glimpse of a vital, exciting collective settlement of over two thousand persons. This was Givat Brenner, the largest *kibbutz* (Hebrew for "group") in Israel. Here the principle of mutual aid is predominant, as every member is responsible for the welfare of every other member and for the welfare of the kibbutz as a whole. A socialistic structure, based on cooperation and equality, prevails. There is no competition, private property, or exploitation. Men and women enjoy an equal status at home and at work. High value is placed on group living and upbringing. Grouping within the kibbutz is based on age, occupation, and interests. Collective education begins very early—from a few days after birth through eighteen years of age.

The process begins when mother and infant return from the hospital. The baby is admitted to the Infants' House where he or she will remain for the first year. Responsibility for overall care of babies and management of the Infant House is carried on by a specially trained nurse, or *metapelet*. The metapelet keeps notes on children, guides young and inexperienced mothers in feeding and care, and supervises a permanent group of infants until their entrance into kindergarten. For the first few months infants don't leave the Infant House but are visited

Summary

1. Encouraging independence helps children become competent and develops initiative, but when children experience frequent failure and criticism about initiating certain activities, a deep sense of guilt can predominate.

2. During early childhood, children's dependency shifts from maintaining nearness to seeking distant relationships in the form of attention, approval, and a parent-child partnership. Three types of parenting styles have been linked to three types of children's personalities: authoritative parents/energetic-friendly children;

in the afternoons by parents and siblings. After six months, infants are brought to their parents' room for an evening visit.

At about fifteen months of age, children are transferred as a group from the Infant House to the Toddlers' House. In some instances the infant metapelet is transferred with them and she remains with the group until they are about five years old. Generally, the children become members of the peer group known as the kindergarten at about five years of age. This new grouping consists of about eighteen children and represents the combining of three groups from the Toddlers' House. The kindergarten is housed in a building of its own and contains bedrooms, each for three or four children, with special "corners" for toys and books intended to stimulate individual and independent activity.

The kibbutz educational authorities have worked out methodological programs designed to develop the child's senses and physical skills. Group activities and creative expression are considered vital. Art, music, and "rhythmics" are important and there is an emphasis on nature study and the natural environment. During this period, the children begin to get acquainted with the kibbutz workaday world. They visit various branches of the economy and begin to take care of small gardens and small animals. The children also make their own beds, set the table at meal time, and do other small chores as part of the day's routine.

The kindergarten stage covers a period of three to four years and includes a transitional period which corresponds to a traditional first grade. It is during this period that the fundamental instruction of the three R's is begun. An attempt is made to incorporate these basic skills in an individual manner and according to the child's level of maturity and development. There is increased emphasis on group activities, mutual aid, discipline, and on social interaction and integration. The pattern of family contact as established during the Toddler period continues throughout childhood.*

Many positive factors of kibbutz child rearing have been reported by social scientists, which can be incorporated in current day-care practices throughout the world. For example, Bettelheim (1969) found that toddlers in the kibbutz experience less separation anxiety than those brought up in traditional family groupings. They get a sense of stability and belonging from the group upbringing. In general, kibbutz child rearing offers what good parenting provides—physical, cognitive, social, and emotional needs are met.

But communal child rearing does appear to have limits. The kibbutz is a heterogeneous community of highly motivated people, but, as Bettelheim notes there are disadvantages to the kibbutz child-rearing system, mainly the loss of the child's individuality and creativity. The system has not been entirely successful. In fact, it seems to be eroding; communal child rearing on the kibbutz is no longer as common as it once was.

---

*Adapted from a manuscript written by Bobbie H. Rowland, Associate Professor of Human Development and Learning, University of North Carolina, Charlotte. Used with permission.

---

authoritarian parents/conflicted-irritable children; and permissive parents/impulsive-aggressive children.

3. Spending more time in peer social interactions aids preschoolers in loosening strong ties from parents and helps them become physically separate as well as socially and emotionally independent. With age, preschoolers become less socially isolated and more socialized in their playgroups.

4. Play is an important avenue for social and emotional development. Six categories of play have been identified as preschoolers move from solitary activity to

playing mostly with peers: unoccupied behavior, onlooker play, solitary play, parallel play, associative play, and cooperative play. In dramatic play, children enjoy acting out scenes they observe from everyday life.

5. Emotional development is increasingly influenced by the larger society as children interact more with peers, watch television, and go to preschool. Aggression, prosocial development, childhood psychosis, and coping with death are particular concerns during early childhood.

6. Preschool children may insist on conformity to sex-role stereotypes that are transmitted through parents, teachers, peers, and the media. But some modern-day parents are calling for an end to sex-role stereotyping and are advocating androgynous child rearing, despite its controversial nature.

Empathetic Activities

■ What feelings did you have as you read The Case of the Parent-Teacher Conference and A Case of Dramatic Play? What feelings do you think Mary Hopkins had? Nicky's mother? Nicky, Roosevelt, and Caroline?

■ What are some things you can do to help youngsters as they watch television? How can you help them understand death?

■ Observe a group of preschool children in their classroom. Write a summary of your observations, using the following guidelines:

  ■ Which types of Parten's play classifications do you notice most often?

  ■ What roles are acted out in the children's dramatic play?

  ■ What theory or philosophy do you see evidenced in this preschool program?

  ■ Do children reinforce each other for sex-stereotypes in their play?

■ Re-read The Case of the Parents' Day Picnic (Chapter 8) and The Case of the Parent-Teacher Conference. Then, review the principles of Erikson, Piaget, the behaviorists, and the humanists (see Chapter 1). Consider each theory separately to explain Nicky's behavior. Then, using the systems approach, combine information from all theories to get a more total understanding of Nicky's behavior.

■ Using information from this chapter, predict how Mary Hopkins might answer the question Nicky's mother desperately asked, "What can I do to help Nicky behave better in school?"

■ Describe how the effects of television on preschoolers provide a good illustration of the larger social system's influence on the *Whole Child*.

■ How does excessive television viewing influence a child's relationships with others?

Related Readings

Kaye, Evelyn. *The ACT guide to children's television: How to treat TV with TLC.* Boston: Beacon Press, 1979. A timely, hard look at the impact of television on young viewers, supported by Action for Children's Television (ACT). Exposes the struggle between big business and the needs of children.

Newson, John, and Newson, Elizabeth. *Toys and playthings: In development and remediation.* New York: Pantheon Books, 1979. A developmental guide for selecting toys from infancy through middle childhood. Includes chapters on toys and playthings for sick or handicapped children. An excellent resource for parents and child development practitioners.

Norris, Gloria, and Miller, Jo Ann. *The working mother's complete handbook: Everything you need to know to succeed on the job and at home.* New York: E. P. Dutton, 1979. Practical tips for wage-earning mothers on how to cope with the everyday pressures of their new role. Research and advice from child development experts dispels any lingering guilt or doubt a working mother might have. Readable and entertaining.

Paluszny, Maria. *Autism: A practical guide for parents and professionals.* Syracuse, N.Y.: Syracuse University, 1980. A well-written, practical, and informative guide for someone interested in the fundamentals of childhood autism. Chapters include characteristics of autism, symptoms, causes, therapeutic approaches, educational responsibilities and approaches, parent involvement, and future planning.

Rubin, Zick. *Children's friendships.* Cambridge, Mass.: Harvard University, 1980. A very readable account of the development of social relationships among toddlers and preschool children. Lots of case examples make reading fun!

V Middle Childhood

(ages 6 to 12)

11 *Middle Childhood: Physical and Cognitive Development*

The Case of the Tree House

With help from their fathers, Brad, Roosevelt, and Scotty planned the amount of wood they would need for a tree house and paid for it with their savings. When the wood was delivered, the boys stacked it neatly in Brad's backyard while his four-year-old brother, Josh, looked on in wonderment. Then the boys sorted bolts and nails into piles according to size and length.

On Friday night, the boys received permission to camp in the backyard so they could begin work on their tree house early Saturday morning.

After gobbling up their breakfast cereal, the boys measured and sawed the wood pieces for their tree house floor. Soon Josh came out. He watched as each boy sawed five pieces of wood. Then he studied the yard and the piles of wood and asked, "When did the truck bring more wood?"

Brad replied with disgust, "Silly, there's no more wood. We just sawed the big pieces into smaller ones. Would you please get lost!"

The boys' skill in sawing and hammering improved throughout the day as they worked with their dads to build the tree house. Soon the house was complete. Their house didn't have two bedrooms or a bath, but the boys were proud of it and they collapsed with exhaustion. Next weekend they planned to ride their bikes over to the dump to look for useful decorations for their new tree house.

Physical Growth

If Kim, Scotty, and their gang were to continue to grow at the rate they did during prenatal development, they would be twenty feet tall at age twenty and weigh much more than the earth (Williams and Stith, 1980)! Fortunately, as you can see in Fig. 11.1, the general body growth rate decreases by age five or six and levels off in middle childhood before spurting ahead again during the adolescent growth spurt (see Chapter 13), which begins late in middle childhood. As arms and legs grow and fat decreases, school children begin to look more like adults—leaving behind the stockiness of early childhood.

Scotty's mother was surprised to note the similar heights and weights of the nine-year-old boys and girls Scotty played with. Early in the school years, patterns of physical development are similar for boys and girls but variations in physical growth are more pronounced among older school children. This is partly because of individual differences in the start of the growth spurt and because girls begin their growth spurt before boys.

HEIGHT AND WEIGHT

During the middle years, most children grow a steady two to two and a half inches per year (Lowrey, 1978). The average height of most six year olds is just four feet, but by adolescence, the average child nears five feet in height (Tanner, 1978).

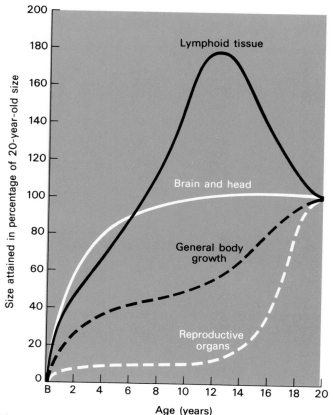

Figure 11.1 **Summary chart of growth and development**

Typically, girls are slightly shorter than boys at age six, equal to them at age nine, and slightly taller at age ten (Hamill, et al., 1977).

Weight increase is fairly constant from age three to the adolescent growth spurt (averaging 4.4 to 5.9 pounds per year). Between ages six and twelve, weight generally doubles—increasing from about forty to eighty pounds. Girls typically weigh less than boys at age six, about the same as them at age eight, and more than them at age nine or ten (Hamill et al., 1977).

STRUCTURAL DEVELOPMENT

Brain and Nervous System. There is little actual increase in the size of the brain during middle childhood—from 90 percent of adult weight at age five to 95 percent of adult weight at age ten. But refinements of the nervous system and the brain continue (Tanner, 1970). New connections develop among nerve cells, brain hemispheres increase in specialization, and nerve tissue connecting the two hemi-

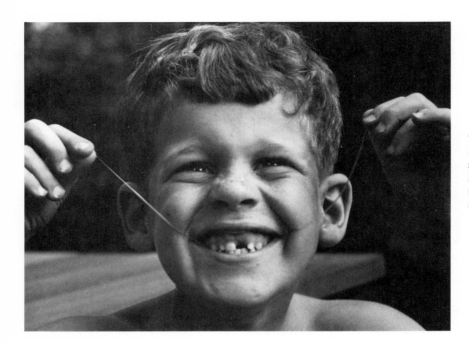

The smile of this young boy is a common sight among school-age children as they lose their "baby" teeth and await the arrival of permanent teeth.

spheres matures by age seven or eight allowing greater communication between the two sides. These nervous system refinements lay the foundation for cognitive development.

Bones and Teeth. Bone growth in middle childhood is particularly obvious in the facial and long arm and leg bones. But children's bones still have proportionally fewer minerals and more water and protein-like material than adults' bones (Williams and Stith, 1980). Children's bones require a larger blood supply than adult bones, ligaments are less firmly attached, and there is more space between bones at joints. These characteristics make the growing child more flexible, more affected by pressures and muscle pulls, and less resistant to bone infections carried by the blood than adults (Breckenridge and Vincent, 1965). Such immature bones and ligaments can be damaged when adults push children too hard to win at organized sports

Girls lose their baby teeth earlier than boys. By age eleven or twelve, both boys and girls have all their permanent teeth except the second and third molars. Children's faces look more adult-like as permanent teeth appear, the jaw lengthens, and facial bones grow.

Muscles and Fat. Fatty tissue does not typically change in middle childhood unless eating habits change. But a gradual increase in muscle mass and strength occurs. It was this increase in strength that allowed the boys to persist in their efforts to build a tree house for almost the whole day on Saturday. Boys have more muscle tissue than girls, apparently because of higher levels of androgen, the male sex hormone (Maccoby, 1980). Because they have more muscle cells, males at all ages are typically stronger than females.

Even though muscle development during the middle years results in greater strength and firmer attachments to bone, muscles still don't function as well as they do in the adult. Awkwardness, inefficient movement, the inability to sit still for long periods of time, and quick fatigue attest to the immaturity of muscle tissue in the middle years. As muscles become stronger, children experience a stronger drive to be active.

Posture

"Scotty, will you please stand up straight!" Scotty's mom pleaded for the third time that day.

"Aw, Mom, can't a guy even relax around here?" complained Scotty.

Good, upright posture requires continuous muscular activity. Poor posture adds an extra burden to bones, ligaments, and joints and may be the result of laziness, poor development of muscles, or illness. Such activities as Little League baseball, ballet dancing, building a treehouse, or riding bikes can be beneficial in improving the posture and muscle tone of the body. But when baseball or ballet dancing are begun too early or carried to extremes, they can cause bone or muscle damage. Little League elbow is a muscular injury related to pitching and severe cases can require surgery. Toe dancing before age thirteen may cause damage to the child's rapidly growing foot.

PHYSICAL GROWTH, PERSONALITY, AND POPULARITY

W. H. Sheldon (1940) identified three types of body build and their corresponding personality traits:

1. *endomorphs*—plump, round individuals who are jolly and calm.
2. *mesomorphs*—muscular, athletic individuals who are bold and outgoing.
3. *ectomorphs*—tall and frail individuals who are shy, withdrawn, and characterized by thoughts instead of action.

It is easy to find examples of individuals having these body types who also have the associated personality traits. For example, Jun has a muscular build and advanced motor skills, and he is a very outgoing individual. But there are many people who don't fit such stereotypes. Velma, for instance, is also mesomorphic. But she tends to have the personality traits associated with ectomorphs—she is withdrawn, weak, and sickly. Sheldon's theory has also been criticized because the three types usually don't appear in pure forms. Instead, most people have a mixture of all three body types and their corresponding personality characteristics—some matching the stereotype more than others.

Body build can affect the child's relationships with others. A poorly coordinated, frail but bright son may be a big disappointment to an athletic father. He may be accepted if his father values scholarly achievements. In one study, parents were asked to rate their preschool children on a series of personality traits, while researchers secretly categorized the children on the three body types (Walker, 1963). Parents viewed their children differently, depending upon the child's body type. Mesomorphs of both sexes were seen as energetic. Endomorphic boys were rated as aggressive and bossy, but endomorphic girls were said to be cooperative and outgoing. Male ectomorphs were viewed as withdrawn, shy, and eager to please, while female ectomorphs were seen as uncooperative and hard to get along with.

Of the three body types, our society generally favors mesomorphs. Boys between six and ten years old rated the mesomorph physique as the ideal for themselves. And they viewed agemates who were overweight or very skinny as less popular than those with athletic builds (Staffieri, 1967).

Whether or not a child is physically attractive also makes a difference in how they are viewed by peers and adults. Generally, when shown photographs of attractive and unattractive children, children and adults gave more desirable ratings to attractive youngsters (Lerner and Lerner, 1977).

Motor Development

Although the motor abilities of school children do not improve as dramatically from age six to twelve as they did from birth to five, there is a gradual increase in ability to perform a variety of complex motor skills. School children, like Scotty, Brad, and Roosevelt, devote time to perfecting motor skills such as sawing wood and hammering nails to build a tree house.

LATERALITY

Laterality involves distinguishing between the left and right sides of the body and preferring one side to another. Laterality improves rapidly in middle childhood.

Most six-year-olds have learned the right/left distinction but have trouble relating their personal body orientation to that of others. That's why teachers learn to turn their backs to children when demonstrating raising the right and left hand. First grade or kindergarten children facing a teacher who raises a right hand are likely to raise their left hand. But by age seven, 75 percent could identify the left and right hands of another person regardless of the direction they faced, and by age eight, 95 percent could do so.

Laterality is an important basis for many kinds of learning (such as noticing the left and right side of the letters b, d, p, and q). Persistent difficulty in laterality can result in problems such as letter reversal and the incorrect placement of letters in words.

By age seven or eight, handedness and laterality are firmly established, with nearly 90 percent of U.S. children being right-handed.

Changing Routines

Upon entering middle childhood, the poor appetite of early childhood gradually fades as the school child begins to eat larger amounts and likes a wider variety of food. Middle childhood is also characterized by good health. But care must be taken to help children avoid accidents.

NUTRITION

Body size does not increase very rapidly during the school years, so calorie needs are not as high as they will be during the adolescent growth spurt.

Nutrition education is important for school children since they decide what they will eat in the school lunchroom and often at home as well. Children often eat breakfast earlier than their parents and also directly influence the food purchases made by their parents. A favored food in this age group is sugared cereal. In one study, children aged five to seven persuaded their mothers to buy snack foods, candy, and soft drinks 38 percent of the time and their own cereal choices 88 percent of the time. Mothers were persuaded by eight- to ten-year-olds' food preferences over 90 percent of the time (Ward and Wackman, 1971). The majority of food advertisements on children's television programs run counter to developing good nutritional habits (Gussow, 1972.). So it is important for parents and educators to guide children's nutritional habits in the lunchroom, classroom, and home. In this way, healthy food patterns can be set for life.

ACCIDENTS AND ILLNESS

Scotty asked for, and received, all of the wood scraps from the boys' tree house. He built a huge ramp over the driveway and planned to jump it on his bicycle like his idol Evel Knievel.

When Scotty's mother came home from work, she absolutely refused to allow Scotty to make the jump. "You don't have the practice and the safety precautions that Evel Knievel has," she argued.

In middle childhood, children's physical-motor skills have advanced enough so that children sometimes become daring and take extraordinary risks. In 1974, accidents accounted for almost half the deaths of children age five to fourteen (Snapper and Ohms, 1977). Half of these accidents were caused by motor vehicles, followed in frequency by drowning and burns. School children are especially prone to accidents when they are tired, distracted, or overeager, and when they attempt feats beyond their skill level.

Some children are particularly accident- or illness-prone. Repeated frustration, hostility toward adults, broken homes, authoritarian discipline, and poor

School-age children are particularly prone to accidents, as their physical skills now enable them to attempt daring feats while their cognitive abilities do not yet allow them to weigh the dangers of such actions.

social adjustment are associated with being accident- or illness-prone (Harmon et al., 1980). Teaching children about traffic rules and safety precautions and alerting them to common household poisons can help prevent many accidents.

Through immunization, such childhood diseases as diphtheria and whooping cough have almost been eliminated. As a result, the school years are typically healthy years. Unfortunately, many parents no longer recognize the need for proper immunization. About 20 percent of American children now lack adequate immunization against diphtheria, tetanus, and whooping cough. Even the number of children being immunized against polio is decreasing. Fearing outbreaks of illness, school districts across the country are beginning to say "No Shots, No School!"

Cognitive Development

As you saw in Chapter 9, the ages from five to seven years mark an important transition period in the way children think (White, 1965). These cognitive changes affect children's functioning in many areas, as you will see in our discussions of memory, reading, intelligence, and creativity.

CONCRETE OPERATIONS

Between the ages of seven and eleven, children's thought is no longer dominated by perception, so they develop the ability to perform many cognitive operations that preschool children cannot. Brad's preoperational egocentrism has disappeared and is replaced by a new form of egocentric thought. School-age Brad can decenter his thought, follow transformations, and reverse his thinking. As a result, he can make logical decisions and solve the conservation problems that baffled him as a preoperational child. Brad is in the **concrete operational period,** the third period of cognitive development described by Piaget in which logical thinking is limited to problems involving concrete or actual objects. Not until adolescence will Brad be able to think logically about abstract problems.

Logical Thinking in Concrete Operational Children
EGOCENTRISM.   As a preoperational child, Brad was not able to take the viewpoint of his mother as he tried to solve the conservation problems she posed and he did not feel a need to validate his own thoughts. In contrast, Brad as a concrete thinker can take other viewpoints and is aware that others can reach different conclusions.

This new awareness comes about largely through social interaction with peers. Instead of the monologues characteristic of preschool children, school children exchange information as they talk with each other. Play also reflects the decreased egocentrism of early childhood. Cooperation and competition emerge.

But egocentrism does not disappear in the concrete operational period. Instead it undergoes a series of changes. As we observe the school age child's attempts to solve more difficult problems, we can see a new form of egocentrism emerge.

The egocentrism of schoolchildren prevents them from thinking about several possible courses of action while testing them systematically. And concrete thinkers often mistake possibility for necessity. As a result, once nine-year-olds have formulated a hypothesis (possibility), they tend to make contradictory facts fit the hypothesis rather than changing the hypothesis to fit the facts.

One experiment examined five- to seventeen-year-olds' thought processes when trying to obtain pieces of candy from a three-knobbed box that served as a type of slot machine (Weir, 1964). Certain knobs had to be pressed in order to obtain the greatest number of pieces. One knob never paid off; one paid off one third of the time; and the third paid off two thirds of the time. Preschoolers proceeded on a trial and error basis and quickly learned to press only the two-third's knob to get the most candy. Adolescents formulated many hypotheses, tested them systematically, and also solved the problem. Concrete thinkers had the most trouble. They typically formed a hypothesis such as *If I win, stick with that knob; if I lose, shift to another.* Once that strategy was chosen, concrete thinkers assumed it was correct, and blamed the machine for being wrong when it didn't pay off according to their hypothesis.

DECENTRATION.   When Brad was nine, his father held out some money in both hands. His right hand contained four quarters; in his left hand were two Susan B. Anthony dollars. Brad was told to choose the hand he wanted. He almost chose the four quarters, but stopped just in time as he noticed the markings on the dollars. Children in the concrete operational period are now capable of **decentration**—Piaget's term for the ability to consider several dimensions of objects or events. Brad was able to decenter his thinking and consider both the markings on the coins and the number of coins as well as the relative importance of markings versus number. Four-year-old Josh would have centered his attention on number alone and chosen the quarters.

ABILITY TO FOLLOW TRANSFORMATIONS.   Preschoolers focus on only the beginning and ending states of a transformation. But Piaget observed that concrete thinkers have the ability to consider and understand the relationship between steps in a transformation (Wadsworth, 1979).

One spring day Brad rode his bicycle to a field where he carefully selected several caterpillars for his terrarium. Over the course of many weeks, Josh, Brad's four-year-old brother, watched the caterpillars eat the leaves Brad gathered. Eventually, the caterpillars spun cocoons and two beautiful butterflies later emerged. Looking into the terrarium one day, Josh called to his brother, ''The caterpillars are gone. But some butterflies got in.'' Brad tried to explain how the caterpillars turned into the butterflies, but Josh insisted the caterpillars were gone, not changed.

REVERSIBLE THOUGHT.   **Reversibility** is Piaget's term indicating the ability to reverse the thought process and return it to its original state. For example, Brad now knows that if closely spaced buttons are moved farther apart, their number doesn't change because the buttons can be moved close together again. Reversibility is important in the areas of logic or ideas. Addition, for example, can be reversed by subtraction, and multiplication by division. School-age Brad learns to check his subtraction problems by adding certain numbers and his division problems by multiplying them.

Cognitive Concepts of Concrete Thinkers

CONSERVATION.   According to Piaget, before children can conserve, they must be able to decenter, follow transformations, and reverse thought. These schemes begin to develop between the ages of five or six but are not completely developed until around age seven—toward the end of the preoperational period. Conservation of number, liquid, length, mass, and area also occur early in the concrete operational period. As you saw in The Case of the Tree House, nine-year-old Brad can conserve length. But as Spotlight 11.1 illustrates, more advanced types of conservation problems such as weight and volume are not solved until the end of concrete operations and the beginning of formal operations (ten to eleven years) (Piaget and Inhelder, 1969). Most children acquire conservation in about the same sequence, though not always at the same age (Fogelman, 1970). Variation among groups also occurs. Middle-class children, for example, typically move into concrete operations earlier than lower-class children (Almy et al., 1966).

Piaget assumed that failure to conserve occurs because of limitations in underlying cognitive structures such as reversibility. But when children were trained not in reversibility but in noticing and telling the difference between objects such as an orange and a banana, their ability to conserve improved (Sigel et al., 1966; Gelman, 1969). Nonconserving children also improved in their ability to conserve through observational learning (Charbonneau et al., 1976; Zimmerman and Lanaro, 1974). Most psychologists substantiate Piaget's notion that preoperational children have trouble with conservation problems. But findings of these studies suggest that attentional or discrimination skills or lack of learning opportunities may have more to do with the inability to conserve than the lack of underlying cognitive structures such as reversibility.

CLASSIFICATION

Brad's understanding of class inclusion has progressed tremendously since age four when he sorted the popcorn at Christmas. The summer Brad was nine, he gathered bagfuls of shells on his vacation and spent hours classifying and labeling them. Brad's mother asked him which shells he had more of—scallops or whelks. "Scallops" was Brad's prompt reply. When his mother then asked "Which do you have more of, scallops or shells?" Brad replied with disgust, "Oh, mother. Of course I have more shells!"

❖ Spotlight 11.1: Conservation Problems

CONSERVATION OF LIQUID (ages 6 to 7). When Brad was five, he stubbornly insisted that his mother's tall, slender glass held more juice than his short, wide cup. He held to his belief even when he watched his mother pour the same amount of juice from the tall glass into the short cup. It appeared to him that the amount decreased because the liquid level was not as high in the cup as in the glass. Now that Brad is nine and can conserve liquid, he scorns his younger brother Josh, who makes the same mistake. *A conserver realizes the amount of liquid isn't changed by the shape of a container.*

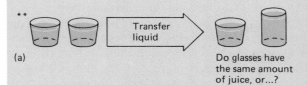

(a) Do glasses have the same amount of juice, or...?

CONSERVATION OF LENGTH (ages 6 to 7). Doreen showed Brad two equally long strings. Brad agreed that an ant would have to walk just as far no matter which string it walked on. When Doreen curved one string, five-year-old Brad thought an ant on the straight string would have to walk farther. But now at age nine, Brad can conserve length and teases Josh by posing many variations of this problem for his little brother. *Conservers realize the length of a string is not affected by its shape or its placement.*

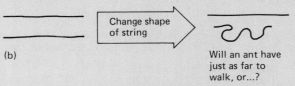

(b) Change shape of string. Will an ant have just as far to walk, or...?

CONSERVATION OF AREA (ages 7 to 8). Two green placemats were put before five-year-old Brad on the kitchen table. Brad's father placed a plastic toy cow on each placemat. Then he told Brad that each cow was in a pasture and asked, "Which cow has more grass to eat?" Brad replied, "They have the same." Then, using red checkers as barns, Brad's father put one barn in each pasture and repeated his question. Brad again responded, "The same." Next Brad's father put three barns in each pasture. In the first pasture the barns are placed far apart. In the second pasture, the barns are placed close together. Asked the question a third time, Brad gave a different answer, as is typical of children who cannot conserve area. He said the cow in the second pasture had more to eat than the cow in the first pasture. Brad maintained this view even when his father pointed out that the barns were the same size. In contrast, nine-year-old Brad, who can conserve area, says both cows have the same amount of grass to eat. *Conservers know that the area covered by an equal number of equal-sized objects is not affected by the arrangement of the objects.*

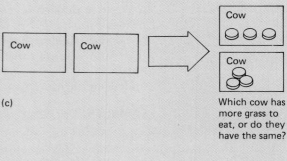

(c) Which cow has more grass to eat, or do they have the same?

CONSERVATION OF MASS OR SUBSTANCE (ages 7 to 8). Dad asked five-year-old Brad to make two balls containing equal amounts of clay. Then, as Brad watched, his father rolled one of the balls into a sausage. Asked whether the amount of clay in the sausage and the ball were the same, Brad replied, "No." Instead, he saw the sausage as containing more clay, even though no clay had been added or taken away. Older and wiser at age nine, Brad now agrees that the amount of clay is the same and laughs at his brother who can't solve the problem. *Conservers know the amount of substance does not change.*

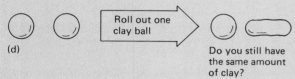

(d)
Roll out one clay ball

Do you still have the same amount of clay?

CONSERVATION OF WEIGHT (ages 9 to 10). Doreen took the same two clay balls and placed them on a balance scale to show Brad that they weighed the same. She then removed them, rolled one into a sausage shape and asked Brad whether they were the same or different weights. At age five, Brad thought the sausage weighed more. But at age nine, Brad cockily replies, "They weigh the same. All you did was roll one out longer, and you could roll it back up again." Brad's answer shows he has achieved reversibility and conservation of weight. *Conservers know a clay ball weighs the same even when its shape is changed.*

CONSERVATION OF VOLUME (ages 11 to 12). One type of conservation problem still cannot be solved by nine-year-old Brad. Doreen again rolls the clay into two equal-sized balls and places them in identical glasses containing equal amounts of water. Brad sees that the water level rises the same amount in both glasses. But when his mother removes the balls from the water and again rolls one into a sausage, Brad answers incorrectly that the sausage shape will cause the water level to rise higher than the ball. Brad thinks the sausage shape will displace more water than the ball. He still can't conserve volume. *Conservers know the volume of water displaced by an object depends on the volume of the object—not its weight, shape, or position.*

(e)
Change shape of one ball

Do the balls of clay weigh the same, or are they different?

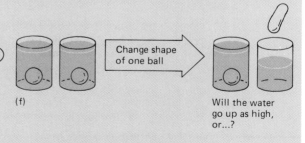

(f)
Change shape of one ball

Will the water go up as high, or...?

Adapted from Piaget and Inhelder (1969) and Labinowicz (1980).

School children love to collect and classify things. The ability to classify or categorize people, objects, events, and ideas saves a tremendous amount of time and makes for a much more efficient memory. This ability gradually develops throughout the middle childhood years and approaches adult abilities by adolescence.

MEMORY

Cognition and memory are closely intertwined and both are important to the perception of and reaction to the world around you. As you experience your world, you gather information through your senses, process it cognitively, then store it through the process called memory. Memory storage in humans consists of three stages: sensory, short-term, and long-term (Atkinson and Shiffrin, 1968; 1971). Immediate sensory impressions enter *sensory storage* momentarily—for less than a second. *Short-term storage* allows you to remember information for a few seconds to a minute. *Long-term storage* allows you to remember information for weeks or years.

Memory Processes.   Rehearsal, organization, and elaboration are *control processes* for storing information in memory (Kagan and Kogan, 1970).

Have you ever thought about what goes on in your head as you try to remember things you read or hear? Ms. Cunningham plays a memory game with her fourth graders that gives some clues on how information is stored and remembered. She begins by saying, ''I have a friend named Susie who likes some things and dislikes others. As I name first her likes and then her dislikes, see how many you can remember from each list.'' *Susie likes:* cheese, books, dresses, skiing, puppies, sheep, lettuce, carrots, cabbage, and kittens. *Susie dislikes:* dogs, ice cream, lambs, candy, cake, cats, reading, sodas, diving, and climbing.

Let's see how Ms. Cunningham's fourth graders used these control processes to help them remember the lists. Brad silently repeated the items and remembered four of Susie's likes and three of her dislikes. *Spontaneous verbal rehearsal*—which Brad used when he simply repeated words to himself—occurs more frequently with older than younger children. And the quality of rehearsal improves with age (Ornstein et al., 1975, Ornstein et al., 1977).

Caroline thought to herself, ''Susie seems to like baby animals instead of adult ones and vegetables but not sweets.'' She remembered five things from each list using *organization*—classifying or organizing material in some way. Caroline partly organized Susie's likes and dislikes by using classification of baby/adult animals and vegetables/sweets. As an aid to memory, this classification process goes hand in hand with concrete operations.

Roosevelt noticed the things Susie likes are all spelled with double letters. Having discovered the overall organizational scheme, he remembered most of the list of ''Likes'' but accidentally added *cookies, swimming* and *summer,* too!

Kim remembered seven items, using *elaboration*—adding to the information in some way to make it easier to remember. She learned to improve her memory by using the technique of story-stacking. She remembered eight items by constructing a mental story about *puppies* and *kittens* eating *cheese* under gigantic *books* upon which *sheep* were grazing on *lettuce, carrots,* and *cabbage!*

Metamemory. Middle childhood is a time when a child's ability to store and retrieve information in memory improves dramatically. Not only are older children and adults better at remembering, they are also more effective at **metamemory**—thinking about how they remember.

In one study, preschool and elementary school children were asked to study a set of items until they could remember them perfectly. Preschoolers failed, while school children had perfect recall (Flavell, 1979). The school children were found to have purposefully rehearsed, organized, or elaborated the list of items in order to remember it.

When told to, younger children will rehearse a list to remember it. But school-age children like Brad, Caroline, Roosevelt, and Kim use metamemory processes spontaneously. Understanding such thought processes and training people to use them efficiently are emerging as important new areas of investigation.

READING

Scotty was excited when a firefighter visited his first-grade class and gave each child a plastic fire hat to wear. Scotty later dictated stories to his teacher about the firefighter's visit and about a fire in his neighborhood that he saw the fire department put out. The teacher typed Scotty's story for him exactly as he told it. Because the syntax and vocabulary were his own, Scotty found the story easy to read and to understand. At the end of the school year, Scotty had a book of his own stories to take home and enjoy reading during the summer months.

Scotty's first-grade teacher was using the **language experience approach** to reading, which utilizes the child's own experiences and language as a basis for learning to read.

In the 1940s, the dominant approach to teaching reading was the **whole word approach,** a technique that stresses the single, whole word as the focus of instruction. Teachers following this approach typically used basal reading textbooks of the Dick, Jane, Baby Sally, and our dog Spot variety. But by the 1950s there was great concern about the many children who weren't reading well.

In 1955, Rudolf Flesch published *Why Johnny Can't Read,* a book attacking the whole-word approach and advocating a return to an old-style **phonics approach,** a technique that emphasizes learning the sounds of letters. Current practices in teaching phonics include having children enthusiastically recite such chants as "Beating heart, beating heart, buh, buh, buh. Hissing snake, hissing snake, s-s-s-s"—which teaches the "b" and "s" sounds. The phonics approach is sometimes called the decoding approach because children learn to "break the code" of the written word.

By 1967, these two approaches were described as the "Great Debate" in teaching reading. On the one side, whole-word-approach advocates argued that "If the purpose of reading is communication, shouldn't meaning be stressed?" (Williams, 1979, p. 918). On the other side, advocates of the phonics approach argued that "English is, after all, based on the alphabetic principle, so shouldn't instruction focus on the correspondence between letters and sounds" (Williams, 1979, p. 918). The debate about which approach is best—language experience, whole word, or phonics—continues without much sign of resolution.

REFLECTIVE AND IMPULSIVE COGNITIVE STYLES

Brad, Nicky, and the other nine-year-old boys in their class participated in an experiment that was like one conducted by Siegelman (1969). The boys completed problems from the Matching Familiar Figures Test (MFF), two of which are shown in Fig. 11.2. In Problem 1, each boy was asked to tell which of the teddy bears in the bottom rows is exactly like the standard one in the top row. The same procedure was followed with Problem 2 and the other items in the test.

Brad took his time and thought carefully about each problem. Like other **reflective children,** Brad considered all the information and the possible solutions before responding to each question. He spent less time looking at the "standard" and more time looking at the possible choices. He compared all the choices and then consulted the standard to see which choice was exactly the same. Reflective children like Brad worry about making mistakes, but they choose harder tasks to work on, stay with tasks longer, and get more answers correct than impulsive children (Kagan, 1965a).

Nicky responded to each problem quickly without thinking it over. Like other **impulsive children,** he ignored details and chose the first solution that looked reasonable. He compared the standard with each choice and made a snap decision as to sameness or difference. Impulsive children like Nicky have more problems with paying attention, reading, reasoning tasks, and schoolwork than reflective children (Kagan, 1965c; Kagan and Kogan, 1970). They also make more errors. Of course, there are those children who are fast and accurate or slow and inaccurate. But we don't know much about them because these groups have usually been disregarded in the research.

Kagan and Kogan (1970) proposed that fear of making a mistake is an important influence on the behavior of reflective and impulsive children. Reflective children don't want to make errors. They believe they can solve the problem and are extra careful with solutions. Impulsive children are more anxious about the testing situation and want to get it over with as soon as possible even if they make mistakes (Zelniker and Jeffrey, 1976).

Some children are born with temperamental characteristics that make them tend to be reflective or impulsive. Reflective and impulsive styles for solving problems are noticed in children as young as five or six (Kagan, 1965b, 1965c, 1966).

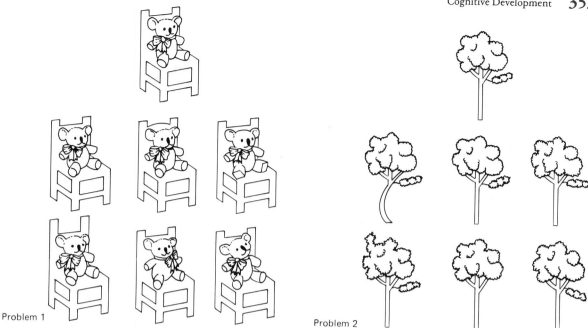

Figure 11.2 Matching familiar figures test (MFF). In each problem, select the object identical to the model shown in the top row.

The tendency to be reflective or impulsive is fairly stable over time and according to situations. You will remember that Brad has usually been thoughtful and reflective and Nicky has been fairly impulsive since kindergarten. As children grow older, they take more time and make fewer errors on such tests as the MFF. In other words, they lose some of their impulsiveness and become more reflective. The response time of American children increases and their errors decrease between the ages of five and twelve (Messer, 1976; Salkind and Nelson, 1980). Because Japanese children are socialized to avoid errors earlier than American children, they are more reflective on the MFF test than their American agemates. It has also been shown that lower-class children in the United States are slightly more impulsive than middle-class children. This may be because lower-class families place less socialization emphasis on making errors on intellectual tasks (Messer, 1976). Some researchers found that teachers could help impulsive children learn to be more reflective through operant conditioning and modeling (Ridberg et al., 1971; Cohen and Przybycien, 1975.) But evidence on the usefulness of training in modifying impulsivity is mixed. Requiring impulsive children to take more time does not reduce their errors (Lange, 1980).

INTELLIGENCE

"Brad's IQ is 111," bragged his mother. "Why, he's very intelligent," replied Grandma Bonnie. "He inherited that from his father!"

Like Grandma Bonnie, many people define intelligence in terms of a single test score—the **IQ** or **intelligence quotient.** The IQ score is the mental age (MA) (which is determined by your score on an intelligence test), divided by the chronological age (CA) and multiplied by 100:

$$IQ = \frac{MA}{CA} \times 100$$

Brad's CA is nine. His mental age is based on the number of items he got correct on an intelligence test and how these results compared with other children of the same age. Brad scored as well as the average ten-year-old, so his MA is ten. Plugging those numbers into the formula, we can calculate Brad's IQ as 111. The average child will have the same MA as the CA and the IQ will be 100. As you can see, Brad has a slightly above average IQ. Grandparents might view this as very exceptional but most others would not. When a child's MA is lower than the CA, the IQ score will be less than 100 and below average.

How Is Intelligence Measured?   Suppose we labeled intelligence as "high," "average," or "low" based on a child's performance on a swimming test. That probably seems ridiculous to you—and it is. Swimming is a test of physical, not intellectual, ability and so is not a valid measure of intelligence. For a test to have **validity,** it must actually measure what it is said to measure. A test should also have **reliability;** that is, it should produce the same results for the same person on two or more occasions. If scores change dramatically when people are retested, the test is not a very useful (reliable) measure of intelligence. Regardless of what you are measuring, you should ask about the validity and reliability of the test being used. As you might imagine, the task of constructing valid and reliable intelligence tests is complicated. Specialists have not agreed upon the types of abilities or skills to test for. They have not even agreed upon a definition of intelligence!

Intelligence tests can be generally categorized as either individual tests—such as the Stanford-Binet and the Wechsler tests—or group tests—such as the Otis-Lennon test. Individual tests are more time-consuming (they take an hour or more to complete), require specially trained examiners, and are more expensive than group tests. But they do provide a somewhat more valid and reliable measure of intelligence than group tests.

THE STANFORD-BINET.   In 1904, Alfred Binet was commissioned by the Minister of Public Instruction in Paris, France, to develop an intelligence test. The purpose of this test was to identify mentally retarded children who could not profit from regular classroom instruction. The test that Binet devised worked. It was successful in predicting who would succeed in school and who would not.

In 1916, Lewis M. Terman of Stanford University revised Binet's test—which then became known as the Stanford-Binet—for use with children in the United States. Terman introduced the term IQ in the scoring of his test. The Stanford-Binet is widely used, especially with children ages three to eight. It is primarily a verbal test. So when children's language differs from standard English, their IQ test scores on the Stanford-Binet reflect this difference.

THE WECHSLER TESTS. The Wechsler Preschool and Primary Scale of Intelligence (WPPSI) is for children aged four to six and a half. The revised version of the Wechsler Intelligence Scale for Children (WISCR) is designed to measure intelligence of children from six to sixteen years old. The Wechsler tests include a balance of verbal and performance items providing two different measures of IQ. Table 11.1 describes the types of items on the Wechsler tests. A low performance IQ may indicate motor/perceptual problems.

THE OTIS-LENNON TESTS. The Otis-Lennon Mental Ability Tests are available on the primary level designed for children in kindergarten and first grade. Children are tested in small groups of ten to sixteen. A booklet containing pictures and drawings is given to each child. Verbal instructions are given, so no reading ability is necessary for the primary level test. Children are evaluated on their ability to classify objects, to demonstrate knowledge of verbal and number concepts and general information, and to follow directions.

Table 11.1
What the Wechsler Tests Measure*

VERBAL SCALE	PERFORMANCE SCALE
1. *General information:* Questions are asked about information most children have been exposed to.	1. *Picture completion:* Children are shown pictures of common objects and asked to tell what is missing in each one.
2. *General comprehension:* Children are asked to tell why certain things are done as they are.	2. *Picture arrangement:* A series of pictures must be placed in the correct order to tell a story.
3. *Arithmetic:* Arithmetic problems ranging from easy to difficult must be solved.	3. *Block design:* Blocks with red, white, or half-red/half-white sides must be arranged to match a pictured design.
4. *Similarities:* Child must tell how two things are alike.	4. *Object Assembly:* Jigsaw-like parts must be assembled to produce a puzzle of a common object.
5. *Vocabulary:* Increasingly difficult words must be defined.	5. *Coding:* Symbols must be matched with numbers according to the code provided.
6. *Digit span:* A series of digits must be repeated in order or in reversed form.	6. *Mazes:* The correct solution must be traced on a maze.

*The WISCR was "standardized" on 2200 children including whites, blacks, Puerto Ricans, Mexican-Americans, American Indians, and Orientals in about the same proportions as they are found in our population.

What Influences Intelligence?   Most researchers attempting to answer this question have defined intelligence as an IQ score. But IQ scores reflect performance on a test and this performance can be affected by all sorts of things. Results of research clearly indicate that heredity plays a part in influencing IQ scores (DeFries and Plomin, 1978). The closer the genetic similarity of individuals, the greater the correlation between their IQ scores. Studies of identical and fraternal twins show greater similarities of IQ scores between identical twins (Erlenmeyer-Kimling and Jarvik, 1963). At age ten, Velma and Thelma (who were introduced in Chapter 4) have IQ scores more similar to each other and to their biological parents than to their adoptive parents, and research studies have found this to be typical (Scarr and Weinberg, 1977). Correlations of scores for unrelated persons are very small—almost 0. Innate temperamental characteristics may also influence performance on intelligence tests (Bell et al., 1971).

We also know that poor environmental conditions can dramatically lower IQ scores and enriched environmental conditions can raise them. Identical twins who have been reared together have more similar IQs than twins who have been reared apart. When unrelated children are reared together, their IQs are more similar than unrelated children reared apart. And the higher the academic emphasis in the home environment, the higher the children's IQs.

Nutritional problems such as hunger can also affect test performance. Hungry children may be lethargic or overactive, and they may not pay attention to the test as well as well-nourished children. Research studies have shown various other findings: Firstborn children generally have higher IQs than laterborns, test scores decrease as the family size increases, and children in one-parent homes have lower test scores than children in two-parent homes (Belmont and Marolla, 1973; Zajonc, 1976).

Children of low socioeconomic status score ten to fifteen IQ points below middle-class children and black children score fifteen to twenty points below white children (Kennedy, 1969). Whether these differences result from heredity or environment continues to be debated. In fact, the nature/nurture debate has never been more intense than when the topic is intelligence.

In the late 1960s, Jensen (1968, 1969) advanced the view that about 80 percent of what is measured by IQ scores is due to heredity and 20 percent is due to environment. Jensen believed the reason blacks score an average of fifteen IQ points lower than whites in our society is due to heredity. Jensen went on to say that those environmental factors that have the most influence on IQ performance are prenatal factors. You can see that if you follow Jensen's views, not much can be done to elevate intellectual performance once a child is born!

Other specialists have severely criticized Jensen's views. For one thing, IQ tests have frequently been culturally biased. And in most cases, low socioeconomic groups and blacks have fewer advantages in the home, poorer nutrition, and larger families than middle-income groups and whites. All these environmental factors have clearly been shown to influence IQ test performance. The data on which Jensen's hypothesis is based was called into question during the late 1960s and early

1970s by researchers claiming that the studies were not planned and conducted appropriately (Bronfenbrenner, 1975). Nevertheless, research supports the view that intelligence is influenced by hereditary factors (Scarr and Weinberg, 1977). In the case of intelligence, as in many other issues, researchers have not taken an either/or stand. Instead, most researchers believe that it is the interaction of hereditary and environmental influences that determines intellectual performance.

CREATIVITY

Piaget (1964) said the basic goal of education should be to produce people who are capable of creativity, invention, and discovery. But what is creativity? Is it related to intelligence? And how can we encourage it?

Who's the more creative, Charlie Brown or Linus? Charlie Brown's descriptions of cloud formations are ordinary ones that most people would give. Linus's descriptions are fluent, flexible, and original. Like Linus, a creative person perceives the world in original ways and can interpret these perceptions to others.

What Is Creativity?   How many ways can you use a brick? This type of open-ended question was asked by Guilford (1954) to measure creativity. To build a house or prop open a door is a usual, noncreative response to the question. But to place a brick in a toilet tank to conserve water is an unusual, creative response thought of by a housewife when one midwestern city was experiencing a water shortage. (The brick reduces the amount of water required to fill the toilet tank.)

Creativity is the ability to solve problems in new and original ways. Like Linus, creative people can interpret their original ideas for others. Creativity involves such characteristics as fluency, flexibility, and originality (Guilford, 1959). A *fluent* person gives many responses on tests for creativity. A *flexible one* gives many different categories of responses. (Using a brick to build a hospital, a fire station, a house, a school, and so on is only one category of response. A creative person would give several categories of responses.) An *original person* gives responses that others taking the test do not. In the cartoon, Linus is fluent, flexible, and original. Charlie Brown is none of these.

A problem with existing tests for creativity is that we don't know how valid they are. Even though the tests measure creative test performance, they may not measure how creative a person is likely to be in everyday life (Anastasi, 1976). As you will see, standard intelligence tests are certainly not valid measures of creativity.

Creativity and Intelligence.   According to Torrance (1962), 70 percent of the most gifted, creative people cannot be identified by standard intelligence test scores. Scotty's creativity was evident in his writing stories and plays but his performance on an IQ test was average. A moderate level of intelligence (which varies for different fields) is required for creativity. Beyond this moderate level, intelligence has no consistent relationship with creativity (Barron, 1961; Chambers, 1969; MacKinnon, 1961; Walberg, 1971). When Wallach and Kogan (1965) gave tests of intelligence and of creativity to 151 fifth graders, they identified four groups; High Intelligence-High Creativity, High Intelligence-Low Creativity, Low Intelligence-High Creativity, Low Intelligence-Low Creativity. An extremely low relationship was found between intelligence and creativity. The researchers also found that children who are both intelligent and creative were not as afraid of errors as other children. They seemed more willing to take a chance and to risk a crazy idea. Intelligent and creative girls seemed to be self-confident and popular in school and in peer relationships. Girls who were intelligent but not creative were sought after but appeared somewhat aloof or cautious in their peer relationships. Low-intelligence, high-creativity girls had little self-confidence and were cautious and hesitant in peer interactions. Boy's creativity did not appear related to social behavior with peers.

Encouraging Creativity.   A series of stages is followed as the creative person attempts to solve a problem (Jackson and Messick, 1967). Ms. Cunningham followed these stages to encourage creative problem solving when she asked her class, "How can children get safely across this big highway in front of the school?" First, she encouraged them to let ideas flow freely. Brad suggested they could be transported across in a balloon; Caroline suggested digging a tunnel under the road; Scotty wanted to build a catapult out of flexible tree limbs and shoot everyone across. At this stage of creative problem solving, all ideas were accepted. Next, the class evaluated the ideas to see which ones were appropriate. Only those ideas that could possibly work were retained at this stage of creative problem solving. Finally, three ideas were selected when the class wrote a letter to the school board recommending possible solutions to the problem: build a tunnel under the road, construct a bridge over it, or post a safety patrol.

Parents who practice tolerance and acceptance, reward creative ideas, use positive rather than punitive disciplinary techniques, have high expectations, and show confidence in their children's ability to behave appropriately are likely to have creative children (Getzels and Jackson, 1962; MacKinnon, 1962). But whether children's creativity caused the parental practices, or whether there are reciprocal causes and effects we cannot yet say.

Those preschoolers who had imaginary playmates tended to be more creative college students (Schaefer, 1969). A child's creative imagination reaches a peak at age four and drops at age five when school attendance begins. E. Paul Torrance (1963, 1970b) says that a child's ability to do creative thinking is highly influenced by what happens in schools. Risk-taking has been correlated with creativity. But many teachers don't associate risk taking and creativity and they don't encourage it among school children (Ritchie, 1981). If we want children to do open-ended, original thinking as opposed to rigid, closed-ended thinking, we must encourage rather than discourage creative behaviors in schools.

Operant conditioning techniques and observational learning have been effective in encouraging creative behavior (Glover and Gary, 1976). There are many ways to encourage creativity, among them removing time limits from activities in which children are very interested; establishing a free, open atmosphere that encourages open expression; taking risks such as being different; allowing children to share ideas and to talk to each other; and reducing levels of stress and anxiety (Maxim, 1980).

EXCEPTIONAL COGNITIVE DEVELOPMENT

Learning Disabilities.   There has been a great deal of controversy regarding the exact definition of learning disability. The following definition was recently published as part of the Education for All Handicapped Act (Public Law 94–142).

> "Specific **learning disability**" means a disorder in one or more of the basic psychological processes involved in understanding or in using language spoken or written, which may manifest itself in an imperfect ability to listen, think, speak, read, write, spell or to do mathematical calculations.

Characteristics of learning disabled youngsters can include impulsiveness, hyperactivity, perceptual-motor difficulties, poor coordination, short attention span, memory or speech disorders, and behavior or emotional problems.

❖ Spotlight 11.2: Learning to Cope with a Learning Disability

Until Alex Roberts started going to school, there was no hint he was any different from any other little boy. "He was well behaved, happy, articulate, with an unusually large vocabulary," said his mother. If there was any area in her son's development that could possibly be classified as slow, it would be his awkwardness at tying shoelaces.

But during the second school year, a pattern began to emerge. Alex wrote slowly and poorly and if he was assigned a story to write about his vacation, it hardly made sense at all. Conferences with his teachers were unsatisfactory and they always resulted in the same frustration.

"The teachers realized he was bright and the only explanation they had for his poor performance was that he was lazy." Alex's mother reported. "We blamed the teachers," she said frankly. Of course, at home the atmosphere was deteriorating. Lectures to the little boy were frequent. "You have your mind on playing, you're not trying," were the words the Roberts found themselves using far too often. And along with the lectures was the gnawing concern that something might be "wrong" with their boy.

"Thank God for Ms. Chandler, Alex's third grade teacher," his mother said. "She mentioned the wonderful work being done at the University of South Carolina Educational Service and the Learn-

ing Disabilities Program and believed Alex might derive great benefit from the service."

After an in-depth study by the service, Alex's problems were pinpointed. Testing established that Alex had difficulty in any task that required sequencing, such as the organization of thought required to write a story concerning his vacation.

The service recommended ways to assist Alex at home to make up the deficit of his learning disability, such as tasks that require a number of activities in carrying out [tasks].

When Alex entered fourth grade this year, his mother said she contemplated having a conference immediately with his teacher but then decided to wait, allowing Alex's teacher to make her own evaluation. The parents were also anxious to give Alex a chance to apply his specialized instructions.

Ms. Roberts asked for a conference with the teacher who expressed amazement that Alex had been diagnosed as having a learning disability. He now works in the top percent of his class.

"It's a very real success story," Ms. Roberts said with understandable pride.

"Family Learns to Cope with Learning Disability" by Mary Jennings Terry, *The State,* Columbia, South Carolina, Nov. 13, 1977. Reprinted by permission.

Disorders of the perceptual system and the nervous system have been named as causes of learning disabilities. Some blame brain injury (Becker, 1975). Others cite biochemical problems related to nutrition or food additives (Wunderlich, 1973; Roberts, 1969; Feingold, 1976). Factors such as emotional disturbances, motivational problems, and improper instruction have also been blamed (Lovitt, 1978). At this point, no one cause has been pinpointed as the villain in the LD mystery. Most likely, learning disabilities can result from different influences. And what causes a learning disability in one child may not affect another, less vulnerable child.

Through extensive assessment, the specific learning disability of a child like Alex may be identified. And as Alex demonstrated, children with learning disabilities *can* learn to cope. Such noted figures as Thomas Edison, Woodrow Wilson, and Nelson Rockefeller have all described the frustrations they felt during their difficult school days because of what we would now label a learning disability.

The Mentally Retarded.   At age seven, Joan can say "Mama," "baw" (for ball), and "bye-bye." Her additional *expressive,* or spoken vocabulary, is limited to grunts and gestures. Joan's *receptive* vocabulary, or the vocabulary she can understand, is much higher.

Today Joan is learning to walk up stairs using alternating feet. Her teacher has taped first a red, than a blue paper foot shape to each step in the stairway. Joan's right shoe has a red dot taped to it and her left shoe has a similar blue dot. Her task is to ascend the stairs, matching the color on each shoe to the appropriate step. When Joan succeeds, the teacher hugs and praises her.

Is this much effort necessary to teach what should be a simple motor skill for a seven-year-old? Yes. Joan is mentally retarded. Her development is characterized by physical, cognitive, social, and emotional delays.

Not so long ago, such terms as idiots, dunces, fools, or imbeciles were applied to the mentally retarded. By 1937, attempts were made to define retardation in less vague and negative ways (Tredgold, 1937). Table 11.2 shows the definition of retardation based on IQ scores. But the current trend is away from classifying a person as mentally retarded on the basis of an IQ test alone. Individuals who can function adequately in the school or community should not be considered mentally retarded even though they score within the retarded range of an IQ test. Persons considered mentally retarded during their school years may not be later if they are able to function successfully on their jobs in the "mainstream" of society (Payne and Thomas, 1978).

Table 11.2
Levels of Retardation

LEVEL	INTELLIGENCE TEST SCORE (IQ)	
	Stanford-Binet	Wechsler
Mildly retarded	68–52	69–55
Moderately retarded	51–36	54–40
Severely retarded	35–20	39–25
Profoundly retarded	19 and under	24 and under

Adapted from Payne and Thomas, 1978, p. 104.

The cause of 94 percent of the cases of mental retardation is unknown or unclassified. Known causes are varied and include such genetic defects as Down's syndrome and PKU as well as prenatal or postnatal disease or injury. In the majority of cases, the cause involves a complex interaction of both hereditary and environmental factors.

Mainstreaming.   Public Law 94–142 was enacted on November 29, 1975 guaranteeing "a free appropriate public education" for all handicapped children aged three to twenty-one, including the mentally retarded, hard of hearing, deaf, speech impaired, visually handicapped, seriously emotionally disturbed, orthopedically impaired, other health impaired, and those with specific learning disabilities as the handicapped. This law requires that free public education will occur in the "least restrictive environment." And the regular public school classroom is suggested as the most natural and least restrictive of the options (Haring, 1978). Nowhere in the law is the term **mainstreaming** mentioned, but it is popularly used when people talk about placing handicapped children in the regular classroom or the "mainstream" instead of in special classrooms for the handicapped.

Public Law 94–142 requires that all children, regardless of their handicaps, receive free public education in the "least restrictive environment."

This same law requires that an Individualized Education Plan (IEP) be developed for each handicapped child. The IEP must include objectives to meet the unique needs of each individual. Long-term and short-term objectives, along with a means of evaluating these objectives, are among those things required in the IEP. Teachers, parents, support staff (such as speech or physical therapists), and, when appropriate, the child should plan the IEP in a joint effort.

The impact of this law on parents, teachers, administrators, school boards, and children is far-reaching. Parents are pleased to finally be able to obtain the services they need for their handicapped child. But some parents of nonhandicapped children are saying, ''Why can't my child have an IEP too?''

The reactions of educators are mixed. Many teachers argue that they haven't been trained to deal effectively with the handicapped. They argue that placing a handicapped child in an already crowded classroom makes it impossible to meet the child's needs and is more than they can manage. Administrators and school boards are worried about finding funds to provide services for children previously placed in special schools.

The impact of mainstreaming on children has not yet been assessed. Some specialists have expressed warnings:

> Mainstreaming can have many positive effects on handicapped children, but this policy will be an empty slogan, with many negative effects, if not accompanied by adequate teacher training and support services. . . . Much more work is needed to determine not just which children, with which handicaps, can benefit from mainstreaming, but also what the environmental nutrients are that promote full development. (Zigler and Muenchow, 1979, p. 995).

The Gifted and Talented.   Who is ''gifted?'' An outstanding scholar? A creative writer? An Olympic gold medal winner? It's not an easy question. Indeed, various definitions of **gifted children** have been suggested. The dominant one has been the child who shows ''consistently remarkable performance in any worthwhile line of endeavor'' (Stephens and Wolf, 1978). This definition includes children who demonstrate outstanding performance in physical-motor, academic, intellectual and/or creative activities as well as those who show outstanding social-emotional development such as leadership skill. Perhaps definitions will always vary since different societies have different values and label those who possess valued skills and abilities as ''gifted.'' When we hear the term ''gifted'' in our society, we typically think of the intellectually or creatively talented.

Terman and Oden (1947, 1959) listed some characteristics of the intellectually gifted: fast learning, interest in reading biographies, reading begins prior to school entrance, good abstract reasoning, good language ability, high IQ (over 130), and so on. Current reseach indicates gifted children are physically, academically, and socially superior (Clark, 1979). People have objected to using IQ scores as the major measure of giftedness, so teacher nomination, parent interviews, school performance, and behavioral checklists are now being used together with test scores.

Teachers of the intellectually gifted must be experienced, emotionally well-adjusted, and intelligent. They must be able to accept challenges from students. Gifted students learn with a minimum of review or drill. A focus on concepts and principles, intellectual initiative, critical thinking, social adjustment, responsibility, leadership, and creativity is generally believed to be the best approach in teaching gifted children (Stephens and Wolf, 1978).

Moral Development

As toddlers, Eve, Scotty, Kim, and Caroline were often eager to share, comfort, and help. But at other times their behavior was not prosocial. When toddler Caroline wanted Eve's toy, she shoved her and took it. Eve cried and Caroline's Mom came to the rescue—reminding Caroline as she returned the toy, "Remember how it hurt when Kim shoved you and took your toy." At age nine, Caroline knew better than to shove. But when she wanted a candy bar and didn't have the money to pay for it, she slipped it into her pocket. Caroline's father, witnessing the theft, had a talk with Caroline. "How did it make you feel when your bicycle was stolen?" he began. Years later, fourteen-year-old Caroline passed a burning house, heard a baby crying, and rushed inside the house to rescue the baby. She was presented with a "Good Citizens Award" by the local radio station.

Moral development is the gradual internalization of society's standards for right and wrong, involving both moral judgments (or reasoning about morality) and prosocial behavior. But it does not occur overnight. It took many years for Caroline to learn not to push others or take things from them and to behave with concern for others even when her parents were absent. Morality requires that you learn to manage conflicts arising when personal needs and social obligations clash (Hoffman, M. L., 1979), as when Caroline placed her personal need for safety secondary to the social obligations she felt to rescue the crying baby.

How children develop—or fail to develop—a moral sense is an increasingly important issue in our society. An escalating crime rate and traumatic public events, such as the American hostage crisis in Iran, have placed questions about morality in the forefront of our thinking. But theorists and researchers have long been interested in the factors influencing moral development.

COGNITIVE INFLUENCES

Piaget's View.   In Piaget's view, moral development occurs in the same way as cognitive development—through experiences with people and things in the environment. As a result, moral reasoning and cognitive development are linked.

To study moral reasoning, Piaget watched children play marbles and listened to what they said about rules (Piaget, 1932). He found that, like adults, what children do and what they say are often contradictory.

Until age three, the actual play behavior of children involves just fooling around with the marbles, manipulating and experimenting with them in various ways. What they say is also consistent with their behavior and shows no understanding of rules. But from ages three to ten, children's verbalizations contradict their actual behavior. At age three, children believe that rules come from some external authority, such as parents or God, and that rules of play are unchangeable. But since they don't really understand rules, these very young children actually change rules whenever it suits their purposes. By age seven or eight, children begin to play in a socialized manner. Rules are mutually agreed upon by the players. But while children agree in principle that the rules are subject to change, in reality they adhere to the rules rigidly at this age. Not until the age of eleven or twelve do children understand the true nature of rules—that they exist to make play possible and can be changed when players agree (Piaget, 1932).

Kohlberg's Theory.   Building on Piaget's work, Lawrence Kohlberg constructed a theory showing how moral reasoning parallels cognitive development. In a series of investigations to examine moral development, Kohlberg presented children and adolescents with hypothetical moral dilemmas. One of these dilemmas went something like this:

> Heinz's wife was dying from cancer. A rare drug might save her, but the druggist—who made the drug for 200 dollars—would not sell it for a penny less than 2000 dollars. Heinz tried hard, but could only raise 1000 dollars. The druggist refused to give Heinz the drug for that price even though Heinz promised to pay the balance later. So Heinz broke into the store to steal the drug. Should he have done that?

Based on children's responses, Kohlberg developed a six-stage theory of moral development, which he divided into three levels: *preconventional, conventional,* and *postconventional,* each of which is divided into two stages (see Table 11.3). Keep in mind that it is not whether the child responds yes or no but the *reason* for the response that determines the level of moral development.

Table 11.3
Levels of Moral Development

Level I. Preconventional Level
- *Stage 1.* "I must do what I'm told so I won't be punished."
- *Stage 2.* "You scratch my back and I'll scratch yours."

Level II. Conventional Level
- *Stage 3.* "I want to do what's nice and to please others."
- *Stage 4.* "I will obey the law."

Level III. Postconventional Level
- *Stage 5.* "Because society has agreed on these laws, I will follow them."
- *Stage 6.* "Do unto others as you would have them do unto you."

Each stage builds on, reorganizes, and includes the one before and provides new insights and criteria for making moral judgments. People in all cultures move through the stages in the same order, varying only in how quickly and how far they progress (Hoffman M. L., 1979). Kohlberg does not give specific ages for the stages, though he did find age trends (see Fig. 11.3). Individuals can move through the stages at different rates and stop in any stage. Kohlberg believes most people in the United States come to a stop by age twenty-five. But as long as a person's moral development continues, the order of stages remains the same.

PRECONVENTIONAL LEVEL.   At the **preconventional level,** children conform to external rules or pressures in order to avoid external punishment or to obtain rewards (Gelfand and Hartmann, 1980). Kohlberg further divides this level into Stage 1 and 2.

Josh illustrates Stage 1 reasoning when he asserts: ''Heinz should steal the drug because if you let your wife die, you will get in trouble'' (adapted from Rest, 1968). A Stage 1 child might also reason: ''Heinz should not steal the drug because he will get in trouble for stealing.'' In Stage 1, Josh obeys rules in order to avoid punishment from powerful ''others.'' He is self-centered and has a strict pleasure/pain orientation.

Reasoning from a Stage 2 orientation, Nicky justifies Heinz's behavior by saying ''You wouldn't get much time even if you got caught; a little time is OK if

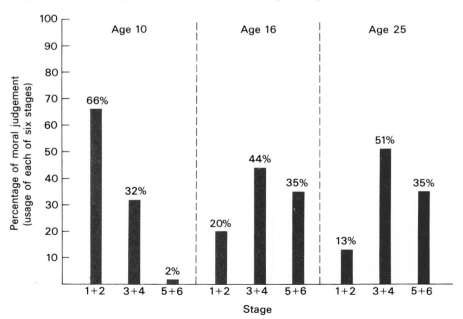

Figure 11.3 **Moral development and age.** (Adapted from Kohlberg and Kramer, 1969).

you have your wife'' (adapted from Rest, 1968). In contrast, a Stage 2 child might also reason, ''Heinz should not steal. Everyone would think he was a thief. His friends will probably help him raise the rest of the money.'' At Stage 2, Nicky's judgments are motivated by anticipated rewards and exchanges. Personal need satisfaction is still the most important consideration. But trade-offs and deals are accepted if Nicky sees something in the deal for himself.

CONVENTIONAL LEVEL.   At the **conventional level,** morality is rule-based and highly conventional. Cognitive advances permit children to internalize standards and to judge actions from the point of view of others. Children want to please peers and adults by following their standards. This level is divided into Stage 3 and 4.

At Stage 3, Heinz's behavior is justified by Kim. She explains: ''People won't think you're bad if you steal it to save your wife, but they'd think you're terrible if you didn't'' (adapted from Rest, 1968). A Stage 3 child might also reason, ''Heinz should not steal the drug because it's not nice to steal and people don't like you when you take things that belong to them.'' Individuals at Stage 3 want to maintain good relations and gain the approval of others. Moral judgments adhere strictly to society's rules.

Caroline, reasoning from a Stage 4 orientation, asserted, ''Heinz should steal the drug. It's his responsibility if his wife dies. He can pay the druggist later.'' Another Stage 4 child might reason, ''It's against the law to steal. Heinz should find some other way to get the drug.'' Reasoning at Stage 4 is based on duty and guilt rather than approval and shame—showing a greater internalization of morality. Children at Stage 4 seek approval of society in general, but they have rigid ideas about rules. Kohlberg (1976) believes Stage 4 responses are typical of most adults in our society. We will discuss Stages 5 and 6 in Chapter 13, since they are more common in adolescence.

HOW MORALITY DEVELOPS.   What causes the movement from stage to stage? Both Kohlberg and Piaget believe there is a genetic factor in human morality. An inherited potential to realize when we are being fair or unfair with each other leads us—when not blocked by social forces—to develop the principle of **social justice,** which states that all human beings are equal in value, and fairness in human relations is essential. When this principle is not blocked, it emerges as a natural result of our relationships with other people. Cognitive development also plays a part. Children who perform at more advanced cognitive levels also perform at more advanced stages of moral judgment (Kurdek, 1978). Cognitive advances allow children to internalize rules, to take the role of others, and eventually to make moral judgments based on abstract ethical principles such as the Golden Rule. Another influence is exposure to people who are at slightly more advanced stages (Hoffman M. L., 1979). Active discussions about moral dilemmas among people at different stages are said to promote change.

CRITICISM OF KOHLBERG'S THEORY.   Much criticism has been leveled at Kohlberg's theory. Some critics claim that the stages don't appear to be homogeneous. In other words, a child may judge one situation at a Stage 4 level but may turn right around and judge a different situation at a Stage 1 level. Stages don't appear to form an unvarying sequence. And no evidence supports the notion that exposure to advanced levels leads to movement through the stages. Also there is very little relationship between moral judgments and moral behavior (Mussen and Eisenberg-Berg, 1977). The theories of both Piaget and Kohlberg include issues such as law, honesty, responsibility, and justice as well as moral development and each of these may have different patterns of development (Turiel, 1975). Another charge is that Kohlberg's theory has a masculine bias—ignoring females in favor of adolescent male morality (Gilligan, 1977).

As a result of such criticism, you might be tempted to discard Kohlberg's notions as useless. And, as a matter of fact, the unvarying, six-stage model is probably not accurate. But despite flaws, Kohlberg's theory has made a substantial contribution to our understanding of moral development and has encouraged educators to make new efforts in moral educaton (Gelfand and Hartmann, 1980).

OTHER INFLUENCES ON MORAL DEVELOPMENT

Cognitive development is not the only influence on moral development. Parents, peers, sex-role socialization, and television as well as emotional development are also important influences.

Parents.   Parents are disciplinarians, affection givers, and models. Caroline's parents used effective disciplinary techniques when they reminded her how she would feel if she were Eve or if someone stole something from her. Such techniques may arouse empathy and guilt, helping children to reduce the conflict between personal needs and social obligations. In addition, parental "dos and don'ts" complete with reasons are more likely to be remembered than spankings. Frequent parental expression of affection outside the disciplinary situation also contributes to internalization of moral rules. Affection may make children more receptive to discipline, emotionally secure enough to be open to needs of others, and likely to model the parent's behavior (Hoffman M. L., 1979).

Peers.   Little theory and research exists on the effects of peers on moral development (Hoffman M. L., 1979). In Piaget's view (1932), unsupervised peer interactions allow children an opportunity to develop a morality based on mutual consent and cooperation among equals. But other researchers suggest that unsupervised peer interaction may release inhibitions and undermine prior socialization. Some studies indicate agreement between peer and adult values (Langworthy, 1959) but others find that peer values undermine parental values (Sherif et al., 1961).

Sex-Role Socialization.   Traditionally, girls have been socialized to give and receive affection and to respond to needs of others more than boys have. High achievement and a success orientation have been more prized for boys than to be humanistic and honest (Johnson, 1963). Parents also use different techniques of discipline and express affection more often with girls than with boys (Zussman, 1978). These and other socialization practices encourage females to become more morally internalized and humanistic than males. According to some research though, women tend to remain at Stage 3 (pleasing others) while men move to Stage 4 (law and order) of Kohlberg's stages. The official morality of the business world is Stage 4, while that of the neighborhood is Stage 3 (Hoffman M. L., 1979). As sex-role socialization practices change and women move more and more into the business world, these findings may change.

Television.   Television is an important influence on several areas of a child's development, including moral development. See Spotlight 10.3 in Chapter 10.

Emotions.   Some research suggests that empathy and guilt are related and together form a basis for moral behavior (Hoffman M. L., 1979). Empathy is assumed to form the basis for helping others. As you remember from our discussion of toddlerhood, even very young children aged two to four show empathetic reactions. Older children also show empathetic reactions and their reactions are typically followed by helping behaviors. Children respond more empathically to others who are similar to them—of the same role, sex, or age. So moral education programs that emphasize similarities among people may promote empathy. Disciplinary techniques that point to the effects of a child's behavior contribute to feelings of guilt. When people feel guilty, they want to help the victim or sometimes resolve to act less selfishly in the future (Hoffman M. L., 1979).

Summary

1. Physical growth levels off during middle childhood before spurting ahead again in adolescence, but body proportions continue to change, and body systems become more refined.

2. Calorie needs are not high during the school years since at this age body size is not increasing rapidly. But the active nature of children involves them in more accidents, and increased interactions with other children exposes them to more infectious diseases.

3. Logical thinking abilities of school children include decentration, the ability to follow transformations, and reversible thought. Children in the concrete operational period also master the concepts of conservation and classification. But a new form of egocentrism emerges, which prevents children from thinking about several possible courses of action while testing them systematically.

4. Memory is the process through which we store information from the environment. Sensory, short term, and long term are three stages of memory storage. The increased metamemory—knowledge of how one remembers—of school-age children helps them store and recall information more effectively.

5. Reflective children take their time and think carefully when solving problems. Impulsive children respond quickly without thinking their answers through.

6. There is much dispute over the definition of intelligence and the validity of intelligence tests, but individual and group intelligence tests, such as the Stanford-Binet, the Wechsler, and the Otis Lennon, are widely used.

7. Creativity—the ability to solve problems in new and original ways—involves such characteristics as fluency, flexibility, and originality. No correlation has been found between creativity and intelligence, but certain situations seem to be associated with increased creativity in children.

8. Several approaches to teaching reading have been widely used over the years. The language experience and whole-word approaches emphasize meaning, while the phonics approach requires that children learn the sounds that correspond to letters of the alphabet. Authorities on reading do not agree on which approach is best.

9. The cognitive development of some children does not follow the standard pattern. Learning-disabled children can have perceptual-motor, emotional, coordination, attention, memory, or speech disorders. In the past, the definition of mental retardation was based on IQ scores alone. Today, a person who functions adequately in the school or community is not considered functionally mentally retarded even though IQ scores are in the retarded range. At the other extreme is the gifted child, an individual who shows ''consistently remarkable performance in any worthwhile line of endeavor.''

10. Both Piaget and Kohlberg have theorized that moral development is tied to cognitive development. Kohlberg's work led him to formulate three levels of moral development (preconventional, conventional, and postconventional) which are in turn divided into a total of six stages. Other researchers have disputed his claims and have pointed to such influences as parents, peers, sex-role socialization, television, and emotions on moral development.

Empathetic Activities

- What feelings did you have as you read the Case of the Tree House and Learning to Cope with a Learning Disability? How would you feel if you were Brad, Roosevelt, or Scotty? Josh? Alex's mother? His teacher? Alex?

- What activities might you provide to encourage school children's creativity? Their moral development? Memory improvement? The gifted and talented?

- Try some of the conservation problems described in Spotlight 11.1 with several preschool and school-age children. Discuss your results with others who complete this activity.

- Use the information in the section on Concrete Operations to analyze the Case of the Tree House at the beginning of the chapter. What skills could the boys perform as schoolchildren that they could not perform as preschool children because of their cognitive advances?

■ Describe what might happen to the *Whole Child* if some aspect of development is out of step, either ahead or behind, other aspects. This often happens when a child is learning disabled, mentally retarded, intellectually gifted, or creatively talented.

■ How do relationships influence moral development?

Related Readings

Beal, Virginia, *Nutrition in the lifespan.* New York: Wiley, 1980. Normal growth and nutrition are presented developmentally. Text covers pregnancy, infancy, preschool years, middle childhood, adolescence, adulthood, and the elderly years. An excellent and readable resource for advanced nursing, home economics, and education students.

Haring, Norris G., ed. *Behavior of exceptional children: An introduction to special education,* 2nd ed. Columbus, Ohio: Charles Merrill, 1978. Excellent, short cases illustrate this introductory textbook. Interesting reading for those who want to learn more about exceptional children.

Galbraith, Ronald E., and Jones, Thomas M. *Moral reasoning: A teaching handbook for adapting Kohlberg to the classroom.* St. Paul, Minn.: Greenhaven Press, 1976. An excellent, clear, and understandable introduction to Kohlberg's theory. A series of moral dilemmas is presented along with specific teaching suggestions for stimulating moral reasoning in the classroom.

Williams, Joyce, and Stith, Marjorie. *Middle childhood: Behavior and development.* 2nd ed. New York: MacMillan, 1980. A practical and readable in-depth examination of development during the middle years. Special sections on the family, school, peers, and guidance of the middle-years child.

12 Middle Childhood: Social and Emotional Development and Relationships

The Case of the Secret Fort

Caroline, Kim, and Eve, now nine years old, are in Ms. Cunningham's fourth grade. Early in the school year, they became "best friends" and they walk home together each afternoon. One day the girls' walk lasted a long time because they were making plans and discussing rules for their new club: "The Secret Fort." They decided on a secret password and handshake. One rule was for certain, "No Boys Allowed!"

Of course, they knew this rule would end up causing them trouble with Caroline's cousin Brad and his pals, Scotty and Roosevelt. The three boys were always trying to interfere with the girls' plans. "Why are boys such pests?" Eve asked Kim.

Caroline agreed, "We'll have to keep our fort secret from those boys or Mom and Dad will make us let them in. Oh, no! Here they come now!"

"Queen, Queen Caroline washed her hair in turpentine, turpentine to make it shine, Queen, Queen Caroline!" Brad, Scotty, and Roosevelt taunted Caroline in unison.

"Sticks and stones may break my bones, but words will never hurt me!" retorted Caroline. But she was mad and tears stung her eyes as the girls hurried past the boys.

At home the girls found Caroline's mother at work in her office. "Hi, Mom!" Caroline yelled. "Can we have something to dig with? We're going to make a secret fort in the backyard. Everyone will have to put something in our treasure."

"Well, let's see," responded Caroline's mom looking up from the books on her desk. "I think there are some gardening tools in the shed. But be sure you dig only behind the garage. We've been working hard on the rest of the lawn all summer."

Equipped with a spade from the toolshed, the girls dug a small hole on the site of the secret fort and raked pine needles into piles to make the club "walls." They carefully placed their treasure (shells, costume jewelry, a few coins, and a secret message) inside a "treasure chest" they had made from a painted and decorated cigar box and buried it in the hole. They were drawing a secret map so they could find their treasure again when who should appear but—yuk!—Brad the Brat and Roosevelt.

"We know about your silly old club," said Brad. "Our Dads helped us build a real tree house. Your club will never be as good as ours."

After they left the girls, Brad and Roosevelt made a secret pact to be blood brothers and never play with girls. Two weeks later, Caroline's mom asked about the girl's secret fort. Caroline looked puzzled for a moment. Then she replied cheerfully, "Oh! That didn't work out. We started a new club called the Animal House. So far we have Kim's kitten, a bird, a goldfish. . . ."

The Schoolchild

After reading the Case of the Secret Fort you may be asking yourself, "What is this business with secret clubs, buried treasure, and girls and boys forming cliques?" This case typifies the social and emotional development and relationships of schoolchildren (ages six to twelve). Children are busy making plans and collections in this stage of personality development, which Erikson calls "industry versus inferiority." Influences on the schoolchild's self-esteem expand to include not just parents but also relationships in the peer group, school, and community. Schoolchildren also begin to rely less on adults to control their behavior as they develop more internal controls.

INDUSTRY VERSUS INFERIORITY

Caroline spent days collecting and cataloging the shells that she proudly shared with her "Secret Fort Club." Brad and Kim are busy working on school committees and playing softball. Thelma is practicing the violin. In other parts of the world, Omblean and Formo are learning to hunt and fish by wielding a spear or a bow and arrow. An Egyptian girl sells fabric in the streets of Cairo. Chinese schoolchildren are developing skills using a lathe. What does this diverse group of school-age children have in common? Let's look to Erikson for an answer.

According to Erikson (1963), school-age children have moved to a stage of personality development that involves the struggle between **industry and inferiority**—the fourth stage of psychosocial development in which success results in a child becoming a competent and productive member of society, while failure results in feelings of inadequacy. During this stage, children want to fix things, demonstrate new physical skills, create, and learn. They might try their hand at a variety of creative skills such as woodworking, clay modeling, or painting. Other favorite pastimes are scouts, swimming, community service, and lending a helping hand at home and at school.

Whether a child develops industry or inferiority is strongly influenced by the support and feedback that comes from important adults and peers. Children benefit when situations are structured so they can be successful in making and doing things they consider worthy. When Caroline and her friends asked, they were provided with tools, a space, and suggestions about building the fort. This helped them succeed. And when children's efforts and products are recognized and approved by adults and peers, feelings of worth and industry result.

But feelings of inferiority or inadequacy can develop when children's efforts are not praised by peers or adults. When frequent failure or disapproval are common, children may come to believe that the results of their work are not worthwhile. According to Erikson, poor work habits and feelings of uselessness could result. In the future, the child may avoid strong competition, do a job only half way, or cease productivity altogether. Stereotyping, labeling, or grouping children in detrimental ways can also suppress a sense of industry. Children who have had

According to Erikson, success in their endeavors results in schoolchildren becoming competent and productive members of society.

unsuccessful experiences in school, for example, are sometimes labeled ''failures'' by teachers and peers. Eventually, such children come to believe the label. Many give up trying to achieve at all.

SELF-ESTEEM

At age nine, Roosevelt felt confident in himself and his judgments. So when he believed he was right, he didn't hesitate to follow his own judgments and disagree with the general wishes of the group. He was an assertive, active leader in his social group, seldom allowing his personal problems to get in his way.

At the same age, Nicky didn't really trust himself and was hesitant about suggesting unpopular ideas or bringing up anything that might not be accepted by the group. He was unwilling to disagree with the group even when he was almost certain he was correct. He lived in the shadows of his social group, yielding to the leadership of peers like Roosevelt. Nicky preferred listening or participating in group settings. Sometimes paralyzed by personal problems, he spent more time dealing with these than interacting with others. As a result, Nicky had very few genuine relationships with children his own age.

During middle childhood, the **self-concept**—how the individual views himself or herself—continues to develop. Children also form judgments of their worth called **self-esteem** which are based on their increased self-awareness and on feedback from important other people around them. Parents, peers, and society as a whole all affect a child's self-esteem. Like other children their age, Roosevelt and Nicky have begun to see themselves as others see them. Roosevelt's self-esteem is characteristic of those who judge themselves very highly. In contrast, Nicky's self-judgments typify poor self-esteem.

Parents' Influence. One of the most important studies of self-esteem in middle childhood was conducted by Coopersmith (1967). He studied eighty-five white boys between the ages of ten and twelve and found that parents of high self-esteem children tended to have high self-esteem themselves. On the other hand, parents of low self-esteem children had low self-esteem. He also found that high-esteem parents dealt with their children differently than did low-esteem parents. High-esteem parents loved and accepted their children but still set firm, though flexible, limits on their children's behavior. They were both supportive and positive. Parents of low-esteem boys wavered between hostility and indifference and set few and inconsistent standards for behavior. These parents appeared less concerned or involved with their children.

Another study (Sears, 1970) confirmed these findings for both boys and girls. Children who had at least one parent who was warm and accepting had higher self-esteem than children of cold, unaccepting parents. It is clear that parents who are warm, involved, and affectionate rear children who have high self-esteem.

The Influence of Peers. It is difficult to tell which comes first—self-esteem or popularity. Children viewed negatively by their peers tend to have lower self-esteem, while those who are viewed positively by peers have higher self-esteem (Horowitz, 1962). In another study, junior high school students who were popular also had positive self-concepts (Chambliss et al., 1978).

Society's Influence. Many people believe that minority-group children such as blacks and Hispanic-Americans have lower self-esteem than middle-class white children—presumably because they have greater difficulty doing schoolwork. Their ways of doing things are also different from society in general. Some studies have supported this idea. For example, Lefley (1974) discovered that American Indian children had lower self-esteem than white children. But in many studies the very opposite occurs—lower-class or minority children think more highly of themselves than white middle-class children. As an illustration, Portuguese-Mexican (Calhoun et al., 1978), black and Puerto Rican (Soares and Soares, 1969), and low income (Trowbridge and Trowbridge, 1972) children all showed higher self-esteem than white, middle-class American children.

Although some researchers believe self-esteem is linked to school achievement, others have found that minority group children—who often do poorly in school—have higher self-esteem than white, middle-class children.

LOCUS OF CONTROL

Locus of control refers to the degree to which people accept responsibility for what happens to them (Chandler et al., 1980). Children who have an **internal locus of control** believe themselves to be in control of what happens to them. But children who have an **external locus of control** believe that fate, luck, or other people control what happens to them. Researchers have found that such diverse factors as socioeconomic class, parental style, and cultural background all affect a child's locus of control.

In one study (Bartel, 1971), two groups started school with no differences in locus of control. But by sixth grade, middle-class children had a higher locus of control than lower-class children. In another study, American-Indian children scored lower than white children on locus of control—perhaps reflecting the poverty and feelings of powerlessness in their everyday life (Tyler and Holsinger, 1975).

Most school-aged children assume more and more personal responsibility for their successes and failures. As a result, an increasing internal locus of control is shown during middle childhood. But the way adults behave toward children encourages an internal or external sense of control (Chandler et al., 1980).

When researchers gave fourth- and fifth-grade boys tasks to do, parents (who had been told to help if they wished) of externally controlled boys were likely to intrude and be directive. Parents of internally controlled boys were likely to be supportive but nondirective (Loeb, 1975).

In another study, nine-year-olds from the United States were more internally controlled than nine-year-olds in a kibbutz. But by the time these children reached age fourteen, there was almost no difference. Greater internal locus of control was evident among Israeli children when they were encouraged to make choices, to organize themselves, and to take responsibility (Lifshitz, 1973).

Schoolchildren and Adult Relationships

Children in the middle years are gradually detaching themselves from their parents but they still need adult direction. Schoolchildren are still profoundly influenced by their relationships with parents, the structure of their family units, and their parents' relationship with each other. But growing contact with the outside world provides important new influences from adults—particularly from teachers.

PARENT-CHILD DETACHMENT

Schoolchildren are able to tolerate—and even initiate—separations from parents for hours or days with little or no insecurity (Marvin, 1977). But schoolchildren continue to depend on parents for attention, affection, and guidance.

Every day parents must make decisions influencing the schoolchild's developing sense of industry and independence. These decisions center around how much freedom and control childen can handle as they venture from family into the larger systems of school and community. Parents must gradually let go as children move from early childhood toward adulthood.

VARIATIONS IN FAMILY STRUCTURE

Even though parent-child detachment is occurring gradually, a schoolchild's development is profoundly influenced by such variations in family structure as birth order, divorce, single parenting, and stepfamilies, though some so-called invulnerable children succeed in life despite difficult backgrounds (see Spotlight 12.1).

Development of the Parent-Child Relationship

Relationship	Developmental Period
Parent-Newborn Synchrony	Newborn (birth–4 weeks)
Parent-Infant Attachment	Infancy (birth–12 months)
Parent-Toddler Dependency	Toddlerhood (1–3 years)
Parent-Preschooler Partnership	Early childhood (3–6 years)
Parent-Child Detachment/Children's Same-Sex Friendships—Schoolchildren need the emotional security and support of their peer group to begin weakening ties from parents. Cliques are formed—almost always with members of the same sex.	Middle childhood (6–12 years)
Parent-Teenager Individuality/Crowd Formation	Adolescence (13–18 years)

❖ Spotlight 12.1: Invulnerable Children

Ross's mother spent years in and out of a mental institution. While she was away, he and his sisters were cared for by a housekeeper who, unfortunately, cared for no one but her dog and her whisky. Ross's alcoholic father was out drinking and carousing almost every night. But when both father and mother were home, things were even worse. There were constant arguments and tension day and night. The verbal aggression frequently turned into physical assault. Ross's parents would yell and scream and bloody each other's faces with their fists. Sometimes they would throw knives, furniture, and glass figurines from the mantle or coffee table. It wasn't unusual for the action to move onto the front porch and even into the front lawn where all the neighbors could see. Once Ross's father ripped the telephone from the wall and threw it into the roaring fire of their fireplace.

Ross was in the midst of it all. He would cry and beg his parents to stop and settle their differences quietly. Sometimes he would stand in between them, trying to keep them apart. But it was like trying to separate two vicious dogs and getting bitten in the scuffle. When Ross interfered, his parents would strike wildly at him or push him away so they could get back to their battle. Other times, feeling humiliated, Ross busied himself closing curtains, windows, and doors to hide the domestic war from neighbors. Whenever he sensed a fight coming on, Ross immediately began hiding dangerous weapons and fragile pieces from the mantle or coffee table.

Eventually, Ross discovered his best course of behavior was to withdraw altogether. So he spent hours alone in his room writing adventure stories. Daybreak was always a welcome sight. As morning finally broke and quiet fell over the house, Ross could breathe a sigh of relief, because he knew his family had made it through another night.

"Whatever happened to Ross?" you might wonder. Did he end up in prison or a mental institution? After all, his upbringing is typical of that found among adult lawbreakers and mental patients. You might be surprised to learn that today Ross leads a highly successful life as a free-lance writer. He has a stable family life and long-term, intimate relationships with friends and loved ones.

For years Ross silently asked himself, "How did I make it through all that craziness and come out relatively free of emotional scars?" Now, the answer to the puzzle has emerged. Ross is among a newly discovered group of children known as *invulnerables*.

Invulnerable children are youngsters reared under the most dire circumstances who somehow do remarkably well, despite their disadvantaged surroundings. The most common characteristic of invulnerable children is their ability to cope and react to stress because of their exceptional competence (Garmezy, 1974; Pines, 1979b). According to experts who observed these children, invulnerables are competent and mentally healthy. That is, they work well, play well, love well, and expect that the future is worth living (Garmezy, 1974).

In every case, invulnerables are brought up in extremely traumatic and stressful surroundings. But they are stress-resistant; they thrive in spite of these disadvantages. Experts accidentally stumbled upon the first reported patterns of invulnerability while studying children who were judged to be high risks to develop adult schizophrenia (Garmezy, 1970). As these children were studied over time, it was noted that a majority of them did not become schizophrenic. In fact, only 10 or 12 percent had difficulty as adults, while the rest were unhurt. Invulnerable children have also been identified among ghetto children (Garmezy, 1970), abused children (Nagera, 1978), children who suffer parental loss (Eisenstadt, 1978), adopted children (McNeil, 1969), and children of divorce (Wallerstein and Kelly, 1980b).

Anthony (1978) describes the differences between children who are vulnerable and those who are invulnerable. To explain the effects, he compares children with three kinds of dolls—a glass, plastic, and steel doll. Glass dolls are shattered by the stressful experiences in childhood. Plastic dolls are permanently dented, and steel dolls are invulnerable—resisting the harmful effects of their surroundings. So glass (vulnerable) children break down completely, plastic children sustain some serious injury, and steel (invulnerable) children thrive on the troubles and turmoil in their world.

Invulnerable children share a number of common characteristics. They have good social skills. They are at ease and make others feel comfortable, too. They are friendly and well liked by classmates and adults. They have positive feelings of self-regard. And they sense a feeling of personal power for influencing events around them (*internal locus of control*). This contrasts with the feelings of helplessness of vulnerable children (*external locus of control*). Not only do invulnerable children feel in control, but they also have an urge to help others needier than themselves.

There is a certain sense of detachment from the stressful surroundings—for example, Ross retreated to his room to write stories. Other children paint, dance, do crafts, read, listen to music, or build models. Along with this self-distancing comes a greater sense of independence and a more objective understanding of what's going on around them.

Invulnerables are successful, usually receiving high grades in school. And later on they become high achievers in their careers. Many invulnerable children become artists, actors, musicians, and, as in the case of Ross, writers. Others become lawyers, politicians, and professors. Some 50 percent of invulnerable children have elements of creative expression in their makeup as adults. Somehow, their intellectual and creative skills are not destroyed by their misfortunes at home. In fact, misfortunes seem to make them more highly motivated to perform well.

The discovery of invulnerable children provides additional evidence for the systems viewpoint of development. Most of these children who experience terrible parents and early turmoil grow up to be competent adults and suffer little or no psychological damage. Some say invulnerables have more genetic insulation or are genetically equipped to cope better with turmoil in their world. Others credit significant events in the environment as leading to invulnerability. For example, a special relationship with one person somehow makes up for the inadequate early family life (Rutter and Madge, 1976; Skolnick, 1978). But the most popular belief is the systems idea that heredity and environment are interacting in some way to produce invulnerability (Erlenmeyer-Kimling, 1978).

Birth Order

Carlos is the firstborn, Tony the secondborn, and Miguel the thirdborn child of Mr. and Mrs. Sanchez. Each of the three children has his own unique personality. Carlos spoke very early and more clearly than his brothers and he is brighter and more successful in school. Tony has the most self-confidence. He is more popular and socially outgoing and finds it easier to make friends than Carlos. Miguel is the least competitive and most immature. He is also the most original and creative child.

The boys in the Sanchez family are typical of children who are firstborn, secondborn, and thirdborn. Researchers have found that birth order makes a difference in personality characteristics.

FIRSTBORNS.   Mr. Sanchez was excited about the birth of his first child, Carlos, "You will see," he said to his wife. "Our Carlos will be a fine doctor someday, and everyone will look up to him!"

Parents often have high educational expectations for their first children and are concerned that they succeed in life. Firstborn children respond by feeling they *must* achieve. And they typically do have greater educational success and fewer academic problems (Gallagher and Cowen, 1977) than their brothers and sisters.

Certainly firstborn children receive more attention from their parents. One study with two-week-old infants found that caregivers interacted more with firstborns than with later-borns (Kilbride et al., 1977). Some researchers (Pulvino and Lupton, 1978) have suggested that this extra interaction and attention during the formative years results in children with a more completely developed intellectual ability. And Zajonc (1976) found that firstborns do have higher IQs than later-borns. Firstborns also develop better verbal skills, perhaps because parents tend to talk more to their first children than to subsequent offspring. So when one uses development of intellectual skills and language as a measuring stick, firstborn children and those reared in small families or with wide age gaps between siblings appear to have an advantage. But so much emphasis on achievement may occur at the expense of social skills in firstborns.

SECONDBORNS.   Friendly and outgoing are the watchwords of secondborn children. Like Tony, they have a personal charm that earns them the label of the agreeable one in the family. And they are generally less aggressive, less tense, and more comfortable to live with than their older siblings (Forer, 1969).

Like other later-born children, secondborns tend to be less achievement-oriented but more socially outgoing and popular than firstborns (Miller and Maruyama, 1976), perhaps because they gain social skills from spending more time with older siblings—an advantage firstborns don't have.

Mothers feel more confident with later-born children, since they have already seen one child through each stage of development. In dealing with problem behaviors, parents of firstborn children more often seek professional help than parents of later-borns, who devise their own means for solving problems (Schaefer and Coie, 1977).

Later-borns also receive less parental attention than firstborns. In a family with more than two children, secondborns can have special problems. Such children sometimes feel ''lost in the middle'' and may have more difficulty developing an identity within the family.

LASTBORNS.   Youngest children, like Miguel, are often the most spontaneous, original, and creative children in the family. While lastborns do not receive the same parental attention firstborns get, they are generally disciplined less. And older siblings tend to give more attention to last borns and to be more protective of them.

But youngest children have their share of difficulties. Sometimes they remain babies all their lives because parents have trouble letting go and allowing them to grow up (Kerns, 1980). And youngest children often find it difficult to compete with the achievements of their older brothers and sisters.

ONLY CHILDREN.   The common notion that only children are ''spoiled brats'' has been contradicted by research (Crase and Crase, 1979). Only children have many of the characteristics of firstborn children. They tend to have a high intelligence level, to be self-sufficient and independent, and to have high aspirations. Yet they are often as socially outgoing and socially accepted by peers as later-born children. This may be because the only child has not suffered the ''dethronement'' that occurs to firstborns when a second child is born. It may also be that an only child has no automatic playmates and must work to develop peer relationships.

Some suggest there are advantages to a one-child family. There is more money available, the child receives more parental attention, and there is less family tension. Mothers of small families tend to spend more time with their children, give them better physical care, and show more interest in their school progress (Terhune, 1976). And when only children grow up, they typically want and have fewer children than those from two-child families.

Divorce.   The following reactions of children involved in divorce are typical of those observed by parents and teachers (Skeen and McKenry, 1980).

''I'm afraid my own marriage will be a failure'' (Jim, age sixteen).

''At first it's so terrible you could really die, but then it gets better'' (Andy, age nine).

''If I'd only kept my room clean (like Daddy asked), he wouldn't have left me'' (Alice, age four).

Silence (Becky, age five).

Without exception, divorce is a stressful event in the life of a child. It is a developmental crisis to which children react in many different ways. The sex of the child can play a role, as boys usually have more difficulty coping with parental divorce for longer periods of time than girls (Hetherington, 1979; Rubenstein, 1980).

And temperamental differences, unique experiences of the child, and the child's developmental status are also contributing factors to differences in reactions (Hetherington, 1979).

But for almost all children, divorce is an emotionally painful experience. As you can see from the comments above, children often feel afraid, guilty, and depressed.

The impact of divorce on preschool children is very strong. Sometimes it has negative effects on self-concept (Rubenstein, 1980) and threatens the child's view of dependable and predictable relationships. Like Nicky, the preschool child may come to mistrust people in his environment. Schoolchildren react to divorce with sadness, fear, anger, and feelings of being deprived (Kelly and Wallerstein, 1976; Wallerstein and Kelly, 1980a). Sometimes they show marked changes in behavior—such as ''acting out'' during school (Cantor, D. W., 1977). Kim began sassing her teacher and bossing the other children when her parents separated. Older school-aged children sometimes have trouble keeping their attention on schoolwork. They also show a shaken sense of identity and loneliness (Wallerstein and Kelly, 1976). Adolescents often have strong feelings of rejection and fear of abandonment. Confused and disillusioned, they suffer from an increase in typical adolescent conflicts and worry about the possibility of their own marriage failure (Sorosky, 1977).

For parents and children, divorce can represent a sense of loss, a sense of failure in interpersonal relationships, and the beginning of a difficult transition to new life patterns (Magrab, 1978). But research shows that what affects children the most is not so much the divorce experience as the parents' personalities, attitudes, and their relationships with their children (Wallerstein and Kelly, 1980a).

Jacobson (1978) found that when fathers spent time with their children during a twelve-month period following divorce, the likelihood of maladjustment decreased. But when fathers did not spend time with their children, the likelihood of maladjustment increased. Sometimes developmental needs of children are unmet because of parental preoccupation with their own needs and parental role conflicts. When compared with parents in intact families, divorced parents were less consistent and effective in discipline, less nurturant, and generally showed less appropriate behavior with their children because of their preoccupation with the divorce process (Hetherington et al., 1976). Divorced parents also communicated less well with their children and made fewer demands for mature behavior than parents in intact families.

But when parents remain supportive of each other following a divorce, the effects on children are decreased (Hetherington, 1979). Sometimes divorce is the most positive solution to destructive family situations. The divorce experience can even have a positive influence on children.

Teachers can be central, stable figures in the lives of children in months following a divorce or separation. Spotlight 12.2 lists some ways classroom teachers can help children and parents cope with divorce.

When parents divorce, the amount of time the absent parent—usually the father—spends with the children can greatly influence their reactions and adjustment to their new situation.

Single-Parent Families.   Nowadays, the American family can be found in many forms in our society. The word ''family'' no longer automatically means father, mother, and children. Instead, single-parent families are rapidly increasing because of divorce, separation, death, desertion, and unmarried and adoptive parenthood. About one-half of the children born in the 1970s will spend some time living in a single-parent family.

Nicky's mother took time off from her job to attend a parent-teacher conference with Ms. Cunningham, Nicky's fourth-grade teacher. ''You know, it's been hard being a single parent for the last six years. But now I'm very happy working as a nurse. And I believe Nicky's adjusting better too,'' she said.

Single parents generally describe their parent-child relationships as very close (Orthner, 1979). In fact, children in single-parent families usually get along better than children in conflict-ridden, intact families (Hetherington, 1979). Nevertheless, problems do arise. Both single fathers and single mothers experience more stress than married parents. One parent must wear two or three hats—parent, housekeeper, and breadwinner. Aside from the difficulties in filling their many roles, single parents also have financial hardships and trouble finding suitable child-care arrangements. Inadequate preparation for the homemaker and caregiver role is often a problem for wifeless fathers. And husbandless mothers may have difficulty disciplining their children, since in two-parent families, fathers can back up the mother's authority (Hetherington, 1979).

❖ Spotlight 12.2: How to Help Children and Parents Adjust to Divorce

Teachers can play a key role in helping children and their parents adjust to divorce. Skeen and McKenry (1980) suggest that teachers try the following:

- Understand that parents are in a crisis situation and may not be able to parent as well as you or they would like.

- Support each parent as an important person about whom you are concerned.

- Provide parents with books about divorce written for both children and adults.

- Assure parents that children will need time to adjust to divorce. Difficulties in their behavior during divorce do not mean they have become permanently disturbed.

- Help lessen guilt by telling parents that many of their children's peers have divorced parents. There is also evidence that children from stable, one-parent families are better off emotionally than children in unstable, conflictual two-parent families.

- Provide an informal atmosphere in which parents can share their problems and solutions about children.

- Correctly address notes to parents. "Dear Parent" can be used when you are not sure if the child's parents are divorced or if the mother might have remarried and have a different name from the child.

- Make a special effort to love the child. Let the child know that he/she is important and worthwhile by smiling, hugging, praising, and paying attention to appropriate behaviors. But avoid "being a mother or father" or allowing the child to become overly dependent upon you since you will leave the child at the end of the year.

Skeen and McKenry also recommend that teachers encourage parents to do the following:

- Help the child recognize and express feelings and resolve conflict through activities such as

Overwhelmed by it all, single parents sometimes feel they are socially isolated. Sometimes feelings of loneliness, lowered self-esteem, depression, and helplessness interefere with parenting abilities (Hetherington et al., 1978). To address this need, groups such as Parents Without Partners, an organization providing social and emotional support for single parents, have sprouted across the country.

SINGLE FATHERHOOD.   About 10 percent of the children of divorced parents live with their fathers (Hetherington, 1979; Wallerstein and Kelly, 1980b). The average age of these fathers is late thirties (Bartz and Witcher, 1978), and most hold professional or semi-professional jobs (Keshet and Rosenthal, 1979). Living with fathers is also more likely to occur with school-aged rather than preschool children (Glick and Norton, 1978). Men who obtain custody must usually fight for it, so most single fathers are highly motivated to be parents. One single father offered this advice: "What is your real basic motive in wanting custody? You should examine way deep down in. Taking a shot at the wife is the wrong reason. If you feel you can do a better job of parenting, then that's a good reason. It's not a piece of cake, so be sure you want to do it." (Bartz and Witcher, 1978, p. 35).

painting or drawing or small doll play, reading books about alternate family styles, free play, woodworking, music, or movement.

- Allow the child solitude and privacy when it is needed.

- Help the child understand the situation, feelings and how they can be expressed, and the consequences of expressing feelings. Many discussions over an extended period of time will be necessary before understanding is achieved.

- Avoid overprotecting the child, always realizing that children must be dealt with patiently and might regress to less mature forms of behavior at times.

- Set firm, reasonable and consistent limits. Even though the child might have problems, he/she should not be allowed to "run wild."

- Be as open and honest as possible with the child about the divorce and related feelings.

- Assure the child that divorce occurs because of problems the parents have. The child did not cause the divorce and cannot reunite parents.

- Work together as much as possible in parenting roles even though the couple role is being dissolved. Attitudes that parents display toward each other and their divorce are important factors in the child's adjustment. Using the child as a messenger or a "pawn" in the couple relationship is particularly harmful to children.

- Establish a meaningful personal life both as a parent and as a productive individual apart from the child. This can be the best gift for a child.

Skeen and McKenry (1980). Reprinted by permission from *Young Children,* copyright © 1980, National Association for the Education of Young Children, 1834 Connecticut Ave. N.W., Washington, D.C. 20009.

In the past, myths about fathers made it difficult for men to obtain custody of their children. Beliefs that fathers seek custody to avoid child-support payments or to hurt their wives, that men don't know how to rear daughters, and that they cannot manage an adequate home life for their children have not been supported by research (Mendes, 1976; Orthner and Lewis, 1979).

When men really want to be parents, they are most likely to adjust to single fatherhood and do a good job (Mendes, 1976). Fathers often report that child custody has a beneficial effect upon their relationships with their children. Some report feelings of more closeness and affection in the father-child relationship (Bartz and Witcher, 1978; Keshet and Rosenthal, 1979).

Of course, some men wouldn't make competent single fathers, just as some women wouldn't make competent mothers. So it is becoming increasingly important that fathers and mothers be judged on their merits and not on notions of sex-role bias (Orthner and Lewis, 1979).

FATHER ABSENCE.   Research findings on single mothers cannot be compared with research on single fathers for several reasons. The 10 percent of fathers who obtain custody of their children are a select group because they have usually chosen their

As the movie *Kramer vs. Kramer* illustrated, despite some difficulties, single fathers can turn out to be competent parents.

role. Their income is also higher than that of single mothers. In addition, custody for men is very recent, so we have research only on their immediate child-rearing practices—not on the long-term consequences on children who have been reared without a mother. Yet the research on the effects of father absence is often contradictory.

On one hand, more antisocial behavior and rebellion against authority and less self-control have been noted among boys in father-absent households (Lynn, 1974; Santrock, 1975). Shinn (1978) reported that children from father-absent homes score lower on achievement tests and do more poorly in schoolwork than children from intact families because children of single mothers receive less attention and interaction with adults than children in two-parent families. Hetherington (1966) found that father absence occurring within the first four years of a boy's life can have long-lasting effects on the child's sex-typed behavior.

While girls have traditionally been viewed as less affected by father absence, according to a study by Hetherington (1972), many adolescent girls who grew up without fathers had difficulty relating to men. Girls whose fathers were absent because of divorce were likely to have problems with heterosexual relations during adolescence. They tended to be overly aggressive and were often sexually promiscuous. Girls whose fathers were absent because of death behaved differently. They were sexually tense, shy, and uncomfortable around men.

Other studies raise questions about the negative effects of father absence. Hetherington (1966) found that after the age of four, the sex-typed behaviors of boys are not generally affected when fathers leave. "When divorced mothers encouraged independent, mature, positive masculine behaviors and had a positive

When Patricia Ebert (twelve children) married David Hunt (eleven children), they faced the problem of blending families on a large scale. Their story was later dramatized in the movie *Yours, Mine, and Ours*.

attitude toward males and ex-husbands, boys in divorced families did not differ from those of nuclear families on measures of sex-typing'' (Hetherington et al., 1977, p. 18).

Several researchers (Bould, 1977; Pedersen, 1976; and Herzog and Sudia, 1968, 1970) have concluded that fathers are important in their children's development, but mothers, too, can raise children successfully as single parents. And Rutter (1971) found that children of single mothers were better adjusted than children from two parent, conflict-ridden homes.

Finally, it is important to remember that many factors influence the outcomes of father absence. Father absence is accompanied by decreased financial resources, stress for the mother, more responsibility for children, and perhaps a move out of a familiar neighborhood. These factors, in addition to the temperamental characteristics, age, and sex of the child and the attitude and behaviors of the mother interact to produce long-term effects—negative or positive—on children in father-absent homes.

Stepfamilies.   Currently 6.5 million children—10 percent of those under eighteen—live in stepfamilies. Sometimes called reconstituted or blended families, stepfamilies may be as simple as a widow with one child marrying a bachelor, or as complex as four divorced individuals, all with joint custody of their children, trying to form two new households. Transitions from unbroken homes to broken homes to stepfamilies aren't easy.

> I was really turned on by her—then I met her kids. They scared the hell out of me. I began to look at them in a very different way after I got serious. I kept asking myself, ''What are they trying to do to me? What am I going to do to them?'' Everybody warned me not to marry a woman with children. They said there'd be problems: There were. But the youngest goes off to college next month and I think we've won. (Bohannan and Erickson, 1978, p. 53)

389

Stepchildren must adjust to one or two new stepparents and still maintain relationships with the biological parent who no longer lives with them. Stepchildren may direct anger for the absent parent toward the new stepparent (Francke and Reese, 1980). Relationships with biological siblings in or out of the home must be maintained. Developing step-sibling relationships can also present adjustment problems (Jacobson, 1980).

Stepparents have their difficulties adjusting, too. Stepfathers tend to be self-critical and unsure of themselves in the stepparenting role, as compared to biological fathers. But research suggests that stepfathers can have positive effects on the personality development of stepsons who would otherwise be without a father figure (Oshman and Manosevitz, 1976). And stepfathers get just as high ratings from their spouses and stepchildren as biological fathers do (Bohannan and Erickson, 1978). In fact, some evidence suggests that stepfathers have better relationships with stepchildren (Duberman, 1973) and adjust more easily to the stepparenting role than stepmothers do (Bowerman and Irish, 1962). Some say that's partly because the Cinderella myth—that stepmothers are wicked—lingers into the 1980s.

Unbroken families have had a lifetime to establish their relationship patterns. But stepparents and children—who may be virtual strangers—are thrown into instant, intimate relationships for which they may not be ready (Kompara, 1980). Stepfamily members have separate histories, memories, and habits. A sense of family togetherness must be established. And status, duties, and privileges must be redefined in the context of the new family system. Remarriage preparation courses, counseling, and honest discussions of feelings among stepfamily members are a few ways stepfamilies can build positive relationships (Jacobson, 1980).

Adoption. Adopted children sometimes secretly fear that their new parents might abandon them. Velma's adoptive parents were aware that this fear might exist so they explained to Velma that her biological parents had reasons for not being able to keep her.

Velma's parents told her she was special to them because they had chosen her. At age twelve, Velma's adoptive parents took her to visit the hospital where she was born. Velma has become curious about her biological parents. Perhaps one day she will seek them out and even discover her twin sister, Thelma, who was adopted by a family in another city.

Adoption agencies, concerned about separation anxiety and the development of attachment, attempt to place newborns as early as possible—most babies being placed before three months of age. Not so long ago, only healthy newborns were likely to be adopted. Newborns' actual parents were matched with adoptive parents on such things as eye and hair color and educational level. As a result, the child would have a good chance of resembling the adoptive parents.

A social trend has now begun to affect such adoption practices: the decision of many unmarried teenagers to keep their babies rather than place them for adoption. As a result, the number of newborn babies who can be carefully matched to adoptive parents has declined. The number of adults who want to adopt has not decreased, only the number of babies available for adoption. Adults who want children are now searching for previously unadoptable children such as war orphans—babies from Korea or Vietnam—or older, handicapped, biracial or other "hard to place" children. Typically, the children are preschool or school-aged. To increase the chances of finding homes for hard-to-place children, interracial adoptions and single parent family adoptions are now being allowed.

CHILD-ADULT RELATIONSHIPS IN SCHOOL AND COMMUNITY

As schoolchildren move outside the home and into the community, they are exposed to the different disciplinary and leadership styles of teachers, camp counselors, church and scout leaders, and heads of various other community organizations. The leadership styles of community leaders—*authoritarian, democratic,* and *laissez-faire*—parallel the parenting styles discussed in Chapter 10—*authoritarian, authoritative,* and *permissive.*

Community leaders and teachers using an *authoritarian style* impose rigid controls and make all decisions and rules. Under such leadership, children have no chance to learn to make the best decisions for themselves. Sometimes Little League ball falls into this leadership category—especially when adults make the rules and insist children follow them.

The *democratic style* allows children more freedom. Decisions and rules are made by the child or children, not imposed by adults. But adults provide choices and general guidance without giving step-by-step instructions. Community leaders and teachers using democratic styles prepare children for autonomy in a rapidly changing society where control of behavior must come from within. Usually, civic organizations such as scouts and youth groups are democratic, although the style used depends upon the personalities of individual group leaders.

The *laissez-faire or permissive style* imposes no limits, guidelines, or structures. Children are left totally on their own and are given complete decision-making authority. But this "anything goes" style can cause children to be uncertain, confused, and unable to make responsible decisions whether in the classroom, on the ballfield, or at home. Examples of this style are poorly guided classroom, neighborhood, or household projects that never seem to get off the ground.

A famous experiment by Lewin and his colleagues organized ten-year-old boys into three different groups, each one under a different leadership style (Lewin et al., 1939). The boys worked together on soap carvings, mural painting, and other activities. Adult leadership styles set the tone for the groups and influenced the children's behavior. In the authoritarian group, children argued and competed against one another rather than working cooperatively. When their leader left for a minute, children had difficulty working constructively. As a whole, the boys in the authoritarian group were disinterested and displeased with their project. In the democratic group, more cooperation toward group goals was observed and morale was high. When the leader left the room, the boys continued their active involvement and interest. The laissez-faire group struggled with problems of disorganization and frustration. Although the boys tried to pull themselves together as a group, they were never successful in establishing a cooperative work situation.

This experiment shows the effects adult leadership can have on the behavior of children. Most teachers and community leaders use all three styles of leadership at one time or another. But we can conclude that under the guide of a democratic, respected adult who provides not only direction but choice, children will learn to make decisions and accept responsibility better than they would under oppressive leadership or no leadership at all.

Schoolchildren and Peer Relationships

Lord of the Flies (Golding, 1959) is a frightening novel that tells the tale of a group of school-aged boys marooned on a remote island. They struggle for leadership roles, split into separate power groups, and devise their own laws. Some of the penalties for breaking laws are extremely harsh—even savage. This is a fictional work that provides one man's shocking view of what would happen if children were left to structure their own ''society,'' but in fact it is just an exaggeration of what really happens in our everyday world.

Schoolchildren have a society all their own within society at large. They have their own set of rules, norms, and folklore passed down from one generation of children to the next. And conformity to these standards is very important to children in this age group.

SAME-SEX FRIENDSHIPS

Peer relationships follow a pattern of development. During early childhood, children's short-term social interactions with other children give them the opportunity to learn the give-and-take that is a basis for later, more long-term relationships. During middle-childhood, children begin spending more time away from parents and with their peers. These early friendships are almost always with members of the same sex. Children need the emotional security and support of their peer group as they gradually begin to weaken ties from parents. Peer groups in the middle years also serve as a screening system through which children filter the values and attitudes of parents—deciding which to keep and which to throw away (Siman, 1977).

School-age peer groups are also based on such commonalities as interests, age, and sometimes socioeconomic status. **Cliques**—peer groups consisting of

Friendships during middle childhood are almost always with members of the same sex and usually with children of the same age, interests, and socio-economic class.

three to eight members who consciously exclude others—can start as early as third grade. But they are typically formed in grades five and six (Dacey, 1979). Although Caroline and her friends called the ''Secret Fort'' a club, their group was really a clique that excluded boys.

An experiment conducted by Sherif and associates (1961) showed patterns of peer group formations based on cooperation and competition of a group of fifth grade boys at summer camp. The boys were divided into two groups before camp opened. None of the boys knew one another. Despite the arbitrary assignment of the boys to the two groups, some interesting patterns emerged. Friendships were mostly confined to the boy's own group. There were feelings of group spirit and unity. When the two groups learned of each other's existence, group solidarity became stronger. Aggression and competition occurred between the groups. But when the two groups were assigned tasks to complete jointly, old barriers disappeared and new friendships were formed across group lines. This experiment showed how important the peer group is to the schoolchild. It limits or defines friendship possibilities, develops group unity, fosters certain attitudes and values, provides a sense of identity, establishes rules, and gives a sense of purpose to children's lives.

Conformity.   According to research on conformity, although none of us are immune to group pressure, a person's behavior in this situation is influenced by age.

Roosevelt's science teacher asked, "How many of you agree that Earth is the fourth planet from the sun?" Almost all the students, including the smartest in class, raised their hands in agreement. But Roosevelt had a funny feeling inside. And his heart began to pound. He felt sure they were wrong—and that Earth is the *third* planet from the sun. But maybe they were right and he was wrong! If he raised his hand in disagreement, he might be wrong and he would really look dumb! If he was right, his classmates might think he's a smart aleck. What should he do?

Children during middle childhood are more apt to conform than at any other period—even though it means giving the wrong answer (Berenda, 1950; Berndt, 1979; Constanzo and Shaw, 1966). This conformity can be explained through Piaget's (1954) notion that children become more rule (or wrongness) conscious, causing them to conform more until about twelve years of age. After age twelve, children have internalized rules and they react more on an individual basis and conform less often.

During the middle years, children desperately want to fit in. They don't want to appear peculiar or too different from their peers—even when the group's behavior is "wrong." Antisocial acts such as rolling a neighbor's yard with toilet tissue, making prank telephone calls, or stealing gum from a local store are not unusual. In fact, children are ready to conform to peer misconduct and often do not defy peer pressure to misbehave until at least the eighth grade (Bixenstine et al., 1976). Peer-group acceptance is even more important than acceptance by adults. This increased need for peer recognition and approval marks the shift from dependency on parents and adults to dependency on peers.

Roosevelt's dilemma was complicated by the fact that the smartest pupils raised their hands. When children view their peers as highly competent, they are more influenced by these peers than children who view their peers as having low competence (Berenda, 1950; Landsbaum and Willis, 1971). So we would expect Roosevelt to deliberately give the wrong answer or be quiet, even though he knew better.

Popularity.   In every group, some children are liked and some disliked more than others. One way to find out the most and least popular person in a group is to draw a **sociogram**—a diagram that plots most preferred and least preferred relationships in a group. Ms. Cunningham asked members in her class to choose one classmate they would like to work with on a class project and one classmate they would not want as a partner. A sociogram showing some of the results is shown in Figure 12.1.

Notice that most children usually chose partners of the same sex and rejected partners of the opposite sex. Among the girls, Caroline and Kim are the "stars" because they were chosen most often. The boy "star" is Brad, receiving choices from most of his male agemates. Best friends are Caroline and Kim and Roosevelt and Brad because they chose each other. Velma and Jun are least friendly because

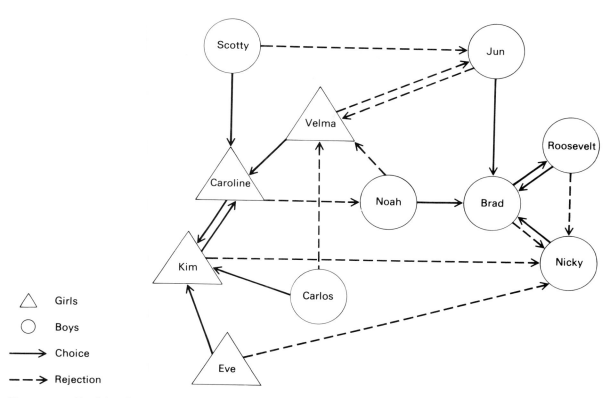

Figure 12.1   **Partial sociogram of Ms. Cunningham's class**

they both rejected each other. The most rejected children in the class are Velma and Nicky—rejection coming from both males and females in the class. Scotty, Eve and Carlos were the isolates—being neither preferred nor rejected by anyone in the class.

What is it about Caroline, Kim, and Brad that make them so popular among their peers? Popular middle-years children are usually well adjusted, enthusiastic, friendly, cooperative and sensitive to the needs of others (Mannerino, 1976). They do well academically, they are bright, and they come from higher socioeconomic levels than unpopular children (Hartup, 1970; Minuchin, 1977). In addition, well-liked children ask questions and show interest in others (Gottman et al., 1975). And as a rule, they have good self-concepts (Horowitz, 1962). Usually, popular children have nicknames from the group (Harre, 1980). Brad is called "grasshopper" because of his long legs and Roosevelt is known as "moose" because of his large size.

But in most childhood groups there are also unpopular children who usually aren't nicknamed (except with malicious names such as "Fatty"), who nobody wants to play with, and who are passed over during namings on class projects. What is it about Velma and Nicky that caused the other children to reject them? Long-term research shows that school-age children who were institutionalized as infants, like Velma, are likely to be less popular and more quarrelsome and attention-seeking than home-reared children (Tizard and Hodges, 1978). Anxious children and those with adjustment problems also tend to be unpopular (Horowitz, 1962). You will remember that both Nicky and Velma had attachment and other adjustment problems as younger children, which could have carried over into middle childhood. Physically handicapped children also receive more unpopular ratings than nonhandicapped children (Richardson et al., 1961). Unpopular children tend to think less well of themselves (Campbell, 1964) and are sometimes emotionally immature, overly aggressive, or withdrawn.

PLAY

Caroline and Kim caught themselves saying the same word at the same time. They immediately hooked their little fingers together and began to chant: ''I wish I may, I wish I might, have this wish come true tonight!'' The girls remained silent, eyes closed, until a third person spoke to them and broke the spell.

Chants are an important part of verbal play and peer interaction among school children. Some chants bring children like Caroline and Kim closer together. Other chants like ''Queen, Queen Caroline, washed her hair in turpentine. . .'' are used for teasing and taunting.

Children learn important social skills through play with other children (Elkind, 1976). Roles and rules in the ''society of childhood'' provide children with opportunities to learn about similar roles and rules in adult society. Feelings of cooperation and competition are developed through play. And concepts such as justice and injustice, prejudice and equality, leading and following, and loyalty and disloyalty begin to take on real and personal meaning. Words and nicknames take on unusual significance:

> ''In these years, children also grasp the power of words to create personal ownership through formulas like ''Dibs on the cake!'' That understanding forms the psychological basis of contracts, values, and other kinds of verbal devises that maintain social order among adults. (Harre, 1980, p. 79).

Rules and Rituals.   School-age children enjoy making up their own rules and rituals and enforcing them in the peer group. An important rule at ''The Secret Fort'' was that everybody who joined had to put something in the treasure. Roosevelt and Brad's ''bloodletting'' ceremony at which they declared their ''blood brother'' relationship is an example of a ritual. Secret maps, passwords, and handshakes are other examples of middle childhood rituals.

Cooperative and Competitive Games.   A 1971 Government survey reported how children ages six to eleven spend their time outside school (Roberts and Baird, 1971). Children enjoyed watching television, working, reading books, and playing alone. But they spent most of their time out of school playing with friends. Group games such as hopscotch, blindman's bluff, chasing games, hide-and-seek, and Red Rover are popular games at this age. These games allow children to let off steam or pent-up energy. They develop physical-motor capacities and build social skills.

As children move through the early elementary grades, favorite games become less cooperative, more organized, and more competitive (Bryan, 1975). Competitive board games such as checkers and Monopoly continue to be favorite pastimes. But children today know fewer games and spend less time in spontaneous play than they used to (Minuchin, 1977). Instead, spontaneous play has sometimes been replaced by more sophisticated, technological games. With his "Pac-Man" game, Brad matches wits with a video computerized game. Electronic games imitate human intelligence and offer challenging interchanges and unpredictable outcomes for children in our technological society (Gardner, 1979).

But active games are still the predominant interest of girls and boys during middle childhood. In fact, a 1961 analysis of changes in children's games over a sixty-year period showed that girls' play had become more competitive and active than it had been because of a loosening of sex-role stereotypes (Sutton-Smith and Rosenberg, 1961).

Humor.   Schoolchildren are also beginning to understand and appreciate humor, though their favorite jokes are not those of the adults around them.

The following joke, which Roosevelt told to both his four-year-old brother and his eighteen-year-old sister, is typical of humor during the middle years:

> Mr. Jones went into a restaurant and ordered a whole pizza for his dinner. When the waiter asked if he wanted it cut into six or eight pieces, Mr. Jones said, "Oh, you'd better make it six, I would never eat eight pieces!" (McGhee, 1973).

"Don't you get it?" Roosevelt chuckled, poking his little brother in the ribs. Looking confused, his brother chuckled with some effort before turning back to his play. Roosevelt's older sister didn't even pretend to laugh. She thought the joke was corny and said so.

HUMOR AND COGNITIVE DEVELOPMENT.   Why didn't Roosevelt's brother and sister appreciate his pizza joke? A child's grasp of humor is related more to the level of cognitive development than to age alone (McGhee, 1979). For humor to be appreciated, children must see it as cognitively challenging (moderately difficult, yet understandable). Children lose interest in humor when it is too easy or too hard (Zigler et al., 1967).

Cooperative and Competitive Play in Middle Childhood

Roosevelt's pizza joke is based on an understanding of the *conservation of mass* (see Chapter 11). Because preoperational children, have not reached this level of cognitive development, they neither understand nor appreciate such jokes (McGhee, 1973). Roosevelt is a concrete operational thinker and has recently achieved conservation—so he finds the joke hilarious! His teenaged sister, long past this stage, does not find the joke a cognitive challenge and so views the joke as more corny than funny.

Concrete operational children also understand humor that contains *logical inconsistencies*—such as a cartoon in which firemen are holding back a woman who wants to run into her burning house to answer the telephone (McGhee, 1971). Preoperational children could not appreciate humor employing such violations of logic because they don't understand the underlying logic.

HUMOR AND LANGUAGE DEVELOPMENT.   An expanding view of the world allows schoolchildren to make transformations of their native languages not possible in early childhood. For the first time, words become objects that can be manipulated. The child's newfound abilities allow an understanding of the humor of wordplays, riddles, and rhymes, and transformations of words, sounds, or phrases to create new effects or double meanings (see Fig. 12.2). Roosevelt's four-year-old brother can no more understand jokes when liberties are taken with words than he can understand the pizza joke.

Wordplays

Reporter: Are you worried about rising food prices?

Farm boy: Naw—if things go bad, we can always eat our Forest Preserves.

City boy: Yeah, and we can eat our Traffic Jams.

Knock-Knock Jokes

"Knock-knock"

"Who's there?"

"Marcella"

"Marcella who?"

"Marcella's (my cellar's) full of water. Call a plumber!"

Riddles

"What's black, white, and red all over?"

"A newspaper"

Rhymes

"Ice cream, you scream,
We all scream for ice cream!"

Transformations of Words to Create New Effects*

"What's one and one?"

"Two"

"What's a word that means also?"

"Too"

"What is the last name of the man who wrote *Tom Sawyer*?"

"Twain"

"Now, can you remember all the answers and say them over again?"

"Two, too, Twain."

"When you get a little older, I'll teach you to say locomotive."

Figure 12.2 **Roosevelt's favorite jokes**
*Adapted from Williams and Stith, 1980.

HUMOR AND EMOTIONAL DEVELOPMENT. Some theorists (Wolfenstein, 1954) have suggested that joking is an instrument for letting out anxiety or other emotional difficulties. They believe children use humor as an outlet for disappointment, to gain temporary release from frustration, or to master difficult or fearful situations. Through their humor children:

> transform the painful into the enjoyable, turn impossible wishes and the envied bigness and powers of adults into something ridiculous, expose adult pretensions, make light of failures, and parody their own frustrated strivings. (Wolfenstein, 1954, p. 12).

A recent study (Fisher and Fisher, 1981) indicates that children who *always* play the clown typically have been overloaded with responsibility and are expected to be adult beyond their years. They go overboard with humor as a way of coping with their burden.

Among Roosevelt's favorite jokes are a series of stories about a mother and her child, "Heinie." Heinie gets lost in a department store. The mother walks up to the store manager and asks, "Sir, have you seen my Heinie?" Startled, the store manager replies, "No madam, and I really don't care to!"

According to Wolfenstein (1954), the "Heinie" jokes are popular with most nine-year-olds. The thought of revealing an intimate part of her body makes Heinie's mother appear sexually loose and silly. Children telling this joke are in a powerful situation because they control the behaviors of the adult through the words in the story. Through jokes, children can deal with forbidden, "off-color" thoughts about the lady's behind. They can also minimize anxiety of feared grown-ups and retaliate against these powerful authority figures by making them appear ridiculous in their jokes.

Scary stories, horror movies, and jokes about death become of interest after nine and ten. At this age, children have gained enough mastery over these fears to enjoy exploring them (Minuchin, 1977). The following familiar childhood chant deals with the feared subject of a parent's death:

> "Help! Murder! Police!
> My mother fell in the grease!
> I laughed so hard,
> I fell in the lard,
> Help! Murder! Police!"

Concerns about being competent (i.e., industry vs. inferiority), being viewed in a good light, and appearing stupid are also reflected in the humor and jokes of middle childhood. That's why children at this age laugh at the mistakes of others, play practical jokes, and enjoy reporting pranks someone else played on a friend (Aho, 1979). That's also why middle-years children enjoy telling and hearing "Little Moron" jokes:

> "Why did Little Moron tiptoe quietly past the medicine cabinet?"
> "So he wouldn't wake the sleeping pills."

School-age children giggle a lot—from embarrassment, from boredom, from the happiness of being alive.

HUMOR AND SOCIAL DEVELOPMENT.   Roosevelt spends a lot of time whispering and giggling with his male friends. This interchange of humor acts as a cementing of social relationships and group belonging. Humor provides a common ground for sharing and communion, which strengthens children's social interactions in school and community. Sometimes children laugh at jokes and sometimes they simply giggle for reasons unknown even to themselves. Adults may become exasperated with such never-ending contagious giggling or laughter. But as giggling reaches its peak during childhood (Williams and Stith, 1980), we must remember that it does serve a purpose.

Giggling can serve to cover up embarrassment or to prevent boredom. When a child does not know the correct answer or understand what is expected, giggling can be a way out of the difficulty. Giggling can also come from the happiness of being alive. Adults will find it easier to live with gigglers if they understand that giggling is normal for schoolchildren (Williams and Stith).

Emotions

As schoolchildren venture into school and society, their emotional development is more influenced by people and experiences outside the home than it was in earlier years. In this section, we will look at some of these influences as we examine fear, hyperactivity, and prejudice in middle childhood.

FEAR

Roosevelt's parents *always* came to his room to say goodnight. But one night they didn't come, so he went to see what was the matter. The kitchen door was ajar. As he peeked inside, he saw his parents sitting at the kitchen table whispering. His father was pounding the table and tears were streaming down his cheeks.

At first, nobody told Roosevelt what was going on. So for a long time he tried to figure it out himself. He worried constantly about his parents, wondering what was wrong. And after that night, things began to change at Roosevelt's house. His father started staying home and his mother started leaving the house each morning. The sudden change of his father not working caused Roosevelt to secretly worry even more about where his family would get enough money to live on. Finally, after noticing his son's bewilderment, Roosevelt's father told him that he had lost his job.

During the middle years of childhood, children's fears reflect their expanding world (Williams and Stith, 1980). For the most part fears center around the school, family, and peer group. Irrational and fantasy fears of earlier periods are replaced by more realistic concerns of everyday life—school, injury, natural events, social interactions (Miller et al., 1974). Fears also become more generalized, taking the form of anxiety or worry (MacFarlane et al., 1954). Children like Roosevelt begin to share the worries of their parents—financial problems, fear of parental illness and death, and difficulties in interpersonal relationships with family, neighbors, and peers. Fears of failing in school, of critical teachers, of bullies, of getting hurt, and of rejection by parents and peers begin to emerge (Wolman, 1978).

When children like Roosevelt view their parents as worried, weak, helpless, and upset, their fears increase (Wolman, 1978). Although a job loss might not be a major catastrophe, it could appear that way in the eyes of a twelve-year-old. Telling Roosevelt about the job loss in a straightforward way would have better prepared him for the change in daily routine and prevented some of his excessive worry. Otherwise, a sensitive nine- or ten-year-old may come to believe he somehow caused his father's job loss (Wolman, 1978).

An occasional unwillingness to go to school is typical among school-aged children. But **school phobia,** an extreme fear of going to school, may appear during this age period. In this instance, the child might refuse to go to school or become overanxious about going to school. Physical symptoms such as headaches, stomachaches, and dizziness are also common. Vomiting sometimes occurs. These physical symptoms are not faked. They are real. Children with school phobia usually do well in school. Their fears emerge more from fear of separation and abandonment from parents (usually the mother) than from fear of scholastic failure (Wolman, 1978). Generally, phobic children fear that accidents or injuries might happen to their mothers while they are away. Parents who are weak and have difficulty making decisions in front of the child produce children who worry about them. And when parents encourage dependence on mother, they contribute to the child's fear of school (Hetherington and Martin, 1972).

> Inconsistent and insecure parents may give the child the impression that *they* fear separation, that *they* need the child's presence. Their unconscious clinging to the child discourages his or her independence and self-assertiveness. Many overdependent and overprotected children develop school phobia, as if they sense the need behind their mother's solicitude for them. Of course, consciously every mother wishes her child to go to school and be independent and outgoing, but unconscious anxieties may make her act in an inconsistent manner that, in turn, fans the child's anxiety and overdependence (Wolman, 1978, p. 160).

It is important that the child with school phobia be returned to school as quickly as possible. Sometimes, too much attention to the phobic child's physical complaints can cause the symptoms to increase. Ignoring tantrums and complaints may be necessary. A friendly, firm, matter-of-fact insistence that the child return to school is a better approach than one of pity or sorrow (Wolman, 1978).

HYPERACTIVITY

Nicky sat restless in his seat, trying to do his arithmetic. But his eyes roamed the room and his feet tapped the beat of a song he remembered from the radio. When he could stand it no longer, his pencil and desk became his drum—accompanying the rhythm of his feet. Then, the head of the child in front of Nicky became the object of his energy as he thumped him in a steady rhythm. Moments later, the two boys tumbled to the floor in a fierce wrestling match.

As you remember, Nicky has been overactive and on the move since early childhood. Sometimes he is explosive and aggressive—jumping up, yelling, or destroying property. Nicky's behavior was influenced by his **hyperactivity**—a behavior disorder characterized by difficulty in paying attention and concentrating, high levels of motor activity, poor impulse control, and attention-seeking behavior (Wolf, 1977). Hyperactivity itself is not a disease or an emotional disturbance. Sometimes hyperactivity accompanies severe emotional or intellectual handicaps. Other times, the hyperactive condition is so stressful that emotional problems result. Hyperactivity—or hyperkineticism as it is sometimes called—affects between 5 and 8 percent of elementary school boys and about 1 percent of girls (Ross and Ross, 1976).

Because they have trouble concentrating, paying attention, and sitting still, hyperactive children have problems doing schoolwork. And as you saw in the Case of the Parent-Teacher Conference (Chapter 10), children like Nicky, become sources of concern for parents and teachers. One survey of children referred to a medical clinic for hyperactivity found that 50 percent were referred directly by schools (Kenny et al., 1971).

Although the cause of hyperactivity remains a mystery, many reasons have been suggested. Damage to the central nervous system (Satterfield and Cantwell, 1976) and genetic causes (Ross and Ross, 1976) have been consistent suggestions of experts. Others have cited diet (Feingold, 1975), temperament (Fine, 1977), and reinforcement of inappropriate behavior (Reith, 1977) as explanations. There are no simple answers to complex questions about hyperactivity. Most likely many factors interact to produce the hyperactive behavior (Fine, 1977).

Since we do not know the cause, there is no "cure". But many treatment techniques have been used. Certain medications (such as Ritalin) have calming effects on hyperactive children. These drugs allow children to concentrate better, to make fewer errors in their work, and to pay attention to one activity for a longer time (Humphries et al., 1978; McManis et al., 1978). But many people are concerned about the possibility of negative side effects of drugs that we know very little about. For this reason, diets—free of sugar, artificial flavorings, and food additives—have become more popular as treatment techniques (Feingold, 1975). Other treatments have included a behavioral management approach (Reith, 1977), and the installation of soft, blue lights in place of regular institutional lighting (Mullen, 1979). All of these techniques have shown some decreases in levels of hyperactivity, allowing children to benefit from counseling and improve their schoolwork. But no cure works consistently for all children. Perhaps the best approach of all is a systems approach in which professionals track down the many influences on hyperactivity and use a variety of treatment approaches instead of just one (Mira and Reece, 1977).

The outlook for hyperactive children like Nicky is not too bad. Most complete high school, some go to college, and most are steadily employed as adults (Borland, 1976). But in cases where psychiatric or intellectual problems accompany hyperactivity, hyperactive adults may not be as successful as other family members (Borland, 1976).

PREJUDICE

Roosevelt, Brad, and Scotty rode their bikes to the dump one Saturday afternoon to shoot their pellet guns. On the way home they were tired and thirsty so they stopped by a fast food restaurant for a soft drink. As they entered the cafe, several boys in a corner booth shouted, "Niggers ain't welcome in here."

The more chances children of different races have to interact, the more likely they are to form interracial friendships.

Roosevelt was obviously hurt and Brad and Scotty wanted to fight the boys. "No," said Roosevelt. "C'mon let's get out of here."

Racial prejudice is not inborn. Prejudice is learned when parents or peers put down people from other races. Prejudice is not always taught directly through words. Facial expressions and body movements also indicate approval or disgust, hate and intolerance toward others. Books, magazines, newspapers, and other media transmit attitudes toward race. Children's judgments and awareness of racial differences are influenced as they become increasingly aware of the attitudes that parents, peers and society have toward other races.

Prejudice is evident in black and white children from the preschool years into the early school years (Morland, 1966; Williams et al., 1975b). For instance, black and white children in the third, fourth, and fifth grades are aware that it is unlikely for a mixed-race couple to get married, for an opposite-race man to join their church, or for an opposite-race woman to become their father's boss (Kleinke and

Nicholson, 1979). Generally, ten-year-olds are more prejudiced than six-year-olds, and during the middle years, children generally prefer friends who are of the same race (Singleton and Asher, 1979).

But interracial friendships are sometimes formed in the early school years (Shaw, 1974). Roosevelt, Brad, and Scotty live in adjoining neighborhoods, attend the same school, and have become the best of pals. Increased contact with children of other races changes racial attitudes of white elementary school children. In fact, interracial friendships occur more often in integrated schools or summer camps (Clore, et al., 1978). Children's liberal racial attitudes are also related to high self-esteem, nonpunitive child-rearing practices, and nonauthoritarian parents (Stephan and Rosenfield, 1978).

Children who belong to a minority group that is viewed negatively by society at large often come to accept society's negative view of their own group. In early studies of racial awareness, both black and white preschool children labeled a black doll as "looking bad." They preferred a white doll instead (Clark, 1955) and were more favorable to white rather than dark-skinned figures (Williams et al., 1975b). Hunsberger (1978) found a similar preference for white over American Indian dolls among Canadian Indian and white five- to nine-year-olds. And American-Chinese children identified less with their race and less often preferred their own race for play than did either white or black children (Fox and Jordan, 1973). Similar feelings were reported among Hispanic-American first- and third-graders (Weiland and Coughlin, 1979).

There is some evidence that prejudice among some children has decreased over the years. This is attributed to society's increasing sensitivity to the harmful effects of racial prejudice and to the emergence of racial pride. A replication of Clark's (1955) study found that black children had increased in identification with their own race and, as a result, more often preferred black to white dolls. And black children's preferences for playing with other children of their own race have increased dramatically (Fox and Jordan, 1973). Such changes in children's views of themselves reflect improved self-images of blacks as well as the long-term effects of the civil rights struggle of the 1960s. The "Black Is Beautiful" campaign appears to have had a positive effect on the personality development of a new generation of black Americans.

Sex-Role Development and Relationships

SEX CONSTANCY

Preschool Caroline's thinking was so rigid, she believed that if a girl wore boy's clothes or got a boyish haircut, the girl's sex would also change. That's because preschool children have not developed **sex constancy**—the understanding that being male or female is a permanent part of a person, regardless of alterations in hair, clothing, or other surface changes. Preschool children believe one's sex can be transformed if there are changes in hair, clothes, and activities (Emmerich et al., 1976). But sex constancy occurs along with other shifts in cognitive development (Gouze and Nadelman, 1980). During the transition from preoperational to concrete operational thinking (around age seven and eight), children realize that masculine and feminine traits can exist separately from physical or biological features (Ullian, 1976). Sex constancy is achieved along with other kinds of conservation as part of the shift from Piaget's preoperational to concrete operational period (Emmerich et al., 1976; Marcus and Overton, 1978). Now a concrete thinker, Caroline laughs hysterically at the thought of a girl's sex changing because she gets a haircut or wears boy's clothes.

SEX-ROLE STEREOTYPING

During elementary school, boys and girls tend to be more positive about their own sex and more negative about the opposite sex than high school students (Parish and Bryant, 1978). They also give higher ratings to male and female peers who excel in subject areas that their sex is known to do well in. In one study, for example, girls who did well in reading and boys who did well in math got higher ratings from fifth- and sixth-grade children than boys who did well in reading and girls who did well in math (Mokros and Koff, 1978).

Increased stereotyped thinking has been noted up until the second grade—around age seven (Williams et al., 1975a). But beginning at age seven or eight, when shifts appear in other aspects of cognitive development, schoolchildren loosen their hold on rigid sex-role stereotypes.

A recent study of two groups of girls between ages six to eight and ten to twelve illustrated this shift in stereotyped thinking (Meyer, 1980). Researchers presented 150 girls with stereotyped male activities such as "be an astronaut," "fix the car," "be the boss" and stereotyped female activities such as "clean the house," "be a librarian," or "babysit." Then, they asked the girls who should do each activity and who could do it better: men, women or both. Younger girls had more sex-stereotyped attitudes and job goals than older girls. And the sex-role attitudes of older girls correlated with their mother's sex-role attitudes and job goals. Differences in sex-stereotypes between the two groups were attributed to different stages of cognitive development.

Progress beyond sex-role stereotyping is important because stereotypes can restrict the child's growth and potential. During middle childhood, parents and teachers can help children begin to move beyond social stereotypes by helping children explore many different occupational roles—regardless of the stereotypes associated with them. Girls can be encouraged to play ball, to use hammers and screwdrivers, and to compete in athletics. Boys can learn to cook and to develop domestic interests as well as athletic skills. Such "trying on" of various roles gives children greater flexibility and prepares them to be competent in many different situations.

RESPONSIBILITIES AND PRODUCTIVITY IN MIDDLE CHILDHOOD

Nine-year-old Manyara, a Nyansango girl from Kenya, Africa is a child nurse. Like other girls her age, she is expected to care for her baby brothers and sisters until they can walk alone. Since she does not attend school, Manyara busies herself all day long feeding, bathing and caring for the children while her mother works in nearby gardens and goes to market. Nyansango children as young as five are given the responsibility of child nurse.

In some parts of Mexico and in Okinawa and India, children also take the role of child nurse during middle childhood or even earlier (Whiting and Whiting, 1975). In Taiwan, some five-year-old girls go to kindergarten with infant siblings strapped to their backs. Taiwanese girls pat, bounce, and talk to the infants, trying to keep them content. In Samoa, mothers turn full responsibility for routine housework and care of younger children over to six- and seven-year-old child nurses: "No mother will ever exert herself to discipline a younger child if an older one can be made responsible." (Mead, 1928. p. 24). It is through these responsibilities that middle-years children in other cultures are themselves disciplined and socialized.

As you can see children in other cultures are given much greater responsibility than their age-mates in the United States—although school-age children in this country are sometimes put in charge of younger children. Manyara's child-nursing responsibilities are very different from Caroline's occasional babysitting with her younger sister or feeding her dog, or Roosevelt's carrying out the trash.

According to Minturn and Lambert (1964), in places like Okinawa and Mexico, children are viewed as irresponsible before six or seven years of age. So in these cultures, children are not assigned chores until middle childhood, the "age of reason." Among the Mixtican people of Juxlahuaca, Mexico, this age marks the time at which children are considered capable of accepting responsibility for doing their part. Before this age, children work whenever they want to and there is no sex-typing in the things they do. In fact, during early childhood, young boys do what is considered "woman's work." But all this changes at the "age of reason."

Although they are not expected to attend school, children are expected to do more work than before around the house. And there is a division of labor based on sex. Girls take care of younger siblings, carry water, sweep the house, wash dishes and clothes, and care for family pigs and chickens. Boys carry firewood, care for burros and goats, and haul fodder for the animals. Through these chores, Mixtican children learn responsibilities and skills they will be required to perform as adults.

In China, factories are associated with schools and schools with factories. Primary school youngsters might be seen gluing boxes and middle-school students operating electric motor equipment. In addition, students are expected to spend time in the country working in the fields (Mahoney, 1978).

PEER AND SIBLING RELATIONSHIPS

Peer and sibling relationships also differ from culture to culture. Before middle childhood, Samoan girls spend time with an older guardian and don't associate much with other children (Mead, 1928). But at age seven, neighborhood children start to form larger groups. Much as in our own culture, these groups are strictly divided by sex. The prohibition that girls must never join a group of boys is rigidly enforced. Similar preferences for close, same-sex friendships have been noted among eight- and nine-year-old children in the Philippines (Minturn and Lambert, 1964).

From middle childhood onward, relationships between brothers and sisters are discouraged in the Samoan culture (Mead, 1928). Beginning at age nine or ten brothers and sisters are not allowed to touch, sit, eat near, or even address one another. They cannot remain in any house together unless a large group of villagers accompany them. And they cannot walk together, use each other's possessions, dance on the same floor, or take part in any of the same activities. This separation continues until old age, when a toothless brother or sister unite by sitting together without feeling ashamed.

Khalapur, India

Juxlahuaca, Mexico

Charleston, South Carolina

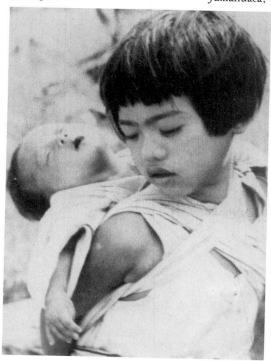

Taira, Okinawa

Nyansango, Kenya

In many cultures, children are routinely expected to care for those younger than themselves. Even in the United States, school-age children are sometimes put in charge of their younger siblings.

Summary

1. The development of industry involves becoming a competent and productive member of society, but when failure and disapproval are frequent, children can develop feelings of inferiority.

2. Many factors influence the child's development of self-esteem: parental traits and behaviors, peer relationships, success and failure in school, ethnic group, and social class membership.

3. School-age children gradually detach from parents as the influence of peers and other adults strengthens.

4. Children's development is still strongly influenced by their role as a member of a family. Such variations in family structure as birth order, divorce, single-parent families, stepfamilies, and adoption make a difference in how the family functions as a whole system.

5. Middle-years children are exposed to a variety of adults besides their parents. The leadership styles of these adults—whether authoritarian, democratic, or laissez-faire—affect children's behavior and development. Although most adults use a combination of all three styles, children function better under democratic guidance than under oppressive guidance or no guidance at all.

6. During middle childhood, children begin spending more time away from parents with their peers—almost always with members of the same sex. Conformity reaches an all-time high, and because children want to fit in, they'll go to practically any extreme to go along with the group. Popular schoolchildren are usually well adjusted, enthusiastic, friendly, and cooperative.

7. The schoolchild's increasing awareness of how words can be manipulated shows up in their humor, which is influenced by cognitive, emotional, and social development.

8. As schoolchildren move into school and society, their emotional development is more influenced by people and experiences outside the family, and fears become less fantasy-based and more tied to the difficulties of everyday life—centering around school, family, and peer group.

9. Hyperactivity is characterized by difficulties in paying attention, excessive motor activity, poor impulse control, and attention-seeking behavior. The cause remains a mystery, but such treatment approaches as drugs, diets, and behavior management have been tried with some success.

10. Influenced by the child's broadening experiences in society, prejudice is evident in black and white children from preschool years into the early school years. But increased contact with children of other races reduces racial attitudes among schoolchildren. Children of minority groups who once viewed themselves negatively, regard themselves in a more favorable light today.

11. Shifts in cognitive development allow school-age children to master the concept of sex constancy and loosen their rigid thinking about sex-role stereotypes.

Empathetic Activities

- What feelings did you have as you read about the following? What feelings do you think the children in these cases had?
  - The Case of the Secret Fort
  - Roosevelt's Conformity Dilemma
  - Nicky's Hyperactivity
  - Roosevelt and Brad's Close Relationship
  - Manyara, the Child Nurse from Kenya, Africa
- As a parent or teacher, what special things would you do to encourage industry? To improve a child's self-esteem? To help a child deal with pressures for conformity, fears, prejudice, and sex-role development?
- Observe children in an elementary school classroom.
  - With the teacher's permission, ask the children to write down their own name, the name of one classmate they like to work with the most and one classmate they do not like to work with.
  - Plot the answers in a sociogram. Compare your sociogram with the teacher's knowlege of the children. How does your sociogram compare to his or her descriptions?
  - Compare the teacher's descriptions of children with the research on popular and unpopular children. How do they match?
- Use information from this chapter to describe the leadership style or styles Caroline's mother used when the girls were planning the Secret Fort. What other styles could she have used?
- Suppose you were a judge charged with deciding whether children in a divorce case should live with the father or mother. What factors would enter into your decision and what information would you need?
- In what ways do social, emotional, and cognitive development interact through the development of humor to illustrate the *Whole Child*?
- How do the social networks of school- and preschool children differ in terms of peer relationships and adult relationships in school and community?

Related Readings

Gatley, Richard H., and Koulack, David. *Single father's handbook: A guide for separated and divorced fathers.* Garden City, N.Y.: Doubleday, 1979. Readable and useful for single fathers. Focuses on the process of becoming a separated father, dealing with changed relationships with children, friends, and in-laws. Many helpful suggestions for "mothering" children.

Ross, Dorothea M., and Ross, Sheila A. *Hyperactivity: Research, theory, and action.* New York: Wiley, 1976. A very readable introduction to research, theory, and treatment of hyperactivity in childhood. Useful for parents, professionals, and students.

Salk, Lee. *What every child would like parents to know about divorce.* New York: Harper & Row, 1978. A must for parents and teachers working with children and families involved in divorce. Considers personal and legal aspects of divorce. Many practical and helpful suggestions for dealing with divorce and its consequences.

Stephens, Joseph H., and Matthews, Marilyn, eds. *Mother-child father-child relationships.* Washington D.C.: National Association for the Education of Young Children, 1978. Easy reading concerning the relationship of mothers and fathers to children. Also considers divorce, minority families, and alternative family styles.

VI Adolescence

(ages 13 to 18)

13 *Adolescence: Physical and Cognitive Development*

The Case of a Weekend Retreat

A sense of nervous excitement filled the air as the Middleton High School seniors piled onto the bus for a weekend retreat. Brad, Eve, Scott, Kim, Roosevelt, Caroline, Nicky, Velma, Carlos, Jun, and Noah had been selected especially to help their teachers, Ms. Gaither and Coach Wilson, develop a curriculum for a new course on adolescence. The course would combine health education, psychology, and home economics. This weekend retreat was to include the first of six rap sessions held at Camp Kalowatchee. Rap sessions were designed so that the students could identify key issues that should be addressed in the new course.

The seniors were somewhat nervous because they weren't exactly sure what to expect from the rap sessions. They knew they were supposed to talk about issues related to the physical, cognitive, social, and emotional development of adolescents and their relationships. But the seniors were secretly shy and afraid of discussing these issues with their friends. However, they knew that hiking, swimming, bicycle riding, a hayride, and campfire were also planned—and these activities sounded like fun!

The tension heightened as the students and teachers arrived at Camp Kalowatchee, unpacked, and assembled for their first meeting. To begin the discussion, Ms. Gaither suggested they discuss the physical changes of adolescence.

Physical Growth

In the past, children in all societies used to become adults without the adolescent transition period. Teenagers were expected to get married and support themselves at an early age. But the Industrial Revolution of the early nineteenth century brought advanced technology, and this required longer schooling. Eventually, industrial societies became wealthy enough to support advanced education for their young adults. Child labor laws and compulsory education expelled young people from the world of work and placed them in schools. Children had lost their economic value as workers. The time between biological maturity and recognition of adult status was lengthened and the stage we now call adolescence emerged. As a result, teenagers in our culture are neither child nor adult. Their physical and cognitive development is adultlike but they are still childlike in their economic dependence on parents.

Jun took pride in describing to the group how his people, the Hopi Indians, traditionally had no transition period such as adolescence to mark the passage from childhood to adulthood. "Indian children were boys or girls one day and the next day they were men or women," he explained. "There was no in-between."

Spotlight 13.1 shows how cultures are unique in defining the end of childhood and the beginning of adulthood. But in all cultures, the stability of growth characteristic of schoolchildren gives way to a period of rapid physical growth and sexual maturation in teenagers. Accompanying this physical growth and sexual maturation are psychological reactions to these changes.

PUBERTY: WHAT IS IT?

People often confuse the terms adolescence and puberty, using both to refer to the teen years. But **puberty**—Latin for "age of manhood," even though it applies to changes in both males and females—is only that period of adolescence marked by a rapid growth spurt and sexual maturation. *Adolescence* is usually defined as the period from the beginning of puberty to the beginning of adulthood.

Many of the characteristic physical changes during puberty are regulated by the pituitary gland, which is a pea-sized organ on the underside of the human brain. Hormones from the pituitary gland stimulate the production of other growth-regulating glands (including the thyroid, adrenals, ovaries, and testes). These glands in turn produce hormones that have already begun to increase in differing kinds and amounts in boys and girls by about age eight or nine. But we don't typically see the results as outward signs of puberty until age ten or eleven among girls and eleven to twelve among boys. The completion of puberty takes between two to four years and marks the beginning of reproductive ability. Girls achieve puberty (marked by the *first menstrual flow*, called **menarche**) at an average age of twelve. Boys' puberty (marked by sperm production) is complete about two years later, at an average age of fourteen.

Puberty comes earlier—the average American girl has her first menstrual period at 12.45 years today compared with 14.2 in 1900—and **menopause** (the end of reproductive capability in women) comes later than it did a hundred years ago. Improved health and nutrition have led to this lengthened reproductive span (Roche, 1979). The adolescent growth spurt and sexual maturation accompany puberty.

Adolescent Growth Spurt. The **adolescent growth spurt** is a period of rapid height and weight increases. It occurs in all children but varies from one child to another in timing, intensity, and duration (Tanner, 1962; Roche, 1976). Growth at this time is more intense and rapid than in any stage in human development except the prenatal period.

"I'm afraid if I keep getting taller and skinnier I'll be a freak or something. I'm already taller than all my friends. I wish I could see a doctor about it. . . ." This was Scotty's silent lament on his thirteenth birthday. As he stared into the mirror, he continued his self-analysis: "My arms seem to drag to the ground when I walk, and I trip over my own legs and feet. And no matter how much I eat, I still look like a string bean!"

❖ Spotlight 13.1: Rites of Passage

Initiation ceremonies called **rites of passage** or puberty rites signal a child's transition into adulthood. Even today, American Indians such as the White Mountain Apaches practice initiation rites.

THE CASE OF NITA QUINTERO: PASSING FROM CHILDHOOD TO WOMANHOOD

We call it Sunrise Dance. It's the biggest ceremony of the White Mountain Apache—when a girl passes from childhood to womanhood. When my time came at fourteen, I didn't want to have one. I felt embarrassed. All my friends would be watching me. But my parents encouraged me, "Then you will live to an old age."

On Friday evening Godmother dressed me and pinned an eagle feather on my head and an abalone shell pendant on my forehead. The feather will help me live until my hair turns gray. The pendant is the sign of Changing Woman, mother of all Apache people.

The most important thing Godmother does is to massage my body. She is giving me all her knowledge. For hours around the fire I follow a dancer who impersonates a protective spirit.

Saturday is like an endurance test. Men begin prayer chants at dawn. Godmother tells me to dance while kneeling on a buckskin pad facing the sun—the creator. In that position, Apache women grind corn. When the time comes for running, I go fast around a sacred cane, so nobody evil will ever catch up with me. Aunt Dolly runs behind me, followed by Godmother. Rain begins, and my ten pound costume gets heavier and heavier. But I don't fall. I don't even get tired.

Cattail pollen is something holy to my people. All the people pick up a handful of pollen from a basket beside me and shake it over my head. They say silent prayers. I am praying to the sun, "Thank you, and bless all these people to have a good life and be happy."

Dolly's daughter wants me to blow in her baby's mouth. That's because during the dance I have power to keep evil spirits away. Next, my father pours candies and corn kernels over me to protect me from famine. My family passes out crates of candy and pop—this means the people will always have food.

My Godfather directs my dancing on Sunday with an eagle feather in each hand. My father holds my sacred cane. When I'm old, I'll use the cane for walking. It's decorated with feathers of the even-

---

In most cases, rapid growth in boys begins during the period from ten and a half to sixteen—the average age being thirteen—and reaches a peak at about fourteen (Tanner, 1970). In girls, the growth spurt begins during the period from seven and a half to eleven and a half—the average age being nine and a half—and reaches a peak at about eleven years eight months (Lipsitz, 1979). During the peak of adolescent growth, girls grow about three and a half inches (Faust, 1977) while boys grow about four to five inches in height per year (Tanner, 1962). Full growth is reached near age nineteen in girls and twenty-one or twenty-two in boys, although there can be small increases after this.

Weight usually doubles during adolescence (Beal, 1980). Increased bone, organ, muscle growth and the development of fatty tissue account for weight

tempered oriole to give me a good disposition. Aunt Dolly stays close to make sure no evil-thinking people touch me.

Godfather paints me from the top of my head to the bottom of my buckskin boots. I am blessed and protected from all four sides. Four is the most important number to the Apache.

On Monday there is more visiting and blessing. I was really strong all the way; I didn't cry like some girls do. I'm really glad I had a Sunrise Dance. It made me realize how much my parents care for me and want me to grow up right. They know my small age is past and treat me like a woman. If I have a daughter, I want her to have a Sunrise Dance too.*

---

* "Coming of Age the Apache Way," by Nita Quintero, *National Geographic*, February 1980, *157*, 262–271. Reprinted with permission.

Jewish boys also traditionally participate in a rite of passage called *bar mitzvah*. At thirteen, a Jewish boy memorizes many religious scriptures and participates in an elaborate ceremony, ending in a celebration with family and friends. From that day on, he is considered a man by the Jewish community (though he may complain his parents still treat him like a child) and is allowed to participate in religious ceremonies with elders in the community. In the conservative and reformed branches of Judaism, girls participate in a similar ceremony called a *bat mitzvah*.

In some Christian churches, the rite of confirmation makes the recipient an adult in church affairs. But for most teenagers today there is no quick, clear evidence of adult status. Instead, the path from childhood to adulthood is a long and often meandering one that leaves many persons well beyond the teen years wondering when—if ever—they will feel like "grown-ups."

gains. We can expect the average boy to gain between twelve and fourteen pounds and the average girl about eleven pounds each year during the peak growth years.

Primary and Secondary Sex Characteristics. **Primary sex characteristics** are the reproductive organs—ovaries, fallopian tubes, uterus, and vagina—in the female and testes, penis, and seminal vesicles in the male. **Secondary sex characteristics** are those traits evident on the surface of the body. In both sexes they include pubic and underarm hair and increased activity of oil-producing glands (which contributes to the acne that causes adolescents so much embarrassment). Secondary sex characteristics in the male also include facial and chest hair and a marked voice change, while in the female they include increased width and depth of the pelvis and breast development.

Table 13.1
Average Age and Sequence of Appearance
of Primary and Secondary Sex Characteristics

AGE	MALES	FEMALES
9–10		Bony pelvis begins to grow; hips begin to widen and nipples begin to bud (enlarge).
10–11	Testes and penis begin growing.	Breasts bud, pubic hair begins to appear.
11–12	Prostate gland becomes active, first ejaculation usually occurs between 11 and 15.	Vaginal lining undergoes changes, external and internal sex organs grow.
12–13	Pubic hair appears.	Nipples become pigmented, breasts begin to fill out, menstruation begins (average age 12 years 9 months for whites and a year earlier for blacks; range 9 to 17).
13–14	Rapid growth of testes and penis.	Underarm hair, menstruation may occur without ovulation for a few years.
14–15	Underarm hair, down on upper lip, voice change, average age of first ejaculation.	Earliest normal pregnancies.
15–16	Mature sperm appear (average age 15; range 11 to 17)	Acne, deepening of voice.
16–17	Facial and body hair, acne.	Arrest of skeletal growth.
21	Arrest of skeletal growth.	

Sources: Wilkins, 1957; Faust, 1977; Katchadourian, 1977; Lipsitz, 1979.

The development and order in which primary and secondary sex characteristics appear is more constant than is the age at which they occur. This development—along with approximate ages—is summarized in Table 13.1. Variability in ages of occurrence is shown in Figure 13.1

THE PSYCHOLOGICAL ASPECTS OF PHYSICAL CHANGE

The conversation at Camp Kalowatchee went on and on as members of the group talked about their personal experiences and reactions to adolescence.

"I'm older than you and it's harder for me to remember my adolescence," Ms. Gaither said. "But I do remember the day I had my first period. No one in my family had ever mentioned menstruation to me. It was hard to call my mother into the bathroom to show her what had happened. When I finally did and mother

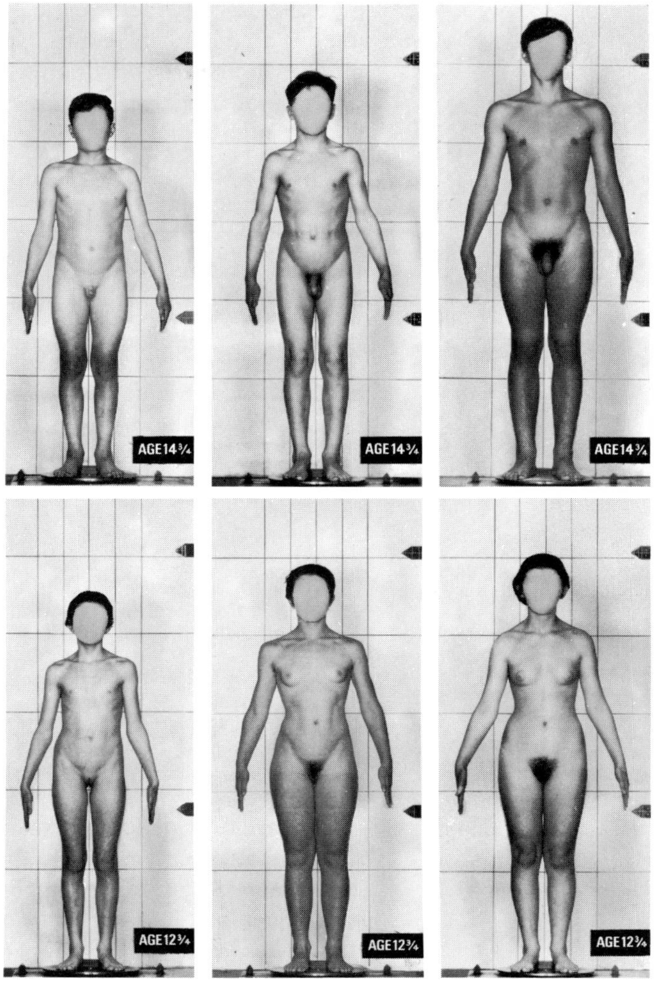

Figure 13.1
Development of sex characteristics. Timing of the development of sex characteristics varies from child to child, as can be seen in these photos of twelve-year-old girls and fourteen-year-old boys.

had shown me how to use a sanitary napkin, I hated the idea of having to menstruate the rest of my life. It was only much later I learned to appreciate the fact that these hated periods were a part of my being a woman!''

Roosevelt remembered an incident similar to Ms. Gaither's about his first **nocturnal emission** or ''wet dream'' (ejaculation of semen during sleep which may or may not accompany an erotic dream). His thoughts drifted back to the day it happened—but he didn't say a word. He remembered how he had been really afraid about what his mother would say. For the first time in his life, he made up his bed as soon as his feet touched the floor in the morning!

Because first menstruation and ejaculation symbolize sexual maturity, it is important that these events be positive ones. When girls and boys have not received accurate information from parents, school personnel, or peers, they may suffer from unnecessary fears (Shainess, 1961; Pomeroy, 1968). A majority of female and male adolescents reported mixed or negative feelings about menstruation (Clark and Ruble, 1978). Only 25 percent of girls said menstruation is something to be happy about. But when parents prepare daughters and sons, first menstruation and first ejaculation can be celebrated rather than feared events.

Early versus Late Maturers.   The rapidity of change during puberty can be threatening and difficult to deal with. When adolescents are "out of step" with their peers because of late or early maturation, life is even more difficult. Because there is great variability in the onset of puberty, some boys and girls are **early maturers** and exhibit the physical changes of puberty at an early age, while others, like Nicky, are **late maturers** and do not reach sexual maturity until much later.

While the group was taking a break, Nicky looked at the other boys resentfully. Roosevelt and Brad were tall and looked like men while he was still a "little shrimp." Roosevelt and Brad were athletic, while Nicky felt like the world's most outstanding ninety-nine-pound weakling. Even those ads in the magazines couldn't provide enough muscle developers to help Nicky. It seemed as if he would never be as big as the rest of the guys. Even now that he had begun to grow, there were problems. Every time he spoke, his voice squeaked! He guessed all his teachers thought he was dumb. When a question was asked, he would never raise his hand—even when he knew the answer. He was too afraid his voice would squeak!

At age fifteen, Nicky, like other late maturers, was small and still looked like a kid. Brad, an early maturer, appeared to be a grown man with broad shoulders, strong muscles, adult-sized sex organs, and a deep voice. The early maturing boy has greater physical strength and size, which makes him superior in athletic ability—an important basis for acceptance and leadership in early adolescent peer groups. Brad's maturation also makes him interested in and interesting to girls in his class who are now looking for interaction with boys. A disadvantage for early maturers like Brad and Roosevelt is that adults may make greater demands of them because of their mature physical status. But in our society today, the early maturing boy's position is generally an advantageous one, and the late maturing boy is at a disadvantage. He is too small to compete effectively in valued male competitive sports. He is ignored or treated as a "kid" by the girls in his class. Most of all, he may be a convenient object of ridicule for other adolescents in a hurry to deny their close connections with childhood.

For girls, the effects of early or late maturation may be different depending on how early or how late the maturation occurs (Conger, 1977). The early maturing girl is handicapped because she feels self-conscious. She "sticks out like a sore thumb'' at a time when it's so important to be like everybody else. Developmentally, she may be three or four years ahead of the boys in her class. She has little time to gradually get used to her rapidly changing body. For example, an early-maturing girl, may suddenly reach nearly all her adult height by age thirteen. She may try to solve the problems of early maturity by escaping into an older peer group. But this can cause social and emotional pressures for which she is unprepared. On the other hand, even though a late-maturing girl may have the personal anxiety of wondering when (and sometimes *if*) she will mature, she has the advantage of time to adjust more gradually to her changing body. She also has the psychological advantage of maturing in step with the boys in her group.

Health-Related Issues

Issues related to health become especially crucial in adolescence since teenagers are growing so rapidly and usually don't rely on their parents in making health-related decisions. Yet adolescents often make their decisions on behaviors such as nutrition, sexual activity, and drug use based on a less reliable but very powerful influence on their lives—their peers. Accidents, homicides, and suicides can also endanger the health of adolescents.

With all the physical changes occurring during adolescence, teenagers spend so much time in front of the mirror partly to keep up with their changing looks.

❊ Spotlight 13.2: The Deadly Diet

Amy was 16 years old when she decided to go on a strict diet. Tired of being described as "cute and bouncy"—which she felt really meant "fat"—Amy was determined to lose fifteen pounds. Already a diligent student, a varsity cheerleader and an active member in her school's drama club, Amy added a vigorous exercise program to her crowded schedule. The excess weight melted off.

But then she decided that fifteen pounds wasn't enough. "I still feel fat," she complained. Her weight continued to drop; her clothes hung on her five-foot five-inch frame. She quit cheerleading and began concentrating on thirty-minute jump-rope sessions.

Amy's mother and the school guidance counselor agreed that something was drastically wrong. Amy had stopped menstruating and had lost nearly forty-five pounds in less than five months; she was no longer seeing most of her friends, and at home she was argumentative, weepy, and depressed. Her family doctor suggested counseling, and Amy began seeing a psychiatrist who told her that she was suffering from a disease called anorexia nervosa. Neither Amy nor any of her friends had ever heard of it.

Anorexia (loss of appetite) nervosa (due to nerves) is a severe psychological problem: victims of the disease, almost always young women, begin losing weight and then can't stop. In pursuit of a seemingly elusive thinness, anorexics starve themselves, sometimes to death. And recent studies note that approximately one out of every one hundred adolescent girls suffers from anorexia.

Although the disease has been discussed in medical circles for nearly three centuries, its underlying causes and proper treatment are still being debated. Most doctors, however, do agree on the symptoms of anorexia. "Any girl who has lost weight and has missed a number of periods should be considered anorexic," explains Dr. Joseph Silverman, an associate clinical professor of pediatrics at New York's Columbia Presbyterian Medical Center.

Other symptoms of anorexia can include the denial or absence of hunger despite not eating, often accompanied by a constant preoccupation with food and dieting. Some anorexics alternate between starving and then gorging on all the foods that they regularly deny themselves. After a food binge they will take quantities of laxatives or make themselves vomit so that the food they've eaten will not affect their weight. Exercising compulsively and the belief that an emaciated body is desirable are also indicative of anorexia.

Although boys have been treated for anorexia, the vast majority of patients are middle- or upper-middle-class young women between the ages of ten and twenty-five. Most are described by their teachers as "bright students," and by their parents as "good children." "And the families of anorexics are often very close, very loving," notes Dr. Joellen Werne, the director of the Stanford Univer-

NUTRITION

Childhood nutrition affects the timing of puberty and adolescent nutrition affects later growth and development. The adolescent girl's nutritional intake for example, is already preparing her for future pregnancy. Adolescents need more nutrients than children in middle childhood because of their rapid growth. The recommended number of calories for girls between twelve and eighteen ranges from 2300 to 2400 and for boys from 2700 to 3000, but this varies greatly from individual to individual and can change at different times (Beal, 1980).

A teenager's nutritional well-being affects personal well-being. Because of their extensive nutritional needs and their rapid growth, adolescents are highly

sity Hospital in-patient treatment program for anorexics in Palo Alto, California. Frequently, however, there are underlying marital or familial tensions that the anorexic may feel responsible for. To relieve those tensions, she tries to conform to the expectations she feels her parents have of her—she may study harder or play more sports—but the confusion and pressures of adolescence cause her to look for something that she alone can control. Her own body fits that definition, and dieting is a way to control its shape and size. "A lot of teen-agers start out by dieting normally; the situation goes haywire when the family responds in a certain way," notes Werne. As the young woman loses weight, she finds that the attention of the whole family is focused on her, attention she wants and fears losing. "Maybe my parents won't love me as much if I gain weight" is a common worry for many anorexics.

Why are adolescents particularly susceptible? "That's the age when a girl and her family are faced with a significant number of new roles, new choices," says Werne. A young woman may feel she is not ready to make the kinds of decisions she associates with growing up. Excessive dieting stunts that growth. "Anorexics don't grow up," explains Werne. "Physically they just stop maturing."

Treating anorexia can take anywhere from a few weeks to a few years. Catching the disease in its earliest stages usually means less time is needed to treat the psychological problems and to reverse the very real physical effects of starvation. Often it's the family doctor who is consulted first. "As a pediatrician, I am usually the first doctor to see an anorexic patient because, after all, what gets a person to a doctor or a hospital is not that they have a psychological problem; it's that they're five feet six inches and weigh seventy-five pounds," says Silverman. It's the delicate job of the doctor and the parents to persuade the patient to eat and to make her understand that eating normally will not make her fat. Often, where counseling is recommended, the whole family is asked to participate.

One question that is often asked of anorexics is why losing weight becomes so important. Amy feels that one reason she so badly wanted to lose weight was because she felt a tremendous pressure to be thin: "Everybody was always talking about dieting. Even the thinnest girls were preoccupied with their weight." Werne agrees. "We're a diet-conscious society, and excessive dieting is considered acceptable. People are caught up in thinking that 'thinner is better,' but in the case of the anorexic thinner can be deadly."

"Anorexia Nervosa: The Deadly Diet" by Brie Quinby, *Family Weekly*, October 14, 1979. Reprinted by permission of *Family Weekly*. Copyright 1979, 641 Lexington Avenue, New York, New York 10022.

sensitive to energy restriction. One symptom of a poor diet is irritability. And since the adolescent period is already a stressful one, it seems sensible that a good diet will help teenagers cope (McWilliams, 1980).

But, the late teen years are a time when dietary problems are likely to occur. A particularly serious problem is **anorexia nervosa,** a severe psychological problem characterized by a refusal to eat (see Spotlight 13.2). Another problem is obesity. Overweight teenagers usually suffer from a poor self-concept, and they are more likely to suffer emotional problems than are average-sized teenagers. Emotional problems can lead to overeating. For many people the two go hand in hand. About 80 percent of obese teenagers remain overweight as adults.

VENEREAL DISEASE

"I was scared to have sex for a while because all I heard from my father about sex was VD, VD, VD—you can get VD from anybody—you can die from it. He never told me anything good about sex." (Sorensen, 1973, p. 329). This confession made by a sixteen-year-old boy is not typical. Most teenagers don't hear about **venereal disease**—sexually transmitted diseases such as gonorrhea, syphilis, herpes simplex 2—from their parents. Many teenagers report, "I'd like to ask my parents for information . . . I'm afraid . . . because they would ask whether I'm having sex" (Sorensen, 1973, p. 338).

Only the common cold is a more commonly "caught" ailment than VD. Eleven percent of nonvirgin boys and 10 percent of nonvirgin girls have had VD—older adolescents more frequently than younger ones (Sorensen, 1973). In 1970, 21 percent of all gonorrhea cases occurred in teens aged fifteen to nineteen (Millar, 1972). Untreated venereal diseases are harmful—the effects ranging from dangers to unborn babies to blindness, brain damage, and death. One prevalent venereal disease, herpes simplex 2, is even incurable. Public education, personal responsibility and honesty, the use of condoms for protection, and prompt medical attention are the ways VD can be combated.

DRUGS

Carlos had hardly said a word all day. But that evening as the group continued, he chose to share some of his feelings about his personal experience with drugs.

"Somewhere along the line I fell into a rough crowd, and by the time I was twelve, I was into drugs pretty heavy. I was suspended from school so often the year I was fifteen that I failed.

"One day I got hold of some new drugs on the street. I didn't know what the pills would do, but my friends were taking them so I popped two. I didn't feel any effects, so pretty soon I popped two more. Then I went home to get something to eat.

"I made myself a peanut butter and jelly sandwich. I put the sandwich on the counter and went to the bathroom. When I came back and started to eat the sandwich, the sandwich started to eat me! I started screaming and my parents came running. I didn't think of putting the sandwich down, I was just scared of it. My mother grabbed the sandwich out of my hand and threw it on the floor. She slapped me in the face and said, 'If I had known you were going to end up like this, I would have killed you in my womb!' Boy, did that throw me.

"Pretty soon, with the help of a counselor, I was able to get myself back on the right track. And then, I started back to school. Now I plan to go to college and major in criminal justice. Maybe I can help some kids like me."

During adolescence, teenagers often experiment with alcohol and a wide variety of drugs. But only about 5 percent develop a *physical addiction*—symptoms such as vomiting, sweating, delusions, anxiety, muscle tremors, and hallucinations that occur when a drug is discontinued. We don't know how many teenagers have *psychological dependence* on drugs—feelings of anxiety or irritation when deprived of a drug.

All age groups—from adolescent to adult—use drugs. Alcohol is usually introduced to adolescents in their homes by parents who also model other drug use when they smoke or take tranquilizers. Most other drugs are introduced to teens by their friends (Dacey, 1979). Nearly everyone in our society consumes caffeine in coffee, tea, chocolate, or soft drinks. But we will focus our attention on those drugs that often cause problems for teens: tobacco, alcohol, marijuana. A small percentage of adolescents become regular users of other drugs such as cocaine, LSD, heroin, "speed," and tranquilizers.

Tobacco. Tobacco is one of the most widely used drugs in our society. Since 1970, there has been a slight decrease in smoking among adolescent boys, but

Peer pressure is a major influence on teens' use of alcohol, tobacco, and other drugs.

Table 13.2
Young-Adult Use of Selected Drugs: Ages 18 to 25

DRUG	HAVE USED	HAVE USED IN PAST MONTH	HAVE NEVER USED
Alcohol	84.2%	70.0%	15.5%
Nicotine (tobacco)	67.6	47.3	30.3
Marijuana and/or hashish	60.1	27.7	39.9
Stimulants (nonmedical use)	21.2	2.5	78.8
Hallucinogens	19.8	2.0	80.1
Cocaine	19.1	3.7	80.9
Sedatives (nonmedical use)	18.4	2.8	81.6
Tranquilizers (nonmedical use)	13.4	2.4	86.6
Inhalants	11.2	*	88.8
Heroin	3.6	*	96.4

*Less than 0.5%

Source: Adapted from National Institute on Drug Abuse, *National survey on drug abuse; 1977. Vol. I: Main findings.* Washington, D.C.: U.S. Government Printing Office, 1977, p. 23.

there has been an increase in smoking among teenage girls (Special Action Office for Drug Abuse Prevention, 1976; *The State,* 1979).

Because of the effects of smoke on lung tissue and heart arteries, even young smokers experience such symptoms as shortness of breath, nagging coughs, and heart problems, and nervous tension. Research also shows that smoking is directly related to heart disease, emphysema, and cancer. It is also psychologically and physically addictive.

Alcohol.   The use—and abuse—of alcohol is becoming a major problem among teenagers. Teenage liquor consumption—particularly beer and wine—has doubled in the past ten years (U.S. Department of Transportation, 1976; Chamberlain, 1978). Experimenting with alcohol is natural in adolescence since this is a time of trying out adult behaviors (though peer pressure and curiosity also play a role). Adolescents also experience stress as a result of rapid physical, cognitive, social, and emotional changes, so they sometimes use alcohol to help them feel more relaxed and self-confident. But alcohol does not provide adolescents with a permanent solution for problems they need to solve. It can be psychologically and physically addictive. And alcohol is implicated in many highway accidents and deaths, especially among teens.

Marijuana.   A study by the National Institute of Drug Abuse found that 22 percent of twelve- to seventeen-year-olds have used marijuana and 15 percent are regular users; 53 percent of high school seniors have used marijuana with 32 percent being regular users (Swift, 1977a). In general, the older the adolescent the greater the use of marijuana. Boys use it more than girls. High academic achievers and those who place a high value on independence have more conservative views on marijuana than others.

Laboratory research has given few conclusive results about the chronic use of marijuana. It appears to be psychologically but not physically addictive. As in the use of alcohol, there is impaired motor performance. And chronic use among young adolescents may affect intellectual development (Secretary of HEW, 1976). In a study of 2000 high school students, Yankelovich (1975) says individuals can be classified into three types of users: nonusers, limited users, and abusers of marijuana. Abusers suffer from fits of depression, anxiety, and frustration—often feeling like misfits. They are likely to leave projects incomplete and find it hard to get through the day. Abusers are likely to have trouble with families and in school. But no one can say whether marijuana abuse causes these problems or whether the problems cause the abuse. Limited users seldom exhibit the same characteristics as

Use of marijuana has increased among adolescents in the United States. Studies show that more than half of high school seniors have at least experimented with it.

abusers. With limited use, the effects of marijuana are apparently no worse and perhaps not as bad as the effects of alcohol.

Other Drugs.   Cocaine is increasing in popularity, which is surprising because it is an expensive drug. In one study, 3 percent of twelve- to seventeen-year-olds and 13 percent of eighteen- to twenty-five-year-olds had used cocaine (Swift, 1977a). Cocaine was once thought to cause physical addiction, but because it does not seem to cause withdrawal symptoms, people have argued it should be placed in the same category as marijuana. Psychological dependence is evident in most users. In general, coke produces hyperstimulation; giving feelings of alertness, power, and euphoria.

Hallucinogens, or **psychedelics** as they are sometimes called, are drugs that alter the physical sensations, emotions, and cognitive patterns of the individual. LSD, mescaline, and psilocybin are examples. The effects produced by these drugs include delusions, hallucinations, and changes in time and space perception. **Narcotics** include opium and opium derivatives—morphine, codeine, and heroin. Narcotics cause a feeling of relaxation and well-being. Under their influence, problems seem to evaporate. Addiction occurs quickly and withdrawal symptoms are severe. **Stimulants** include drugs such as caffeine and amphetamines. They increase alertness and activity, reduce hunger, and can provide a lift for a tired person. But they are also addictive. Long-term use may lead to physical exhaustion, tremors, itching, muscle pains, and tension. **Sedatives** include drugs such as the barbiturates and tranquilizers. They help reduce anxiety and excitement and they are useful in treating psychiatric disorders, high blood pressure, and pain from peptic ulcers. But a spokesperson for the federal government reported that more people die from misuse of barbiturates than all other drugs combined. Suicide, accidental overdoses taken by children, and inadvertent overdoses taken by adults—especially when combined with alcohol—cause the barbiturate deaths (*Boston Globe*, 1977).

Conflicting Attitudes about Drugs.   Differing attitudes about drugs have caused many controversies between adults and adolescents. Adult concern for the welfare of the adolescent is an important aspect of this adult/adolescent conflict—but this is only part of the problem. Drugs have come to symbolize a lifestyle that challenges the basic values of our society. A dedication to the values of the Protestant ethic—which emphasizes competition, aggressiveness, delayed gratification, and material success—is directly challenged by the lifestyle of drug users. Marijuana, for example, tends to induce passivity, pleasure for pleasure's sake, and soul searching rather than action. Adult condemnation of adolescent drug use is likely to occur while the adult stands at a cocktail party with a drink in one hand and a cigarette in the other. Adolescents argue that research has proved that alcohol and cigarettes contribute to early death, disability, and addiction, while the harmful effects of marijuana have yet to be proved (Conger, 1977). Objective research can be difficult to find and carry out on this subject. And even when valid information is obtained, the results are rejected by the group whose views are not upheld.

ACCIDENTS, HOMICIDES, AND SUICIDES

According to a United States Surgeon General's report, it is becoming more dangerous to be an American adolescent (*The State*, 1979). In 1960, there were 106 deaths per 100,000 American youths aged fifteen to twenty-four. In 1977, the figure had climbed to 117, resulting in 48,000 adolescent deaths in 1977. Accidents, homicides, and suicides, in that order, account for three fourths of these deaths, with the death rate for young men almost three times that of young women. Behavior patterns characterized by errors of judgment, aggression, and ambivalence about whether to live or die were judged responsible for the high death rate. Alcohol use, drug abuse, and teenage pregnancy also contribute.

Adolescent Suicide.   Suicide is rare in childhood and in young adolescence. But between ages fifteen and nineteen the reported suicide rate increases rapidly. It has doubled since 1955—now averaging about 5000 per year for young people (Committee on Adolescence, 1980). Among American Indians, the suicide rate is five times the national average and is the leading cause of death among Indian youth (Farris, 1973). Attempted suicides are greater among females, but completed suicides are three times more common among male adolescents than females. Firearms or explosives account for the greatest number of completed suicides. But drugs or poisons account for the greatest number of attempted suicides (Committee on Adolescence, 1980).

Why do adolescents attempt suicide? Erikson (1968) has suggested that adolescents who do not gain a sense of identity (see Chapter 14) feel so worthless that they withdraw from reality—or even from life. Feelings of isolation from meaningful relationships are frequent among adolescents who attempt suicide. Separation from parents or friends, family or personal illness, disruptive family interaction patterns, school problems, poor social skills, developmental problems such as lack of preparation for puberty and emotional problems can also make adolescents vulnerable to suicide (Green, 1979). Most suicidal adolescents don't really want to die. They just want to change their lives enough so they can continue to live (Cantor, P., 1977). But people who talk about suicide often *do* take their own lives. They say such things as "You'll be sorry when I'm dead," or "I'd be better off dead." So talk of suicide should not be ignored. Warning signals include depression, eating or sleeping disturbances, problems with school performance, social withdrawal, communication breakdowns, and previous accidents or suicide attempts (Jacobs, 1971).

Therapy can help teens with emotional difficulties. Treatment includes working with immediate and long-standing problems. Warmth and true concern by a therapist can provide adolescents with the type of relationships they have been searching for. A therapist must show that the suicide attempt is being taken seriously, acknowledge that real problems exist, and convince the adolescent that solutions can be found for problems. And because suicide attempts are usually related to family relationships, it is desirable for parents and siblings to be involved in the therapy (McKenry and Tishler, 1979).

Cognitive Development

One morning, following the pledge of alliegiance to the flag, Eve remarked to the group, "You know, it's funny. I've been saying the pledge of allegiance since I was five or six. But just the other day I realized how differently I say it now.

"My little sister is going into first grade and I've been teaching her the pledge. She's learned the words, sort of. But when I asked her if she knew what 'indivisible' meant, she said 'Of course. I see the invisible man on TV every week.'

"I don't think she understood when I tried to explain that indivisible meant that the country could never be torn apart. She just said it was silly to think anyone was big enough to tear the country apart."

Eve's definition of the highly abstract concept of indivisibility shows she is doing the kind of thinking Piaget says is characteristic of adolescents and adults starting between the ages of eleven and fifteen. Changes in cognitive development during adolescence are as dramatic as those in physical development. During the **formal operational** period, Piaget's fourth period of cognitive development, the cognitive structures—schemes—reach maturity and adolescent thought becomes radically different from child thought (Inhelder and Piaget, 1958). Adolescents in formal operations no longer need to rely on the concrete. Abstract, symbolic, and true scientific thought are possible. Formal thinkers can use their new cognitive abilities to solve complex verbal, hypothetical, and combinatorial problems related to the past, present, or future in a systematic and objective way.

SCIENTIFIC THOUGHT

The development of formal operations allows adolescents to think like scientists and to systematically solve problems that could be solved only by trial and error during the preoperational period or with concrete objects during the concrete operational period of cognitive development.

Inhelder and Piaget (1958) presented fifteen experimental tasks—the pendulum problem shown in Figure 13.2 was one of them—to children from age five to fifteen. When preoperational children tried to solve the pendulum problem, the experiments they devised revealed no overall pattern. They made random tests that offered little in the way of valuable information. Preoperational children might begin by swinging a long pendulum with a light weight, then a short pendulum with a heavy weight. Their observations were often inaccurate and their first guesses biased them about the answer. And their conclusions were inaccurate due to faulty reasoning.

Concrete operational children showed considerable improvement in using scientific investigation. But they still did not design their experiments scientifically. They were more analytic and objective than preoperational children in

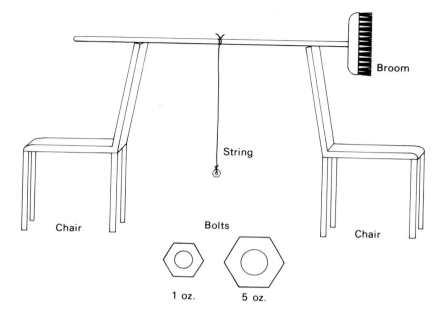

Figure 13.2

The pendulum problem. What controls the frequency of the pendulum swing: the length of the string, the weight of the bolt, or a combination of both?

investigating variables that could control the swing. But many features of their procedures were illogical. They generally were unbiased and observed results accurately. They sometimes discovered the right answer, but often drew the wrong conclusions from correctly observed results.

The adolescents in the formal operational period used a systematic, scientific process to approach the task. When adolescent Brad was asked to solve the pendulum problem by recreating the experiment, three characteristics of formal operational thought were obvious. First, he designed the experiment systematically. Second, he observed the results accurately—without bias. (Even though he thought that heavier weights would swing faster, he still tried out all possible combinations). Third, based on his observations, he drew the correct logical conclusions—the shorter the string, the more frequent the swing, regardless of the weight of the bolt.

IS THE FORMAL OPERATIONAL LEVEL UNIVERSAL?

Inhelder and Piaget's (1958) research on formal operations is among the most original and interesting. Other experts following similar procedures suggest that some people never attain the formal operational level and that most people attain it only part of the time (Martorano, 1974; Neimark, 1975). In several studies, more than 50 percent of college-educated adults were at the formal operational level, but less than 50 percent of young adolescents operated at that level (Mar-

✤ Spotlight 13.3: Problems Formal Thinkers Can Solve

Formal operational thinkers are able to use true scientific reasoning to solve a variety of problems, including complex verbal problems, "pretend" or hypothetical problems, problems dealing with the past, present, or future, and combinatorial problems (Wadsworth, 1979; Flavell, 1977; Ginsburg and Opper, 1979). The following are examples of some of these problems.

Complex Verbal Problems. Children without formal operations have difficulty solving such complex verbal problems as the following: If Edith is fairer than Suzanne, and Edith is darker than Lili, who is darkest, Edith, Suzanne, or Lili? (Piaget, 1964). When Ginger, Coach Wilson's eight-year-old child, was asked this question, she said "Who are those people anyway, friends of yours?" As soon as the problem was posed using people who were present, Ginger solved it right away. A formal thinker could solve such complex verbal problems whether or not the people or objects were present.

Hypothetical Problems. Consider this hypothetical problem: All cows are purple. If a purple cow gives birth to a calf, what color will the calf be? Ginger would not try to solve the problem because "Cows are not purple!" Ginger, like other concrete thinkers, was not able to consider the logic of the problem (if all cows are purple, of course the calf would be purple) because it contradicts what she knows to be true about cows. For concrete thinkers, logic can only be applied to real things—not to

torano, 1977; Roberge and Flexer, 1979). In some non-Western cultures, this type of thinking seems to be missing altogether—even in adults (Ginsburg and Opper, 1979). Why the apparent lack of universality?

Piaget's adolescents were affluent and well trained in science. Their stimulating environments may have contributed to early development of formal operations. Adolescents without such stimulation might develop at a slower rate, with formal operations not appearing until adulthood. But Piaget himself favored another interpretation. He suggested that adolescents and adults may use formal operations only in situations that interest them. Individuals not trained in science would be capable of formal operational thinking only in those areas for which they are trained.

Consider the following example of research on Kalahari Bushmen. These men are expert hunters. Instead of administering a problem like the pendulum problem, Tulkin and Konner (1973) set up a seminar to discuss hunting. In this seminar, the adult male Kalahari showed a high level of formal operational thought. When tracking animals, these hunters must draw conclusions based on logical reasoning, test hypotheses, and observe complexities that would tax the best capacities of the human mind. "Determining from tracks, the movements of animals, their timing, whether they are wounded and if so how, and predicting how far they will go and in which direction and how fast, all involve" developing hypothetical things such as purple cows. On the other hand, the adolescent in the formal operational period has no trouble dealing with the logic of statements separate from their hypothetical content.

Combinatorial Problems. The adolescent in formal operational period can imagine all possible variables and combinations of variables involved in the solution of a problem. When Brad was given the pendulum problem, he considered all possible variables (long or short string and one or five ounce weight). Brad also thought of all possible combinations of lengths and weights (one ounce weight and short string, five ounce weight and short string, one ounce weight and long string, five ounce weight

and long string) before conducting tests to find out that the variable of length was the real solution. This ability to consider possibility separately from reality is an important characteristic of adolescent thought.

When presented with the pendulum problem, the concrete thinker plunges in and randomly tests variables without considering all possibilities. In contrast, formal thinkers like Brad consider a possibility before testing it against reality. As a matter of fact, when the pendulum problem was presented to another group, they sat around talking about the possibilities for fifteen minutes and then wanted us to tell them the real solution instead of conducting the experiments to determine the reality.

hypotheses, testing them against new information, considering old information about animal movements, rejecting hypotheses that do not stand up, and finally getting everything to fit logically, "which adds up to meat in the pot" (Tulkin and Konner, 1973, pp. 35, 36).

EGOCENTRISM

Egocentrism, as you have seen, goes hand in hand with cognitive development, occurring in some new form at each new period (Elkind, 1976). At first, the child's ability to use the new cognitive abilities developed in each new period is limited by the egocentrism of that period.

With the new cognitive ability to think abstractly, adolescents begin to think about their own thoughts and the thoughts of others. Being able to think about the thoughts of others allows adolescents to see themselves as they think others see them and encourages a kind of egocentrism known as the **"imaginary audience"** (Elkind, 1978). The adolescent may feel that "everyone out there is looking at me. I am always on stage. I am never alone. Everything counts, everything that I do, everything that I wear, everything that I say." (Lipsitz, 1979, p. 5).

The *"personal fable"* is another type of adolescent egocentrism. The personal fable goes like this: "I am alone, no one understands me, I am unique, no

The personal fable of immortality is often tragically disproved when risk-taking by teenagers in automobiles leads to injury and death on the highway.

one experiences what I am experiencing. My story is my own, unique to me.'' (Lipsitz, 1979, p. 6).* The personal fable type of egocentrism leads adolescents to think, ''I won't be affected by things that happen to others because I am unlike others.'' (Elkind, 1978). Caroline thinks ''I won't become pregnant.'' Roosevelt is convinced, ''I won't crash in this car or become addicted to drugs.'' A sense of immortality often accompanies the personal fable—''I won't die.'' Adolescent risk-taking behaviors can be amusing, frustrating, or disturbing to adults and dangerous to adolescents. But these behaviors are a normal part of the adolescent egocentrism.

Adolescents in the formal operational period also demonstrate their egocentrism when they fail to distinguish between what is logical and ideal to them versus what is real. They are ''hooked'' on their new powers of logical thought and think the world should match their conception of an ideal world, run by logic (Inhelder and Piaget, 1958). As an adolescent, Brad had difficulty understanding why ''all men do not love each other'' and was angered by unfairness such as racism and poverty. He wanted to remove all injustice and make all people brothers and sisters. Many hours were spent discussing such issues with friends and Brad joined an organization committed to his ideas.

---

* Reprinted by permission.

When adolescents learn to use logic in terms of the real world instead of an idealized version, egocentrism subsides (Wadsworth, 1979). But this does not happen until the adolescent enters the occupational world or begins serious professional training. "The adolescent becomes an adult when he undertakes a real job. It is then that he is transformed from an idealistic reformer to an achiever." (Inhelder and Piaget, 1958, p. 346). Adolescents are then able to consider the point of view of others within the context of a realistic world.

Moral Development

Kohlberg used the same moral dilemma about Heinz, his dying wife, and the druggist described in Chapter 11 to examine the moral judgments of adolescents.

At the **postconventional level,** individuals operate from general moral principles that have been examined and accepted. Moral decisions are controlled internally and decisions are based on what is "known" to be right rather than on externally applied punishments, rewards, or social sanctions.

One sixteen-year-old boy operating at the postconventional level said, "By the law of society he (the husband) was wrong but by the law of nature or of God the druggist was wrong and the husband was justified. Human life is above financial gain. Regardless of who was dying, if it was a total stranger, man has a duty to save him from dying" (Kohlberg, 1969, p. 244).

The adolescent quoted had internalized the principle that "man has the duty to save others from dying." His decision was not based on whether or not the druggist or Heinz would be punished or rewarded or judged to be good or bad. Instead, his decision was based on an internalized, universal principle of right. Kohlberg's postconventional level contains two stages—Stage 5 and Stage 6.

In the first part of Stage 5, morality is thought of in terms of general rights agreed upon by society. Later in Stage 5, there is an increasing orientation toward internal decisions based on conscience.

The sixteen-year-old showed he understood the morality of Stage 5 when he said, "By the law of society he was wrong. . . ." In Stage 6, morality reaches its highest—and least likely to be achieved—state. At this point, behavior is guided by abstract ethical principles such as the Golden Rule. And one conforms to these principles to avoid self-condemnation. The sixteen-year-old was operating at this level, as you can tell by his statement "but by the the law of nature or of God the druggest was wrong. . . ." According to Kohlberg, people can understand the levels below those where they are operating, but not the levels above them.

We said earlier that not all adolescents in our society attain true formal operational thinking. Even fewer reach the postconventional level of moral development. Only about 10 percent of the adolescents over the age of sixteen studied by Kohlberg showed the "clear principled" thinking of the postconventional level, and all 10 percent were formal thinkers (Kohlberg and Gilligan, 1971; 1972).

Kohlberg concludes that only young persons capable of formal operational thought are likely to reach the postconventional level. But being a formal thinker doesn't guarantee reaching this level. A person may be a theoretical chemist operating on the highest level of formal operations, but may still be operating on the lowest level of moral development.

Summary

1. In many primitive or nonindustrialized societies, there is no adolescent period to separate childhood from adulthood. But technological advances have required longer schooling and an extended adolescence.

2. Puberty—the Latin word for ''age of manhood''—is the start of adolescence and is marked by the menarche in girls and the production of sperm in boys.

3. Height and weight increase and sexual maturation occurs during the adolescent growth spurt.

4. Sexual maturation includes maturation of the primary and secondary sex characteristics. The development and order in which the primary and secondary sex characteristics appear are more constant than their age of occurrence.

5. Variations in the timing of sexual maturation can cause early and late maturers to feel different from their peers, but the effects of such time discrepancies are partially dependent on the individual's sex.

6. Nutrition and venereal disease are important health-related issues in adolescence. Nutritional well-being affects personal well-being. VD can be combated through public education and personal responsibility.

7. Adolescent drug use is influenced by adult models, personal feelings of stress, curiosity, and peer pressure. Tobacco, alcohol, and marijuana are three commonly used drugs that can cause problems. Other drugs that also cause problems include cocaine, hallucinogens, narcotics, stimulants and sedatives.

8. Adolescents (and adults) who are in the formal operational period can form abstractions and can use scientific reasoning. They can design experiments systematically, observe results accurately, and draw logical conclusions.

9. At the postconventional level, individuals operate from general moral principles that have been examined and accepted. According to Kohlberg, not all individuals reach this stage of moral development.

Empathetic Activities

■ What were some feelings you experienced while reading about Nita Quintero? Ms. Gaither, Nicky, and the others at the retreat? If you were in the same situation as some of these individuals, would you feel as they did?

- What might you do to help an adolescent on drugs?
- Ask children of different ages to solve the pendulum problem described in Fig. 13.2. Summarize what you learned.
- Write a case describing your adolescence. Then analyze it using the information from this chapter. Follow only the cognitive empathy part of the empathetic process as described in the Prologue. Remember to include information about puberty, the adolescent growth spurt, psychological reactions to the physical changes in adolescence, health-related issues, cognitive, and moral development. As a summary, explain how an understanding of your own adolescence has increased as a result of this analysis.
- How can the fact that physical, cognitive, social, and emotional growth are all interrelated affect the development of the *Whole Adolescent*?
- Discuss how different experiences in adolescence can influence intergenerational relationships. Interview a parent, grandparent, or other older person and/or a member of another culture for information about adolescence in their generation or cultural setting.

Related Readings

Conger, John J. *Adolescence and youth: Psychological development in a changing world,* 2nd ed. New York: Harper and Row, 1977. An extensive and authoritative discussion of adolescence.

Dacey, John S. *Adolescents today.* Santa Monica, Calif.: Goodyear Publishing, 1979. Fun to read with lots of interesting activities to do related to adolescents.

Elkind, David. *A sympathetic understanding of the child: Birth to sixteen,* 2nd ed. Boston: Allyn and Bacon, 1978. Short but excellent description of the personal, social, and mental development of children. Very good ''age profiles'' of children from six to sixteen years old, with brief overviews of children at each age.

Hass, Aaron. *Teenage sexuality: A survey of teenage sexual behavior.* New York: Macmillan, 1979. The results of interviews with more than six hundred teenagers from southern California. Discusses teenagers' attitudes and behaviors concerning such topics as masturbation, orgasm, virginity, homosexuality.

Katchadourian, Herant. *The biology of adolescence.* San Francisco: W.H. Freeman, 1977. A fascinating description of a potentially boring subject. Puberty, the adolescent growth spurt, sexual maturation, and health hazards are discussed in a detailed but digestible fashion.

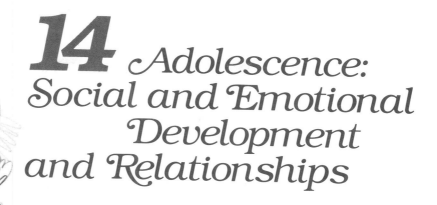

14 Adolescence: Social and Emotional Development and Relationships

The Case of the Campfire

When the Middleton High School students and their teachers returned to Camp Kalowatchee shortly after the Easter break from school, feelings were mixed. Graduation would be in two months and plans for the future were being finalized. The crowd built a campfire to roast wieners and marshmallows. After eating, they sat around the campfire talking about old times and sharing their plans for the future.

Kim reminded Caroline and Eve how they excluded Brad, Roosevelt, Scott, and other boys from their Secret Fort Club. "Boy, we didn't know what we were missing!" Kim said laughingly. "Now, we all run around in the same crowd. And Scott and I are planning to be married after graduation. I plan to work full-time at the bank where I worked last summer. Of course, Scott's parents are giving us a hard time, they want Scott to be a doctor and think that I'm going to prevent that."

Roosevelt told about his plans to study law at the nearby university. "Of course I've got to make it through my undergraduate degree first," he joked.

Brad began to tell the other students about his plans. "I was really excited when I pulled my car into the parking lot at the Middleton airport. I had never been up in a plane before, and now I was going up with members of a local skydiving club. I wasn't planning to jump! But, I was covering the skydiving club for the sports department of our local paper. That was when I was a junior. Then I started to cover games for our school. Now, I'm covering the games of a local college. There is no doubt in my mind about what I want to do. I want to be a sportswriter."

Caroline was very quiet during the campfire chatter. She didn't know what she would do. "Who am I? Where am I going? What occupation will I choose?" she thought to herself.

Eve's parents wanted her to take a secretarial course. "That is a good career for a woman they said." Eve had different ideas. She wanted to study child development at the community college. "Being a secretary was good enough for your mother, it's good enough for you," her father argued.

Soon Coach Wilson called a halt to the campfire discussion. We must get an early start tomorrow, he reminded them.

The Adolescent

IDENTITY VERSUS ROLE CONFUSION

As we have already seen, physical changes occur rapidly during adolescence. And more mature cognitive development allows adolescents to ask questions about themselves. They may be unsure what they want from life—and what parents, peers, and society want from them. This is the fifth stage of psychosocial development, which Erikson (1974) called **identity versus role confusion**. He termed this struggle—not only for a sense of self, but for an outlook on life that is acceptable to the individual and to society—an **identity crisis**. Caroline summarized the adolescent identity crisis in a nutshell. ''My body is not a kid's body anymore. And my mind won't let me be a kid anymore. But it's hard to know what I want to do or be'' (after Cottle 1979). Resolving this conflict of identity versus role confusion involves satisfactory answers to many questions: ''Who am I?'' ''Where am I going?'' ''What occupation will I choose?''

Role confusion is common during the beginning stages of identity formation. Young adolescents try on many roles—one week they are the studious, intellectual type, the next week a high fashion type.

As one teenager put it, ''Your mind sort of tells you to act old, and so do your body and your teacher and your parents, so you act old. . . . You think, 'Hey, I *know* I'm not old, but it's fun to try, because if I want, I can fail miserably at it.' You can pull off this big mask of yours and say, 'Hi, everybody, it's really me and I'm really a kid. Fooled you, though, huh?' '' (Cottle, 1979). By trying on various adult roles and over-identifying with peers and idols such as movie stars or football players, adolescents are able to experiment with a variety of identities, thereby reducing role confusion.

In the search for who and what they are, adolescents sometimes develop a negative identity and adopt dress and behavior patterns that shock and outrage their parents.

❖ Spotlight 14.1: Theories of Adolescence

G. Stanley Hall was the first psychologist to develop a theory of adolescence and to use scientific methods to study adolescents. He thought humans pass through all the stages of their past evolution as they develop from a fertilized egg into an adult. According to Hall (1916), adolescent "storm and stress" represents a transitional and particularly turbulent stage in the development of the human race. All humans are genetically programmed to "recapitulate" or reenact this turbulent stage during adolescence. As you can see, Hall's view is that adolescent storm and stress inevitably results from our heredity as humans.

In contrast to Hall's views, Margaret Mead took an environmentalist position in explaining adolescence. Mead and other anthropologists discovered that adolescence is not a stormy, stress-ful, or turbulent event in all cultures (or even in ours for most adolescents). When societies permit children to learn their adult roles by engaging in sexual activity, watching babies being born, contributing to meaningful adult work, and other adult tasks, childhood and adulthood are not disconnected, and children can more easily take up their adult roles (Mead, 1953). In Mead's view, biological factors underlie the adolescent transition, but cultural factors determine how stressful or peaceful it is.

Social learning theorists like Bandura and Walters (1959) also take an environmentalist position on adolescence. For these theorists, the same learning principles that explain child development also explain adolescent development. They have suggested that adult society is punishing for teen-

When the situation becomes too confusing, adolescents may try to resolve it by developing a *negative identity*. An adolescent whose parents constantly stress the importance of college may adopt a negative identity by refusing to do well in school or even quitting school. Or a student living in a world where neatness and physical appearances are valued may decide that inner neatness is what counts and refuse to conform to social notions about cleanliness, body odor, and hair length. Negative identity experiences can be positive if they are short-lived and allow the person to gain insight. But when adolescents get labeled as "bad" or are harshly punished by authoritarian adults, they may rebel even further by permanently assuming a negative identity.

Identity cannot be given to the child by society, nor does it automatically appear as a result of maturation, like pubic hair. It must be acquired through an ongoing personal struggle. Failure to resolve the struggle for identity means continued role confusion—not knowing who you are or being unable to find a satisfactory vocation. The results of such a failure vary: negative feelings about self and doubts about the future, drug abuse, delinquent or psychotic behavior, or suicide attempts. But adolescents who have resolved the struggle and have developed a positive identity move into adulthood knowing who they are and where they are going. They have found a role in society, and society accepts them as responsible adult members.

agers. So teens quit interacting with adults in favor of the more reinforcing peer group. In adolescence, heroes from the media and peers are chosen as models for such things as hairstyles, language, social values, and behavior. Adolescents learn aggression through modeling of parents, peers, and others. Bandura (1964) has gone so far as to suggest that a stressful adolescence is no more than a self-fulfilling prophecy. In other words, because we expect adolescents to have an identity crisis, they do! Actually, most adolescents are happy and well adjusted. We just pay more attention to the deviant 10 percent of the adolescent population.

Earlier you read Piaget's and Erikson's theories of adolescence. Now you know the views of Hall, Mead, and Bandura. No one view of adolescence is entirely right or wrong. Instead, each has contributed to our understanding of this stage of life. Even though no modern theorist takes Hall's theory seriously, we recognize that biological factors and physical changes in adolescence have a tremendous influence on development. Piaget helps us understand adolescent thought while Erikson contributes to our understanding of adolescent identity formation. Mead, Bandura, and Walters among others encourage us to pay attention to the environmental factors influencing adolescent development. Each view gives us a slightly different picture of adolescents. And each is useful in helping us piece together a more comprehensive and accurate view of the whole adolescent.

Adolescents and Adult Relationships

THE GENERATION GAP: MYTH OR REALITY?

The term **generation gap** was coined to refer to the differences in values held by members of different generations. In the 1960s, our society was in the midst of significant political and social changes—from the Vietnam War to the civil rights movement. It was simple to depict the young as agents of change and the non-young as opponents to change. But in fact, the parents of the young people who demonstrated radical political views in the 1960s were usually political liberals themselves (Block et. al., 1968). Major differences of opinion in our society "have far more to do with social class, education, race, and religious background than with age" (Adelson, 1979, p. 33). The idea that there was or is a wide generation gap between the majority of adolescents and adults in our society is simply a myth. Other myths and realities about adolescence are discussed in Table 14.1.

PARENT-ADOLESCENT RELATIONSHIPS

At one of their weekend retreats in February, Coach Wilson made a startling suggestion to the group of seniors. "Ms. Gaither and I want to arrange for your parents to come along next time to discuss parent-adolescent relationships." A tor-

Table 14.1
Adolescents Today: Myths and Realities

MYTH	REALITY
1. Adolescence is a pathological time of extreme "storm and stress."	1. Adolescence is not a pathological but a normal time of development. Most adolescents cope with the rapid change and growth of adolescence remarkably well.
2. Adolescents are all alike. One thirteen-year-old is no different than another thirteen-year-old.	2. No more variable group exists than adolescents—especially young adolescents. There can be a six-year span in physical development between a quickly developing girl and a slowly developing boy. And just as much variability occurs in cognitive, social, and emotional development.
3. Adolescents are children.	3. Some adolescents are children, some are sexually mature adults.
4. Growth is continuous, uniform, synchronized.	4. Physical, cognitive, social and emotional growth are not synchronized. Boys and girls who experience an early physical maturation are not necessarily as socially or emotionally mature as their looks would lead us to believe. And those adolescents who are physically late maturers may be treated as children socially and emotionally long after they are ready to assume adult responsibilities.
5. The problems adolescents face need not concern us—they will grow out of it!	5. Adolescence is no more transitional than any other time of life. All stages are marked by growth and change, so we shouldn't discount the problems of adolescents as transitional and a passing phase.

Adapted from Lipsitz, 1979.

rent of muttering and grumbling swept the room at once. "Come on now, let's at least consider the idea. Remember, parents have feelings and thoughts about things too. What do you think?" After much discussion, the seniors agreed, and the next weekend the parents began by talking about their feelings and concerns:

"I love Velma," her father said. "But we can't seem to communicate. What I want from her is some straight answers. When I ask her a question she always sulks or makes some smart remark. I don't understand why children today can't show some respect for their parents.''

Nicky's mom sounded exasperated when she spoke: ''Nicky has always been a handful for me. And now that he's an adolescent, I am even more worried about him. I want him to make something of himself—be a doctor or something. But he just won't listen to me. I recently married a man with two boys of his own. I thought Nicky would listen better to a father. But, now he just seems resentful. Of course Nicky is really good at making things. He made me a lovely table for Christmas.''

Doreen, Brad's mom, seemed depressed. ''I don't know what I'll do when Brad leaves for college. I'm proud of Brad. He's bright. And he writes quite good articles for the sports section of the newspaper. When he leaves, I'll have only one boy left. I have to figure out what to do for the rest of my life.''

Roosevelt's father reported worrying about his son: ''There's so much more meanness kids can get into today than when I was growing up. Why just last week two boys from our neighborhood were killed in a car accident. And that Roosevelt

Many parents hope their children will follow in their footsteps and are angry or disappointed when their offspring have other plans.

wants to be out in the car every day. To tell the truth, the reason I worry so much about Roosevelt is that I know how much trouble I got into when I was a kid his age. If my old man had known half the stuff I did he would have killed me.''

''Carlos has really come a long way,'' his father said. ''He got involved with drugs at one time. That really shook his mom and me up. Right now he's a lot more responsible—earns his own spending money. I just wish he'd save some of the money he makes. He says he wants to go to college. Looks like he'd try to save some money to help pay his way.''

''Kim's grades worry me. She is really a bright child—always did well in elementary school. Now she's involved in so many social things. She dances, plays in band, and goes out on dates. If she'd just spend some of her time studying, I know she'd do better in school.''

When the teenagers' turn to talk came, they had frustrations to vent, too.

''I think adults should take a look at their *own* behavior before they talk to their teenagers,'' Velma remarked. ''When my dad sits around drinking beer and watching TV on weekends, I have a hard time listening to his advice on the subject of drinking.''

''Honesty is important to me,'' said Brad. ''And that my parents—and other adults, too—really listen to me and try to understand me.''

''And I think parents should remember we teenagers have ideas too,'' Nicky continued. ''We should have discussions about things affecting our lives. Not lectures.''

''The problem with my parents is that they get all over my case when they start talking about anything,'' Roosevelt reported. ''We will start to have a discussion about borrowing the car and the next thing you know I will be hearing about my clothes, my hair, and the decay of morality and manners in today's teenagers. Oh, sure, I know my parents love me—and I love them too. It's just that they don't seem to trust me.''

Carlos was thoughtful, ''I want my parents to love and accept me. Once I ran away from home because I felt like my parents could never accept me for who I am. Of course, I'm not perfect. Now I know they accept me even when they don't like my ideas or the way I act.''

''I know that my parents are really interested in me,'' said Kim. ''Some parents are always too busy, or too tired, or gone. I play basketball on the high school team and my parents came to our games all last year.''

By adolescence, children and parents have a long history of interaction. But as teenagers assume more responsibility for their own activities, their relationship with their parents undergoes changes. Unfortunately, sometimes parents are often having their own problems when adolescents need them most.

Sexual Identity Crisis.   Both parents and adolescents are dealing with a sexual identity crisis (Burr, 1970). Adolescent girls are trying to adjust themselves to bodily changes including menstruation. Boys are also adjusting to dramatic bodily changes. And teenage girls and boys are dealing with their new sexuality. At the same time, mothers are adjusting to menopause and the loss of youthful attractiveness. One mother of an adolescent expressed a common feeling when she said, ''I find myself competitive and jealous of my teenage daughter. She grows more luscious, and I feel like I am drying up.'' (Ponzo, 1978). Fathers, too, are becoming sensitive about increased weight, baldness, and the fear of a decline in sexual capacity.

Role Crisis.   Roles are also important to adolescents and parents alike (Rollins and Feldman, 1970). Adolescents are trying to resolve their role confusion by deciding on a vocational role. Fathers are worried about their accomplishments and future security. Sometimes full-time mothers try to hold on to their adolescent children so they won't have to give up their role of mother. Parents may pressure adolescents to assume roles they wanted but could not attain. Scotty's father, who always wanted to study medicine but couldn't afford medical school had been saving money for years so that his son could go to medical school.

Independence-Dependence Struggle.   Another crisis for adolescents and parents revolves around the independence-dependence struggle. Parents are used to having authority over their dependent children. But adolescents feel the need for increased independence. Adolescents must eventually win the independence-dependence struggle if they are to achieve a personal identity. Yet the adolescent has ambivalence about playing the game. The increased privileges of adulthood bring increased responsibility. And this increased responsibility can be scary.

When parents remember their own difficulties in the struggle for independence, they may try to protect their children from experiencing the same problems by trying to maintain the degree of control they had when their children were younger—which may cause adolescents to rebel against such restrictions, going ''overboard'' to assert their independence. But when parents give in and allow the independence being demanded, their teenager may interpret this as ''my parents not caring.'' When teens can count on support and love from parents who will let go, then they can make the transition to independence more easily (Ausubel et. al., 1980).

Value Conflicts.   Value conflicts can arise as adolescents try to choose personal value systems. Parents have years of experience with which to judge and measure current events in the world—from the crisis in Poland to registration for the draft. Because of their greater perspective, adults tend to be more realistic than their idealistic adolescents and are likely to stress thought and caution before action (Elkind, 1978). Adolescents may press for action based on their ideals, scorning their parents' tendency toward more realism and caution.

Letting Go.   As a result of the similar crises they are experiencing, adolescents and parents often feel confused. And sometimes each generation is so involved with their own problems, they tend to overlook those of the other. But increasing

Keeping the lines of communication open is important in adolescent-parent relationships.

research data indicate that the single most important influence aiding or hindering the average adolescent in accomplishing the developmental tasks of adolescence is his or her parents (Martin, 1975; Walters and Stinnett, 1971).

"How can parents help adolescents accomplish the necessary developmental tasks without excessive turmoil, extremely disrupted parent-child relations, extraordinary psychological difficulties, and with a fair amount of immunity to destructive external pressures?" (Conger, 1977). As a guide, parents of adolescents can show they are interested, keep lines of communication open, provide for independence within limits, love and accept their teenagers, trust them, set a good example, and be democratic (Rice, 1978).

PARENTS VERSUS PEERS

You may think that as adolescents gradually achieve independence from the home, parents lose their influence—particularly when compared with the influence of peers. Actually, this is untrue. Adolescents see parents and peers as important in different areas (Kandel and Lesser, 1969). Parental advice is likely to be taken in areas dealing with society in general and adolescents are likely to adopt their parents' moral and social values. Peer advice will be taken in areas such as fashion, language, peer interaction, and activities where peer conformity is impor-

---

Development of the Parent-Child Relationship

Relationship	Developmental Period
Parent-Newborn Synchrony	Newborn (birth–4 weeks)
Parent-Infant Attachment	Infancy (birth–12 months)
Parent-Toddler Dependency	Toddlerhood (1–3 years)
Parent-Preschooler Partnership	Early Childhood (3–6 years)
Parent-Child Detachment/Children's Same-Sex Friendships	Middle Childhood (6–12 years)

Parent-Teenager Individuality/Crowd Formation—Adolescents struggle to achieve an individual identity apart from parents. They become involved in larger peer groups called crowds. Crowd formation makes it possible for children to move from the same-sex cliques in middle childhood into the heterosexual cliques of adolescence.

Adolescence (13–18 years)

---

tant. Similarities in family backgrounds of peer group members have often produced similar values and ideas, so peer influence may well reinforce parental influence. The more difficult and serious the choice, the more adolescents look to parents for advice. But parental influence is highest when parent-adolescent affection is high, when parents are involved, and when parents have strong value systems.

Adolescents and Peer Relationships

During adolescence, the peer group continues to increase in importance for a number of reasons. It is a major source of self-esteem for adolescents. Adolescents need the emotional security and support provided by their peer group as they build their own identity and continue breaking ties from parents. Teenagers bounce ideas and actions off their peers and receive feedback as they test out various roles, commitments, and relationships (Lipsitz, 1979). Relating with peers serves as a model for later social relationships and follows a pattern similar to the pattern of crowd formation.

CROWD FORMATION

The deep attachments between same-sex friends that began in the pre-crowd stage of middle childhood persist during early adolescence. But gradually, adolescents become involved in larger groups called **crowds**—loosely knit groups made up of several cliques.

Early Adolescence

Stage 1:   Pre-crowd stage. Isolated same-sex cliques.

Stage 2:   The beginning of the crowd. Same-sex cliques in group-group interaction.

Stage 3:   The crowd in transition. Same-sex cliques with upper status members forming a heterosexual clique.

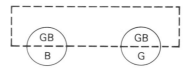

Stage 4:   The fully developed crowd. Heterosexual cliques in close association.

Stage 5:   Beginning of crowd disintegration. Loosely associated groups of couples.

Late Adolescence

G = Girls   B = Boys   GB = Girls and boys

Figure 14.1 **Crowd formation during adolescence.** (Adapted from Dunphy, 1963).

A principle function of the crowd is to make possible transitions from same-sex cliques of middle childhood and early adolescence to the heterosexual cliques of later adolescence. The development of crowds is shown in Figure 14.1

Even though conformity begins to decline in adolescence, it continues to be a necessary "membership card" in the adolescent peer group. Whatever the clique decides to do—wear saddle oxfords or work boots, get "punk" haircuts or none at all, dress up or wear jeans—the individual members are also supposed to do. Group identity is accomplished through unique group behavior, dress, hairstyles, and language. But if the unique behavior is adopted by other groups, the group changes its behavior.

The unique behavior of three crowds in a suburban high school in the Northeast was described by Leona (in Dacey, 1979). The "jocks" were good at athletics, drank a lot (mostly beer), and almost never smoked dope. Examples of their language included "going guzzling" or "getting buzzed" for going drinking. The "motorheads" were mostly males noted for their interest in cars, leather jackets, low grades, and unusual hair styles. Their language included "cruising" for driving around town, "frosties" for cans of beer. "Flea bags" were a group of male and female students who used drugs regularly—mostly marijuana. Their language included "joint," "j's," "bone" for marijuana cigarettes; getting "wasted," "high," "baked" for feeling the effect of smoking a lot of marijuana.

Some adolescents—either by choice or (most frequently) rejection—don't fit into any group. Nicky and Velma never did seem to be part of a crowd. And even though some adolescents are showing more tolerance and empathy for loners like Nicky and Velma, many adolescents can be remarkably indifferent or cruel to adolescents who don't fit in. Isolated teenagers typically lack self-confidence and often try to overconform to peer values. This lack of confidence and overconformity leads to further rejection by the peer group. Isolated teenagers are also more likely to become mentally ill or delinquent (Rogers, 1977). They are often underachievers since doing well in school (grade C or better) is motivated by membership in cliques (Damico, 1975).

FRIENDSHIPS, DATING, AND MARRIAGE

Same-Sex Friendships.   In early adolescence, finding out about one's body and learning culturally defined "masculine" or "feminine" behaviors is more easily done by modeling and communicating with same-sex peers. It is easier to identify with others of the same sex because they are affected by similar concerns and physical changes. And since girls are usually two years ahead of boys in maturation, adolescent females and males of the same age have little in common because of differences in interests and activities. Besides, newly awakened sexual impulses along with related physical and psychological changes cause self-consciousness and anxiety about opposite-sex peers. Same-sex friendships and antagonisms toward

Adolescence: Social and Emotional Development and Relationships

the opposite sex help to affirm girls as ''feminine'' and boys as ''masculine.'' Such antagonisms also prevent early sexual relationships with members of the opposite sex.

Dating. Nowadays, adolescents leave the stage of same-sex friendships and begin dating earlier than they used to (Dunphy, 1972). This trend is partly due to media stereotypes and the pressure for children to grow up too quickly (Elkind, 1981). Dating too early or overemphasizing dating penalizes adolescents in many ways. One study showed that girls who started dating and going steady early (eleven to fourteen) tended to be active, energetic, and self-confident (Conger, 1977). But they were also immature, superficial, unimaginative, and limited in ideas and friendships. This finding suggests it is important to explore one's own identity through interaction and identification with same-sex peers. Later relationships with the opposite sex are built on this foundation.

Strong emotional feelings toward members of the opposite sex emerge during adolescence.

Marriage.   Adolescents do not agree with the idea that "marriage is out of date" and most eventually plan to marry and have children. But marriage role requirements are complex and difficult in our society and adolescent marriage receives little social reward or support (Dreyer, 1975). Along with their continuing search for personal identity, adolescent husbands and wives have the added problems of managing a house, surviving economically, meeting job demands, and dealing with complicated social relationships (Cannon-Bonventre and Kahn, 1979). Personal freedom is restricted and adjustment to the wishes and habits of a spouse is difficult. Our society's unrealistic emphasis on marriage as "and they lived happily after" romance tends to complicate an already difficult situation when adolescents marry (Sebald, 1968).

Adolescent marriages are often further complicated by pregnancy. When childbirth occurs before the wedding, the divorce rate is more than twice the average rate. If expectant couples marry before the baby is born, the divorce rate is not so high.

ADOLESCENTS AND SEX

Sexual behavior has changed more than most aspects of human behavior in the current century. Until recently, it was popularly believed that, "they're talking more about sex now, but not really doing more about it." This may have been true before 1951, but not today. Virtually all available data indicate an increase in sexual interests and behavior during adolescence (Phipps-Yonas, 1980). The increase in sexual activities among teenagers began before the "sexual revolution" of the 1960s and is continuing (Zelnik and Kantner, 1978). Masturbation, premarital intercourse, pregnancy and adolescent parenthood are among the issues related to the increase in teenage sexual activity.

Masturbation.   Masturbation is defined as the act of stroking one's own sex organs in order to gain pleasure. In one study of almost 400 adolescents aged thirteen to eighteen, 58 percent of boys and 39 percent of girls said they had masturbated (Sorensen, 1973). Children, in general, are masturbating at an earlier age than in the past. Most boys reported having their first experience before or during their thirteenth year, most girls before or during their twelfth year. No other sexual practice discussed in the Sorensen study produced more defensiveness and secrecy than masturbation. But younger adolescents were more frank about it than older adolescents.

Premarital Intercourse and Pregnancy.   In 1976, 66 percent of adolescent girls reported having sexual intercourse before age nineteen as compared to 55 percent in 1971—and the intercourse was almost always premarital. One fifth of teens aged thirteen to fourteen have had intercourse. But few (one third) of these sexually active teenagers used contraceptives (Rich, 1979; House Select Committee on Population, 1979).

In a survey of more than 400 black, white, and Hispanic male youths between thirteen and nineteen, only 15 percent of the 69 percent who were sexually active reported they "always" used contraception (Finkel and Finkel, 1978). Most adolescents felt that "if a girl uses birth control pills or other methods of contraception it looks as if she were planning to have sex" (Sorensen, 1973). Nearly half of the girls having intercourse without using birth control believe that if a girl truly does not want to have a baby, she won't—even if she doesn't use birth control. Myths and ignorance about contraception are surprisingly widespread among adolescents (Walters et al., 1979) and contribute to the nonuse of contraceptives.

Out-of-wedlock births increased 75 percent between 1961 and 1974 for teens aged fourteen to seventeen (Lipsitz, 1979). Teenage pregnancies currently exceed one million each year and thirty thousand of the pregnant girls are under age fifteen (Lipsitz, 1979). Many girls have miscarriages or abortions, but about 600,000 give birth annually (Cannon-Bonventre and Kahn, 1979; Rich, 1979). And only 10 percent of out-of-wedlock babies are being offered for adoption, compared with 90 percent offered for adoption ten years ago. This poses serious problems for society, since teenage motherhood has negative effects on both the mother and child (see Spotlight 14.2).

Homosexuality.   Sexual attraction during adolescence is not always confined to the opposite sex. Sometimes homosexual experiences occur, too.

As the discussion of dating, marriage, and sex continued, Noah's mind began to wander far from what was happening at the retreat. He felt the same way he usually felt in the shower room after a game. Other guys on the team would kid each other about being "queers" and "fags." But he always kept quiet. The kidding made him feel like an outsider. And that's how he felt right now—like an outsider.

Noah started daydreaming about summer camp. Suddenly, he realized he was sexually aroused. At first, he couldn't figure out why. Then he realized the things he remembered from camp were the things he did with a guy he met there—swimming, canoeing, hiking, archery. He also remembered a night they went camping and slept in a double sleeping bag. That night Noah had his first sexual experience with his friend. Then, all he could think about was the guy from camp and what a terrific time they had together. Before he knew it, Noah was daydreaming just about his male friend—not about summer camp.

The way Noah felt toward his male friend could be a passing phase. Or it could be the beginning of a permanent homosexual orientation that will remain an important part of his identity and relationships for the rest of his life. Noah's situation is not at all unusual for adolescent males. The Kinsey research of the 1940s made us aware that the incidence of homosexuality among men and women is more common than we had thought (Kinsey, et al., 1948). Kinsey and his colleagues reported that more than half of adult males remembered some type of preadolescent homosexual sex play. In fact, among preadolescent boys, homosexual play was more frequent than heterosexual play (Kinsey et al., 1953). And one third of females reported engaging in same-sex play at some time during their lives—usually adolescence. But most males and females who engage in homosexual activity in adolescence do not continue a homosexual lifestyle as adults.

Despite Kinsey's findings, our society continued to view homosexuality as a disease—something in need of cure. But in 1973, the American Psychiatric Association stated that homosexuality is neither a disease, nor a mental disturbance, nor a psychiatric disorder. In fact, more recent research indicates that today the average homosexual reports positive parental upbringing (Robinson et al., 1982) and is just as psychologically well adjusted as the average heterosexual (Bell and Weinberg, 1978).

No one knows for sure what causes homosexuality. Some claim it results from domineering mothers and cold, rejecting fathers. Others believe hormones and genetics play a role. The Kinsey Institute for Sex Research (1982) recently concluded from a study of 1000 homosexuals and 500 heterosexuals that sexual preference results from many factors but begins with an early (probably biological) tendency toward homosexuality or heterosexuality. Regardless of the causes, homosexuality exists. Homosexuals are now expressing themselves more openly and homosexuality is now being received with more openness and tolerance from society than ever before. But hostility still exists among some people.

Support groups for gays, which help counteract such hostility and promote healthy growth of members, are now quite prevalent. Parents of gays are also forming groups to help members deal with their questions and concerns.

Adolescents and Society

Parents and peer relations are not the only influences on adolescents. Teenagers are increasingly being influenced by society in general. School occupies much of the adolescent's time and a vocation must be chosen and prepared for. Minority group adolescents face special problems at school and in their vocational choices. The legal system now shares with parents the responsibility for setting rules for behavior. When adolescents break these rules, they may be labeled delinquent.

ADOLESCENTS AND SCHOOLS

Adolescents spend many waking hours in schools. Peer groups are largely formed at school, and many models for adolescent behavior are found at school. Physical, cognitive, moral, social, emotional, religious, and vocational education have all been placed in the hands of the schools. But how well schools are accomplishing those tasks is an issue for debate. Some researchers claim that schools are not meeting the needs of teenagers and may even be harmful to them (Friedenberg, 1959; Goodman, 1960).

Spotlight 14.2: Adolescent Parenthood

CONSEQUENCES FOR PARENTS

Three adolescents share difficulties they had as young adults:

> "Once we didn't have any money and I ran out of food stamps. So I went to my mother and grandpa and they gave me money for food."
>
> "I didn't know where to find friends. My old friends were gone away to school or were just too busy."
>
> "I was going to school nights to try to pass the test for my high school diploma. I got afraid on the math. I wanted to finish but I was afraid." (Cannon-Bonventre and Kahn, 1979).

According to this study, financial difficulty was the most frequently reported problem of teenage parents (Cannon-Bonventre and Kahn, 1979). And poverty worsened all their other problems, which included isolation, inadequate child care, decreased educational opportunities, and substandard housing. Isolation and loneliness was the next most frequently noted problem. Old friends were no longer available and new ones were hard to find. This absence of a friendship network contributed to the likelihood of child abuse and neglect, depression, suicide, and marital problems. Infant and child-care arrangements were difficult to locate. "My mother sits for us when she feels like it. We'll plan on her for two weeks. Then she won't feel like it," said one frustrated teen parent. "My husband had to leave his job because we had no babysitter," said another. Early childbearing is also associated with significant educational losses. Women who had their first child at age fifteen or less completed an average of nine years of school. And these young mothers did not "catch up" on their schooling in later years. Instead, the educational gap between them and their peer group widened (Moore et. al., 1979). Little is known about adolescent fathers because they usually don't live with mother and child. But the social and psychological problems associated with adolescent motherhood are similar for teenage fathers who do live with their wives and babies (Barret and Robinson, 1982; Earls and Siegel, 1980).

CONSEQUENCES FOR CHILDREN

Recent evidence indicates that the typical pregnant teenager is biologically ready for pregnancy and childbirth if she receives good prenatal care and nutrition. But according to Phipps-Yonas (1980), these conditions are frequently not met. As a result of these and other factors, they cite high rates of health problems among infants born to teenage women: 6 percent of first children and 10 percent of second children born to mothers under fifteen die before their first birthday—three to five times the rate for other American babies.

Teenage mothers are more likely than older mothers to abuse their children (Kinard and Klerman, 1980). In terms of social relationships, preschool children are as isolated as their teenage parents (Cannon-Bonventre and Kahn, 1979). Some studies have found problems such as hostility, overactivity, and impulsiveness in children of teenage parents. Others have found no relationship between social-emotional behavior and maternal age (Baldwin and Cain, 1980). Children of teenagers have lower scores on the Bayley developmental scale (see Chapter 4) at eight months, lower Stanford-Binet scores at age four, and lower WISC scores at age seven (Phipps-Yonas, 1980). But after home-based infant stimulation programs, babies score higher on developmental tests. (Field, T. et al., 1980). And children who stayed in day-care settings or with grandmothers did better on preschool tests than those who stayed with their teenage mothers (Baldwin and Cain, 1980).

Having children during the teen years can pose special problems for young mothers and fathers, regardless of whether or not they wed.

HELP AND HOPE FOR TEENAGE PARENTS

Supportive measures can be taken to help teenagers adjust to their parenting role:

- Building a good self-concept and feelings of worth along with education about contraception and the consequences of teenage parenthood can help prevent unwanted pregnancies.

- Health problems or deaths of infants of teenage mothers can be decreased when the mother receives good prenatal care and nutrition.

- Feelings of isolation can be decreased when a social network is established and maintained. Adults in the neighborhood, peers, or social workers can form the necessary support group.

- Home-based infant stimulation programs can serve to educate teens about parenthood,

decrease isolation, and encourage the infant's development.

In one study, premature infants of mothers from severely deprived socioeconomic backgrounds were given extra stimulation in the hospital. Social workers visited the home weekly for a period of two years—providing instruction and guidance in infant care techniques. Mothers were interested in the social worker's help and sought her advice on personal problems and feelings of depression as well as infant care. The experimental group showed better weight gains and higher scores on the Brazelton Infant Development Scale after four to six weeks than a comparison group. At the age of one year, the infants in the experimental group had average IQ scores of almost ten points higher than the comparison group (Scarr-Salapatek and Williams, 1973).

Isolation.   Schools are increasing adolescent isolation in our society. Spending many hours with their own age group in settings preparing them for adult society—but not clearly relevant to it—leaves some adolescents feeling removed from the mainstream. Adolescents are denied access to a variety of adult models and the feeling of making a meaningful contribution to society. The high school years allow adolescents to concentrate on forming an identity and to select and prepare for an adult vocational role. But critics argue that by remaining full-time students, teenagers are isolated from the world of work and prevented from forming a sense of identity (Dye, 1979).

Lack of Relevance.   Young people in schools in the United States are tested through written examinations far removed from real-life experience. But a young Australian aborigine is tested on his knowledge and skills as a contributor to the tribe in a rite of passage. After receiving survival training skills for most of his life, the sixteen-year-old male must leave the village and live on his own. During his ''walkabout'' the teenager must stay alive and behave with competence, confidence, and courage (Gibbons, 1974).

In 1974, Phi Delta Kappa (an honorary fraternity of educators) set up a task force to study the possibility of establishing an Americanized version of the walkabout to help make our high schools less isolated and more relevant. Such ''walkabouts'' would be self-initiated, take place outside schools, and contain opportunities for individual and group work. They would be well planned, but promote the unexpected. Schools in other parts of the nation are encouraging students to take vocational training and also to work part-time in the community.

Discipline.   Many people believe that the most important problem in schools today is discipline (Gallup, 1978). Yearly vandalism costs about the same as textbooks (500 million dollars). Assaults on teachers increased by 77 percent in a five-year period, causing 70,000 serious accidents in 1975. Assaults on students by students rose 85 percent. Robberies, rapes, and attempted rapes increased almost 40 percent. Homicides increased 18 percent and weapons confiscated increased by about 50 percent. This increase in violence and vandalism leveled off in the 1970s (National Institute of Education, 1977).

The public response to such delinquency has become more and more punitive. But psychologists have evidence against the use of punishment as a primary means of changing behavior (Hyman, 1979). Educators and psychologists have proposed various positive approaches to discipline in the schools.

Conflict negotiation is one positive approach to handling many problems. In conflict negotiation, all parties state their perception of the issue, agree on a common written statement of the issue, and bargain to achieve a resolution. Written plans to carry out the negotiated settlement are included in a final agreement. Conflict negotiation requires time, but it can lead to a deeper understanding of the democratic process and to emotional as well as cognitive development. Students learn to improve interpersonal relations, to deal with anger in socially acceptable ways, and to resolve present and future conflicts.

Solving School Problems.   To combat such problems as isolation, lack of relevance, and discipline in schools, Wynne (1978) suggests we return to the types of schools we had thirty or forty years ago when society was more cohesive. We should move toward neighborhood schools, lower costs, more authority given to the school principal, more personalized grading of students, smaller educational units, more emphasis on the development of school spirit, greater parental control, and less reliance on technology.

Other educators believe that although we should not attempt to return to the organization of schools in the past, we should return to an earlier goal—teaching basic skills. The Denver public schools now test basic skills competencies in all four grades of high school. Students who do not pass are given individualized instruction and prescriptions for study so that they may pass in the next year. Students who do not pass by the senior year are given a certificate of attendance rather than a diploma. But they may later retake the test and receive their diploma.

Vocational Choice.   What will I be when I grow up? What will I do when I am no longer in school? These questions become critical during adolescence since the time is approaching when adolescents must choose an occupation. Such questions and decisions related to work are important in the adolescent's search for identity (Douvan and Adelson, 1966; Erikson, 1968). Work opportunities can provide adolescents with a sense of purpose and responsibility, allow them to participate in society in a realistic way, and help them practice communicating with adults.

A major recommendation of the youth panel of the President's Science Advisory Committee (Coleman, 1974) was that young people be given opportunities to become involved in work experiences. Proposals from the panel included providing half a day of work and half a day of school; alternating between school and work for a semester; extending educational programs to provide academic credit for work; and offering opportunities for public service (Coleman, 1974).

Many adolescents recognize the independence that comes with a job. But adolescents typically have only a vague idea of what jobs they are skilled enough to do, which they would enjoy doing, what training is required, or what present and future demands will be for workers in various jobs. Unfortunately, adolescents in our society have little opportunity to learn a vocation through an apprenticeship like Brad's newspaper job. Because of our societal myths that adolescents are children and that adolescence is a pathological time, we don't give teenagers an opportunity to try out socially responsible roles and commitments when they need to (Bronfenbrenner, 1979; Lipsitz, 1979). This is particularly true of minority teens, who have the highest unemployment rate in the United States today.

Work Experience and Occupational Training in Adolescence

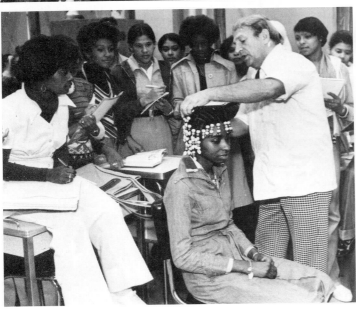

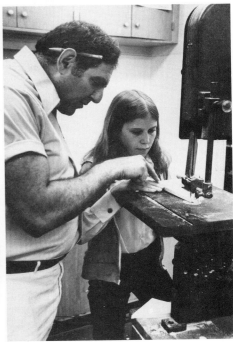

The Case of Cleveland

Cleveland Wilke's family in Providence, Rhode Island, has never had much money; both he and his parents know what unemployment can do to a family. Nevertheless, Cleveland, who is seventeen, is referred to by his friends as the Dresser because of his penchant for startling clothes—especially shoes. What little money he manages to scrape together is all channeled into maintaining his style. In conversation, Cleveland may grow quite animated, but he always has time to check the press of his trousers or smooth the wrinkles of his sleeves:

"Take the kids around here; they ain't all alike. This one worries about this, another one, he'd like to bust the hell out of this place. I got a sister talking about going to college. She may do it, too, man. You can't tell. I seen stranger things going on.

"Saw a man get knifed once . . . person stuck him so many times doctor came and couldn't figure out which hole to stop 'im up with first. Tell you, man, the dude was lying on the street, wasn't an inch of him didn't have blood coming out of him. Bunch of cats, we was watching the whole thing, ten feet away.

"Whole world floats by around here. This here's the whole world, only in miniature, like they call it. There ain't nothin' you can't see in these streets. Only thing we don't have is the thing we need the most of: jobs. Ain't no jobs for us over here. Not a one, man, and I know too, because I been looking for three years, and I ain't all that old. *Act* old, but I ain't old. *Seen* things old people seen, but I ain't old. Next week I may be old; next year I sure am fixin' on being old if I don't find no work. I'd take anything, too, man, *anything* they got for me.

"Country got no use for me, folks around here neither. Ain't nobody care too much what happens to us. Tell us, 'Ain't you boys got nothing better to do than stand around all day? What you find to talk about all these hours? And ain't you supposed to be in school? Ain't you supposed to be doing this or doing that? I tell them, 'Hey, listen to me, turkey. I ain't *supposed* to be doing nothin' if I don't want to. You hear me? Ain't supposed to be nowhere, helping no one.'

"I can *hear* my brain rotting it's been so long I ain't done nothin'. How they let this happen in a country like this, having all these kids walking around the streets, got their hands jammed down in their pockets, head down, like their necks was bent in half? What do folks think these kids gonna do, when they go month after month, year after year without nothing that even *smells* like a job. Not even no part-time affair. Hell, they might get to the point to where they'll waste some kid working for the cleaners, waste the kid and take his job. Folks do it when they ain't got enough food, and they'll start doing it for jobs, too.''*

---

* "Listening to a Brain Rotting" by T. J. Cottle, *Psychology Today*, Feb. 1979, p. 44. Reprinted from *Psychology Today Magazine*. Copyright © 1979, Ziff-Davis Publishing Company.

Most adolescents occasionally feel "out of it"—that they don't fit in, that nobody loves them. But some teens have strong, long-term feelings of **alienation**—a loss or absence of desired relationships (Keniston, 1960).

Much attention was focused on this problem in the late 1960s and early 1970s, when it became widespread among middle- and upper-class youths. Signs of generalized alienation today can be found in the "punk" style adopted by some teens. Blacks, Mexican-Americans, Puerto Ricans, American Indians, Appalachain Whites—social groups that are born into the "culture of poverty"—can become alienated from the affluent society they see all around them and on their television screens. Middle- or upper-class youth may feel alienated from a society that they view as preoccupied with materialism, social status, and financial gain. Sometimes privileged youth become alienated and reject certain aspects of society—as they did in the 1960s during the Vietnam War—while others become alienated because they feel the whole social system is rotten.

Today's youth are not as likely to be alienated from society as the youth of the 1960s. Instead, they are more anxious and conservative (Dye, 1979). Current parenting practices are likely to result in **"hurried" children**—children who grow up too fast socially and psychologically—and this hurried development can be as stressful as alienation. Some of the premature social and psychological maturity may be attributed to exposure to tele-

MINORITY-GROUP ADOLESCENTS

Nonwhite adolescents, especially those from poor families, have more difficulties with the system—school, vocational, social—than white youngsters. For such youth, the American Dream can become a nightmare. It is not surprising to find such underprivileged youth alienated (see Spotlight 14.3) from a society that has given them nothing but crumbs (Baughman, 1971).

But, even worse than alienation from society is alienation from self. Such alienation comes from the poor identity development and self-esteem that results from life-long discrimination. Self-esteem among blacks is improving. But low self-esteem still characterizes American Indians and Hispanic-Americans—probably explaining in part the greater incidence of suicides among American Indians. Alienation also helps explain Carlos' drug problems (see Chapter 13). Hispanic-Americans tend to have a negative self-identity and child-rearing practices in their culture do not encourage autonomy, initiative, or independence.

There are growing indicators that minority groups are taking more pride in their own ethnic culture and attempting to preserve their art, music, dance, crafts, literature, and folk heroes. Asserting their rights to a cultural identity and to a share in economic, educational, and vocational opportunities is a sign that culturally deprived youth are dealing with the alienation that has been their birthright. Pride in cultural heritage is important in reducing adolescent identity and role confusion. A study of Mexican-Americans in Los Angeles showed that youths who had first identified with their own subculture and its heritage showed a better

vision and peer pressure. But social changes are also involved.

As was the case long ago, children today are being dressed like miniature adults. Working mothers and fathers have generated another trend: very young children are placed in day care and teenagers are left at home alone after school to tend to their own clothing, meals, and hygiene. And the financial pressures of life in inflationary times has caused parents and society to stress the need for a good job and a good income and for the education and good grades needed to achieve them. Children are pressured to learn in kindergarten what they once learned in first grade. And most college students have turned from the protest of the 60s to studying.

Hurried children achieve in adult ways but also acquire the tensions that accompany the pressure to achieve. Symptoms of hurried children sometimes take the form of severe anxiety about academic achievement. This anxiety may result in drug use when failure occurs. Drugs may also be used as an escape by those who do achieve but at too great a cost. Hurried young people may resent parents' lack of support and participate in activities to hurt them. They may do poorly in school or drop out. Teenage pregnancy, running away, committing delinquent acts or suicides are other symptoms of hurried children. Others turn anger inward and try to escape through drugs or charismatic religions (Elkind, 1979).

sense of personal identity and eventually adapted better in the total society. They had fewer school failures and arrests and maintained more respect for authority than a comparable group who had not identified with their cultural heritage (Derbyshire, 1968).

DELINQUENT BEHAVIOR

When Scott was thirteen, he and some friends broke into their school after hours and took money from the ice cream and milk machines. After four break-ins, one boy was caught and he told on the rest. Scotty's parents were called in to talk with the principal. After many hours of discussion and weeks of probation, Scott finished paying the money back from his own earnings. Is Scott a delinquent?

Young people under sixteen or eighteen years of age who behave in ways punishable by law are termed juvenile delinquents in our society. The number of arrests for juveniles under eighteen rose 27.5 percent between 1968 and 1977, but this includes both status and serious offenses.

About 80 percent of all delinquent crimes are **status offenses**—they cause no harm to others and would not even be considered against the law if the individual were an adult. Examples of such offenses would be drinking and running away from home. It has been suggested that status offenders not be prosecuted. But today we *are* prosecuting such offenders. **Serious offenses** are more serious crimes such as theft, rape, vandalism, and murder. Youths eighteen years and under committed almost half of serious offenses, which include crimes such as shoplifting and bicycle theft, in 1977 even though they made up only 16 percent of the population (Lipsitz, 1979).

Most young people have at one time or another committed an act that could be labelled as delinquent. But some are caught and some are not. When lower-class children are caught, they are more likely to become entangled in the web of law than middle-class children like Scott. Scott would be labelled delinquent by the legal definition. But since he was taken home and allowed to be disciplined by his parents, he escaped being officially labeled a delinquent.

The better the family relationships, the less the likelihood of delinquency (Bachman, 1970). Parents of delinquents are usually not democratic in discipline techniques. Instead, they use permissive, inconsistent, or authoritarian discipline. They are more likely to use physical punishment than reasoning. Parents of delinquents are often hostile or indifferent toward school and have personal problems of their own. Broken homes are also associated with delinquency. But the likelihood of delinquency is much higher in intact, hostile, and ignoring homes than in broken, affectionate, and supportive homes (Ahlstrom and Havinghurst, 1971).

Sex differences are seen in the frequency and nature of delinquency. Boys are four to five times more likely than girls to be delinquent (Gold, 1970). And boys tend to be more involved in active or aggressive delinquent behaviors such as malicious mischief, burglary, auto theft, and drug usage. Girls are more likely to commit status offenses—being "uncontrollable," running away, or engaging in sexual activity.

Changes in the social system that contribute to feelings of alienation also contribute to delinquency. When the sense of "community" disappears along with the extended family, delinquency increases. Suburbs characterized by high social and geographic mobility have seen the greatest increases in delinquency. Delinquency rates are highest in slum districts of large cities and lowest in rural areas.

Treatment of delinquency is receiving a great deal of attention. But authorities are divided on the best approach to take. One approach to reduce rising juvenile crime is to imprison offenders. But placing youthful offenders in jail or training schools does not rehabilitate them. Instead, detention tends to produce rather than prevent adult criminal behavior.

A more effective approach, it is argued, is to rehabilitate delinquents or prevent delinquency. A national conference on juvenile delinquency suggested we need to "return to the community and foster a sense of belonging and mutual responsibility. . . . It is important to establish a relationship with youth based on equality, trust, and openness, rather than based on authority. We must give them the opportunity to make an investment in the community and its programs, and let them see the payoff." (Kinch, 1978, pp. 9–10). Involvement of youth on local youth service boards, community and private sector involvement, and increased volunteerism were seen as powerful deterrents for juvenile offenders.

Adolescent prostitution becomes a way of life for runaways—both male and female—who have run out of money. Here Jodie Foster plays a prostitute in the movie *Taxi Driver*.

RUNAWAYS

Children have always been running away from other countries—to escape poverty, unhappy families, or work situations or to seek adventure, romance, or fortune. American immigrants in the Colonial days included runaways. But only when the runaway youth problems touched middle-class America during the 1960s did running away attract much attention (Libertoff, 1980). An estimated 733,000 youths ran away in 1975 (Opinion Research Corporation, 1976). Most runaways are between fourteen and seventeen years of age (Lipsitz, 1979) and about half of them are girls (Ambrosino, 1971). Running away can mean many things. It can be just a lark, a message of distress, or a grim determination to escape parental authority, boredom, or demands from parents or school.

Most runaways don't run very far or stay away very long (Nye and Edelbrock, 1980). Some runaways may find a place to build a new life. Homes for runaways, for example, provide counseling and attempt to reconcile parent and child. If this is impossible, school or job placement is sought. Finding a home is not the typical

Finding a safe place to run *to* poses a major problem for runaway youth.

pattern for runaways. At one time runaways could find shelter with "hippies." Since the hippie culture is much less prevalent today, runaways usually have no place to run to. So they are in need of shelter, protection, counseling, and health care. Alone, in a strange city, with no money or food, these teens are ready victims of street gangs, drug pushers, and others (Bayh, 1973). Runaways often turn to a life of prostitution. When caught, runaways are typically jailed and their resentment of this plus exposure to criminals often lead them into additional criminal behavior (Bayh, 1973).

Help for troubled adolescents and runaways may be obtained through hot lines that provide information and a chance for young people to just talk with someone (Ambrosino, 1971). Some cities are also providing centers for runaways. But in a twelve-year follow-up study (Olson et al., 1980), runaways reported turbulent and painful childhood relationships and still report more pressure from parents than their nonrunaway siblings. In contrast with their siblings, runaways have limited education, training, work options, and mobility.

Emotions

As children move from infancy through childhood and into adolescence, certain conditions no longer arouse the same emotions they once did. Childhood fears of strange noises and persons no longer exist. Instead, fears have become more tied to reality. And many things that used to cause emotional excitement are no longer thrilling. Motor and intellectual skill development no longer provide the joy they once did.

Cognitive development that occurs during adolescence also widens the range of possible emotions. Young children—still dealing with the concrete—can love mother and father and hate spinach. Adolescents can use their advanced cognitive skills to deal with abstracts—to love freedom and independence and to hate tyranny and injustice.

FEAR

Adolescent fears tend to be more realistic than childhood fears. Even though adolescents may sometimes keep a childhood fear—such as fear of the dark, of strangers, or of animals—most of their fears are associated with the demands of adolescence. Common fears of adolescents include a fear of growing up and plans for the future. Facing new experiences like meeting a new peer group, going to camp, school promotion, or taking a job can also arouse fear (Senn and Solnit, 1968). Fears relating to sexuality and to death are also common. An adolescent with a sequence of life-threatening illnesses may fear death and an adolescent who has been rejected by the peer group may fear rejection.

AFFECTION AND LOVE

Adolescents are at times swept with love for parents, home, a pet—but the most dramatic instance of adolescent love involves love with a member of the opposite sex. Adolescent love is a desire for relationships with significant others who will be accepting (Scarlett, 1975). And the adolescent in love tends to use new cognitive abilities to construct a romance around that love (Piaget and Inhelder, 1961).

Broderick (1966) found that in a study of 1000 adolescents, a large proportion of the ten- and eleven-year-olds reported being in love within the past year. Half of the twelve- to thirteen-year-olds said they had been in love in the past two years. By age sixteen to seventeen two thirds of adolescents reported being in love during the previous year. Erikson (1968) suggests these first love relationships help the adolescent form an identity. Love partners serve as mirrors, against which teens can see themselves more clearly. So a large part of young love is conversation and experimentation with self-image. True love—with dedication to the other person—will not be possible until after identity formation has occurred.

RITES OF PASSAGE

Rites of passage differ from society to society. Isolation or attention, fasting or feasting, terrible consequences or tremendous benefits, brief or lengthy preparation are some of the contrasts noted by anthropologists who study such rites (Brown, 1963).

Among the Bemba of Africa, young girls know how to cook and grind, but after the "chisungu" rite, they must do their work in a different way. According to the Bemba, "a girl can idle in the garden if she likes and her mother will shrug her shoulders and say 'she is not grown up' " (Richards, 1956, p. 128–129). After the chisungu, the girl must do things with a new spirit and sense of responsibility. "Before, if they were called to work they could go slowly, now they have to run" (Richards, 1956, p. 128–129).

Male rites of passage are often more complicated than female rites—perhaps reflecting the greater demands for independence among males (Conger, 1977). Young Zunis are taught to fear "scare Kachinas," the punitive masked gods that appear in tribal ceremonies. At about age fourteen, a boy is ceremonially whipped with yucca strands by the Kachinas to exorcise bad happenings and to make the future favorable. Afterwards the Kachina mask is placed upon the boy's head and he learns that the masked Kachinas are neighbors and relatives—not supernaturals from the Sacred Lake. Now he knows that mortals must perform all functions he formerly believed were performed by supernaturals (Benedict, 1934).

ADOLESCENT SEXUALITY

Cultures vary from permissive to restrictive in their practices concerning childhood and adolescent sexuality. Samoans are permissive (Mead, 1928). Samoan adolescents spend a great deal of time in secret sexual experimentation. In fact, a Samoan girl's first love affair is considered the high point of her sexual pleasure.

The Chewa of Africa believe that children must exercise themselves sexually from early childhood in order to be fertile. Older children build huts and play husband and wife. Exchanging mates is allowed until marriage occurs. The Lepcha of India also allow sex play—including mutual masturbation and attempts at intercourse among children. Girls are thought to be immature unless they engage in sexual intercourse and most of them do so by age eleven or twelve (Conger, 1971).

Restrictive practices occur among the Cuna who live on the northwest coast of South America. Cuna children are kept ignorant of sexual matters until the marriage ceremony. Even watching animals give birth is forbidden (Conger, 1971). In Africa, the Ashanti consider sexual intercourse with a girl who has not completed the puberty rites so dangerous that both partners can be put to death.

Sometimes adolescent male sexuality is expected or encouraged and female sexuality is forbidden. In the Admiralty Islands north of New Guinea, the adolescent male's sex drive is expected, but sexual intercourse is taboo until marriage. Sexual release among boys occurs through secret homosexual activity or masturbation surrounded by shame. But girls in this culture are taught that sex is not gratifying. Instead, it's loathsome and shameful (Ausubel, et al., 1954).

ESTABLISHING INDEPENDENCE

Establishing independence is not as difficult in some cultures as it is in ours. Among the Arapesh of New Guinea and the Mixtecan Indians of Mexico, a very gradual change occurs from dependence and nurturance in infancy and early childhood to increased independence as the child grows older. No noticeable spurt in independence is expected nor does it occur at adolescence (Mead, 1939; Minturn and Lambert, 1964). An Arapesh adolescent gradually takes over much of the responsibility for supporting and managing the household. A girl is chosen by her future husband's parents many years before she is married and she wanders at will back and forth between her home and her future husband's home. Similarly, Arapesh boys work the

As a part of a circumcision ceremony marking their passage to manhood, these boys of the Warusha tribe in Tanzania, Africa, have their faces painted.

family garden with increasing responsibility. When marriage occurs the couple has known and adjusted to each other for a long period (Mead, 1939). No dramatic break with parents occurs.

Remember Omblean and his people, the Mundugumor (see Prologue)? Because the Mundugumor socialize their young to be extremely hostile towards members of the same sex, adolescent Omblean views his father as an enemy. Husband and wife relationships are also negative (Mead, 1939). Even sexual relations reflect the Mundugumor emphasis on aggression and competition. As a result, like other Mundugumor families, Omblean and his mother have teamed up against his father and sister. Rivalry and distrust characterize relationships between the two subfamilies. So Omblean enters adolescence psychologically close to his mother, hostile to his father, and distrustful of girls his age. Girls enter adolescence resentful toward mothers, close to fathers, and distrustful of boys their age. And jealous fathers maintain a hold on their daughters as long as possible. Because of the hostility and lack of tenderness in the Mundugumor people, children develop independence early. But since such great demands for independence are placed on the Mundugumor adolescent, establishing independence is very stressful (Conger, 1977).

SEX-ROLE LEARNING

Many cultures have established rigid sex roles for children by the time they are teenagers. Generally (but not always) girls are expected to be caregivers. Boys are expected to be hunters and food gatherers and warriors.

As soon as Samoan girls are strong enough to carry heavy loads, their child-care responsibilities are shifted to younger girls. Instead of baby-tending, adolescent Samoan girls spend their time learning to weave baskets, fans, and floor mats and to make cloth from bark. A girl's chances of marriage are badly damaged if it becomes known that she is lazy and cannot do domestic work (Mead, 1928). Adolescent girls do not specialize vocationally except for midwifery and medicine, which are usually monopolized by older women.

Most cooking in Samoa is done by boys. At seventeen, Samoan males learn to fish, make dugout canoes, and maneuver boats. They become members of a society of men referred to as "the strength of the village." Samoan male adolescents specialize in home building, fishing, oration, or wood carving. Such vocational specialization is important to males who aspire to membership in the Fono, an assembly of leaders that admits the most promising youths of each family (Mead, 1928).

Sex-Role Development and Relationships

Roosevelt's parents were proud when he told them he had decided to go to law school. "A man can make a good living as a lawyer in today's world!" they said. Caroline's parents were equally proud when, having resolved her uncertainty after much "soul searching" at the retreat, she announced that she would pursue a career as an architect. "Architecture has been dominated by men for too long. It's time more women entered the field!" her parents said.

The process of sex typing has been gradually defining sex-role identity since infancy and is well established by age three. By adolescence, a great deal of what is culturally defined as feminine or masculine has been internalized. But physical changes of puberty make the fact "I am female" or "I am male" inescapable. Acceptance of a female or male body is related to previous and present acceptance of sex role. A child who has rejected the assigned sex identity can no longer do so. Adolescents also feel the need to combine their various identities into an integrated whole and so their attention is consciously focused on their sex-role identity (Chilman, 1978).

In early adolescence, the strong need to define oneself as "female" or "male" emerges as a bond with like-sex peers. The peer group functions to help define and strengthen culturally defined sex-appropriate behavior. Women are "supposed" to be yielding, shy, affectionate, understanding, compassionate, soft-spoken, tender, and gentle. Men are "supposed" to be self-reliant, athletic, assertive, forceful, authoritative, daring, dominant, aggressive, competitive, and ambitious (Bem, 1974). So desired activities and characteristics for the sex-segregated peer groups of early adolescence become quite different for girls and boys.

With the beginning of formal thought, adolescents begin to see sex-role behaviors as existing independently of society's sex-role standards. Adolescents like Caroline are aware of sex-role stereotypes, but they no longer view these stereotypes as fixed. Older adolescents can come to adopt a set of universal sex-role standards that incorporate principles of equality and human freedom. It may be considered acceptable, even desirable, for men to become child rearers or nurses and for women to become architects and doctors. And male-female relationships can be considered equal and fair. But even though adolescents accept or even defend the right of males and females to choose nontraditional sex-role identities, they often choose to conform to traditional sex-role patterns.

In our society, with its increasing freedom of individual choice, resolving the adolescent sex-role identity crisis is more difficult than in societies where everyone knows what it means to be man or woman. The cultural trend of more androgynous sex roles may increase the possibility of confusion in the area of sex roles. Adult models may be providing so many different roles that adolescent choices may be too varied for easily accepting a sex-role identity. This is not necessarily a negative trend. When more choices are available, individuals can assume roles that suit them best. But having to make such a choice also increases the pressure on the adolescent who already has many questions about sex-role identity.

As the final retreat weekend drew to a close, the group said its farewells. "Well, group," Ms. Gaither announced," I guess it's time to go now. Thanks for sharing yourselves and helping develop the new course on adolescence. I have learned a great deal and hope you have too."

As the teenagers were seated on the bus for home, they glanced behind them as the sun set over Camp Kalowatchee. But in their minds they looked ahead to their upcoming graduation and the future.

Summary

1. Successful resolution of the identity crisis means finding satisfactory answers to many questions: Who am I? Where am I going? What occupation will I choose? Failure results in role confusion—adolescents not knowing who they are or being able to find a satisfactory vocation.

2. Adolescents continue to rely on parents, though to a lesser degree. But parent-teenager relationships can be complicated when parents are involved in their own middle-age identity crisis during their adolescent's identity crisis. Areas in which adolescents and their parents experience conflicts are sexual identity, roles, independence-dependence, and values.

3. Adolescents gradually become involved in large groups called crowds, which are made up of the same-sex cliques of middle childhood. At first, heterosexual interaction occurs only within the security of the crowd. Then upper-status members of the same-sex clique begin dating, forming heterosexual cliques. The fully developed crowd consists of heterosexual cliques in close association.

4. Adolescents today leave the stage of same-sex friendships and begin dating earlier than they used to. When adolescents marry, their relationship can be complicated by complex role requirements, lack of support, and pregnancy.

5. Sexual behavior has changed more than most aspects of human behavior. Virtually all data indicate an increase in sexual interests and behavior.

6. Problems adolescents have in schools include isolation, lack of relevance, and disciplinary problems. Solutions suggested include decreasing isolation and increasing relevance, making discipline more positive, and returning to "neighborhood" schools or the "basics."

7. Vocational choice is important in the adolescent's search for identity, but in our society, we tend to exclude adolescents from the world of work.

8. Nonwhite adolescents have more difficulties than white youngsters with the system—school, vocational, social. But there are growing indications that minority groups are taking more pride in their own cultures.

9. Young people who behave in ways punishable by law are termed delinquent in our society. Status offenses are delinquent acts that do not harm others. Serious offenses are what we consider crimes in adults—theft, rape, vandalism, murder, etc.

10. Cognitive development that occurs during adolescence widens the range of possible emotions and changes the adolescent's perception of fear, affection, and love.

11. Physical changes of puberty make the fact of being a male or female inescapable. Acceptance of this fact is related to previous and present acceptance of sex role.

Empathetic Activities

Kingsley Davis *

- What feelings did you have as you read about the case of the campfire? Noah's daydream? The case of Cleveland?

- Interview your friends about the generation gap. Find out if they think a generation gap exists between themselves and their parents. Try to determine through questioning why they think a gap does or does not exist.

- Read a book about adolescents in a culture other than yours. Brody's book in the suggested readings or Mead's books listed in the references are good choices. Compare what you know from personal experience and reading about adolescence in your culture with adolescence in another culture. Is adolescence in your culture a more difficult transition? Why or why not?

- In Chapter 13, you were asked to write a case describing your own adolescence. Extend that case and analyze it using information from each section of this chapter. Follow only the cognitive empathy part of the empathetic process (see Prologue).

- Explain Erikson's ideas on the identity crisis. Tell how the identity crisis involves the *Whole Adolescent*.

- Describe peer relationships in your own high school. Did they follow the pattern described in the "crowd formation" section of this chapter? Why or why not?

Related Readings

Administration for Children, Youth, and Families; Children's Bureau. *Children today: Focus on youth—Parts 1 and 2*. Washington, D.C.: Government Printing Office, 1979. Myths and realities of adolescent development, health care, teenage motherhood, adolescent prostitution, youth employment, and runaways.

Brody, Eugene B. *Minority group adolescents in the United States*. Huntington, N.Y.: Krieger, 1968. A book of readings providing research-based descriptions of identity formation in minority-group adolescents. Interesting, medium-difficulty reading.

Konopka, Gisela. *Young girls: A portrait of adolescence.* Englewood Cliffs, N.J.: Prentice-Hall, 1976. A sensitive description of the views of a thousand adolescent girls on life goals, sexuality, adults, friends, loneliness, drugs and alcohol, school, youth organizations, and social-political concerns. Includes case reports and poems by adolescents.

Mead, Margaret. *Culture and commitment: The new relationships between the generations in the 1970s.* New York: Columbia University, 1978. The generation gap from the perspective of the 1960s and 1970s. A fairly difficult, philosophical book.

Rogers, Dorothy. *Adolescence: A psychological perspective,* 2nd ed. Monterey, Calif.: Brooks/Cole, 1978. A lively presentation of authentic case material. Examines family and sex, youth and culture, education and vocation in adolescence.

Epilogue:
Research in Child
Development

The Case of the Effects of Aircraft Noise on Schoolchildren

A team of psychologists (Cohen, et al., 1980) had a *question:* "Does the constant noise of aircraft affect children's health and behavior?" They *gathered information* about their question and found that other researchers working in laboratories had studied the effects of noise pollution. Their studies showed that it causes hearing loss, elevated blood pressure, decreased motivation and sensitivity to others, and decreased persistence and success in completing a task such as working puzzles. In these laboratory studies, participants were exposed to high-intensity noise only temporarily. Cohen and his colleagues then *hypothesized* that they would find similar negative effects on health and behavior if they studied the influence of constant, naturally occurring noise pollution caused by airplanes in the community.

To *test their hypothesis,* the investigators studied two *samples* of third- and fourth-grade children living in Los Angeles. Children in the "noisy" group attended school bombarded by the roar and vibration of planes departing from or arriving at the Los Angeles International Airport every two minutes during school hours. Children in the "quiet" group attended similar schools except there was no unusual noise. Children in the two groups were matched for parent's occupational and educational level, ethnic group, race, and percentage receiving public financial assistance. The investigators set up an insulated, noise-free trailer outside both the quiet and noisy schools and measured each child's blood pressure, ability to concentrate, and ability to persist and successfully solve puzzle tasks. They found that children in the noisy schools had higher blood pressure, less ability to concentrate, and less persistence and success in solving the puzzles than children attending the quiet schools. When tested again two years later, the children had not become used to the noise. Instead, they were even more easily distracted. The blood pressure of children in the noisy school had dropped somewhat, but still remained higher than that of students in quiet schools.

When the investigators *evaluated their hypothesis* that negative health and behavior effects would result from continual exposure to noise, they found it was confirmed. Children exposed to continual noise pollution did indeed show negative effects on health and behavior. And the similarity of the results to earlier findings obtained in laboratory studies were said to be "striking."*

Systematic Research

All child development research begins with human experience (Ryan, 1979). A teacher, parent, nurse, home economist, social worker, researcher, you—somebody—begins the research process when he or she has a question about some as-

---

* Adapted from Cohen et al., 1980.

pect of child behavior and development. You might make observations, ask your friends, or look in books to find the answers to your questions about children. The difference between you and social scientists is that they ask and answer research questions in systematic ways using the research process.

As you can see from the case of airplane noise effects on children, systematic research involves several steps:

1. Ask a question—what is the behavior or situation to be studied?
2. Do preliminary investigation; this includes gathering information from theories and previous studies of the topic.
3. Make the best guess about an answer to the question. Scientists call a good guess a **hypothesis**—an explanation to be tested that is based upon theory and/or research.
4. Test the hypothesis, using scientific methods.
5. Evaluate the hypothesis. How do the results of the study compare with the results predicted by the hypothesis?

Answers obtained using the research process are likely to be more efficient and accurate than answers obtained in less systematic ways.

Now that we have reviewed the research process, let's take a look at the question ''Whom do researchers study?'' Then we will examine various strategies for studying children and developmental comparisons. Finally, we will consider a systems approach to research.

Whom Do Researchers Study?

To answer their ''what'' and ''why'' questions (see Chapter 1) about child development, scientists study different types and numbers of people and animals in a variety of settings. To illustrate, we can study about children and animals anywhere we can find them: in playgrounds, jungles, schools, homes, skating rinks, or in laboratories.

The types and numbers of participants selected for a study depend upon the kinds of research questions asked and the research strategies chosen to answer the questions. Sometimes investigators study one individual in detail for a long time. Other researchers examine large groups of people to look for common patterns and individual differences.

SAMPLING

It is impossible, as well as unnecessary, for us to study the behavior of all children. But if we carefully **sample**—that is study only some scientifically selected children—we can learn about large groups of people by directly studying only a few individuals. Sampling in research is similar to sampling a pie. That is, we don't have to eat the whole pie to know how it tastes. Random sampling is a sampling technique that allows us to study only a portion of a large group of people and to consider the results as characteristic of the whole group.

In **random sampling** the subjects are selected from the whole group in such a way that all members of the group have an equal chance of being chosen. Suppose we are interested in studying the effects of noise on the reading performance of first-graders and we locate a total of ninety first-graders in a nearby school. If we place their names in a hat and draw forty names out for inclusion in the study, each child would have an equal opportunity to be chosen for the study and the selection of one person wouldn't affect the selection of another.

Sometimes we study a sample just because it is convenient, but this is not really the best way to do research. White, middle-class children have been the participants in most research studies done in the United States. Serious questions must be raised about whether the results of such studies also apply to nonwhite children as well as those from the lower and upper income levels. Additional research questions can be studied and more accurate conclusions can be drawn when observations are made on random samples and when samples are from not one but several cultures.

Research Strategies for Studying Children

Researchers have developed different research strategies—methods of collecting information—as they try to answer questions about child development. All research strategies have advantages and disadvantages and no one strategy is always best. Researchers must choose the strategy that best suits the purposes of their study. We will examine five different research strategies: naturalistic, self-report, clinical, correlational, and experimental.

NATURALISTIC STRATEGIES

Naturalistic studies such as case studies and naturalistic observation are concerned with what children do every day. No effort is made to control their behavior or change the situation in any way.

Case Study.   A **case study** is an intensive study of a single child over a long period of time. It includes assessments of a child's physical, cognitive, social, and emotional development, as well as family, school, physical environment, and medical history. Based on these assessments—often done by a team of professionals and parents—recommendations are made for those who work or live with the child. A case study allows researchers to get a picture of the whole child and how the child functions with the family and society and in the physical environment.

Sometimes researchers use special devices—such as one-way mirrors—so they can observe children's behavior in as natural a setting as possible.

Naturalistic Observation.   In **naturalistic observation** the observer records the behavior of a child, noting in detail exactly what the child is doing. Barker and Wright (1951) emphasize that an observer should not look for specific behaviors but should write a detailed description of the child's total behavior and world. One example of a naturalistic observation is **running notes,** a written, objective description of an incident. The idea is to present a verbal picture as similar as possible to a videotape of an incident or a behavior. The written record should precisely describe—without interpretations—the actions of the child and other people involved, including what is said and done—postures, gestures, and so forth. A week or so of taking running notes provides a picture of the child's world. Such observations show how children react to everyday situations, what play materials they choose, how they play with other children, and how they interact with teachers and parents. Running notes can be especially helpful in pinpointing problems in a child's development. Anthropologists such as Margaret Mead often use this method in their naturalistic research strategy.

One of the problems with naturalistic research is that it is hard to observe every behavior. In most situations behavior occurs quickly and interactions are complex. It can be helpful to use a technique called **time sampling,** in which behavior is recorded at regular intervals for a specified length of time. For example, suppose we were interested in a teacher's reinforcement of children's use of language. Instead of counting each time reinforcement occurred all day, we would observe for only one hour during each day for a week. Or the observation might be made for only ten minutes each hour. But time sampling does not solve all our problems with naturalistic observation. It is also difficult to know which of the many factors in the situation is causing the behavior. So we must be extremely cautious in answering "why" questions based upon naturalistic observation.

SELF-REPORT STRATEGIES

Much information can be obtained from large numbers of children and adults when using **self-report measures** in which participants are asked to respond orally or in writing to carefully designed and systematic questions that encourage objective reporting of feelings, attitudes, perceptions, and behaviors. Responses of various participants can then be compared.

Interviews, Questionnaires, Surveys. Self-reports such as interviews, questionnaires, and surveys allow us to collect a large amount of information from many people in a relatively short time. They are more often used with older children and adults than young children.

There are several problems with self-reports: they rely on what people think or say about themselves rather than on actual behaviors; the ratings on self-reports don't always match real-life behaviors; and the ways in which questions are posed can influence the respondent's answers. Additional problems arise when respondents are dishonest, careless, or forgetful, or when they misunderstand the questions.

Standardized Tests. Standardized tests have been developed to measure such variables as intelligence, aptitude, physical skills, attitudes, intellectual functioning, and personality. A **standardized test** is "standardized" on one group of children. That is, it is given to one large group of children to identify typical responses from this particular group. The same test is then given to similar groups of children whose scores are compared with those of the original group. But there are problems of reliability, validity, and fairness involved in the use of standardized tests.

CLINICAL STRATEGIES

In the **clinical strategy** approach, the investigator uses different types of interview techniques to get individual children to talk about or act out ways they think, feel, and relate to their world. Two commonly used clinical approaches are Piaget's clinical method and projective techniques.

Piaget's Clinical Method.   Jean Piaget studied children through in-depth interviews combined with observations. In **Piaget's clinical method,** questions are tailored to the individual and are different from child to child. The investigator listens to the child's answers and then asks the next question based on the previous answer. The following is an example of a Piagetian interview (Piaget, 1966, p. 144):

Interviewer:	What is a lie?
MAB (age 6):	When you talk nonsense.
Interviewer:	You tell me about something that is a lie.
MAB:	A boy once said he was a little angel, and it wasn't true.
Interviewer:	Why did he say that?
MAB:	For a joke.
Interviewer:	Are we allowed to tell lies?
MAB:	No.
Interviewer:	Why not?
MAB:	Because it's a sin and God doesn't want us to sin.
Interviewer:	A boy told me that two plus two equals five. Is it true?
MAB:	No, it makes four.
Interviewer:	Was it a lie or did he make a mistake?
MAB:	He made a mistake.
Interviewer:	Is making a mistake the same as telling a lie or different?
MAB:	The same.

Projective Techniques.   With **projective techniques,** ambiguous or unstructured situations are used to encourage individuals to reveal their feelings and thoughts while interpreting a situation. In the Rorschach ink blot test, respondents are asked to tell what they see in a series of ink blots. In other projective techniques, the person sometimes makes up stories about pictures or finishes an incomplete story or sentence such as "I feel . . .", "My mother is . . .", "Things to be afraid of are . . . ." Games and play materials representing such things as family members, police officers, teachers, animals, houses, furniture, and cars are also often used—particularly with young children. Children can also project feelings, attitudes, and needs through their artwork. The colors and type of strokes they use, the size of the figures in relation to one another, and their behavior suggest how children organize their cognitive and emotional world. As children project feelings, they can work out their problems and the clinician can gather useful, diagnostic information.

Problems with Clinical Strategies.   There are certain problems in carrying out clinical studies. The investigator must be a good observer of human behavior and a capable therapist. It is also important to have a good memory and skill in asking questions that are well grounded in knowledge about child development. Problems with any one of these can interfere with making accurate observations and interpretations. And with projective techniques, one cannot be certain as to whether children are actually projecting their own feelings or whether they are guessing what someone else is feeling.

CORRELATIONAL STRATEGIES

By allowing us to describe behavior, correlational research answers some of the ''what'' questions. That is, correlational research tells us about the strength and direction of relationships between variables or factors we are studying. Suppose we are interested in the relationship or association between the variables of a pregnant mother's smoking and a baby's birth weight. A **positive correlation** means that as one variable increases the other increases, or as one variable decreases the other decreases. Suppose a mother's smoking and the baby's birth weight were positively correlated. We could say that as the cigarette smoking increases, the birth weight also increases. If a **negative correlation** is found, it means that as one variable increases the other decreases. And this is what actually happens—as smoking increases, birthweight decreases. So we can say maternal smoking is *negatively correlated* with infant birth weight. Correlations are expressed as a number within the range from − 1 to 0 to + 1. A correlation near + 1 or − 1 indicates a strong positive or negative relationship. But a correlation near 0 shows a weak relationship and a correlation of 0 indicates no relationship at all between the variables under study.

When we say that maternal smoking is negatively correlated with infant birth weight, we are describing the relationship between the two variables. In the case of smoking, you might be tempted to say smoking causes low birth weight. But correlational studies don't allow us to make such causal statements. Let's look at another example. There is a high positive correlation between birth rate and amount of melted tar in New York streets. It would, of course, be absurd to assume that the higher birth rate caused more tar to melt or that increased melting tar caused a higher birth rate. The birth rate happens to increase in summer when the temperature is also higher. It is probably obvious to you that the increased summer temperature—not the increased birth rate—causes more tar to melt. Even though they can't tell us about causes, correlational studies do allow us to make predictions about behavior or relationships with a certain amount of confidence. For example, we can predict with some assurance that when cigarette smoking occurs, birth weight of babies will be lower than normal. But we don't know that one causes the other. Some additional, undiscovered variable may be found to cause both the smoking and the lower birth weights.

In summary, correlational studies answer ''what'' questions and tell us about the direction and strength of a relationship—not about causes or answers to our ''why'' questions. In order to determine causes for behavior and development, we must turn to experimental strategies.

EXPERIMENTAL STRATEGIES

Let's look at an example of what an experiment is and is not. Suppose we had worked for years to design a fantastic new reading program—at least by our standards. Hoping to make our fortune and retire at an early age, we eagerly present the program to the school board in our local community. The school board members wisely insist we must test the new program before they will even consider it for their district, much less pay us for it!

We arrange to have a group of first-graders complete the program and then we test their reading skills. Just as we expect, reading performance of the group that completed our program is superior to that of a group across town who did not complete the program but from which we were able to obtain test scores. Could we say the improved reading performance was *caused* by our special curriculum? It is probably obvious to you that we could not. Children from one school could differ widely from children in another school in terms of socioeconomic status or educational level of parents. The poorer readers could have been continually bombarded by the noise of airplanes while being tested. The better readers may have performed better than the poorer readers even before we introduced our reading program. No self-respecting school board is going to accept our findings as proof of the value of our curriculum.

To accurately evaluate the effectiveness of our reading program on reading abilities we should rule out—by controlling them—the effects of variables such as socioeconomic status, educational level of parents, noise level, and all other variables *except* our reading program. We could do this by treating two "alike" groups (randomly selected) exactly the same way except for whether they did or did not complete our special curriculum. In one group (the **experimental group**), children receive special treatment in the area being studied. In this case, the experimental group should be enrolled in our special reading program. In a second group (the **control group**), children are treated just like the experimental group in every way except for receiving the special treatment in the area being studied. So in this case, they would not participate in the reading program. If after completing such an experiment we found that the experimental group performed significantly better on tests of reading performance, we could assume that the special reading curriculum did indeed cause the difference in the two groups. After obtaining results from this type experiment, we could put on our most professional looking clothes, return to the school board with the results of our test . . . again with the carefully hidden hope of making an early fortune and retiring!

The objective of experiments is to determine the *effect* of the independent variable (special reading program in this case) on the dependent variable (reading performance). The **dependent variable** is the behavior being studied, and it is measured by the researcher. The **independent variable** is systematically manipulated by the experimenter. That is, the experimenter decides what the independent variable will be and how it will be used in the experiment. Everything else is carefully controlled. So the presence or absence of the independent variable can be said to cause any changes in the dependent variable. For example, if all children were treated exactly alike in our experiment and the reading program were the only difference between the groups, the researcher could conclude that presence or absence of the special reading program caused differences in reading test scores.

Experiments differ in the amount of control investigators can have over the independent variable. Maximum control can be achieved in a laboratory setting where everything—including noise, room temperature, and color of the walls—can be controlled. But because it's *so* controlled, the situation becomes artificial. Behaviors observed in laboratory experiments are not necessarily what people do in everyday life (Bronfenbrenner, 1977a, 1979). Many researchers are now emphasizing the importance of conducting experiments in more natural settings. In the natural experiment we described in the case of the airplane noise, investigators took advantage of the aircraft noise (independent variable) occurring naturally in the children's world and measured its effect on health and behavior (dependent variables). Investigators lose some control in natural settings, but the situations studied are more life-like.

Developmental Comparisons

Suppose you were interested in finding out how behavior and development change as children grow older. How and why is a one-year-old different from a three-year-old? Longitudinal, cross-sectional, and cross-sectional/short-term longitudinal comparisons could help you answer such questions.

LONGITUDINAL COMPARISONS

In a **longitudinal comparison,** the same children are studied repeatedly over a period of several years. Differences found at various ages are assumed to be developmental—appearing as the child gets older. For example, Gesell studied approximately one hundred children over a period of ten years, and found that physical behaviors appear in the same sequence and at similar ages for most children. Longitudinal research is particularly useful in studying sequences of development such as physical and language development. Longitudinal comparisons can also be used to find out how early experiences influence later development: For example, what happens to later personality and intellectual development if babies are deprived of satisfactory mothering or if they are given extra intellectual stimulation?

Despite many advantages, longitudinal studies pose problems too. First, changes we observe in a longitudinal study might be due to societal changes or a child's particular life experience instead of developmental changes. Traditional sex-role stereotypes are not as rigidly enforced as they once were. Observations of girls playing with dolls at age four and Little League ball at age eleven may reflect changes in societal attitudes about sex roles—not developmental changes.

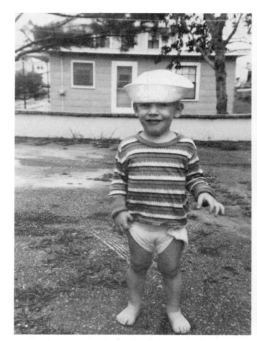

Longitudinal studies help us understand how children change or remain the same as they grow and develop. How he looks is important for this boy as a toddler and as an adolescent.

A second problem is decreased flexibility. A longitudinal study that spans fifteen years cannot take advantage of newly developed instruments or procedures. Once instruments and procedures are decided on, the researcher must stick with them for the remainder of the study so that exact age comparisons can be made throughout the entire investigation.

A third problem with longitudinal studies is that children often drop out for reasons such as illness or a family move. If children who drop out are different in important ways from children who remain, findings of the study will be biased and unreliable. Also, subjects can become test wise—they "figure out" the test. After taking the same tests several times, children score better simply because they learn how to take the test—not because they are any more mature.

Finally, researchers conducting longitudinal studies must have a great deal of time, money, and persistence. Because of these problems, many researchers now do **short-term longitudinal comparisons**—studying the same children for short time spans of between six and twelve months—which reduces many of these problems.

CROSS-SECTIONAL COMPARISONS

Most research information about developmental changes comes from cross-sectional rather than longitudinal studies because they are quicker, easier to manage, and cheaper. Instead of following the same group of children for several years, the

cross-sectional method follows the development of a number of different-aged children at the same time. For example, tests are given to groups of four-year-olds, six-year-olds, eight-year-olds, and so forth. Researchers can, in a short time, see how behavior differs at various ages. Differences in the various age groups are assumed to be developmental.

But as with the longitudinal approach, there are problems with the cross-sectional approach. First, it's difficult to know if changes from one group to the next are occurring because children are getting older. Children may be different because they grew up in different historical periods and had life experiences peculiar to their age group. Suppose we were studying a group of children when television was invented. The younger children would have television in their homes at an earlier age than the older children, and this could make a difference in how both groups develop. Developmental changes might result from the influence of television—or other historical events—not from age at all. A second problem is that change from one group to another does not necessarily represent growth sequences of individual children. And cross-sectional findings are not valid if subjects differ on important factors such as intelligence, cultural background, and so forth.

Short-term longitudinal comparisons reduce the likelihood of problems such as children dropping out, staff turnover, and out-of-date measures and procedures. But they still allow researchers to study children's development over time.

Research can make life better for all of us by helping us understand, predict, and enhance human development. But there are ethical issues involved when we study people and researchers must be sensitive to the individual's rights and welfare. Experiments that separate children from parents or purposely starve them are obviously unethical and most researchers wouldn't do such things. Ethics in other research studies are not as clear-cut. Should researchers be able to observe people in natural settings such as in a bar or at a ball game without their consent? And just how do we determine whether an experiment has long-lasting or harmful effects on subjects? Our current standards for conducting research are higher than in the past. Universities, hospitals, and research facilities now have ethics advisory committees made up of representatives from different areas of human interest. All research proposals with human beings must be approved in advance by these committees.

Ethical research is particularly important with children since they are especially vulnerable to harmful practices. Children don't have the cognitive ability to understand experiments and possible risks involved. If conducted improperly, experiments involving aggression, self-esteem, failure, or guilt could have harmful, long-term effects. So,

since a child cannot give informed consent, researchers must obtain it from parents or guardians who clearly understand all procedures involved in the research.

The American Psychological Association (1973) and the Society for Research in Child Development (1973) developed standards that apply to children. Ethics committees and researchers following these standards must ensure that children and parents be guaranteed the following:

Full information about the purposes and procedures of the study.

The opportunity to refuse participation and have the refusal honored.

The right to remain anonymous.

Protection from physical or psychological harm.

The right to stop participation at any time they choose.

Pay as a research subject, even if withdrawal from participation occurs before completion of the project.

Information on the results of the study.

The opportunity to ask and receive answers for questions.

CROSS-SECTIONAL/SHORT-TERM LONGITUDINAL COMPARISONS

One way to have the best of both cross-sectional and longitudinal designs is to combine them. A researcher can select groups of several different ages such as four and six and six and eight (cross-sectional) and follow each age group for short periods of time (short-time longitudinal).

A Systems Approach to Research

Human behavior and development are remarkably complex. Physical, cognitive, social, and emotional factors interact and influence each other continually. From a researcher's point of view, it is nearly impossible to study all of the parts of the total child system at the same time. Imagine how much more difficult it is to study the child within the family, peer group, school, society, and physical environment. It is even harder to consider how all these systems interact. Social scientists still have not perfected the research tools that will make studies of complex systems completely possible. But researchers who study child development are beginning to place more and more emphasis on studying children in their everyday worlds. And scientists are beginning to develop more sophisticated research tools that allow us to study a child as a system within the larger systems of family, peers, school, and society.

Summary

1.   Child development is a science in which questions about children are raised and answered systematically. The research process includes the following steps: (a) formulate a question, (b) locate information, (c) formulate a hypothesis, (d) test the hypothesis, (e) evaluate the hypothesis.

2.   Instead of studying every child's behavior, researchers study a sample that represents a large group of children. Random sampling helps the researcher choose representative samples.

3.   In naturalistic research strategies, researchers observe what children do in their everyday worlds. Through self-report strategies such as interviews, questionnaires, surveys, and standardized tests the researcher tries to compare thoughts and/or reported feelings. Clinical strategies such as Piaget's clinical method, and projective techniques use interview techniques with individual children. Correlational strategies allow the researcher to describe relationships between variables while experimental strategies allow for explanations of cause.

4.   In longitudinal comparisons, observations and measurements are made repeatedly on the same children over a period of several years. Cross-sectional comparisons examine a number of different age groups at the same time. In cross-sectional/short-term longitudinal comparisons, the researcher selects children of several ages and follows them for short periods of time.

5.   When conducting research, it is useful to think of the child as a system, behaving and developing within the larger systems of family, peers, school, society, and physical environment. But it is extremely difficult to consider such complex systems in research.

Empathetic Activities

■ What feelings did you have as you read The Case of the Effects of Aircraft Noise on Schoolchildren? What feelings do you think the children had? Their parents? Their teachers?

■ Find the following study in the library: Perry, D. G. and Perry, L. C. "Denial of suffering in the victim as a stimulus to violence in aggressive boys." *Child Development*, 1974, *45*, 55–62. In this study on aggression, fifth, sixth, and seventh grade boys were told to push buttons (numbered one to ten) to indicate to a schoolmate whether his answers to number problems were "right" or "wrong." The boy pushing the buttons was told that button one caused a soft noise in the earphones worn by the schoolmate "victim." As the numbers on the buttons went up so did the noise, causing the victim's ears to hurt more and more. Actually, the victim was not hurt at all, but he sometimes pretended to the boy pushing the buttons that he was hurting. It was found that boys who were rated as aggressive by their classmates before the study demonstrated more aggression (pushed higher numbered buttons) when the victim reported little pain than when the victim reported great pain (Perry and Perry, 1974). Since the boys were deceived in being told they were hurting their schoolmates, the experimenter debriefed the boys and explained the nature of the experiment upon its completion. Discuss the study in terms of your values and the discussion of ethics in this chapter.

- Ask friends if you might observe their child. Before you begin your observation, write down at least two things you would like to observe. Observe the child on the playground, at home, in a school setting or at the grocery store. How does the child's behavior appear to be affected by the different settings?

- Use information from this chapter to do the following:

    - List the steps in the research process used by researchers in The Case of the Effects of Aircraft Noise on Schoolchildren.

    - Write down a question you have or a problem you want to solve. Use the scientific research process to find the answer.

- How does the aircraft noise case relate to a systems approach for studying children and the *Whole Child* concept?

- How might a child's relationship with parents, teachers, peers, and their usual physical environment cause research findings in the laboratory to be different from those in home and school environments?

Related Readings

Barker, R. G., and Wright, H. F. *One boy's diary: A specimen record of behavior.* New York: Harper and Row, 1951. A good example of observational research.

Earle, Patty, Cosby, Rogers, and Jean Wall. *Child development: An observation manual.* Englewood Cliffs, N. J.: Prentice-Hall, 1982. An excellent observation workbook designed for use as a supplement to child development courses. A unique developmental approach to the observational activities with units on infancy, toddlerhood, preschool age, and middle childhood.

Irwin, D. Michelle, and Margaret M. Bushnell. *Observational strategies for child study.* New York: Holt, Rinehart, and Winston, 1980. A "hands-on" lab manual for observing children. Observational strategies—presented along with laboratory assignments—makes learning to observe interesting and fun.

Medinnus, Gene R. *Child study and observation guide.* New York: Wiley, 1976. A handy guide for learning more about how to observe and study children in highly structured or unstructured situations. Excellent discussion questions and observation activities are provided within each chapter.

Vasta, Rosso. *Studying children: An introduction to research methods.* San Francisco: W. H. Freeman, 1979. The scientific method, research designs and methods, and ethics are discussed in a straightforward fashion.

Glossary

Accommodation. Piaget's term for the process of changing schemes so that different or contradictory information can be taken in (or assimilated).

Adolescent growth spurt. A period of rapid increase in height and weight characteristic of puberty.

Advanced babbling. Prelanguage activity that begins at about eight months; characterized by repetition of sounds the baby has heard and speech that sounds adult-like although adult words are not actually used.

Afterbirth. The term used for the umbilical cord and the attached placenta after the birth of a baby; expelled during the third stage of labor.

Alienation. Feelings of loss or absence of desired relationships.

Amniocentesis. A medical technique used to determine evidence of abnormalities in the unborn child. Amniotic fluid is withdrawn, cells are cultured, and a karyotype of the chromosomes is made.

Amniotic fluid. The liquid in the amniotic sac that surrounds the embryo or fetus.

Amniotic sac. A protective, fluid-filled sac in the uterus in which the fetus develops.

Anal stage. The second stage of psychosexual development (two to three years) described by Freud. These are the toilet-training years in which the libido is focused on the anal area.

Androgyny. The blending of both masculine and feminine traits in an individual's personality.

Animism. Piaget's term for attributing life or human qualities to nonhuman objects or animals.

Anorexia nervosa. A severe psychological problem characterized by a refusal to eat.

Anoxia. Oxygen loss to the body.

Antibodies. Substances produced by the body that attack disease or other foreign agents and provide the newborn infant with some immunity to disease.

Anxiety. According to Freud, nervousness or tension with no real or logical basis, resulting from the conflict between the id and the superego.

Anxious-ambivalent attachment. Refers to infants who are anxious even when the attachment figure is present and become extremely upset when that figure is absent.

Anxious-avoidant attachment. Refers to infants who show few signs of being attached to an attachment figure at all.

Apgar scale. A test that rates the newborn's adjustment to the outside world; used to detect problems so treatment can be started immediately.

Apnea. Periods during sleep when breathing temporarily stops; common among infants.

Assimilation. Piaget's term for the process of incorporating new information into existing schemes without changing those schemes.

Associative play. A type of preschool play. The child plays at similar activities with peers but each child acts as he or she wishes.

Attachment. The establishment of an intimate tie that is formed in later infancy between a baby and another person, binding them together and lasting over time.

Attention span. The amount of time spent paying attention to an activity.

Authoritarian parents. Parents who believe children have few rights and should adhere unquestioningly to authority.

Authoritative parents. Parents who use affection and positive reinforcement but little punishment in interaction with children.

Autonomy. Erikson's term for a form of independence in which toddlers develop a will of their own.

Autonomy versus shame and doubt. The second stage of psychosocial development (toddlerhood) described by Erikson. Successful resolution of the conflict results in the child's independence and positive sense of self; failure results in self-doubt.

Autosomal dominant. The hereditary traits manifested when one or two dominant genes are passed from either parent to the child.

Autosomal recessive. The hereditary traits manifested when two recessive genes are passed to the child—one from each parent.

Autosomes. All chromosome pairs except the sex chromosomes.

Babbling. See **Advanced babbling** and **Random babbling.**

Basic trust versus basic mistrust. The first stage of psychosocial development (infancy) described by Erikson. Successful resolution of the conflict results in the infant's feeling safe and trusting others; failure results in a distrustful attitude.

Bilingual-bicultural education. Incorporation of the language and culture of non–English-speaking children into the English-language and middle-class school curriculum.

Binocular vision. The ability to perceive a single image with both eyes.

Birthing room. A warm, homelike, and intimate labor and delivery room set up within some hospitals.

Black English. A dialect spoken mostly by blacks living in low-income areas.

Blastocyst. A fluid-filled, bubble-like ball resulting from the cell division of the zygote.

Body type. See **Phenotype.**

Bonding. The formation of a strong, close relationship between individuals.

Bonding room. An area within some hospitals where mother, father, and newborn can be alone immediately after birth to get acquainted with no outside interference.

Bradley method. See **Husband-coached childbirth.**

Breech birth. An abnormal feet-first presentation of the fetus at birth.

Carrier. A person whose genetic makeup includes a defective recessive gene, although the person does not exhibit this defect, offspring may if the person's spouse has the same recessive gene.

Cases. Descriptions of real events drawn from newspapers, magazines, books, movies, tape recordings, and personal experiences.

Case study. An intensive study of one individual over a long period of time.

Centration. Piaget's term indicating the tendency of preoperational children to center on one dimension of an object or event, instead of on all dimensions simultaneously.

Cephalo-caudal principle. The theory that physical growth begins with the head and proceeds toward the lower part of the body. For example, infants acquire control over their heads before their legs.

Cervix. The opening of the uterus, which dilates during birth.

Cesarean birth. Delivery of the fetus by abdominal surgery instead of the normal vaginal route.

Child abuse. Any action against or neglect of a child that harms or threatens to harm the welfare of that child.

Childhood psychosis. A severe emotional disturbance in which a child loses or refuses contact with reality.

Childhood schizophrenia. A type of childhood psychosis characterized by withdrawal from the outside world, although such withdrawal is typically less severe than in infantile autism.

Chromosomes. Microscopic, rod-shaped particles composed of DNA (deoxyribonucleic acid) housed in the nucleus of all cells.

Classical conditioning. A type of learning in which the person or animal has an initial response (unconditioned response) to a given stimulus (unconditioned stimulus)—for example, Albert's fear of loud noises and his subsequent crying. The learner is later trained or learns to respond in the same way (conditioned response) to a different stimulus (conditioned stimulus), just as Albert learned to cry when he saw the white rat.

Class inclusion. Piaget's term for the realization that the sum of the subclasses equals the whole class.

Classification. Piaget's term for the grouping of objects into categories based on some common characteristic such as color or shape.

Clinical strategy. A technique in which different types of interview techniques are used to get individuals to talk about or act out ways they think, feel, and relate to their world.

Cliques. Peer groups consisting of three to eight members who consciously exclude others.

Cloning. A type of genetic experimentation in which a whole new organism is produced from just one cell of one parent.

Cognitive empathy. The use of information derived from research and theory to explain and predict the behavior of people in a particular situation.

Colostrum. The first food from the mother's breast; it has a laxative effect and contains antibodies.

Conception. The beginning of development when one sperm from the father penetrates one egg from the mother; also called **Fertilization.**

Concrete operational period. The third period of cognitive development (seven to eleven years) described by Piaget in which logical thinking abilities are limited to problems involving concrete or actual objects.

Conditioned response. Any reaction elicited by a conditioned stimulus. See **Classical conditioning.**

Conditioned stimulus. See **Classical conditioning.**

Conscience. See **Superego.**

Conservation. Piaget's term for the understanding that basic properties of objects (mass, number, etc.) stay the same (are conserved) even though their outward appearance changes.

Control group. A group treated like an experimental group in every way except for receiving the special treatment that is of interest to a researcher.

Conventional level. The second level of moral development described by Kohlberg; children's morality is rule-based and conventional with family, peers, and other social relations seen as highly important.

Convergence. The process in which both eyes turn slightly inward to see a near object.

Cooing. Prelanguage activity beginning at about two months; characterized by extended vowel sounds and vocal play.

Cooperative play. A type of preschool play. The child plays in groups organized for the purpose of attaining some common goal.

Corrective gene therapy. The use of technology to manipulate genes so that certain defects can be corrected.

Couvade. A custom observed in some cultures in which the husband shows some symptoms of pregnancy, goes into seclusion, or restricts activities during childbirth.

Crawling. Locomotor movement in which a baby's stomach remains on the floor.

Creeping. Locomotor movement in which a baby uses hands and knees to move about.

Cretinism. A thyroid disorder that produces physical and mental deficiencies.

Crib death. See **Sudden infant death syndrome.**

Critical period. A crucial time when environmental influences have their greatest effects on development.

Cross-sectional method. A research technique in which a number of different-aged children are studied at the same time.

Crowd. Loosely knit groups made up of several cliques.

Crowning. The time during the delivery process when the top of the baby's head becomes visible.

Decentration. Piaget's term for the ability concrete operational children have to consider several dimensions of objects or events.

Deductive reasoning. Reasoning from the general to the particular, as in "All humans have eyes. I am a human. Therefore I have eyes."

Deep structure. According to Chomsky's theory of transformational grammar, the basic meaning or idea a sentence conveys.

Deoxyribonucleic acid. See **Chromosome.**

Dependent variable. The characteristic or behavior that is being studied and is measured by the experimenter in a research study.

Deprivation dwarfism. Stunted growth resulting when a child's body reacts to emotional distress by switching off the growth hormone.

Developmental norms. Behavioral sequences that occur at common ages in children.

Dizygotic twins. See **Fraternal twins.**

DNA (deoxyribonucleic acid). See **Chromosome.**

Dominant gene. The outranking or controlling gene in a pair of genes, which normally determines the appearance of a trait.

Down's syndrome (mongolism). A birth defect resulting when the twenty-first pair of chromosomes contains an extra chromosome.

Dramatic play. A type of play in which children act out scenes from everyday life.

Early maturer. An adolescent who exhibits the physical changes of puberty at an early age.

Ego. Identified by Freud as the rational or reasoning part of the personality.

Egocentric speech. Piaget's term referring to preoperational children's practice of talking aloud to themselves without attempting to convey a message.

Egocentrism. Piaget's term referring to how children see things only from their own point of view and cannot take the point of view of others.

Elaborated code. A mode of speaking in which sentences tend to be long, grammatically complex, and precise.

Electra complex. According to Freud, a conflict around age four to five when the female child becomes attracted to her father and hostile to her mother.

Embryo. The second stage of prenatal development; occurs between two weeks and the end of the second month.

Emotional empathy. Actually feeling the same feelings that another person experiences.

Empathetic approach. Use of personal reactions and emotional and cognitive empathy to explain and predict behavior.

Episiotomy. An incision made during childbirth in the area between the vagina and rectum to allow for a quicker delivery and to eliminate the possible tearing of vaginal and periteneal tissues.

Equilibration. Piaget's term for the balance between assimilation and accommodation as an individual interacts with the environment.

Ethology. The study of the behavior of animals and humans in their natural environments.

Exceptional children. Children who are developmentally delayed or handicapped or who are developmentally advanced or gifted.

Experimental group. A group that receives special treatment of particular interest to a researcher in a research study.

External locus of control. The belief that fate, luck, or other people are in control of what happens to an individual.

Failure to thrive syndrome (FTTS). The failure of an infant to achieve normal physical growth rate, despite the absence of any neurological or physical abnormality.

Fallopian tube. The passageway between the uterus and ovary where fertilization normally occurs.

FAS. See **Fetal alcohol syndrome.**

Fertilization. See **Conception.**

Fetal alcohol syndrome (FAS). A condition afflicting the babies of many women who drink large amounts of alcohol during pregnancy.

Fetus. The third stage of prenatal development, between three months and birth.

Fine motor activity. Movements using the small muscles, usually the separate fingers and toes.

Fixed action patterns. Biologically determined behaviors commonly called instincts.

Fontanelles. Soft, connective tissue that covers depressions in the skull of the newborn.

Forceps delivery. Birth assisted by a double-pronged surgical instrument that eases the newborn from the birth canal.

Formal operational period. Fourth period of cognitive development (age eleven to adulthood) described by Piaget in which abstract, symbolic, and true scientific thought become possible.

Fraternal (dizygotic) twins. Two children who are the result of two eggs being fertilized by two sperm. Their heredity is as similar or different as that of any other brothers and sisters because they result from different zygotes.

FTTS. See **Failure to thrive syndrome.**

Gene. The segment of a chromosome that transmits hereditary traits.

General movements to specific movements principle. A growth principle stating that generalized physical movements develop before a specific, controlled physical movement.

Generation gap. Term referring to the differences in values held by members of different generations.

Genetic counselor. A specialist who determines a couple's chances of producing children with birth defects.

Gene type. See **Genotype.**

Genital stage. Identified by Freud, the fifth and last stage of psychosexual development (twelve to eighteen years) in which the focus returns to the sexual organs, usually in relation to members of the opposite sex.

Genotype (gene type). The inherited genetic pattern of an individual.

Gestation period. Development from conception to birth; for humans, it covers approximately 266 days or nine months.

Gifted children. Children who generally demonstrate superior performance in any notable endeavor.

Grammar. The set of rules that structures a language.

Gross motor activity. Movements using the large body muscles, usually arms and legs.

Habituation. The ability to get used to repeated stimuli or events so that little or no attention is paid to the stimuli.

Hallucinogens (psychedelics). Drugs that alter the physical sensations, emotions, and cognitive patterns of the individual.

Handedness. A preference for using one hand more often than the other.

Hemophilia (free bleeding). A disorder in which the blood does not clot properly; caused by an X-linked genetic defect.

Heredity. Genetic characteristics transmitted from parent to child.

Holophrases. One-word sentences used at about one year of age.

Home birthing center. A clinic with a homelike atmosphere where nurse midwives and obstetricians are on hand to assist as needed in the birth process.

Hurried child. A child who ''grows up'' too fast socially and psychologically.

Husband-coached childbirth (Bradley method). A childbirth method in which expectant parents attend classes to learn about nutrition, exercise, and physiology, and how to select childbirth services. Parents decide where and how childbirth will occur.

Hyperactivity. A behavior disorder characterized by difficulty in concentrating, high levels of motor activity, poor impulse control, and attention-seeking behavior.

Hypothesis. An explanation to be scientifically tested that is based upon theory and/or research.

Id. Identified by Freud as the inborn component of the human personality that contains basic instinctual drives and is pleasure seeking.

Identical (monozygotic) twins. Two children having exactly the same heredity. Results when one zygote splits into two identical zygotes.

Identification. Patterning behavior after that of another person. According to Freud, a characteristic of the phallic stage, in which children aged four to five resolve their Oedipus or Electra complexes by adopting the behavior of their same-sex parent.

Identity crisis. Erikson's term for a struggle for a sense of self and for an outlook on life that is acceptable to the individual and to society; typical of adolescence.

Identity versus role confusion. The fifth stage of psychosocial development (adolescence) described by Erikson. Successful resolution of the conflict results in finding answers to such questions as "Who am I?," Where am I going?," "What occupation will I choose?" Failure can result in confusion about one's role.

Imaginary audience. A kind of egocentrism typical of adolescents; the belief that "everyone is looking at me, I am always on stage."

Imitation. See **Observational learning.**

Imprinting. Instinctual, early learning that occurs during critical periods of development.

Impulsive children. Those children who tend to respond quickly with the first thought that comes to mind rather than deliberating carefully.

Independent variable. The characteristic that is systematically manipulated by the experimenter in a research study.

Inductive reasoning. Reasoning from the specific to the general, as in "These creatures all have wings and fly. Birds have wings and fly. Therefore these creatures are birds."

Industry versus inferiority. The fourth stage of psychosocial development (middle childhood) described by Erikson. Successful resolution of the conflict results in the child's becoming a competent and productive member of society; failure results in feelings of inadequacy and inferiority.

Infantile autism (autism). A type of childhood psychosis in which the child is totally withdrawn from the outside world and does not communicate meaningfully with others.

Initiative versus guilt. The third stage of psychosocial development (early childhood) described by Erikson. Successful resolution results in the child's being competent and initiating; failure results in feelings of guilt and over-controlling of "self" by some children.

Inner speech. Thinking in word meanings or using language as a tool for reasoning.

Instinct. See **Fixed action patterns.**

Intelligence quotient (IQ). An individual's mental age (MA) divided by his or her chronological age (CA) and multiplied by 100.

Internal locus of control. The belief that individuals are in control of what happens to them.

Invulnerable children. Youngsters reared under dire circumstances who somehow do remarkably well, despite their miserable early lives.

IQ. See **Intelligence quotient.**

Irreversible thought. Piaget's term for the inability of pre-operational children to reverse their thinking.

Jargon. Unintelligible jabber that sounds like actual conversation because of the intonations used; appears around twelve months and increases until about eighteen months.

Karyotype. A chart used to identify genetic defects. Consists of photographs of chromosomes arranged in pairs and numbered.

LAD. See **Language acquisition device.**

Lamaze prepared childbirth. A childbirth method involving preparation, limited medication, and active participation by both parents.

Language acquisition device (LAD). According to Chomsky, an inborn device that contains all the universal rules governing language behavior.

Language-deficit hypothesis. The belief that Black English is inferior or lacking some of the essential characteristics that exist in the language of middle-class white children.

Language-different hypothesis. The belief that Black English is not inferior to, but merely different from, the language of middle-class white children.

Language experience approach. Use of the child's own experiences and language as a basis for learning to read.

Lanugo. The fine downy hair covering the skin of the fetus at about six months after conception.

Late maturer. An adolescent who matures physically at a later age than most.

Latent stage. Identified by Freud, the fourth stage of psychosexual development (six to twelve years) in which the libido is not focused on any particular part of the body.

Laterality. The ability to discriminate between the left and right sides of the body and to prefer one side to another.

Lay midwife. Individuals who assist in delivering babies at home but have no formal medical training.

Learning disability. A disorder causing impaired ability to understand or use spoken or written language.

Leboyer childbirth. A gentle childbirth method designed to ease the baby's entry into the world.

Libido. Freud's term for the positive, loving, ''sexual'' impulses of the id.

Locomotor movement. The ability to move about.

Locus of control. The degree to which people accept responsibility for what happens to them.

Longitudinal comparisons. A research technique in which the same people are studied repeatedly over a period of several years.

Low-birth-weight. Refers to infants weighing less than five and a half pounds (2500 grams) at birth.

Mainstreaming. The placing of handicapped children in regular classrooms (the ''mainstream'') instead of special classrooms for the handicapped.

Masturbation. Act of stroking one's own sex organs in order to gain pleasure.

Maturation. Inherited patterns of growth that occur at about the same time in all people.

Meconium. The first stool of the neonate. Contains intestinal secretions, bile, mucus, and products of cellular breakdown that accumulate before birth.

Menarche. The first menstrual flow.

Metamemory. Thinking about how one remembers.

Modeling. See **Observational learning.**

Mongolism. See **Down's syndrome.**

Monozygotic twins. See **Identical twins.**

Moral development. The gradual internalization of society's standards for right and wrong, involving both moral judgments and behavior.

Myelin. A soft white substance that coats each nerve cell, insulating it and allowing messages to be transmitted from the brain to other parts of the body.

Narcotics. Addictive drugs that cause temporary feelings of relaxation and well-being. They include opium and opium derivations—morphine, codeine, and heroin.

Naturalistic observation. A research technique in which the observer records the behavior of an individual, noting in detail exactly what the individual is doing; observation takes place in the individual's natural setting.

Nature vs. nurture. Centuries-old controversy that focuses on whether biological factors (nature) or environmental factors (nurture) control human development.

Negative correlation. A relationship between variables; as one variable increases the other decreases.

Negative reinforcement. The removal or avoidance of an unpleasant stimulus that serves to increase the behavior it follows.

Neonate. The newborn baby during the first four weeks of life.

Nocturnal emission. Ejaculation of semen during sleep, which may or may not accompany an erotic dream.

Nurse midwife. A qualified nurse with special obstetrical training who delivers babies in problem-free births under the supervision of an obstetrician and also works with the family before and after delivery.

Object constancy. The ability to recognize that size, shape, or other attributes remain the same, even though they appear to change and the retinal image does change.

Object permanence (person permanence). The understanding that objects and people exist even though they cannot be seen.

Observational learning. The learner copies behavior that has been observed without receiving direct rewards or punishment; also called modeling or imitation.

Oedipus complex. According to Freud, a conflict around age four or five when the male child becomes attracted to his mother and hostile toward his father.

One-to-one correspondence. Piaget's term for the ability to match objects one to one.

Onlooker play. A type of preschool play. The child spends time watching others play, often asking questions and giving suggestions but seldom joining the actual play.

Operant conditioning. Type of learning in which the behavior of a person or animal is controlled by the consequences—negative or positive—of that behavior.

Oral stage. Identified by Freud, the first stage of psychosexual development (birth to two years) during which attention is focused on the mouth.

Ossification. The process that occurs when cartilage hardens into bone.

Ovulation. Expulsion of a single ovum (or sometimes more than one) from one of a woman's two ovaries around the fourteenth day of the menstrual cycle.

Ovum (plural, Ova). Female sex cell or egg; also the first stage of prenatal development, from conception to the second week.

Parallel play. A type of preschool play. The child plays independently but alongside other children.

Permissive parents. Parents who exercise practically no control over their children, allowing them to behave mostly as they please.

Personal reactions. Feeling (emotional "gut-level" reactions), thought (ideas, facts, and information), and behavior (actions taken in response to feelings, thoughts, and situations).

Phallic stage. Identified by Freud, the third stage of psychosexual development (four to five years), when the libido is focused on the genital area.

Phenotype (body type). The actual appearance of a genetic pattern in physical traits or behavior.

Phonics approach. A reading technique that emphasizes learning the sounds of letters, which thereby allows the child to "break the code" of the written word.

Piaget's clinical method. A technique in which questions are tailored to the individual and the investigator asks the next question based on the previous answer.

Placenta. A disk-shaped organ attached to the uterus through which the fetus receives nourishment and discharges waste.

Positive correlation. A relationship between variables; as one variable increases the other increases, or as one variable decreases the other decreases.

Positive reinforcement. Any consequence that is pleasurable to the subject and serves to increase the behavior it follows.

Postconventional level. The third level of moral development described by Kohlberg, in which morality consists of conforming to personally accepted and internalized universal principles.

Preconventional level. The first level of moral development described by Kohlberg, in which children conform to external standards and decisions are based on anticipated punishments and rewards.

Premature. Refers to infants born either preterm or of low birth weight.

Preoperational period. The second period of cognitive development (two to seven years) described by Piaget, in which symbolic representation characterizes the child's thought.

Preterm. Refers to infants having a gestation period of thirty-seven weeks or less instead of the usual forty full-term weeks.

Primary sex characteristics. The reproductive organs of the male (testes, penis, and seminal vesicles) and female (ovaries, fallopian tubes, uterus, and vagina).

Projective techniques. Clinical techniques in which ambiguous or unstructured situations (such as pictures or doll play) are used to encourage individuals to reveal feelings and thoughts.

Prosocial behaviors. Helping, sharing, and comforting abilities.

Proximo-distal principle. The principle that physical development begins along the innermost parts of the body and continues developing toward the outermost parts.

Psychedelics. See **Hallucinogens.**

Puberty. The period of adolescence marked by rapid growth spurt and sexual maturation.

Puberty rites. See **Rites of passage.**

Punishment. Any stimulus that serves to decrease the behavior it follows.

Random babbling. Prelanguage activity, beginning at about six months, characterized by erratic, unsystematic vowel, consonant, and vowel/consonant combinations.

Random sampling. A technique in which subjects selected from the whole group are selected in such a way that all members of the group have an equal chance of being chosen.

Rapid eye movement (REM) sleep. Irregular sleep state characterized by rapid fluttering of the eyeballs under closed eyes.

Recessive gene. The outranked gene in a pair of genes. A recessive gene will affect a trait only if it is paired with another recessive gene.

Reflective children. Children who tend to respond after careful deliberation rather than on impulse.

Reflexes. Automatic, inborn behaviors.

Reflexive smiling. The early smiles of newborns, which are reflexes associated with the infant's internal state rather than reactions to specific people.

Reinforcement. Any stimulus that increases the likelihood that a behavior will be repeated.

Reliability. The extent to which a test produces the same results for the same person on two or more occasions.

REM sleep. See **Rapid eye movement sleep.**

Restricted code. A mode of speaking in which sentences tend to be short, grammatically simple, and concerned with the present.

Reversibility. Piaget's term for the ability to reverse the thought process and return it to its original state.

RH factor. A blood component which can endanger the fetus when that of the mother is negative and that of the fetus is positive.

Rites of passage (puberty rites). Initiation ceremonies signifying transition from childhood to adulthood in many cultures.

Rooming in. Arrangements in some hospitals that allow the newborn to stay in the mother's hospital room instead of the nursery.

Running notes. A naturalistic observation technique in which a written, objective description of a behavior is made while actually observing the behavior.

Sample. A research procedure that allows investigations to learn about large groups of people by directly studying only some specially selected people.

Schemes. Piaget's term for the organized patterns of behavior that guide the way individuals act on and organize information.

School phobia. An extreme fear of going to school, which emerges more from fear of separation and abandonment from parents than from fear of scholastic failure.

Secondary sex characteristics. Those traits characteristic of the physically mature adult, which are evident on the body surface. They include breast development, pubic and underarm hair, increased activity of oil-producing glands, marked voice change, etc.

Secular trend. The tendency for today's children to grow taller and reach their adult height earlier than children who lived a century ago.

Secure attachment. A healthy sign of attachment shown, for example, by infants who are secure enough to venture away from the attachment figure without great distress.

Sedatives. Drugs such as barbiturates and tranquilizers that help reduce anxiety and excitement.

Selected attention. A response to some things while others are shut out, depending on the interests, needs, and abilities of the individual.

Self-actualization. The development of an individual's unique inner potential to its fullest.

Self-concept. How individuals view themselves.

Self-demand feeding schedule. Feeding a baby when the baby is hungry rather than on a rigid schedule of every so many hours.

Self-esteem. Judgments about self-worth.

Self-report measures. Research techniques such as interviews, questionnaires, and surveys in which individuals are asked to respond orally or in writing to carefully designed questions that encourage objective reporting of feelings, attitudes, perceptions, and behaviors.

Semantics. Those rules of grammar that determine the meanings of words.

Sensitive period. See **Critical period.**

Sensorimotor period. Piaget's term for the first period of cognitive development (birth to two years); involves the child's use of motor and sensory means to learn about the world.

Sensory linkages. Connections among the five senses, thought to be inborn.

Separation anxiety. The fear of being separated from a parent or loved one; closely tied to the development of object permanence.

Seriation. Piaget's term for the ability to order objects in a sequence or series along some dimension.

Serious offenses. Serious crimes such as theft, rape, vandalism, and murder.

Sex constancy. The understanding that being male or female is a permanent part of a person and does not change with alterations in hair, clothing, etc.

Sex-role identity. Understanding that the sexual classification of male or female carries certain behavioral requirements.

Sex-role stereotyping. The belief that it is only natural and fitting for males and females to adhere to traditional sex-role patterns.

Sex typing. Treating children differently because of their sex.

Short-term longitudinal comparisons. A research technique in which the same children are studied for short time spans (six to twelve months for example).

Sibling rivalry. Antagonism or resentment toward a brother or sister.

SIDS. See **Sudden infant death syndrome.**

Socialization. The process through which children learn to behave in ways considered acceptable by their society.

Social justice. A principle stating that all human beings are equal in value and that fairness in human relations is essential.

Social smiling. Smiles appearing between two and eight weeks of age directed toward human faces and voices.

Social speech. Piaget's term for communicative speech.

Sociobiology. The systematic study of the biological basis for all social behavior.

Sociogram. A diagram that plots the most and least preferred relationships in a group.

Solitary play. A type of preschool play in which the child plays alone with toys.

Sperm (spermatozoan; plural, spermatozoa). The male sex cell.

Standardized test. A test given to one large group of children to identify typical responses; the same test can then be given to similar groups whose scores are compared with the original group.

Status offenses. Delinquent crimes that do not cause harm to others (such as drinking and running away from home) and would not be considered crimes if the individual were an adult.

Stimulants. Drugs such as caffeine and amphetamines that increase alertness and activity.

Stranger anxiety. The crying and signs of distress shown by infants in the presence of newcomers.

Subsystem. A part of a larger system. See **System.**

Sudden infant death syndrome (SIDS). Also called crib death; this mysterious killer is the largest cause of death, for infants between one week and one year of age. Its cause is not yet known.

Superego. Identified by Freud as the personality component concerned with the rules of right and wrong learned primarily from and enforced by parents; typically called the conscience.

Surface structure. According to Chomsky's theory of transformational grammar, the way in which words are arranged to look, sound like, and be a sentence. See also **Deep structure.**

Sutures. Gaps running between the bones of the skull in the neonate.

Symbolic thought. Observed in Piaget's preoperational period; refers to the child's use of mental images to represent actions and objects.

Syntax. The rules of grammar that govern how words are combined to build phrases and sentences.

System. A set of parts (**Subsystems**) and the interactions or relationships among those parts.

Tabula rasa. The belief that an infant's mind is a blank slate, easily affected by environmental factors.

Telegraphic speech. Appearing around eighteen months, two-word telegram-like sentences that consist of only essential words.

Temperament. A person's unique style of interacting with others.

Teratogens. Environmental agents that disturb fetal development, such as disease, drugs, chemicals, and radiation.

Thanatos. Freud's term for the aggressive, destructive impulses of the id.

Theory. A group of general truths or principles that are related in an organized way and allow people to explain past and present behaviors and to predict future behaviors.

Time sampling technique. An observational research technique in which a behavior is recorded at regular intervals for a specified length of time.

Toxemia. A "poisoning" of unknown cause occurring in some pregnant women, which can endanger the life of both mother and infant.

Transductive reasoning. Reasoning from the particular to the particular, without considering the general, characteristic of young children. For example: "A dog has four legs and a tail. An elephant has four legs and a tail. Therefore an elephant is also a dog."

Transformation. Piaget's term for the process in which one state is changed to another; preoperational children are unable to follow transformations.

Transformational grammar. Chomsky's theory that every sentence has two different levels of syntax or structure—a surface structure and a deep structure.

Ultrasound. A special device responding to sound waves, which instantly transmits a visible outline of the fetus on a video screen; used to determine problems in fetal development.

Umbilical cord. A cord attached to the placenta and the fetus through which nourishment and wastes from the fetus are carried.

Unconditioned response. See **Classical conditioning.**

Unconditioned stimulus. See **Classical conditioning.**

Unoccupied behavior. A type of preschool play. The child is not actually playing but is occupied with anything that is of fleeting interest.

Validity. The extent to which a test measures what it is designed to measure.

Venereal disease (VD). Sexually transmitted disease such as gonorrhea, syphillis, and herpes simplex 2.

Vernix. A waxy, waterproof cream that coats the fetus during the last months of pregnancy. It is formed by oil secreted from the skin glands in combination with dead outer skin cells.

Vertex presentation. A normal presentation of the fetus at birth—head first and facing the mother's back.

Visually guided reach. Appearing at about five months, the infant's ability to keep the eyes on an object target and reach for it at the same time.

Weaning. The transition from breast- or bottle-feeding to eating solid foods and drinking from a cup.

Whole word approach. A reading technique that stresses the single, whole word as a focus of instruction.

X-linked genes. The genes found on the X (female) chromosome, which do not have a counterpart on the shorter Y (male) chromosomes.

Zygote. A one-celled organism formed when the sperm penetrates the ovum.

Bibliography

Abramovitch, R., Corter, C., and Lando, B. Sibling interaction in the home. *Child Development,* 1979, *50,* 997–1003.

Acord, L. T. One five-year-old-boy's use of play. *Maternal-Child Nursing Journal,* 1980, *9,* 29–35.

Ad Hoc Committee on the Effect of Trace Anesthetics on the Health of Operating Room Personnel, American Society of Anesthesiologists. Occupational disease among operating room personnel. *Anesthesiology,* 1974, *41,* 321–340.

Adelson, J. Adolescence and the generalization gap. *Psychology Today,* 1979, *12,* 33–37.

Adler, R. P. *Research on the effects of television advertising on children.* Washington, D.C.: National Science Foundation, 1978.

Ahlstrom, W. M., and Havinghurst, R. J. *400 losers.* San Francisco: Jossey-Bass, 1971.

Aho, M. L. Laughing with children. *Childhood Education,* 1979, *56,* 12–15.

Ainsworth, M. D. *Infancy in Uganda: Infant care and the growth of love.* Baltimore: Johns Hopkins Press, 1967.

Ainsworth, M. D. The development of infant-mother attachment. In B. M. Caldwell and H. M. Ricciuti (Eds.), *Review of child development research* (Vol. 3). Chicago: University of Chicago, 1973.

Ainsworth, M. D. Infant-mother attachment. *American Psychologist,* 1979, *34,* 932–937.

Ainsworth, M. D., Blehar, M. C., Waters, E., and Wall, S. *Patterns of attachment: A psychological study of the strange situation.* Hillsdale, N.J.: Erlbaum, 1978.

Albert, M. L., and Obler, L. K. *The bilingual brain.* New York: Academic Press, 1978.

Almy, M., Chittenden, E., and Miller, P. *Young children's thinking.* New York: Teacher's College Press, 1966.

Ambrose, J. A. The development of the smiling response in early infancy. In B. M. Foss (Ed.), *Determinants of infant behavior.* New York: Wiley, 1961, pp. 179–201.

Ambrosino, L. *Runaways.* Boston: Beacon Press, 1971.

American Academy of Pediatrics Committee Statement. The ten-state nutrition survey: A pediatric perspective. *Pediatrics,* 1973, *51,* 1095–1099.

American Academy of Pediatrics. Feeding the new baby: An update for new parents on current advice. *Changing Times,* 1980, *34,* 41–43.

American Psychological Association, Committee on Ethical Standards in Psychological Research. *Ethical principles in the conduct of research with human participants.* Washington, D.C.; Author, 1973.

Anastasi, A. *Psychological testing* (4th ed.). New York: MacMillan, 1976.

Anderson, C. W. Attachment in daily separations: Reconceptualizing day care and maternal employment issues. *Child Development,* 1980, *51,* 242–245.

Anglin, J. M. *The growth of word meaning.* Cambridge, Mass.: M.I.T. Press, 1970.

Anthony, E. J. A new scientific region to explore. In E. J. Anthony, C. Koupernik, and C. Chiland (Eds.), *The child and his family: Vulnerable children,* vol. 4. New York: Wiley, 1978.

Apgar, V. Proposal for a new method of evaluating the newborn infant. *Anesthesia and Analgesia,* 1953, *32,* 260–267.

Apgar, V., and Beck, J. *Is my baby all right? A guide to birth defects.* New York: Trident Press, 1972.

Arganian, M. Sex differences in early development. In J. C. Westman (Ed.), *Individual differences in children.* New York: Wiley, 1973.

Aries, P. *Centuries of childhood.* New York: Alfred Knopf, 1962.

Arms, S. *Immaculate deception: A new look at women and childbirth in America.* Boston: Houghton-Mifflin, 1975.

Aronfreed, T. *Conduct and conscience: The socialization of internalized control over behavior.* New York: Academic Press, 1968.

Aronson, E., and Rosenbloom, S. Space perception in early infancy: Perception within a common auditory-visual space. *Science,* 1971, *172,* 1161–1163.

Aslin, R. N. *Development of binocular fixation and convergent eye movements in human infants.* Paper presented at the meeting of the Association for Research in Vision and Ophthalmology, Sarasota, Fla. April 1976.

Atkinson, R. C., and Shiffrin, R. M. Human memory: A proposed system and its control processes. In K. W. Spence and J. T. Spence (Eds.), *The psychology of learning and motivation* (Vol. 2). New York: Academic Press, 1968.

Atkinson, R. C., and Shiffrin, R. M. The control of short-term memory. *Scientific American,* 1971, *225,* 82–90.

Ausubel, D. P. *Theory and problems of adolescent development.* New York: Grune and Stratton, 1954.

Ausubel, D. P., Sullivan, E. V., and Ives, S. W. *Theory and problems of child development* (3rd ed.). New York: Grune and Stratton, 1980.

Bachman, J. G. *Youth in transition (Vol. 2): The impact of family background and intelligence on tenth-grade boys.* Ann Arbor, Mich.: Survey Research Center, Institute for Social Research, 1970.

Baldwin, A. L. The effect of home environment on nursery school behavior. *Child Development,* 1949, *20,* 49–62.

Baldwin, W., and Cain, V. The children of teenage parents. *Family Planning Perspectives,* 1980, *12,* 34–43.

Bandura, A. The stormy decade: Fact or fiction? *Psychology in the School,* 1964, *1,* 224–231.

Bandura, A. The self system in reciprocal determinism. *American Psychologist,* 1978, *33,* 344–358.

Bandura, A., Grusec, J. E., and Menlove, F. Vicarious extinction of avoidance behavior. *Journal of Personality and Social Psychology,* 1967, *5,* 16–23.

Bandura, A., Ross, D., and Ross, S. A. Transmission of aggression through imitation of aggressive models. *Journal of Abnormal and Social Psychology,* 1961, *63,* 575–582.

Bandura, A., and Walters, R. H. *Adolescent aggression.* New York: Ronald Press, 1959.

Bankart, C., and Anderson, C. C. Short-term effects of prosocial television viewing on play of preschool boys and girls. *Psychological Reports,* 1979, *44,* 935–941.

Barahal, R. M. A comparison of parent-infant attachment and interaction patterns in day-care and non–day-care family groups. *Dissertation Abstracts International,* 1978, *38,* 5639.

Baratz, J. C. Language abilities of black Americans, review of research. In K. Miller and R. Dreger (Eds.), *Comparative studies of blacks and whites in the United States.* New York: Seminar Press, 1973.

Baratz, S. S., and Baratz, J. C. Early childhood intervention: The social science base of institutional racism. *Harvard Educational Review,* 1970, *40,* 29–50.

Barker, R. G., and Wright, H. F., *One boy's day: A specimen record of behavior.* New York: Harper and Row, 1951.

Barrera, M. E., and Maurer, D. Recognition of mother's photographed face by the three-month-old infant. *Child Development,* 1981, *52,* 714–716.

Barret, R. L., and Robinson, B. E. A descriptive study of unwed, expectant teenage fathers. *Family Relations: Journal of Applied Family and Child Studies,* 1982, *31,* in press.

Barron, F. Creative vision and expression in writing and painting. In D. W. MacKinnon (Ed.), *The creative person.* Berkeley: Institute of Personality Assessment Research, University of California, 1961.

Bartel, N. R. Locus of control and achievement in middle- and lower-class children. *Child Development,* 1971, *42,* 1099–1107.

Bartz, K. W., and Witcher, W. C. When father gets custody. *Children Today,* 1978, *7,* 2–6.

Baruch, G. K. Maternal influences upon college women's attitudes toward women and work. *Developmental Psychology,* 1972, *6,* 32–37.

Bateman, B. D. Visually handicapped children. In N. G. Haring and R. L. Schiefelbusch (Eds.), *Methods in special education.* New York: McGraw-Hill, 1967.

Baughman, E. E. *Black Americans: A psychological analysis.* New York: Academic Press, 1971.

Baum, B. Cesarean birth a joyous event for mom, dad. *The Charlotte Observer,* June 17, 1980.

Baumrind, D. Child care practices anteceding three patterns of preschool behavior. *Genetic Psychology Monographs,* 1967, *75,* 43–48.

Baumrind, D. Current patterns of parental authority. *Developmental Psychology Monographs*, 1971, *1*, 1–103.

Baumrind, D. Some thoughts about childrearing. In U. Bronfenbrenner (Ed.), *Influences on human development* (2nd ed.). Hillsdale, Ill.: Dryden, 1975.

Baumrind, D. New directions in socialization research. *American Psychologist*, 1980, *35*, 639–652.

Baumrind, D. Are androgynous individuals more effective persons and parents? *Child Development*, 1982, *53*, 44–75.

Bayh, B. *Runaway youth*. Washington, D.C.: U.S. Government Printing Office, 1973.

Bayley, N. The development of motor abilities during the first three years. *Society for Research in Child Development Monographs*, 1935, *1*, 1–26.

Bayley, N. Comparisons of mental and motor test scores for ages 1 to 15 months by sex, birth order, race, geographic location, and education of parents. *Child Development*, 1965, *36*, 379–412.

Beal, V. A. *Nutrition in the life span*. New York: Wiley, 1980.

Becker, R. D. Minimal brain dysfunction. *Journal of Learning Disabilities*, 1975, *8*, 429–431.

Beckwith, J. B. The Sudden Infant Death Syndrome (DHEW Publication No. HSA 77–5251). Rockville, Bureau of Community Health Services, 1978.

Beckwith, L., and Cohen, S. E. Preterm birth: Hazardous obstetrical and postnatal events as related to caregiver-infant behavior. *Infant Behavior and Development*, 1978, *1*, 403–411.

Bee, H. L., Van Egeren, L. F., Streissguth, A. P., Nyman, B. A., and Leckie, M. S. Social class differences in maternal teaching strategies and speech patterns. *Developmental Psychology*, 1969, *6*, 726–734.

Bell, A. P., and Weinberg, M. S. *Homosexualities: A study of diversity among men and women*. New York: Simon and Schuster, 1978.

Bell, R. Q. Relations between behavior manifestations in the human neonate. *Child Development*, 1960, *31*, 463–477.

Bell, R. Q. Parent, child, and reciprocal influences. *American Psychologist*, 1979, *34*, 821–826.

Bell, R. Q., and Harper, L. V. *Child effects on adults*. Hillsdale, N.J.: Erlbaum, 1977.

Bell, R. Q., Weller, G. M., and Waldrop, M. F. Newborn and preschooler: Organization of behavior and relations between periods. *Monographs of the Society for Research in Child Development*, 1971, *36* (4, Serial No. 142).

Bell, R. R. *Marriage and family interaction*. Homewood, Ill.: Dorsey Press, 1979.

Bell, S. M. The development of a concept of object as related to infant-mother attachment. *Child Development*, 1970, *41*, 291–311.

Beller, E. K. Early intervention programs. In J. D. Osofsky (Ed.), *Handbook of infant development*. New York: Wiley, 1979.

Bellugi, U. Learning the language. *Psychology Today*, 1970, *3*, 33–66.

Belmont, L., and Marolla, F. A. Birth order, family size and intelligence. *Science*, 1973, *182*, 1096–1101.

Belsky, J., and Steinberg, L. D. The effects of day care: A critical review. *Child Development*, 1978, *49*, 929–949.

Bem, S. L. The measurement of psychological androgyny. *Journal of Consulting and Clinical Psychology*, 1974, *42*, 155–162.

Bem, S. L., and Lenney, E. Sex-typing and the avoidance of cross-sex behavior. *Journal of Personality and Social Psychology*, 1976, *33*, 48–54.

Benedict, R. *Patterns of culture*. Boston: Houghton-Mifflin, 1934.

Berenda, R. W. *The influence of the group on the judgements of children*. New York: King's Crown Press, 1950.

Berezin, N. *The gentle birth book: A practical guide to Leboyer family-centered delivery*. New York: Simon and Schuster, 1980.

Berndt, T. J. Developmental changes in conformity to peers and parents. *Developmental Psychology*, 1979, *15*, 608–616.

Bernstein, B. A socio-linguistic approach to socialization with some references to educability. In J. J. Gumperz and D. Hymes (Eds.), *Direction in sociolinguistics*. New York: Holt, Rinehart and Winston, 1972.

Bettelheim, B. *Symbolic wounds*. New York: Free Press, 1954.

Bettelheim, B. *The children of the dream*. New York: Macmillan, 1969.

Bigge, J., and Sirvis, B. Children with physical and multiple disabilities. In N. G. Haring (Ed.), *Behavior of exceptional children* (2nd ed.). Columbus, Ohio: Charles E. Merrill, 1978.

Bixenstine, V. E., DeCorte, M. S., and Bixenstine, B. A. Conformity to peer-sponsored misconduct at four grade levels. *Developmental Psychology*, 1976, *12*, 226–236.

Blanchard, R. W., and Biller, H. B. Father availability and academic performance among third grade boys. *Developmental Psychology*, 1971, *4*, 301–305.

Bledsoe, C. The manipulation of Kpelle social fatherhood. *Ethnology*, 1980, *19*, 29–45.

Block, J. H., Haan, N., and Smith, M. B. Activism and apathy in contemporary adolescents. In J. F. Adams (Ed.), *Understanding adolescence: Current developments in adolescent psychology*. Boston: Allyn and Bacon, 1968, pp. 198–231.

Bloom, L. *Language development: Form and function in emerging grammars.* Cambridge, Mass.: M.I.T. Press, 1970.

Bloom, L. Why not pivot grammar? *Journal of Speech and Hearing Disorders,* 1971, *36,* 40–50.

Bloom, L. Language development review. In F. D. Horowitz (Ed.), *Review of child development research* (Vol. 4). Chicago: University of Chicago Press, 1975.

Bloom, L. Developmental change in the use of single-word utterances. In L. Bloom (Ed.), *Readings in language development.* New York: Wiley, 1978.

Bloom, L., Hood, L., and Lightbown, P. Imitation in language development: If, when, and why. *Cognitive Psychology,* 1974, *6,* 380–420.

Bluestein, N., and Acredolo, L. Developmental changes in map-reading skills. *Child Development,* 1979, *50,* 691–697.

Bohannan, P., and Erickson, R. Stepping in. *Psychology Today,* 1978, *11,* 53–59.

Borland, B. L. Hyperactive boys and their brothers. *Archives of General Psychiatry,* 1976, *33,* 669–675.

Bosma, J. F., and Showacre, J. Symposium on development of upper respiratory anatomy and function: Implications for Sudden Infant Death Syndrome. Superintendent of Documents, U.S. Government Printing Office, Washington, D.C.: Stock No. 617–046–000–33–1, 1971.

Boston Globe, Barbiturates next on hit list? March 30, 1977, p. 2.

Bottoms, S. F., Rosen, M. G., and Sokol, R. J. The increase in the cesarean birth rate. *New England Journal of Medicine,* 1980, *302,* 559–563.

Bould, S. Female-headed families: Personal fate control and the provider role. *Journal of Marriage and the Family,* 1977, *39,* 339–349.

Bowen, G. L. Death education with kindergarten–first grade groups. *Journal of Pediatric Psychology,* 1977, *2,* 77–78.

Bower, T. G. R. *A primer of infant development.* San Francisco: W. H. Freeman, 1977.

Bowerman, C. E., and Irish, D. P. Some relationships of stepchildren to their parents. *Marriage and Family Living,* 1962, *24,* 113–121.

Bowerman, M. *Early syntactic development: A cross-linguistic study with special reference to Finnish.* London: Cambridge University Press, 1973.

Bowes, W. A., Jr., Brackbill, Y., Conway, E., and Steinschneider, A., The effects of obstetrical medication on fetus and infant. *Monographs of the Society for Research in Child Development,* 1970, *35* (4, Serial No. 137).

Bowlby, J. The nature of the child's tie to his mother. *International Journal of Psychoanalysis,* 1958, *39,* 350–373.

Bowlby, J. Separation anxiety. *International Journal of Psychoanalysis,* 1960, *41,* 89–113.

Bowlby, J. *Attachment and loss: Attachment* (Vol. 1). New York: Basic Books, 1969.

Bowley, A. H. *The natural development of the child.* London: Livingstone, 1963.

Brackbill, Y. Acoustic variation and arousal level in infants. *Psychophysiology,* 1970, *6,* 517–526.

Brackbill, Y. Obstetrical medication and infant behavior. In J. Osofsky (Ed.), *The handbook of infant development.* New York: Wiley, 1979.

Bradbard, M., and Endsley, R. The importance of educating parents to be discriminating day-care consumers. In *Advances in early education and day care* (Vol I). Greenwich, Conn.: JAI Press, 1979.

Braine, M. D. S. Children's first word combinations. *Monographs of the Society for Research in Child Development,* 1976, *41* (1, Serial No. 164).

Brazelton, T. B. *Infants and mothers.* New York, Delta, 1969.

Brazelton, T. B. Implications of infant development among the Mayan Indians of Mexico. *Human Development,* 1972, *15,* 90–111.

Brazelton, T. B. *Neonatal behavioral assessment scale.* Philadelphia: Lippincott, 1973.

Brazelton, T. B. *Toddlers and parents: A declaration of independence.* New York: Delacorte Press, 1974.

Brazelton, T. B. How to tame the TV monster: A pediatrician's advice. In E. Kaye (Ed.), *How to treat TV with TLC: The ACT guide of children's television.* Boston: Beacon Press, 1979.

Brazelton, T. B., Koslowski, B., and Tronick, E. Neonatal behavior among urban Zambians and Americans. *Journal of the American Academy of Child Psychiatry,* 1976, *15,* 97–107.

Breckenridge, M. E., and Murphy, M. N. *Growth and development of the young child.* Philadelphia: W. B. Saunders, 1969.

Breckenridge, M. E., and Vincent, E. L. *Child development* (5th ed.). Philadelphia: W. B. Saunders, 1965.

Bridges, K. Emotional development in early infancy. *Child Development,* 1932, *3,* 324–341.

Broderick, C. B. Socio-sexual development in a suburban community. *The Journal of Sex Research,* 1966, *2,* 1–24.

Brody, S. Daddy's gone to Colorado: Male-staffed child care for father-absent boys. *The Counseling Psychologist,* 1978, *7,* 33–36.

Bronfenbrenner, U. Developmental research, public policy, and the ecology of childhood. *Child Development,* 1974, *45,* 1–5.(a)

Bronfenbrenner, U. *Is early intervention effective: A report on longitudinal evaluation and pre-school programs,* vol. 2. Washington, D.C.: Office of Child Development, U.S. Department of HEW, 1974. (b)

Bronfenbrenner, U. The origins of alienation. *Scientific American*, 1974, *231*, 53–61. (c)

Bronfenbrenner, U. Is 80% of intelligence genetically determined? In U. Bronfenbrenner and M. A. Mahoney (Eds.), *Influences on Human Development* (2nd ed.). Hinsdale, Ill.: Dryden Press, 1975.

Bronfenbrenner, U. Ecological factors in human development in retrospect and prospect. In H. McGurk (Ed.), *Ecological factors in human development*. Amsterdam: North-Holland Publishing, 1977. (a)

Bronfenbrenner, U. Nobody home: The erosion of the American family. *Psychology Today*, 1977, *10*, 40. (b)

Bronfenbrenner, U. Another world of children. In *Readings in human development 78/79*. Guilford, Conn.: Dushkin, 1978, pp. 291–297.

Bronfenbrenner, U. *The ecology of human development*. Cambridge, Mass.: Harvard University Press, 1979.

Brown, C. J. Reactions of infants to their parents' voices. *Infant Behavior and Development*, 1979, *2*, 295–300.

Brown, J. K. A cross-cultural study of female initiation rites. *American Anthropologist*, 1963, *65*, 837–853.

Brown, R. Linguistic determinism and the part of speech. *Journal of Abnormal and Social Psychology*, 1957, *55*, 1–5.

Brown, R. *A first language: The early stages*. Cambridge, Mass.: Harvard University Press, 1973.

Brown, R., and Bellugi, U. Three processes in the child's acquisition of syntax. In E. H. Lenneberg (Ed.), *New directions in the study of language*. Cambridge, Mass.: M.I.T. Press, 1964.

Brown, R., and Hanlon, C. Derivation complexity and order of acquisition in child speech. In J. Hayes (Ed.), *Cognition and the development of language*. New York: Wiley, 1970.

Browne, G. Y., Rosenfield, H. M., and Horowitz, F. D. Infant discrimination of facial expressions. *Child Development*, 1977, *48*, 555–562.

Bryan, J. H. Children's cooperation and helping behaviors. In E. M. Hetherington (Ed.), *Review of child development research* (Vol 5). Chicago: University of Chicago Press, 1975.

Burke, P. M. Swallowing and the organization of sucking in the human newborn. *Child Development*, 1977, *48*, 523–531.

Burr, W. R. Satisfaction with various aspects of marriage over the life cycle: A random middle class sample. *Journal of Marriage and the Family*, 1970, *32*, 29–37.

Butler, A. L., Gotts, E. E., and Quisenberry, N. L. *Play as development*. Columbus, Ohio: Charles E. Merrill, 1978.

Caldwell, B. M., Wright, C. M., Honig, A. S., and Tannenbaum, J. Infant day care and attachment. *American Journal of Orthopsychiatry*, 1970, *40*, 397–412.

Calhoun, G., Sheldon, S. R., Serran, R., and Cooke, D. An ethnic comparison of self-esteem in Portuguese-Mexican and Anglo-American pupils. *Journal of Psychology*, 1978, *98*, 11–14.

Caliendo, M. A., Sanjur, D., Wright, J., and Cummings, G. Nutritional status of preschool children. *Journal of the American Dietetic Association*, 1977, *71*, 20–25.

Campbell, J. D. Peer relations in childhood. In M. Hoffman and L. Hoffman (Eds.), *Review of child development research*. New York: Russell Sage, 1964.

Cannon-Bonventre, K., and Kahn, J. R. *The ecology of help-seeking behavior among adolescent parents*. Cambridge, Mass.: American Institute for Research, 1979.

Cantor, D. W. School-based groups for children of divorce. *Journal of Divorce*, 1977, *1*, 183–187.

Cantor, P. Suicide and attempted suicide among students: Problem, prediction and prevention. In P. Cantor (Ed.), *Understanding a child's world*. New York: McGraw-Hill, 1977.

Caplan, F. *The first twelve months of life*. New York: Grosset and Dunlap, 1973.

Carter, D., and Welch, D. Parenting styles and children's behavior. *Family Relations: Journal of Applied Family and Child Studies*, 1981, *30*, 191–195.

Cattell, P. *The measurement of intelligence of infants and young children*. New York: The Psychological Corporation, 1947.

Chacon, M. A., and Tildon, J. T. Elevated values of tri-iodothyronine in victims of Sudden Infant Death Syndrome. *Journal of Pediatrics*, 1981, *99*, 758–760.

Chamberlain, T. Teen drinking—rampant and reckless. *Boston Globe*, October 13, 1978.

Chambers, J. A. A multidimensional theory of creativity. *Psychological Reports*, 1969, *25*, 779–799.

Chambliss, J., Muller, D., Hulnick, R., and Wood, M. Relationship between self-concept, self-esteem, popularity, and social judgements of junior high school students. *Journal of Psychology*, 1978, *98*, 91–98.

Chandler, T. A., Wolf, F. M., Cook, B., and Dugovics, D. A. Parental correlates of locus of control in fifth graders: An attempt at experimentation in the home. *Merrill-Palmer Quarterly*, 1980, *26*, 183–195.

Charbonneau, C., Robert, M., Bourassa, G., and Gladu-Bissonette, S. Observational learning of quantity conservation and Piagetian generalization tasks. *Developmental Psychology*, 1976, *12*, 211–217.

Chilman, C. S. *Adolescent sexuality in a changing American society*. Bethesda, Maryland: U.S. Department of Health, Education, and Welfare, 1978.

Chisholm, J. S. Swaddling, cradleboards, and the development of children. *Early Human Development*, 1978, *2*, 255–275.

Chomsky, C. *The acquisition of syntax from 5 to 10*. Cambridge, Mass.: M.I.T. Press, 1969.

Chomsky, N. *Syntactic structures*. The Hague: Mouton, 1957.

Chomsky, N. *Aspects of a theory of syntax*. Cambridge, Mass.: M.I.T. Press, 1965.

Chomsky, N. Stages of language development and reading exposure. *Harvard Educational Review*, 1972, *42*, 1–33.

Christensen, C., Frederickson, C., and McNeil, J. Language, motor, and socioemotional development from 12 to 30 months. Unpublished manuscript. Institute for Family and Child Study, Michigan State University, 1978.

Clark, A. E., and Ruble, D. N. Young adolescents' beliefs concerning menstruation. *Child Development*, 1978, *49*, 231–235.

Clark, B. *Growing up gifted*. Columbus, Ohio: Charles E. Merrill, 1979.

Clark, H. H., and Clark, E. V. *Psychology and language: An introduction to psycholinguistics*. New York: Harcourt Brace Jovanovich, 1977.

Clark, K. B. *Prejudice and your child*. Boston: Beacon Press, 1955.

Clark, K. B. Empathy: A neglected topic in psychological research. *American Psychologist*, 1980, *35*, 187–190.

Clarke-Stewart, K. A. And daddy makes three. *Child Development*, 1978, *49*, 466–478.

Clay, M. M. Exploring with a pencil. *Theory into Practice*, 1977, *16*, 334–341.

Clifton, C. Language acquisition. In T. D. Spencer and N. Kass (Eds.), *Perspectives in child psychology*. New York: McGraw-Hill, 1970.

Clore, G. L., Bray, R. M., Itkin, S. M., and Murphy, P. Interracial attitudes and behavior at a summer camp. *Journal of Personality and Social Psychology*, 1978, *36*, 107–116.

Coates, B., Anderson, E. P., and Hartup, W. W. Interrelations in the attachment behavior of human infants. *Developmental Psychology*, 1972, *6*, 218–230.

Cofer, L. K., Stein, A., Kipnis, D., Susman, E. J., and Clewett, A. S. Environmental enhancement of prosocial television content: Effects on interpersonal behavior, imaginative play, and self-regulation in a natural setting. *Developmental Psychology*, 1979, *15*, 637–646.

Cohen, L., and Campos, J. Father, mother, and strangers as elicitors of attachment behaviors in infancy. *Developmental Psychology*, 1974, *10*, 146–154.

Cohen, L. B., DeLoache, J. S., and Strauss, M. S. Infant visual perception. In J. D. Osofsky (Ed.), *Handbook of infant development*. New York: Wiley, 1979.

Cohen, S., Evans, G. W., Krantz, D. S., and Stokols, D. Physiological, motivational, and cognitive effects of aircraft noise on children: Moving from the laboratory to the field. *American Psychologist*, 1980, *35*, 231–243.

Cohen, S., and Przybycien, C. A. Some effects of sociometrically selected peer models on the cognitive styles of impulsive children. *Journal of Genetic Psychology*, 1975, *124*, 213–220.

Coleman, J. C. *Relationships in adolescence*. Boston: Routledge and Kegan Paul, 1974.

Commitee on Adolescence of the American Academy of Pediatrics. Teenage suicide. *Pediatrics*, 1980, *66*, 144–146.

Condon, W. S., and Sander, L. W. Neonate movement is synchronized with adult speech: Interactional participation and language acquisition. *Science*, 1974, *183*, 99–101.

Condry, J., and Condry, S. Sex differences: A study of the eye of the beholder. *Child Development*, 1976, *47*, 812–819.

Conger, J. J. A world they never knew: The family and social change. *Daedalus*, 1971, *1*, 1105–1138.

Conger, J. J. *Adolescence and youth: Psychological development in a changing world* (2nd ed.), New York: Harper and Row, 1977.

Constanzo, P. R., and Shaw, M. E. Conformity as a function of age level. *Child Development*, 1966, *37*, 967–975.

Cook, J. V., and Bowles, R. T. *Child abuse*. Ontario, Canada: Butterworths, 1980.

Coopersmith, S. *The antecedents of self-esteem*. San Francisco: W. H. Freeman, 1967.

Cordell, A. S., Parke, R. D., and Sawin, D. B. Fathers' views on fatherhood with special reference to infancy. *Family Relations: Journal of Applied Family and Child Studies*, 1980, *29*, 331–338.

Cordua, G. D., McGraw, K. O., and Drabman, R. S. Doctor or nurse: Children's perception of sex-typed occupations. *Child Development*, 1979, *50*, 590–593.

Corter, C. The nature of the mother's absence and the infant's response to brief separation. *Developmental Psychology*, 1976, *12*, 428–434.

Corter, C., Trehub, S., Boukydis, C., Ford, L., Celhoffer, L., and Minde, K. Nurses' judgements of the attractiveness of premature infants. *Infant Behavior and Development*, 1978, *1*, 373–380.

Cottle, T. J. Adolescent voices. *Psychology Today,* 1979, *12,* 40–44.

Craig, K. E. Gainful employment for women: The facts. *Journal of Home Economics,* 1977, *69,* 23–25.

Crain, W. C. *Theories of development: Concepts and applications.* Englewood Cliffs, N.J.: Prentice-Hall, 1980.

Crase, D. R., and Crase, D. Helping children understand death. *Young Children,* 1976, *32,* 20–25.

Crase, D. R., and Crase D. Onlies are o.k. *Childhood Education,* 1979, *56,* 97–99.

Cratty, B. J. *Perceptual and motor development in infants and children.* New York: Macmillan, 1970.

Crinella, F. M., Beck, F. W., and Robinson, J. W. Unilateral dominance is not related to neuropsychological integrity. *Child Development,* 1971, *42,* 2033–2045.

Crook, C. K. Taste perception in the newborn infant. *Infant Behavior and Development,* 1978, *1,* 52–69.

Crook, C. K., and Lipsitt, L. P. Neonatal nutritive sucking: Effects of taste stimulation upon sucking rhythm and heart rate. *Child Development,* 1976, *47,* 518–522.

Cryan, J. R., and Surbeck, E. *Early childhood education: Foundations for lifelong learning.* Bloomington, Ind.: Phi Delta Kappa Educational Foundation, 1979.

Csermely, H. Perinatal anoxic changes in the central nervous system. *Acta Paediatrica Academiae Scientiarum Hungaricae,* 1972, *13,* 283–299.

Cummings, E. M. Caregiver stability and day care. *Developmental Psychology,* 1980, *16,* 31–37.

Dacey, J. S. *Adolescents today.* Santa Monica, Calif.: Goodyear, 1979.

Dale, P. S. *Language development: Structure and function* (2nd ed.). New York: Holt, Rinehart and Winston, 1976.

Damico, S. B. The effects of clique membership upon academic achievement. *Adolescence,* 1975, *10,* 93–100.

Davids, A., DeVault, S., and Talmadge, M. Anxiety, pregnancy, and childbirth abnormalities. *Journal of Consulting Psychology,* 1961, *25,* 74–77.

Dawkins, R. *The selfish gene.* New York: Oxford University Press, 1976.

Deal, A. W., and Bordeaux, B. R. The phenomenon of SIDS. *Pediatric Nursing,* 1980, *5,* 48–50.

DeCasper, A. J., and Fifer, W. P. Of human bonding: Newborns prefer their mothers' voices. *Science,* 1980, *208,* 1174–1176.

DeChant, E. *Improving the teaching of reading* (2nd ed.). Englewood Cliffs, N.J.: Prentice-Hall, 1970.

DeFrain, J. Androgynous parents tell who they are and what they need. *The Family Coordinator,* 1979, *28,* 237–243.

DeFries, J. C., and Plomin, R. Behavioral genetics. *Annual Review of Psychology,* 1978, *29,* 473–515.

DeLoache, J. S., Rissman, M. W., Cohen, L. R. An investigation of the attention-getting process in infants. *Infant Behavior and Development,* 1978, *1,* 11–25.

DeMause, L. *The history of childhood.* New York: The Psychohistory Press, 1974.

DeMott, R. M. The visually handicapped. In N. C. Haring (Ed.), *Behavior of exceptional children* (2nd ed.). Columbus, Ohio: Charles E. Merrill, 1978.

Dennis, W. The effect of cradling practices upon the onset of walking in Hopi children. *Journal of Genetic Psychology,* 1940, *56,* 77–86.

Derbyshire, R. L. Adolescent identity crisis in urban Mexican Americans in East Los Angeles. In E. B. Brody (Ed.), *Minority group adolescents in the United States.* Baltimore: Williams and Wilkins, 1968.

Derdiarian, J., and Snipper, A. *Effects of maternal employment and sex-role orientation, behavior, and attitudes.* Paper presented at the Society for Research in Child Development, San Francisco, April 1979.

Deutsch, M. The role of social class in language development and cognition. *American Journal of Orthopsychiatry,* 1965, *25,* 75–88.

deVilliers, J. G., and deVilliers, P. A. *Language acquisition.* Cambridge, Mass.: Harvard University Press, 1978.

deVries, M. *East African toilet training readiness.* Paper presented at the Society for Research in Child Development, New Orleans, March 1977.

Dickson, S. Incipient stuttering symptoms and spontaneous remission of stuttered speech. *ASHA,* 1965, *10,* 371 (abstract). Cited in M. E. Wingate, *Stuttering: Theory and treatment.* New York: Wiley, 1976.

Dishotsky, N. I., Loughman, W. D., Mogar, R. E., and Lipscomb, W. R. LSD and genetic damage. *Science,* 1971, *172,* 431–440.

Douvan, E. A., and Adelson, J. *The adolescent experience.* New York, Wiley, 1966.

Drabman, R. S., Cordua, G. D., Hammer, D., Jarvie, G. J., and Horton, W. Developmental trends in eating rates of normal and overweight preschool children. *Child Development,* 1979, *50,* 211–216.

Dreyer, P. H. Sex, sex roles, and marriage among youth in the 1970s. In R. J. Havinghurst and P. H. Dreyer (Eds.), *Youth: The seventy-fourth yearbook of the National Society for the Study of Education.* Chicago: University of Chicago Press, 1975, pp. 194–233.

Drillien, C. M. Prevention of handicap in infants of very low birth weight. In D. A. A. Primrose (Ed.), *Proceedings of the Third Congress of the International Association for the Scientific Study of Mental Deficiency.* Warsaw: Polish Medical, 1975.

Drive to open up more careers for women. *U.S. News and World Report,* January 14, 1974, *76,* 69–70.

Duberman, L. Step-kin relationships. *Journal of Marriage and the Family,* 1973, *35,* 283, 292.

Dubnoff, S. J., Veroff, J., and Kulka, R. A. *Adjustment to work: 1957–1976.* Paper presented at the meeting of the American Psychological Association, Toronto, Canada, August 1978.

Duff, R. S. Care in childbirth and beyond. *The New England Journal of Medicine,* 1980, *302,* 685–686.

Dunn, J., and Kendrick, C. The arrival of a sibling: Changes in interaction between mother and firstborn child. *Journal of Child Psychology and Psychiatry,* 1980, *21,* 119–132.

Dunphy, D. C. The social structure of urban adolescent peer groups. *Sociometry,* 1963, *26,* 230–246.

Dunphy, D. C. Peer group socialization. In F. J. Hunt (Ed.), *Socialization in Australia.* Sydney: Angus and Robertson, 1972, pp. 200–217.

Dye, L. L. Youth as a national resource. *Children Today,* 1979, *8,* 2–5.

Earls, F., and Siegel, B. Precocious fathers. *American Journal of Orthopsychiatry,* 1980, *50,* 469–480.

Easterbrooks, M. A., and Lamb, M. E. The relationship between quality of infant-mother attachment and infant competence in initial encounters with peers. *Child Development,* 1980, *50,* 380–387.

Eckerman, C. O., Whatley, J. L., and Kutz, S. L. Growth of social play with peers during the second year of life. *Developmental Psychology,* 1975, *11,* 42–49.

Edwards, U. N. Check with mother: Did she take DES? *Today's Child,* 1980, *28,* 6.

Egeland, B., and Vaughn, B. Failure of "bond formation" as a cause of abuse, neglect, and maltreatment. *American Journal of Orthopsychiatry,* 1981, *51,* 78–84.

Ehrlich, P. R., Holm, R. W., and Brown, I. L. *Biology and society.* New York: McGraw-Hill, 1976.

Eichorn, D. H. Physical development: Current foci of research. In J. D. Osofsky (Ed.), *Handbook of infant development.* New York: Wiley, 1979.

Eisenstadt, J. M. Parental loss and genius. *American Psychologist,* 1978, *33,* 211–223.

Elardo, R., Bradley, R., and Caldwell, B. M. A longitudinal study of the relation of infants' home environments to language development at age three. *Child Development,* 1977, *48,* 595–603.

Elkind, D. *A sympathetic understanding of the child 6 to 16.* Boston: Allyn and Bacon, 1971.

Elkind, D. *Child development and education: A Piagetian perspective.* New York: Oxford University Press, 1976.

Elkind, D. Understanding the young adolescent. *Adolescence,* 1978, *13,* 127–134.

Elkind, D. Growing up faster. *Psychology Today,* 1979, *12,* 38–45.

Elkind, D. *The hurried child: Growing up too fast too soon.* Reading, Mass.: Addison-Wesley, 1981.

Elkind, D., Koegler, R. R., and Koegler, E. G. Studies in perceptual development: II. Part-whole perception. *Child Development,* 1964, *35,* 81–90.

Emde, R. N., Campos, J., Reich, J., and Gaensbauer, T. J. Infant smiling at five and nine months: Analysis of heartrate and movement. *Infant Behavior and Development,* 1978, *1,* 26–35.

Emde, R., Gaensbauer, T., and Harmon, R. Emotional expression in infancy: A biobehavioral study. *Psychological Issues Monograph Series,* 1976, *10,* (Monograph No. 37).

Emmerich, W., Goldman, K. S., Kirsh, B., and Sharabany, R. *Development of gender constancy in economically disadvantaged children.* Report of the Educational Testing Service, Princeton, N.J., 1976.

Endsley, R. C., and Bradbard, M. R. *The wise guide to quality day care: A guide for parents and students.* New York: Spectrum Books, 1981.

Engen, T., Lipsitt, L. P., and Peck, M. B. Ability of newborn infants to discriminate sapid substances. *Developmental Psychology,* 1974, *10,* 741–744.

Engen, T., Lipsitt, L. P., and Robinson, D. O. The human newborn's sucking behavior for sweet fluid as a function of birthweight and maternal weight. *Infant Behavior and Development,* 1978, *1,* 118–121.

Erikson, E. H. *Group processes: Transactions of the second conference.* New York: Josiah Macy Foundation, 1956.

Erikson, E. H. Growth and crises of the healthy personality. *Psychological Issues,* 1959, *1,* 50–100. (a)

Erikson, E. H. *Identity and the life cycle: Selected papers.* Psychological Issues Monograph Series I., No. 1. New York: International Universities Press, 1959. (b)

Erikson, E. H. *Childhood and society* (2nd ed.). New York: Norton, 1963.

Erikson, E. H. *Identity, youth and crisis.* New York: Norton, 1968.

Erikson, E. H. Autobiographic notes on identity crisis. *Daedalus,* 1970, *99,* 730–759.

Erikson, E. H. *Dimensions of a new identity.* New York: Norton, 1974.

Erlenmeyer-Kimling, L. Vulnerability research: A behavior genetics point of view. In E. J. Anthony, C. Koupernik, and C. Chiland (Eds.), *The child and his family: Vulnerable children* (Vol. 4). New York: Wiley, 1978.

Erlenmeyer-Kimling, L., and Jarvik, L. F. Genetics and intelligence: A review. *Science,* 1963, *142,* 1979.

Ervin, S. M. Imitation and structural change in children's language. In E. H. Lenneberg (Ed.), *New directions in the study of language.* Cambridge, Mass.: M.I.T. Press, 1964.

Etzel, B. C., and Gewirtz, J. L. Experimental modification of caretaker-maintained high rate operant crying in a 6- and a 20-week-old infant: Extinction of crying with reinforcement of eye contact and smiling. *Journal of Experimental Child Psychology,* 1967, *5,* 303–317.

Fagan, J. F., and Shepherd, P. A. Infants' perception of face orientation. *Infant Behavior and Development,* 1979, *2,* 227–234.

Fagot, B. I. Sex differences in toddler's behavior and parental reaction. *Developmental Psychology,* 1974, *10,* 554–558.

Fagot, B. I., and Patterson, G. R. An in vivo analysis of reinforcing contingencies for sex-role behaviors in the preschool child. *Developmental Psychology,* 1969, *1,* 563–568.

Fantz, R. L. The origin of form perception. *Scientific American,* 1961, *204,* 66–72.

Fantz, R. L. Visual perception and experience in early infancy: A look at the hidden side of behavioral development. In H. Stevenson, E. Hess, and H. Rheingold (Eds.), *Early behavior: Comparative and developmental approaches.* New York: Wiley, 1967.

Fantz, R. L., and Nevis, S. Pattern preferences and perceptual-cognitive development in early infancy. *Merrill-Palmer Quarterly,* 1967, *13,* 88–108.

Farran, D. C., and Ramey, C. T. Infant day care and attachment. *Child Development,* 1977, *48,* 1112–1116.

Farris, C. E. A White House conference on the American Indian. *Social Work,* 1973, *18,* 80–86.

Faust, M. S. Somatic development of adolescent girls. *Monographs of the Society for Research in Child Development,* 1977, *42* (1, Serial No. 169).

Favorito, J., Pernice, J., and Ruggiero, P. Apnea monitoring to prevent SIDS. *American Journal of Nursing,* 1979, *79,* 101–104.

Fein, G. G. Pretend play: New perspectives. *Young Children,* 1979, *34,* 61–66.

Fein, G. G., and Apfel, N. Some preliminary observations on knowing and pretending. In N. Smith and M. B. Franklin (Eds.), *Symbolic functioning in childhood.* Hillsdale, N.J.: Erlbaum, 1979.

Feingold, B. F. *Why your child is hyperactive.* New York: Random, 1975.

Feingold, B. F. Hyperkinesis and learning disabilities linked to the ingestion of artificial food colors and flavors. *Journal of Learning Disabilities,* 1976, *9,* 551–559.

Feitelson, D. *Mother tongue or second language?* Newark, Delaware: International Reading Association, 1979.

Fenson, L., Kagan, J., Kearsley, R., and Zelazo, P. The developmental progression of manipulative play in the first two years. *Child Development,* 1976, *47,* 232–236.

Feshbach, N. D., Dillman, A. S., and Jordan, T. S. Children and television advertising: Some research and some perspectives. *Journal of Clinical Child Psychology,* 1979, *8,* 26–30.

Feshbach, S., and Singer, R. D. *Television and aggression: An experimental field study.* San Francisco: Jossey-Bass, 1971.

Field, J. Relation of young infants' reaching behavior to stimulus distance and solidity. *Developmental Psychology,* 1976, *12,* 444–448.

Field, J., Muir, D., Pilon, R., Sinclair, M., and Dodwell, P. Infants' orientation to lateral sounds from birth to three months. *Child Development,* 1980, *51,* 295–298.

Field, T., Dempsey, J. R., and Shuman, H. H. Developmental assessment of infants surviving the respiratory distress syndrome. In T. Field, A. Sostek, S. Goldberg, and H. Shuman (Eds.), *Infants born at risk.* New York: Spectrum, 1979.

Field, T., Widmayer, S. M., Stringer, S., and Ignatoff, E. Teenage, lower-class black mothers and their preterm infants: An intervention and developmental follow-up. *Child Development,* 1980, *51,* 426–436.

Fine, M. J. (Ed.). *Principles and techniques of intervention with hyperactive children.* Springfield, Ill.: Charles C. Thomas, 1977.

Finkel, M., and Finkel, D. Male adolescent contraceptive utilization. *Adolescence,* 1978, *13,* 443–451.

Finkelstein, N. W., Dent, C., Gallacher, K., and Ramey, C. T. Social behavior of infants and toddlers in a day-care environment. *Developmental Psychology,* 1978, *14,* 257–262.

Fisher, S., and Fisher, R. L. *Pretend the world is funny and forever: A psychological analysis of comedians, clowns, and actors.* New York: Lawrence Erlbaum, 1981.

Flaste, R. Scientists wonder what's on a baby's mind. *New York Times,* August 27, 1976.

Flavell, J. H. *Cognitive development.* Englewood Cliffs, N.J.: Prentice-Hall, 1977.

Flavell, J. H. Metacognition and cognitive monitoring: A new area of cognitive-developmental inquiry. *American Psychologist,* 1979, *34,* 906–911.

Flesch, R. *Why Johnny can't read and what you can do about it.* New York: Harper and Row, 1955.

Fogelman, K. R. *Piagetian tests for the primary school.* London: National Foundation for Educational Research in England and Wales, 1970.

Forer, L. K. *Birth order and life roles.* Springfield, Illinois: Charles C. Thomas, 1969.

Fouts, G., and Atlas, P. Stranger distress: Mother and stranger as reinforcers. *Infant Behavior and Development,* 1979, *2,* 309–317.

Fox, D. J., and Jordan, V. B. Racial preference and identification of black, American Chinese, and white children. *Genetic Psychology Monographs,* 1973, *88,* 229–286.

Fraiberg, S. *Insights from the blind.* New York: Basic Books, 1977.

Francke, L. B., and Reese, M. After remarriage. *Newsweek,* February 11, 1980, p. 6.

Frankenburg, W. K., and Dodds, J. B. The Denver developmental screening test. *Journal of Pediatrics,* 1967, *71,* 181–191.

Freud, A., and Dann, S. An experiment in group upbringing. *Psychoanalytic Study of the Child,* 1951, *6,* 127–168.

Friedenberg, E. Z. *The vanishing adolescent.* New York: Random House, 1959.

Friedrich, L. K., and Stein, A. H. Aggressive and prosocial television programs and the natural behavior of preschool children. *Monographs of the Society for Research in Child Development,* 1973, *38* (4, Serial No. 151).

Frisch, H. L. Sex stereotypes in adult-infant play. *Child Development,* 1977, *48,* 1671–1675.

Frodi, A. M., and Lamb, M. E. Child abusers' responses to infant smiles and cries. *Child Development,* 1980, *51,* 238–241.

Frodi, A. M., Lamb, M. E., Leavitt, L. A., and Donovan, W. L. Fathers' and mothers' responses to infant smiles and cries. *Infant Behavior and Development,* 1978, *1,* 187–198.

Frost, J. Language development in children. In P. Lamb (Ed.), *Guiding children's language learning.* Dubuque, Iowa: W. C. Brown, 1971.

Fullard, W., and Reiling, A. M. An investigation of Lorenz's "babyness." *Child Development,* 1976, *47,* 1191–1193.

Furth, H. G. Linguistic deficiency and thinking: Research with deaf subjects, 1964–1969. *Psychological Bulletin,* 1971, *75,* 58–72.

Gadberry, S. *Televiewing, amount and school grades.* Paper presented at the Society for Research in Child Development, New Orleans, April 1977.

Gadberry, S. Effects of restricting first graders' TV-viewing on leisure time use, IQ change, and cognitive style. *Journal of Applied Developmental Psychology,* 1980, *1,* 45–57.

Gaines, R., Sandgrund, A., Green, A. H., and Power, E. Etiological factors in child maltreatment: A multivariate study of abusing, neglecting, and normal mothers. *Journal of Abnormal Psychology,* 1978, *87,* 531–540.

Gallagher, R., and Cowen, E. L. Birth order and school adjustment problems. *Journal of Individual Psychology,* 1977, *33,* 70–77.

Gallup, G. H. The tenth annual Gallup poll of the public's attitudes toward public schools. *Phi Beta Kappan,* 1978, *60,* 33–45.

Galst, J. P. Television food commercials and pro-nutritional public service announcements as determinants of young children's snack choices. *Child Development,* 1980, *51,* 935–938.

Galton, L. Special treatment for obese children. *Parade Magazine,* February 26, 1978, p. 13–14.

Garbarino, J., and Sherman, D. High-risk neighborhoods and high-risk families: The human ecology of child maltreatment. *Child Development,* 1980, *51,* 188–198.

Garcia, E. E. Bilingualism in early childhood. *Young Children,* 1980, *35,* 52–66. (a)

Garcia, E. E. Language switching in bilingual children: A national perspective. In E. Garcia and M. S. Vargas (Eds.), *The Mexican American child: Language, cognitive and social development.* South Bend, Ind.: Notre Dame University Press, 1980. (b)

Gardner, H. Encounter at Royaumont. *Psychology Today,* 1979, *13,* 14–17. (a)

Gardner, H. Toys with a mind of their own. *Psychology Today,* 1979, *13,* 93–101. (b)

Gardner, L. I. Deprivation dwarfism. *Scientific American,* 1972, *227,* 76–82.

Garmezy, N. Vulnerability research and the issue of primary prevention. *American Journal of Orthopsychiatry,* 1970, *41,* 101–105.

Garmezy, N. The study of competence in children at risk for severe psychopathology. In *Child and his family: Children at psychiatric risk.* Vol. 3 of the International Yearbook of the International Association for Child Psychiatry and Allied Professions. New York: Wiley, 1974.

Garn, S. M. Body size and its implications. In L. W. Hoffman and N. L. Hoffman (Eds.), *Review of child development research.* New York: Russell Sage Foundation, 1966, pp. 529–561.

Garn, S. M., and Clark, D. C. Trends in fatness and the origins of obesity. *Pediatrics,* 1976, *57,* 443–456.

Garnets, L., and Pleck, J. H. Sex-role identity, androgyny, and sex-role transcendence: A sex-role strain analysis. *Psychology of Women Quarterly,* 1979, *3,* 270–283.

Garvey, C. Some properties of social play. *Merrill Palmer Quarterly,* 1974, *20,* 163–180.

Gearing, J. Facilitating the birth process and father-child bonding. *The Counseling Psychologist,* 1978, *7,* 53–55.

Geisler, M., and Kleindbredt, J. Cytogenetic and histologic analyses of spontaneous abortions. *Human Genetics,* 1978, *45,* 239–251.

Gelfand, D. M., and Hartmann, D. P. *The development of prosocial behavior and moral judgment.* Santa Monica, Calif.: Goodyear, 1980.

Gelles, R. J. Violence toward childen in the United States. *American Journal of Orthopsychiatry,* 1978, *48,* 580–592.

Gelman, J. L. A learning analysis of the effects of normal stimulation, privation, and deprivation on the acquisition of social motivation and attachment. In B. M. Foss (Ed.), *Determinants of infant behavior.* New York: Wiley, 1961, pp. 213–299.

Gelman, R. Conservation acquisition: A problem of learning to attend to relevant attributes. *Journal of Experimental Child Psychology,* 1969, *7,* 167–187.

Gerbner, G., and Gross, N. Demonstration of power. *Journal of Communication,* 1978, *29,* 177–184.

Gesell, A. *The first five years of life.* New York: Harper and Brothers, 1940.

Gesell, A., and Amatruda, C. S. *Developmental diagnosis: Normal and abnormal child development, clinical methods and pediatric applications* (2nd ed.), New York: Hoeber, 1947.

Gesell, A., and Ilg, F. L. *The child from 5 to 10.* New York: Harper and Row, 1946.

Gesell, A., and Thompson, H. Learning and growth in identical infant twins: An experimental study of the method of co-twin controls. *Genetic Psychology Monographs,* 1929, *6,* 1–25.

Getzels, J. W., and Jackson, P. W. *Creativity and intelligence: Explorations with gifted students.* New York: Wiley, 1962.

Gewirtz, J. L. The course of infant smiling in four child-rearing environments in Israel. In B. M. Foss (Ed.), *Determinants of infant behavior* (Vol. 3). London: Methuen, 1965.

Gibbons, M. Walkabout: Searching for the right passage from childhood and school. *Phi Delta Kappan,* 1974, *55,* 596–602.

Gibson, E. J. Development of perception: Discrimination of depth compared with discrimination of graphic symbols. *Monograph of the Society for Research in Child Development,* 1963, *28,* (2, Serial No. 86).

Gibson, E. J. *Principles of perceptual learning and development.* New York: Appleton-Century-Crofts, 1969.

Gibson, E. J., and Walk, R. D. The "visual cliff." *Scientific American,* 1960, *202,* 64–71.

Gilligan, C. In a different voice: Women's conceptions of self and of morality. *Harvard Educational Review,* 1977, *47,* 481–517.

Ginsburg, H., and Opper, S. *Piaget's theory of intellectual development* (2nd ed.). Englewood Cliffs, N.J.: Prentice-Hall, 1979.

Glick, P. G., and Norton, A. J. Marrying, divorcing and living together in the U.S. today. *Population Bulletin,* 1978, *32,* 3–38.

Glover, J., and Gary, A. L. Procedures to increase some aspects of creativity. *Journal of Applied Behavior Analysis,* 1976, *9,* 79–84.

Gold, D., and Andres, D. Comparisons of adolescent children with employed and nonemployed mothers. *Merrill-Palmer Quarterly,* 1978, *24,* 243–254.

Gold, M. *Delinquent behavior in an American city.* Belmont, Calif.: Brooks/Cole, 1970.

Goldberg, M. E., Gorn, G. J., and Gibson, W. TV messages for snack and breakfast foods: Do they influence children's preferences? *Journal of Consumer Research,* 1978, *5,* 73–81.

Goldberg, S. Infant care and growth in urban Zambia. *Human Development,* 1972, *15,* 77–89.

Goldberg, S., and Lewis, M. Play behavior in the year-old infant: Early sex differences. *Child Development,* 1969, *40,* 21–31.

Goldblatt, A., Strauss, S., and Hess, P. A replication and extension of findings about the development of visual acuity in infants. *Infant Behavior and Development,* 1980, *3,* 179–182.

Goldfarb, W. Effects of psychological deprivation in infancy and subsequent stimulation. *American Journal of Psychiatry,* 1945, *102,* 18–33.

Golding, W. *Lord of the flies.* New York: Capricorn, 1959.

Goldin-Meadow, S., Seligman, M. E. P., and Gelman, R. Language in the two-year-old. *Cognition,* 1976, *4,* 189–202.

Goldstein, K. M., Caputo, D. V., and Taub, H. B. The effects of prenatal and perinatal complications on development at one year of age. *Child Development,* 1976, *47,* 613–621.

Goodenough, F. L. *Anger in young children.* Minneapolis, Minn.: University of Minnesota Press, 1931.

Goodman, K. Reading: A psycholinguistic guessing game. *Journal of the Reading Specialist*, 1967, *4*, 126–235.

Goodman, K. *Reading: A conversation with Kenneth Goodman.* Glenview, Illinois: Scott Foresman, 1976.

Goodman, P. *Growing up absurd.* New York: Random House, 1960.

Gordon, I. Analyzing parent power. In E. Grotberg (Ed.), *Critical issues in research related to disadvantaged children.* Princeton, N.J.: Educational Testing Service, 1969.

Gottfried, A. W. Intellectual consequences of perinatal anoxia. *Psychological Bulletin*, 1973, *80*, 231–242.

Gottfried, A. W., and Rose, S. A. Tactile recognition memory in infants. *Child Development*, 1980, *51*, 69–74.

Gottman, J., Gonso, J., Rasmussen, B. Social interaction, social competence, and friendship in children. *Child Development*, 1975, *46*, 709–718.

Gouze, K. R., and Nadelman, L. Constancy of gender identity for self and others in children between the ages of three and seven. *Child Development*, 1980, *51*, 275–278.

Green, E. C. A modern Appalachian folk healer. *Appalachian Journal*, 1978, *6*, 2–15.

Green, M. A challenge for the 1980s: Adolescent health care. *Children Today*, 1979, *8*, 8–11.

Greenberg, J. H. *Language universals.* The Hague: Mouton, 1966.

Greenberg, M., and Morris, N. Engrossment: The newborn's impact upon the father. *American Journal of Orthopsychiatry*, 1974, *44*, 520–531.

Greenfield, P. M., and Smith, J. H. *The structure of communication in early language development.* New York: Academic Press, 1976.

Gregg, C. L., Haffner, M. E., and Korner, A. F. The relative efficacy of vestibular-proprioceptive stimulation and the upright position in enhancing visual pursuit in neonates. *Child Development*, 1976, *47*, 309–314.

Grusec, J. E., and Kuczynski, L. Direction of effect in socialization: A comparison of the parent's versus the child's behavior as determinants of disciplinary techniques. *Developmental Psychology*, 1980, *16*, 1–9.

Guilford, J. P. A factor analytic study across the domains of reasoning, creativity, and evaluation, I: Hypothesis and description of tests. In *Reports from the psychology laboratory.* Los Angeles: University of Southern California, 1954.

Guilford, J. P. Three faces of intellect. *American Psychologist*, 1959, *14*, 469–479.

Gunnar, M. R., and Donahue, M. Sex differences in social responsiveness between six months and twelve months. *Child Development*, 1980, *51*, 262–265.

Gussow, J. D. Counternutritional messages of TV ads aimed at children. *Journal of Nutrition Education*, 1972, *48*, 4.

Guthrie, H. *Introductory nutrition* (3rd ed.). St. Louis: Mosby, 1975.

Haaf, R. Complexity and facial resemblance as determinants of response to face-like stimuli by 5- and 10-week-old infants. *Journal of Experimental Child Psychology*, 1976, *22*, 155–160.

Haaf, R., and Brown, C. J. Infants' response to facelike patterns: Developmental changes between 10 and 15 weeks of age. *Journal of Experimental Child Psychology*, 1976, *22*, 155–160.

Hagman, R. R. A study of fears of children of preschool age. *Journal of Experimental Education*, 1932, *1*, 110–130.

Hall, G. S. *Adolescence.* New York: Appleton, 1916.

Halonen, J. S., and Passman, R. H. Pacifiers' effects upon play and separations from the mother for the one-year-old in a novel environment. *Infant Behavior and Development*, 1978, *1*, 70–78.

Hamill, P. V. V., Drizd, T. A., Johnson, C. L., Reed, R. B., and Roche, A. F. *NCHS growth curves for children birth to 18 years.* United States DHEW Publ. No. (PHS) 78-1650. Supt. of Documents, U.S. Government Printing Office, Washington, D.C., 1977.

Hamilton, J. S. *Crying behavior and the "nonviolent" Leboyer method of delivery.* Paper presented at the Society for Research in Child Development, San Francisco, April 1979.

Haney, W. The follow-through planned variation experiment. In *A technical history of the national follow-through evaluation* (Vol. 5). Cambridge, Mass.: The Huron Institute, 1977.

Hanson, D. R., and Gottesman, I. I. The genetics, if any, of infantile autism and childhood schizophrenia. *Journal of Autism and Childhood Schizophrenia*, 1976, *6*, 209–234.

Haring, N. G. (Ed). *Behavior of exceptional children* (2nd ed.). Columbus, Ohio: Charles E. Merrill, 1978.

Harlow, H. F. The nature of love. *American Psychologist*, 1958, *13*, 673–685.

Harlow, H. F., and Harlow, M. H. Learning to love. *American Scientist*, 1966, *54*, 244–272.

Harmon, C., Furrow, D., Gruendel, J., and Zigler, E. Childhood accidents: An overview of the problem and a call for action. *SRCD Newsletter*, 1980, Spring, 5.

Harre, R. What's in a nickname? *Psychology Today*, 1980, *13*, 79–84.

Hartley, R. E. *Sex roles from a child's viewpoint.* Paper presented at the annual meeting of the American Orthopsychiatric Association, San Francisco, 1966.

Hartup, W. W. Peer interaction and social organization. In P. H. Mussen (Ed.), *Carmichael's manual of child psychology* (3rd ed., vol. 2). New York: Wiley, 1970, pp. 457–558.

Haskins, R., Farran, D. C., and Sanders, J. Making the day-care decision. *Early Childhood Education,* 1979, *1,* 35–38.

Heathers, G. Emotional dependence and independence in nursery school play. The *Journal of Genetic Psychology,* 1955, *87,* 37–57.

Hendin, D., and Marks, J. *The genetic connection.* New York: New American Library, 1979.

Herbst, A. L., Kurman, R. J., Scully, R. E., and Poskanzer, D. D. Clear-cell adenocarcinoma of the genital tract in young females. *New England Journal of Medicine,* 1972, *287,* 1259–1264.

Herzog, E., and Sudia, C. E. Fatherless homes: A review of the research. *Children,* 1968, *15,* 177–182.

Herzog, E., and Sudia, C. E. *Boys in fatherless families.* U.S. Department of HEW, Youth and Child Studies Branch. Washington, D.C.: U.S. Government Printing Office, 1970.

Hess, R. D., and Shipman, V. C. Early experience and the socialization of cognitive modes in children. *Child Development,* 1965, *36,* 869–886.

Hetherington, E. M. Effects of paternal absence on sex-typed behaviors in Negro and white preadolescent males. *Journal of Personality and Social Psychology,* 1966, *4,* 87–91.

Hetherington, E. M. Effects of father absence on personality development in adolescent daughters. *Developmental Psychology,* 1972, *7,* 303–326.

Hetherington, E. M. Divorce: A child's perspective. *American Psychologist,* 1979, *34,* 851–858.

Hetherington, E. M., Cox, M., and Cox, R. Divorced fathers. *The Family Coordinator,* 1976, *25,* 417–428.

Hetherington, E. M., Cox, M., and Cox, R. *The development of children in mother-headed families.* Paper presented at the Families in Contemporary America Conference, George Washington University, June 1977.

Hetherington, E. M., Cox, M., and Cox, R. The aftermath of divorce. In J. H. Stevens and M. Matthews (Eds.), *Mother/child-father/child relationships.* Washington, D.C.: National Association for the Education of Young Children, 1978.

Hetherington, E. M., and Martin, B. Family interaction and psychopathology in children. In H. C. Quay and J. S. Weery (Eds.), *Psychopathological disorders of childhood.* New York: Wiley, 1972, pp. 32–82.

Hildebrandt, K. A., and Fitzgerald, H. E. Facial feature determinants of perceived infant attractiveness. *Infant Behavior and Development,* 1979, *2,* 329–339.

Hildreth, G. The development and training of hand dominance: II. Developmental tendencies in handedness. *Journal of Genetic Psychology,* 1949, *75,* 221–254.

Hock, E. Working and nonworking mothers with infants: Perceptions of their careers, their infants' needs, and satisfaction with mothering. *Developmental Psychology,* 1978, *4,* 37–43.

Hock, E. Working and nonworking mothers and their infants: A comparative study of maternal caregiving characteristics and infant social behavior. *Merrill-Palmer Quarterly,* 1980, *26,* 79–101.

Hock, E., Christman, K., and Hock, M. Career-related decisions of mothers of infants. *Family Relations: Journal of Applied Family and Child Studies,* 1980, *29,* 325–330.

Hoffman, L. W. Mothers' enjoyment of work and effects on the child. *Child Development,* 1961, *32,* 187–197.

Hoffman, L. W. Maternal employment: 1979. *American Psychologist,* 1979, *34,* 859–865.

Hoffman, M. L. Developmental synthesis of affect and cognition and its implications for altruistic motivation. *Developmental Psychology,* 1975, *11,* 607–622. (a)

Hoffman, M. L. Moral internalization, parental power, and the nature of parent-child interaction. *Developmental Psychology,* 1975, *11,* 228–239. (b)

Hoffman, M. L. Development of moral thought, feeling, and behavior. *American Psychologist,* 1979, *34,* 958–966.

Holmberg, M. C. The development of social interchange patterns from 12 to 42 months. *Child Development,* 1980, *51,* 448–456.

Honig, A. S., and Oski, F. A. Developmental scores of iron deficient infants and the effects of therapy. *Infant Behavior and Development,* 1978, *1,* 168–176.

Hooker, D. (Ed.). *The prenatal origin of behavior.* Lawrence, Kans.: University of Kansas Press, 1952.

Hoorweg, J., and Stanfield, J. P. The effects of protein energy malnutrition in early childhood on intellectual and motor abilities in later childhood and adolescence. *Developmental Medicine and Child Neurology,* 1976, *18,* 330–350.

Horn, J. Easing a baby's way in the world. *Psychology Today,* 1977, *10,* 34.

Horowitz, A. B. Habituation and memory: Infant cardiac responses to familiar and discrepant auditory stimuli. *Child Development,* 1972, *43,* 43–53.

Horowitz, F. D. The relationship of anxiety, self-concept, and sociometric status among fourth, fifth, and sixth grade children. *Journal of Abnormal and Social Psychology*, 1962, *65*, 212–214.

House Select Committee on Population. Illegitimate births to teenagers doubled since 1960, panel finds. *The Charlotte Observer*, April 25, 1979.

Humphries, T., Kinsbourne, M., and Swanson, J. Stimulant effects on cooperation and social interaction between hyperactive children and their mothers. *Journal of Child Psychology and Psychiatry*, 1978, *19*, 13–22.

Hunsberger, B. Racial awareness and preference of white and Indian Canadian children. *Canadian Journal of Behavioral Science*, 1978, *10*, 176–180.

Huntington, D. S. Supportive programs for infants and parents. In J. D. Osofsky (Ed.), *Handbook of infant development.* New York: Wiley, 1979.

Hutt, C. J. *Males and females.* Baltimore, Maryland: Penguin, 1972.

Hutt, S. J., Lenard, H. G., and Prechtl, H. F. R. Psycho-physiological studies in newborn infants. In L. P. Lipsitt and H. W. Reese (Eds.), *Advances in child development and behavior.* New York: Academic Press, 1969, *4*, 127–172.

Huttenlocker, J. The origins of language comprehension. In R. L. Solso (Ed.), *Theories in cognitive psychology.* Hillsdale, N.J.: Erlbaum, 1974.

Hyman, I. A. Psychology, education, and schooling. *American Psychologist*, 1979, *34*, 1024–1029.

Hyson, M. C. Lobster on the sidewalk: Understanding and helping children with fears. *Young Children*, 1979, *34*, 54–60,

Inhelder, B., and Piaget, J. *The growth of logical thinking from childhood to adolescence.* Translated by Anne Parsons and Stanley Milgram. New York: Basic Books, 1958.

Izard, C. E., Huebner, R. R., Risser, D., McGinnes, G. C., and Dougherty, L. M. The young infant's ability to produce discrete emotion expressions. *Developmental Psychology*, 1980, *16*, 132–140.

Jacklin, C. N., and Maccoby, E. E. Social behavior at 33 months in same-sex and mixed-sex dyads. *Child Development*, 1978, *49*, 557–569.

Jacklin, C. N., Snow, M. E., and Maccoby, E. E. Tactile sensitivity and strength in newborn boys and girls. *Infant Behavior and Development*, 1981, *4*, 261–268.

Jackson, P. W., and Messick, S. The person, the product, and the response: Conceptual problems in the assessment of creativity. In J. Kagan (Ed.), *Creativity and learning.* Boston: Houghton-Mifflin, 1967.

Jacobs, J. *Adolescent suicide.* New York: Wiley, 1971.

Jacobson, D. S. The impact of marital separation/divorce on children: Parent-child separation and child adjustment. *Journal of Divorce*, 1978, *1*, 341–360.

Jacobson, D. S. Stepfamilies. *Children Today*, 1980, *9*, 2–6.

James, W. *The principles of psychology.* New York: Holt, 1890.

Jay, S., and Farran, D. *Socioeconomic differences in mother-child interaction.* Paper presented at the American Psychological Association, Los Angeles, August 1981.

Jensen, A. R. Social class, race, and genetics: Implications for education. *American Educational Research Journal*, 1968, *5*, 1–42.

Jensen, A. R. How much can we boost IQ and scholastic achievement? *Harvard Educational Review*, 1969, *39*, 1–123.

Jensen, K. Differential reactions to taste and temperature stimuli in newborn infants. *Genetic Psychology Monographs*, 1932, *12*, 361–479.

Jensen, M. A., and Hanson, D. A. Helping young children learn to read: What research says to teachers. *Young Children*, 1980, *36*, 61–71.

Jersild, A. T., and Holmes, F. B. Children's fears. *Child Development Monographs*, 1935, *6* (Serial No. 20).

Johnson, A. R., Hood, R. L., and Emery, J. L. Biotin and the Sudden Infant Death Syndrome. *Nature*, 1980, *285*, 159–160.

Johnson, M. J. Sex-role learning in the nuclear family. *Child Development*, 1963, *34*, 319–333.

Johnson, W. A. A study of the onset and development of stuttering. In W. Johnson and R. R. Leutenegger (Eds.), *Stuttering in children and adults.* Minneapolis, Minn.: University of Minnesota Press, 1955.

Jonas, G. *Stuttering: The disorder of many theories.* New York: Farrar, Straus, and Giroux, 1977.

Jordan, T. E. *Development in the preschool years: Birth to age five.* New York: Academic Press, 1980.

Kagan, J. Impulsive and reflective children: Significance of conceptual tempo. In J. D. Krumboltz (Ed.), *Learning and the educational process.* Chicago: Rand McNally, 1965. (a)

Kagan, J. Individual differences in the resolution of response uncertainty. *Journal of Personality and Social Psychology*, 1965, *2*, 154–160. (b)

Kagan, J. Reflection impulsivity and reading ability in primary grade children. *Child Development*, 1965, *36*, 609–628. (c)

Kagan, J. Generality and dynamics of conceptual tempo. *Journal of Abnormal Psychology*, 1966, *71*, 17–24.

Kagan, J. Attention and psychological change in the young child. *Science*, 1970, *170*, 826–832.

Kagan, J. *Change and continuity in infancy.* New York: Wiley, 1971.

Kagan, J. Do infants think? *Scientific American,* 1972, *226,* 74–82.

Kagan, J. Discrepancy, temperament, and infant distress. In M. Lewis and L. Rosenblum (Eds.), *The origins of fear.* New York: Wiley, 1975.

Kagan, J. Emergent themes in human development. *American Scientist,* 1976, *64,* 186–196.

Kagan, J., Kearsley, R. B., and Zelazo, P. R. *The effects of infant day care on psychological development.* Paper presented at a symposium on "The effect of early experience on child development," American Association for the Advancement of Science, Boston, February 1976.

Kagan, J., and Klein, R. E. Cross-cultural perspectives on early development. *American Psychologist,* 1973, *28,* 947–961.

Kagan, J., and Kogan, N. Individual variation in cognitive processes. In P. H. Mussen (Ed.), *Carmichael's manual of child psychology,* (3rd ed, vol.1). New York: Wiley, 1970.

Kagan, J., Rosman, B. L., Day, D., Albert, J., and Phillips, W. Information processing in the child: Significance of analytic and reflective attitudes. *Psychological Monographs,* 1964 (Whole No. 578).

Kamin, L. J. *The science and politics of IQ.* Potomac, Md.: Erlbaum, 1974.

Kandel, D. B., and Lesser, G. S. Parental and peer influences on educational plans of adolescents. *American Sociological Review,* 1969, *34,* 213–223.

Kaplan, B. J. Malnutrition and mental deficiency. *Psychological Bulletin,* 1972, *78,* 321–335.

Kaplan, L. The status and function of men teachers in urban elementary schools. Unpublished doctoral dissertation, University of Southern California, Los Angeles, 1947.

Katchadourian, H. *The biology of adolescence.* San Francisco: W. H. Freeman, 1977.

Kay, P. The imaginary companion: Review of the literature. *Maternal-Child Nursing Journal,* 1980, *9,* 7–11.

Kaye, E. *How to treat TV with TLC: The ACT guide to children's television.* Boston: Beacon Press, 1979.

Keister, M. E. *Demonstration project: Group care of infants. Final report.* Greensboro, N.C.: University of North Carolina, Greensboro, 1970.

Keister, M. E. Discipline: The secret heart of child care. Unpublished manuscript, University of North Carolina, Greensboro, 1973.

Kelin, R., and Pertz, D. Nutrition and learning. *Academic Therapy,* 1978, *13,* 527–532.

Kelly, J. B., and Wallerstein, J. S. The effects of parental divorce: Experiences of the child in early latency. *American Journal of Orthopsychiatry,* 1976, *46,* 20–32.

Keniston, K. *The uncommitted: Alienated youth in American society.* New York: Dell, 1960.

Kennedy, W. A. A follow-up normative study of Negro intelligence and achievement. *Monographs of the Society for Research in Child Development,* 1969, *34* (2, Serial No. 126).

Kennell, J. H. Parent and infant bonding: The coming revolution in maternity care. Speech presented at Groves Conference, Grossinger, New York, May 5, 1977.

Kennell, J. H., Voos, D. K., and Klaus, M. H. Parent-infant bonding. In J. D. Osofsky (Ed.), *Handbook of infant development.* New York: Wiley, 1979.

Kenny, T. J., Clemmens, R. L., Hudson, B. W., Lenz, G. A., Cicci, R., and Nair, P. Characteristics of children referred because of hyperactivity. *Journal of Pediatrics,* 1971, *79,* 618–622.

Kerns, R. *Birth order and Adlerian theory.* Paper presented at the First Annual Child and Family Development Conference, University of North Carolina, Charlotte, May 1980.

Keshet, H. F., and Rosenthal, K. M. Fathers: A new study. *Children Today,* 1979, *7,* 13–17.

Kessen, W. Research in the psychological development of infants: An overview. In F. Rebelsky and L. Dorman (Eds.), *Child development and behavior* (2nd ed.). New York: Knopf, 1973.

Kessen, W., Levine, J., and Wondrich, K. A. The imitation of pitch in infants. *Infant Behavior and Development,* 1979, *2,* 93–99.

Kessen, W., Williams, E. J., and Williams, J. P. Selection and test of response measures in the study of the human newborn. *Child Development,* 1961, *32,* 7–24.

Kilbride, H. W., Johnson, D. L., and Streissguth, A. P. Social class, birth order, and newborn experience. *Child Development,* 1977, *48,* 1686–1688.

Kinard, E. M., and Klerman, L. V. Teenage parenting and child abuse: Are they related? *American Journal of Orthopsychiatry,* 1980, *50,* 481–488.

Kinch, R. (Ed.). *Youth development and juvenile delinquency: The changing role of county government.* Wisconsin: The Johnson Foundation, 1978.

Kinsey, A. C., Pomeroy, W. B., Martin, C. E., and Gebhard, P. H. *Sexual behavior in the human male.* Philadelphia: Saunders, 1948.

Kinsey, A. C., Pomeroy, W. B., Martin, C. E., and Gebhard, P. H. *Sexual behavior in the human female.* Philadelphia: Saunders, 1953.

Kinsey Institute for Sex Research. A Kinsey report. *American Orthopsychiatric Association Newsletter,* 1982 (Winter), 18.

Kitano, M. K. Early education for Asian American children. *Young Children*, 1980, *35*, 13–26.

Klaus, M. H., Jerauld, R., Kreger, N. C., McAlpine, W., Steffa, M., and Kennell, J. H. Maternal attachment: Importance of the first post-partum days. *New England Journal of Medicine*, 1972, *286*, 460–463.

Klaus, M. H., and Kennell, J. H. *Maternal-infant bonding*. St. Louis: C. V. Mosby, 1976.

Kleinke, C. L., and Nicholson, T. A. Black and white children's awareness of de facto race and sex differences. *Developmental Psychology*, 1979, *15*, 84–86.

Klemer, R. H., and Smith, R. M. *Teaching about family relationships*. Minneapolis: Minn.: Burgess, 1975.

Knittle, J. L. Basic concepts in the control of childhood obesity. In M. Winick (Ed.), *Childhood obesity*. New York: Wiley, 1975.

Koblinsky, S. G., Cruse, D. F., and Sugawara, A. I. Sex-role stereotypes and children's memory for story content. *Child Development*, 1978, *49*, 452–458.

Kohlberg, L. A cognitive-developmental analysis of sex-role concepts and attitudes. In E. Maccoby (Ed.), *The development of sex differences*. Stanford, Calif.: Stanford University Press, 1966.

Kohlberg, L. Moral education in the schools: A developmental view. In R. E. Grinder (Ed.), *Studies in adolescence: A book of readings in adolescent development*. New York: Macmillan, 1969, pp. 237–258.

Kohlberg, L. Moral stages and moralization: The cognitive-developmental approach. In T. Lickona (Ed.), *Moral development and behavior: Theory, research, and social issues*. New York: Holt, Rinehart, and Winston, 1976.

Kohlberg, L, and Gilligan, C. The adolescent as a philosopher: The discovery of the self in a postconventional world. *Daedalus*, 1971, *100*, 1051–1086.

Kohlberg L., and Gilligan, C. The adolescent as a philosopher: The discovery of the self in a postconventional world. In J. Kagan and R. Coles (Eds.), *12 to 16: Early adolescence*. New York: Norton, 1972.

Kohlberg, L. and Kramer, R. Continuities and Discontinuities in Childhood and Adult Moral Development. *Human Development*, 1969, *12*, 93–120.

Kompara, D. R. Difficulties in the socialization process of step-parenting. *Family Relations: Journal of Applied Family and Child Studies*, 1980, *29*, 69–73.

Koocher, G. P. Childhood, death, and cognitive development. *Developmental Psychology*, 1971, *9*, 369–375.

Koocher, G. P. Talking with children about death. *American Journal of Orthopsychiatry*, 1974, *44*, 404–411.

Kopp, C. B., and Parmelee, A. H. Prenatal and perinatal influences on infant behavior. In J. D. Osofsky (Ed.), *Handbook of infant development*. New York: Wiley, 1979.

Korner, A. F. Some hypotheses regarding the significance of individual differences at birth for later development. In R. S. Eissler (Ed.), *The psychoanalytic study of the child*. New York: International Universities Press, 1964, 58–72.

Kratochwill, T., and Goldman, J. Developmental changes in children's judgements of age. *Developmental Psychology*, 1973, *9*, 358–362.

Kuczaj, S. A. Children's judgments of grammatical and ungrammatical irregular past-tense verbs. *Child Development*, 1978, *49*, 319–326.

Kuhn, D., Nash, S. C., and Brucken, L. Sex-role concepts of two- and three-year-olds. *Child Development*, 1978, *49*, 445–451.

Kurdek, L. A. Perspective-taking as the cognitive basis of children's moral development: A review of the literature. *Merrill-Palmer Quarterly*, 1978, *24*, 3–28.

LaBarbera, I. C., Vietze, P., and Parisi, S. Four- and six-month-old infants' visual responses to joy, anger, and neutral expressions. *Child Development*, 1976, *47*, 535–538.

Labinowicz, E. *The Piaget primer: Thinking, learning, teaching*. Reading, Mass.: Addison-Wesley, 1980.

Labov, W. The logic of nonstandard English. In F. Williams (Ed.), *Language and poverty*. Chicago: Markham, 1970.

Lamb, M. E. *Development and function of parent-infant relationships in the first two years of life*. Paper presented at the Biennial Meeting of the Society for Research in Child Development, New Orleans, March 1977. (a)

Lamb, M. E. The development of parental preferences in the first two years of life. *Sex Roles*, 1977, *3*, 495–497. (b)

Lamb, M. E. Father-infant and mother-infant interaction in the first year of life. *Child Development*, 1977, *48*, 167–181. (c)

Lamb, M. E. The development of sibling relationships in infancy: A short-term longitudinal study. *Child Development*, 1978, *49*, 1189–1196. (a)

Lamb, M. E. Influence of the child on marital quality and family interaction during the prenatal, perinatal, and infancy periods. In R. M. Lerner and G. B. Spanier (Eds.), *Child influences on marital and family interactions: A life-span perspective*. New York: Academic, 1978. (b)

Lamb, M. E. Interactions between eighteen-month-olds and their preschool-aged siblings. *Child Development*, 1978, *49*, 51–59. (c)

Lamb, M. E. Paternal influences and the father's role: A personal perspective. *American Psychologist*, 1979, *34*, 938–943.

Lamb, M. E., and Roopnarine, J. L. Peer influences on sex-role development in preschoolers. *Child Development,* 1979, *50,* 1219–1222.

Landcranjan, I. Genital system—men. In *Occupational safety and health encyclopedia* (Vol. 1). Geneva: International Labor Organization, 1971.

Landcranjan, I. Reproductive ability of workmen occupationally exposed to lead. *Archives of Environmental Health,* 1975, *30,* 396–402.

Landesman-Dwyer, S., Ragozin, A. S., and Little, R. *Behavioral correlates of prenatal exposure to alcohol and nicotine.* Paper presented at the Society for Research in Child Development, San Francisco, 1979.

Landsbaum, J. B., and Willis, R. H. Conformity in early and late adolescence. *Developmental Psychology,* 1971, *4,* 334–337.

Lange, G. Personal communication from Dr. Garrett Lange, University of North Carolina at Greensboro, 1980.

Languis, M., Sanders, T., and Tipps, S. *Brain and learning: Directions in early childhood education.* Washington, D.C.: NAEYC, 1980.

Langworthy, R. L. Community status and influence in a high school. *American Sociological Review,* 1959, *24,* 537–539.

Lawson, K. R. Spatial and temporal congruity and auditory-visual integration in infants. *Developmental Psychology,* 1980, *16,* 185–192.

Lechtig, A., Habicht, J. P., Delgado, H., Klein, R. E., Yarbrough, C., and Martorell, R. Effect of food supplementation during pregnancy on birth weight. *Pediatrics,* 1975, *56,* 508.

Lefkowitz, M. M. Smoking during pregnancy: Long-term effects on offspring. *Developmental Psychology,* 1981, *17,* 192–194.

Lefkowitz, M. M., Eron, L. D., Walder, L. O., and Huesmann, L. R. Television violence and child aggression: A follow-up study. In G. A. Comstock and E. A. Rubenstein (Eds.), *Television and social behavior.* Washington, D.C.: U.S. Government Printing Office, 1972.

Lefley, H. P. Social and familial correlates of self-esteem among American Indian children. *Child Development,* 1974, *45,* 829–833.

Leiderman, P. H., and Leiderman, G. F. Affective and cognitive consequences of polymatric infant care in the East African highlands. In A. Pick (Ed.), *Minnesota symposium on child development* (Vol.8). Minneapolis, Minn.: University of Minnesota Press, 1974.

Leiderman, P. H., Tulkin, S. R., and Rosenfeld, A. (Eds.). *Culture and infancy: Variations in the human experience.* New York: Academic, 1977

Leifer, A. D., Lederman, P. H., Barnett, C., and Williams, J. Effects of mother-infant separation on maternal attachment behavior. *Child Development,* 1972, *43,* 1203–1218.

Leitch, S. M. *A child learns to speak: A guide for parents and teachers of preschool children.* Springfield, Ill.: Charles C. Thomas, 1977.

LeMasters, E. E. *Parents in modern America.* Homewood, Ill.: Dorsey, 1974.

Lenneberg, E. H. Understanding language without ability to speak: A case report. *Journal of Abnormal and Social Psychology,* 1962, *65,* 419–425.

Lenneberg, E. H. Language disorders in childhood. *Harvard Educational Review,* 1964, *34,* 152–177. (a)

Lenneberg, E. H. (Ed.). *New directions in the study of language.* Cambridge, Mass.: M.I.T. Press, 1964. (b)

Lenneberg, E. H. *Biological foundations of language.* New York: Wiley, 1967.

Lenneberg, E. H., Nichols, I. A., and Rosenberger, E. F. Primitive stages of language development in mongolism. *Proceedings of the Association Res. Nerv. Ment. Disease,* 1964, *42,* 119–137.

Lerner, R. M., and Lerner, J. Effects of age, sex and physical attractiveness on child-peer relations, academic performance, and elementary school adjustment. *Developmental Psychology,* 1977, *13,* 585–590.

Lesser, G. S. *Children and television: Lessons from Sesame Street.* New York: Random House, 1974.

Lester, B. M. Spectrum analysis of the cry sounds of well-nourished and malnourished infants. *Child Development,* 1976, *47,* 237–241.

Lester, B. M., Kotelchuck, M., Spelke, E., Sellers, M. J., and Klein, R. E. Separation protest in Guatemalan infants: Cross-cultural and cognitive findings. *Developmental Psychology,* 1974, *10,* 79–85.

Lester, B. M., and Zeskind, P. S. The organization and assessment of crying in the infant at risk. In T. M. Field, A. M. Sostek, S. Goldberg, and H. H. Shuman (Eds.), *Infants born at risk.* New York: Spectrum, 1979.

Levenstein, P. Learning through (and from) mothers. *Childhood Education,* 1971, *48,* 130–134.

LeVine, R. A. Child-rearing as cultural adaptation. In P. H. Leiderman, S. R. Tulkin, and A. Rosenfeld (Eds.), *Culture and infancy: Variations in the human experience.* New York: Academic, 1977.

Lewin, K., Lippit, R., and White, R. K. Patterns of aggressive behavior in experimentally created "social climates." *Journal of Social Psychology,* 1939, *10,* 271–299.

Lewis, M., and Brooks-Gunn, J. *Self, other and fear: The reactions of infants to people.* Paper presented at the annual meeting of the Eastern Psychological Association, April 1972.

Lewis, M., and Rosenblum, L. A. *The effect of the infant on its caregiver.* New York: Wiley, 1974.

Lewis, M. M. *Infant speech.* New York: Arno Press, 1975.

Libertoff, K. The runaway child in America. *Journal of Family Issues,* 1980, *1,* 151–164.

Lieberman, A. F. Preschoolers' competence with a peer: Relations with attachment and peer experience. *Child Development,* 1977, *48,* 1277–1287.

Liebert, R. M., and Baron, R. A. Some immediate effects of televised violence on children's behavior. *Developmental Psychology,* 1972, *6,* 469–475.

Lifshitz, M. Internal-external locus-of-control dimension as a function of socialization milieu. *Child Development,* 1973, *44,* 538–546.

Lindholm, K. J., and Padilla, A. M. Child bilingualism: Report on language mixing, switching and translations. *Linguistics,* 1979, *211,* 23–44.

Lipsitt, L. P. Learning processes of newborns. *Merrill-Palmer Institute,* 1966, *12,* 45–71.

Lipsitt, L. P. Critical conditions in infancy: A psychological perspective. *American Psychologist,* 1979, *34,* 973–980.

Lipsitt, L. P., and Levy, N. Electrotactual threshold in the neonate. *Child Development,* 1959, *30,* 547–554.

Lipsitt, L. P., Sturner, W. Q., and Burke, P. Perinatal indicators and subsequent crib death. *Infant Behavior and Development,* 1979, *2,* 325–328.

Lipsitz, J. S. Adolescent development: Myths and realities. *Children Today,* 1979, *8,* 2–7.

Litoff, J. B. *American midwives.* Westport, Conn.: Greenwood, 1978.

Loeb, R. C. Concomitants of boys' locus of control examined in parent-child interactions. *Developmental Psychology,* 1975, *11,* 353–358.

Londerville, S., and Main, M. Security of attachment, compliance, and maternal training methods in the second year of life. *Developmental Psychology,* 1981, *17,* 289–299.

Lovitt, T. C. The learning disabled. In N. G. Haring (Ed.), *Behavior of exceptional children* (2nd ed.). Columbus, Ohio: Charles E. Merrill, 1978.

Lowery, G. H. *Growth and development of children* (6th ed.). Chicago: Medical Year Book, 1973.

Lowery, G. H., *Growth and development of children* (7th ed.). Chicago Medical Year Book, 1978.

Lundsteen, S. W. On developmental relations between language learning and reading. *The Elementary School Journal,* 1977, *77,* 193–203.

Lyberger-Ficek, S., and Sternglanz, S. H. *Innate sex differences in crying: Myth or reality?* Paper presented at the meeting of the Society for Research in Child Development, Denver, Colo., April 12, 1975.

Lynn, D. B. *The father: His role in child development.* Monterey, Calif.: Brooks/Cole, 1974.

Lyons-Ruth, K. Binocular perception in infancy. Response to auditory-visual incongruity. *Child Development,* 1977, *48,* 820–827.

Maccoby, E. E. *Social development: Psychological growth and the parent-child relationship.* New York: Harcourt Brace Jovanovich, 1980.

Maccoby, E. E., and Feldman, S. S. Mother-attachment and stranger-reactions in the third year of life. *Monographs of the Society for Research in Child Development,* 1972, *37* (1, Serial No. 146).

Maccoby, E. E., and Jacklin, C. N. *The psychology of sex differences.* Stanford: Stanford University Press, 1974.

Macfarland, A. *The psychology of childbirth.* Cambridge, Mass.: Harvard University Press, 1977.

MacFarlane, J., Allen, L., and Honzik, M. P. *A developmental study of behavior problems of normal children between twenty-one months and fourteen years.* Berkeley, Calif.: University of California Press, 1954.

MacKinnon, D. W. Creativity in architects. In D. W. MacKinnon (Ed.), *The creative person.* Berkeley, Calif.: Institute of Personality Assessment Research, University of California, 1961.

MacKinnon, D. W. The nature and nurture of creative talent. *American Psychologist,* 1962, *17,* 484–495.

Magenis, R. E. Parental origin of the extra chromosome in Down's syndrome. *Human Genetics,* 1977, *37,* 7–16.

Magrab, P. R. For the sake of the children: A review of the psychological effects of divorce. *Journal of Divorce,* 1978, *1,* 233–245.

Mahoney, D. A look at education in the People's Republic of China. *PTA Communique,* 1978, *2,* 1–3.

Maier, H. W. *Three theories of child development* (3rd ed.). New York: Harper and Row, 1978.

Malinowski, B. *The father in primitive psychology.* New York: Norton, 1966.

Mandell, F., McAnuity, E., and Reece, R. M. Observations of paternal response to sudden unanticipated infant death. *Pediatrics,* 1980, *65,* 221–225.

Mann, A. J., Harrell, A., and Hurt, M. *A review of Head Start research since 1969 and an annotated bibliography*. Washington, D.C.: Department of Health, Education, and Welfare, 1977.

Mannerino, A. P. Friendship patterns and altruistic behavior in preadolescent males. *Developmental Psychology*, 1976, *12*, 555–556.

Manosevitz, M., Prentice, N. M., and Wilson, F. Individual and family correlates of imaginary companions in preschool children. *Developmental Psychology*, 1973, *8*, 72–79.

Marcus, D. E., and Overton, W. F. The development of cognitive gender constancy and sex-role preferences. *Child Development*, 1978, *49*, 434–444.

Martin, B. Parent-child relations. In F. D. Horowitz and E. M. Hetherington (Eds.), *Review of child development research*. Chicago: University of Chicago Press, 1975.

Martin, J. A. A longitudinal study of the consequences of early mother-infant interaction: A microanalytic approach. *Monographs of the Society for Research in Child Development*, 1981, *46*, (3, Serial No. 190).

Martorano, S. C. The development of formal operational thought. Unpublished doctoral dissertation, Rutgers University, 1974.

Martorano, S. C. A developmental analysis of performance on Piaget's formal operations tasks. *Developmental Psychology*, 1977, *13*, 666–672.

Marvin, R. S. An ethological-cognitive model for the attenuation of mother-child attachment behavior. In T. Alloway, P. Pliner, and L. Krames (Eds.), *Attachment behavior*. New York: Plenum Publishing, 1977.

Maslansky, E. Survey of infant feeding practices. *American Journal of Public Health*, 1974, *64*, 780–785.

Maslow, A. H. *Toward a psychology of being*. Princeton, N.J.: Van Nostrand, 1968.

Masters, J. C. Effects of social comparison upon the imitation of neutral and altruistic behaviors by young children. *Child Development*, 1972, *43*, 131–142.

Masters, J. C., and Wellman, H. M. The study of infant attachment: A procedural critique. *Psychological Bulletin*, 1974, *81*, 218–237.

Mattingly, I. C. *Reading, linguistic awareness, and language acquisition*. Paper presented at Seminar on Linguistic Awareness and Learning to Read, Victoria, British Columbia, June 1979.

Maurer, D., and Lewis, T. L. Peripheral discrimination by three-month-old infants. *Child Development*, 1979, *50*, 276–279.

Maxim, G. W. *The very young: Guiding children from infancy through the early years*. Belmont, Calif.: Wadsworth, 1980.

Mayo, L. W. *A proposed program for national action to combat mental retardation*. Report of the President's Committee on Mental Retardation. Washington, D.C.: U.S. Government Printing Office, 1962.

McCown, D. TV and violence: Aggression in children. *Pediatric Nursing*, 1979, *5*, 17–19.

McGhee, P. E. The role of operational thinking in children's comprehension and appreciation of humor. *Child Development*, 1971, *42*, 733–744.

McGhee, P. E. *Children's appreciation of humor: A test of the cognitive-congruency principle*. Paper presented at the Society for Research in Child Development, Philadelphia, March 1973.

McGhee, P. E. *Humor: Its origin and development*. San Francisco: W. H. Freeman, 1979.

McGhee, P. E., and Frueh, T. Television viewing and the learning of sex-role stereotypes. *Sex Roles*, 1980, *6*, 179–188.

McGraw, M. B. *Growth: A study of Johnny and Jimmy*. New York: Appleton, 1935.

McGurk, H. Infant discrimination of orientation. *Journal of Experimental Child Psychology*, 1972, *14*, 151–164.

McHenry, P. C., and Tishler, C. L. Adolescent suicide: An overview of the problem with implications for practitioners. *Family Perspective*, 1979, *13*, 189–196.

McIntire, W. G., Nass, G. D., and Battistone, D. L. Female misperceptions of male parenting attitudes and expectancies. *Youth and Society*, 1974, *6*, 104–111.

McKenzie, B. E., Toctell, H. E., and Day, R. H. Development of visual size constancy during the first year of human infancy. *Developmental Psychology*, 1980, *16*, 163–174.

McLaren, D. S., and Burman, D. *Textbook of pediatric nutrition*. New York: Churchill, Livingstone, 1976.

McManis, D. L., McCarthy, M., and Koval, R. Effect of a stimulant drug on extraversion level in hyperactive children. *Perceptual and Motor Skills*, 1978, *46*, 88–90.

McNeil, T. F. The relationship between creative ability and recorded mental illness. Unpublished master's thesis. University of Michigan, Ann Arbor, 1969

McNeill, D. The development of language. In P. H. Mussen, (Ed.), *Carmichael's manual of child psychology* (3rd. ed.). New York: Wiley, 1970.

McNeill, D. *The acquisition of language: The study of developmental psycholinguistics*. New York: Harper and Row, 1972.

McWilliams, M. *Nutrition for the growing years* (3rd ed.). New York: Wiley, 1980.

Mead, M. *Coming of age in Samoa*. New York: Morrow, 1928.

Mead, M. *From the south seas: Part III. Sex and temperament in three primitive societies.* New York: Morrow, 1939.

Mead, M. *Male and female: A study of the sexes in a changing world.* New York: Morrow, 1952.

Mead, M. *Growing up in New Guinea.* New York: Mentor, 1953.

Mead, M. Fatherhood. In S. A. Richardson and A. F. Guttmacher (Eds.), *Childbearing—Its social and psychological aspects.* Baltimore: Wilkins and Wilkins, 1967.

Mehrabian, A., and Epstein, N. A measure of emotional empathy. *Journal of Personality,* 1972, *40,* 525–543.

Meltzoff, A. N., and Moore, M. K. Imitation of facial and manual gestures by human neonates. *Science,* 1977, *198,* 75–78.

Mendelson, M. J., and Haith, M. M. The relation between audition and vision in the human newborn. *Monographs of the Society for Research in Child Development,* 1976, *41* (4, Serial No. 167).

Mendes, H. Single fathers. *Family Coordinator,* 1976, *25,* 439–444.

Messer, S. B. Reflection—impulsivity: A review. *Psychological Bulletin,* 1976, *83,* 1026–1052.

Métraux, A. Ethnology of Easter Island. *Bernice Bishop Museum Bulletin* (Honolulu, Hawaii), 1940, *7,* 1–432 (Bulletin No. 160).

Meyer, B. The development of girls' sex-role attitudes. *Child Development,* 1980, *51,* 508–514.

Meyer, W. J. *Developmental effects of infant day care: An empirical study.* Paper presented at the American Educational Research Association, San Francisco, April 1979.

Milewski, A. E., and Siqueland, E. R. Discrimination of color and pattern novelty in one-month human infants. *Journal of Experimental Child Psychology,* 1975, *46,* 696–700.

Millar, J. D. *The national venereal disease problem.* Paper presented at the Second International Symposium on Venereal Disease, St. Louis, 1972.

Miller, L. C., Barrett, C. L., and Hampe, E. Phobia of childhood in a prescientific era. In A. Davids (Ed.), *Child personality and psychopathology: Current topics.* New York: Wiley, 1974.

Miller, N., and Maruyama, G. Ordinal position and peer popularity. *Journal of Personality and Social Psychology,* 1976, *33,* 123–131.

Minde, K., Trehub, D., Corter, C., Boukydis, C., Celhoffer, L., and Marton, P. Mother-child relationships in the premature nursery: An observational study. *Pediatrics,* 1978, *61,* 373–379.

Minturn, L., and Lambert, W. W. *Mothers of six cultures: Antecedents of child-rearing.* New York: Wiley, 1964.

Minuchin, P. P. *The middle years of childhood.* Monterey, Calif.: Brooks/Cole, 1977.

Mira, M., and Reece, C. A. Medical management of the hyperactive child. In M. J. Fine (Ed.), *Principles and techniques of intervention with hyperactive children.* Springfield, Ill.: Charles C. Thomas, 1977.

Mittler, P. *The study of twins.* Baltimore: Penguin, 1971.

Mokros, J. R., and Koff, E. Sex-stereotyping of children's success in mathematics and reading. *Psychological Reports,* 1978, *42,* 1287–1293.

Money, J. Ablatiopenis: Normal male infant sex-reassignment as a girl. *Archives of Sexual Behavior,* 1975, *4,* 65–72.

Money, J., Hampson, J. G., and Hampson, J. L. Imprinting and the establishment of gender role. *Archives of Neurology and Psychiatry,* 1957, *77,* 333–336.

Montagu, A. *Learning nonaggression.* New York: Oxford University Press, 1978.

Moore, K. A., Hofferth, S. L., and Wertheimer, R. Teenage motherhood: Its social and economic costs. *Children Today,* 1979, *8,* 12–16.

Moore, K. L. *The developing human: Clinically oriented embryology.* Philadelphia: Saunders, 1973.

Moore, S., Considerateness and helpfulness in young children. *Young Children,* 1977, *32,* 73–76. (a)

Moore, S. The effects of television on the prosocial behavior of young children. *Young Children,* 1977, *32,* 60–65. (b)

Morland, J. A. Comparison of race awareness in northern and southern children. *American Journal of Orthopsychiatry,* 1966, *36,* 22–31.

Moss, J., and Solomons, H. C. Swaddling then, there, and now: Historical, anthropological, and current practices. *Maternal-Child Nursing Journal,* 1979, *8,* 137–151.

Moss, H. A. Sex, age, and state as determinants of mother-infant interaction. *Merrill-Palmer Quarterly,* 1967, *13,* 19–36.

Mowrer, O. H. *Learning theory and the symbolic process.* New York: Wiley, 1960.

Mueller, E., and Lucas, T. A. Developmental analysis of peer interaction among toddlers. In M. Lewis and L. A. Rosenblum (Eds.), *Friendship and peer relations.* New York: Wiley, 1975.

Mueller, E., and Rich, A. Clustering and socially directed behaviors in a toddler's play group. *Journal of Child Psychology and Psychiatry,* 1976, *17,* 315–322.

Mullen, D. Effects of blue light conditions on hyperactivity level. Unpublished masters thesis, University of North Carolina, Charlotte, 1979.

Munroe, R. L., Munroe, R. H., and Whiting, J. The couvade: A psychological analysis. *Ethos*, 1973, *1*, 30–74.

Murphy, D. P. *Congenital malformation* (2nd ed.). Philadelphia: University of Pennsylvania Press, 1947.

Murray, J. P. *Television and youth: 25 years of research and controversy.* Boys Town, Nebraska: The Boys Town Center for the Study of Youth Development, 1980.

Mussen, P., and Eisenberg-Berg, N. *Roots of caring, sharing, and helping.* San Francisco: W. H. Freeman, 1977.

Naeye, R. L. Effects of maternal cigarette smoking on the fetus and placenta. *British Journal of Obstetrics and Gynecology*, 1978, *85*, 732–737.

Naeye, R. L. Medical news. *Journal of the American Medical Association*, 1979, *241*, 867–868.

Nagera, H. The imaginary companion: Its significance for ego development and conflict solution. In A. Freud (Ed.), *The psychoanalytic study of the child.* New York: International Universities Press, 1969.

Nagera, H. Vulnerability and role of stimulation in psychological development in early life. In E. J. Anthony, C. Koupernik, and C. Chiland (Eds.), *The child and his family: Vulnerable children* (Vol. 4), New York: Wiley, 1978.

National Institute of Education. *The safe school study report to Congress: Executive summary.* Washington, D.C.: Author, 1977.

National Research Council. *Maternal nutrition and the course of pregnancy.* Washington, D.C.: National Academy of Science, 1970.

Neimark, E. Intellectual development during adolescence. In F. D. Horowitz (Ed.), *Review of child development research* (Vol. 4.). Chicago: University of Chicago Press, 1975.

Nelson, C. A., Morse, P. A., and Leavitt, L. A. Recognition of facial expressions by seven-month-old infants. *Child Development*, 1979, *50*, 1239–1242.

Nelson, K. Structure and strategy in learning to talk. *Monographs of the Society for Research in Child Development*, 1973, *38* (1–2, Serial No. 149).

Nelson, N. M., Enkin, M. W., Saigal, S., Bennett, K. J., Milner, R., and Sackett, D. L. A randomized clinical trial of the Leboyer approach to childbirth. *New England Journal of Medicine*, 1980, *302*, 655–660.

Nelson, W., Vaughan, V., and McKay, R. J. *Textbook of pediatrics* (10th ed.). Phiadelphia: Saunders, 1975.

Nicolich, L. Beyond sensorimotor intelligence: Assessment of symbolic maturity through analysis of pretend play. *Merrill-Palmer Quarterly*, 1977, *23*, 89–99.

Niven, M. Failure to thrive: The nutritionist's role. *Clinical Proceedings, Children's Hospital National Medical Center*, 1977, *33*, 206–208.

Nowlis, G. H., and Kessen, W. Human newborns differentiate differing concentrations of sucrose and glucose. *Science*, 1976, *191*, 865–866.

Nurss, J. R. Linguistic awareness and learning to read. *Young Children*, 1980, *35*, 57–66.

Nye, F. I., and Edelbrock, C. Some social characteristics of runaways. *Journal of Family Issues*, 1980, *1*, 147–150.

O'Connor, M. The nursery school environment. *Developmental Psychology*, 1975, *11*, 556–561.

Office on Smoking and Health. Highlights of the 1979 Surgeon General's report on smoking and health. *Journal of the Medical Association of Georgia*, 1979, *68*, 5.

Olson, L., Liebow, E., Mannino, F. V., and Shore, M. F. Runaway children twelve years later. *Journal of Family Issues*, 1980, *1*, 165–188.

Opinion Research Corporation. *National statistical survey on runaway youth.* Princeton, N.J.: Opinion Research Corporation, 1976.

Ornstein, P. A., Naus, M. J., and Liberty, C. Rehearsal and organizational processes in children's memory. *Child Development*, 1975, *46*, 818–830.

Ornstein, P. A., Naus, M. J., and Stone, B. P. Rehearsal training and developmental differences in memory. *Developmental Psychology*, 1977, *13*, 15–24.

Orthner, D. K. *Single parent men and women: Similarities and differences in experience.* Paper presented at the North Carolina Family Life Council, High Point, N.C., 1979.

Orthner, D. K., and Lewis, K. Evidence of single-father competence in child-rearing. *Family Law Quarterly*, 1979, *13*, 27–47.

Osborn, K. *Early childhood education in historical perspective.* Athens, Ga.: Education Associates, 1980.

Osborn, K., and Osborn, J. Television violence revisited. *Childhood Education*, 1977, *54*, 309–311.

Oshman H. P., and Manosevitz, M. Father absence: Effects of stepfathers upon psychosocial development in males. *Developmental Psychology*, 1976, *12*, 479–480.

Osofsky, J. D. Neonatal characteristics and mother-infant interaction in two observational situations. *Child Development*, 1976, *47*, 1138–1147.

Paluszny, M. J. *Autism: A practical guide for parents and professionals.* New York: Syracuse University Press, 1979.

Papousek, H. Experimental studies of appetitional behavior in human newborns and infants. In H. W. Stevenson, E. H. Hess, and H. L. Rheingold (Eds.), *Early behavior: Comparative and developmental approaches.* New York: Wiley, 1967, pp. 58–72.

Parish, T., and Bryant, W. T. Mapping sex group stereotypes of elementary and high school students. *Sex Roles,* 1978, *4,* 135–140.

Parke, R. D. Emerging themes for social-emotional development: Introduction to the section. *American Psychologist,* 1979, *34,* 930–931. (a)

Parke, R. D. Perspectives on father-infant interaction. In J. D. Osofsky (Ed.), *Handbook of infant development.* New York: Wiley, 1979. (b)

Parke, R. D. *Fathers.* Cambridge, Mass.: Harvard University Press, 1981.

Parke, R. D., Hymel, S., Power, T. G., and Tinsley, B. R. Fathers and risk: A hospital based model of intervention. In D. B. Sawin, R. C. Hawkins, L. L. Walker, and J. H. Penticuff (Eds.), *Exeptional infant: Psychosocial risks in infant-environment transactions.* New York: Brunner/Mazel, 1979.

Parke, R. D., and Sawin, D. B. *Infant characteristics and behavior as elicitors of maternal and paternal responsibility in the newborn period.* Paper presented at the Society for Research in Child Development, Denver, Colo., April, 1975.

Parten, M. B. Social participation among preschool children. *Journal of Abnormal Psychology,* 1932, *27,* 243–269.

Parton, D. A. Learning to imitate in infancy. *Child Development,* 1976, *47,* 14–31.

Passman, R. H., and Erck, T. W. Permitting maternal contact through vision alone: Films of mothers for promoting play and locomotion. *Developmental Psychology,* 1978, *14,* 512–516.

Passman, R. H., and Weisberg, P. Mothers and blankets as agents for promoting play and exploration in a novel environment: The effects of social and nonsocial attachment objects. *Developmental Psychology,* 1975, *11,* 170–177.

Pastor, D. L. The quality of mother-infant attachment and its relationship to toddlers' initial sociability with peers. *Developmental Psychology,* 1981, *17,* 326–335.

Patten, B. M. *Human embryology.* New York: McGraw-Hill, 1946.

Payne, J. S., and Thomas, C. The mentally retarded. In N. G. Haring (Ed.), *Behavior of exceptional children* (2nd ed.). Columbus, Ohio: Charles E. Merrill, 1978.

Pedersen, F. A. Does research on children reared in father-absent families yield information on father influences? *The Family Coordinator,* 1976, *25,* 459–464.

Peel, E. A. *The pupil's thinking.* London: Oldbourne, 1960.

Peiper, A. *Cerebral function in infancy and childhood.* Translated by B. Nagler from the 3rd German edition original publication, 1961. New York: Consultant Bureau, 1963.

Pelton, L. H. Child abuse and neglect: The myth of classlessness. *American Journal of Orthopsychiatry,* 1978, *48,* 608–617.

Perkins, E. Children's behavior in early childhood settings: A review of the literature on the influence of physical space and materials. Paper presented at the American Educational Research Association, San Francisco, April 1979.

Perry, D. G., and Perry, L. C. Denial of suffering in the victim as a stimulus to violence in aggressive boys. *Child Development,* 1974, *45,* 55–62.

Pflaum, S. W. *The development of language and reading in the young child.* Columbus, Ohio: Charles E. Merrill, 1974.

Phillips, R. Searching for role models in the classroom. *The Chicago Tribune,* December 16, 1979.

Phipps-Yonas, S. Teenage pregnancy and motherhood: A review of the literature. *American Journal of Orthopsychiatry,* 1980, *50,* 403–431.

Piaget, J. *The moral judgment of the child.* New York: Harcourt, 1932.

Piaget, J. *The language and thought of the child.* London: Routledge and Kegan Paul, 1952. (a)

Piaget, J. *The origins of intelligence in children.* New York: International Universities Press, 1952. (b)

Piaget, J. *The moral judgment of children.* New York: Basic Books, 1954.

Piaget, J. *Judgment and reasoning in the child.* Paterson, N.J.: Littlefield, Adams and Co., 1964.

Piaget, J. *The moral judgment of the child.* New York: Free Press, 1966.

Piaget, J. *Six psychological studies.* New York: Vintage Books, 1967.

Piaget, J. Piaget's theory. In P. H. Mussen (Ed.), *Carmichael's manual of child psychology* (3rd ed.). New York: Wiley, 1970.

Piaget, J. *Understanding causality.* Translated by D. Miles and M. Miles. New York: Norton, 1974.

Piaget, J., and Inhelder, B. *The growth of logical thinking from childhood to adolescence.* New York: Basic Books, 1961.

Piaget, J., and Inhelder, B. *The psychology of the child.* New York: Basic Books, 1969.

Pieroy, S., Chandavasu, O., and Wexler, I. Withdrawal symptoms in infants with the fetal alcohol syndrome. *Journal of Pediatrics,* 1977, *90,* 630–633.

Piggott, L. R. Overview of selected basic research in autism. *Journal of Autism and Developmental Disorders,* 1979, *9,* 199–217.

Pines, M. Invisible playmates. *Psychology Today,* 1978, *12,* 38–42.

Pines, M. Good samaritans at age two? *Psychology Today,* 1979, *13,* 66–77. (a)

Pines, M. Superkids. *Psychology Today,* 1979, *12,* 53–63. (b)

Pines, M. Update/Only isn't lonely (or spoiled or selfish). *Psychology Today,* 1981, *15,* 15–19.

Pipes, P. L. *Nutrition in infancy and childhood.* St. Louis, C. V. Mosby, 1977.

Pitkin, R. M. Nutrition during pregnancy: The clinical approach. In M. Winick (Ed.), *Nutritional disorders of American women.* New York: Wiley, 1977.

Pleck, J. H. Masculinity-femininity: Current and alternative paradigms. *Sex Roles,* 1975, *1,* 161–178.

Podolner, M. *A man in the early childhood classroom.* Paper presented at the National Association for the Education of Young Children, New York, August 1978.

Polo, M. *The description of the world.* London: Routledge and Sons, 1938.

Pomeroy, W. B. *Boys and sex.* New York: Delacorte Press, 1968.

Ponzo, Z. Age prejudice of "act your age." *Personnel and Guidance Journal,* 1978, *57,* 140–143.

Portnoy, F. C., and Simmons, C. H. Day care and attachment. *Child Development,* 1978, *49,* 239–242.

Potts, M., Carlson, P., Cocking, R., and Copple, C. *Structure and development in child language: The preschool years.* Ithaca, N.Y.: Cornell University Press, 1979.

Pratt, K. C., Nelson, A. K., and Sun, K. H. *The behavior of the newborn infant.* Columbus, Ohio: Ohio State University Press, 1930.

Pulvino, C. J., and Lupton, P. E. Superior students, family size, birth order and intellectual ability. *Gifted Child Quarterly,* 1978, *22,* 212–216.

Quintero, N. Coming of age the Apache way. *National Geographic,* 1980, *157,* 262–271.

Rader, N., Bausano, M., and Richards, J. E. On the nature of the visual-cliff-avoidance response in human infants. *Child Development,* 1980, *51,* 61–68

Radin, N., and Kamii, C. The child-rearing attitudes of disadvantaged Negro mothers and some educational implications. *Journal of Negro Education,* 1965, *34,* 138–146.

Ragozin, A. S. Attachment behavior of day-care children: Naturalistic and laboratory observations. *Child Development,* 1980, *51,* 409–415.

Ramsay, D. S., Campos, J. J., and Fenson, L. Onset of bimanual handedness in infants. *Infant Behavior and Development,* 1979, *2,* 69–76.

Rebecca, M., Hefner, R., and Oleshansky, B. A model of sex-role transcendence. *Journal of Social Issues,* 1976, *32,* 197–206.

Rebelsky, F. G., Starr, R. H., and Luria, Z. Language development: The first four years. In Y. Brackbill (Ed.), *Infancy and early childhood.* New York: The Free Press, 1967.

Rees, A. H., and Palmer, F. H. Factors related to change in mental test performance. *Developmental Psychology Monographs,* 1970, *3,* 1–57.

Reisenger, K., Rogers, K. D., and Johnson, O. Nutrition survey of Lower Greasewood, Arizona, Navajos. In W. M. Moore, M. M. Silverberg, and O. M. S. Read (Eds.), *Nutrition, growth, and development of North American Children.* DHEW Publication No. (NIH) 72–26, 1972.

Reiser, J., Yonas, A., and Wikner, K. Radial localization of odors by human newborns. *Child Development,* 1976, *47,* 856–859.

Reiss, I. L. The sexual renaissance in America. *Journal of Social Issues,* 1966, *22,* 123–137.

Reiss, I. L. *The family system in America.* New York: Holt, Rinehart and Winston, 1971.

Reith, H. J. A behavioral approach to the management of hyperactive behavior. In M. J. Fine (Ed.), *Principles and techniques of intervention with hyperactive children.* Springfield, Ill.: Charles C. Thomas, 1977.

Resnik, J. L., Resnik, M. B., Packer, A. B., and Wilson, J. Fathering classes: A psycho/educational model. *The Counseling Psychologist,* 1978, *7,* 56–60.

Rest, J. R. Development hierarchy in preference and comprehension of moral judgment. Unpublished doctoral dissertation, University of Chicago, 1968.

Restak, R. M. *The brain: The last frontier.* Garden City, N.Y.: Doubleday, 1979.

Rheingold, H. L. The modification of social responsiveness of institutional babies. *Monographs of the Society for Research in Child Development,* 1956, *21,* (2, Serial No. 63).

Rheingold, H. L. The effect of environmental stimulation upon social and exploratory behavior in the human infant. In B. M. Foss (Ed.), *Determinants of infant behavior.* New York: Wiley, 1961.

Rheingold, H. L., and Cook, K. The contents of boys' and girls' rooms as an index of parents' behavior. *Child Development,* 1975, *46,* 459–463.

Rheingold, H. L., Gewirtz, J., and Ross, H. Social conditioning of vocalizations in the infant. *Journal of Comparative Physiological Psychology*, 1959, *52*, 68–73.

Rheingold, H. L., Hay, D. F., and West, M. J. Sharing in the second year of life. *Child Development*, 1976, *47*, 1148–1158.

Rice, F. P. *The adolescent: Development, relationships, and culture* (2nd ed.). Boston: Allyn and Bacon, 1978.

Rich, S. Survey shows teens having sex earlier. *The Charlotte Observer*, August 3, 1979.

Richards, A. I. *Chisungu: A girl's initiation ceremony among the Bemba of Northern Rhodesia*. New York: Grove Press, 1956.

Richardson, S. Ecology of malnutrition: Nonnutritional factors influencing intellectual and behavioral development. In *Nutrition, the nervous system, and behavior*. Pan American Health Organization Scientific Publication #251, 1972.

Richardson, S. A., Goodman, U., Hastorf, A. H., and Dornbusch, S. A. Cultural uniformity in reaction to physical disabilities. *American Sociological Review*, 1961, *26*, 241–247.

Ridberg, E. H., Parke, R. D., and Hetherington, E. M. Modification of impulsive and reflective cognitive styles through observation of film mediated models. *Developmental Psychology*, 1971, *5*, 369–377.

Rimland, B. *Infantile autism: The syndrome and its implications for a neural theory of behavior*. New York: Appleton-Century-Crofts, 1964.

Ritchie, S. The relationship between risk taking and creativity. Unpublished doctoral dissertation, University of North Carolina, Greensboro, 1981.

Roberge, J. J., and Flexer, B. K. Further examination of formal operational reasoning abilities. *Child Development*, 1979, *50*, 478–484.

Roberts, H. A. A clinical and metabolic reevaluation of reading disability. In *Selected papers on learning disabilities, fifth annual convention, Association for Children with Learning Disabilities*. San Rafael, Calif.: Academic Therapy Publication, 1969.

Roberts, I. F., West, R. J., Ogilvio, D., and Dillon, M. J. Malnutrition in infants receiving cult diets: A form of child abuse. *British Medical Journal*, 1979, *1*, 296–298.

Roberts, J., and Baird, J. T. *Parent ratings of behavioral patterns of children. Vital and Health Statistics. Data from the National Health Survey.* Series 11, No. 108. Washington, D.C.: U.S. Government Printing Office, 1971.

Robinson, B. E. Changing views on male early childhood teachers. *Young Children*, 1981, *36*, 27–32.

Robinson, B. E., and Canaday, H. Sex-role behaviors and personality traits of male day care teachers. *Sex Roles*, 1978, *4*, 853–865.

Robinson, B. E., Skeen, P., and Flake-Hobson, C. Sex-stereotyped attitudes of male and female child-care workers: Support for androgynous child care. *Child Care Quarterly*, 1980, *9*, 233–242.

Robinson, B. E., Skeen, P., Flake-Hobson, C., and Herrman, M. Gay's perception of early family life and their relationships with parents. *Family Relations: Journal of Applied Family and Child Studies*, 1982, *31*, 79–83.

Robson, K. S., and Moss, H. A. Patterns and determinants of maternal attachment. *Journal of Pediatrics*, 1970, *77*, 976–985.

Roche, A. F. Some aspects of adolescent growth and maturation. In J. I. McKigney and H. N. Munro (Eds.), *Nutrient requirements in adolescence*. Cambridge, Mass.: M.I.T. Press, 1976.

Roche, A. F. Secular trends in human growth, maturation, and development. *Monographs of the Society for Research in Child Development*, 1979, *44* (3–4, Serial No. 179).

Rogers, D. *The psychology of adolescence* (3rd ed.). Englewood Cliffs, N.J.: Prentice-Hall, 1977.

Rollins, B. C., and Feldman, H. Marital satisfaction over the family life cycle. *Journal of Marriage and the Family*, 1970, *32*, 20–28.

Romer, N., and Cherry, D. Developmental effects of preschool and school-age maternal employment on children's sex role concepts. Unpublished manuscript, Brooklyn College of the City University of New York, 1978.

Rosch, E. On the internal structure of perceptual and semantic categories. In T. E. Moore (Ed.), *Cognitive development and the acquisition of language*. New York: Academic Press, 1973.

Rose, S. A. Enhancing visual recognition memory in preterm infants. *Developmental Psychology*, 1980, *16*, 85–92.

Rosen, G. Reversible growth and developmental retardation in the first year of life. *Clinical Proceedings, Children's Hospital National Medical Center*, 1977, *33*, 193–205.

Rosinski, R. R. *The development of visual perception*. Santa Monica, Calif.: Goodyear, 1977.

Ross, D. M., and Ross, S. A. *Hyperactivity: Research, theory, and action*. New York: Wiley-Interscience, 1976.

Ross, G., Kagan, J., Zelazo, P., and Kotelchuck, M. Separation protest in infants in home and laboratory. *Developmental Psychology*, 1975, *11*, 256–257.

Rothbart, M. K. Laughter in young children. *Psychological Bulletin*, 1973, *80*, 247–256.

Rowland, B. H. *Infant-toddler guidebook*. Nashville, Tenn.: Methodist Church Clearinghouse, 1980.

Rubenstein, C. The children of divorce as adults. *Psychology Today*, 1980, *13*, 74–75.

Rubin, K., Watson, K., and Jambor, T. Free-play behaviors in preschool and kindergarten children. *Child Development,* 1978, *49,* 534–536.

Rubin, Z. *Children's friendships.* Cambridge, Mass.: Harvard University Press, 1980.

Rubinstein, E. Television and the young viewer. *American Scientist,* 1978, *66,* 685–693.

Ruble, D. N., Balaban, T., and Cooper, J. Gender constancy and the effects of sex-typed televised toy commercials. *Child Development,* 1981, *52,* 667–673.

Rudel, R. G., and Teuber, H. L. Discrimination of direction of line in children. *Journal of Comparative Physiological Psychology,* 1963, *56,* 892–897.

Rugh, R., and Shettles, L. B., with Einhorn, R. N. *From conception to birth: The drama of life's beginnings.* New York: Harper and Row, 1971.

Russell, G. The father role and its relation to masculinity, femininity, and androgyny. *Child Development,* 1978, *49,* 1174–1181.

Russell, M. J. Human olfactory communication. *Nature,* 1976, *260,* 520–522.

Rutter, M. Parent-child separation: Psychological effects on the children. *Journal of Child Psychology and Psychiatry,* 1971, *12,* 233–260.

Rutter, M. Maternal deprivation, 1972–1978: New findings, new concepts, new approaches. *Child Development,* 1979, *50,* 283–305.

Rutter, M., and Madge, N. *Cycles of disadvantage: A review of research.* London: Heinemann, 1976.

Ryan, J. Early language development: Towards a communicational analysis. In M. P. M. Richards (Ed.), *The integration of a child into a social world.* London: Cambridge University Press, 1974.

Ryan, J. P. Personal communication, July 15, 1979.

Sagi, A., and Hoffman, Y. L. Empathic distress in the newborn. *Developmental Psychology,* 1976, *12,* 175–176.

Salkind, N. J., and Nelson, C. F. A note on the developmental nature of reflection-impulsivity. *Developmental Psychology,* 1980, *16,* 237–238.

Sameroff, A. Can conditioned responses be established in the newborn infant: 1971? In F. Rebelsky and L. Dorman (Eds.), *Child development and behavior.* New York: Knopf, 1973.

Sameroff, A. J., and Cavanagh, P. J. Learning in infancy: A developmental perspective. In J. D. Osofsky (Ed.), *Handbook of infant development.* New York: Wiley, 1979.

Sameroff, A. J., and Chandler, J. J. Reproductive risk and the continuum of caretaking causality. In F. D. Horowitz (Ed.), *Review of child development research* (Vol. 4). Chicago: University of Chicago Press, 1975.

Santrock, J. W. Father absence, perceived maternal behavior, and moral development in boys. *Child Development,* 1975, *46,* 753–757.

Sapir, E. Language and environment. In D. G. Mandelbaum (Ed.), *Selected writings of Edward Sapir in language, culture, and personality.* Berkeley, Calif.: University of California Press, 1958.

Satterfield, J. H., and Cantwell, D. P. Pathophysiology of the hyperactive child syndrome. *Archives of General Psychiatry,* 1976, *31,* 839–844.

Scarf, M. The anatomy of fear. *The New York Times Magazine,* June 12, 1974.

Scarlett, G. Adolescent thinking and the diary of Anne Frank. In J. J. Conger (Ed.), *Contemporary issues in adolescent development.* New York: Harper and Row, 1975.

Scarr, S., and Weinberg, R. A. Intellectual similarities within families of both adopted and biological children. *Intelligence,* 1977, *1,* 170–191.

Scarr-Salapatek, S., and Williams, M. L. The effects of early stimulation on low–birth weight infants. *Child Development,* 1973, *44,* 94–101.

Schaefer, C. E. Imaginary companions and creative adolescents. *Developmental Psychology,* 1969, *1,* 747–749.

Schaefer, R., and Coie, J. D. *Maternal reactions to problem behavior and ordinal position of child.* San Francisco: ERIC (Document Reproduction No. ED 149 234), 1977.

Schaffer, H. R. Some issues for research in the study of attachment behavior. In B. M. Foss (Ed.), *Determinants of infant behavior.* New York: Wiley, 1963.

Schaffer, H. R. *The origins of human social relations.* New York: Academic Press, 1971.

Schaffer, H. R., and Callender, W. M. Psychologic effects of hospitalization in infancy. *Pediatrics,* 1959, *24,* 528–539.

Schaffer, H. R., and Emerson, P. The development of social attachments in infancy. *Monographs of the Society for Research in Child Development,* 1964, *29* (3, Serial No. 94).

Schaller, J., Carlsson, S. G., and Larsson, K. Effects of extended postpartum mother-child contact on the mother's behavior during nursing. *Infant Behavior and Development,* 1979, *2,* 319–324.

Schiffman, P. L., Westlake, R. E., Santiago, T. V., and Edelman, N. H. Ventilatory control in parents of victims of Sudden Infant

Death Syndrome. *The New England Journal of Medicine*, 1980, *302*, 486–491.

Schmitt, M. H. Superiority of breast-feeding: Fact or fancy? *American Journal of Nursing*, 1970, 1488–1493.

Schopler, E., Andrews, C. E., and Strupp, K. Do autistic children come from upper-middle-class parents? *Journal of Autism and Developmental Disorders*, 1979, *9*, 139–141.

Schopler, E., and Reichler, R. J. Parents as cotherapists in the treatment of psychotic children. *Journal of Autism and Childhood Schizophrenia*, 1971, *1*, 87–102.

Schuman, W. Ultrasound: Exploring life in the womb. *Parents*, 1980, *55*, 56–61.

Schweinhart, L., and Weikart, D. *Young children grow up.* Ypsilanti, Mich.: High/Scope Educational Research Foundation, 1981.

Scott, E. P., Jan, J. E., and Freeman, R. D. *Can't your child see?* Baltimore: University Park Press, 1977.

Scrimshaw, N. S. Malnutrition, learning and behavior. *American Journal of Clinical Nutrition*, 1967, *26*, 493–502.

Sears, R. R. Relation of early socialization experience to self-concepts and gender role in middle childhood. *Child Development*, 1970, *41*, 267–290.

Sears, R. R., Maccoby, E. E., and Levin, H. *Patterns of child-rearing.* Evanston, Ill.: Row, Peterson, 1957.

Sebald, H. *Adolescence: A sociological analysis.* Englewood Cliffs, N.J.: Prentice-Hall, 1968.

Secretary of HEW. *Marihuana and health. Report to the U.S. Congress.* Washington, D.C.: U.S. Government Printing Office, 1976.

Segal, J., and Yahraes, H. Bringing up mother. *Psychology Today*, 1978, *12*, 90–96.

Self, P. A., Horowitz, F. D., and Paden, L. Y. Olfaction in newborn infants. *Developmental Psychology*, 1972, *7*, 349–363.

Senn, M. J. E., and Solnit, A. J. *Problems in child behavior and development.* Philadelphia: Lea and Febiger, 1968.

Serunian, S. A., and Broman, S. H. Relationship of Apgar scores and Bayley mental and motor scores. *Child Development*, 1975, *46*, 696–700.

Shainess, N. A. A re-evaluation of some aspects of femininity through a study of menstruation: A preliminary report. *Comprehensive Psychiatry*, 1961, *2*, 20–26.

Shaw, M. E. Changes in sociometric choices following forced integration of an elementary school. *Journal of Social Issues*, 1974, *29*, 143–157.

Sheldon, H. H. *The varieties of human physique.* New York: Harper and Brothers, 1940.

Sherif, M., Harvey, O. J., White, B. J., Hood, W. R., and Sherif, C. W. *Intergroup conflict and cooperation: The Robbers Cave experiment.* Norman, Okla.: University of Oklahoma Press, 1961.

Sherrod, L. R. Social cognition in infants: Attention to the human face. *Infant Behavior and Development*, 1979, *2*, 279–294.

Shinn, M. Father absence and children's cognitive development. *Psychology Bulletin*, 1978, *85*, 295–324.

Shirley, M. M. *The first two years; A study of 25 babies (Vol. 2): Intellectual development.* Minneapolis, Minn.: University of Minnesota Press, 1933, 1961.

Sidel, R. *Women and child care in China.* New York: Hill and Wang, 1972.

Siegel, L. S. Infant tests as predictors of cognitive and language development at two years. *Child Development*, 1981, *52*, 545–557.

Siegelman, E. Reflective and impulsive observing behavior. *Child Development*, 1969, *40*, 1213–1222.

Sigel, I. E., Roeper, A., and Hooper, F. H. A training procedure for acquisition of Piaget's conservation of quantity: A pilot study and its replication. *British Journal of Educational Psychology*, 1966, *36*, 301–311.

Silberberg, N., Iverson, I., and Silberberg, M. The predictive efficiency of the Gates Reading Readiness Tests. *Elementary School Journal*, 1968, *68*, 213–218.

Siman, M. L. Application of a new model of peer group influence to naturally existing adolescent friendship groups. *Child Development*, 1977, *48*, 270–274.

Simner, M. L. Newborn's response to the cry of another infant. *Developmental Psychology*, 1971, *5*, 136–150.

Sinclair, C. B. *Movement of the young child: Ages two to six.* Columbus, Ohio: Charles C. Merrill, 1973.

Singleton, L. C., and Asher, S. R. Racial integration and children's peer preferences: An investigation of developmental and cohort differences. *Child Development*, 1979, *50*, 936–941.

Siqueland, E. R. Reinforcement patterns and extinction in human newborns. *Journal of Experimental Child Psychology*, 1968, *6*, 431–442.

Skeels, H. M. Adult status of children with contrasting early life experience. *Monographs of the Society for Research in Child Development*, 1966, *31* (3, Serial No. 105).

Skeen, P., and McKenry, P. The teacher's role in facilitating a child's adjustment to divorce. *Young Children*, 1980, *35*, 3–12.

Skinner, B. F. *Verbal behavior.* New York: Appleton-Century-Crofts, 1957.

Skinner, B. F. Autobiographic sketch. In E. G. Boring and G. Lindzey (Eds.), *A history of psychology in autobiography* (Vol. 5). New York: Appleton-Century-Crofts, 1967.

Skinner, L. *Motor development in the preschool years.* Springfield, Ill.: Charles C. Thomas, 1979.

Skolnick, A. The myth of the invulnerable child. *Psychology Today,* 1978, *11,* 56–65.

Slater, A. M., and Findlay, J. M. Binocular fixation in the newborn baby. *Journal of Experimental Child Psychology,* 1975, *20,* 248–273.

Slobin, D. I. *Psycholinguistics.* Glenview, Ill.: Scott, Foresman, 1971.

Slobin, D. I. They learn the same way all around the world. In *Readings in Human Development 1977/1978.* Guilford, Conn.: Dushkin, 1977.

Smith, F. *Reading without nonsense.* New York: Teachers College Press, 1979.

Smith, M. E. An investigation of the development of the sentence and the extent of vocabulary in young children. *University of Iowa Studies in Child Welfare,* 1926, *3,* 268–269.

Smith, P. K., and Daglish, L. Sex differences in parent and infant behavior in the home. *Child Development,* 1977, *48,* 1250–1254.

Snapper, K. J., and Ohms, J. S. *The status of children 1977.* Washington, D.C.: U.S. DHEW Publication No. (OHDS) 78–30133, 1977.

Soares, A. T., and Soares, L. M. Self-perceptions of culturally disadvantaged children. *American Educational Research Journal,* 1969, *6,* 31–45.

Society for Research in Child Development. Ethical standards for research with children. *SRCD Newsletter,* 1973(Winter), 3–4.

Sontag, L. W. Difference in modifiability of fetal behavior and physiology. *Psychosomatic Medicine,* 1944, *6,* 151–154.

Sorensen, R. C. *Adolescent sexuality in contemporary America.* New York: World Publishing, 1973.

Sorenson, E. R. Growing up as a Fore is to be "in touch" and free. *Smithsonian,* 1977, *8,* 106–115.

Soroka, S. M., Corter, C. M., and Abramovitch, R. Infants' tactual discrimination of novel and familiar tactual stimulation. *Child Development,* 1979, *50,* 1251–1253.

Sorosky, A. D. The psychological effects of a divorce on adolescents. *Adolescence,* 1977, *12,* 123–136.

Sousa, M. *Childbirth at home.* New York: Harper & Row, 1977.

Spar, K. (Ed.). Failing to help abused, neglected children. *Report on Preschool Education,* 1980, *12,* 5.

Special Action Office for Drug Abuse Prevention. *Q and A.* Washington, D.C.: Executive Office of the President (GPO: 1975 0–576–576), 1976.

Speech Foundation of America. *Stuttering: Its prevention.* Memphis, Tenn.: Author, 1962.

Spelke, E. S., and Owsley, C. J. Intermodal exploration and knowledge in infancy. *Infant Behavior and Development,* 1979, *2,* 13–27.

Spezzano, C. Prenatal psychology: Pregnant with questions. *Psychology Today,* 1981, *15,* 49–57.

Spezzano, C., and Waterman, J. The first day of life. *Psychology Today,* 1977, *11,* 110–116.

Spitz, R. A. Hospitalism: A follow-up report. In *The psychoanalytic study of the child* (Vol. 2). New York: International Universities Press, 1946.

Sroufe, L. A. Socio-emotional development. In J. D. Osofsky (Ed.), *Handbook of infant development.* New York: Wiley, 1979.

Staffieri, J. R. A study of social stereotypes of body image in children. *Journal of Personality and Social Psychology,* 1967, *7,* 101–104.

Starr, R. H. Child abuse. *American Psychologist,* 1979, *34,* 872–878.

The State. Califano warns teenage smokers risking lives. Columbia, S.C., April 27, 1979.

Staub, E. A child in distress: The influence of nurturance and modeling on children's attempts to help. *Developmental Psychology,* 1971, *5,* 124–132.

Stayton, D. J., Hogan, R., and Ainsworth, M. Infant obedience and maternal behavior: The origins of socialization reconsidered. *Child Development,* 1971, *42,* 1057–1069.

Steele, B. F., and Pollock, C. B. A psychiatric study of parents who abuse infants and small children. In R. E. Helfer and C. H. Kempe (Eds.), *The battered child* (2nd ed.). Chicago: University of Chicago Press, 1974.

Stein, A. H. The effects of maternal employment and educational attainment on the sex-typed attributes of college females. *Social Behavior and Personality,* 1973, *1,* 111–114.

Stein, A. H., and Friedrich, L. K. Impact of television on children and youth. In E. M. Hetherington (Ed.), *Review of child development research* (Vol. 5). Chicago: University of Chicago Press, 1975.

Stephan, W. G., and Rosenfield, D. Effects of desegregation on racial attitudes. *Journal of Personality and Social Psychology,* 1978, *36,* 795–804.

Stephens, T. M., and Wolf, J. S. The gifted child. In N. G. Haring (Ed.), *Behavior of exceptional children* (2nd ed.). Columbus, Ohio: Charles E. Merrill, 1978.

Stern, C. *Principles of human genetics* (3rd ed.). San Francisco: W. H. Freeman, 1973.

Stern, D. N. Mother and infant at play: The dyadic interaction involving facial, vocal and gaze behaviors. In M. Lewis and L. A. Rosenblum (Eds.), *The effect of the infant on its caregiver.* New York: Wiley, 1974.

Stoneman, Z., and Brody, G. H. Peers as mediators of television food advertisements aimed at children. *Developmental Psychology,* 1981, *17,* 853–858.

Stoneman, Z., and Brody, G. H. The indirect impact of child-oriented advertisements on mother-child interactions. *Journal of Applied Developmental Psychology,* 1982, in press.

Stotland, E. Exploratory investigations of empathy. In L. Berkowitz (Ed.), *Advances in experimental social psychology* (Vol. 4). New York: Academic Press, 1969.

Strain, B. A., and Vietze, P. M. *Early dialogues: The structure of reciprocal infant-mother vocalization.* Paper presented at the meeting of the Society for Research in Child Development, Denver, Colo. April 1975.

Strang, R. *An introduction to child study* (4th ed.). New York: Macmillan, 1969.

Strayer, J. A naturalistic study of empathic behaviors and their relation to affective states and perspective-taking skills in preschool children. *Child Development,* 1980, *51,* 815–822.

Streissguth, A. P., Herman, C. S., and Smith, D. W. Intelligence, behavior, and dysmorphogenesis in the fetal alcohol syndrome: A report on 20 patients. *Journal of Pediatrics,* 1978, *92,* 363–367.

Sutton-Smith, B., and Rosenberg, B. G. Sixty years of historical change in the game preferences of American children. *Journal of American Folklore,* 1961, *74,* 17–46.

Svejda, M. J., Campos, J. J., and Emde, R. N. Mother-infant "bonding": Failure to generalize. *Child Development,* 1980, *51,* 775–779.

Swift, P. Drug stabilization. *Parade Magazine,* February 20, 1977, *5,* 6. (a)

Swift, P. Inner city teens. *Parade Magazine,* September 18, 1977, *5,* 11. (b)

Tanner, J. M. *Growth at adolescence* (2nd ed.). Oxford: Blackwell, 1962; Philadelphia: David, 1962.

Tanner, J. M. The regulation of human growth. *Child Development,* 1963, *34,* 817–847.

Tanner, J. M. Growth and endocrinology of the adolescent. In J. J. Gariner (Ed.), *Endocrine and genetic diseases of childhood.* Philadelphia: Saunders, 1969.

Tanner, J. M. Physical growth. In P. H. Mussen (Ed.), *Carmichael's manual of child psychology* (3rd ed. vol. 1). New York: Wiley, 1970.

Tanner, J. M. *Fetus into man: Physical growth from conception to maturity.* Cambridge, Mass.: Harvard University Press, 1978.

Taylor, D. C. Differential rates of cerebral maturation between sexes and between hemispheres. *Lancet,* 1969, *2,* 140–142.

Teeple, J. Physical growth and maturation. In M. V. Risenour (Ed.), *Motor development: Issues and applications.* Princeton, N.J.: Princeton Book Company, 1978.

Terhune, K. W. *The paradoxical status of the only child.* American Psychological Association, 1976. (ERIC Document No. ED 130 764)

Terman, L. M., and Oden, M. *The gifted child grows up.* Stanford, Calif.: Stanford University Press, 1947.

Terman, L. M., amd Oden, M. *The gifted group at mid-life.* Stanford, Calif.: Stanford University Press, 1959.

Terry, S. G., Sorrentino, J. M., and Flatter, C. H. *Children: Their growth and development.* New York: McGraw-Hill, 1979.

Thoman, E. B. Sleep and wake behavior in neonates: Consistencies and consequences. *Merrill-Palmer Quarterly,* 1975, *21,* 295–314.

Thomas, A., and Chess, S. *Temperament and development.* New York: Brunner/Mazel, 1977.

Thomas, A., and Chess, S. *The dynamics of psychological development.* New York: Brunner/Mazel, 1980.

Thomas, A., Chess, S., and Birch, H. G. The origin of personality. *Scientific American,* 1970, *233,* 102–108.

Thomas, R. M. *Comparing theories of child development.* Belmont, Calif.: Wadsworth, 1979.

Tizard, B. *Adoption: A second chance.* London: Open Books, 1977.

Tizard, B., and Hodges, J. The effect of early institutional rearing on the development of eight-year-old children. *Journal of Child Psychology and Psychiatry,* 1978, *19,* 99–118.

Tizard, B., and Rees, J. The effect of early institutional rearing on the behaviour problems and affectional relationships of four-year-old children. *Journal of Child Psychology and Psychiatry,* 1975, *16,* 61–74.

Torrance, E. P. *Guiding creative talent.* Englewood Cliffs, N.J.: Prentice-Hall, 1962.

Torrance, E. P. Adventuring in creativity. *Childhood Education,* 1963, *40,* 79.

Torrance, E. P. Broadening concepts of giftedness in the '70s. *Gifted Child Quarterly,* 1970, *4,* 199–208. (a)

Torrance, E. P. *Encouraging creativity in the classroom.* Dubuque, Iowa: W. C. Brown, 1970. (b)

Traisman, A. S., and Traisman, H. S. Thumb and finger sucking: A study of 2650 infants and children. *Journal of Pediatrics,* 1958, *53,* 566.

Trause, M. A. Stranger responses: Effects of familiarity, stranger's approach, and sex of infant. *Child Development,* 1977, *48,* 1657–1661.

Tredgold, A. F. *A textbook of mental deficiency.* Baltimore: Wood, 1937.

Trotter, R. J. LeBoyer's babies. In *Readings in human development 1978/1979.* Guilford, Conn.: Dushkin, 1978.

Trowbridge, H., and Trowbridge, L. Self-concept and socio-economic status. *Child Study Journal,* 1972, *2,* 123–139.

Tubbs, E. V. More men teachers in our schools. *School and Society,* 1946, *63,* 394.

Tulkin, S. R., and Kagan, J. Mother-child interaction in the first year of life. *Child Development,* 1972, *42,* 31–41.

Tulkin, S. R., and Konner, M. J. Alternative conceptions of intellectual functioning. *Human Development,* 1973, *16,* 33–52.

Turiel, E. The development of social concepts: Mores, customs, and conventions. In D. J. DePalma and J. M. Foley (Eds.), *Moral development: Current theory and research.* Hillsdale, N.J.: Erlbaum, 1975.

Tyler, J. D., and Holsinger, D. N. Locus of control differences between rural American Indian and white children. *Journal of Social Psychology,* 1975, *95,* 149–155.

Ullian, D. Z. The development of conceptions of masculinity and femininity. In B. Lloyd and J. Archer (Eds.), *Exploring sex differences.* New York: Academic Press, 1976.

Ullian, D. Z. *Why boys will be boys: A structural perspective.* Paper presented at the National Association for the Education of Young Children, Atlanta, November 1979.

Ungerer, J. A., Brody, L. R., and Zelazo, P. R. Long-term memory for speech in 2- to 4-week-old infants. *Infant Behavior and Development,* 1978, *1,* 177–186.

U.S. Department of Transportation. *How to talk to your teenager about drinking and driving.* Washington, D.C.: National Highway Traffic Safety Administration (GPO 1976 0–625–636), 1976.

Valdes-Dapena, M. A. *Sudden unexplained infant death.* Rockville, Md.: Bureau of Community Health Services (DHEW Publication No. (HSA) 78–5255), 1978.

Vaughan, V. C. Growth and development in the infant and child. In W. E. Nelson (Ed.), *Textbook of Pediatrics* (8th ed.). Philadelphia: Saunders, 1964.

Visher, E. B., and Visher, J. S. *Stepfamilies: A guide to working with stepparents and stepchildren.* New York: Brunner/Mazel, 1979.

Von Mickwitz, M. The effect of type and amount of familiarization training on pattern recognition. Unpublished doctoral dissertation, University of Pittsburgh, 1973.

Vulliamy, D. G. *The newborn child.* Baltimore: Williams and Wilkins, 1972.

Vurpillot, E. The development of scanning strategies and their relation to visual differentiation. *Journal of Experimental Child Psychology,* 1968, *6,* 632–650.

Vygotsky, L. S. *Thought and language.* Translated by E. Hanfmann and G. Vakar. Cambridge, Mass.: M.I.T. Press, 1962.

Vygotsky, L. S. Play and its role in the mental development of the child. *Soviet Psychology,* 1967, *5,* 6–18.

Wadsworth, B. J. *Piaget for the classroom teacher.* New York: Longman, 1978.

Wadsworth, B. J. *Piaget's theory of cognitive development.* New York: David McKay, 1979.

Walberg, H. J. Varieties of adolescent creativity and the high school environment. *Exceptional Children,* 1971, *38,* 111–116.

Walker, R. N. Body build and behavior in young children. Body build and parents' ratings. *Child Development,* 1963, *34,* 1–23.

Wallach, M. A., and Kogan, N. *Modes of thinking in young children.* New York: Holt, Rinehart and Winston, 1965.

Wallerstein, J. S., and Kelly, J. B. The effects of parental divorce: Experience of the child in later latency. *American Journal of Orthopsychiatry,* 1976, *46,* 256–269.

Wallerstein, J. S., and Kelly, J. B. California's children of divorce. *Psychology Today,* 1980, *13,* 67–76. (a)

Wallerstein, J. S., and Kelly, J. B. *Surviving the break-up: How children actually cope with divorce.* New York: Basic Books, 1980. (b)

Walters, J., McKenry, P., and Walters, L. H. Adolescents' knowledge of childbearing. *The Family Coordinator,* 1979, *28,* 163–172.

Walters, J., and Stinnett, N. Parent-child relationships: A decade review of research. *Journal of Marriage and the Family,* 1971, *33,* 70–110.

Ward, S., and Wackman, D. B. Television advertising and intrafamily influence: Children's purchase influence attempts and parental yielding. Unpublished paper, Harvard Graduate School of Business Administration, 1971.

Warren, N. Malnutrition and mental development. *Psychological Bulletin,* 1973, *80,* 324–328.

Wasserman, M. Oestrogens. In *Occupational safety and health encyclopedia* (Vol. 2). Geneva: International Labor Organization, 1971.

Waters, E. The reliability and stability of individual differences in infant-mother attachment. *Child Development,* 1978, *49,* 483–494.

Waters, E., Vaughn, B. E., and Egeland, B. R. Individual differences in infant-mother attachment relationships at age one: Antecedents in neonatal behavior in an urban, economically disadvantaged sample. *Child Development,* 1980, *51,* 208–216.

Watkins, B., Calbert, S., Huston-Stein, A., and Wright, J. C. Children's recall of television material: Effects of presentation mode and adult labeling. *Developmental Psychology,* 1980, *16,* 672–674.

Watson, E. H., and Lowrey, G. H. *Growth and development of children.* Chicago: Year Book Publishers, 1967.

Watson, J. B. *Behaviorism.* Chicago: University of Chicago Press, 1925.

Watson, J. B., and Rayner, R. Conditioned emotional reactions. *Journal of Experimental Psychology,* 1920, *3,* 1–14.

Watson, J. S. Smiling, cooing and "the game." *Merrill-Palmer Quarterly of Behavior and Development,* 1972, *18,* 323–339.

Weiland, A., and Coughlin, R. Self-identification and preferences: A comparison of white and Mexican-American first and third graders. *Journal of Cross-Cultural Psychology,* 1979, *10,* 356–365.

Weininger, O. Young children's concepts of dying and dead. *Psychological Reports,* 1979, *44,* 395–407.

Weinraub, M., and Frankel, J. Sex differences in parent-infant interaction during free play, departure, and separation. *Child Development,* 1977, *48,* 1240–1249.

Weinraub, M., and Lewis, M. The determinants of children's responses to separation. *Monographs of the Society for Research in Child Development,* 1977, *42* (4, Serial, No. 172).

Weir, M. W. Development changes in problem-solving strategies. *Psychological Review,* 1964, *71,* 473–490.

Weir, R. H. *Language in the crib.* The Hague: Mouton, 1962.

Weisberg, P. Social and nonsocial conditioning of infant vocalizations. *Child Development,* 1963, *34,* 377–388.

Weisler, A. and McCall, R. B. Exploration and play: Resume and redirection. *American Psychologist,* 1976, *31,* 492–508.

Werner, E. E. *Cross-cultural child development: A view from the planet earth.* Monterey, Calif.: Brooks/Cole, 1979.

Werner, J. S., and Siqueland, E. R. Visual recognition memory in the preterm infant. *Infant Behavior and Development,* 1978, *1,* 72–94.

Werner, J. S., and Wooten, B. R. Human infant color vision and color perception. *Infant Behavior and Development,* 1979, *2,* 241–274.

Wertz, R. W., and Wertz, D. C. *Lying-in: A history of childbirth in America.* New York: The Free Press, 1977.

West, M. J., and Rheingold, H. L. Infant stimulation of maternal instruction. *Infant Behavior and Development,* 1978, *1,* 205–215.

Westinghouse Learning Corporation. *The impact of Head Start.* Athens, Ohio: Ohio University Press, 1969.

White, B. L. An experimental approach to the effects of experience on early human behaviors. In J. P. Hill (Ed.), *Minnesota symposia on child psychology* (Vol. 1). Minneapolis, Minn.: University of Minnesota Press, 1967.

White, B. L. *The first three years of life.* Englewood Cliffs, N.J.: Prentice-Hall, 1975.

White, B. L., and Castle, P. W. Visual exploratory behavior following postnatal handling of human infants. *Perceptual Motor Skills,* 1964, *18,* 497–502.

White, B. L., Castle, P. W. and Held, R. Observation on the development of visually directed reaching. *Child Development,* 1964, *35,* 349–365.

White, E., Elsom, B., and Prawat, R. Children's conceptions of death. *Child Development,* 1978, *49,* 307–310.

White, S. H. Evidence for a hierarchical arrangement of learning processes. In L. P. Lipsitt and C. C. Spiker (Eds.), *Advances in child development and behavior* (Vol. 2). New York: Academic Press, 1965.

Whitehurst, G. J., and Vasta, R. Is language acquired through imitation? *Journal of Psycholinguistic Research,* 1975, *4,* 37–59.

Whiting, B. B. (Ed.). *Six cultures: Studies of child rearing.* New York: Wiley, 1963.

Whiting, B. B., and Whiting, J. *Children of six cultures: A psycho-cultural analysis.* Cambridge, Mass.: Harvard University Press, 1975.

Whiting, J., and Child, I. L. *Child training and personality: A cross-cultural study.* New Haven, Conn.: Yale University Press, 1953.

Whorf, B. *Language, thought, and reality.* New York: Wiley, 1956.

Widdowson, E. M. Mental contentment and physical growth. *Lancet,* 1951, *1,* 1316–1318.

Wilkins, L. (Ed.). *The diagnosis and treatment of endocrine disorders in childhood and adolescence.* Springfield, Ill.: Charles C. Thomas, 1957.

Willemsen, E. *Understanding infancy.* San Francisco: W. H. Freeman, 1979.

Williams, J. Reading instruction today. *American Psychologist,* 1979, *34,* 917–922.

Williams, J., Bennett, S., and Best, D. Awareness and expression of sex stereotypes in young children. *Developmental Psychology,* 1975, *11,* 635–642.

Williams, J. E., Best, D. L., and Boswell, D. A. The measurement of children's racial attitudes in the early school years. *Child Development,* 1975, *46,* 494–500.

Williams, J. W., and Stith, M. *Middle childhood: Behavior and development* (2nd ed.). New York: Macmillan, 1980.

Wilson, E. O. *Sociobiology: The new synthesis.* Cambridge, Mass.: Harvard University Press, 1975.

Wilson, R. M. Head Project Follow Through: Personal telephone conversation, Washington, D.C., 1980.

Wing, L. W. *Autistic children: A guide for parents.* New York: Brunner/Mazel, 1972.

Wingate, M. E. *Stuttering: Theory and treatment.* New York: Wiley, 1976.

Winick, M. *Malnutrition and brain development.* New York: Oxford University Press, 1976.

Witelson, S. F. Sex and the single hemisphere: Specialization of the right hemisphere for spatial processing. *Science,* 1976, *193,* 425.

Wolf, C. W. Transactional analysis and the management of hyperactivity. In M. J. Fine (Ed.), *Principles and techniques of intervention with hyperactive children.* Springfield, Ill.: Charles C. Thomas, 1977.

Wolfenstein, M. *Children's humor: A psychological analysis.* Glencoe, Ill.: The Free Press, 1954.

Wolff, P. H. Observations on the early development of smiling. In B. M. Foss (Eds.), *Determinants of infant behavior* (Vol. 2). New York: Wiley, 1963.

Wolff, P. H. The causes, controls, and organization of behavior in the neonate. *Psychological Issues,* 1966, *5* (1, Whole No. 17), 1–105.

Wolff, P. H. The natural history of crying and other vocalizations in early infancy. In B. M. Foss (Ed.), *Determinants of infant behavior* (Vol. 4). London: Methuen, 1969.

Wolman, B. B. *Children's fears.* New York: Grosset and Dunlap, 1978.

Woods, N. B. The unsupervised child of the working mother. *Developmental Psychology,* 1972, *6,* 14–25.

Wright, J. C., and Vlietstra, A. G. The development of selective attention: From perceptual exploration to logical search. In H. W. Reese (Ed.), *Advances in child development and behavior* (Vol. 10). New York: Academic Press, 1975, pp. 195–239.

Wunderlich, R. C. Treatment of the hyperactive child. *Academic Therapy,* 1973, *8,* 375–390.

Wyatt, G. E. Studying the black mother-child interaction: Issues and alternatives. *Young Children,* 1977, *33,* 16–22.

Wynn, R. L. *The effect of a playmate on day-care and home-reared toddlers in a strange situation.* Paper presented at the Society for Research in Child Development, San Francisco, April 1979.

Wynne, E. Beyond the discipline problem: Youth suicide as a measure of alienation. *Phi Delta Kappan,* 1978, *59,* 307–315.

Yankelovich, D. Drug users vs. drug abusers: How students control their drug crisis. *Psychology Today,* 1975, *9,* 39–42.

Yarrow, L. J. Maternal deprivation: Toward an empirical and conceptual reevaluation. *Psychological Bulletin,* 1961, *58,* 459–590.

Yarrow, L. J. Research in dimensions of maternal care. *Merrill-Palmer Quarterly,* 1963, *9,* 101–114.

Yarrow, L. J. Separation from parents during early childhood. In *Review of child development research* (Vol. 1). New York: Russell Sage Foundation, 1964.

Yarrow, L. J. Emotional development. *American Psychologist,* 1979, *34,* 951–957.

Yarrow, L. J., Rubeinstein, J. L., Pedersen, F. A., and Jankowski, J. J. Dimensions of early stimulation and their differential effects on infant development. *Merrill-Palmer Quarterly,* 1972, *18,* 205–218.

Yarrow, M. R., and Waxler, C. Z. *The emergence and functions of prosocial behaviors in young children.* Paper presented at the Society for Research in Child Development, Denver, Colo., 1975.

Yarrow, M. R., and Waxler, C. Z. Dimensions and correlates of prosocial behaviors in young children. *Child Development,* 1976, *47,* 118–125.

Yarrow, M. R., and Waxler, C. Z. The emergence and functions of prosocial behaviors in young children. In R. C. Smart and M. S. Smart (Eds.), *Readings in child development and relationships* (2nd ed.). New York: Macmillan, 1977.

Yussen, S. R., and Santwik, J. W. Comparison of the retention of preschool and second grade performers under three verbalization conditions. *Child Development,* 1974, *45,* 821–824.

Zahn-Waxler, C., Radke-Yarrow, M., and King, R. A. Child-rearing and children's prosocial initiations toward victims of distress. *Child Development,* 1979, *50,* 319–330.

Zajonc, R. B. Family configuration and intelligence. *Science,* 1976, *197,* 227–236.

Zajonc, R. B. Feeling and thinking: Preferences need no inference. *American Psychologist,* 1980, *35,* 151–175.

Zambrana, R. E., Hurst, M., and Hite, R. L. The working mother in contemporary perspective: A review of the literature. *Pediatrics,* 1979, *64,* 862–870.

Zaslow, M., and Kramer, E. *Postpartum depression in new fathers.* Paper presented at the Society for Research in Child Development, Boston, April 1981.

Zelnik, M., and Kantner, J. Contraceptive patterns and premarital pregnancy among women aged 15–19 in 1976. *Family Planning Perspectives,* 1978, *10,* 135–142.

Zelniker, T., and Jeffrey, W. E. Reflective and impulsive children: Strategies of information processing underlying differences in problem solving. *Monographs of the Society for Research in Child Development,* 1976, *41*(5, serial no. 168).

Zentella, M. Codeswitching in elementary level Puerto Rican children. *Working Papers in Sociolinguistics,* 1978, *43.*

Zeskind, P. S. Adult responses to crises of low and high risk infants. *Infant Behavior and Development,* 1980, *3,* 167–177.

Zeskind, P. S., and Ramey, C. T. *Fetal malnourishment: Evidence for a transactional model of infant development.* Paper presented at the Society for Research in Child Development, San Francisco, April 1979.

Zigler, E., and Heller, K. A. On day care standards. *Newsletter for the Society for Research in Child Development,* 1979(Winter), 5.

Zigler, E., Levine, J., and Gould, L. Cognitive challenge as a factor in children's humor appreciation. *Journal of Personality and Social Psychology,* 1967, *6,* 332–336.

Zigler, E., and Muenchow, S. Mainstreaming: The proof is in the implementation. *American Psychologist,* 1979, *34,* 993–996.

Zimmerman, B. J., and Lanaro, P. Acquiring and retaining conservation of length through modeling and reversibility cues. *Merrill-Palmer Quarterly,* 1974, *20,* 145–161.

Zivin, G. Removing common confusions about egocentric speech, private speech, and self-regulation. In G. Zivin (Ed.), *The development of self-regulation through private speech.* New York: Wiley, 1979.

Zussman, J. U. Relationship of demographic factors to parental discipline techniques. *Developmental Psychology,* 1978, *14,* 685–686.

Credits

PHOTOS

12 Elizabeth Crews 17 Library of Congress 21 Erika Stone 23 Herbert Gehr, *Life Magazine,* ©
1949, Time, Inc. 24 Mary Evans/Sigmund Freud copyrights 26 Harvard University News Office
photograph 27 Yves De Braine/Black Star 29 Christopher S. Johnson/Stock, Boston 34 Brandeis
University, Office of Public Affairs 38 top right, Thomas Kujawski; others, Erika Stone 39 top left,
Leo de Wys, Inc.; top right, Culver Pictures; center, U.P.I.; bottom left, Elizabeth Crews; bottom
right, Bryan Robinson 59 Erika Stone 68 Wide World Photos 74 Bryan Robinson 76 American
Cancer Society 80 U.P.I. 90 Mary Ellen Mark/Archive Pictures 94 John H. Kennell 102 top,
Elizabeth Crews/Stock, Boston; center, Lew Merrim/Monkmeyer Press Photo Service; bottom, Ellis
Herwig/Stock, Boston 103 top, Eve Arnold/Magnum Photos; center, Bryan Robinson; bottom,
Nolan Patterson/Black Star 109 Bryan Robinson 125 Bryan Robinson 127 UNICEF photo by
Wolff 130–131 Elizabeth Crews 133 Bryan Robinson 142 Wayne Miller/Magnum Photos 145
Bryan Robinson 151 Bryan Robinson 153 Florence Sharp 157 Erica Stone 161 top left, Costa
Manos/Magnum Photos; top center, Loren McIntyre/Woodfin Camp & Associates; top right, William
Hubbell/Woodfin Camp & Associates; bottom, Michal Heron/Woodfin Camp & Associates 172
Bryan Robinson 175 Florence Sharp 178 Brent Petersen/Parade 179 Thomas Hopker/Woodfin
Camp & Associates 181 Paul S. Conklin/Monkmeyer Press Photo Service 185 Erika Stone 187 In
J. E. Jan, R. Freeman, and E. Scott, *Visual impairment in children and adolescents.* New York: Grune
& Stratton, 1977. Reprinted by permission of Grune & Stratton, Inc. and the author. 194 Erika
Stone 197 Elizabeth Crews 204 Bryan Robinson 209 Paul S. Conklin/Monkmeyer Press Photo
Service 212 René Barri/Magnum Photos 220 Erika Stone 223 Florence Sharp 227 Florence
Sharp 230 Alan Hui 233 Bryan Robinson 236 Erika Stone/Photo Researchers, Inc. 239 *The Bos-
ton Globe* 241 E. Richard Sorenson, *The edge of the forest: Land, childhood, and change in a New
Guinea protoagricultural society.* © Smithsonian Institution Press: Washington, D.C., 1976, p.
168. 254 Wide World Photos 260 left, Elizabeth Crews; right, © 1981 *The Gastonia Gazette* 261
left, Elizabeth Crews; top right, Owen Franken/Stock, Boston; bottom right, Patricia Hollander
Gross/Stock, Boston 262 Anna Kaufman Moon/Stock, Boston 264 Erika Stone 266 Elizabeth
Crews 267 Elizabeth Hamlin/Stock, Boston 275 Erika Stone 280 Florence Sharp 283 Bryan
Robinson 291 Wide World Photos 293 Elizabeth Crews 303 Elizabeth Hamlin/Stock, Boston 307 Bryan Robinson 308 U.P.I. 312 top, Myron Papiz/Photo Researchers, Inc.; bottom,

Alice Kandell/Photo Researchers, Inc.   **313** bottom right, Alice Kandell/Photo Researchers, Inc.; others, Ken Heyman   **317** The Charlotte Montessori School   **318** Elaine M. Ward   **324** Elizabeth Crews   **329** Elizabeth Crews   **340** Erika Stone   **343** Elizabeth Crews   **344** Erika Stone   **362** President's Committee on Mental Retardation   **376** S. Oristaglio/Photo Researchers, Inc.   **378** Elizabeth Crews   **385** Bryan Robinson   **388** Courtesy Columbia Pictures. Copyright © 1981.   **389** U.P.I.   **393** J. Berndt/Stock, Boston   **398** top left, © 1981 *The Gastonia Gazette;* top right, Erika Stone; bottom, Elizabeth Crews   **401** Florence Sharp   **405** Ed Lettau/Photo Researchers, Inc.   **409** top right, Bryan Robinson; others, reprinted by permission of the publication. From B. B. Whiting and J. Whiting, *Children of six cultures: A psychocultural analysis.* Cambridge, Mass.: Harvard University Press, © 1975   **423** Bryan Robinson   **427** The South Carolina Department of Youth Services   **429** Bryan Robinson   **436** Wide World Photos   **443** Michael Uffer/Photo Researchers, Inc.   **447** Anestis Diakopoulos/Stock, Boston   **450** Bryan Robinson   **454** Bryan Robinson   **459** left, Christopher Brown/Stock, Boston; right, Rick Smolan/Stock, Boston   **462** top left, Wide World Photos; top right, Mimi Forsyth/Monkmeyer Press Photo Service; bottom left, Susan Kuklin/Photo Researchers, Inc.; bottom right, Michal Heron/Monkmeyer Press Photo Service   **467** Museum of Modern Art, Film Stills Archive. Courtesy Columbia Pictures, copyright © 1976   **468** The South Carolina Department of Youth Services   **471** George Holton/Photo Researchers, Inc.   **481** Hugh Rogers/Monkmeyer Press Photo Service   **487** left, Glenda Loftin; right, Bryan Robinson   **488** Bryan Robinson

CARTOONS

18 © 1955 United Feature Syndicate, Inc.   **31** *Dennis the Menace* (R), reprinted courtesy of Hank Ketcham, © by Field Enterprises, Inc.   **287** *The Family Circus,* reprinted courtesy of The Register and Tribune Syndicate, Inc.   **322** © 1978 by Sidney Harris/Wall Street Journal   **327** Used with permission from *Day Care and Early Education*   **357** © 1960 United Feature Syndicate, Inc.

FIGURES

1.2 Thomas McAvoy, *Life Magazine* © 1955 Time, Inc.

2.1 Dr. Everett Anderson.

2.3 Dr. Landrum B. Shettles.

2.6 Mohr, O. L. Woolly hair a dominant mutant character in man. *Journal of Heredity,* 1932, *23,* 345. Published by permission of the American Genetic Association.

2.8 Photo Researchers

2.9 Moore, K. L. *The developing human. Clinically oriented embryology,* 2nd ed., 1977. Courtesy of W. B. Saunders Co.

3.4 A. Meltzoff and K. Moore, *Science,* 1977, *198,* 75–78.

3.5 David Linton, *Scientific American.*

4.1 Reprinted by permission of Yale University Press from C. M. Jackson, Some Aspects of Form and Growth. In W. J. Robbins, S. Brody, A. F. Hogan, C. M. Jackson, and C. W. Green, eds., *Growth.* New Haven: Yale University Press, 1929, p. 118.

4.2 From *Human Embryology* by Bradley M. Patten. Copyright © 1968 by McGraw-Hill, Inc. Used with permission of McGraw-Hill Book Company.

4.3 Thomas S. England, *People Weekly,* © 1980 Time, Inc.

4.4 William Vandivert, *Scientific American.*

4.5 Harry F. Harlow, University of Wisconsin Primate Laboratory.

5.1 Vivienne, Photo Researchers, Inc.

6.2 From M. D. S. Braine, Children's first word combinations. *Monographs of the Society for Research in Child Development,* 1976, *41* (Serial No. 164), Table 1, p. 7. Reprinted by permission of the Society for Research in Child Development, Inc. © 1976.

7.1 *A primer of infant development* by T. G. R. Bower. W. H. Freeman and Company © 1977.

8.1 Louise Skinner, *Motor development in the preschool years,* 1979. Courtesy of Charles C. Thomas, Publisher, Springfield, Ill.

9.2 *Piaget for the classroom teacher* by Barry Wadsworth. Copyright © 1978 by Longman Inc. Reprinted with permission of Longman Inc., New York.

11.1 Adapted from J. M. Tanner, Physical growth. In P. H. Mussen, ed., *Carmichael's Manual of Child Psychology,* vol. 1, 3rd ed. New York: Wiley, 1970. Used with permission.

11.2 Kagan, J., Rosman, B. L., Day, D., Albert, J., and Phillips, W. Information processing in the child: Significance of analytic and reflective attitudes. Psychological Monographs (Whole No. 578). © 1964 by the American Psychological Association. Reprinted by permission.

12.2 Adapted from Williams and Stith, 1980.

13.1 Tanner, J. M. Growth and endocrinology of the adolescent. In L. J. Gardner, *Endocrine and Genetic Diseases of Childhood.* Philadelphia: W. B. Saunders, 1969. By permission.

FIGURES IN SPOTLIGHTS

Page 132 From Shirley, *The First Two Years: A Study of Twenty-five Babies,* vol. II, Institute of Child Welfare Monograph Series No. 7, University of Minnesota Press, Minneapolis, Copyright © 1933, 1961 by the University of Minnesota.

Page 133 From W. K. Frankenburg and J. B. Dodds, The Denver Developmental Screening Test. *Journal of Pediatrics,* 1971, *71,* 181–191. Used with permission.

Author Index

Feingold, B. F., 360, 404
Feitelson, D., 290
Feldman, H., 449
Feldman, S. S., 149, 222, 306
Fenson, L., 197
Feshbach, N. D., 321
Field, J., 105
Field, T., 94, 458
Findlay, J. M., 104
Fine, M. J., 404
Finkel, D., 456
Finkel, M., 456
Finkelstein, N. W., 230, 231
Fisher, R. L., 400
Fisher, S., 400
Fitzgerald, H. E., 149
Flaste, R., 154
Flavell, J. H., 351, 434
Flesch, R., 351
Flexer, B. K., 434
Flinchum, B. M., 271
Forer, L. K., 382
Forisha, B. E., 41
Forman, G. E., 297
Fouts, G., 147
Fox, D. J., 406
Fraiberg, S., 185
Francke, L. V., 390
Frankel, J., 162
Frankenburg, W. K., 134, 173
Freeman, R. D., 189
Freud, A., 24, 225–227
Freud, S., 24, 25
Friedenberg, E. Z., 457
Friedrich, L. K., 320, 321
Frisch, H. L., 159
Frodi, A. M., 148, 255
Frost, J., 144
Frueh, T., 326
Fullard, W., 148
Furth, H. G., 213

Gadberry, S., 321
Gaines, R., 255
Galbraith, R. E., 371
Gallagher, R., 382
Gallup, G. H., 460
Galst, J. P., 322
Galton, L., 182
Garbarino, J., 255
Garcia, E. E., 290
Gardner, H., 397
Gardner, L. I., 152
Garmezy, N., 380, 381
Garn, S. M., 182
Garnets, L., 326
Garvey, C., 237

Gary, A. L., 359
Gatley, R. H., 411
Gearing, J., 111
Geisler, M., 65
Gelfand, D. M., 366, 368
Gelles, R. J., 255
Gelman, R., 347
Gerbner, G., 320
Gesell, A., 21, 22, 23, 134
Getzels, J. W., 359
Gewirtz, J. L., 158
Gibbons, M., 460
Gibson, E. J., 138, 263, 265
Gibson, J., 138
Gilligan, C., 368, 437
Ginsburg, H., 277, 279, 434
Glick, P. G., 386
Glover, J., 359
Gold, D., 309
Gold, M., 466
Goldberg, M. E., 21, 135, 160, 322
Goldberg, S., 158, 160, 162
Goldfarb, W., 153
Goldin-Meadow, S., 205
Golding, W., 392
Goldman, J., 282
Goldstein, K. M., 95
Gonzalez-Mena, J., 164
Goodenough, F. L., 231, 234
Goodman, K., 268, 269, 457
Gordon, I., 317
Gottesman, I. I., 323
Gottfried, A. W., 95, 139
Gottman, J., 395
Gouze, K. R., 407
Green, E. C., 47
Green, M., 431
Greenberg, J. H., 211
Greenberg, M., 91
Greenfield, P. M., 212
Gregg, C. L., 104
Gresh, S., 114
Gross, N., 320
Grusec, J. E., 304
Guilford, J. P., 358
Gunnar, M. R., 159
Gussow, J. D., 343
Guthrie, H., 250
Guttmacher, A. F., 83

Haaf, R., 104, 136
Hagman, R. R., 236
Haith, M. M., 105
Halfar, C., 296
Hall, G. S., 444, 445
Halonen, J. S., 228
Hamill, P. V. V., 339

Hamilton, J. S., 90
Haney, W., 317
Hanlon, C., 208
Hanson, D. A., 267, 268
Hanson, D. R., 323
Haring, N. G., 371
Harlow, H. F., 150, 225, 227
Harlow, M. H., 225
Harmon, C., 345
Harper, L. V., 108, 219
Harre, R., 395, 396
Hartley, R. E., 309
Hartmann, D. P., 366, 368
Hartup, W. W., 395
Haskins, R., 308
Hass, A., 439
Havinghurst, R. J., 466
Heathers, G., 222
Heller, K. A., 308
Hellugi, U., 210
Hendin, D., 64, 67
Herbst, A. L., 78
Herzog, E., 389
Hess, R. D., 289
Hetherington, E. M., 240, 383, 384, 385, 386, 388, 389, 403
Hildebrandt, K. A., 149
Hill, F., 297
Hock, E., 308, 309
Hodges, J., 152, 396
Hoffman, L. W., 309
Hoffman, M. L., 232, 364, 366, 367, 368, 369
Hoffman, Y. L., 233
Holmberg, M. C., 230, 231
Holmes, F. B., 235
Holsinger, D. N., 378
Honig, A. S., 183
Hooker, D., 106
Hoorweg, J., 183
Horn, J., 89
Horowitz, A. B., 104
Horowitz, F. D., 377, 395, 396
Humphries, T., 404
Hunsberger, B., 406
Huntington, D., 109, 302
Hutt, C. J., 102, 250
Huttenlocher, J., 199
Huxley, A., 82, 83
Hyman, I. A., 460
Hyson, M. C., 235

Inhelder, B., 282, 347, 349, 432, 433, 436, 437, 469
Irish, D. P., 390
Irwin, D. M., 491
Izard, C. E., 156

Subject Index

Crawling, 132
Creativity, 357–359
  defined, 358
Creeping, 132
Cretinism, 72
Crib death (Sudden Infant Death
  Syndrome), 121–124
Crisis, in Erikson's stage theory, 27
  identity, 443, 449
  role, 449
  sexual, 449
Critical (sensitive) periods, 32, 106
  in prenatal development, 70
Cross-cultural development and
  relationships, 80, 330–331, 408,
  470–471
Cross-sectional comparisons, 487–488,
  489
Crowd formation, 451–453
Crowning, 87
Crying, 144, 157
  in neonates, 99, 112
Cultures, 160
  differences in, 135
  and language development, 205

Dating, 453–455
Day care, 228–229
Death, coping with, 323–325
  crib (Sudden Infant Death Syndrome),
  121–124
Decentration, 346
Deductive reasoning, 279
Deep structure of sentence, 210
Defects, birth. See Birth defects
  genetic, 61–65
Deficiencies, iron, 183
  protein, 183
  vitamin, 122, 183
Delayed language, 293, 294
Delinquent behavior, 465–466
Delivery. See Birth
Democratic leadership style, 391
Deoxyribonucleic acid (DNA), 57
Dependence, 147
  vs. independence, 449
  parent-toddler, 222
  proximity-seeking, 149
  psychological, 427
Dependent variable, 485
Depression, 124
Deprivation dwarfism, 152
Depth perception, 138
DES (diethylstilbestrol), 78, 79
Despair, 227
Detachment, parent-child, 379
  as reaction to parental absence, 227

Determination of sex, 59
Development, anal stage of, 25
  autonomy, 220–221
  bone, 340
  brain, 250
  brain cell, 183
  cognitive. See Cognitive development
  comparisons in, 486–489
  concrete operational, 28
  cross-cultural, 80, 330–331, 408,
  470–471
  emotional. See Emotional development
  exceptional, 121–124
  formal operational, 28
  genital stage of, 25
  language. See Language development
  latent stage of, 25
  locomotor, 257
  moral. See Moral development
  motor, 20, 21, 129–133, 173–176,
  185–187, 256–257, 342
  muscle, 250
  operational. See Operational
  development
  oral stage of, 25
  of parent-child relationship, 112, 154,
  223, 305, 379
  patterns in, 119–120
  perceptual. See Perceptual
  development
  personality, 26
  phallic stage of, 25
  physical. See Physical development
  prenatal. See Prenatal development
  preoperational. See Preoperational
  children
  psychosexual, 24
  sensorimotor. See Sensorimotor
  development
  sex-role, 158–162, 238–241, 325–329,
  406–407, 472–473
  social. See Social development
  social speech, 288–289
  of specific emotions, 156
  structural. See Structural development
  vocabulary, 205, 284–285
Developmental norms, 23
  uses and abuses of, 134–135
Diabetes, 74, 75
Dialects, 290
Diethylstilbestrol (DES), 78, 79
Differences between sexes, 158–159
Differentiated listening, 267
Difficulties, language, 293–295
  perceptual-motor, 359
"Difficult" infants, 108, 161
Digestive system in neonates, 99

Dilemmas, 365, 437
Disabilities in learning. See Learning
  disabilities
Discipline in schools, 460–461
Discrimination, 264–265
  auditory, 268
  letter, 269
  visual, 268
Disease. See also Illness; specific diseases
  childhood, 20
  in mother, 74
  venereal, 75, 426
Disorders, memory, 359
  nervous system, 360
  perceptual system, 360
  speech, 359
Distance judgments, 282
Distress, emotional, 152
  generalized, 156
Divorce, 383–384
  adjustment to, 386–387
Dizygotic (fraternal) twins, 50
DNA (deoxyribonucleic acid), 57
Dominance of males, 58
Dominant genes, 60
  autosomal, 64
Doubt, 221–222
Down's syndrome, 65, 68, 362
  and genetic counseling, 67
  piggy-back, 67
Dramatic play, 310–313
Dreams, 315
  wet (nocturnal emission), 421
Drives. See Instincts
Drowsy state in neonates, 99
Drugs, 426–430. See also specific drugs
  addiction to, 427
  addictive, 77
  and childbirth, 92
  conflicting attitudes about, 430
  during childbirth, 88, 92, 93
  during pregnancy, 75–78
  hallucinogenic (psychedelic), 430
  pain-relieving, 93
  physical addiction to, 427
  psychological dependence on, 427
Dwarfism, 152

Early-contact mothers, 107
Early maturers vs. late maturers, 422–423
Easter Island, 110
Easter Seal Society for Crippled Children
  and Adults, 294
Eating, 125, 180
Ebert, P., 389
Economic Opportunity Act of 1964, 316
Ectoderm, 52

Noah is a strong-willed child, but he is also sensitive to the needs and feelings of others. Noah is a contemplative child and his friends consider him a deep thinker.

Velma spent most of her first year in an orphanage before being adopted. She is withdrawn, dependent, and insecure, with few friends. As a school-aged child, Velma is attention-seeking and quarrelsome.

Thelma is Velma's twin sister, though neither is aware of the other's existence. Unlike her sister, Thelma was adopted at birth. She is well-adjusted, of average intelligence, and generally well-liked by adults and other children. Thelma is more outgoing than her twin.